Contents

PART I INTRODUCTION

PART II PERSPECTIVES ON CORPORATE SOCIAL RESPONSIBILITY

PART III CRITIQUES OF CORPORATE SOCIAL RESPONSIBILITY

PART IV ACTORS AND DRIVERS

PART V MANAGING CORPORATE SOCIAL RESPONSIBILITY

PART VI CORPORATE SOCIAL RESPONSIBILITY IN GLOBAL CONTEXT

PART VII FUTURE PERSPECTIVES AND CONCLUSIONS

LIST OF FIGURES

Editor Biographies

Andrew Crane is the George R. Gardiner Professor of Business Ethics in the Schulich School of Business at York University. He has a Ph.D. in Management from the University of Nottingham, and was previously Chair in Business Ethics and Director of the UK's first MBA in CSR in the International Centre for Corporate Social Responsibility at Nottingham University Business School.

Abagail McWilliams (Ph.D., Ohio State University) is a Professor in the College of Business, University of Illinois at Chicago and since 2002 has been a Visiting Professor in the International Centre for Corporate Social Responsibility, University of Nottingham. Her research on CSR has appeared in *Academy of Management Journal*, *Academy of Management Review*, *Strategic Management Journal*, and *Journal of Management Studies*.

Dirk Matten holds the Hewlett-Packard Chair in Corporate Social Responsibility at the Schulich School of Business, York University, Toronto. He holds a doctoral degree and the habilitation from Heinrich-Heine-University Düsseldorf, Germany. He is interested in CSR, business ethics, and comparative management. He has published widely, including in *Academy of Management Review*, *Journal of Management Studies*, *Organization Studies*, and *Business Ethics Quarterly*.

Jeremy Moon is Professor and Director of the International Centre for Corporate Social Responsibility at Nottingham University Business School. Recent publications include *Corporations and Citizenship* (Cambridge University Press) and papers in *Academy of Management Review* and *British Journal of Management*. He is a Fellow of the Royal Society for the Arts.

Donald Siegel is Dean and Professor at the School of Business, University of Abany, SUNY. Recent publications include *Innovation, Entrepreneurship, and Technological Change* (Oxford University Press), the *Handbook of University Technology Transfer* (University of Chicago Press, forthcoming), and articles on CSR in *Academy of Management Review*, *Journal of Management Studies*, *Journal of Economics and Management Strategy*, and *Leadership Quarterly*. He is editor of the *Journal of Technology Transfer*, an associate editor of the *Journal of Business Venturing* and the *Journal of Productivity Analysis*, and serves on the editorial boards of the *Journal of Management Studies*, *Academy of Management Perspectives*, *Academy of Management Learning & Education*, and *Strategic Entrepreneurship Journal*.

AUTHOR BIOGRAPHIES

Ruth V. Aguilera is an Associate Professor at the College of Business and the Institute of Labor and Industrial Relations at the University of Illinois at Urbana-Champaign. She received her Ph.D. in Sociology from Harvard University. Her research interests fall at the intersection of economic sociology and international business, specifically in the field of comparative corporate governance.

Jay B. Barney, Professor of Management and Chase Chair for Excellence in Corporate Strategy at the Max M. Fisher College of Business, The Ohio State University, received his doctorate in Administrative Science and Sociology from Yale University. Professor Barney's research focuses on the relationship between firm skills and capabilities and sustained competitive advantage. He has published over 75 articles and books and consulted widely. Awards include an honorary doctorate degree from the University of Lund and honorary visiting professor positions in New Zealand, China, and the United Kingdom. He was elected Fellow in the Academy of Management, where he received the Irwin Outstanding Educator Award in the Business Policy and Strategy Division.

Jill A. Brown (Ph.D., University of Georgia) is Assistant Professor of Management at Lehigh University's College of Business and Economics. Her research, focusing on corporate governance and business ethics, has been published in the *Journal of Management Studies* and *Business and Society: Ethics and Stakeholder Management* (Archie B. Carroll and Ann K. Buchholtz eds.).

Ann K. Buchholtz (Ph.D., New York University) is an Associate Professor in the Terry College of Business at the University of Georgia. She has authored numerous articles on business ethics, social issues and corporate governance, and she serves as the inaugural ethics adjudication chair for the Academy of Management.

Archie B. Carroll is Director of the Nonprofit Management and Community Service Program and Professor Emeritus in the Terry College of Business, University of Georgia. He received his doctorate in management from The Florida State University. His research interests include corporate social responsibility and business ethics. He is senior co-author of *Business and Society: Ethics and Stakeholder Management*, 6th edn., 2006, and a former President of the Society for Business Ethics.

Barry A. Colbert (Ph.D., York University) is an Assistant Professor of Policy at the School of Business and Economics at Wilfred Laurier University in Canada. His work has been published in *Academy of Management Review*, the *Journal of General Management*, and *Human Resource Planning*. His research is centered on the ways and means by which organizations align a vision for sustainability, business strategy, and the strategic development of human capital.

Stanley Deetz (Ph.D., Ohio University) is Director of Peace and Conflict Studies at the University of Colorado. He has written several books on corporate relations to society, organizational communication, and micropractices of power. He was a Senior Fulbright Scholar and is a National Communication Association Distinguished Scholar.

Thomas Donaldson (Ph.D., University of Kansas) is the Mark O. Winkelman Professor, and Director of the Wharton Ph.D. Program in Ethics and Law at the Wharton School, University of Pennsylvania. He has published more than ten books and 70 articles and has consulted widely. He is the current President of the Social Issues in Management Division of the Academy of Management and is past President of the Society for Business Ethics.

Thomas W. Dunfee served as President of the Academy of Legal Studies in Business (1989–90), and the Society for Business Ethics (1995–6). Tom was the author or editor of several books (published by e.g. Harvard Business School Press, McGraw-Hill, Prentice-Hall, Wiley and Kluwer) and published articles in many management, ethics and law journals (e.g. *Academy of Management Review*, *Academy of Management Journal*, *Business Ethics Quarterly*, *California Law Review*, *Economics and Philosophy*, *Journal of Business Ethics*, *Journal of Marketing*, and the *Northwestern Law Review*). He died in 2008.

William C. Frederick is Professor Emeritus, Katz Graduate School of Business, University of Pittsburgh. His principal scholarly interest is the social and ethical responsibilities of business corporations, as reflected in his books, *Corporation, Be Good! The Story of Corporate Social Responsibility* (2006) and *Values, Nature, and Culture in the American Corporation* (1995). His Ph.D. in economics and anthropology is from the University of Texas-Austin. Additional information is at his website: <http://www.williamcfrederick.com>.

Gerard Hanlon is a Professor of Organizational Sociology, at the School of Business and Management, Queen Mary College, University of London. He holds a Ph.D. in Sociology from Trinity College, University of Dublin. His research interests include social theory, the nature of capitalist societies, the relationship between the state and the market, critique of political economy, the work of the middle class, professional organizations, and industrial sociology. Professor Hanlon is the author of *Commercialization of Accountancy: Flexible Accumulation* *and the Transformation of the Service Class* (Macmillan, 1994) and *Lawyers, the State and the Market: Professionalism Revisited* (Macmillan, 1998). He has published numerous papers, and has recently completed two Economic and Social Research Council projects: one on corporate social responsibility and a second on innovative health technologies with particular reference to telemedicine—see <http://www.esrc.ac.uk/ESRCInfoCentre/index.aspx>.

Pursey P. M. A. R. Heugens is Professor of Organization Theory at RSM Erasmus University. He holds a Ph.D. in Management from RSM Erasmus University (2001). Research interests include Business Ethics and Positive and Normative Organization Theory. Pursey Heugens has published some 30 articles in journals like the *Academy of Management Review, Strategic Organization, Organization Studies, Journal of Business Ethics,* and *Journal of Management Studies.* He serves on the editorial board of six scholarly journals, and is a representative at large of the Academy of Management's Social Issues in Management Division.

Bryan W. Husted a Professor and Erivan K. Haub Chair in Business and Sustainability, Schulich School of Business, York University Toronto. He holds a Ph.D. in Business and Public Policy from the University of California at Berkeley. His work focuses on corporate social responsibility and sustainability.

Rami Kaplan, Ph.D. candidate, Department of Sociology and Anthropology, Tel Aviv University.

Timothy Kuhn is an Associate Professor, University of Colorado and holds a Ph.D. in Communication from Arizona State University. His research centers on understanding firms—particularly knowledge-intensive firms—as complex discursive systems, a conceptual move that directs his attention to processes of corporate governance, knowledge development, and personal identity construction. His research has appeared in a variety of outlets, including Organization Studies, Management Communication Quarterly, and Communication Monographs.

Lloyd Kurtz is a senior portfolio manager with Nelson Capital Management of Palo Alto, California. He is a Chartered Financial Analyst and holds an MBA in Finance from Babson College. He serves as a Research Fellow at the University of California's Haas School of Business, and maintains the sristudies.org online database of studies of socially responsible investment.

Elizabeth C. Kurucz (Ph.D., York University) is Assistant Professor of Organizational Behaviour and Sustainable Commerce in the Department of Business, College of Management and Economics at the University of Guelph. Her research in Organizational Behaviour spans business, government, and civil society, and is focused on how organizational mindsets facilitate or inhibit progress toward more sustainable practice.

David L. Levy is Professor of Management at the University of Massachusetts, Boston. He received a DBA from Harvard Business School, and his research examines strategic contestation over the governance of controversial global issues, with a focus on climate change. His most recent book, co-edited with Peter Newell, is *The Business of Global Environmental Governance* (MIT Press, 2005).

Alison Mackey is an Assistant Professor of Management at the Orfalea College of Business at California Polytechnic State University. She received her Ph.D. from The Ohio State University. Her current research interests include corporate social responsibility and executive selection, compensation, and performance measurement.

Tyson B. Mackey is an Assistant Professor of Management at the Orfalea College of Business at California Polytechnic State University. He received his Ph.D. in Business Policy from The Ohio State University. His current research interests include the relationship between diversification and firm value as well as corporate social responsibility.

Domènec Melé is Professor of Business Ethics and holds the Chair of Economics and Ethics at IESE Business School, University of Navarra, Spain. He holds a Doctorate in Industrial Engineering (Polytechnic University of Catalonia, Spain) and in Theology (University of Navarra, Spain). He is the author or editor of several books on Business Ethics and related topics, apart from numerous articles and contributions to books. Currently he is working on a book on Business Ethics from a human values perspective.

Andrew Millington is Deputy Dean of the School of Management, and Professor of Business and Society, at the University of Bath. His current research interests include supply chain management in China and international comparative studies of ethical supply chain management. His publications include papers in the *Journal of International Business Studies, Journal of Management Studies, Human Relations, International Journal of Operations and Production Management,* and *Business & Society*. He received his Ph.D. in European Studies from the University of Bath.

Brendan O'Dwyer is Professor and Head of Accounting at the University of Amsterdam Business School. He holds a Ph.D. in Accounting from the University of Dundee. His research interests encompass: sustainability reporting assurance practice; corporate and non-governmental organization (NGO) accounting and accountability; social and ethical accounting and reporting; corporate stakeholder engagement; corporate social responsibility; and professional accounting ethics and disciplinary procedures.

Marc Orlitzky (Ph.D., University of Iowa) is Associate Professor of Management, Division of Business and Engineering, Pen State Univesity. His research interests include corporate social responsibility, business ethics, strategic human resource management, and organizational and small-group performance. He serves on the editorial review boards of the *Academy of Management Journal* and *Encyclopedia of Business Ethics and Society* and has published several empirical studies of corporate social performance in a variety of publication outlets.

David L. Owen BA ACA FRSA. David is a Professor of Social and Environmental Accounting at the International Centre for Corporate Social Responsibility, Nottingham University Business School. Professor Owen's main research interests lie in the fields of corporate social and environmental accounting, auditing, and reporting. His most recent work has focused on the issue of corporate capture of the 'sustainability' agenda and the appropriation of its potential radical edge by managerial interests.

Guido Palazzo is Professor at the Faculty of Management and Economics at the University of Lausanne. Guido holds a doctorate in philosophy from the University of Bamberg in Germany. His research interests are in the area of CSR, ethical decision-making, political theory, and branding. Key publications include:

- Guido Palazzo and Andreas Scherer (2006), 'Corporate Legitimacy as Deliberation. A Communicative Framework', *Journal of Business Ethics*, 66: 71–88.
- Andreas Scherer, Guido Palazzo, and Dorothée Baumann (2006), 'Global Rules and Private Actors—Towards a New Role of the TNC in Global Governance', *Business Ethics Quarterly*, 16(4): 505–32.
- Kunal Basu and Guido Palazzo, 'Corporate Social Responsibility: A Process Model of Sensemaking', *Academy of Management Review* (forthcoming).

Peter Pruzan, Professor Emeritus, Department of Politics, Management and Philosophy, Copenhagen Business School and Visiting Professor, Sri Sathya Sai University, India. Highest degrees: Dr.Polit. (Economics, University of Copenhagen, Denmark) and Ph.D. (Operations Research, Case-Western Reserve, USA). Current research: spiritual-based leadership; see e.g. *Leading with Wisdom: Spiritual-Based Leadership in Business* (Greenleaf Publishing, UK, 2007).

José Salazar is a titular professor at the Economics Department of Tecnológico de Monterrey (Mexico). He received his Ph.D. in Social Sciences from Universidad Autónoma de Nuevo León (Mexico). His actual research is on corporate social responsibility and international trade.

Andreas Georg Scherer is Director of the Institute of Organization and Administrative Science (IOU) at the University of Zurich. He received his degrees from the University of Erlangen-Nuremberg. Research interests include: business ethics, international management, organization theory, and theories of the firm. He has published in *Academy of Management Review, Business Ethics Quarterly, Journal of Business Ethics, Organization, Organization Studies.*

Kareem M. Shabana is an Assistant Professor of Management at Indiana University, Kokomo. He is finalizing his dissertation, entitled 'Two Essays on the Nature and Practice of Corporate Social Responsibility,' at the University of Georgia. Kareem's research interests include Corporate Social Responsibility, Corporate Social Performance, and Corporate Social Reporting.

N. Craig Smith is the INSEAD Chaired Professor in Ethics and Social Responsibility at INSEAD in Fontainebleau, France. He was previously on the faculties of London Business School, Georgetown University, and Harvard Business School. His current research projects examine ethical consumerism, deception in marketing, marketing ethics, and strategic drivers of corporate responsibility. His recent publications appear in the *Journal of Marketing, Business Ehics Quarterly, Sloan Management Review, California Management Review,* and the *Journal of Business Ethics.* He consults on business and marketing ethics and corporate responsibility, and serves on the Scientific Committee of Vigeo (a social responsibility rating agency) and the Advisory Board of Carbon Clear (a carbon offset company). Smith was the winner of the Beyond Grey Pinstripes' 2005 European Faculty Pioneer Award for his work on social and environmental issues in business.

Ulrich Steger (Ph.D., Ruhr University) holds the Alcan Chair of Environmental Management at IMD. Professor Steger is Director of IMD's research project on Corporate Sustainability Management. He is Director of Building High Performance Boards and other major partnership programs including the DaimlerChrysler and Allianz Excellence Program. He is the author or editor of numerous publications including, most recently *Managing Complex Mergers* (2004) and *Mastering Global Corporate Governance* (2004).

Diane L. Swanson, the von Waaden Professor at Kansas State University, holds a Ph.D. in Business from the University of Pittsburgh and publishes widely on corporate social responsibility. She is the recipient of the 2001 Award for Best Article in Business and Society and the 2004 Best Ethics Educator Award.

J. (Hans) van Oosterhout is a Professor of Corporate Governance and Responsibility at RSM Erasmus University. He holds an MA in Political Science from Leiden University, and a Ph.D. in Organization Theory from Erasmus University. His research interests pertain to the positive and normative theory of organizations and institutions, corporate governance, and the relationship between economic, legal, and political institutions in general.

Wayne Visser is founder and CEO of CSR International, a Visiting Professor in CSR at Manhein University, Germany and Senior Associate and Internal Examiner at the University of Cambridge Programme for Industry, UK. Wayne holds a Ph.D. in Corporate Social Responsibility, Nottingham University Business School. His research interests include: CSR in developing countries, corporate governance in

Africa, leadership for sustainability, and the purpose of business. Key publications include: author/editor of four books on CSR and sustainable business, including most recently *Corporate Citizenship in Africa* (Greenleaf, 2006) and *The A to Z of CSR: An Encyclopaedia of Corporate Social Responsibility* (Wiley, 2007). He is a former Director of Sustainability Services for KPMG South Africa; and has lectured on CSR and sustainable business in Finland, South Africa, and the UK.

David Vogel is the Solomon Lee Professor of Business Ethics and Professor of Political Science at the University of California, Berkeley. He holds a doctorate in political science from Princeton University. His research focuses on business–government and business–society relations. He is the author or editor of ten books, including *The Market for Virtue: The Potential and Limits of Corporate Social Responsibility*.

David Wheeler is Dean of Management, Dalhousie University, Nova Scotia, Canada. He holds a Ph.D. in Applied Microbiology from the University of Surrey (UK). Dr Wheeler's research interests focus on the role of the private sector in international development, corporate strategy, governance and sustainability, and organizational change and sustainability. He was the principal author of *The Stakeholder Corporation* (Pitman), and has published more than 70 articles in the Science, Medicine, and Management literatures. Dr. Wheeler is currently Co-chair of the United Nations Development Program Project on case writing in private sector development. He is Chair of the Foundation for Sustainable Enterprise and Development and a board member of Zero Footprint.

Cynthia A. Williams (J.D., NYU School of Law) is a Visiting Professor and Osler Chair in Business Law at Osgoode Hall Law School, York University, Toronto, Canada. Her research interests include corporate law, securities, comparative corporate governance, and CSR, based on interdisciplinary collaborations in anthropology, business, economics, and organizational psychology.

Duane Windsor is Lynette S. Autrey Professor in the Jones Graduate School of Management, Rice University. His Ph.D. in Political Economy and Government is from Harvard University. His research emphasizes corporate social responsibility and stakeholder management. 'Corporate Social Responsibility: Three Key Approaches' appeared in *Journal of Management Studies* (January 2006).

PART I

INTRODUCTION

CHAPTER 1

THE CORPORATE SOCIAL RESPONSIBILITY AGENDA

ANDREW CRANE

ABAGAIL McWILLIAMS

DIRK MATTEN

JEREMY MOON

DONALD SIEGEL

INTRODUCTION

CORPORATE social responsibility (CSR) has experienced a journey that is almost unique in the pantheon of ideas in the management literature. Its phenomenal rise to prominence in the 1990s and 2000s suggests that it is a relatively new area of academic research. However, the scholarly literature dates to at least the 1950s and commentators on business have written about the subject for considerably longer (see Carroll, Chapter 2). The basic questions at the heart of CSR are as old as business itself, such as what is a business for and what contribution does it make to society (Handy, 2002)? There is, it has to be said, no shortage of history to dwell on in the debate about CSR even if those who write about the subject rarely acknowledge as much.

The story of CSR is interesting because its rise to prominence has not been at all a smooth one, considering that along the way, CSR has been quite frequently discredited, written off, marginalized, or simply overlooked in favor of new or supposedly better ways of conceptualizing the business and society interface (there are by now a whole host of competing labels that cover the same or similar territory as CSR, including corporate citizenship, sustainable business, corporate responsibility, and corporate social performance). Until the 1990s, publications on CSR came in peaks and troughs, rather than a steady rise (De Bakker *et al.*, 2005). And even since then, knowledge on CSR has arguably been more expansive than accumulative. For a subject that has been studied for so long, it is unusual to discover that researchers still do not share a common definition or set of core principles, that they still argue about what it means to be socially responsible, or even whether firms should have social responsibilities in the first place. Empirical researchers have been similarly unable to agree on the answer to the one question that has dominated CSR research probably more than any other over the past 30 years, which is whether CSR is good for business or not. Thus, a subject that even its proponents regard as 'that most naïve of concepts' (Mintzberg, 1983: 14), and which its critics acknowledge has 'won the battle of ideas' (Crook, 2005), has become a major area of research despite a degree of ambiguity and disagreement that might ordinarily be expected to lead to its demise (Hirsch and Levin, 1999).

The prominence now afforded to CSR as an academic field in part reflects the growing attention to the subject in the arenas of business, civil society, and government across the globe. This higher profile of CSR has been manifested in several ways. It has acquired distinctive organizational status within companies (e.g. in the designations of managers, staff teams, board-level responsibilities, etc.), from where an outpouring of CSR programs, reports, and other forms of corporate communications has issued in recent years. Evidence suggests that 90% of the largest European companies now publish substantial information on their social and environmental impacts (Context, 2006), whilst more than 50% of the largest firms globally produce a stand-alone CSR report under one label or another (KPMG, 2005). CSR campaigns have long been a significant feature of major Western multinationals such as BP, McDonald's, Nike, and Shell, but have also been manifested in Asian, African, and Latin American corporations, as well as small and medium-sized enterprises (Crane *et al.*, 2007).

Another factor increasing the importance of CSR is the substantial increase in socially responsible investment (SRI) funds that has occurred over the past decade (see Kurtz, Chapter 11). More generally, there has been a mushrooming of dedicated CSR consultancies and service organizations, as well as a burgeoning number of CSR standards, watchdogs, auditors, and certifiers aiming at institutionalizing and harmonizing CSR practices globally (see Ethical Performance, 2007; Leipziger, 2003). Governmental and intergovernmental organizations have also attempted to encourage investment in CSR, better reporting of social impacts by corporations, and the implementation of CSR initiatives that complement broader public policies. Similarly, various activists and NGOs have sought not only to promote CSR, but also to bring critical perspectives to bear and to raise CSR standards. Finally, there has been an increase in attention to CSR in mainstream print and electronic media as well as the emergence of dedicated CSR business publications, email lists, and newsletters.

What exactly these developments in the CSR 'movement' mean, of course, remains open to debate: whilst some see it as a management trend, others view it as a framework of 'soft regulation' that places new demands on corporations, whilst others present it as a way for corporate actors to assist in social and economic development (Sahlin-Andersson, 2006). However, given the current interest in CSR, as well as the unusual path that the development of the literature has taken, it is, we would suggest, timely now to pause and reflect on what, if anything, we have learnt about CSR over the past decades. With a cornucopia of concepts, theories, and evidence emerging to ostensibly make sense of CSR, there is a clear need to establish some markers in the field to identify where we have got to, where we have come from, and where the future might take us in thinking and writing about CSR.

This Handbook seeks to offer such a critical reflection on some of the major debates that coalesce around the subject of CSR. Bringing together a range of voices from within, across, and around the management literature, the book is intended to be the most authoritative account available of the CSR literature as it stands today, from the world's leading scholars in the area. In this introduction, we will provide an overview of CSR as a subject of academic inquiry, discuss the institutionalization of the CSR literature, and outline the guiding principles that we have adopted in assembling the *Handbook* and selecting the contributors.

CSR as a Field of Academic Inquiry: Definitions and Boundaries

Few subjects in management arouse as much controversy and contestation as CSR. As will become clear in reading the chapters in this volume, definitions of the term abound to the extent that even now 'there is no strong consensus on a definition for CSR' (McWilliams *et al.*, 2006). If, like corporate citizenship, CSR is an 'essentially contested concept' (Moon *et al.*, 2005), this may be inevitable. Archie Carroll (see Chapter 2) provides an extensive overview of some of these definitions, but even if we compare just two early examples, we can see a great deal of variation in different authors' assumptions about what firms should be responsible for. Whilst Milton Friedman (1970) contends that 'the social responsibility of the firm is to increase its profits', Keith Davis (1973: 312) argues that CSR requires 'consideration of issues beyond the narrow economic, technical, and legal requirements of the firm'. Similarly, in the current volume, the definitions provided by the chapter authors range from CSR as an 'obligation to respond to the externalities created by market action' (Salazar and Husted, Chapter 6), to CSR as 'discretionary spending in furtherance of an explicit measurable social objective consistent with relevant social norms and laws' (Dunfee, Chapter 15), and CSR as entailing 'an additional political responsibility to contribute to the development and proper working of global governance' (Scherer and Palazzo, Chapter 18). Many of our contributors understandably discuss problems in reaching a concrete definition of CSR in this context, whilst others perhaps wisely avoid the matter entirely and deliberately choose to focus on specific elements only.

What is clear then is that defining CSR is not just a technical exercise in describing what corporations do in society. Definitional work in CSR is also a normative exercise in setting out what corporations should be responsible for in society, or even an ideological exercise in describing how the political economy of society should be organized to restrain corporate power (Marens, 2004). In this context, it is understandable that the status of CSR as a well-defined and widely agreed upon concept in the management literature remains elusive. Indeed, without clear agreement on its core tenets, it would seem unwarranted and probably unnecessary even to classify CSR as a theoretical construct or concept in the first place.

We would suggest, therefore, that for the purposes of this *Handbook*, CSR is best understood not as a concept, a construct, or a theory but as a *field of scholarship* (Lockett *et al.*, 2006). The reason for this is that although various authors have developed important and influential concepts, constructs, and theories of CSR, these are competing with many other concepts, constructs, and theories of CSR. Thus, a comprehensive overview of CSR has to accommodate such difference rather than eschew it in favor of a closely defined term. That said, we might at least suggest that at the core of these debates is the subject of the social obligations and impacts of corporations in society.

Bibliometric analyses of the CSR literature show that despite its identifiable set of core concerns, not to mention its relatively long history, CSR is still a developing field of research. De Bakker *et al.*'s (2005) analysis of over 500 articles on CSR from the last 30 years led them to conclude that 'the field is vibrant and developing', but that 'a refinement and further operationalization of the general central concepts' is not evident. Similarly, Lockett *et al.* (2006: 133) recently concluded from a study of the CSR literature over a ten-year period that 'CSR knowledge could best be described as in a *continuing state of emergence*. While the field appears well established . . . it is not characterised by the domination of a particular theoretical approach, assumptions and method.' It is, they suggested, 'a field without a paradigm'.

The lack of a clear paradigm for CSR research should not necessarily be seen as a weakness for a field that is still in a state of emergence. However, it does mean that anyone looking for a field marked by clarity, consensus, and cohesiveness is likely to be disappointed. The field of scholarship that CSR represents is a broad and diverse one, encompassing debates from many perspectives, disciplines, and ideological positions. It is located at an intersection of many contributing disciplines. Its natural home is arguably in the management literature, but even here, CSR has been approached from a variety of subdisciplines such as strategy, marketing, accounting, operations management, and organizational behavior. Notably, work on CSR has also increasingly originated from other sources, such as law, economics, political science, development studies, geography, area studies, sociology, and history, amongst others. This brings to the literature a diversity of theoretical perspectives, conceptual approaches, and empirical traditions that does little to engender consensus around core concepts, but does much to enrich and enliven the debate.

Institutionalization of CSR as a Field of Scholarship

The relative ambiguities discussed earlier in this chapter regarding the definition and clear identity of CSR as an area of academic inquiry are also reflected in the institutional infrastructure of CSR, most notably the journals where CSR research is published, the societies and conferences which facilitate scholarly debate, and the institutionalization of CSR as a field of academic teaching.

Table 1.1 provides an overview of the key specialist journals that would typically be considered as the most likely places to find published CSR research. Conspicuously, with one fairly recent exception, none of the journals has CSR in its title. Rather the debate has taken place under the broader umbrella of 'business and society' or with a more disciplinary focus under the label of 'business ethics'. While these journals would be considered the main specialist CSR journals, and indeed many important contributions can be found in these journals, we would like to add three important observations. First, a considerable number of—often even seminal—contributions have been published in so-called mainstream management journals (Lockett *et al.*, 2006), such as the *Academy of Management Journal*, the *Academy of Management Review, California Management Review*, or *Harvard Business Review*. In a similar vein, we have seen a considerable number of special

Table 1.1 Academic journals in the field of Corporate Social Responsibility

Journal name	Formation date	Current editor based in
Business & Society (Sage)	1960	USA
Business and Society Review (Blackwell)	1972	USA
Journal of Business Ethics (Springer)	1982	Canada
Business Ethics Quarterly (Society for Business Ethics)	1991	USA
Business Ethics: A European Review (Blackwell)	1991	UK
Corporate Governance: the International Journal of Business in Society (Emerald)	2001	UK
Journal of Corporate Citizenship (Greenleaf)	2001	UK
Corporate Social Responsibility and Environmental Management (previously *Ecomanagement and Auditing*, Wiley)	2002	China (Hong Kong)

issues dedicated to CSR in mainstream journals, such as the *Journal of International Business Studies* (vol. 37, no. 6) or the *Journal of Management Studies* (vol. 43, no. 1). These developments towards mainstream acceptance of CSR as an academic field of scholarship apply not only to US-based management journals but also to some of the more critical organization theory journals in Europe, such as *Organization Studies* or *Organization*, which have recently started to publish more CSR-related research.

Second, even though the journals in Table 1.1 can be considered the main CSR journals, there are a number of outlets close to the topic which many scholars interested in CSR would consider a natural outlet for their work. Journals focusing on sustainability and environmental management, such as *Organization & Environment*, *Business Strategy and the Environment*, or *Sustainable Development* have all published research which—with a focus on the natural environment—could also be considered to be a contribution to the wider CSR debate. Next to environmental management, the field of accounting has also made a considerable contribution to CSR knowledge, in particular the journals *Accounting, Organizations and Society*, *Accounting, Auditing and Accountability Journal*, and *Critical Perspectives on Accounting*. Many papers published in these journals today would be considered as core contributions to the CSR literature. A similar overlap can be witnessed in the area of corporate governance, where for instance *Corporate Governance: An International Review* and *Journal of Management and Governance* have published a considerable number of papers and special issues on governance-related aspects of CSR. Another neighboring area would be public management and public affairs, where for instance the *Journal of Public Affairs* has published a sizeable number of papers on classic topics of CSR. In addition to these neighboring fields in management studies, there is also a considerable debate on CSR in journals in economics, politics, international relations, law, and sociology which clearly reflects the interdisciplinary nature of the emerging CSR field.

A third observation would be that while most of these main journals are published in North America and the UK there is a considerable debate on CSR going on in various non-English languages. Examples are the Italian *Etica degli Affari e delle Professione* (founded 1988), the French *Revue Ethique des Affaires* (1995), the German *Zeitschrift für Wirtschafts- und Unternehmensethik* (2000), or most recently and more pronounced in CSR, the French *Revue de l'Organisation Responsible— Responsible Organization Review* (2005).

Beyond the world of academic journal publishing, it is also worth noting that we have lately witnessed a growing number of edited collections on key topics in CSR. While this *Oxford Handbook of Corporate Social Responsibility* for the first time attempts to take stock of the entire debate, similar efforts have been undertaken in specific topics of CSR, such as stakeholder management (Andriof *et al.*, 2002, 2003), sustainability (Sharma and Starik, 2002; Starik and Sharma, 2005), global aspects of CSR (Doh and Stumpf, 2005) or corporate citizenship (Scherer and Palazzo, forthcoming). In a similar category, we should also mention the books in the series Research in Corporate Social Performance and Policy (JAI Press, started in 1978), which for many years published some of the key contributions to the CSR literature.

An important indicator of the institutionalization of CSR can also be seen in the growing number of conferences and learned societies interested in CSR. Among the most longstanding are we could mention the Society for Business Ethics (SBE) and the Social Issues in Management-Division of the Academy of Management (SIM), both of which bring together many scholars from all over the world in their annual meetings in North America. Similarly, the International Association for Business and Society (IABS) serves as a platform for CSR research with a specific mission to bring together scholars from both sides of the Atlantic. More focused on business ethics is the International Society for Business, Ethics and Economics (ISBEE), which understands itself as a global organization, and hosts a large international conference every four years in a different continent. There are also more regionally focused initiatives, such as the European Business Ethics Network (EBEN) or, more recently and more focused on CSR, the European Academy of Business in Society (EABiS, founded in 2002), both of which have annual conferences, and a plethora of smaller workshops and seminars. Many of the more recent initiatives, such as the Hong Kong- and Singapore-based CSR Asia or the German national chapter of EBEN, the *Deutsches Netzwerk Wirtschaftsethik* (DNWE), have a large involvement by practitioners and industry, reflecting the growing demand for CSR expertise in many companies in the respective countries and regions. Given the recent surge in interest in CSR outside the United States we witness a growing number of initiatives in many European countries and beyond, such as the French *Association pour le Développement de l'Enseignement et de la Recherche sur la Responsabilité Sociale de l'Entreprise* (ADERSE), or a growing number of national chapters of EBEN, to establish national learned societies facilitating scholarly exchange in CSR.

Traditionally, CSR research has often been established at universities in special units, centers, or institutes. US examples include the Center for Business Ethics at Bentley College or the Olsson Centre for Applied Ethics at the University of Virginia. The growth in interest in CSR globally is reflected by a considerable surge in new research units dedicated to CSR at many universities in Europe (e.g. International Centre for Corporate Social Responsibility, Nottingham; Department for Business-Society Management, Rotterdam), Australia (e.g. Corporate Citizenship Research Unit, Deakin), India (e.g. Centre for Corporate Governance and Citizenship, Indian Institute of Management, Bangalore), China (e.g. CSR Asia, Hong Kong), and South Africa (e.g. African Institute of Corporate Citizenship, UNISA).

Relatedly, many of those who contribute to the CSR research are educators, and mainly business or management school educators. As Windsor (Chapter 22) outlines, there has been considerable debate about the general role of business school education for responsible management and about the status and nature of CSR education therein. Notwithstanding earlier claims of an intellectual bias against business ethics in business schools (e.g. Hosmer, 1999), there is some evidence of a greater interest in consolidating the CSR field in at least certain business schools around the world as presented by the *Beyond Grey Pinstripes* reports (World Resources Institute, various years).

However, the focus remains quite heterogeneous. A study of CSR education in Europe (Matten and Moon, 2004) confirmed our general finding of the variety of underlying meanings of CSR scholarship. Programs and modules described as CSR were offered under a range of labels including business ethics, CSR, environmental management, and sustainable development.

All of this points to a burgeoning and multifaceted field of scholarship. Our tasks in this book are to try and provide a comprehensive overview of this field, offer ways of navigating through the academic terrain of corporate social responsibility, and set out some markers for where we are, where we have come from, and where we are going as academics working in the field.

THE SCOPE OF THE CONTRIBUTIONS IN THIS VOLUME

The range of contributions and the variety of backgrounds of the contributors to this volume provide an impressive overview of the debate on CSR. First, there are a number of contributors who count among the main voices in CSR and have informed our fundamental understanding of the concept and the wider field. Among these are *Archie Carroll, Tom Dunfee, Bill Frederick,* and *David Vogel,* who for the last four decades have published on CSR and who, among others, can be considered among the most longstanding contributors to this area of research. Besides these leading voices, the authors brought together in this volume also showcase the breadth and variety of disciplinary backgrounds which are necessary to understand CSR. This pertains, first, to management or business studies as a discipline itself, where CSR cuts across all the usual specializations—as such, this volume brings together perspectives from accounting, business ethics, critical management, finance, international business, marketing, organizational theory, strategy, and sustainability. As we have already noted, there has also always been a lively debate on the role and responsibilities of business in neighboring disciplines. This volume therefore reflects the interdisciplinary nature of the subject of CSR and brings together perspectives from a large variety of social sciences, most notably cultural studies, economics, international relations, law, philosophy, politics, and sociology. In assembling such a variety of perspectives the contributions in this volume demonstrate the need for an inter- and trans-disciplinary approach to CSR.

It has often been argued that CSR is an essentially American idea that reflects a specific understanding of the role of markets, governments, business, and civil society. As this is certainly true with regard to the origins of the CSR debate, it does not come as a surprise that the majority of contributions in this volume are authored by scholars based at academic institutions in the United States. The range of authors, however, also reflects the recent global spread of CSR, bringing together scholars based in, or with close links to, Canada, Denmark, Germany, Israel, Mexico, Spain, South Africa, Switzerland, and the United Kingdom.

KEY BUILDING BLOCKS OF CSR

The book is structured into seven substantive parts. After this introductory part, Part II is dedicated to mapping out the perspectives on CSR. These have varied over time, by academic discipline, and among national business systems. The purpose of this part is therefore to provide an overview of these different perspectives and to explain how they relate to, complement, or challenge one another.

In Chapter 2 *Archie Carroll* provides a comprehensive historical overview of the main practices and ideas in CSR over the last 50 years. This demonstrates a significant legacy of disparate conceptual work in the area, which in Chapter 3 *Domènec Melé* takes stock of to provide a state-of-the-art review of CSR theory.

In contrast to Chapter 2, which provides an historical overview, this chapter is structured more analytically in order to group and distinguish specific theoretical approaches to the subject. While many see CSR as an imperative based on non-economic, most notably ethical and social grounds, a vast amount of the CSR literature has aimed at showing that socially responsible behavior in fact can also make very good business sense. This debate is addressed by *Elizabeth Kurucz, Barry Colbert*, and *David Wheeler* in Chapter 4 who discuss the basic arguments around the business case for CSR. In fact, this literature is one of the most developed areas in CSR and has led to a debate around the social and financial performance of the corporation and ways in which these can be measured and managed—which is the focus of Chapter 5 by *Marc Orlitzky*.

Even where there is agreement about the meaning of CSR, its application and scope are often contested in both normative and empirical terms. Conspicuously, one of the key features of CSR has always been its contested nature. Even at the early stages of its emergence as a business practice in the United States it solicited the most heated antagonism and venomous critique, illustrated most famously by Milton Friedman's (1970) landmark newspaper article as well as, more recently, a skeptical survey on CSR in *The Economist* in 2005 (Crook, 2005). Part III therefore takes stock of the critiques of CSR, starting with Chapter 6 by *José Salazar and Bryan Husted* who examine the Friedman critique and refine it with a more nuanced view of agency from an economic perspective. CSR, though, has not only been met with skepticism from right-wing economists such as Friedman but also from the left of the political spectrum. Chapter 7 by *Gerry Hanlon* provides an overview of the latter debate, highlighting, for example, elements of the Marxist critique of CSR. Chapter 8 by *Tim Kuhn* and *Stan Deetz* goes on to examine CSR from the angle of critical theory while in Chapter 9 *Hans van Oosterhout* and *Pursey Heugens* refute the underlying conceptual need for CSR in the first place. All told, these critiques offer some serious challenges to the CSR field, although the conclusions reached by each of the contributors differ as to their degree of optimism or pessimism regarding its potential.

Part IV turns to the multifaceted arena in which CSR is enacted by corporations and provides a detailed analysis of the key actors and their roles in driving CSR. First, in Chapter 10, *Diane Swanson* looks at managers and their role and motivation in driving CSR. Chapter 11 by *Lloyd Kurtz* looks at shareholder activism and the industry that has emerged around socially responsible investment, which has put pressure on publicly listed companies to comply with basic ethical and social standards. In a similar vein, Chapter 12 by *Craig Smith* surveys the potential and limits of consumers in demanding socially responsible behavior through their decisions at the checkout. Finally, Chapter 13 by *Jeremy Moon* and *David Vogel* examines the role of governments and civil society in shaping and encouraging CSR.

As we have argued above, there has been quite controversy about the status of CSR as a 'subject', 'management discipline', or 'field', much of which is fuelled by the fact that claims to more socially responsible behavior reach the corporation in nearly every aspect of its operations. Thus, it is rather difficult to establish a distinct set of management concepts, tools, and areas which are unique to CSR as such. There are however some aspects of management where CSR might arguably claim to provide a distinct contribution to the arsenal of management concepts and tools. The discussion in Part V then starts with the area of corporate governance, where CSR thinking has arguably had the biggest impact. Chapter 14 by *Ann Buch-holtz, Jill Brown*, and *Kareem Shabana* outlines the relationship between corporate governance and CSR. *Tom Dunfee* in Chapter 15 provides a basic understanding of stakeholder thinking, arguably one of the very few theoretical frameworks generated by the CSR literature itself, to explore the management challenges of CSR. *Andrew Millington* in Chapter 16 then provides a comprehensive overview of one of the main areas where CSR issues have impacted upon firms across the globe, namely the supply chain. Probably one of the most distinct management areas which CSR can claim to have created over the last years is the area of social and environmental accounting. *David Owen* and *Brendan O'Dwyer* map out this area of corporate involvement in CSR in Chapter 17.

From the early 1970s—in the context of Western corporations' role in apartheid South Africa—up to the very recent time—linked to debates on sweatshop labor, fair trade, or the global fight against HIV/AIDS—the CSR agenda has been decisively pushed by international issues. Part VI turns attention to this arena. First, in Chapter 18 *Andreas Scherer* and *Guido Palazzo* analyze the advent of globalization and delineate its impact on the corporation and its social responsibilities. They suggest that the corporation, as a responsible actor at the global level, positions business next to governments and NGOs in the arena of global governance. Chapter 19 by *David Levy* and *Rami Kaplan* provides a basic understanding of this critical issue by providing theoretical perspectives, mostly drawn from politics and international relations, to understand the new challenges for the corporate world at the global level. As we argued above, the main debate on CSR over the last 50 years has been strongly focused on North America, but the more recent attention to its global diffusion suggests the need to understand CSR in comparative perspective. Thus, in Chapter 20, *Cynthia Williams* and *Ruth Aguilera* go on to explore how CSR can reflect wider national business and governance systems, such as market structures and rules, institutional norms, and respective responsibilities of governments, corporations and other social actors. A particularly exposed role, most notably for multinational corporations from the global north, is emerging for corporations in developing countries. *Wayne Visser* maps out the crucial role and responsibilities for business in fighting poverty and acting responsibly in developing countries in Chapter 21.

While the area of CSR is mature enough to warrant the effort of a comprehensive overview in the Oxford Handbook series, it is still a relatively young and currently a very dynamic area. The final part invites the reader to share some of the expectations and visions of thought leaders in CSR with regard to future developments in the field. This pertains, first of all, to its role as an established element in the curriculum of (business) education. In Chapter 22 *Duane Windsor* discusses the current status of CSR in MBA education (as the flagship product of business schools) and assesses the state-of-the-art as well as the demands for future curriculum development. With five short essays by *Bill Frederick*; *Alison Mackey*, *Tyson Mackey*, and *Jay Barney*; *Tom Donaldson*; *Peter Pruzan*; and *Ulrich Steger*, the book then finishes with personal impressions on the future of CSR by well-known experts from both sides of the Atlantic. The book closes with some conclusions by the editors.

This *Handbook* is an attempt to try and make sense of these interweaving, yet disparate strands of literature in so far as they help us to understand the messy and multifaceted reality of CSR. We do not seek as much as to clear up the confusion that characterizes the field, but more to identify the core areas of research activity and establish the key themes, arguments, and findings that may be relevant to those areas. The book is intended to be a milestone in setting out where the CSR literature has come from, and where it is (or could be) going to in order to provide some kind of coherent overview or orientation for scholars working in the field.

REFERENCES

ANDRIOF, J., WADDOCK, S., HUSTED, B., and SUTHERLAND RAHMAN, S. (eds.). 2002. *Unfolding Stakeholder Thinking 1: Theory, Responsibility and Engagement.* Sheffield: Greenleaf.

————————(eds.). 2003. *Unfolding Stakeholder Thinking 2: Relationships, Communication, Reporting and Performance.* Sheffield: Greenleaf.

Context. 2006. 'Global Corporate Responsibility Trends'. London: Context.

CRANE, A., MATTEN, D., and SPENCE, L. 2007. *Corporate Social Responsibility: Readings and Cases in Global Context.* London: Routledge.

CROOK, C. 2005. 'The Good Company'. *The Economist*, 374, 22 Jan.: 20 pp.

DAVIS, K. 1973. 'The Case for and against Business Assumption of Social Responsibilities'. *Academy of Management Journal*, 16(2): 312–22.

DE BAKKER, G. A., GROENWEGEN, P., and DEN HOND, F. 2005. 'A Bibliometric Analysis of 30 years of Research and Theory on Corporate Social Responsibility and Corporate Social Performance'. *Business & Society*, 44(3): 283–317.

DOH, J. P., and STUMPF, S. A. (eds.). 2005. *Handbook on Responsible Leadership and Governance in Global Business.* Northampton, Mass.: Edward Elgar.

ETHICAL PERFORMANCE. 2007. *CSR Professional Services Directory 2007.* Canterbury: Dunstans Publishing.

FRIEDMAN, M. 1970. 'The Social Responsibility of Business is to Increase its Profits'. *The New York Times Magazine*, 13 Sept. 1970: 32–3, 124–6.

HANDY, C. 2002. 'What's a Business For?' *Harvard Business Review*, 80(12): 49–56.

HIRSCH, P. M., and LEVIN, D. Z. 1999. 'Umbrella Advocates versus Validity Police: A Life-Cycle Model'. *Organization Science*, 10(2): 199–212.

HOSMER, L.T. 1999. 'Somebody out There Doesn't Like us: A study of the Position and Respect of Business Ethics at Schools of Business Administration'. *Journal of Business Ethics*, 22(1): 91–106.

KPMG. 2005. *International Survey of Corporate Responsibility Reporting*. Amsterdam: KPMG.

LEIPZIGER, D. 2003. *The Corporate Responsibility Code Book*. Sheffield: Greenleaf.

LOCKETT, A., MOON, J., and VISSER, W. 2006. 'Corporate Social Responsibility in Management Research: Focus, Nature, Salience and Sources of Influence'. *Journal of Management Studies*, 43(1): 115–36.

MCWILLIAMS, A., SIEGEL, D. S., and WRIGHT, P. M. 2006. 'Corporate Social Responsibility: Strategic Implications'. *Journal of Management Studies*, 43(1): 1–18.

MARENS, R. 2004. 'Wobbling on a One-Legged Stool: The Decline of American Pluralism and the Academic Treatment of Corporate Social Responsibility'. *Journal of Academic Ethics*, 2: 63–87.

MATTEN, D., and MOON, J. 2004. 'Corporate Social Responsibility Education in Europe'. *Journal of Business Ethics*, 5(4): 323–37.

MINTZBERG, H. 1983. 'The Case for Corporate Social Responsibility'. *Journal of Business Strategy*, 4(2): 3–15.

MOON, J., CRANE, A., and MATTEN, D. 2005. 'Can Corporations be Citizens? Corporate Citizenship as a Metaphor for Business Participation in Society'. *Business Ethics Quarterly*, 15(3): 427–51.

SAHLIN-ANDERSSON, K. 2006. 'Corporate Social Responsibility: A Trend and a Movement, but of What and For What?' *Corporate Governance*, 6(5): 595–608.

SCHERER, A. G., and PALAZZO, G. (eds.). Forthcoming. *Handbook of Research on Corporate Citizenship* Cheltenham: Edward Elgar.

SHARMA, S., and STARIK, M. (eds.). 2002. *Research in Corporate Sustainability*. Cheltenham: Edward Elgar.

STARIK, M., and SHARMA, S. (eds.). 2005. *New Horizons in Research on Sustainable Organisations: Emerging Ideas, Approaches and Tools for Practitioners and Researchers*. Sheffield: Greenleaf.

World Resources Institute. Various years. *Beyond Grey Pinstripes: Preparing MBAs for Social and Environmental Stewardship*. World Resources Institute, available at <http://www.beyondgreypinstripes.org/index.cfm>.

PART II

PERSPECTIVES
ON CORPORATE
SOCIAL
RESPONSIBILITY

....

A HISTORY OF CORPORATE SOCIAL RESPONSIBILITY

CONCEPTS AND PRACTICES

....

ARCHIE B. CARROLL

THOUGH the roots of the concept that we know today as corporate social responsibility have a long and wide-ranging history, it is mostly a product of the twentieth century, especially from the early 1950s up to the present time. In spite of its recent growth and popularity, one can trace for centuries evidence of the business community's concern for society. To help appreciate the context in which corporate social responsibility (CSR) grew and flourished, we will consider the late 1800s, or the Industrial Revolution, as a reasonable beginning point for purposes of discussion.

The purpose of this chapter on corporate social responsibility concepts and practices, referred to as just 'social responsibility' (SR) in the period before the rise and dominance of the corporate form of business organization, is to provide an overview of how the concept and practice of SR or CSR has grown, manifested itself, and flourished. In addition to considering how the concept has changed and grown in terms of its *meaning*, we will consider its *practice* as well. That is, we will consider how the concept has, in practice, expanded from its focus on a few stakeholders, close at hand, to be more far reaching and inclusive, eventually becoming global in scope.

In addition, we will briefly consider what organizational activities and changes have taken place to accommodate these new initiatives, to the point at which it has become fully institutionalized today. It will become apparent that today, well into the first decade of the 2000s, CSR in many firms is moving towards full integration with strategic management and corporate governance. This has included firms developing management and organizational mechanisms for reporting and control on business's socially conscious policies and practices. It will also become apparent that the range of stakeholders and issues defining CSR has broadened, especially in the past several decades.

Formal writings on social responsibility are largely a product of the twentieth century, especially the past 50 years or so. Though it is possible to see evidence of CSR throughout the world, mostly in the developed countries, most early writings have been most obvious in the United States where a sizable body of literature has accumulated (Cavrou, 1999). In the past decade, however, Europe has become captivated with CSR and there is considerable evidence that scholars and practitioners in Europe are taking seriously this social concern, often manifested in the form of formal writings, research, conferences, and consultancies. More recently, countries in Asia have begun increasing their attention to CSR policies and practices. At the same time, it must be acknowledged that CSR and related notions have been developed in practice and thought in a number of other countries and at different times. With this background in mind, this review of CSR's history will focus primarily on developments in the United States and Europe.

Social Initiatives and Practices
Prior to 1950

Since a good argument can be made that CSR began to take form in the 1950s, it is useful to consider some developments before that time in the way of providing context rather than detailed content. It is beneficial to begin with some of the activities and practices originating in the Industrial Revolution as a useful starting point. In examining the mid-to-late 1800s, it is apparent that emerging businesses were especially concerned with *employees* and how to make them more productive workers. Then, and now, it is sometimes difficult to differentiate what organizations are doing for business reasons, i.e. making the workers more productive, and what the organizations are doing for social reasons, i.e. helping to fulfill their needs and make them better and more contributing members of society.

According to management historian, Daniel A. Wren, there were criticisms of the emerging factory system in Great Britain, particularly regarding the employment of women and children, and these same issues occurred in America as well. Reformers in both countries perceived the factory system to be the source of numerous social problems, including labor unrest, poverty, slums, and child and female labor. Wren depicted the industrial betterment/welfare movement of this early period as an uneven mixture of humanitarianism, philanthropy, and business acumen. He points to industrialists such as John H. Patterson of National Cash Register as one executive instrumental in setting the course for the industrial welfare movement. Welfare schemes emanating from this movement sought to prevent labor problems and improve performance by taking actions which could be interpreted as both business and social. Examples included the provision of hospital clinics, bathhouses, lunch-rooms, profit sharing, recreational facilities, and other such practices (Wren, 2005: 269–70). Was the creation of these schemes to improve the workers' conditions appropriately thought of as business decisions or social decisions? Did they reflect companies taking some responsibility for their workers that extended beyond normal business requirements? It is impossible to decisively answer these questions, though both motives were apparently evident.

In addition to concern for employees, *philanthropy* was appearing on the scene in the late 1800s, but sometimes it was difficult to determine whether the philanthropy of such individuals as Cornelius Vanderbilt or John D. Rockefeller was *individual* philanthropy or *business* philanthropy. Muddying the waters were activities of questionable character that led to these individuals and others being dubbed 'robber barons' for some of their unscrupulous practices.

As Wren noted, many of these early business leaders were very generous and such philanthropy by business people had origins that began centuries earlier, including patrons of the arts, builders of churches, endowers of educational institutions, and providers of money for various community projects. Wren also pointed out that one of the major issues of the day was a legal question. Could the idea of (1) limited charter powers and (2) the concept of management as trustee of the stockholders' property work together to create the nineteenth-century legal basis for *corporate* philanthropy (pp. 109–10)?

Two cases cited by Wren depicted the ongoing debate over this legal question. The first occurred in Great Britain in 1883 when the West Cork Railroad Company tried to compensate its employees for job losses brought about by the dissolution of the corporation. In this case, Lord Justice Byron ruled that charity had no business at the table of the board of directors and that they could spend the company's money only for purposes of carrying on the business.

In another case involving Steinway, by contrast, the court permitted the piano manufacturer to buy an adjoining tract of land to be used for a church, library, and school for its employees. In this case, the court saw 'improved employee relations' as a major benefit accruing to the company. These are some of the early struggles with corporate philanthropy and it would be decades later before company managements could engage in philanthropy that provided benefits to the general community or community groups (p. 110). In spite of this, individual entrepreneurs and business owners for years gave of their own money to support social causes that today might be categorized as socially responsible.

Another early practice illustrated how business people were thinking about social causes and striving to do something about them within the context of their businesses. Morrell Heald illustrated how company expenditures on community causes were quite evident in the late 1800s. He cites the case of the R. H. Macy Company of New York City that might have reflected a social sensitivity on the part of its management. The firm's records show that there were enough cases of company assistance rendered to social agencies to document a sense of relationship to the community that extended beyond the walls of the company. In 1875, Macy's contributed funds to an orphan asylum. In 1887, company gifts to charities were listed under Miscellaneous Expenses in the company's books (Heald, 1970: 7).

Heald highlights two other early programs at the turn of the century that suggested some degree of social responsibility was being taken on by companies, though they were never called social responsibility. First, there was the example of *paternalism*. An excellent example of paternalism was manifested in what historians have called the Pullman experiment. In 1893, a model industrial community at Pullman was created south of Chicago. George M. Pullman of the Pullman Palace Car Company created a community town that was quite a showplace and was considered by some to be an example of enlightened business policy. The town was built with standards of housing, appearance, lighting, and maintenance that were far more advanced than the times. The community was populated by parks, playgrounds, a church, an arcade, a theatre, a casino, and a hotel. One person who knew Pullman, and who had visited the town often, testified to George Pullman's genuine interest in improving living conditions for his employees and their families as well as creating an improved capacity for attracting and retaining employees (Heald, 1970: 7–9).

Second, Heald cites the case of the YMCAs (Young Men's Christian Associations) as a good example of early social responsibility initiatives. Begun in London in 1844, the YMCA movement quickly spread to the United States. The YMCAs were supported not only by individuals, but by companies as well. Just before World War I, there appeared growth of company giving for community-related welfare and social programs became closely associated with the YMCAs, especially linked to the railroad companies (Heald, 1970: 13–14).

During the period 1918–29, Heald has suggested that the 'community chest movement' also helped to shape business views of philanthropy, one of the earliest forms of CSR. As business executives came into contact with social workers, new views of corporate responsibility began to emerge. Business leaders began to be exposed to others' views as to what constituted social problems in society and became somewhat conscious of the mission of social agencies. As professional voices arose from the social service communities, business people were hearing from individuals whose education and professional training merited respect, and their views on the relationship between business and society could not be easily dismissed (pp. 118–19).

Though there was some evidence of socially responsible business behavior as noted above, this was not always the general case. Nicholas Eberstadt has observed that in the late 1800s a charter of incorporation was a favor bestowed only on those businesses that were socially useful. But, by the end of the Civil War, charters were available under any business pretext, and were nearly impossible to revoke. Large corporations began to dominate the economy and many of these firms had the power of governments. Concentrated economic power was drawn into the hands of a few, and this raised up a corporate ruling class with almost limitless power. Power corrupted, and many business leaders and captains of industry began holding their fellow citizens and the government in contempt. The monopolies and trusts that these leaders were able to create and cultivate frequently defied the rules of market pricing and even stockholders were sometimes cheated by these business leaders. Eberstadt observed that 'indeed, business might never have turned back toward responsibility and accountability if the culmination of corporate irresponsibility had not been the collapse of the economic system' (Eberstadt, 1973: 21–2). What followed, of course, was the Great Depression and massive unemployment and business failure and the post-Depression period ushered in the next period of business and society relationships.

Robert Hay and Ed Gray characterized the period we have been describing up to this point in time as the 'profit maximizing management' phase in the development of social responsibility. The second phase, which they dubbed the 'trusteeship management' phase, emerged in the 1920s and 1930s, resulting from changes occurring both in business and society. Trusteeship, in their view, saw corporate managers taking on the responsibility for both maximizing stockholder wealth and creating and maintaining an equitable balance among other competing claims, such as claims from customers, employees, and the community (Hay and Gray, 1974). Thus, the manager started to be viewed as the 'trustee' for the various groups in relationship with business and were not seen just as agents of the company. Hay and Gray believed two major trends brought these changes about: (1) the mounting diffusion of stock ownership, and (2) a gradually more pluralistic society.

Philanthropy, or corporate contributions, have assumed a central role in the development of CSR since the beginning of the time periods being examined. According to Sophia Muirhead (1999) in a research report for The Conference Board, the period of the 1870s to 1930s should be considered the 'prelegalization period' of corporate contributions. Prior to the 1900s, corporate contributions were perceived by many in a negative light, being seen as giving away stockholders' assets without their approval. Also, corporate contributions were legally restricted to causes that benefited the company. During this period, the beneficiaries were primarily related to World War I, to include the YMCA/YWCA, United Way Campaign, Boy Scouts, Salvation Army, and Community/War Chests.

In the increasingly 'corporate period,' (1930 to the present), according to Eberstadt, the corporations began to be seen as institutions, like the government, that had social obligations to fulfill (Eberstadt, 1973: 22). As business grew in the 1940s, and World War II, Eberstadt argued that companies thought they were being socially responsible by standing up as an anti-Communist institution.

If we consider the writings on social responsibility that were influential in the pre-1950s consideration of the topic, it should be noted that references to a concern for social responsibility appeared, for example, during the 1930s and 1940s in the United States. Works from this period worth noting included Chester Barnard's *The Functions of the Executive* (1938), J. M. Clark's *Social Control of Business* (1939), and Theodore Kreps's *Measurement of the Social Performance of Business* (1940), to point out just a few.

From a more practical point of view, it should be noted that as early as 1946 business executives (they were called *businessmen* in those days) were polled by *Fortune* magazine asking them about their social responsibilities. The results of this survey suggest what was developing in the minds of business people in the 1940s. One question asked the businessmen whether they were responsible for the consequences of their actions in a sphere wider than that covered by their profit-and-loss statements. Specifically, the question was 'do you think that businessmen should recognize such responsibilities and do their best to fulfill them?' Of those polled, 93.5% said 'yes'. Second, they were asked 'about what proportion of the businessmen you know would you rate as having a social consciousness of this sort?' The most frequent responses were in the categories of 'about a half' and 'about three quarters' (*Fortune*, Mar. 1946, 197–8, cited in Bowen, 1953: 44.). These results seem to support the idea that the concept of trusteeship or stewardship was a growing phenomenon among business leaders.

There is no easy way to summarize how the concept of social responsibility was growing in the industrialized world prior to the 1950s. The previous discussion, however, touched upon some of the developing themes and examples which set the stage for CSR's formal birth and growth in the 1950s.

CSR TAKES SHAPE IN THE 1950S

Before discussing the 1950s, it is useful to set forth what Patrick Murphy (*University of Michigan Business Review*, 1978) classified as four CSR eras that embraced the period before and after the 1950s. In a simplified scheme, Murphy argued that the period up to the 1950s was the 'philanthropic' era in which companies donated to charities more than anything else. The period 1953–67 was classified as the 'awareness' era, in which there became more recognition of the overall responsibility of business and its involvement in community affairs. The period 1968–73 was termed the 'issue' era in which companies began focusing on specific issues such as urban decay, racial discrimination, and pollution problems. Finally, in the 'responsiveness' era, 1974–8, and, continuing beyond, companies began taking serious management and organizational actions to address CSR issues. These actions would include altering boards of directors, examining corporate ethics, and using social performance disclosures. Though it is difficult to delineate specific dates regarding such era classifications, Murphy's interpretation is useful and generally consistent with our discussion to this point and to come.

As stated previously, corporate social responsibility was often referred to more as social responsibility (SR) than corporate social responsibility (CSR) for many years. This may be because the age of the modern corporation's prominence and dominance in the business sector had not yet occurred nor been noted. Howard R. Bowen's publication of his landmark book *Social Responsibilities of the Businessman* (1953) best marks the beginnings of the modern period of literature on this subject. As the title of Bowen's book suggests, there apparently were no business*women* during this period, or at least they were not acknowledged in formal writings.

Bowen's treatment of CSR proceeded from the belief that the several hundred largest businesses at the time were vital centers of power and decision making and that the actions of these firms touched the lives of citizens in many ways. Among the many questions raised by Bowen, one is of special relevance here. He inquired: 'What responsibilities to society may businessmen reasonably be expected to assume?' (p. xi). Interestingly, we are still asking this same question today.

What did Bowen mean by SR or CSR? Bowen was one of the first to articulate a definition as to what SR means. He set forth an initial definition of the social responsibilities of businessmen as follows:

It (SR) refers to the obligations of businessmen to pursue those policies, to make those decisions, or to follow those lines of action which are desirable in terms of the objectives and values of our society. (p. 6)

Bowen's book was specifically concerned with the doctrine of social responsibility. Thus it is easy to see how it commenced the modern, serious discussion on the topic. Bowen goes on to argue that social responsibility is no panacea for all business social problems, but that it contains an important truth that must guide business in the future. Because of Bowen's early and seminal work, Carroll has argued that Howard Bowen should be called the 'Father of Corporate Social Responsibility' (Carroll, 2006: 5).

Bowen's book and definition represented the most noteworthy literature from the 1950s.

For further evidence of the extent to which business people were adopting and practicing CSR during this time, and earlier, Morrell Heald's (1970) *The Social Responsibilities of Business: Company and Community, 1900–1960*, is a thorough source. Though Heald does not succinctly state definitions of social responsibility, he provides an interesting and provocative discussion of the theory and circumstances surrounding CSR during the first half of the twentieth century.

It is clear from Heald's discussions that CSR was defined consistently with the Bowen characterization previously presented. Other important literature from the 1950s included Selekman's *Moral Philosophy for Management* (1959); Heald's 'Management's Responsibility to Society: The Growth of an Idea' (1957), and Eels's *Corporate Giving in a Free Society* (1956).

In summarizing what CSR meant in the 1950s, William C. Frederick, one of the early pioneers of CSR, asserted that there were three core ideas in the 1950s: the idea of corporate managers as public trustees, the idea of balancing competing claims to corporate resources, and the acceptance of philanthropy as a manifestation of business support of good causes (Frederick, 2006). The idea of trusteeship commenced in the 1920s and matured as it was practiced into the 1950s. The idea of balancing competing claims prefigured the stakeholder era. Philanthropy, probably one of the most tangible CSR practices, grew into popularity from the Community Chest movement, later called the United Way. It, too, began in about the 1920s.

Philanthropy, or corporate contributions as manifestations of CSR, was said by Muirhead, who wrote a history of corporate contributions, to be in a period of 'innovation and legalization' during the 1940s and 1950s. During this period, giving continued to be ad hoc, somewhat subject to executive whim, and primarily in response to requests by beneficiary organizations. Recipients included the YMCA, American Red Cross, local community chests, and local hospitals (Muirhead, 1999: 15).

The decade of the 1950s was one of more 'talk' than 'action' with respect to CSR. It was a period of changing attitudes, with business executives learning to get comfortable with CSR talk. There were very few corporate actions, beyond philanthropy, to report that stood out in terms of accommodating this new theme, though Howard Bowen demonstrated how he was ahead of his time by calling for specific management and organizational changes for improving business responsiveness to the growing social concern. Bowen's proposals included changes in the composition of boards of directors, greater representation of the social viewpoint in management, use of the social audit, social education of business managers, development of business codes of conduct, and further research in the social sciences (Bowen, 1953: 151–63). There was not much evidence that any of this was done in the 1950s, or even soon thereafter, but Bowen placed on the table for further thought and reflection a number of interesting management strategies that years later would surface and become standard practices with respect to managing CSR.

CSR CONCEPTS AND PRACTICES
PROLIFERATE IN THE 1960S

If there was limited evidence of CSR thought in the 1950s and before, the decade of the 1960s marked a momentous growth in attempts to formalize or more precisely state what CSR meant. In the 1960s, we began to see scholars striving to best state what CSR meant. One of the first, and most prominent, writers in this period to define CSR was Keith Davis, who later extensively wrote about the topic in his business and society textbooks, later revisions, and articles. Davis set forth his definition of social responsibility by arguing that it refers to: 'Businessmen's decisions and actions taken for reasons at least partially beyond the firm's direct economic or technical interest' (Davis, 1960: 70). Davis argued that social responsibility was a nebulous idea but should be seen in a managerial context. Further, he asserted that some socially responsible business decisions can be justified by a long, complicated process of reasoning as having a good chance of bringing long-run economic gain to the firm, thus paying it back for its socially responsible viewpoint (p. 70). Davis was on the cutting edge with this insight, inasmuch as this view became commonly accepted by the late 1970s and 1980s. Davis's contributions to early definitions of CSR were so important that he should be considered as the runner-up to Howard Bowen for the 'Father of CSR' designation.

Another influential contributor to the early definitions of social responsibility was William C. Frederick (1960, 1978, 1998). One of his views is stated below:

Social responsibility in the final analysis implies a public posture toward society's economic and human resources and a willingness to see that those resources are utilized for broad social ends and not simply for the narrowly circumscribed interests of private persons and firms. (1960: 60)

Clarence C. Walton, an important thinker on business and society, in a book entitled *Corporate Social Responsibilities* (1967), addressed many facets of CSR in a book series addressing the role of the business firm and the business person in modern society. In this significant book, he presents a number of different varieties, or models, of social responsibility. His fundamental definition of social responsibility is found in the following quote:

In short, the new concept of social responsibility recognizes the intimacy of the relationships between the corporation and society and realizes that such relationships must be kept in mind by top managers as the corporation and the related groups pursue their respective goals. (p. 18).

Walton goes on to emphasize that the essential ingredients of the corporation's social responsibilities include a degree of voluntarism, as opposed to coercion, an indirect linkage of certain other voluntary organizations to the corporation, and the acceptance that costs are involved for which it may not be possible to gauge any direct measurable economic returns (p. 18).

Philanthropy continued as the most noticeable manifestation of CSR during the 1960s. In fact, Muirhead (1999) categorized the period from the mid-1950s to mid-1980s as a period of 'growth and expansion' of corporate contributions. Many previous groups continued to be supported, and gifts expanded to groups representing health and human services, culture and the arts, and civic and community (1999: 15).

Towards the end of the 1960s, business practices that might be categorized as social responsibility embraced such topics as philanthropy, employee improvements (working conditions, industrial relations, personnel policies), customer relations, and stockholder relations (Heald, 1970: 276). In the 1960s, there was still more talk than action on the CSR front (McGuire, 1963).

CSR ACCELERATES IN THE 1970S

Morrell Heald's path-breaking book, *The Social Responsibilities of Business: Company and Community, 1900–1960* (Heald, 1970) ushered in the 1970s. Though Heald does not provide a succinct definition of the social responsibility concept, it is clear that his understanding of the term was in keeping with the definitions presented during the 1960s and earlier. In the Preface to his book, he asserted that he was concerned with the idea of social responsibility 'as businessmen themselves have defined and experienced it' (p. xi). He goes on to say that the 'meaning of the concept of social responsibility for businessmen must finally be sought in the actual policies with which they were associated' (ibid.). He then describes in an historical fashion community-oriented programs, policies, and views of business executives. His accounts suggest that business people during this period were significantly preoccupied with corporate philanthropy and community relations.

Harold Johnson's *Business in Contemporary Society: Framework and Issues* (1971), another of the first books of this decade to address CSR, presents a variety of definitions or views of CSR. Johnson then proceeds to critique and analyze them. Johnson first presents what he terms 'conventional wisdom'. Following is a definition that describes this conventional wisdom:

A socially responsible firm is one whose managerial staff balances a multiplicity of interests. Instead of striving only for larger profits for its stockholders, a responsible enterprise also takes into account employees, suppliers, dealers, local communities, and the nation. (p. 50)

It is worth noting that Johnson is alluding to a precursor of the stakeholder approach as he references a 'multiplicity of interests' and actually names several of these specific interests (groups). It is clear that the interests of employees and philanthropy-recipients are no longer exclusive with respect to company's CSR initiatives.

A ground-breaking contribution to the concept of CSR came from the Committee for Economic Development (CED) in its 1971 publication, *Social Responsibilities of Business Corporations*. The CED introduced this topic by observing that 'business functions by public consent and its basic purpose is to serve constructively the needs of society—to the satisfaction of society' (p. 11). The CED noted that the *social contract* between business and society was changing in substantial and important ways:

Business is being asked to assume broader responsibilities to society than ever before and to serve a wider range of human values. Business enterprises, in effect, are being asked to contribute more to the quality of American life than just supplying quantities of goods and services. Inasmuch as business exists to serve society, its future will depend on the quality of management's response to the changing expectations of the public. (p. 16)

The CED went on to articulate a three concentric circles notion of social responsibility:

The *inner circle* includes the clear-cut basic responsibilities for the efficient execution of the economic function—products, jobs and economic growth.

The *intermediate circle* encompasses responsibility to exercise this economic function with a sensitive awareness of changing social values and priorities: for example, with respect to environmental conservation; hiring and relations with employees; and more rigorous expectations of customers for information, fair treatment, and protection from injury.

The *outer circle* outlines newly emerging and still amorphous responsibilities that business should assume to become more broadly involved in actively improving the social environment. (For example, poverty and urban blight). (p. 15)

What was especially influential about the CED's views of CSR was that the CED was composed of business people and educators and thus reflected an important practitioner view of the changing social contract between business and society and businesses' newly emerging social responsibilities. It is useful to note that the CED may have been responding to the times in that the late 1960s and early 1970s was a period during which social movements with respect to the environment, worker safety, consumers, and employees were poised to transition from special interest status to formal government regulations.

George Steiner was another significant writer on corporate social responsibility in the 1970s. In the first edition of his textbook, *Business and Society* (1971), Steiner wrote at length on the subject. Steiner deferred to Davis's and

Frederick's definitions of CSR but he did state his opinion on the subject as follows:

Business is and must remain fundamentally an economic institution, but...it does have responsibilities to help society achieve its basic goals and does, therefore, have social responsibilities. The larger a company becomes, the greater are these responsibilities, but all companies can assume some share of them at no cost and often at a short-run as well as a long-run profit. (p. 164)

Steiner did not dwell on definitions, but he extended the meaning and circumstances under which CSR might be interpreted and applied. For example, he discussed specific spheres in which CSR might be applied and presented models for determining the social responsibilities of business (p. 157). He also presented criteria for determining the social responsibilities of business (pp. 159–63).

Keith Davis again entered the discussion of CSR in his landmark article presenting the case for and against business assumption of social responsibilities (Davis, 1973). In the introduction of the article he quotes two well-known economists and their diverse views on the subject. First, he quotes Milton Friedman whose famous objection is familiar to most. Friedman contended that 'few trends could so thoroughly undermine the very foundations of our free society as the acceptance by corporate officials of a social responsibility other than to make as much money for their stockholders as possible' (1962: 133). However, Davis counters this view with a quote by Paul Samuelson, another distinguished economist, who argued that 'a large corporation these days not only may engage in social responsibility, it had damn well better try to do so' (1971: 24). Beyond these observations, Davis in 1973 defined CSR as follows: 'For purposes of this discussion it [CSR] refers to the firm's consideration of, and response to, issues beyond the narrow economic, technical, and legal requirements of the firm' (p. 312). Davis then goes on to present and discuss the arguments to date both for and against businesses being socially responsible (pp. 313–21). Davis made other contributions to CSR theory in the 1960s (Davis, 1967).

Though Richard Eels and Clarence Walton addressed the CSR concept in the first (1961), edition of their volume *Conceptual Foundations of Business*, they elaborated on the concept at length in their third edition (1974). Their favorite topics were business history, the concept of the corporation, ownership, and governance. However, they dedicate a chapter to 'recent trends' in corporate social responsibilities. Like Steiner, they do not focus on definitions, per se, but rather take a broader perspective on what CSR means and how it evolved. They observe:

In its broadest sense, corporate social responsibility represents a concern with the needs and goals of society which goes beyond the merely economic. Insofar as the business system as it exists today can only survive in an effectively functioning free society, the corporate social responsibility movement represents a broad concern with business's role in supporting and improving that social order (p. 247).

Eels and Walton go on to provide an extensive discussion of the CSR movement and the various ways in which academics and practitioners were coming to regard the topic at this point in time.

In the 1970s we find reference increasingly being made to corporate social *responsiveness* (Ackerman, 1973; Ackerman and Baner, 1976), corporate social *performance* (CSP), as well as corporate social *responsibility* (CSR). One major writer to make this distinction was S. Prakash Sethi. In a classic article (1975), Sethi discussed 'dimensions of corporate social performance', and in the process distinguished between corporate behaviors that might be called 'social obligation', 'social responsibility', and 'social responsiveness'. In Sethi's schema, social obligation is corporate behavior 'in response to market forces or legal constraints' (p. 70). The criteria here are economic and legal only. Social responsibility, by contrast, goes beyond social obligation. He states: 'Thus, social responsibility implies bringing corporate behavior up to a level where it is congruent with the prevailing social norms, values, and expectations of performance' (p. 62).

Sethi goes on to say that while social obligation is proscriptive in nature, social responsibility is prescriptive in nature. The third stage in Sethi's model is social *responsiveness*. He regards this as the *adaptation* of corporate behavior to social needs. This stage is anticipatory and preventive.

In a book titled *Private Management and Public Policy: The Principle of Public Responsibility* (1975), Lee Preston and James Post sought to direct attention away from the concept of CSR and toward a notion of *public* responsibility. Their recitation of Dow Votaw's commentary on social responsibility is worth repeating. Votaw (1973) articulated the concern that many writers in this era had with CSR. He stated:

> The term [social responsibility] is a brilliant one; it means something, but not always the same thing, to everybody. To some it conveys the idea of legal responsibility or liability; to others, it means socially responsible *behavior* in an ethical sense; to still others, the meaning transmitted is that of 'responsible for', in a causal mode; many simply equate it with a charitable contribution; some take it to mean socially conscious; many of those who embrace it most fervently see it as a mere synonym for 'legitimacy', in the context of 'belonging' or being proper or valid; a few see it as a sort of fiduciary duty imposing higher standards of behavior on businessmen than on citizens at large. (p. 11)

Preston and Post, following Votaw's thinking, said the following about social responsibility:

> In the face of the large number of different, and not always consistent, usages, we restrict our own use of the term social responsibility to refer only to a vague and highly generalized sense of social concern that appears to underlie a wide variety of ad hoc managerial policies and practices. Most of these attitudes and activities are well-intentioned and even beneficent; few are patently harmful. They lack, however, any coherent relationship to the managerial unit's internal activities or to its fundamental linkage with its host environment. (p. 9)

Preston and Post then go on to state that they prefer the term *public responsibility* which is intended to define the functions of organizational management within the specific context of public life (pp. 9–10). They state that in the principle of public responsibility, 'the scope of managerial responsibility is not unlimited, as the popular conception of 'social responsibility' might suggest, but specifically defined in terms of primary and secondary involvement areas' (p. 95). They go on to say that they prefer the word *public* rather than *social*, 'in order to stress the importance of the public policy process, rather than individual opinion and conscience, as the source of goals and appraisal criteria' (p. 102). Though providing an important perspective, the term public responsibility has not supplanted the term social responsibility in the literature, and it has seldom been suggested as having an 'unlimited' scope.

Two examples of early research on corporate social responsibility were published in the mid-1970s. First, Bowman and Haire (1975) conducted a study striving to understand CSR and to ascertain the extent to which companies were engaging in CSR. Though they never really defined CSR in the sense we have been discussing, the researchers chose to operationalize CSR by measuring the proportion of lines of prose devoted to the topic of social responsibility in the annual reports of the companies they studied. While not providing a formal definition of CSR, they illustrated the kinds of topics that represented CSR as opposed to those that were strictly 'business' (p. 50). The topics they used were usually subheads to sections in the annual report. Some of these subheads were as follows: corporate responsibility, social responsibility, social action, public service, corporate citizenship, public responsibility, and social responsiveness. A review of their topical approach indicates that they had a good idea of what CSR generally meant, given the kinds of definitions we saw developing in the 1970s.

Another research study in the mid-1970s was conducted by Sandra Holmes in which she sought to gather 'executive perceptions of corporate social responsibility' (1976). Like Bowman and Haire, Holmes had no clear definition of CSR. Rather, she chose to present executives with a set of statements about CSR, seeking to find out how many of them agreed or disagreed with the statements. Like the Bowman and Haire 'topics', Holmes's statements addressed the issues that were generally felt to be what CSR was all about during this time period. For example, she sought executive opinions on businesses' responsibilities for making a profit, abiding by regulations, helping to solve social problems, and the short-run and long-run impacts on profits of such activities (p. 36). Holmes further added to the body of knowledge about CSR by identifying the 'outcomes' which executives expected from their firms' social involvement (ibid. 38) and the 'factors' executives used in selecting areas of social involvement.

In terms of specific issues that business executives thought were important CSR issues in the early 1970s, a survey conducted by Eilbirt and Parket (1973: 11) revealed a list of activities along with the percentage of large firms engaged in that activity (see Table 2.1).

Table 2.1 Important CSR issues in the early 1970s

CSR Activity	Percent of Firms Engaged
Minority hiring	100
Ecology (concern for environment)	95
Minority training	91
Contributions to education	91
Contributions to the arts	83
Hard-core hiring	79
Hard-core training	66
Urban renewal	62
Civil rights	58

Source: Eilbirt and Parket (1973: 11).

This list gives us a general picture of what businesses thought CSR was all about in the 1970s. Other important CSR activities were found to be: developing understandable accounting statements, truth in advertising, product defects, consumer complaints, consumer-oriented label changes, and guarantees and warrantees. In the late 1970s, Sandra Holmes identified the following issues to be popular CSR causes on the part of companies: pollution control, charities, community affairs, recruitment/development of minorities, and support of education (1978). Gerald Keim presented an analysis of the enlightened self-interest model (1978).

In 1979, Archie B. Carroll proposed a four-part definition of corporate social responsibility which was embedded in a conceptual model of corporate social performance (CSP) (Carroll, 1979). His basic argument was that for managers or firms to engage in CSP they needed to have (1) a basic *definition* of CSR that identified the different types of CSR businesses had; (2) an understanding/enumeration of the *issues* for which a social responsibility existed (or, in modern terms, stakeholders to whom the firm had a responsibility, relationship, or dependency) and (3) a specification of the *philosophy (or strategy) of responsiveness* to the issues (p. 499). Let us restrict our discussion here to the basic CSR definition.

Carroll offered the following definition:

The social responsibility of business encompasses the economic, legal, ethical, and discretionary expectations that society has of organizations at a given point in time. (Carroll, 1979: 500)

Though Carroll's definition includes an economic responsibility, many today still think of the economic component as what the business firm *does for itself* and the legal, ethical, and discretionary (or philanthropic) components as what business *does for others*. While this distinction is attractive, Carroll's argument is that economic viability is something business does for society as well, in perpetuating the business system, though we seldom look at it in this way. It is for this reason that the economic responsibility was included in Carroll's definition of the firm's CSR. His basic definition of CSR, embracing economic, legal, ethical, and discretionary/philanthropic responsibilities was later depicted as a 'pyramid of CSR' with the economic responsibility forming the base or foundation of the pyramid (Carroll, 1991).

The 1970s was a decade during which there began many writings suggesting the importance of a *managerial approach* to CSR (Carroll, 1977). A managerial approach to CSR is one in which business managers applied the traditional management functions to dealing with CSR issues. Thus, it was recommended that companies *forecast and plan* for CSR, *organize* for CSR, *assess social performance*, and *institutionalize corporate social policy and strategy*. As observed before, there was more talk, especially among academics, than action on the part of companies, but legislative initiatives during the 1970s mandated that companies create organizational mechanisms for complying with federal laws dealing with the environment, product safety, employment discrimination, and worker safety.

COMPLEMENTARY THEMES TO CSR ASCEND IN THE 1980S

In the 1980s, the focus on developing new or refined definitions of CSR gave way to research on CSR and a splintering of writings on alternative or complementary concepts and themes such as corporate social *responsiveness*, corporate social *performance*, public policy, business ethics, and stakeholder theory/management, just to mention a few. The interest in CSR did not die out; rather, the core concerns of CSR began to be 'recast' into alternative or complementary concepts, theories, models, or themes. In the ever present quest to discover and accurately elucidate 'truth', this should not be too surprising. For our purposes here, we will continue to focus on the development of CSR in thought and action.

Thomas M. Jones entered the CSR discussion in 1980 with an interesting perspective. First, he defined CSR as follows:

Corporate social responsibility is the notion that corporations have an obligation to constituent groups in society other than stockholders and beyond that prescribed by law and union contract. Two facets of this definition are critical. First, the obligation must be *voluntarily adopted*; behavior influenced by the coercive forces of law or union contract is not voluntary. Second, the obligation is a *broad* one, extending beyond the traditional duty to shareholders to other societal groups such as customers, employees, suppliers, and neighboring communities. (Jones, 1980: 59–60)

Jones then went on to summarize the CSR debate by listing the various arguments that have been presented both for and against it (p. 61). One of Jones's major contributions in this article is his emphasis on CSR as a *process*. Arguing that it is very difficult to reach consensus as to what constitutes socially responsible behavior, he posits that CSR ought to be seen not as a set of outcomes, but as a process (p. 65). Perceiving CSR as a process is what Jones refers to as a revised or redefined concept. In a discussion of implementing CSR, he then goes on to illustrate how a firm could engage in a process of CSR decision making that should constitute CSR behavior (p. 66). Jones's contribution was an important one; however, it would not end the debate regarding the content and extent of CSR expected of business.

Frank Tuzzolino and Barry Armandi (1981) sought to develop a better mechanism for assessing CSR by proposing a need-hierarchy framework patterned after Maslow's need hierarchy. The authors accepted Carroll's 1979 definition as 'appropriate' for their purposes (p. 21), and then proceeded to say that it would be helpful to have an analytical framework to facilitate the *operationalization* of CSR. Their organizational need hierarchy did not redefine CSR; however, it sought to suggest that organizations, like individuals, had criteria that needed to be fulfilled, or met, just as people do as depicted in the Maslow hierarchy. The authors proceeded to illustrate how organizations have physiological, safety, affiliative, esteem, and self-actualization needs that parallel those of humans as depicted by Maslow. The authors presented the hierarchy as a 'conceptual tool whereby socially responsible organizational performance could be reasonably assessed' (p. 24). To some extent, Carroll's pyramid of CSR unfolded the firm's social responsibilities (economic, legal, ethical, discretionary) in a hierarchical way that somewhat resembled the Maslow hierarchy of priorities.

One excellent example of the quest in the 1980s to 'go beyond' CSR was the growing acceptance of the notion of 'corporate social *performance*' as a more comprehensive theory under which CSR might be classified or subsumed. We saw earlier references to CSP in the 1970s (for example, Sethi, 1975; Preston, 1978; Carroll, 1979), but the idea of a CSP 'model' continued to draw interest. In 1985, therefore, Steven Wartick and Philip Cochran presented their 'evolution of the corporate social performance model' which extended the three-dimensional integration of responsibility, responsiveness, and social issues that Carroll (1979) had previously introduced and Donna Wood (1991) had refined (Wartick and Cochran, 1985: 758). One of the major contributions of these two authors was to recast Carroll's three aspects—corporate social responsibilities, corporate social responsiveness, and social issues—into a framework of principles, processes, and policies. They argued that Carroll's CSR definition embraced the ethical component of social responsibility and should be thought of as *principles*, social responsiveness should be thought of as *processes*, and social issues management should be thought of as *policies* (p. 767).

Edwin M. Epstein (1987) provided an explanation of CSR in his quest to relate social responsibility, responsiveness, and business ethics. He pointed out that these three concepts dealt with closely related, even overlapping, themes and concerns (p. 104). He said:

Corporate social responsibility relates primarily to achieving outcomes from organizational decisions concerning specific issues or problems which (by some normative standard) have beneficial rather than adverse effects upon pertinent corporate stakeholders. The normative correctness of the *products* of corporate action have been the main focus of corporate social responsibility. (ibid.)

In addition to expounding on CSR, Epstein defined corporate social responsiveness and business ethics and then brought them together into what he called the *corporate social policy process*. He went on to say that 'the nub of the corporate social policy process is the institutionalization within business organizations of the following three elements . . . business ethics, corporate social responsibility and corporate social responsiveness' (p. 106).

Though it is difficult to catalog the CSR issues that business thought were most important during the 1980s, a 'social responsibility agenda for the 1980s' was set forth by William C. Frederick (2006: 58), and this agenda closely corresponds with, or was slightly ahead of, business concerns and practices during this period. The issues embraced as important for the 1980s included business practices with respect to environmental pollution, employment discrimination, consumer abuses, employee health and safety, quality of work life, deterioration of urban life, and questionable/abusiveness practices of multinational corporations. Another important research topic became research on the relationship between corporate social responsibility and firm profitability (Aupperle *et al.*, 1985).

Two very important 'alternative themes' to CSR that developed during the 1980s were *stakeholder theory* and *business ethics*. R. Edward Freeman published his classic book on stakeholder theory in 1984. Though the book was classified as one focusing on strategic management, it had its most substantial impact in later years in the fields of business and society, corporate social responsibility, and eventually, business ethics. The other alternative theme to appear and grow in the 1980s was business ethics. The 1980s was a period of widely reported ethical scandals that brought the public's attention to managerial and corporate wrong-doing. Examples of these scandals included the infant-formula controversy that spanned most of the 1970s and half of the 1980s, the 1984 Union Carbide Bhopal explosion in India, killing thousands of people, the controversy over companies doing business in South Africa, in apparent support of apartheid, and the Ivan Boesky insider trading scandal of the mid-to-late 1980s. Not coincidentally, perhaps, it has been argued that the fictional character of business executive-bad guy Gordon Gekko in the 1987 blockbuster movie, *Wall Street*, was patterned after a speech made by Boesky in which he argued that greed was good. Picking up on this same theme, the decade of the 1980s was frequently portrayed as the decade of 'greed' or of 'me', accounting for the self-absorption that was so evident during this period.

CSR Serves as Basepoint for Complementary Themes in the 1990s

As a generalization, it should be observed that very few unique contributions to the concept of CSR occurred in the 1990s. More than anything else, the CSR concept served as the basepoint, building block, or point-of-departure for other complementary concepts and themes, many of which embraced CSR thinking and were quite compatible with CSR. The prominent themes which continued to grow and take center stage in the 1990s included the following: corporate social performance (CSP), stakeholder theory, business ethics, sustainability, and corporate citizenship. A fair amount of research sought to examine the relationship between corporate social performance and financial performance (Griffin and Mahon, 1997). Swanson (1995) sought to reorient the basic CSP model. We will not explore these themes in detail as they are outside the realm of our present scope of focusing on CSR concepts and practice, and each of these thematic frameworks has its own extensive literature.

Corporate citizenship, more than any other, became a concept that competed with CSR. Whether corporate citizenship actually becomes a distinct area of study, or simply another way of articulating or framing CSR, remains to be seen. Corporate citizenship may be broadly or narrowly conceived. Depending on which way it is defined, the notion seems to overlap more or less with the previously mentioned themes or theories. Sustainability was another important complementary theme that attracted significant interest in the 1990s. Though initially defined in terms of the natural environment, it evolved into a more encompassing concept that embraced the larger social and stakeholder environment. Each of these themes or topics has its own extensive literature, however, and it is beyond the scope of this chapter to provide a summary of each of these areas of research (Carroll, 1994).

The 1990s was concluded with a special issue of the *Academy of Management Journal* on the subject of 'stakeholders, social responsibility, and performance' (October 1999). This issue continued the quest to link CSR with other concepts such as stakeholders but added no new definitions to the CSR literature. Harrison and Freeman provided an overview of six excellent efforts to tackle fundamental ideas about stakeholders, social responsibility, and performance (Harrison and Freeman, 1999).

During the late 1980s and into the 1990s, philanthropy expanded considerably. Muirhead (1999) characterized this period of corporate contributions as 'diversification and globalization'. More global companies appeared in the economy, and management positions dedicated to corporate giving began proliferating on the organization charts of major companies. Managers of corporate giving, corporate social responsibility, and public/community affairs, became commonplace. The Ethics Officer Association was founded in the early 1990s. New concepts, such as global social investment, corporate reputation, community partnerships, corporate social policy, and others, became evident in large companies. In terms of management philosophy or policy, strategic giving, cause-related marketing, international donations, employee volunteerism, sustainability, and global corporate citizenship, emerged to characterize many CSR initiatives. The beneficiaries of CSR initiatives included the following: education, culture and the arts, health and human services, civic and community, international donees, community partners, and NGO partners (Muirhead, 1999: 15). During the 1990s, many of these beneficiaries had become global.

The most significant advances to CSR in the 1990s came in the realm of business practice. In 1992, a nonprofit organization called Business for Social Responsibility (BSR) formed to represent the initiatives and professionals having responsibility for CSR in their companies. BSR's web page (<http://www.bsr.org>) describes the organization in the following way:

Business for Social Responsibility (BSR) is a global organization that helps member companies achieve commercial success in ways that respect ethical values, people, communities and the environment. Through socially responsible business policies and practices, companies can achieve viable, sustainable growth that benefits stakeholders as well as stockholders. By providing tools, training and custom advisory services, BSR enables its members to leverage corporate social responsibility as a competitive advantage.

As the leading global resource for corporate social responsibility (CSR), BSR equips its member companies with the expertise to design, implement and evaluate successful, socially responsible business practices. Membership provides an extensive set of practical resources including training programs, technical assistance, research and business advisory services accessible through face-to-face sessions, custom publications and via the Web at www.bsr.org.

BSR defines CSR rather broadly to include topics such as business ethics, community investment, environment, governance and accountability, human rights, marketplace, and workplace. It also states that a variety of terms are used often interchangeably to talk about corporate social responsibility, and these terms include business ethics, corporate citizenship, corporate accountability, and sustainability. Taking a practical, managerial point-of-view, BSR asserts that 'CSR is viewed as a comprehensive set of policies, practices and programs that are integrated into business operations, supply chains, and decision-making processes through the company'.

In addition to the growth and acceptance of BSR, another major trend that characterized the 1990s and continues today is the emergence of many different companies that have developed excellent reputations for CSR practices. Though some of these companies have gotten some skepticism questioning the sincerity or nature of some of their practices, companies such as The Body Shop, Ben & Jerry's ice cream, Patagonia, Esprit de Corp, Aveda, and Stonyfield Farms represent some of the smaller companies that grew larger while embracing CSR practices. Larger companies that developed CSR-related reputations included IBM, Johnson & Johnson, Nike, Merck, Prudential Insurance, Levi Strauss & Co., Coca-Cola, UPS, McDonald's, and Herman Miller.

THE TWENTY-FIRST CENTURY: REFINEMENTS, RESEARCH, ALTERNATIVE THEMES, MANAGEMENT PRACTICE, AND GLOBAL EXPANSION

By the 2000s, the emphasis on *theoretical* contributions to the concept and meaning of CSR had given way to *empirical research* on the topic and a splintering of interests away from CSR and into related topics such as stakeholder theory, business ethics, sustainability, and corporate citizenship. Some developmental and empirical research continued on the CSR construct, however. Time will need to pass before broad generalizations can accurately be made concerning the early 2000s. However, a mix of conceptual and empirical work provides a flavor for some of the developments in the early 2000s.

Bryan Husted (2000) presented a contingency theory of corporate social performance (CSP). He argued that CSP is a function of the fit between the nature of the social issue and its corresponding strategies and structures. This fit then leads to an integration of elements such as corporate social responsiveness, issues management, and stakeholder management. Husted's contributions would best be termed theoretical and applied.

In a special issue of *Business & Society* (December 2000) titled 'Revisiting Corporate Social Performance', a number of different perspectives, if not definitions, of CSR were set forth. In most instances, these were studies manifesting CSR as well as CSP. Rowley and Berman (2000) presented 'a brand new brand of corporate social performance'. The authors argued that the future direction of CSP needed to be built not on an overall concept of CSP but rather by reducing CSP to operational measures. Griffin (2000) discussed 'CSP: Research Directions for the 21st Century'. She argued that existing research in related disciplines (e.g. marketing, human relations) can help accelerate our understanding of CSP.

The period 2001–2 was dominated not by new concepts of CSR but rather empirical research linking CSR or CSP to other relevant variables. A few studies are illustrative. In an event study of family-friendly firms, Jones and Murrell (2001) examined how a firm's public recognition for exemplary social performance can serve as a positive signal of the firm's business performance to shareholders. Smith *et al.* (2001) examined the extent to which diversity characteristics and stakeholder role influenced corporate social orientation (CSO) perceptions on the part of individuals surveyed. Zyglidopolous (2001) studied the impact of accidents on firms' reputation for social performance. He found that accidents and their complexity play a role in social performance reputation perceptions. Backhaus *et al.* (2002) explored the relationship between corporate social performance and employer attractiveness. The researchers found that job seekers do consider CSP to be important in their assessment of firms and they found that the most important CSP dimensions were environment, community relations, employee relations, diversity, and product issues. The researchers did not have a conceptual model of CSP, but rather used a listing of relevant CSP dimensions as forming the construct.

On the conceptual front, Schwartz and Carroll (2003) presented a three-domain approach to corporate social responsibility. The three-domain approach took Carroll's (1979, 1991) four categories of CSR and reduced them to three: economic, legal, and ethical. The model, presented as a venn diagram, offered an alternative to his earlier conceptualizations of CSR. The three-domain approach, deemed to be especially useful in discussions of business ethics, collapsed the philanthropic category into the ethical category and argued that philanthropy could be conceptualized in both ethical and discretionary terms. The three-domain model then more thoroughly discussed each of the three domains and suggested how each section of the venn diagram represented a set of organizational characteristics that could be useful in analyzing firms. By altering the size and dominance of each element of the model (economic, legal, and ethical), the authors visualized different CSR 'portraits' that could serve as benchmarks in analyzing companies.

From a business point-of-view, the interest in CSR 'best practices' moved center-stage. This was consistent with the relentless call on the part of the business community for the 'business case' for CSR. A major book cataloging these best practices, targeted at a business audience, was written by Philip Kotler and Nancy Lee (2005). The authors set out to demonstrate how the CSR approach establishes a new way of doing business that combines the success and the creation of value with a respectful and proactive attitude towards stakeholders (Perrini, 2005). The authors present 25 best practices that may well assist companies with their CSR programs. These best practices are categorized into six major types of social initiatives, along with practical examples, that frame effectively what CSR is all about in the 2000s. The categories include: (1) cause promotion (increasing awareness and concern for social causes); (2) cause-related marketing (contributing to causes based on sales); (3) corporate social marketing (behavior change initiatives); (4) corporate philanthropy (contributing directly to causes); (5) community volunteering (employees donating time and talents in the community); and (6) socially responsible business practices (discretionary practices and investment to support causes) (Kotler and Lee, 2005; Perrini, 2005).

For the previous 20 years, but especially in the 2000s, the CSR movement has been a global phenomenon. The interest and growth of CSR has been most evident in the European Community. According to a report prepared by the Organization for Economic Co-operation and Development (OECD, 2001), voluntary initiatives in corporate social responsibility have been a major trend in international business in recent years. The OECD project on private initiatives for corporate responsibility revealed a number of key findings about CSR. Some of the important findings are worth noting. CSR is definitely a global phenomenon, though there are important intra-regional variations in practice. Some initiatives are more voluntary than others as some companies have been under legal and regulatory pressure to adopt them. There appear to be divergences of commitment and management practice, even in narrow areas of application such as labor standards, environment, human rights, and fighting bribery. First steps have been taken towards the development of consensus on social norms of business conduct, though the conversation is ongoing (OECD, 2001).

Considerable management expertise in legal and ethical compliance is being achieved. This is due partially to the institutionalized support that is emerging in terms of day-to-day company practices, management standards, professional societies, and specialized consulting and auditing services. The OECD did not reach definite conclusions on the costs of CSR initiatives, but the benefits for companies and for society have been established to be numerous. Finally, it was concluded that the effectiveness of CSR initiatives, especially in Europe, is closely associated with the effectiveness of broader systems of private and public governance (p. 10).

Jeremy Moon's discussion of how CSR evolved in the UK gives one significant example of its development in the European Union (Moon, 2005). He presents CSR as part of societal governance in the UK, embedded in a system intended to give direction to society. The roots of CSR in the UK may be found in nineteenth century business philanthropy, as previously described in the United States. Moon argues that although CSR was discussed in the 1970s, it was the period of high unemployment, urban decay, and social unrest of the early 1980s that was a defining moment for CSR in the UK. In the 1990s, the concept of CSR broadened from community involvement to an eventual and abiding concern for socially responsible products, processes, and employee relations. The explicit concern for CSR in the UK and among companies was characterized by growth in CSR staffs in companies, embedding of CSR in corporate systems via standards and codes, increased social reporting, and growing partnerships between companies and NGOs or governmental organizations (pp. 56–7). In addition, these initiatives were augmented by the emergence and expansion of CSR umbrella organizations, the CSR consultancy industry, interest in the investment community, and growth of CSR initiatives in higher education. The institutionalization of CSR by corporate managements in the UK has paralleled that in the United States and in other developed countries of the world: senior level management and board-level responsibilities, reporting and organizational systems, and increased external stakeholder relations (p. 60).

A major volume, *Corporate Social Responsibility across Europe* (2005), edited by Habisch *et al.*, documents the spread of CSR across Europe as part of an intense debate about sustainability and globalization. They claim CSR was virtually unknown about a decade before, but now it is one of the most important topics for discussion for business people, politicians, trade unionists, consumers, NGOs, and researchers.

What is the future for CSR around the world? The most optimistic perspective seems to prevail and it is depicted well by Steven D. Lydenberg in his book *Corporations and the Public Interest: Guiding the Invisible Hand*. Lydenberg sees CSR as 'a major secular development, driven by a long-term reevaluation of the role of corporations in society' (Teach, 2005: 31.) Lydenberg says this re-evaluation is more evident in Europe, where the stakeholder responsibility notion is more readily assumed, but that US business people are more skeptical of this assumption. He goes on to argue, however, that the European influence will be very hard to resist over the long run (Teach, 2005).

By contrast with the optimistic perspective, David Vogel is genuinely skeptical of CSR and he develops this argument in his book, *The Market for Virtue: The Potential and Limits of Corporate Social Responsibility*, in which he critiques CSR's influence and success. Vogel is very much of the mind that CSR will not be successful until mainstream companies begin reporting some aspect of CSR as being critical to the company's past or future performance (Teach, 2005). In other words, CSR is successful only to the extent that it adds to the bottom line and can be specifically delineated as having made such an impact. In reacting to Vogel's skepticism, it must be observed that this convergence of financial and social objectives characterizes the trajectory that CSR has taken in the past two decades.

It is clear from CSR trends and practices that social responsibility has both an ethical or moral component as well as a business component. In today's world of intense global competition, it is clear that CSR can be sustainable only so long as it continues to add value to corporate success. It must be observed, however, that it is society, or the public, that plays an increasing role in what constitutes business success, not just business executives alone, and for that reason, CSR has an upbeat future in the global business arena. The pressures of global competition will continue to intensify, however, and this will dictate that the 'business case' for CSR will always be at the center of attention.

REFERENCES

ACKERMAN, R. W. 1973. 'How Companies Respond to Social Demand's. *Harvard Business Review*, 51(4): 88–98.

—— and BAUER, R. A. 1976. *Corporate Social Responsiveness*. Reston, Va.: Reston Publishing Co.

AUPPERLE, KENNETH E., CARROLL, ARCHIE B., and HATFIELD, JOHN D. 1985. 'An Empirical Investigation of the Relationship between Corporate Social Responsibility and Profitability'. *Academy of Management Journal*, 28: 446–63.

BACKHAUS, KRISTIN B., STONE, BRETT A., and HEINER, KARL. 2002. 'Exploring the Relationship between Corporate Social Performance and Employer Attractiveness'. *Business & Society*, 41(3), Sept.: 292–318.

BARNARD, CHESTER I. 1938. *The Functions of the Executive*. Cambridge, Mass.: Harvard University Press.

BOWEN, HOWARD R. 1953. *Social Responsibilities of the Businessman*. New York: Harper & Row.

BOWMAN, EDWARD H., and HAIRE, MASON. 1975. 'A Strategic Posture toward Corporate Social Responsibility'. *California Management Review*, 18: 49–58.

Business for Social Responsibility. 2006. <http://www.bsr.org>.

CARROLL, ARCHIE B. (ed.) 1977. *Managing Corporate Social Responsibility*. Boston: Little, Brown and Co.

—— 1979. 'A Three-Dimensional Conceptual Model of Corporate Social Performance'. *Academy of Management Review*, 4: 497–505.

—— 1981. *Business and Society: Managing Corporate Social Performance*. Boston: Little, Brown and Co.

—— 1991. 'The Pyramid of Corporate Social Responsibility: Toward the Moral Management of Organizational Stakeholders'. *Business Horizons*, 34, July–Aug.: 39–48.

—— 1994. 'Social Issues in Management Research: Experts' Views, Analysis and Commentary'. *Business and Society*, 33, Apr.: 5–29.

—— 1999. 'Corporate Social Responsibility: Evolution of a Definitional Construct'. *Business and Society*, 38(3), Sept.: 268–95.

—— 2006. 'Corporate Social Responsibility: A Historical Perspective', in Marc J. Epstein and Kirk O. Hanson (eds.), *The Accountable Corporation*, vol. 3. Westport, Conn.: Praeger Publishers, 3–30.

—— and BUCHHOLTZ. 2006. *Business and Society: Ethics and Stakeholder Management*, 6th edn. Cincinnati, Oh.: South-Western College Publishing/International Thompson Publishing.

CLARK, J. M. 1939. *Social Control of Business*. New York: McGraw-Hill.

Committee for Economic Development (CED). 1971. *Social Responsibilities of Business Corporations*. New York: CED.

DAVIS, KEITH. 1960. 'Can Business Afford to Ignore Social Responsibilities?' *California Management Review*, 2, spring: 70–6.

—— 1967. 'Understanding the Social Responsibility Puzzle: What does the Businessman Owe to Society?' *Business Horizons*, 10, winter: 45–50.

—— 1973. 'The Case for and against Business Assumption of Social Responsibilities'. *Academy of Management Journal*, 16: 312–22.

EBERSTADT, NICHOLAS N. 1973. 'What History Tells us about Corporate Responsibilities'. *Business and Society Review/Innovation*, autumn: 76–81.

EELS, RICHARD. 1956. *Corporate Giving in a Free Society*. New York: Harper.

—— and WALTON, CLARENCE. 1974. *Conceptual Foundations of Business*, 3rd edn. Homewood, Ill.: Richard D. Irwin, Inc.

EILBERT, HENRY, and PARKET, I. ROBERT. 1973. 'The Current Status of Corporate Social Responsibility'. *Business Horizons*, 16, Aug.: 5–14.

EPSTEIN, EDWIN M. 1987. 'The Corporate Social Policy Process: Beyond Business Ethics, Corporate Social Responsibility, and Corporate Social Responsiveness'. *California Management Review*, 29: 99–114.

FREDERICK, WILLIAM C. 1960. 'The Growing Concern over Business Responsibility'. *California Management Review*, 2: 54–61.

—— 1978. 'From CSR1 to CSR2: The Maturing of Business and Society Thought'. Graduate school of business: University of Pittsburgh. Working paper no. 279.

—— 1998. 'Moving to CSR4: What to Pack for the Trip'. *Business & Society*, 37(1), Mar.: 40–59.

—— 2006. *Corporation Be Good: The Story of Corporate Social Responsibility*. Indianapolis: Dog Ear Publishing.

FREEMAN, R. EDWARD. 1984. *Strategic Management: A Stakeholder Approach*. Boston: Pitman.

FRIEDMAN, MILTON. 1962. *Capitalism and Freedom*. Chicago: University of Chicago Press.

GRIFFIN, JENNIFER J. 2000. 'Corporate Social Performance: Research Directions for the 21st Century'. *Business & Society*, 39(4), Dec.: 479–91.

—— and MAHON, JOHN F. 1997. 'The Corporate Social Performance and Corporate Financial Performance Debate: Twenty-Five Years of Incomparable Research' *Business & Society*, 36, Mar.: 5–31.

HABISCH, ANDRÉ, JONKER, JAN, WEGNER, MARTINA, and SCHMIDPETER, RENÉ (eds.) 2005. *Corporate Social Responsibility across Europe*. Berlin: Springer Berlin Heidelberg.

HARRISON, JEFFREY S., and FREEMAN, R. EDWARD. 1999. 'Stakeholders, Social Responsibility, and Performance: Empirical Evidence and Theoretical Perspectives'. *Academy of Management Journal*, Oct.: 479–85.

HAY, ROBERT and GRAY, ed. 1974. 'Social Responsibilities of Business Managers'. *Academy of Management Journal*, 17: 1.

HEALD, MORRELL. 1957. 'Management's Responsibility to Society: The Growth of an Idea'. *Business History Review*, 31: 375–84.

—— 1970. *The Social Responsibilities of Business: Company and Community, 1900–1960*. Cleveland: The Press of Case Western Reserve University.

—— 1978. 'Adapting corporate Structure for social Responsiveness'. *California Management Review*, 21(1), 51.

HOLMES, SANDRA L. 1976. 'Executive Perceptions of Corporate Social Responsibility'. *Business Horizons*, 19, June: 34–40.

HUSTED, BRYAN W. 2000. 'A Contingency Theory of Corporate Social Performance'. *Business & Society*, 39(1), Mar.: 24–48.

JOHNSON, HAROLD L. 1971. *Business in Contemporary Society: Framework and Issues*. Belmont, Calif.: Wadsworth Publishing Co., Inc.

JONES, RAY and MURRELL, AUDREY J. 2001. 'Signaling Positive Corporate Social Performance: An Event Study of Family-Friendly Firms'. *Business & Society*, 40(1), Mar.: 59–78.

JONES, THOMAS M. 1980. 'Corporate Social Responsibility Revisited, Redefined'. *California Management Review*, spring: 59–67.

KEIM, GERALD D. 1978. 'Corporate Social Responsibility: An Assessment of the Enlightened Self-Interest Model'. *Academy of Management Review*, 3: 32–9.

KOTLER, PHILIP, and LEE, NANCY. 2005. *Corporate Social Responsibility: Doing the Most Good for Your Company and Your Cause*. Hoboken, NJ: John Wiley & Sons, Inc.

KREPS, T. J. 1940. *Measurement of the Social Performance of Business: In an Investigation of Concentration of Economic Power for the Temporary National Economic Committee*. Monograph No. 7. Washington: Government Printing Office.

LYDENBERG, STEVEN D. 2005. *Corporations and the Public Interest: Guiding the Invisible Hand*. San Francisco: Berrett-Koehler Publishers, Inc.

MCGUIRE, JOSEPH W. 1963. *Business & Society*. New York: McGraw-Hill.

MOON, JEREMY. 2005. 'An Explicit Model of Business-Society Relations', in Habisch *et al.* (2005), 51–65.

MUIRHEAD, SOPHIA A. 1999. *Corporate Contributions: The View from 50 Years*. New York: The Conference Board.

MURPHY, PATRICK E. 1978. 'An Evolution: Corporate Social Responsiveness'. *University of Michigan Business Review*, Nov.

Organization for Economic Co-operation and Development (OECD). 2001. *Corporate Responsibility: Private Initiatives and Public Goals*. Paris: OECD.

PERRINI, FRANCESCO. 2005. Book Review of *Corporate Social Responsibility: Doing the Most Good for Your Company and Your Cause*. *Academy of Management Perspectives*, May: 90–3.

PRESTON, LEE E. (ed.) 1978. *Research in Corporate Social Performance and Policy*, vol. 1. Greenwich, Conn.: JAI Press.

——— and POST, JAMES E. 1975. *Private Management and Public Policy: The Principle of Public Responsibility*. Englewood Cliffs, NJ: Prentice-Hall.

ROWLEY, TIM, and BERMAN, SHAWN. 2000. 'A Brand New Brand of Corporate Social Performance'. *Business & Society*, 39(4), Dec.: 397–418.

SAMUELSON, P. A. 1971. 'Love that Corporation'. *Mountain Bell Magazine*, spring.

SCHWARTZ, MARK S., and CARROLL, ARCHIE B. 2003. 'Corporate Social Responsibility: A Three-Domain Approach'. *Business Ethics Quarterly*, Oct.: 503–30.

SELEKMAN, B. 1959. *A Moral Philosophy for Business*. New York: McGraw-Hill.

SETHI, S. PRAKASH. 1975. 'Dimensions of Corporate Social Performance: An Analytic Framework'. *California Management Review*, 17, spring: 58–64.

SMITH, WANDA J., WOKUTCH, RICHARD E., HARRINGTON, K. VERNARD, and DENNIS, BRYAN S. 2001. 'An Examination of the Influence of Diversity and Stakeholder Role on Corporate Social Orientation'. *Business & Society*, 40(3), Sept.: 266–94.

STEINER, GEORGE A. 1971. *Business and Society*. New York: Random House.

SWANSON, DIANE L. 1995. 'Addressing a Theoretical Problem by Reorienting the Corporate Social Performance Model'. *Academy of Management Review*, 20: 43–64.

TEACH, EDWARD. 2005. 'Two Views of Virtue'. *CFO*. Dec.: 31–4.

TUZZOLINO, FRANK, and ARMANDI, BARRY R. 1981. 'A Need-Hierarchy Framework for Assessing Corporate Social Responsibility'. *Academy of Management Review*, 6: 21–8.

VOGEL, DAVID. 2005. *The Market for Virtue: The Potential and Limits of Corporate Social Responsibility*. Washington: The Brookings Institution.

VOTAW, DOW. 1973. 'Genius becomes Rare', in Dow Votaw and S. P. Sethi (eds.), *The Corporate Dilemma*. Englewood Cliffs, NJ: Prentice-Hall.

WALTON, CLARENCE C. 1967. *Corporate Social Responsibilities*. Belmont, Calif.: Wadsworth Publishing Co, Inc.

WARTICK, STEVEN L., and COCHRAN, PHILIP L. 1985. 'The Evolution of the Corporate Social Performance Model'. *Academy of Management Review*, 10: 758–69.

WOOD, DONNA J. 1991. 'Corporate Social Performance Revisited'. *Academy of Management Review*, 16: 691–718.

WREN, DANIEL A. 2005. *The History of Management Thought*, 5th edn. Hoboken, NJ: John Wiley & Sons, Inc.

ZYGLIDOPOULOS, STELIOS C. 2001. 'The Impact of Accidents on Firms' Reputation for Social Performance'. *Business & Society*, 40(4), Dec.: 416–41.

....

CHAPTER 3

CORPORATE SOCIAL RESPONSIBILITY THEORIES

....

DOMÈNEC MELÉ

INTRODUCTION

....

IN order to consider Corporate Social Responsibility (CSR) theories, the first difficulty is how to identify with and organize the great variety of existing approaches on CSR. Even the concept of CSR itself is far from being unanimous. Carroll (1999) has reviewed and discussed over 25 different ways that CSR is defined in the academic literature. Some of them are wider while others are narrower in their contents, but most definitions contain certain similarities. Some proposals of CSR are presented as a vague notion or even as a belief. Others, however, respond to a more or less elaborate theory on the firm and the purpose of business in society, in which CSR is a part. Those theories generally include a certain vision of the human being and society within a social philosophy framework, although sometimes in an implicit manner.

Among the attempts to classify CSR theories, three studies can be pointed out. Klonoski (1991) distinguishes three different kinds of theories. He calls the first group 'fundamentalism'. It includes all positions that, in one way or another, claim that corporations are only legal artifacts and the only social responsibility of business is increasing profits in compliance with the laws. The second group is made up of those theories which defend the corporation's moral personhood and point to its moral agency. Consequently, corporations can be held morally responsible for their actions. The third group considers theories in which the social dimension of the corporation is particularly relevant. The roots of these theories are in political and ethical theories.

Windsor (2006) understands that there are three key approaches to CSR: (1) *ethical responsibility theory*, which presents strong corporate self-restraint and altruistic duties and expansive public policy to strengthen stakeholders' rights, (2) *economic responsibility theory*, which advocates market wealth creation subject only to minimalist public policy and perhaps customary business ethics, and (3) *corporate citizenship*, which language invokes a political metaphor which provides neither true intermediate positioning nor theoretical synthesis.

In a third study, Garriga and Melé (2004) distinguish four groups of CSR theories, considering their respective focus on four different aspects of the social reality: economics, politics, social integration, and ethics. The first one focuses on economics. Here the corporation is seen as a mere instrument for wealth creation. The second group focuses on the social power of the corporation and its responsibility in the political arena associated with its power. The third group focuses on social integration. It includes theories which consider that business ought to integrate social demands. The fourth group of theories focuses on ethics, including theories which consider that the relationship between business and society should be embedded with ethical values. Garriga and Melé have classified theories considering the main focus of each one, although they point out that in some cases this is not too easy, since some theories seem to focus on more than one aspect. In addition, they suggest that 'the concept of business and society relationship must include these four aspects or dimensions and some connection among them must exist.' (2004: 64)

This chapter follows this last study by discussing four theories of CSR, or more precisely, four theories about the responsibilities of business in society, which can be considered contemporary mainstream theories:

1. Corporate Social Performance, a theory basically grounded in sociology. This theory has some relation to the second group of Klonoski (1991).
2. The theory sometimes called 'Shareholder Value Theory' or 'Fiduciary Capitalism', which comes from a particular economic theory. There is close relationship with what Klonoski calls 'fundamentalism' and Windsor 'economic responsibility theory'.
3. Stakeholder theory, which in its normative version is based on ethical perspectives. It can be related to 'ethical responsibility theory' of Wilson and with some theories included in the third group of Klonoski.

4. Corporate Citizenship theory (or approach), whose roots are on political studies. Windsor mentions it as one of the key approaches and Klonoski considers it as one of the theories included in his third group.

In describing each theory we will commence with an overview, followed by a brief historical background, including the milestones of its development. Then, we will outline the conceptual bases of the theory, concluding with a brief discussion on the strengths and weaknesses of each theory.

CORPORATE SOCIAL PERFORMANCE

Overview

Corporate Social Performance (CSP) theory has evolved from several previous notions and approaches. In one of its prominent versions, Corporate Social Performance is understood as 'the configuration in the business organization of principles of social responsibility, processes of response to social requirements, and policies, programs and tangible results that reflect the company's relations with society' (Wood, 1991b: 693). This theory maintains that business, apart from wealth creation, also has responsibilities for social problems created by business or by other causes, beyond its economic and legal responsibilities. This includes ethical requirements and discretionary or philanthropic actions carried out by business in favor of society. In other words, improving corporate social performance 'means altering corporate behavior to produce less harm and more beneficial outcomes for society and their people' (Wood, 1991a: 68).

In order to determine specific responsibilities, many authors insist on the importance of paying attention to social expectations regarding the firm's performance and concern for social needs. Among other arguments for assuming CSR, it is stressed that business has power and power requires responsibility. It is also emphasized that society gives license to business to operate and, consequently, business must serve society not only by creating wealth, but also by contributing to social needs and satisfying social expectations towards business.

It also emphasizes the risk to which a company would be vulnerable if its performance was contrary to the expectations of those people who constitute the company's social environment (Davis, 1975). In a positive sense, corporate reputation is also related to the acceptance of the community where a company is operating (Lewis, 2003). Nevertheless, the long-term economic consequences for the company, which are not always easy to evaluate, are not the main consideration for many authors, who point out that assuming social responsibilities is not considered primarily an economic question but a social and ethical matter: being responsible is doing the right thing.

Historical Background

Howard R. Bowen marked the beginning of the modern period of CSR literature with his book *Social Responsibility of the Businessman*, published in 1953. He started by asking the following: 'What responsibility to society may businessmen reasonably be expected to assume?' Then, he explained that the social responsibility of businessmen [at this time the presence of women in management was rare] 'refers to the obligation of businessmen to pursue those policies, to make decisions, or to follow those lines of action which are desirable in terms of the objectives and values of our society' (1953: 6). In a more detailed and pragmatic way, the Committee for Economic Development (1971) (USA) defined CSR as related to (i) products, jobs, and economic growth, (ii) societal expectations, and (iii) activities aimed at improving the social environment of the firm.

In the 1970s, new directions appeared in the business and society literature. They arose within a context of protests against capitalism and business and growing social concerns, which led to an increasing government regulatory procedures and formal requirements. At this time, Ackerman (Ackerman, 1973; Ackerman and Bauer, 1976), Sethi (1975), and others started to pay attention toward what was called 'corporate responsiveness', or adaptation of corporate behavior to social needs and demands, even acting in a pro-active manner. Sethi (1975) set out a three-level model, which was a predecessor of the current 'corporate social performance' theory. This model included: (i) social obligations, as response to legal and market constraints, (ii) societal responsibility, that is, congruent with societal norms, and (iii) social responsiveness (adaptive, anticipatory, and preventive).

The concept of 'social responsiveness' was soon widened to the concept 'issues management'. The latter includes the former but emphasizes social and political issues which may impact significantly upon the process of corporate response. Considering 'issues management' attempts to minimize the 'surprises' which accompany social and political change by serving as an early warning system for potential environmental threats and opportunities.

Preston and Post (1975) introduced the notion of 'public responsibility'. With this notion, they tried to define the function of organizational management within the specific context of public life. The term 'public' rather than 'social' was chosen 'to stress the importance of the public process, rather than individual opinion and conscience, as the source of goals and appraisal criteria' (1975: 112).

This approach provoked controversy among defenders of 'corporate responsiveness' which emphasizes the process rather than the content. Jones (1980) posited that social responsibility ought not to be seen as a set of outcomes but as a process.

From this perspective, he was critical of abstract concept of CSR and particularly with the concept of 'public responsibility' proposed by Preston and Post. The latter replied to Jones by updating their main thesis and presenting practical applications (Preston and Post, 1981).

Carroll (1979), who first introduced the concept of 'corporate social performance', made a synthesis of the basic principle of social responsibility, the concrete issues for which social responsibility exists, and the specific philosophy of response to social issues. Carroll suggested that an entire range of obligations that business has to society must embody the economic, legal, ethical, and discretionary (philanthropic) categories. He included them in a 'Pyramid of Corporate Social Responsibility' (Carroll, 1991). More recently, Schwartz and Carroll (2003) have proposed an alternative approach based on three core domains (economic, legal, and ethical responsibilities) and a Venn model framework. The Venn framework yields seven CSR categories resulting from the overlap of the three core domains. The model is more complex but the essential concepts remain. In a global context, Carroll has applied his 'pyramid' understanding that 'economic responsibility' is to do what is required by global capitalism, 'legal responsibility' is to do what is required by global stakeholders, 'ethical responsibility' is to do what is expected by stakeholders, and 'philanthropic responsibility' is to do what is desired by global stakeholders (Carroll, 2004).

Wartick and Cochran (1985) extended the Carroll approach suggesting that corporate social involvement rests on the principles of social responsibility, the process of social responsiveness, and the policy of issues management. A new development came with Wood (1991b), whose model we will discuss next. This is probably the most complete approach on Corporate Social Performance considering social expectations. However, the Wood model has some limitations. Swanson (1995) has revised this model integrating business ethics perspectives.

In recent times, the social expectations considered in this model have become more specific in terms of actors, processes, and contents. Actors have multiplied. Immediate stakeholders, non-governmental organizations (NGOs), activists (sometimes even 'shareholders' activists'), media, communities, governments, and other institutional forces asking for what they consider corporate responsible practices. Some companies are establishing processes of dialogue with stakeholders in order to determine what should be an appropriate corporate social behaviour. Besides, more and more corporations are being pro-active in publishing reports on economic, social, and environmental performance, following the idea of triple-bottom line (Elkington, 1998). The Global Initiative Report (GIR) has become more and more popular as have certifications or reports, such as the UN Global Compact, the AA1000, SA8000, and others. All of this introduces more complexity into the corporate social performance models but, in essence, the conceptual foundations of this theory remain unalterable.

Conceptual Bases

The CSP model presented by Wood (1991*b*) is probably one of the most representative within this theory. It is a synthesis which includes: (i) principles of CSR, expressed on three levels: institutional, organizational, and individual; (ii) processes of corporate social responsiveness, and (iii) outcomes of corporate behavior.

The 'Institutional Principle' is also called 'the Principle of Legitimacy' and its origin is in Davis (1973). Davis presented interesting arguments based on ethics (human values and responsibility), social legitimacy (what society considers responsible), and a pragmatic vision of business through considering the consequences of an irresponsible use of power. He began his approach by emphasizing that responsibility goes with power, and business has power which has social impact (Davis, 1960). Consequently, business has to assume corresponding responsibility. He remarked that the factors that give rise to the social power of the firm are not completely internal to the firm but also external and their locus is unstable and shifting all the time from the economic to the social forum, and from there to the political forum and vice versa. Business needs social acceptance. 'Because society changes'—he wrote—'evidence suggests that the continued vigor of business depends upon its forthright acceptance of further socio-human responsibilities' (1960: 76).

Davis formulated 'the power-responsibility equation' in these terms: 'social responsibility of businessmen arises from the amount of social power they have' (1967: 48), an 'equation' which goes along with the 'Iron Law of Responsibility', which states that 'those who do not take responsibility for their power, ultimately shall lose it' (Davis and Blomstrom, 1966: 174; Davis, 1967: 50). Finally, he applied these ideas to business by saying: 'Society grants legitimacy and power to business. In the long run, those who do not use power in a manner which society considers responsible will tend to lose it' (Davis, 1973: 314).

Davis distinguished two types of social responsibilities for business people: first, socio-economic responsibility for general economic welfare; and second, socio-human responsibility for preserving and developing human values. However, he rejected two extreme positions: first, those who defend businesses having 'no responsibility' for what they are doing, that is, business stays in power but accepts no responsibility; and second, he also refused a sense of 'total responsibility', that is, business is responsible for 'everything' (Davis, 1967).

Wood understood the 'Organizational Principle' or 'Principle of Public Responsibility' following Preston and Post (1975, 1981), who proposed the public responsibility principle, that is 'widely shared and generally acknowledged principles directing and controlling actions that have broad implications for society at large or major portions thereof' (Preston and Post, 1975: 56). In accordance with this view, business should adhere to the standards of performance in law and the existing public policy process.

At the core of the 'Public Responsibility' approach presented by these scholars lies the idea that business and society are two interpenetrating systems. They emphasized the interdependence between social institutions. This differs from the functional theory of the business–society relationship, in which every social institution (family, school, business, etc.) is mono-functional. Considering business and society are interpenetrating systems, firms should be socially responsible, because they exist and operate in a shared environment.

For Preston and Post standards come from public policy, but understanding that 'public policy includes not only the literal text of law and regulation but also the broad pattern of social direction reflected in public opinion, emerging issues, formal legal requirements and enforcement or implementation practices' (Preston and Post, 1981: 57). They recognized that discovering the content of the principle of public responsibility is a complex and difficult task, variable over time, which requires substantial management attention.

At the same time, Preston and Post are in favor of business intervention in the public policy process especially with respect to areas in which specific public policy is not yet clearly established or is in transition: 'It is legitimate—and may be essential—that affected firms participate openly in the policy formation' (Preston and Post, 1981: 61).

Wood (1991*b*), without accepting in full Preston and Post's theory, understands business and society relations in a similar way, as 'interwoven rather than being distinct entities'. Hence, social expectations have direct influence on the shaping of CSR.

Preston and Post (1975) analyzed the scope of managerial responsibility in terms of the 'primary' and 'secondary' involvement of the firm in its social environment. *Primary involvement* includes the essential economic tasks of the firm, such as locating and establishing its facilities, procuring suppliers, engaging employees, carrying out its production functions, and marketing products. It also includes legal requirements. *Secondary involvements* follow (e.g. career and earning opportunities for individuals), arising from the primary activity of selection and advancement of employees.

The 'Individual Principle' is, for Wood, 'the Principle of Managerial Discretion'. Since managers are moral actors, they are obliged to exercise such discretion, within the very domain of CSR, as is available to them, towards socially responsible outcomes. In other words, this principle implies that 'because managers possess discretion, they are personally responsible for exercising it and cannot avoid this responsibility through reference to rules, policies, or procedures' (Wood, 1991*b*: 699).

Within the 'Processes of Corporate Social Responsiveness', Wood (1991*b*) includes 'environmental assessment', adapting the organization to its environment in order to survive, 'stakeholder management', analyzing stakeholder relationships and processes in order to manage interdependences and relations correctly, and 'issues management', which includes external issues, such as public–private partnership, community involvement, social strategies, etc. and internal issues such as corporate ethical programs, corporate codes of ethics, etc. Finally, 'outcomes of corporate behavior' include studies on social impacts, social programs, and social policies.

Strengths and Weaknesses

The CSP model is a synthesis of relevant developments on CSR up to the 1980s. Actually, it 'provides a coherent structure for assessing the relevance of research topics to central questions in the business and society field' (Swanson, 1995: 43). However, this model suffers from several weaknesses. The first comes from the vagueness of the concept of CSR. However, this is not the most important, since this can be partially solved by integrating stakeholder perspectives within those traditional approaches (Carroll, 1991, 2004).

More important is the weakness of the lack of integration between ethical normative aspects and business activity. Wood's institutional principle, which searches for legitimacy, does not advocate the moral motivation of respect (Swanson, 1995: 48). But, apart from that, this theory only emphasizes the social control of business by paying attention to public responsibility. As Freeman and Liedtka (1991) have suggested, CSR appears exclusively to give a human face to capitalism, but with a complete separation of economics and ethics.

Actually, from the very beginning, proponents of this model struggled for a business respectful to all people, defending human rights and human conditions in the workplace. In spite of the ethical content of these goals, many pioneers in CSR literature were reluctant to connect CSR with ethics, maybe because of the dominant ethical relativism in those days or to avoid discussing what is morally right or wrong. Instead, they preferred to use terms such as 'values of our society', 'social expectation', 'performance expectation', and so forth, instead of 'ethical duties' or equivalent expressions. Thus, as we have seen above, Bowen (1953) talked about 'objectives and values of our society'. Similarly, Frederick affirmed that social responsibility 'means that businessmen should oversee the operations of an economic system that fulfills the expectations of the public' (1960: 60), and Sethi considered that CSR 'has to be congruent with the prevailing social norms, values, and expectations of performance' (Sethi, 1975: 62). Archie B. Carroll (1979) also emphasized the role of the changing expectations of society on the contents of the CSR. Even when he talked about ethics responsibilities he meant the kinds of behaviors and ethical norms that society expects business to follow (Carroll, 1999: 283 and 1979: 500).

Other early scholars, however, without forgetting social expectations and demands, took into consideration ethical requirements as well. Thus, Eells *et al.*, wrote that 'when people, talk about corporate social responsibilities they are thinking in terms of the problems that arise when the corporate enterprise casts its shadow on the social scene, and of the ethical principles that ought to govern the relationships between the corporation and society' (1961: 457–8). Likewise, Davis, who was a great champion of CSR in the 1960s and 1970s, asserted that 'the substance of social responsibility arises from concern for the ethical consequences of one's acts as they might affect the interest of others' (1967: 46). Reference to ethical principles and ethical values became more frequent after the business ethics movement started by the late 1970s, and some relevant scholars, such as Frederick (1986), advocate for normative ethical foundation of CSR.

Because the CSP model does not integrate economic and duty-aligned perspectives, some attempts have been made to solve this problem (Swanson, 1995, 1999). However, and in spite of some advances, we are still far from having a sound 'integrated theory' of CSP.

SHAREHOLDER VALUE THEORY

Overview

Shareholder Value Theory (SVT) or Fiduciary Capitalism holds that only social responsibility of business is making profits and, as the supreme goal, increasing the economic value of the company for its shareholders. Other social activities that companies could engage in would only be acceptable if they are prescribed by law or if they contribute to the maximization of shareholder value. This is the theory that underlies neoclassical economic theory, primarily concerned with shareholder utility maximization. The Nobel laureate Milton Friedman is the paramount representative of this view. He wrote, with his wife Rose Friedman: 'In such an economy, there is one and only one social responsibility of business—to use resources and engage in activities designed to increase its profits so long as it stays within the rules of the game, which is to say, engages in open and free competitions, without deception or fraud' (Friedman and Friedman, 1962: 133).

In a famous article published in the *New York Times Magazine* in 1970, Friedman repeated and completed this approach by saying: 'the only one responsibility of business towards the society is the maximization of profits to the shareholders, within the legal framework and the ethical custom of the country' (1970).

This approach, which currently is presented as 'shareholder value-oriented', usually takes shareholder value maximization as the supreme reference for corporate governance and business management. Generally, 'shareholder value-oriented' goes along with the Agency Theory (Ross, 1973; Jensen and Meckling, 1976), which has been dominant in many business schools in the last few decades. In this theory, owners are the principal and managers are the agent. The latter bear fiduciary duties towards the former, and are generally subject to strong incentives in order to align their economic interests with those of the owners, and with the maximization of shareholder value.

Historical Background

The SVT has been quite common in the USA and other Anglo-Saxon countries, supported by the law, at least until the mid-twentieth century.

In the 1960s and 1970s a big debate took place between Friedman and others who defended the business enterprise as being responsible only for making as much profit as possible, always in compliance with the law, and in contrast, scholars including Davis (1960, 1973), Walton (1967), and Andrews (1971) who argued that corporations had much power and power entails responsibility, therefore, corporations had responsibilities beyond the economic and legal.

Friedman's position was clearly against the concept of social responsibility currently held in the 1960s, emphasizing the responsibility of business facing social problems, including those such as pollution created by companies themselves. He wrote: 'Few trends could so thoroughly undermine the very foundations of our free society as the acceptance by corporate officials of a social responsibility other than to make as much money for their stockholders as possible' (Friedman and Friedman, 1962: 133). Likewise, Theodor Levitt, who was editor of *Harvard Business Review*, wrote about the danger of corporate social responsibilities. In his own words: 'Corporate welfare makes good sense if it makes good economic sense—and not infrequently it does. But if something does not make economic sense, sentiment or idealism ought not to let it in the door' (1958: 42).

Since then, and in line with Friedman, some economists have argued that the market, instead of managers, should have control over the allocation of resources and returns. The starting point was the belief that the market is always superior to organizations in the efficient allocation of resources, and managers may lead companies in favor of their own interests and not of shareholder interests. If the rate of return on corporate stock was taken as the measure of a superior performance and managers' remuneration reflects this rate, opportunistic behaviors of managers would be avoided. In this view shareholders are seen as the principal and managers as agents of this principal. The expected role of the manager is exclusively to serve the principal interests. Thus agency theory, and the maximization of shareholder value, became a new creed (Lazonick and O'Sullivan, 2000), reinforcing the

Friedman position. Under this philosophy, from the late 1970s, merger and takeover activity was widely employed, especially in American and British companies, to discipline managers who failed in their responsibility to enhance shareholder value.

Adherents of this view considered CSR as a threatening dragon for shareholder value creation. However, an interesting answer came from Peter Drucker. This well-known management 'guru', who had already mentioned social responsibility of business (1954), reintroduced this topic three decades later, stressing the idea that profitability and responsibility were compatible, and the challenge was to convert business social responsibilities into business opportunities. He wrote: '...the proper "social responsibility" of business is to tame the dragon, that is, to turn a social problem into economic opportunities and economic benefit, into productive capacity, into human competence, into well-paid jobs, and into wealth' (1984: 62). A similar view was held by Paul Samuelson, another Nobel laureate, arguing that 'a large corporation these days may not only engage in social responsibility, it had damn well better try to do so' (1971: 24, quoted by Davis, 1973).

Subsequently, others have insisted that social contributions can be profitable, presenting CSR as a question of enlightened self-interest (Keim, 1978). As a result, arguments have been made for cause-related marketing (Murray and Montanari, 1986; Varadarajan and Menon, 1988; Smith and Higgins, 2000), corporate philanthropy in a competitive context (Porter and Kramer, 2002, 2006), and strategies for the bottom of the economic pyramid, that is, strategies which can simultaneously serve the poor and make profits (Prahalad, 2003).

Today, it is commonly accepted that under certain conditions the satisfaction of social interests contributes to maximizing shareholder value and most large companies pay attention to CSR, particularly in considering the interests of people with a stake in the firm (stakeholders). In this respect, Jensen (2000) has proposed what he calls 'enlightened value maximization'. This concept specifies long-term value maximization or value-seeking as the firm's objective, which permits some trade-offs with relevant constituencies of the firm.

However, it is hard to affirm that all practices of CSR are profitable. Burke and Logsdon (1996) have proposed the concept of 'Strategic Corporate Social Responsibility' (SCSR) to refer to policies, programes, and processes which yield 'substantial business related benefits to the firm, in particular by supporting core business activities and thus contributing to the firm's effectiveness in accomplishing its mission' (p. 496). On this perspective, there is an 'ideal' level of CSR determinable by cost-benefit analysis and depending on several factors (McWilliams and Siegel, 2001). In this way, CSR becomes compatible with Friedman's vision, if one carefully calculates what the optimal level of social output for maximizing shareholder value is in each situation (Husted and Salazar, 2006).

Conceptual Bases

Milton Friedman, in his *New York Times Magazine* article, made several references to values such as: 'free society', 'free-enterprise', 'private-property system', and, before stating that the only responsibility of business is to increase profits, he establishes as a condition: 'In a free society . . .'.

Again, when he explains that a corporate executive is an employee of the owners, he gives as a premise: 'In a free-enterprise, private-property system . . .'. In the same sense, Friedman's criticisms of his counterparts who defend corporate social responsibilities appeal to the fact that their theories 'undermine the basis of a free society'; they are a 'fundamental subversive doctrine'. He adds that those who spread the idea of business as not concerned 'merely' with profits 'are preaching pure and unadulterated socialism'. It is a doctrine—he said—that 'harms the foundation of a free society'. Talking about voluntary cooperation you find the same logic: 'In an ideal free market resting on private property, no individual can coerce any other, all cooperation is voluntary . . .'.

Shareholder Value Theory contains several philosophical assumptions. Those tend to originate in the seventeenth century, particularly from the British philosopher John Locke, who, from an atomistic vision of society, wrote extensively on 'natural' laws of liberties for the individual and the necessity of social contracts for living together, as buyers and sellers, and championing of a limited government. These ideas arrived in America in the eighteenth century and had an enormous influence on the US Constitution and, to a great extent, served as an economic and business framework along with Adam Smith's ideas on a free market economy.

Human beings are seen as individuals with desires and preferences. Some civic rights such as the rights to life, private property, and freedom are particularly emphasized. Society is no more than the sum of the individuals and the good of society is only the agreement on individual interests. This individualism is compatible with a sense of 'equality' understood as 'equal opportunity' and with the formation of 'interest group pluralism' as a key means of directing society.

Private property is considered practically as an absolute right, limited only by a few legal restrictions to avoid abuses. Private property is crucial, since it is considered the best guarantee of individual rights. The right of property is traditionally seen as a concept that assures individual freedom from predatory powers of sovereign. Thus, Sternberg (2000) strongly defends property rights, and argues that owners are legally entitled to the (residual) fruits of their financial investment and any other use is unjust.

Regarding the concept of the firm, SVT generally accepts that 'a corporation is an artificial person', that is to say, a creation of the law (Friedman, 1970), which establishes duties and rights for the corporation. Frequently, the firm is seen 'a nexus of contracts', especially in the economic neoclassical literature (Williamson and Winter, 1991). In the agency theory, contracts adopt a relation of principal-agent (Jensen and Meckling, 1976).

This vision of the corporation comes from legal fiction or from a hypothesis employed in economic and financial theory. But, to some extent, it is also a part of the reality one can observe everywhere: those who own business corporations hire people to manage them and these in turn hire labor to work in them. Managers and workers are employees of the owners of the business. On behalf of the company managers establish a set of contracts with suppliers, creditors, and buyers. So it seems unquestionable that in the firm there is a net of contracts and as Friedman points out, 'the persons among whom a voluntary contractual arrangement exists are clearly defined' (1970).

Coinciding with other theories, SVT accepts as a matter of fact democracy, market economy, and liberties included in economic activity, such as freedom of contract, freedom of association, freedom to start up a business, to hire labor, for choose products and to trade. More controversial is another assumption implicit in this theory: a full separation of the functions of the public and private spheres. So business is considered as a private and autonomous activity only restricted by the regulations of the government, without responsibility other than to make profits and create wealth. This mono-functional view leads to the rejection of responsibilities for the consequences of business activities. Thus, responsibility for the pollution of a factory has to be taken into account only if there is a legal requirement to avoid it. Friedman literally says that it is not acceptable 'to make expenditures on reducing pollution beyond the amount that is in the best interests of the corporation or that is required by law in order to contribute to the social objective of improving environment' (1970). In other words, the public good has to be pursued exclusively by public servants and politicians, but not by private businesses. So in Friedman's view, if the corporate executive assigns corporate resources to 'social objectives' that means that he or she is imposing 'taxes' on shareholders.

As a consequence of property rights, those who own the means of production hire managers, who have to defend the owners' interests. This raises a crucial point: corporate management has fiduciary duties towards the owners. These fiduciary duties, as Friedman (1970) stated, come from considering that 'a corporate executive is an employee of the owners of the business'. Consequently, 'he [or she] has direct responsibility to his employers'.

The purpose of business in society, according to Friedman (1970), is to generate profits. This purpose is expressed by this criticism towards those who state that 'business is concerned 'merely' with profits.' That is the exclusive responsibility of business. In his own words: 'there is one and only social responsibility of business: ... increase its profits' (Friedman, 1970). Nowadays, it is expressed in a wider way by saying the corporation has to be oriented to 'maximizing shareholder value'.

In the SVT there are two basic normative standards: the fiduciary duties of corporate executives and the compliance with the law, with a minimalist public policy. The fiduciary duties of corporate executives towards the shareholders or the company's owners become an important standard for responsibilities. According to Friedman (1970), 'a corporate executive is an employee of the owners of the business' and therefore 'he has a direct responsibility to his employers'. His or her responsibility is to conduct the business in accordance with the owners' desires, which generally will be to make as much money as possible.

Corporate structure in shareholder theory generally includes a decision-making structure based on principal-agency theory and to facilitate the fiduciary duties of executives towards shareholders. Likewise, the role of the corporate governance is seen basically to defend the shareholders' interests. Managerial systems also have to be designed in order to maximize shareholder wealth.

The second standard covers observance of the 'rules of the game' of open and free competition and abiding the law. Some defend a mitigated theory in which some other voluntary responsibilities can also be acceptable, according to a customary ethics.

Strengths and Weaknesses

Those who support shareholder theory usually emphasize the efficiency of this model for creating wealth. Managing and governing a company towards maximization of shareholder value is not only to enrich the shareholders, but also to achieve a better economic performance of the whole system. It is argued that conducting business for self-interest, presenting profits as the supreme goal, and operating under conditions of free and competitive markets within a minimalist public policy are the best conditions for wealth creation. For Jensen (2000), two centuries of experience strongly support this thesis. The above-mentioned conditions provide incentives for innovation, cutting costs and prices, producing products with economic added value, and having capital for future investments. At the same time, the tax system permits a part of the wealth generated to be shared by society through governmental mediation. The negative social impacts of business can be avoided through appropriate laws and government actions along with private charity, which can deal with inequalities and other social problems created by markets.

This approach is widely supported by the law and many companies are running under the guidance of this model, especially in Anglo-Saxon countries. However, there are also many critics who point out several weaknesses of this theory.

To begin with, economic performance is not the whole public good. Profits can go up, while workers are exploited, natural resources are irreversibly exhausted and the environment seriously damaged.

Adam Smith talked about the 'invisible hand' which provides public good, and the idea is still latent in many approaches supporting Shareholder Value Theory. Kenneth Arrow (1973), who criticized both the efficiency of markets and the factual separation of political and economical power, argues that the effects of externalities through asymmetric information (and for social purposes) destroys the invisible hand of Adam Smith and the connection between the micro and macro levels, and therefore the efficiency of markets.

In practice, shareholder maximization value frequently reflects short-term profits, such as a reduction in personnel expenses, rather than long-term profitability. There is increasing evidence that economic success in the long run cannot be achieved unless management takes into account not only shareholder interests, but also those of employees, customers, suppliers, local communities, and other groups with a stake in companies' activities (stakeholders). A successful business firm needs much more than self-interest and concern for profits. It requires trust, a sense of loyalty, and good relationships with all stakeholders and, as a consequence, an enduring cooperation among those who are involved in or are interdependent with the firm (Hosmer, 1995; Kay, 1993; Kotter and Heskett, 1992).

Alienating managers with shareholder interests, through high remuneration strongly connected with share value (stocks, stock options), is not always best for the company (Delves, 2003). Merger and takeover activities, regardless of their effects on disciplining managers, can cause economic instability and insecurity (Porter, 1992).

Property rights considered almost as an absolute right, which is pivotal to Shareholder Value Theory, have also been criticized as not acceptable for modern theories of property (Donaldson and Preston, 1995). Handy (1997) argues that the old language of property and ownership no longer serves us in the modern world because it no longer describes what a company really is. Capital is neither the only asset nor the main asset of a company. People who work in the corporation are, increasingly, its principal asset.

Regarding constraints introduced by the law, critics remember that laws are imperfect and their effects limited. It is neither possible nor convenient to regulate everything in business life. Furthermore, laws generally come after some undesirable impact occurs. Moreover, loopholes can easily be found in the law and many regulations strangle business creativity and entrepreneurial initiatives. In addition, a strong interventionism with laws, rules, and other governmental actions is opposed to minimalist regulation of markets, also required for strong free competition.

Last, but not least, some criticisms have been made of this theory, and particularly of Friedman's approach, for its narrow view of human beings, limited to freedom of election and self-interest, the atomistic vision of society, and the autonomous conception of business activity within society (Davis, 1960; Preston and Post, 1975; Sethi, 1975; Grant, 1991; among others).

STAKEHOLDER THEORY

Overview

In contrast to the 'Shareholder Theory', the 'Stakeholder Theory' takes into account the individuals or groups with a 'stake' in or claim on the company. In a very general sense, stakeholders are groups and individuals who benefit from or are harmed by corporate actions. From this perspective, the notion of CSR means that 'corporations have an obligation to constituent groups in society other than stockholders and beyond that prescribed by law or union contact' (Jones, 1980: 59–60).

However, not everybody describes business responsibilities towards the firm's stakeholders as CSR. For instance, Freeman and Liedtka (1991), who defend the stakeholder approach, maintain that CSR is not a useful idea and ought to be abandoned. They stated that the question of social responsibility just doesn't come up if stakeholders are broadly defined to include suppliers, community, employees, customers, and financiers. They wrote: 'Once we come to see each of these groups, and the individuals within them, as legitimate partners in the dialogue about 'what is this corporation going to be,' the social responsibility of the resulting entity is moot'. Instead, they suggested corporations have responsibility to all the parties affected by business activity, that is, *responsibilities towards the stakeholders* of the firm.

More recently Freeman and collaborators have insisted that the authentic responsibility is to create value for stakeholders, including the local community. Thus, Freeman and Velamuri (2006) have suggested that the main goal of CSR is to create value for stakeholders fulfilling the firm's responsibilities to them, without separating business from ethics. Consequently, they have proposed replacing CSR with 'company stakeholder responsibility', not just as a semantic change but as a different interpretation of the CSR meaning. Previously Wheeler *et al.* (2003) presented a proposal to reconcile the stakeholder approach, CSR, and sustainability with the creation of value (economic, social, and ecologic) for constituencies of the firm, not only economic value for shareholders. Apart from this clarification, there is no doubt that this 'stakeholder value-oriented' is a different theory for understanding the responsibilities of business, and is therefore relevant here.

Although there are a variety of approaches to the 'stakeholder theory', a sound definition of this theory could be the following: 'The firm is a system of stakeholders operating within the larger system of the host society that provides the necessary legal and market infrastructure for the firm activities. The purpose of the firm is to create wealth or value for its stakeholders by converting their stakes into goods and services' (Clarkson, 1995).

Stakeholder theory was first presented as a managerial theory. 'The stakeholder concept' wrote Freeman in 1984, 'provides a new way of thinking about strategic management—that is, how a corporation can and should set and implement direction. By paying attention to strategic management executives can begin to put a corporation back on the road to success.' (p. vi). However, it is also a normative theory which requires management to have a moral duty to protect the corporation as a whole and, connected with this aim, the legitimate interests of all stakeholders. In Evan and Freeman's words: 'management, especially top management, must look after the health of the corporation, and this involves balancing the multiple claims of conflicting stakeholders' (1988: p. 151).

In the stakeholder theory, the corporation ought to be managed for the benefit of its stakeholders: its customers, suppliers, owners, employees, and local communities, and to maintain the survival of the firm (Evan and Freeman, 1988) The decision-making structure is based on the discretion of top management and corporate governance, and frequently it is stated that such governance should incorporate stakeholder representatives.

In spite of these arguments, if we take CSR in a broad sense, then stakeholder theory can be considered a CSR theory, because it provides a normative framework for responsible business towards society.

Historical Background

The word 'stakeholder' was used for the first time in 1963 in an internal memorandum at the Stanford Research Institute, although the concept of constituencies of a company had existed before (Freeman, 1984; Preston and Sapienza, 1990). In 1983, Freeman and Reed contrasted the notions of 'stockholder' and 'stakeholder' in the context of corporate governance. In 1984, R. Edward Freeman published the landmark book *Strategic Management: A Stakeholder Approach* as a new conceptual framework for management. Four years later, Evan and Freeman presented a normative stakeholder theory based on a Kantian approach. In 1995, Donaldson and Preston examined in depth the foundations of the normative stakeholder theory. Since then, this model has spread considerably and Freeman, alone or with collaborators, has deepened his initial work, enlarging it, clarifying some aspects, and introducing some modifications (Freeman and Evan, 1990; Freeman and Liedtka, 1991; Freeman and Gilbert, 1988; Wicks *et al.*, 1994; Freeman, 1994, 1995,

1997, 1999; Freeman and Phillips, 2002; Phillips *et al.*, 2003; Freeman *et al.*, 2004; Dunham *et al.*, 2006; Freeman and Velamuri, 2006; among others). Other authors have also made further developments. Phillips (2003*a*) echoed some of these works.

Conceptual Bases

The term 'stakeholder', closely related to 'stockholder', was meant by Freeman 'to generalize the notion of stockholder as the only group to whom management needs to be responsible' (1984: 31). 'Stakeholder' can be taken in two senses: in a narrow sense, the term stockholder includes those groups who are vital to the survival and success of the corporation; in a wide sense this includes any group or individual who can affect or is affected by the corporation (Freeman and Reed, 1983; Freeman, 1984). Thus, 'stakeholders are identified by their interests in the affairs of the corporation' and it is assumed that 'the interests of all stakeholders have intrinsic value' (Donaldson and Preston, 1995: 81).

The stakeholder theory basically shares the same convictions as the shareholder theory regarding democracy and market economy principles. However, on other points they are quite divergent. The firm is seen as an 'abstract entity' where a variety of interests converge rather than as a 'set of contracts'. The purpose of the firm is related to the interests of different individuals or groups who affect or are affected by the activities of the firm. In other words, the purpose of the firm is 'to serve as a vehicle for coordinating stakeholder interests' (Evan and Freeman, 1988: 151).

Evan and Freeman base the legitimacy of the stakeholder theory on two ethical principles, respectively called by these authors: 'Principle of Corporate Rights' and 'Principle of Corporate Effects'. Both principles take into account Kant's dictum of respect for persons. The former establishes that 'the corporation and its managers may not violate the legitimate rights of others to determine their future'. The latter focuses on the responsibility for consequences by stating that 'the corporation and its managers are responsible for the effects of their actions on others'.

Two more principles come to guide managerial decision-making known as P1 and P2 'Stakeholder Management Principles' (Evan and Freeman, 1988):

P1: The corporation ought to be managed for the benefit of its stakeholders: its customers, suppliers, owners, employees and local communities. The rights of these groups must be ensured, and, further the groups must participate, in some sense, in decisions that substantially affect their welfare.

P2: Management bears a fiduciary relationship to stakeholders and to the corporation as an abstract entity. It must act in the interests of the stakeholders as their agent, and it must act in the interest of the corporation to ensure the survival of the firm, safeguarding the long-term stakes of each group.

Donaldson and Preston (1995) argue that property rights must be based upon an underlying principle of distributive justice. They also contend that all the critical characteristics underlying the classical theories of distributive justice are present in stakeholder theories. They conclude that the normative principles which support the contemporary pluralistic theory of property rights provide the foundation for stakeholder theory.

Several authors, accepting the basic stakeholder framework, have used different ethical theories to elaborate different approaches to the stakeholder theory, among others, Feminist Ethics (Wicks, Gilbert, and Freeman, 1994; Burton and Dunn, 1996), the Common Good Theory (Argandoña, 1998), the Integrative Social Contracts Theory (Donaldson and Dunfee, 1999), and the Principle of Fairness (Phillips, 1997). Freeman accepted a pluralistic ethical approach by presenting the stakeholder model as a metaphor where different ethical theories find room (Freeman, 1994). Balancing stakeholders' interests could be quite complex. Carson (1993: 174) made an interesting distinction which helps us to deal with those different interest:

Business executives have positive duties to promote the interests of all stakeholders. (These are *prima facie* duties.) But the duties to some stakeholders are more important than the duties to other stakeholders. Thus, sometimes lesser interests of more important stakeholders take precedence over the greater interests of less important stakeholders. Positive duties to stakeholders are constrained by negatives duties not to lie or break the law, etc.

In order to make this theory practical, seven Principles of Stakeholder Management have been proposed by The Clarkson Center for Business Ethics (1999):

Principle 1: Managers should acknowledge and actively monitor the concerns of all legitimate stakeholders, and should take their interests appropriately into account in decision-making and operations.

Principle 2: Managers should listen to and openly communicate with stakeholders about their respective concerns and contributions, and about the risks that they assume because of their involvement with the corporation.

Principle 3: Managers should adopt processes and modes of behavior that are sensitive to the concerns and capabilities of each stakeholder constituency.

Principle 4: Managers should recognize the interdependence of efforts and rewards among stakeholders, and should attempt to achieve a fair distribution of the benefits and burdens of corporate activity among them, taking into account their respective risks and vulnerabilities.

Principle 5: Managers should work cooperatively with other entities, both public and private, to insure that risks and harms arising from corporate activities are minimized and, where they cannot be avoided, appropriately compensated.

Principle 6: Managers should avoid altogether activities that might jeopardize inalienable human rights (e.g. the right to life) or give rise to risks which, if clearly understood, would be patently unacceptable to relevant stakeholders.

Principle 7: Managers should acknowledge the potential conflicts between (a) their own role as corporate stakeholders, and (b) their legal and moral responsibilities for the interests of all stakeholders, and should address such conflicts through open communication, appropriate reporting and incentive systems and, where necessary, third party review.

These principles propose a normative model for management. It is not a rigid code to be applied but a set of guidelines respecting stakeholders' legitimate interests and rights. They combine both the above-mentioned philosophical principles and some 'best managerial practices'.

Strengths and Weaknesses

Several strengths can be mentioned regarding stakeholder theory. First, this theory seems ethically superior to maximizing shareholder value because it takes into consideration stakeholder rights and their legitimate interests, and not only what is strictly required by law in manager–stakeholder relations. Consequently, managerial duties are wider than management fiduciary duties to the shareholders. In addition, the consideration of property rights fit better with justice requirements than the Shareholder Value Theory. Finally, this theory, at least in its original formulation, is more respectful of human dignity and rights.

It also contributes to a pedagogical language more in accordance with recognizing such dignity than other kinds of business language which tend to suggest people are mere human resources and a corporation simply a matter of ownership, which is bought and sold, sometimes without considering that the corporation is basically formed by persons. It is in line with Handy's argument that 'the language and the measures of business need to be reversed. A good business is a community with purpose, and a community is not something to be "owned". A community has members, and those members have rights, including the right to vote or express their views on major issues' (Handy, 2002: 52).

A second strength, is that the stakeholder theory superseded the conceptual vagueness of CSR by addressing concrete interests and practices and visualizing specific responsibilities to specific groups of people affected by business activity (Blair, 1995; Clarkson, 1995).

As a third strength, it can be pointed out that this is not a mere ethical theory disconnected from business management, but a managerial theory related to business success. The normative approach comes later and is closely connected with managerial decision-making. Stakeholder management is well accepted in many companies and provides a guideline which can lead to business success in the long term (e.g. see Royal Society of Arts, 1995; Collins and Porras, 1994), although to establish sound conclusions on the relationship between stakeholder theory and financial performance requires further research (Berman *et al.*, 1999).

Along with these strengths, this theory also has weaknesses, or at least, some critics. Criticisms, sometimes take the form of critical distortions, and at other times of friendly misinterpretations (Phillips *et al.*, 2003). Among the latter are those who consider that the stakeholder theory is socialism and refers to the entire economy or interpret it as a comprehensive moral doctrine. It is also a misinterpretation to apply stakeholder theory only to corporations and to think that this theory requires legal changes.

Some critics of stakeholder theory argue that it cannot provide a sufficiently specific objective function for the corporation, since the balancing of stakeholder interests abandons an objective basis for evaluating business actions (Jensen, 2000; Sundaram and Inkpen, 2004). This does not seem a strong objection since objective functions, algorithms, and mathematics, though useful in some respects, are not sufficient as a guide for human life, including business. In addition, stakeholder management is not necessarily against shareholders. As Freeman *et al.* (2004) note: (i) the goal of creating value for stakeholders is decidedly pro-shareholder, (ii) creating value for stakeholders creates appropriate incentives for managers to assume entrepreneurial risks, (iii) having one objective function will make governance and management difficult, if not impossible, (iv) it is easier to make stakeholders out of shareholders rather than vice versa, and (v) in the event of a breach of contract or trust, shareholders, compared with stakeholders, have protection (or can seek remedies) through mechanisms such as the market price per share.

Stakeholder theory has also been accused of being an excuse for managerial opportunism (Jensen, 2000; Marcoux, 2000; and Sternberg, 2000). A manager is able to justify self-serving behavior by appealing to the interests of those stakeholders who benefit. Hence the stakeholder theory, states Sternberg, 'effectively destroys business accountability … because a business that is accountable to all, is actually accountable to none' (2000: 51. f) Phillips *et al.* (2003) reply that managerial opportunism is a problem, but it is no more a problem for stakeholder theory than the alternatives. Furthermore, because a manager can attempt to justify self-serving behavior by reference to some stakeholder group does not mean that the justification is a persuasive or viable one. They also argue that stakeholder groups, in certain conditions, will maintain managerial accountability.

Another criticism is that stakeholder theory seems to be primarily concerned with the distribution of final outputs (Marcoux, 2000). However, this is more than questionable. Actually, 'stakeholder theory is concerned with who has input in decision-making as well as with who benefits from the outcomes of such decisions. Procedure is as important to stakeholder theory as the final distribution' (Phillips *et al.*, 2003: 487).

Several criticisms come from accepting that managers bear a fiduciary duty to all stakeholders and that all of them ought to be treated equally, balancing their interests (Marcoux, 2000, 2003; Sternberg 2000). Marcoux (2003) argues that stakeholder–manager relations contemplated by stakeholder theorists are necessarily non-fiduciary, while shareholder–manager relations possess the features that make fiduciary duties morally necessary to those relations. He concludes that stakeholder theory is morally lacking because (i) it fails to account for shareholders being owed fiduciary duties, and (ii) it treats all stakeholders' interests equally despite shareholders' legitimate claim to managerial partiality as required by the fiduciary duties owed to them. Here there could be some misunderstanding regarding legitimacy (Phillips, 2003b). Only legitimate interests should be considered in stakeholder theory. Gioia (1999) adds that managers do not find credible a normative theory based on voices shouting from the sidelines that organizational decision-makers should do the right thing. He believes that stakeholders do not adequately represent the complex social, economic, and organizational realities managers face.

It has also been objected that stakeholder theory admits a pluralistic set of interpretations (e.g. feminist, ecological, fair contracts, etc.). Hummels (1998) argues that 'each interpretation provides us with a different set of stakeholders and stresses the importance of specific values, rights and interests. Hence, different stakeholder interpretations lead to different distribution of benefits and burden, of pleasures and pain, of values, rights and interests' (p. 1404). This could be a more serious problem if stakeholder theory does not adopt a sound ethical theory and if the manager does not act properly.

Another weakness of this theory concerns stakeholder representation in corporate decision-making. This point has difficulties in both justification and implementation. Etzioni (1998) argues that although the theory can justify stakeholders taking part in corporate governance, it cannot be implemented without affecting the common good: 'while all stakeholders and not only shareholders have fair claims to a voice in corporate governance, recognizing such claims may be damaging to the well-being of the economy, and hence injurious to the common good. It might be further maintained that such consideration should outweigh the fairness claim' (Etzioni, 1998: 688).

To sum up, the normative 'stakeholder theory' or 'company stakeholder responsibility' needs some improvements, but it seems a powerful theory of the business–society relationship.

CORPORATE CITIZENSHIP

Overview

For decades, business leaders have been involving their companies in philanthropic activities and donations to the community where businesses operated. This has been understood as an expression of good corporate citizenship. This meaning is still accepted by some people. Thus, for Carroll, 'be a good corporate citizen' includes 'actively engaging in acts or programs to promote human welfare or goodwill' (1991: 42) and 'be a good global corporate citizen' is related to philanthropic responsibility, which 'reflects global society's expectations that business will engage in social activities that are not mandated by law nor generally expected of business in an ethical sense' (2004: 118). However, since the 1990s and even earlier this concept has expanded from its traditional meaning, and the language of corporate citizenship (CC) has frequently been used as equivalent to CSR (Wood and Logsdon, 2002, and Matten *et al.*, 2003, among others). But beyond these two meanings, in the last few years, some scholars have suggested that the notion of corporate citizenship is actually a different way of understanding the role of business in society. Thus, Birch (2001) sees CC as an innovation. While CSR is more concerned with social responsibilities as an external affair, CC suggests that business is a part of the society. Logsdon and Wood believe that 'this linguistic change [from corporate social responsibility to corporate citizenship] contains a profound change in normative understanding of how business organization should act in respect to stakeholders' (2002: 155). Similarly, Windsor thinks of 'corporate citizenship as a managerial movement that effectively substitutes a different conception, as well as language, for responsibility' (2001*b*: 239). For their part, Moon *et al.* (2005) suggest that corporate citizenship is a metaphor for business participation in society.

Historical Background

The term 'corporate citizenship' was introduced in the 1980s into the business and society relationship mainly through practitioners (Altman and Vidaver-Cohen, 2000; Windsor, 2001*a*). However, the idea of the firm as citizen had already been floated by several pioneers in the CSR field, including McGuire (1963) and Davis (1973). The latter, for instance, wrote that 'social responsibility begins where the law ends. A firm is not socially responsible if it merely complies with the minimum required of the law, because this is what a good citizen would do' (1973: 313). Eilbirt and Parket, in the 1970s, sought a better understanding of what social responsibility really meant, using the expression 'good neighborliness', which is not too far from being a 'good citizen'. Eilbirt and Parket explained that 'good neighborliness' entails two meanings. First, 'not doing things that spoil the neighborhood' and, second, 'the commitment of business, or Business, in general, to an active role in the solution of board social problems, such as racial discrimination, pollution, transportation, or urban decay' (1973: 7).

In the late 1980s, a respected scholar in the business and society field explained that 'good (corporate) citizenship . . . as reflected in company assistance to community well-being through its financial and non-monetary contribution was deemed for many years to be the quintessence of socially responsible business behavior' (Epstein, 1989: 586).

In the 1990s the concept of 'corporate citizenship' attracted positive business attention (e.g. Alperson, 1995; McIntosh *et al.*, 1998). The increasing popularity of the corporate citizenship concept has been due, at least in part, to certain factors that have had an impact on the business and society relationship, such as globalization, the crisis of the welfare state, and the power of large multinational companies.

Concern for communities where companies operate has extended progressively to a global concern due to intense protests against globalization, mainly since the end of the 1990s. Facing this challenge, 34 CEOs of the world's largest multinational corporations signed a document during the World Economic Forum in New York in 2002: *Global Corporate Citizenship: The Leadership Challenge for CEOs and Boards.* For the World Economic Forum, '*Corporate citizenship* is about the contribution a company makes to society through its core business activities, its social investment and philanthropy programmes, and its engagement in public policy'.[1]

Academic work on corporate citizenship, both empirical and conceptual, began in the late 1990s (Tichy *et al.*, 1997; McIntosh *et al.*, 1998: Andriof and McIntosh, 2001; Wood and Logsdon, 2001).

In the last few years, some scholars have undertaken the task of developing normative theories of corporate citizenship or similar concepts. Although a full theory of 'corporate citizenship' is not yet available, some valuable academic work has been done, among others, by Wood, Logsdon, and co-authors (Wood and Logsdon, 2001; Logsdon and Wood, 2002, Wood *et al.*, 2006, among other articles) who have developed the concept of 'Global Business Citizenship' and by Matten, Crane, and Moon (Matten *et al.*, 2003; Matten and Crane, 2005; Crane and Matten, 2005, and Moon *et al.*, 2005). Matten *et al.* (2003) have presented an extended view of corporate citizenship derived from the fact that, in some places, corporations enter the arena of citizenship at the point of government failure to protect citizenship. Then, business fulfills a role similar to that of government in solving social problems.

Conceptual Bases

The term 'citizenship', taken from political science, is at the core of the 'corporate citizenship' notion. The notion of citizen evokes individual duties and rights within a political community. However, it also contains the more general idea of being part of a community. In the Aristotelian tradition, business firms are seen as an integral part of society and for this reason they ought to contribute to the common good of society, first of all to the community where companies are operating, as good citizenship. In this tradition, the key concept of citizen is 'participation' rather than individual rights, as occurs in the current liberal state.

For Aristotle, being a citizen is basically to have 'the right to participate in the public life of the sate, which was more in the line of a duty and a responsibility

---

[1] See <http://www.weforum.org/en/initiatives/corporatecitizenship/index/htm>. Accessed on 10 Aug. 2006.

to look after the interest of the community' (Eriksen and Weigård, 2000: 15). Whether or not this view is accepted, theories on and approaches to 'corporate citizenship' are focused on rights, but even more on duties, responsibilities, and possible partnerships of business with societal groups and institutions.

Although, corporate citizenship is sometimes related to social expectation, it is mostly adopted from an ethical perspective. Thus, Solomon states:

> The first principle of business ethics is that the corporation itself is a citizen, a member of the larger community and inconceivable without it ... Corporations like individuals are part and parcel of the communities that created them, and the responsibilities they bear are not the products of argument or implicit contracts, but intrinsic to their very existence as social entities (1992: 184).

Solomon contrasts this perspective with current models of CSR which frequently implicitly concur with the Friedmanian assumption that corporations are autonomous, independent entities although they consider their obligations to the surrounding community (Solomon, 1992: 184).

For Waddock and Smith (2000), 'citizenship, fundamentally, is about the relationships that a company develops with its stakeholders' (p. 48). They understand that being a good corporate global citizen, basically, is respect for others. At the same time, this 'involves building good relationships with stakeholders and that such citizenship is the very same thing as doing business well' (p. 59).

Proponents of corporate citizen theory insist that application of the concept of citizenship to business should be undertaken cautiously, since citizenship primarily refers to individuals. Thus, Logsdon and Wood, the main proponents of 'Global Business Citizenship' (GBC), started their theory by analyzing the concept of 'citizen' and then considering possible meaning of 'corporate citizen' and then 'business citizenship'. For them 'business citizenship cannot be deemed equivalent to individual citizenship—instead it derives from and is secondary to individual citizenship' (2002: 86).

Wood and Logsdon (2002) found especially useful the distinction introduced by Parry (1991) between three views of 'citizenship': minimalist, communitarian, and universal rights. In the minimalist view of citizenship, citizens are merely residents of a common jurisdiction who recognize certain duties and rights. The communitarian view embeds citizens in a particular social context, where the rules, traditions, and culture of own community are highly significant, along with the participation in such a community. The universal human rights perspective of citizenship is based on the moral assumption of rights as necessary for the recognition of human dignity and for the achievement of human agency. Wood and Logsdon (2002, and in other cited works) think that, although business organizations can be seen from any of these perspectives, only the last seems to them suitable for business operating in a global arena. Thus, based on universal human rights and on the 'integrative social contracts theory' (Donaldson and Dunfee, 1994, 1999),

Logsdon, Wood, and others have developed an innovative theory of business and society relationship, called Global Business Citizenship (GBC).

In GBC theory, business organizations are vehicles for manifesting human creativity. They permit the creation of surplus value, allowing people and societies to do more with resources. The interests of the firm and their actions span multiple locales and cannot be completely captured in contracts. Each firm is seen as a participant in a network of stakeholder relationships. Because firms can be considered as citizens, although with a secondary status to individuals, they have derivative or weaker rights and duties.

To sum up, Global Business Citizenship can be described as 'a set of policies and practices that allow a business organization to abide by a limited number of universal ethical standards (called hypernorms), to respect local cultural variations that are consistent with hypernorms, to experiment with ways to reconciliate local practice with hypernorms when they are not consistent, and to implement systematic learning processes for the benefit of the organization, local stakeholders, and the larger global community' (Logsdon and Wood, 2005b). Thinking specifically about multinational companies, Logsdon and Wood explain that 'a global business citizen is a multinational enterprise that responsibly implements duties to individuals and to societies within and across national and cultural borders' (Wood and Logsdon, 2002: 82).

The GBC process requires (1) a set of fundamental values embedded in the corporate code of conduct and in corporate policies that reflect universal ethical standards; (2) implementation throughout the organization with thoughtful awareness of where the code and policies fit well and where they might not fit stakeholder expectations; (3) analysis and experimentation to deal with problem cases; and (4) systematic learning processes to communicate the results of implementation and experiments internally and externally (Logsdon and Wood, 2005a).

Matten and Crane (2005) presents a different perspective, which they call 'extended theoretical conceptualization of Corporate Citizenship'. They start to examine the notion of citizenship from the perspective of its original political theory and some significant recent developments in political studies. They also consider that forces of globalization have changed the relative roles of governments and corporations in administering citizenship rights, with corporations assuming this role: '(1) where government ceases to administer citizenship rights, (2) where government has not yet administered citizenship rights, and (3) where the administration of citizenship rights may be beyond the reach of the nation-state government' (2005: 172).

Matten and Crane state that corporations are 'active in citizenship and exhibit citizenship behavior' (2005: 175), but the corporation is neither a citizen itself (as individuals are) nor does it have citizenship. Thus Matten and Crane describe CC as 'the role of the corporation in administering citizenship rights for individuals' (2005: 173). This leads 'towards the acknowledgement that the corporation administers certain aspects of citizenship for other constituencies. These include traditional stakeholders, such as employees, customers, or shareholders, but also include wider constituencies with no direct transactional relationships to the company' (p. 173).

In explaining how the corporation administers citizenship rights, especially in countries where governments fail in their responsibilities, Matten and Crane distinguish a triple social role by considering three types of rights (social, civil, and political) recognized in democratic societies. First, the corporations is a *provider of social rights* (by supplying or not supplying individuals with social services which provide the individual with the freedom to participate in society, such as education, health care, and other aspects of the welfare). Second, the corporation is an *enabler of civil rights* (enabling or constraining citizens' civil rights, which provide freedom from abuses and interference by third parties). Third, the corporation is a *channel for political rights* (being an additional conduit for the exercise of individual' political rights, which permit active participation in society).

The proposal of Matten and Crane is descriptive, not normative. In fact, they question whether this triple role of corporations is acceptable, since the administration of these rights is a non-mandatory aspect of managerial discretion. If corporations act as CC in the way described, there arises the question of corporate accountability towards society. However, this is also problematic. 'Governments are accountable to their citizens and, in principle, could be approved or discharge of their responsibilities through an electoral process. Similar mechanisms, however, do not exist with regard to corporations' (Matten and Crane, 2005: 176).

Strengths and Weaknesses

A first strength of the corporate citizenship and global business citizenship concepts is probably the name itself. While some practitioners can see concepts such as 'business ethics' and 'social responsibilities' as opposed to business, corporate citizenship 'can be said to highlight the fact that the corporation sees—or recaptures—its rightful place in society, next to other 'citizens' with whom the corporation forms a community' (Matten *et al.*, 2003: 111).

A second point is in overcoming the narrow functionalist vision of business which reduces it to an economic purpose. Without forgetting the basic economic responsibility of business, the notion of corporate citizenship emphasizes the social and ethical dimensions of business and its role in respecting and defending human rights and in contributing to social welfare and human development within society.

A third good quality is its global scope, which seems especially appropriate in the current business globalization. From an economic perspective, it is emphasized that citizenship activities avoid risks, enhance corporate reputation, and hence long-term financial performance (Vidal, 1999). Gardberg and Fombrun (2006) argue that citizenship programs are strategic investments comparable to R&D and advertising. In certain conditions, they can help globalizing companies neutralize their alien futures by strengthening community ties and by enhancing their reputation among potential local employees, customers, and regulators.

A general criticism of the notion of corporate citizenship notion is that it is a diffuse concept, which includes many different topics: public–private partnership, corporate contributions, corporate ethical practices, corporate community economic development, corporate voluntarism, corporate community involvement and corporate brand, image and reputation management (Windsor, 2001a: 39 and 41). Probably a further theoretical development would give unity and coherence to several practices now presented under the umbrella of 'corporate citizenship'.

These two particular approaches presented above, the GBC and the extended theory of corporate citizenship, have received criticisms in their specific approaches. Moon et al. (2005) recognize that the work of Logsdon and Wood marks a major turning point in the corporate citizenship literature; nevertheless, they argue that their approach severely limits this important new potential. First, they argue that Logsdon and Wood fail to adequately examine the underlying metaphorical nature of the application of Citizenship Corporation. Second, they rely on fairly simplistic and dated notions of citizenship that do not allow them to explore the normative and conceptual potential of the term. Third, Logsdon and Wood's approach doesn't add anything to our understanding of business–society relations. Fourth, they do not offer any new normative base for the social role of corporations, being essentially voluntaristic. Fifth, because of their narrow view, the scope of corporate activities is substantially limited. More specifically, the Logsdon and Wood' model is not able to examine actions such as corporate political donations, lobbying, and involvement in rule-making. Finally, Moon and co-authors argue that the application of notions of citizen to corporations also requires a clearer elucidation of the specific conditions under which the status of citizenship could be reasonably extended to corporate bodies.

The extended theory of corporate citizenship has also been criticized (Van Oosterhout, 2005) because Matten and Crane's conceptualization of CC is considered highly speculative with little empirical support and because their approach fails to discuss corporate rights along with responsibilities. In addition, it is not clear why and how CC can emerge and be sustained and what corporations may want in return for assuming the responsibilities included in the concept of CC. Crane and Matten (2005) have responded to these criticisms by clarifying some points and giving further explanations.

Another concern about CC is its dependency on managerial discretion and the philanthropic ideology of this approach (Windsor, 2001a, 2001b). Windsor believes that those who use this concept are taking advantage of rising social expectations of corporate benefits in an age of government cutbacks and of a strategic management aimed at value creation in all functions and activities of a firm. The accusation of CC as a philanthropic ideology is spoiled by considering a broarder vision of business as a member of the society and the above-mentioned definition of business citizenship or global business citizenship, more dosely related to moral duties. Furthermore, even when some specific programs of corporate citizenship have to do with philanthropy this can have beneficial effects and can even bring about value creation in the long term. In addition, GBC is not, in the first place, about philanthropy but about universal human rights.

Regarding its managerial ideology, corporate citizenship is certainly, managerial-centered, but this is not necessarily a negative characteristic, and to avoid abuses some effective accountability and social controls may be established, although this is not an easy task, especially in a global context. This point deals with the concern expressed by Matten and Crane (2005) about how to make corporate accountability effective.

Another point which could be considered a weakness, or at least an unsolved question, in this theory, is the lack of clarity about who is responsible for creating the standards for global citizenship (Munshi, 2004). However, this point can be addressed if one considers that sets of universal standards and principles already exist, such us the UN Universal Declaration of Human Rights, the UN Global Compact, the Roundtable Principles, and so forth. Furthermore, there is also an increasing interest in discovering common grounds in religions and wisdom traditions, and some have indeed been found (Lewis, 1987, appendix; Moses, 2001; see also Melé, 2006).

A final weakness is that, although universal human rights can be a first step towards a corporate citizenship notion based on relational stakeholder networks, one can object that this approach is minimalist. A sound relationship with stakeholders should require solidarity with them, which is more than respect for other people's rights. Many would agree that a good society must be respectful of human rights, but this is probably not sufficient to build up a good society. On this point further developments will be necessary.

To summarize, 'corporate citizenship' and the related notion of 'global business citizenship' are powerful notions for business and society relationships, but they need further development to become more robust and overcome some current concerns and criticisms.

CONCLUSION

After reviewing these four theories, one may wonder which theory is the best. The first answer is: it depends on what you are looking for. All these theories can be used to explain what companies are actually doing. But, most of them can also be understood as normative theories showing what companies should do to maintain appropriate behavior in society. From this latter perspective, theories give us reasons why firms ought to assume, and principles for implementing certain responsibilities toward society.

It goes without saying that not all theories which can be proposed are equally acceptable. While a descriptive theory is established as valid after a significant number of tests, a normative theory is accepted as a consequence of its rationality and internal consistency. In practice, many companies, especially in the USA, are probably better described as following the shareholder model, while in other countries (Japan, Europe) the social behavior of many companies is closer to the stakeholder model. However, one can also find anywhere some companies which respond to the corporate social performance model. Furthermore, an increasing number may adopt the corporate citizenship model, particularly among transnational companies.

If we consider these theories as normative, the answer to what is the best is not easy. We have discussed some strengths and weakness in each of them, and we have found reasons in favor of and against each one. A first problem is that every theory comes from a different field of knowledge, with their corresponding premises. Corporate Social Performance is related to sociology, Shareholder Theory to economic theory, Stakeholder Theory is rooted in several ethical theories, and Corporate Citizenship comes from the political concept of citizen.

A good normative theory needs a good philosophical foundation, which has to include a correct view of human nature, business, and society, and the relationship between business and society. In future one may hope for further philosophical developments in order to reach a more convincing normative theory of business and society relations.

References

ACKERMAN, R. W. 1973. 'How Companies Respond to Social Demands'. *Harvard University Review*, 51(4): 88–98.

——— and BAUER, R. 1976. *Corporate Social Responsiveness*. Reston, Va.: Reston Publishing Co.

ALPERSON, M. 1995. *Corporate Business Strategy that Add Business Value*. New York: Conference Board.

ALTMAN, B. W., and VIDAVER-COHEN, D. 2000. 'Corporate Citizenship in the New Millennium: Foundation for an Architecture of Excellence'. *Business and Society Review*, 105(1): 145–69.

ANDREWS, K. R. 1971. *The Concept of Corporate Strategy*. Homewood, Ill.: H. Dow Jones-Irwin.

ANDRIOF, J., and McINTOSH, M. (eds.). 2001. *Perspectives on Corporate Citizenship*. Sheffield: Greenleaf.

ARGANDOÑA, A. 1998. 'The Stakeholder Theory and the Common Good'. *Journal of Business Ethics*, 17: 1093–102.

ARROW, K. J. 1973. 'Social Responsibility and Economic Efficiency'. *Public Policy*, 21, summer.

BERMAN, S. L., WICKS, A. C. KOTHA, S., and JONES, T. M. 1999. 'Does Stakeholder Orientation Matter? The Relationship between Stakeholder Management Models and Financial Performance'. *Academy of Management Journal*, 42(5): 488–506.

BIRCH, D. 2001. 'Corporate Citizenship—Rethinking Business beyond Social Responsibility', in M. McIntosh (ed.), *Perspectives on Corporate Citizenship*. Sheffield: Greenleaf, 53–65.

BLAIR, M. M. 1995. *Ownership and Control: Rethinking Corporate Governance for the Twenty-First Century*. Washington: Brookings Institution.

BOWEN, H. R. 1953. *Social Responsibilities of the Businessman*. New York: Harper & Row.

BURKE, L., and LOGSDON, J. M. 1996. 'How Corporate Social Responsibility Pays Off'. *Long Range Planning*, 29(4): 495–502.

BURTON, B. K., and DUNN, C. P. 1996. 'Feminist Ethics as Moral Grounding for Stakeholder Theory'. *Business Ethics Quarterly*, 6(2): 133–47.

CARROLL, A. B. 1979. 'A Three-Dimensional Conceptual Model of Corporate Performance'. *Academy of Management Review*, 4: 497–505.

—— 1991. 'The Pyramid of Corporate Social Responsibility: Towards the Moral Management of Organizational Stakeholders'. *Business Horizons*, July–Aug.: 39–48.

—— 1999. 'Corporate Social Responsibility: Evolution of Definitional Construct'. *Business & Society*, 38(3): 268–95.

—— 2004. 'Managing Ethically with Global Stakeholders: A Present and Future Challenge'. *Academy of Management Executive*, 18(2): 114–20.

CARSON, T. L. 1993. 'Does the Stakeholder Theory Constitute a New kind of Social Responsibility?' *Business Ethics Quarterly*, 3(2): 171–6.

CLARKSON, M. B. E. 1995. 'A Stakeholder Framework for Analyzing and Evaluating Corporate Social Performance'. *Academy of Management Review*, 92: 105–8.

Clarkson Center for Business Ethics. 1999. *Principles of Stakeholder Management*. Toronto: Joseph L. Rotman School of Management, available at <http://www.mgmt.utoronto.ca/%7Estake/Principles.htm>.

COLLINS, J. 2001. *Good to Great: Why Some Companies make the Leap and Others Don't*. New York: HarperCollins.

—— and PORRAS, J. 1994. *Built to Last*. New York: Harper Business.

Committee for Economic Development. 1971. *Social Responsibilities of Business Corporations*. New York: Committee for Economic Development.

CRANE, A., and MATTEN, D. 2005. 'Corporate Citizenship: Missing the Point or Missing the Boat? A Reply to van Oosterhout'. *Academy of Management Review*, 30(4): 681–4.

DAVIS, K. 1960. 'Can Business Afford to Ignore Social Responsibilities?' *California Management Review*, 2(3): 70–6.

—— 1967. 'Understanding the Social Responsibility Puzzle'. *Business Horizons*, 10(4): 45–51.

DAVIS, K. 1973. 'The Case For and Against Business Assumption of Social Responsibilities'. *Academy of Management Journal*, 16: 312–22.

—— 1975. 'Five Propositions for Social Responsibility'. *Business Horizons*, 18(3): 19–24.

Davis, K., and Blomstrom, R. L. 1966. *Business and its environment*. New York: McGraw-Hill.

Delves, D. P. 2003. *Stock Options & The New Rules of Corporate Accountability. Measuring, Managing and Rewarding Executive Performance*. New York: McGraw-Hill.

Donaldson, T., and Dunfee, T. W. 1994. 'Towards a Unified Conception of Business Ethics: Integrative Social Contracts Theory'. *Academy of Management Review*, 19: 252–84.

————1999. *Ties that Bind: A Social Contracts Approach to Business Ethics*. Boston: Harvard Business School Press.

——and Preston, L. E. 1995. 'The Stakeholder Theory of the Corporation: Concepts, Evidence, and Implications'. *Academy of Management Review*, 20(1): 65–91.

Drucker, P. 1954. *The Practice of Management*. New York: Harper.

——1984. 'The New Meaning of Corporate Social Responsibility'. *California Management Review*, 26: 53–63.

Dunham, L., Freeman, R. E., and Liedtka, J. 2006. 'Enhancing Stakeholder Practice: A Particularized Exploration of the Community'. *Business Ethics Quarterly*, 16(1): 23–42.

Eells, R., Walton, C., and Fox, S. 1961. *Conceptual Foundations of Business: An Outline of Major Ideas Sustaining Business Enterprise in the Western World*. Homewood, Ill.: R. D. Irwin.

Eilbert, H., and Parket, I. R. 1973. 'The Current Status of Corporate Social Responsibility'. *Business Horizons*, 16(4): 5–14.

Elkington, J. 1998. *Cannibals with Forks: The Triple Bottom Line of 21st Century Business*. Gabriola Island, Canada: New Society Publishers.

Epstein, E. M. 1989. 'Business Ethics, Corporate Good Citizenship and the Corporate Social Policy Process: A View from the United States'. *Journal of Business Ethics*, 8(8): 583–95.

Erisksen, E., and Weigård, J. 2000. 'The End of Citizenship?' in C. McKinnon and I. Hampsher-Monk (eds.), *The Demands of Citizenship* London: Continuum, 13–24.

Etzioni, A. 1998. 'A Communitarian Note on Stakeholder Theory'. *Business Ethics Quarterly*, 8(4): 679–91.

Evan, W. M., and Freeman, R. E. 1988. 'A Stakeholder Theory of the Modern Corporation: Kantian Capitalism'. in T. Beauchamp and N. Bowie (eds.), *Ethical Theory and Business*. Englewood Cliffs, NJ: Prentice Hall, 75–93.

Frederick, W. C. 1960. 'The Growing Concern Over Business Responsibility'. *California Management Review*, 2: 54–61.

——1986. Theories of Corporate Social Performance: Much Do, More to Do. Pittsburgh: Working Paper, Graduate School of Business, University of Pittsburgh.

Freeman, R. E. 1984. *Strategic Management: A Stakeholder Approach*. Boston: Pitman.

——1994. 'The Politics of Stakeholder Theory: Some Future Directions'. *Business Ethics Quarterly*, 4(4): 409–29.

——1995. 'Stakeholder Thinking: The State of the Art', in J. Nasi (ed.), *Understanding Stakeholder Thinking*. Helsinki: LSR-Julkaisut Oy, 35–46.

——1997. 'A Stakeholder Theory of the Modern Corporation', in T. L. Beauchamp and N. E. Bowie (eds.), *Ethical Theory and Business*, 5th edn.: Englewood Cliffs, NJ: Prentice Hall, 66–76.

——1999. 'Divergent Stakeholder Theory'. *Academy of Management Review*, 24(2): 233–6.

——and Evan, W. M. 1990. 'Corporate Governance: A Stakeholder Interpretation'. *Journal of Behavioral Economics*, 19(4): 337–59.

—— and GILBERT JR., D. R. 1988. *Corporate Strategy and the Search for Ethics*. Englewood Cliffs, NJ: Prentice-Hall.

—— and LIEDTKA, J. 1991. 'Corporate Social Responsibility: A Critical Approach'. *Business Horizons*, 34(4): 92–9.

—— and PHILLIPS, R. A. 2002. 'Stakeholder Theory: A Libertarian Defense'. *Business Ethics Quarterly*, 12(3): 331–49.

—— and REED, D. 1983. 'Stockholders and Stakeholders: A New Perspective on Corporate Governance', in C. Huizinga (ed.), *Corporate Governance: A Definitive Exploration of the Issues*. Los Angeles: UCLA Extension Press.

—— and VELAMURI, R. 2006. 'A New Approach to CSR: Company Stakeholder Responsibility', in A. Kakabadse and M. Morsing (eds.), *Corporate Social Responsibility (CSR): Reconciling Aspirations with Application*. Basingstoke Palgrave Macmillan, 9–23.

—— WICKS, A. C., and PARMAR, B. 2004. 'Stakeholder Theory and "The Corporate Objective Revisited" '. *Organization Science*, 15(3): 364–9.

FRIEDMAN, M. 1970. 'The Social Responsibility of Business is to Increase its Profits'. *New York Times Magazine*, 13 Sept.: 32–3, 122, 126.

—— and FRIEDMAN, R. 1962. *Capitalism and Freedom*. Chicago: University of Chicago Press.

GARDBERG, N. A., and FOMBRUN, C. 2006. 'Corporate Citizenship: Creating Intangible Assets across Institutional Environments'. *Academy of Management Review*, 31(2): 329–46.

GARRIGA, E., and MELÉ, D. 2004. 'Corporate Social Responsibility Theories: Mapping the Territory'. *Journal of Business Ethics*, 53(1–2), Aug.: 51–71.

GIOIA, D. A. 1999. 'Response: Practicability, Paradigms, and Problems in Stakeholder Theorizing'. *Academy of Management Review*, 24(2): 228–32.

GRANT, C. 1991. 'Friedman Fallacies'. *Journal of Business Ethics*, 10: 907–14.

HANDY, C. 1997. 'The Citizen Corporation (Looking Ahead: Implications of the Present)'. *Harvard Business Review*, 75(5), Sept.–Oct.: 26–8.

—— 2002. 'What's a Business For?' *Harvard Business Review*, 80(12): 49–55.

HOSMER, L. T. 1995. 'Trust: The Connecting Link between Organizational Theory and Philosophical Ethics'. *Academy of Management Review*, 20(2): 373–97.

HUMMELS, H. 1998. 'Organizing Ethics: A Stakeholder Debate'. *Journal of Business Ethics*, 17: 1403–19.

HUSTED, B. W., and SALAZAR, J. D. 2006. 'Taking Friedman Seriously: Maximizing Profits and Social Performance'. *Journal of Management Studies*, 43(1): 75–91.

JENSEN, M. C. 2000. 'Value Maximization, Stakeholder Theory, and the Corporate Objective Function', in M. Beer and N. Nohria (eds.), *Breaking the Code of Change*. Boston: Harvard Business School Press, 37–58.

—— and MECKLING, W. 1976. 'Theory of the Firm: Managerial Behavior, Agency Cost, and Capital Structure'. *Journal of Financial Economics*, 3, Oct.: 305–60.

JONES, T. M. 1980. 'Corporate Social Responsibility Revisited, Redefined'. *California Management Review*, 22(2): 59–67.

KAY, J. 1993. *The Foundations of Corporate Success*. Oxford: Oxford University Press.

KEIM, G. D. 1978. 'Corporate Social Responsibility: An Assessment of the Enlightened Self-Interest Model'. *Academy of Management Review*, 3(1): 32–40.

KLONOSKI, R. J. 1991. 'Foundational Considerations in the Corporate Social Responsibility Debate'. *Business Horizons*, 34(4): 9–18.

KOTTER, J., and HESKETT, J. 1992. *Corporate Culture and Performance*. New York: Free Press.

LAZONICK, W., and O'SULLIVAN, M. 2000. 'Maximizing Shareholder Value: A New Ideology for Corporate Governance'. *Economy and Society*, 29(1): 13–35. Reprinted in: T. Clarke (ed.). 2004. *Theories of Corporate Governance: The Philosophical Foundations of Corporate Governance*. London and New York: Routledge, 290–303.

LEVITT, T. 1958. 'The Dangers of Social Responsibility'. *Harvard Business Review*, 36(5): 41–50.

LEWIS, C. S. 1987. *The Abolition of Man*. London: Curtis Brown.

LEWIS, S. 2003. 'Reputation and Corporate Responsibility'. *Journal of Communication Management*, 7(4): 356–64.

LOGSDON, J. M., and WOOD, D. J. 2002. 'Global Corporate Citizenship: From Domestic to Global Level of Analysis'. *Business Ethics Quarterly*, 12(2): 155–87.

———— 2005a. Global Business Citizenship and Voluntary Codes of Ethical Conduct'. *Journal of Business Ethics*, 59(1–2): 55–67.

———— 2005b. Implementing Global Business Citizenship: Multi-Level Motivations', in J. Hooker (ed.), *International Corporate Responsibility: Exploring the Issues*. Pittsburgh: Carnegie Mellon University Press.

MCGUIRE, J. W. 1963. *Business and Society*. New York: McGraw-Hill.

MCINTOSH, M., LEIPZIGER, D., JONES, K., and COLEMAN, G. 1998. *Corporate Citizenship: Successful Strategies for Responsible Companies*. London: *Financial Times*.

MCWILLIAMS, A., and SIEGEL, D. 2001. 'Corporate Social Responsibility: A Theory of the Firm Perspective'. *Academy of Management Review*, 26(1): 117–27.

MARCOUX, A. M. 2000. 'Balancing Act', in J. R. DesJardins and J. J. MacCall (eds.), *Contemporary Issues in Business Ethics*, 4th edn. Belmont, Califf.: Wadsworth, 1–24.

—— 2003. 'A Fiduciary Argument against Stakeholder Theory'. *Business Ethics Quarterly*, 13(1): 1–24.

MATTEN, D., and CRANE, A. 2005. 'Corporate Citizenship: Towards an Extended Theoretical Conceptualization'. *Academy of Management Review*, 30(1): 166–79.

———— and CHAPPLE, W. 2003. 'Behind the Mask: Revealing the True Face of Corporate Citizenship'. *Journal of Business Ethics*, 45(1–2): 109–20.

MELÉ, D. 2006. 'Religious Foundations of Business Ethics', in M. J. Epstein and K. O. Hanson (eds.), *The Accountable Corportion*. London: Praeger, 11–43.

MOON, J., CRANE, A., and MATTEN, D. 2005. 'Can Corporations be Citizens? Corporate Citizenship as a Metaphor for Business Participation in Society, *Business Ethics Quarterly*, 15(3), 429–53.

MOSES, J. 2001. *Oneness: Great Principles Shared by All Religions*. New York: Ballantine.

MUNSHI, N. V. 2004. 'Conversations on Business Citizenship'. *Business and Society Review*, 109(1): 89–93.

MURRAY, K. B., and MONTANARI, J. B. 1986. 'Strategic Management of the Socially Responsible Firm: Integrating Management and Marketing Theory'. *Academy of Management Review*, 11(4): 815–27.

PARRY, G. 1991. 'Paths to Citizenship', in U. Vogel and M. Moran (eds.), *Frontiers of Citizenship*. New York: St Martin Press.

PHILLIPS, R. A. 1997. 'Stakeholder Theory and a Principle of Fairness'. *Business Ethics Quarterly* 7(1): 51–66.

—— 2003a. *Stakeholder Theory and Organizational Ethics*. San Francisco: Berrett-Koehler.

—— 2003b. 'Stakeholder Legitimacy'. *Business Ethics Quarterly*, 13(1): 25–41.

—— FREEMAN, E., and WICKS, A. C. 2003. 'What Stakeholder Theory Is Not'. *Business Ethics Quarterly*, 13(1): 479–502.

PORTER, M. E. 1992. 'Capital Disadvantage: America's Falling Capital Investment System'. *Harvard Business Review*, Sept.–Oct.: 65–82.

—— and KRAMER, M. R. 2002. 'The Competitive Advantage of Corporate Philanthropy'. *Harvard Business Review*, 80(12): 56–69.

—— —— 2006. 'Strategy & Society: The Link between Competitive Advantage and Corporate Social Responsibility'. *Harvard Business Review*, 84(12): 78–92.

PRAHALAD, C. K. 2003. 'Strategies for the Bottom of the Economic Pyramid: India as a Source of Innovation'. *Reflections: The SOL Journal*, 3(4): 6–18.

PRESTON, L. E., and POST, J. E. 1975. *Private Management and Public Policy. The Principle of Public Responsibility*. Englewood Cliffs, NJ: Prentice Hall.

—— —— 1981. 'Private Management and Public Policy'. *California Management Review*, 23(3): 56–63.

—— and SAPIENZA, H. J. 1990. 'Stakeholder Management and Corporate Performance'. *Journal of Behavioral Economics*, 19: 361–75.

ROSS, S. 1973. 'The Economy Theory of the Agency: The Principal's Problem'. *American Economic Review*, 63: 134–9.

Royal Society of Acts. 1995. *Tomorrow's Company Inquiry Final Report*. London: Royal Society of Arts.

SAMUELSON, P. A. 1971. 'Love that Corporation'. *Mountain Bell Magazine*, spring.

SCHWARTZ, M. S., and CARROLL, A. B. 2003. 'Corporate Social Responsibility: A Three-Domain Approach'. *Business Ethics Quarterly*, 13(4): 503–30.

SETHI, S. P. 1975. 'Dimensions of Corporate Social Performance: An Analytical Framework'. *California Management Review*, 17(3): 58–64.

SMITH, W., and HIGGINS, M. 2000. 'Cause-Related Marketing: Ethics and the Ecstatic'. *Business and Society*, 39(3): 304–22.

SOLOMON, C. R. 1992. *Ethics and Excellence: Cooperation and Integrity in Business*. New York: Oxford University Press.

STERNBERG, E. 2000. *Just Business: Business Ethics in Action*, 2nd edn. Oxford: Oxford University Press.

SUNDARAM, A. K., and INKPEN, A. C. 2004. 'The Corporate Objective Revisited'. *Organization Science*, 15(3): 350–63.

SWANSON, D. L. 1995. 'Addressing a Theoretical Problem by Reorienting the Corporate Social Performance Model'. *Academy of Management Review*, 20(1): 43–64.

—— 1999. 'Toward an Integrative Theory of Business and Society: A Research Strategy for Corporate Social Performance'. *Academy of Management Review*, 24(3): 506–21.

TICHY, N. M., McGILL, A. R., and ST CLAIR, L. (eds.). 1997. *Corporate Global Citizenship*. San Francisco: The New Lexington Press.

VAN OOSTERHOUT, J. H. 2005. 'Corporate Citizenship: An Idea Whose Time Has Not Yet Come'. *Academy of Management Review*, 30(4): 677–81.

VARADARAJAN, P. R., and MENON, A. 1988. 'Cause-Related Marketing: A Coalignment of Marketing Strategy and Corporate Philanthropy'. *Journal of Marketing*, 52(3): 58–74.

VIDAL, D. J. 1999. 'The Link between Corporate Citizenship and Financial Performance. *Report No. 1234*. New York: Conference Board.

WADDOCK, S., and SMITH, N. 2000. 'Relationships: The Real Challenge of Corporate Global Citizenship'. *Business & Society Review*, 105(1): 47–62.

WALTON, C. C. 1967. *Corporate Social Responsibilities*. Belmont, Calif.: Wadsworth.

WARTICK, S., and COCHRAN, P. L. 1985. 'The Evolution of Corporate Social Performance Model'. *Academy of Management Review*, 10(4): 758–69.

WHEELER, D., COLBERT, B., and FREEMAN, R. E. 2003. 'Focusing on Value: Reconciling Corporate Social Responsibility, Sustainability and a Stakeholder Approach in a Network World'. *Journal of General Management*, 28(3): 1–28.

WICKS, A. C., GILBERT, D. R., JR., and FREEMAN, R. E. 1994. 'A Feminist Reinterpretation of the Stakeholder Concept'. *Business Ethics Quarterly*, 4(4): 475–97.

WILLIAMSON, O. E., and WINTER, S. G. (EDS.). 1991. *The Nature of the Firm: Origins, Evolution, and Development*. New York: Oxford University Press.

WINDSOR, D. 2001a. 'Corporate Citizenship: Evolution and Interpretation', in Andriof and McIntosh (2001), 39–52.

——2001b. 'The Future of Corporate Social Responsibility'. *International Journal of Organizational Analysis*, 9(3): 225–56.

——2006. 'Corporate Social Responsibility: Three Key Approaches'. *Journal of Management Studies*, 43(1): 93–114.

WOOD, D. J. 1991a. 'Toward Improving Corporate Social Performance', *Business Horizons*, 34(4): 66–73.

——1991b. 'Corporate Social Performance Revisited'. *Academy of Management Review*, 16: 691–718.

——and LOGSDON, J. M. 2001. 'Theorizing Business Citizenship: From Individuals to Organizations', in Andrioff and McIntosh (2001), 83–103.

————2002. 'Business Citizenship: From Individuals to Organizations', *Business Ethics Quarterly* Ethics and Entrepreneurship (special issue on), The Ruffin Series No. 3: 59–94.

————LEWELLYN, P. G., and DAVENPORT, K. 2006. *Global Business Citizenship: A Transformative Framework for Ethics and Sustainable Capitalism*. Armonk, NY: Sharpe.

World Economic Forum. 2002. *Global Corporate Citizenship: The Leadership Challenge for CEOs and Boards*. Geneva: World Economic Forum and The Prince of Wales Business Leaders Forum.

CHAPTER 4

....

THE BUSINESS CASE FOR CORPORATE SOCIAL RESPONSIBILITY

....

ELIZABETH C. KURUCZ

BARRY A. COLBERT

DAVID WHEELER

The old thinking was that if you make money you can do this positive social and environmental stuff—but I think the true philosophy of sustainability is the interdependence. It's not about charity; it's about the fact that if you do the right things in the community, the community will do the right things for you. If you do the right things for the environment, you'll have a stronger business so that you can make more money. It's not about sort of a condescending view...I don't know if that's subtle or if people don't get it, but it's very important. It's about interdependence rather than balance. It's about mutual dependence or interdependence, rather than charity. It's fundamental.

(Manufacturing Executive, 2005).

IN business practitioner terms, a 'business case' is a pitch for investment in a project or initiative that promises to yield a suitably significant return to justify the expenditure. In what has become known as the 'business case for Corporate Social Responsibility (CSR)' the pitch is that a company can 'do well by doing good': that is, can perform better financially by attending not only to its core business operations, but also to its responsibilities toward creating a better society. A long tradition of scholars have examined this proposition, both theoretically (Carroll, 1979; Swanson, 1995, 1999; Wood, 1991), and empirically (Cochran and Wood, 1984; Graves and Waddock, 1994; Mattingly and Berman, 2006; Russo and Fouts, 1997), primarily with a focus on conceptualizing, specifying, and testing some relationship between corporate social performance (CSP) and corporate financial performance (CFP). The results are decidedly mixed: a firm that dedicates resources to fulfilling what are perceived to be its social responsibilities will financially perform either better, worse, or the same as it might have done otherwise, depending on which studies we line up and consult.

In a meta-analysis of CSP–CFP studies correcting for sampling error and measurement error, Orlitzky et al. (2003) found support for a generally positive relationship between CSP and CSF across industries and study contexts, and Preston and O'Bannon (1997) found evidence that positive financial performance either lagged or occurred synergistically with positive social performance. At the level of the individual firm, however, the question persists for both academics and practicing managers: is there a generalizable 'business case' for CSR, and if so, what are its dimensions?

The purpose of this chapter is to provide a general summary of the key value propositions evident in the research on the business case for CSR, described as four general 'types' of the business case, or four modes of value creation. We will then present a critique of these approaches (including identifying some problems inherent in the construct of CSR itself) and offer some principles for constructing a 'better' business case. Our intent is not to conduct a thorough review of studies analysing the relationship between CSR and financial performance, as that has been well done elsewhere (Griffin and Mohon, 1997; Orlitzky et al., 2003; Vogel, 2005). Rather we seek to unearth assumptions underlying dominant approaches in an effort to build a more robust business case for CSR that can move beyond existing limitations.

We take the view that managing a business enterprise is an increasingly complex task in an era of globalized trade and competition, exponentially faster information flow, highly fluid capital markets, and greater interconnectedness among civil society groups. Factors bearing upon the successful operation of a business are multiple, often non-linear and stochastic (and therefore largely unpredictable), and inextricably entwined with the needs of a global society—as described by the executive business practitioner in the opening quote from recent research. If ever the separation of business concerns from those of society generally was real and justified—and we concur with those who contend that it is, and has always been, a false distinction—such a separation is now not only conceptually invalid, but is pragmatically untenable. Principles for constructing a better 'business case' for CSR must reflect the changing conditions for business at a global level.

This chapter is structured as follows: first we will draw on existing reviews and models to construct an overview of four general types of business case for CSR, where each type rests on a broad value proposition for corporate social responsiveness and performance; the four are: *cost and risk reduction, competitive advantage, reputation and legitimacy*, and *synergistic value creation*, focused on creating value on multiple fronts simultaneously. Here we attempt to organize much of the literature under these four value creation categories. Next we outline some underlying characteristics and basic assumptions of each general type of CSR business case. Third, we consider key critiques of the business case as highlighted in the broader CSR literature. Finally, we offer ideas toward addressing these limitations, toward building more compelling business cases for contemporary organizations operating in a complex global environment.

FOUR GENERAL TYPES OF THE BUSINESS CASE FOR CSR

While there have been numerous reviews of the business case for CSR (Haigh and Jones, 2006; Margolis and Walsh, 2001; Salzmann *et al.*, 2005; Smith, 2003; Vogel, 2005), most are focused on organizing and evaluating the evidence for establishing a link between corporate social responsibility and financial performance (Griffin and Mohon, 1997; Orlitzky *et al.*, 2003, Roman *et al.*, 1999). Over 120 studies have examined this link over the past 30 years with mixed results (Margolis and Walsh, 2003), which has left some scholars in the field of CSR to question whether there is really any clear market motivation for firms to engage in socially responsible behaviour (Vogel, 2005). It would appear then that in the real world of strategic management a solid business case cannot be built by depending solely on locating an irrefutably established causal connection between CSP and financial performance.

Given these diverse reviews, this chapter will take a different approach. Although this mixed evidence might suggest that there is no a priori reason to develop a business case for CSR, there are growing calls for business to adopt a wider range of social and environmental responsibilities—from business associations such as the World Business Council for Sustainable Development and Business for Social Responsibility (Smith, 2003) and from governments and business leaders (Wheeler and Grayson, 2001). As the economic, political, and social power of business has grown relative to other societal institutions (governments, organized religion, for example), some argue that corporate social responsibility has expanded to the provision of the kind of services that used to be offered by governments and community organizations (Perrow, 2002; Solomon, 1997), including the function of guarding and enabling citizens' rights (Crane *et al.*, 2004; Matten *et al.*, 2003).

So here we have an apparent paradox: critics of business—and global business leaders themselves—are calling for an increased role for business in social and environmental affairs, yet there is mixed evidence of a positive 'business case' for CSR. Perhaps that is because most business cases seek justification on purely economic grounds. We support those who have argued that some kind of business case *must* be made in order to call attention and garner support from the business sector (Joyner and Payne, 2002; Schmidt Albinger and Freeman, 2000), but we suggest that the case to be made is qualitatively different from the one that currently dominates the literature.

A necessary step towards advancing a robust business case for CSR is a close exploration of the fundamental underlying assumptions of dominant approaches, so that we can move beyond the stalemate between economic or ethical models of CSR (Driver, 2006; Matten *et al.*, 2003), and build a more 'nuanced' business case for virtue (Vogel, 2005). While there is no universal definition of CSR (Carroll, 1999; Driver, 2006; Garriga and Melé, 2004; Smith, 2003; Van Marrewijk, 2003) this in itself is not problematic; like CSR, 'sustainability' has often been referred to as a 'contested concept' (Jacobs, 1999) and in this field of alternate meanings lies opportunity for forward-thinking businesses that adopt this frame (Colbert *et al.*, forthcoming 2008; Hart, 2005). We suggest that what is needed is a set of questions for unearthing the underlying assumptions of the various approaches in order to build a *better* (more robust, multidimensional, more compelling) business case for CSR, in order to address the growing need for business to become engaged in creating value on multiple fronts. In so doing we add to the call for the development of more integrative models of CSR (Driver, 2006; Swanson, 1995, 1999; Freeman, 2000), and make advances in that direction by offering a set of criteria that will begin to enable a move beyond economic and ethical conceptions of the business case through a focus on modes of value creation and the various dimensions that underlie this construct.

This section presents findings from our review of the literature focusing on the business case for CSR, which we have organized as four general types of business cases, each embodying a proposition for value creation: *cost and risk reduction, profit maximization and competitive advantage, reputation and legitimacy,* and *synergistic value creation.* As with other classification schemes, there may be disagreement on the placement of a topic under one category or another, but we hold with Bowie and Dunfee (2002) who emphasized the pragmatic usefulness of offering a classification scheme over an ad hoc approach. We do not present these as mutually exclusive categories—a firm may be involved in all four at once through a variety of policies and initiatives—but in our review of the business case for CSR literature, we identified these as predominant themes emphasized across the field of theories and studies.

In the following sections we describe these four general types of CSR business cases in terms of the *focus of the approach*, the *topics* of empirical studies and theory papers that characterize the type, as well as by the underlying assumptions about *how value is created and defined* in each domain.

Cost and Risk Reduction: Optimization Subject to Constraints

The focus of this approach is that the firm chooses to engage, or not, in CSR related activities in order to reduce costs and risks to the firm. A number of areas of inquiry typify this general approach to building a business case for CSR, including: the *trade-off hypothesis*, the *available funds hypothesis* or *slack resources theory*, and *enlightened value maximization*. Each of these hypotheses can be seen as embodying a view of value creation as some form of *trading* interests among social, environmental, and economic concerns.

The trade-off hypothesis, which most explicitly displays this view of value creation, was polemically defined by Milton Friedman (1962, 1970), who made a clear distinction between what he considered to be the real obligations of corporate executives: to work solely in the interests of the firm's owners, customers, and employees, and to eschew any urge toward diverting funds to improving the general social good, which he deemed 'taxation without representation'—grounds for another revolution. His succinct libertarian view set a firm dichotomy in the debate between fulfilling fiduciary duties and social responsibility, and established a benchmark statement on the negative trade-off view of CSR and costs to the firm: by increasing social performance for reasons of managerial whimsy, firms incur unnecessary costs and reduce their profitability—a view supported in a few subsequent studies in CSR (Kedia and Kuntz, 1981; Lerner and Fryxell, 1988). Some studies under this approach have identified an inverted U relationship which suggests that there is an optimal level of environmental and social performance, beyond which the corporation is incurring unnecessary costs and reductions in profitability (Salzmann *et al.*, 2005; Lankoski, 2000). The available funds hypothesis or slack resources theory (Waddock and Graves, 1997*a*), also assumes a trade-off view of CSR and financial performance by suggesting that when organizations are enjoying superior financial performance, or slack resources, they are able to dedicate additional resources to CSR activities. The implication in this approach is that firms perceive CSR as an additional cost and thus can only afford to pursue these activities when they are not in a situation where they need to minimize costs. In terms of Carroll's characterization (1979, 1991) of four categories of responsibilities (economic, legal, ethical, and discretionary or philanthropic), the slack resources theory addresses primarily the discretionary responsibilities.

A focus on enlightened value maximization (Jensen, 2002) implies that long-term corporate value maximization occurs through the appropriate management of trade-offs between stakeholders. Managerial decision trade-offs are driven by the 'agency solution', that is, the alignment of managerial interests with those of company owners through executive compensation weighted with stock options. High incentive plans can lead to the managerial opportunism hypothesis (Aklhafaji, 1989; Posner and Schmidt, 1992; Preston and O'Bannon, 1997), which identifies the potential for executives to reduce social and environmental spending, even when funds are available, in order to maximize personal compensation linked to short-term financial performance. Instrumental stakeholder management (Berman *et al.*, 1999; Donaldson and Preston, 1995; Quinn and Jones, 1995) describes how the firm is affected by stakeholder relations with a view to risk and cost reduction through trading off stakeholder concerns in the firm's decision-making process. Firms view stakeholders as part of the environment to be managed, rather than as driving corporate strategic decisions (Berman *et al.*, 1999), and attention to stakeholder concerns helps to reduce corporate risk by avoiding decisions that will push stakeholders to oppose the organization's objectives (Bowie and Dunfee, 2002). Establishing trusting relationships with key stakeholders is seen from this perspective as having the potential to significantly lower costs of the firm (Barney and Hansen, 1994; Hill, 1995; Jones, 1995; Wicks *et al.*, 1999; Godfrey, 2005). A focus on developing CSR standards and auditing CSR practices is a focus of the risk management approach aimed at building confidence among stakeholders (Story and Price, 2006; Kok *et al.*, 2001); research that presents a 'trading' managerial view positions CSR as separate from and secondary to economic performance (Adams, 2002) and strategic management (Dick-Forde, 2005). How organizations respond to expressions of morality in markets is influenced by a desire to avoid consumer boycotts, liability suits, increased labour costs, and short-term losses in market capitalization (Bowie and Dunfee, 2002).

Under a cost and risk reduction perspective of the CSR business case, the primary view is that the demands of stakeholders present potential threats to the viability of the organization, and that corporate economic interests are served by mitigating those threats through a threshold level of social or environmental performance.

Competitive Advantage: Adapting and Leveraging Opportunities

In this general case, CSR initiatives are conceived strategically as conferring competitive advantage on the firm over industry rivals. A number of topics relate to this area of focus, including: the *supply and demand theory* of the firm, *base of the pyramid* approaches, a *natural resource-based view* of the firm, and *including stakeholders for competitive advantage*. What is common to these perspectives is the characterization of value creation occurring through the firm *adapting* to its external context in order to optimize the organization's competitive advantage in its respective industry.

The supply and demand theory of corporate CSR (McWilliams and Siegel, 2001; Anderson and Frankle, 1980; Aupperle *et al.*, 1985; Freedman and Jaggi, 1982) takes an adaptation perspective toward the external environment by suggesting that firms will supply only the level of environmental and social performance that is demanded of them, with a view to profit maximization. Base of the pyramid approaches (Hart and Christensen, 2002; Prahalad, 2004; Prahalad and Hammond, 2002; Prahalad and Hart, 2002) examine how multinational firms might adapt to global drivers for change, such as population growth and poverty, in order to capitalize on the 'fortune at the bottom of the pyramid' (Prahalad and Hart, 2002). Similarly, adaptations of the traditional resource-based view of strategic management (Barney, 1991) are the 'natural resource based view' (Hart, 1995), natural capitalism (Lovins *et al.*, 1999) and the sustainable value framework (Hart, 1997; Hart and Milstein, 1999, 2003) that challenge managers to adapt to global drivers of change using an appropriate set of 'sustainability lenses' that allow a firm to segment shareholder value creation strategies. Also in line with the resource-based view, social and ethical resources and capabilities (Harrison and St John, 1996; Hillman and Keim, 2001; Litz, 1996; Petrick and Quinn, 2001) are conceived in this approach as internal organizational resources that build competitive advantage by enabling a strategic adaptation to the external environment. Approaches advocating stakeholder inclusion in strategy-making (Hart and Sharma, 2004; Mitchell *et al.*, 1997; Ogden and Watson, 1999; Wheeler and Sillanpää, 1998) also take an adaptation perspective toward creation of investor value. Competitive strategic positioning is the focus of Porter and Van der Linde's (1995) view of CSR as a competitive driver to be resourced by the firm. Social investments in a competitive context (Porter and Kramer, 1999, 2002) or strategic philanthropy (Bruch and Walter, 2005; Smith, 1994) also fall under this approach where firms elect to engage in philanthropic efforts that are supported by the core competencies of their organization, adapting to stakeholder expectations in order to generate sustainable performance with regard to stakeholder needs and their own competitive advantage.

In sum, *adaptive* approaches to building a business case for CSR focus on building firm competitive advantage through strategically orienting and directing resources toward the perceived demands of stakeholders. Stakeholder demands are viewed less as constraints on the organization, and more as opportunities to be leveraged for the benefit of the firm.

Reputation and Legitimacy: Building a Responsible Brand

The business case built in this domain is focused on exploiting CSR activities in order to build value through gains in firm reputation and legitimacy. Frames of inquiry associated with this view include: *licence to operate, social impact hypothesis, cause-related marketing*, and *socially responsible investing*. These approaches are characterized by a focus on value creation by leveraging gains in reputation and legitimacy made through *aligning* stakeholder interests.

Licence to operate concepts can be linked to Davis's (1973) 'iron law of responsibility' with the idea that a business organization is a social entity that must exercise responsible use of its power, or risk having it revoked, and thereby lose control over its own decision making and external interactions (Sethi, 1979). Social impact hypothesis (Cornell and Shapiro, 1987; Pava and Krausz, 1996; Preston and O'Bannon, 1997) focuses on the importance of alignment by suggesting that failure to meet stakeholder needs has a negative impact on firm reputation and thus suggests that the costs of CSR activities are much less than the potential benefits. Other studies focus on the positive link between a firm's corporate social performance and reputation (Fombrun and Shanley, 1990; Turban and Greening, 1997). Social cause-related marketing (Drumwright, 1996; Varadarajan and Menon, 1988; Murray and Montanari, 1986) highlights the alignment of stakeholder and firm interests by linking corporate philanthropy and marketing, showcasing socially and environmentally responsible behavior of the firm in order to generate reputational gains. Studies on ethical purchasing behavior and green consumerism (Crane, 2001; Frankel, 1998; Peattie, 1998), an extension of consumer sovereignty arguments that have been employed to model citizenry behaviour in political markets (Haigh and Jones, 2006; Jones, 1995), consider how a strong product brand or reputation acts as a marketing differentiation strategy for firms that can impact financial performance through enhancing reputation (Smith, 1990; Bhattacharya and Sen, 2004; Brown and Dacin, 1997; Sen and Bhattacharya, 2001).

Socially responsible investing (Barnett and Salomon, 2003; Domini, 2001; Kinder *et al.*, 1993) and ethical investing (Mackenzie and Lewis, 1999) emphasize an alignment between a potential investor's ethics and expectations of corporate social performance, suggesting a relationship with reputation and market value. Studies on the attractiveness of corporations as prospective employers (Schmidt Albinger and Freeman, 2000; Waddock *et al.*, 2002; Riordan *et al.*, 1997; Turban and Greening, 1997; Stigler, 1962) emphasize the alignment between a firm's reputation in the area of CSR and its ability to attract talent. Reputation and legitimacy is also the focus of intrinsic stakeholder approaches (Calton and Lad, 1995; Jones, 1995) that compare the approach a firm uses to interact with one stakeholder group, and its effects on stakeholder groups' perceptions. Isomorphic pressure for social responsibility is explored for its role in motivating CSR where an organization might gain first mover advantage and reap the rewards of reputational gains with dominant stakeholders (Bansal and Roth, 2000) or within industry-specific CSR initiatives (King and Lenox, 2000). The potential performance benefits granted through enhanced legitimation from corporate CSR disclosures (Gelb and Strawser, 2001; King and Lenox, 2001) is another area of inquiry in this general type of business case for CSR. Supply chain pressures on firms to seek social or environmental certification in order to support their legitimacy (Cashore, 2002) is another topic area that supports a business case for CSR through concerns with impact on firm reputation.

In summary, these topics and studies, organized under an *aligning* perspective, focus on building competitive advantage by enhancing the reputation and legitimacy of the organization through firm CSR initiatives.

Synergistic Value Creation: Seeking Win-Win-Win Outcomes

The focal point of this approach is in finding win-win-win outcomes by seeking out and connecting stakeholder interests, and creating pluralistic definitions of value for multiple stakeholders simultaneously. Topics gathered under this approach to the business case include: *positive synergy* or '*virtuous circle*', *sustainable local enterprise networks*, *value-based networks*, and *societal learning*. A focus underlying these approaches is the view that creating connections between stakeholders by *relating* common interests will open up heretofore unseen opportunities for multi-point value creation.

Positive synergy or the 'virtuous' circle' approach (Pava and Krausz, 1996; Preston and O'Bannon, 1997; Stanwick and Stanwick, 1998; Waddock and Graves, 1997*b*) highlights positive gains generated through combining slack resources and good management. The sustainable local enterprise networks (Wheeler *et al.*, 2005) model emerged from examining 50 case studies of successful and self-reliant sustainable enterprise-based activities in developing countries, resulting in virtuous cycles of reinvestment in human, social, financial, and ecological capital. The value-based networks conception (Wheeler *et al.*, 2003) describes how communities and social networks united by a sense of what is valuable create new opportunities for mutual gain. The concept of the triple bottom line of sustainability (Elkington, 1998) emphasizes synergies that can emerge for organizations, environment, and societies through integrating efforts across these domains.

Societal learning is defined as articulating new paradigms that can alter the perspectives, goals, and behaviours of social systems larger than particular organizations (Brown and Ashman, 1998). Of the three types of learning—single, double, and triple loop (Argyris and Schon, 1978)—societal learning deals with triple-loop learning (rethinking the rules of the business and society relationship), although it often is stymied at double-loop learning (reflection on how to play the current game better) (Waddell, 2002).

In summary, approaches advocating synergistic value creation are focused on seeking opportunities to unearth, relate, and synthesize the interests of a diverse set of stakeholders, broadly conceived. Because many of these emerging ideas fall outside of traditional business models, they are the least represented in our framework of value creation approaches.

Summary of Section: Four General Types of the Business Case

The business case for CSR is conceived under a wide range of topical and theoretical approaches. We have offered a typology of the chief approaches according to the basic value proposition embodied in each.

There are subtle but distinct differences between some approaches we have categorized under one type of business case or another. For example, one could argue for *base of the pyramid* (BoP) approaches to be situated under a *synergistic value creation* instead of *competitive advantage* view. Our rationale is that BoP advocates typically exhort multinational corporations (MNCs), primarily situated in more developed nations, to enter less developed geographies and find business opportunity by alleviating social problems, but with much of the financial value captured by the MNC. *Sustainable local enterprise networks*, by comparison, assume a more organic, grassroots, relativistic approach, and work with existing networks. The private sector is one player that can extract value but not necessarily the key player.

Our intent here is to draw some broad second-level CSR value creation categories in order to examine some of the basic assumptions underpinning the various business case pitches. The next section highlights some general characteristics of each type of business case, along with some basic underlying assumptions.

UNDERLYING CHARACTERISTICS AND BASIC ASSUMPTIONS OF THE FOUR TYPES OF CSR BUSINESS CASE

Each general type of CSR business case we have constructed embodies a number of characteristics and is underpinned by some basic assumptions. Our assessment of these underpinnings is necessarily broad, with the aim of sketching the general contours of each approach—to step back from the trees and describe the shape of the forest of CSR business case research. Characteristics we highlight are: the

Table 4.1 Four types of business case value creation

	Cost and risk reduction	Competitive advantage	Reputation and legitimacy	Synergistic value creation
Key Value Proposition	Trading: Engaging in CSR to reduce costs and risks to the firm	Adapting: A strategic approach to CSR to build relative competitive advantage	Aligning: Exploiting CSR activities to build value through gains in firm reputation and legitimacy	Relating: Integrating stakeholder interests to create value on multiple fronts
Central role of business	Economic Actor	Economic Actor	Political Actor	Social Actor
Level of Theory	Organization	Industry	Political and Cultural System	Societal
Assumed Nature of Interactions	Linear	Complicated	Complex	Self-Organizing
Dominant Logic	Normative Economic	Normative Economic	Normative Political	Cognitive Social
Ontological stance	Unequivocal	Unequivocal	Equivocal	Equivocal but grounded (language, history, culture)
Epistemological stance	Positivism	Post-Positivism	Social Construction (Structuralist to Interactionist)	Pragmatism

fundamental proposition for *how value is created* (and for whom); emphasis regarding a particular *role for business*; a preferred *level of theorizing* on which it is focused; and a *dominant logic* under which the basic proposition is grounded. Basic assumptions include the underlying *ontological stance* and *epistemological stance* of each of these approaches, which we will highlight in order to identify opportunities to bridge traditional debates in CSR. The general shape of each type is outlined in Table 4.1.

Key Proposition for Value Creation

The four general types of CSR business case we have described differ in their key value propositions based on the approach to dealing with elements in the organizational environment (stakeholder interests, competitive pressures, or other), each of which is succinctly captured under our four active descriptors: trading, adapting, aligning, or relating. Business cases framed as *cost and risk reduction* focus on *trading* among what are viewed generally as competing interests; *competitive advantage* business cases describe payoffs accrued through *adapting* to the competitive environment; a CSR proposition based on building *reputation and legitimacy* advocates aligning with political and social norms and expectations; and *synergistic value creation* approaches are aimed at *relating* disparate elements in the operating domain, and integrating those elements in novel ways.

Central Actor Role for Business

Across the theories underpinning these four broad propositions for business value creation there are, implied and explicit, a number of 'actor roles' for business institutions to play in society. Garriga and Melé (2004) mapped the territory of CSR theory and offered a set of four groups: instrumental theories, in which the organization is seen only as an instrument for wealth creation; political theories, which are concerned with the use of corporate power in the political arena; integrative theories, which focus on the satisfaction of social demands; and ethical theories, which are based on the responsibilities of corporations to society. These groups of theories correspond roughly to Carroll's (1991) categories (a pyramid of economic, legal, ethical, and philanthropic responsibilities) though his morality-based perspective would fit into the latter of the theoretical groups.

If we consider these groups of general theories and responsibilities in the CSR field at large, and we view 'business' (we use this term in the general sense to mean the private business sector, focusing mainly on public corporations) as a value-creating actor in the world, we can draft various actor roles that business is purported to play in global society. Both the *cost and risk reduction* and *competitive advantage* approaches take the explicit view that business is primarily an *economic actor*—the chief (or in the extreme, only) function of business is to efficiently convert inputs to products and services and to create financial wealth, and CSR activities are admitted as a means to that narrow end. Business cases based on a *reputation and legitimacy* approach highlight the *political actor* role for business. This includes and extends the economic role to include a complex mix of political and economic interests and dynamics. The power and position of the corporation in society is the central concern; the organization accepts social duties and rights or participates in some form of social cooperation (Garriga and Melé, 2004) as an expected part of doing business. *Synergistic value creation* approaches focus on the firm as an integrative *social actor*, which we define to embrace both the *economic* and *political* roles for business, and also extend to improving general social well-being. This is not a new idea, but one based on the reasonable presumption that economics and politics are human constructs, and therefore integral to the broad societal domain. This conception is consistent with the 'concentric circles' depiction of corporate responsibility issued by the Committee for Economic Development (CED), based on the notion that 'business functions by public consent and its basic purpose is to constructively serve the needs of society' (1971: 11, cited in

Carroll 1999). The first circle holds the economic and efficiency function of a corporation, the second contains the responsibility to execute the economic function with sensitivity to context, including changing social values and priorities, and the outer circle holds the responsibility to actively improve the general social environment, including the natural environment. The outer circle contains the inner two, and is not separable. This view is all the more relevant in an increasingly globalizing business environment.

Main Level of Theorizing

The level of theory (Klein *et al.*, 1994) is the organizational level that the researcher is attempting to depict or describe, and is the level to which the findings are purported to be generalizable. The four general types of CSR business case vary across theoretical levels; that is, each includes and describes interactions and effects at various levels in the business system. Theorizing in the *cost and risk reduction* view is centered on the organization, with key variables such as CSP and CFP distinctly attached to the firm; *competitive advantage* approaches necessarily include consideration of the relevant industry dynamics; *reputation and legitimacy* business cases address elements in the political and cultural context; and *synergistic value creation* approaches take a wide view of all components of the societal context. Again here, these are not mutually exclusive categories; there is an accumulative expansion of variables under consideration moving left to right.

Assumed Nature of System Interactions

As the level of theory is raised above the organization level there is a corresponding assumption regarding the nature of system interaction effects across the four general types. *Cost and risk reduction* approaches, often involving linear regression of CSF dependent variables on CSP/CSR independent variables, generally assume linear effects; *competitive advantage* approaches typically involve mediating or moderating strategic variables, complicating direct linear effects; a *reputation and legitimacy* view acknowledges non-linear complex effects in qualitative reputational narratives; and synergistic value creation approaches emphasize the self-organizing tendency of complex interactive variables. 'Complex' in this instance 'means more than just "complicated"; it describes a system whose component agents operate with some measure of autonomy, as well as in relation to other system components, i.e. independently and interdependently. That interaction gives rise to emergent properties that are irreducible, that exist only in relationship. As Cilliers (1998) has noted, an airliner is merely *complicated*; a mayonnaise is *complex*' (Colbert 2004: 349).

Dominant Logic Frame

The dominant logic frame describes the grounds for logical justification in each of the four general CSR business case types. A key debate in the literature turns on how to justify CSR-related corporate activity, which we address in the next section on key critiques. In our construction of four general types we deliberately have not separated out a purely 'moral business case', as we adopt the assumption that morality and ethics are embedded within constructs of economy and politics: to suggest that these are value-free realms is absurd, despite the distinctions made in much of the CSR literature. The four general types constructed here are justified on normative economic grounds, normative political grounds, or on grounds of cognitive social integration—that is, of unearthing and connecting notions of value and values in the broad social domain. The *cost and risk reduction* and the *competitive advantage* approaches appeal exclusively to economic logic and norms; the reputation and legitimacy cases find grounding in political logic—in the relative power dynamics operating in the prevailing social system, in the service of economic ends; and the *synergistic value creation* approach is grounded in cognitive social integration.

Relevant Ontological and Epistemological Stance

Economics-based descriptive research, which includes the *cost and risk reduction* and *competitive advantage* business cases, is primarily founded on a realist ontology that sees reality as objective and unequivocal (Wicks and Freeman, 1998). Both predominantly embody a positivist epistemological stance, which relies 'on the assumption of an objective world external to the mind that is mirrored by scientific data and theories' (Gephart, 2004: 456). A degree of relativism is admitted under a *competitive advantage* approach through a post-positivist epistemological stance, which holds that reality can only be known probabilistically; plurality is typically introduced in taking stakeholder constructions into strategy formulation processes.

Reputation and legitimacy approaches are built on an equivocal, constructivist ontology and epistemology. The social construction of reality means that social existence is a human construction, while at the same time human perspectives are shaped by social factors (Berger and Luckmann, 1966). There are two main streams of social construction: an interactionist approach and a structuralist approach (Pfeffer, 1985). The interactionist position is one of extreme relativism, with each event knowable only from the perspective of the individual experiencing it, whereas the structuralist sees patterns of meaning shaped by roles and shared paradigms, which both structure and constrain the interpretations that are given to interaction patterns. Reputation and legitimacy are constructs that can be framed from both an interactionist and a structuralist view.

The *synergistic value creation* view holds an equivocal, or relativist, ontology, but adopts a pragmatic stance that sees intersubjective realities as mediated by language, history, and culture (Wicks and Freeman, 1998). A pragmatic epistemology rejects the categorical distinctions of positivism, and the absolute relativism of anti-positivism, and assesses research not on grounds of 'truth', however constructed, but on grounds of usefulness (Wicks and Freeman, 1998)—in this case, usefulness applies to the level and range of value creation through corporate CSR activities.

Underlying Characteristics and Assumptions: Summary

The characteristics and assumptions described above and displayed in Table 4.1 help to illustrate some key differences across the four types of CSR business case. Differences across the *central role of business*, and the *level of theorizing* point to an opportunity to broaden the scope of business-case making to explicitly include consideration of value creation at various levels—levels that are cumulatively integrated, or exist as nested systems. The range of the *assumed nature of system interactions* and variations in the *dominant logic* taken together suggest there are alternate ways in which a business case can be framed. There are also alternate ways in which one might be received by managers and stakeholders, once we admit a wider variety of sense-making frames and processes of meaning creation. And finally, the variation in *ontological* and *epistemological* stances indicates that the methods by which we attempt to describe and justify a business case for CSR could be broader than they are typically. And finally, acknowledging the variation in *ontological* and *epistemological* grounds opens opportunities to describe and justify a CSR business case more broadly than is typical.

GENERAL CRITIQUES OF THE BUSINESS CASE FOR CSR

Building a 'business case' for CSR implies we are building a coherent justification for a corporation to invest in CSR-defined initiatives. The central debates and critiques in the CSR literature, as they relate to a business case for CSR, are therefore problems of justification. Three key problems that recur in CSR critiques are: the *level* of justification (organization and society); the *logic* of justification (economic, ethical, political, social); and the *grounds* of justification (positivist, anti-positivist, and pragmatist).

Level of Justification: Organization and Society

The search for definitive causal connections between CSP and CFP has yielded inconclusive results (Griffin and Mohon, 1997), and some have argued that the search is pointless, because there logically cannot be a consistently positive relationship between these two constructs: the working assumption of CSP research is that corporate social and financial performance are universally related, and it is an extreme, untenable proposition to assert that any management initiative is *always* positively correlated with financial results under any conditions (Rowley and Berman, 2000). While generalizable justification at the level of the single organization might inherently not be possible, meta-studies have found a positive correlation overall between CSP and CFP indicators (Orlitzsky *et al.*, 2003; Preston and O'Bannon, 1997). This suggests that CSR business case arguments might be more appropriately framed at multiple levels simultaneously: we might see 'the projects of "self-creation" and 'community creation' as two sides of the same coin, and see in institutions many possibilities for different ways of living together to pursue the joint ends of individual and collective good' (Freeman and Liedtka, 1991: 96).

Logic of Justification: Economic, Ethical, Political, Social

The problem with the logic of justification is most often characterized as a schism between economic and ethical justifications for CSR—the implication being that economic evidence is not normative, is value free. This problem is perpetuated due to an inherent defect in the construct of CSR itself: by asserting that corporations must attend to 'social responsibilities' in addition to 'business responsibilities', we admit that the two are distinct and separable. This distinction is further amplified when we attempt to justify CSR with a 'business case', i.e. when we attempt to express the value of socially responsible practices in purely financial terms, which says that financial performance stands as sufficient justification for CSR-related activity.

Swanson (1995) described several theory-building problems with 'economic' and 'duty-aligned' (ethical, political, social) perspectives of CSP research: incompatible value outcomes, a focus on individual choice, and narrow value orientations. Others have argued that CSR justified on economic models presents a too-narrow idea of the corporation and of the interests of investors (Gioia, 2003; Stormer, 2003), for whom, presumably, a business case for CSR is built.

Burrell and Morgan described a *unitary* view of organizations as one that tends to stress that the corporation is a cooperative enterprise united in the pursuit of a common goal. A *pluralist* view stresses the diversity of individual goals and interests—the formal goals of an organization are seen as 'little more than a legitimizing façade, an umbrella under which a host of individual and group interests are pursued as ends in themselves' (1979: 202–3). Debate between economic and ethical justifications for CSR is a debate between two fundamental conceptions of *what is a corporation*: a disconnected, simple entity with unidimensional, stable interests, or an interconnected, complex self with multidimensional, dynamic interests, taking responsibility for a greater common good (Driver, 2006).

Throughout the CSR literature, economic and ethical justifications are separated, and the latter are called 'normative'; we rejected that separation in our overview of the underlying characteristics of business case arguments, and used the terms *normative economic* and *normative political* to foreground the integration of ethics and values into those paradigms. All management research is normative in the sense that every paradigm rests on some (often unstated, unchallenged) assumptions about what is good and valuable and worth pursuing; CSR researchers hold that firms have real obligations to a broad set of stakeholders, and because this runs counter to the dominant ideology of shareholder primacy, they appeal to ethical arguments to substantiate their preferences (de Bakker *et al.*, 2005); this creates the appearance of a separation between ethics and economics where none exists, as the dominant view is just as ethically laden. This false separation is perpetuated when we attempt to justify positive social behaviour in economic terms, rather than as valuable in itself, and as integral to a healthy capitalist business system.

Grounds of Justification: Positivist, Anti-positivist, and Pragmatist

A further critique occurs on epistemological grounds of justification for CSR: what has been called the 'integration dilemma' (Swanson 1999: 507), of bringing together empirical (descriptive) and normative (prescriptive) approaches. Empirical inquiry investigates measurement, explanation, and prediction, while normative inquiry focuses on moral evaluation, judgment, and prescription of human action (Trevino and Weaver, 1994). Positivistic approaches place a sharp distinction between describing and prescribing: in descriptive work, researchers stand as neutral observers, using scientific methods to make contact with 'reality', to report to managers 'in an unbiased way what empirical forces are to be reckoned with in a given context' (Wicks and Freeman, 1998: 125). When prescription is undertaken, as it often is in the strategy discipline, it is done so on the grounds of assumed goals such as corporate efficiency and wealth maximization. An anti-positivist epistemology (including interpretive, constructivist, and morally normative approaches) admits an intersubjective, multi-vocal plurality to the grounds of justification, but is in danger of collapsing under the weight of the relativist dilemma, where nothing useful can be said to advance organizational practice, lest one view be privileged over another. The pragmatist approach employs the criterion of 'usefulness'—though not in the utilitarian sense of 'the greatest good for the greatest possible number'. Rather, useful 'in the sense of helping people to cope with the world or to create better organizations' (Wicks and Freeman, 1998: 129). A pragmatic epistemology admits multi-vocality, but finds evaluative criteria in higher order humanistic goals.

Summary

These three problems: the *level, logic,* and *grounds of justification* are critical issues to be addressed in formulating research in the business case for CSR. These problems are at some level irresolvable, and are exacerbated by the construct of CSR itself. Rather than attempt resolution, we will next offer ideas toward building more expansive conceptions of the CSR business case to embrace these apparent paradoxes.

Building a Better Business Case for CSR: Addressing the Critiques and Embracing a Social Actor Role for Business

We suggest that progression toward a more integral approach to CSR, with a focus on *modes of value creation,* would assist with developing a more robust rationale for why CSR matters to business theorists and practitioners. To set out some recommendations in this regard, it would first be helpful to consider three 'eras' of CSR research (Van Marrewijk, 2003), and how we might envisage different incarnations of the business case for CSR in relation to those eras. We consider how research in CSR might shift in order to enable the development of a 'postconventional' view of the business case for corporate social responsibility. Our recommendations will address the ontological (rational to pluralistic to integral), epistemological (reductive to fragmented to integrative), and methodological (positivist to constructivist to pragmatic) transitions that we argue are required for this new 'era' of the business case in CSR to be fully realized.

Three Eras in CSR Research and the Business Case for Social Responsibility

Different authors have outlined historical eras in CSR in terms of a sequence of approaches (Carroll, 1999; Freeman, 1984; Van Marrewijk, 2003). Rather than take this as a succession of eras, where the shareholder approach was replaced by the stakeholder approach and so on, we suggest that these approaches exist simultaneously, one building on the next and necessitating a broader business case be built (this is a matter of shifting emphasis: 'stakeholder'-focused management has existed since the beginning of the Industrial Revolution,[1] what is novel is that this view has been named and described, and has moved to the mainstream of management thought and practice). The first era of *shareholder primacy* is characterized by a view of organizations as primarily accountable to shareholders, evidenced most clearly in the *cost and risk reduction* approach, and to some degree in the *competitive advantage* view to building a business case for CSR. The second era of *stakeholder management* broadens the locus of reference for the firm toward incorporation of, and adaptation to, a variety of stakeholder interests. In the general types of the business case for CSR, *competitive advantage* and *reputation and legitimacy* approaches demonstrate thinking in this 'era' by extending the role of business beyond that of an economic actor, toward acknowledging a dual role for business: as both economic and political actor. This approach thus builds on the perspective of the previous era, rather than negating it, developing a richer and fuller view of the organization in context. The third era of *social integration*, or a societal approach, is represented by a move away from thinking about social responsibility toward thinking about *societal* responsibility (Gioia, 2003). CSR theory and research that builds the business case for *synergistic value creation* begins to advance into this era by incorporating a view of business as an economic, political, and social actor (all of which embrace ethics). Each of these eras co-exists in the *social integration* approach to CSR, with 'eras' representing waves of influence in the dominant approaches, rather than temporally distinct conceptions. In fact, the social integration perspective was embodied in the CED (1971) description of CSR more than 35 years ago, and thus does not represent a modern 'era', so much as a worldview toward social systems as holistic and contextually sensitive.

Eras of CSR and Development in Human Systems

In order to explore this more fully, we follow Van Marrewijk (2003) and invoke Ken Wilber's thinking on levels of development in human systems. The four value propositions identified earlier as four general types of the business case for CSR can be conceived of as *four modes of value creation*, underlain by several dimensions. These dimensions can be mapped across the three eras of general CSR research in order to describe a new form of the business case for CSR, one that holds the promise of advancing the field. In his map of 'human possibilities', Wilber (2000) describes the evolution of social systems and related evolution in culture and

---

[1] The first examples of 'cooperative' enterprise occurred in the early years of the 19th century in Scotland and England (Wheeler and Sillanpää, 1997).

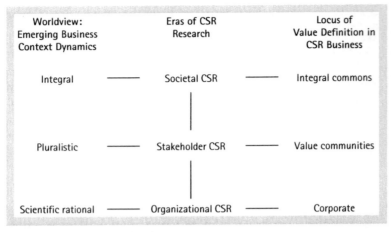

Fig. 4.1 CSR value holarchy

worldview in terms of preconventional, conventional, and postconventional states, and these can map onto the different eras of CSR. Shareholder primacy typifies the preconventional 'corporate states' approach to social systems reflected in a scientific rational worldview. Stakeholder approaches can be seen as the conventional state, organizing society in terms of 'value communities' that are embodied within a pluralistic perspective. Finally, the postconventional approach of societal integration portrays a view of social systems as an integral commons, coextensive with an integral worldview—a creative space (physical, cognitive, or virtual) to foster the coming together of humanistic interest and intention.

In this progression, nothing is lost, but there is an increase in integrative capacity that facilitates a move toward holism—the progression is not 'hierarchical', but 'holarchical'. Figure 4.1 depicts a CSR value holarchy. Each stage can be viewed as 'higher or deeper, meaning more valuable and useful for a wider range of interactions' (Wilber, 1998: 59).

While acknowledging that the 'pluralistic relativism' of stakeholder management is a positive progression, it must be viewed as a precursor to moving to the ground for integration, or be found irrelevant; without integration, pragmatic action is stymied. Within the stakeholder management era then, the move away from dealing with a few individual stakeholders that are powerful, legitimate, and urgent (Mitchell *et al.*, 1997) and the increasing trend toward acknowledging a wider range of 'fringe stakeholders' (Hart and Sharma, 2004) holds great potential for enhancing contextual sensitivity. However, there is the danger that this new radical pluralism will collapse to fragmentation and challenge any action beyond individual agency. It is necessary to view this as a stage of development toward integralism. For business organizations, integralism occurs when deep and broad social needs are put to the foreground in re-imagination of business strategies—when strategic planning exercises are driven from an intensive

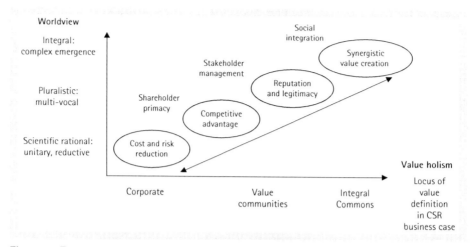

Fig. 4.2 Four modes of value creation in the CSR business case

exploration and understanding of real human needs, versus commercially created wants. This move honours that difference but creates a healthy tension between *agency* and *communion*, in order to avoid what Wilber calls the 'pathology' of fragmentation.

In our analysis of the business case for CSR, this integral commons is approached in the move from stakeholder management to social integration through a focus on value-based networks, with modes of value creation forming the business case for corporate social responsibility (see Fig. 4.2). We describe the dimensions of these modes of value creation more fully in the following three recommendations for building a better business case for CSR; that is, one that has more integrative capacity, is more holistic and allows for emergence, and thus is more valuable and useful for a wider range of interactions.

Recommendations for Building a Better Case for CSR: Dimensions of Modes of Value Creation

In this section we will discuss three recommendations for building a better business case for CSR: acknowledging complexity, building integrative capacity, and encouraging pragmatism.

Acknowledge Complexity and Allow for Emergence

To overcome the difficulty in conceiving a business case for CSR, it is essential to broaden the locus of reference for business away from an organization-centric to an organization-and-society view. We argue that CSR research needs to move beyond the reductive approach of the rational view, and the fragmented challenges of radical pluralism, to a view of the organization as part of an integral complex network, 'interdependent and complexly interactive' (Wilber, 1998: 57).

Causal effects in complex systems are both linear and non-linear, and complex living systems pursue multiple goals (Frederick, 1998; Colbert, 2004). Frederick (1998) suggests that a paradigm shift in which we move beyond existing stakeholder concepts to a view of social systems that draws on insights from complex natural systems is essential for the field to respond to urgent questions facing business and society. This complexity perspective would focus more on non-linear emergent outcomes, rather than on more reductive or linear relationships.

Build Integrative Capacity for a more Holistic Approach

Our second recommendation for building a better business case for CSR is to focus on enhancing the integrative capacity of business in order to encourage holism. CSR needs to move beyond the economic/ethical divide through a decreased emphasis on reductive or fragmented approaches to a more integrative perspective. This integrative capacity is characterized by a move from corporate states, to value communities to a view of the integral commons—that is, by a capacity for members of the organization to view themselves and their work as a part of something larger, whether purpose-bound or value-chain-defined, and then to assess whether that larger purpose is satisfactory.

Frederick (1998) comments on the 'pre-Copernican' state of dominant CSR research and theorizing, advocating a move away from the organization as the central focus of CSR analysis that has led much of this research to a dead end. He draws on complexity theorist Stuart Kauffman (1992) to describe how it is essential to broaden the context within which we consider human relations and 'decenter' the corporation away from the normative reference for the field of social issues in management. In a similar fashion, Gioia (2003) advocates moving from the concept of 'social responsibility' to that of 'societal responsibility'. This shift would emphasize the move away from creating organizational wealth, to the organization as an instrument for creating broader societal value. This view of business as an *interdependent* system is essential for recognizing the complexity of globalization and the interaction of systems, so that CSR becomes the foundation for strategic action rather than an add-on (Stormer, 2003). This requires moving beyond the stakeholder model of the firm to an inter-systems model of business (Stormer, 2003): shifting the assumption of corporations as autonomous or independent entities, which secondarily consider their obligations to the community, toward a view of firms as part of the communities that created them (Solomon, 2004) as an essential element of this critique. This is characterized by a shift from the 'egoic' view of the self as alienated and autonomous toward the 'post-egoic' view of the organization self as interdependent (Driver, 2006). Rather than focusing exclusively on the 'responsibilities' piece of the term, which emphasizes an 'atomistic individualism' (Solomon, 2004: 1029) there is a need to emphasize the social aspect as well. We argue that in order to address critiques of the dominant approaches to the business case for CSR, we need to return to some more fundamental questions about the self and communities that will allow us to envision new forms of social and economic life (Freeman and Liedtka 1991).

Encourage Pragmatism to Enhance Value Creation

Our final recommendation for building a more robust business case for CSR deals with the importance of moving beyond positivist and constructivist epistemologies to embrace a pragmatic perspective. We have argued that each stage in the eras of development is deeper, more valuable, and useful for a wider range of interactions. From the pragmatic perspective, becoming more integral through acknowledging complexity and enabling emergence, and more integrative through building capacity and encouraging holism, is more *useful* because it enables a broader view of value creation, supported by this wider range of interactions. While value from this perspective may be hard to measure with traditional quantitative approaches that have an ontological view of reality that is unequivocal, more qualitative, narrative perspectives may assist with apprehending the worth of these approaches to support a business case for social responsibility.

CONCLUSIONS

We began with the view that managing a business enterprise is an increasingly complex task: that factors bearing upon the successful operation of a business are multiple, often non-linear (and therefore unpredictable), and inextricably entwined with the needs of a global society. We suggested that a 'better business case' for CSR must reflect the changing conditions for business at a global level. We have drawn three recommendations in this chapter for conceiving a more robust, nuanced, and compelling CSR business case: acknowledge system complexity (move from reductive, to pluralistic, to integral conceptions of the business and value creation), build integrative capacity (in conceiving of the locus of value creation, from corporate, to value-based communities, to seeking an integral commons), and taking a pragmatic approach (encouraging managerial experimentation with new business models for value creation).

   If the four modes of value creation in CSR are viewed along a holarchic progression, where each is inclusive of the last, and if CSR objectives are defined integratively, as creating simultaneous value for organizations and society, and if the business case for CSR is framed as a pragmatic, experimental pursuit toward a better society and better organizations, then the business case for CSR would be a relevant concept, and would look quite different than it does currently. The case for socially responsible thinking *and action* would extend beyond the economic business case. It would attempt to connect the identity of the organization and of individual members, and it would be an argument for a more richly and deeply conceived notion of value creation.

REFERENCES

ADAMS, C. A. 2002. 'Internal Organizational Factors Influencing Corporate Social and Ethical Reporting: Beyond Current Theorising'. *Accounting, Auditing and Accountability Journal*, 15(2): 223–50.

ALKHAFAJI, A. F. 1989. *A Stakeholder Approach to Corporate Governance: Managing in a Dynamic Environment*. New York: Quorum.

ANDERSON, J. C., and FRANKLE, A. W. 1980. 'Voluntary Social Reporting: An Iso-Beta Portfolio Analysis'. *The Accounting Review*, 55: 467–79.

ARGYRIS, C., and SCHON, D. A. 1978. *Organizational Learning: A Theory of Action Perspective*. Reading, Mass.: Addison-Wesley.

AUPPERLE, K. E., CARROL, A. B., and HATFIELD, J. D. 1985. 'An Empirical Examination of the Relationship between Corporate Social Responsibility and Profitability'. *Academy of Management Journal*, 28(2): 446–63.

BANSAL, P., and ROTH, K. 2000. 'Why Companies Go Green: A Model of Ecological Responsiveness'. *Academy of Management Journal*, 43: 717–36.

BARNETT, M. L., and SALOMON, R. M. 2003. 'Throwing a Curve at Socially Responsible Investing Research'. *Organization & Environment*, 16(3): 381–9.

BARNEY, J. B. 1991. 'Firm Resources and Sustained Competitive Advantage'. *Journal of Management*, 17(1): 99–120.

——and HANSEN, M. H. 1994. 'Trustworthiness as a Source of Competitve Advantage'. *Strategic Management Journal*, 15: 175–90.

BERGER, P. L., and LUCKMANN, T. 1966. *The Social Construction of Reality: A Treatise in the Sociology of Knowledge*. Garden City, NY: Doubleday.

BERMAN, S. L., WICKS, A. C., KOTHA, S., and JONES, T. M. 1999. 'Does Stakeholder Orientation Matter? The Relationship between Stakeholder Management Models and Firm Financial Performance'. *Academy of Management Journal*, 42(5): 488–506.

BHATTACHARYA, C. B., and SEN, S. 2004. 'Doing Better at Doing Good: When, Why, and How Consumers Respond to Corporate Social Initiatives'. *Californial Management Review*, 47(1): 9–24.

BOWIE, N. E., and DUNFEE, T. W. 2002. 'Confronting Morality in Markets'. *Journal of Business Ethics*, 38(4): 381–93.

BROWN, L. D., and ASHMAN, D. 1998. 'Social Capital, Mutual Influence and Social Learning in Intersectoral Problem Solving', in D. D. Cooperrider (ed.), *Organizational Dimensions of Global Change*. Beverly Hills, Calif.: Sage: 139–67.

BROWN, T. J., and DACIN, P. A. 1997. 'The Company and the Product: Corporate Associations and Consumer Product Responses'. *Journal of Marketing*, 61: 68–84.

BRUCH, F., and WALTER, F. 2005. 'The Keys to Rethinking Corporate Philanthropy'. *MIT Sloan Management Review*, 47(1): 49–55.

BURRELL, G., and MORGAN, G. 1979. *Sociological Paradigms and Organizational Analysis*. Aldershot: Ashgate Publishing.

CALTON, J. M., and LAD, L. J. 1995. 'Social Contracting as a Trust-Building Process of Network Governance'. *Business Ethics Quarterly*, 5: 271–96.

CARROLL, A. 1979. 'A Three Dimensional Conceptual Model of Corporate Social Performance'. *Academy of Management Review*, 4: 497–505.

—— 1991. 'The Pyramid of Corporate Social Responsibility: Toward the Moral Management of Organizational Stakeholders'. *Business Horizons*, 34: 39–48.

—— 1999. 'Corporate Social Responsibility: Evolution of a Definitional Construct'. *Business & Society*, 38(3): 268–95.

CASHORE, B. 2002. 'Legitimacy and the Privatization of Environmental Governance: How Non-state Market Driven (NSMD) Governance Systems Gain Rule-Making Authority'. *Governance*, 15(4): 503–29.

CILLIERS, P. 1998. *Complexity and Postmodernism: Understanding Complex Systems*. New York: Routledge.

COCHRAN, P. L., and WOOD, R. A. 1984. 'Corporate Social Responsibility and Financial Performance'. *Academy of Management Journal*, 27: 42–56.

COLBERT, B. A. 2004. 'The Complex Resource-Based View: Implications for Theory and Practice in Strategic Human Resource Management'. *Academy of Management Review*, 29(3): 341–58.

COLBERT, B. A., KURUCZ, E. C. and WHEELER, D., forthcoming 2008. *Sustainability Conversations: Contested Conceptions and Mesodynamic Tensions*. Wilfrid Laurier University.

Committee for Economic Development (CED) 1971. *Social Responsibilities of Business Corporations*. New York: Committee for Economic Development.

CORNELL, B., and SHAPIRO, A. C. 1987. 'Corporate Stakeholders and Corporate Finance'. *Financial Management*, 16: 5–14.

CRANE, A. 2001. 'Unpacking the Ethical Product'. *Journal of Business Ethics*, 30(4): 361–73.

—— MATTEN, D., and MOON, J. 2004. 'Stakeholders as Citizens? Rethinking Rights, Participation and Democracy'. *Journal of Business Ethics*, 53: 107–22.

DAVIS, K. 1973. 'The Case for and against Business Assumption of Social Responsibilities'. *Academy of Management Journal*, 16: 312–22.

DE BAKKER, F. G. A., GROENEWEGEN, P., and HOND, F. DEN 2005. 'A Bibliometric Analysis of 30 Years of Research and Theory on Corporate Social Responsibility and Corporate Social Performance'. *Business and Society*, 44: 283–317.

DICK-FORDE, E. 2005. 'Democracy Matters in Corporate Accountability: A Carribean Case Study'. Critical Perspectives on Accounting Proceedings, City University of New York.

DOMINI, A. 2001. *Socially Responsible Investing: Making a Difference and Making Money*. Chicago: Dearborn Trade.

DONALDSON, T., and PRESTON, L. E. 1995. 'The Stakeholder Theory of the Corporation: Concepts, Evidence, Implications'. *Academy of Management Review*, 20(1): 65–91.

DRIVER, M. 2006. 'Beyond the Stalemate of Economics versus Ethics: Corporate Social Responsibility and the Discourse of the Organizational Self'. *Journal of Business Ethics*, 66: 337–56.

DRUMWRIGHT, M. 1996. 'Company Advertising with a Social Dimension: The Role of Non-economic Criteria'. *Journal of Marketing*, 60: 71–87.

ELKINGTON, J. 1998. *Cannibals with Forks*. Gabriola Island, BC: New Society.

FOMBRUN, C. J., and SHANLEY, M. (1990). 'What's in a Name? Reputation Building and Corporate Strategy'. *Academy of Management Journal*, 33: 233–58.

FRANKEL, C. 1998. *In Earth's Company*. Gabriola Island, BC: New Society Publishers.

FREDERICK, W. 1998. 'Creatures, Corporations, Communities, Chaos, Complexity: A Naturalogical View of the Corporate Social Role'. *Business Ethics*, 37(4): 358–89.

FREEDMAN, M., and JAGGI, B. 1982. 'Pollution Disclosures, Pollution Performance and Economic Performance'. *Omega*, 10(2): 167–76.

FREEMAN, R. E. 1962. *Capitalism and Freedom*. Chicago: University of Chicago Press.

—— 1984. *Strategic Management: A Stakeholder Approach*. Englewood Cliffs, NJ: Prentice-Hall.

—— 2000. 'Business Ethics at the Millennium'. *Business Ethics Quarterly*, 10(1): 169–80.

—— and LIEDTKA, J. 1991. 'Corporate Social Responsibility: A Critical Approach'. *Business Horizons*, 34: 92–8.

—— 1970. 'The Social Responsibility of Business is to Increase its Profits'. *New York Times Magazine*: 32–3, 122, 124, 126.

GARRIGA, E., and MELÉ, D. 2004. 'Corporate Social Responsibility Theories: Mapping the Territory'. *Journal of Business Ethics*, 53: 51–71.

GELB, D. S., and STRAWSER, J. A. 2001. 'Corporate Social Responsibility and Financial Disclosures: An Alternative Explanation for Increased Disclosure'. *Journal of Business Ethics*, 33(1): 1–13.

GEPHART, R. 2004. 'Qualitative Research and the Academy of Management Journal'. *Academy of Management*, 47(4): 454–62.

GIOIA, D. 2003. 'Business Organzation as Instrument of Social Responsibility.' *Organization*, 10(3): 435–8.

GODFREY, P. 2005. 'The Relationship between Corporate Philanthropy and Shareholder Wealth: A Risk Management Perspecitve'. *Academy of Managment Review*, 30(4): 777–98.

GRAVES, S. B., and WADDOCK, S. A. 1994. 'Institutional Owners and Corporate Social Performance'. *Academy of Management Journal*, 37: 1034–46.

GRIFFIN, J. J., and MOHON, J. F. 1997. 'The Corporate Social Performance and Corporate Financial Performance Debate: Twenty-Five Years of Incomparable Research'. *Business and Society*, 36(1): 5–31.

HAIGH, M., and JONES, M. T. (2006). 'The Drivers of Corporate Social Responsibility: A Critical Review'. *The Business Review, Cambridge*, 5(2): 245–51.

HARRISON, J. S., and ST JOHN, C. H. (1996). 'Managing and Partnering with External Stakeholders'. *Academy of Management Executive*, 10(2): 46–61.

HART, S. L. 1995. 'A Natural-Resource-Based View of the Firm'. *Academy of Management Journal*, 20(4): 986–1014.

—— 1997. 'Beyond Greening: Strategies for a Sustainable World'. *Harvard Business Review*, 75(1): 66–76.

—— 2005. *Capitalism at the Crossroads: The Unlimited Business Opportunities in Solving the World's most Difficult Problems*. Upper Saddle River, NJ: Wharton School Publishing.

—— and CHRISTENSEN, C. M. 2002. 'The Great Leap: Driving Innovation from the Base of the Pyramid'. *MIT Sloan Management Review*, 44(1): 51–7.

—— and MILSTEIN, M. B. 1999. 'Global Sustainability and the Creative Destruction of Industries'. *Sloan Management Review*, 41(1): 23–33.

———— 2003. 'Creating Sustainable Value'. *Academy of Management Executive,* 17(2): 56–69.

—— and SHARMA, S. 2004. 'Engaging Fringe Stakeholders for Competitive Imagination'. *Academy of Managment Executive,* 18(1): 7–18.

HILL, C. W. L. 1995. 'National Institutional Structures, Transaction Cost Economizing and Competitive Advantage: The Case of Japan'. *Organization Science,* 6: 119–31.

HILLMAN, A. J., and KEIM, G. D. 2001. 'Shareholder Value, Stakeholder Management, and Social Issues: What's the Bottom Line?' *Strategic Management Journal,* 22: 125–39.

JACOBS, M. 1999. 'Sustainable Development as a Contested Concept', in A. Dobson (ed.), *Fairness and Futurity: Essays on Environmental Sustainability and Social Justice.* Oxford: Oxford University Press, 21–45.

JENSEN, M. C. 2002. 'Value Maximization, Stakeholder Theory and the Corporate Objective Function'. *Business Ethics Quarterly,* 12(2): 235–56.

JONES, T. M. 1995. 'Instrumental Stakeholder Theory: A Synthesis of Ethics and Economics'. *Academy of Management Review,* 20: 404–37.

JOYNER, B. E., and PAYNE, D. 2002. 'Evolution and Implementation: A Study of Values, Business Ethics and Corporate Social Responsibility'. *Journal of Business Ethics,* 41: 297–311.

KAUFFMAN, S. A. 1992. *Origins of Order: Self-Organization and Selection in Evolution.* Oxford: Oxford University Press.

KEDIA, B., and KUNTZ, E. C. 1981. 'The Context of Social Performance: An Empirical Study of Texas Banks', in L. E. Preston (ed.), *Research in Corporate Social Performance and Policy.* Greenwich, CT: JAI.

KINDER, P., LYDERBERG, S., and DOMINI, A. 1993. *Investing for Good: Making Money while Being Socially Responsible.* New York: Harper-Business.

KING, A., and LENOX, M. 2000. 'Industry Self-regulation without Sanctions: The Chemical Industry's Responsible Care Program'. *Academy of Management Journal,* 43(4): 698–716.

———— —— 2001. 'Does it Really Pay to be Green? An Emprical Study of Firm Environmental and Financial Performance'. *The Journal of Industrial Ecology,* 5(1): 105–16.

KLEIN, K. J., DANSEREAU, F., and HALL, R. J. 1994. 'Levels Issues in Theory Development, Data Collection and Analysis'. *Academy of Management Review,* 19(2): 195–229.

KOK, P., VAN DER WIELE, T., McKENNA, R., and BROWN, A. 2001. 'A Corporate Social Responsibility Audit within a Quality Management Framework'. *Journal of Business Ethics,* 31(4): 285–97.

LANKOSKI, L. 2000. 'Determinants of Environmental Profit: An Analysis of the Firm-Level Relationship between Environmental Performance and Economic Performance'. *Department of Industrial Engineering and Management.* Helsinki: University of Technology.

LERNER, L. D., and FRYXELL, G. E. 1988. 'An Empirical Study of the Predictors of Corporate Social Performance: A Multi-dimensional Analysis'. *Journal of Business Ethics,* 7: 951–9.

LITZ, R. A. 1996. 'A Resource-Based View of the Socially Responsible Firm: Stakeholder Interdependence, Ethical Awareness and Issue Responsiveness as Strategic Assets'. *Journal of Business Ethics,* 15: 1355–63.

LOVINS, A., LOVINS, L. H., and HAWKEN, P. 1999. 'A Road map for Natural Capitalism'. *Harvard Business Review,* May: 145–58.

MACKENZIE, C., and LEWIS, A. 1999. 'Morals and Markets: The Case of Ethical Investing'. *Business Ethics Quarterly,* 9(3): 439–52.

McWilliams, A., and Siegel, D. 2001. 'Corporate Social Responsibility: A Theory of the Firm Perspective'. *Academy of Management Review*, 26(1): 117–27.

Margolis, J. D., and Walsh, J. P. 2001. *People and Profits? The Search for a Link between a Company's Social and Financial Performance*. Mahwah, NJ: Lawrence Erlbaum.

———— 2003. 'Misery Loves Companies: Rethinking Social Initiatives by Business'. *Adminstrative Science Quarterly*, 48: 268–305.

Matten, D., Crane, A., and Chapple, W. 2003. 'Behind the Mask: Revealing the True Face of Corporate Citizenship'. *Journal of Business Ethics*, 44(1–2): 109–20.

Mattingly, J. E., and Berman, S. L. 2006. 'Measurement of Corporate Social Action: Discovering Taxonomy in the Kinder Lydenburg Domini Ratings Data'. *Business and Society*, 45(1): 20–46.

Mitchell, R., Agle, B. and Wood, D. 1997. 'Toward a Theory of Stakeholder Identification and Salience: Defining the Principle of Who and What Really Counts'. *Academy of Management Review*, 22(4): 853–86.

Murray, K. B., and Montanari, J. R. 1986. 'Strategic Management of the Socially Responsible Firm: Integrating Management and Marketing Theory'. *Academy of Management Review*, 11(4): 815–28.

Ogden, S., and Watson, R. 1999. 'Corporate Performance and Stakeholder Management: Balancing Shareholder and Customer Interests in the U.K. Privatized Water Industry'. *Academy of Managment Journal*, 42(5): 526–38.

Orlitzky, M., Schmidt, F. L., and Rynes, S. 2003. 'Corporate Social and Financial Performance: A Meta-Analysis'. *Organization Studies*, 24: 403–42.

Pava, M. L., and Krausz, J. 1996. 'The Association between Corporate Social Responsibility and Financial Performance: The Paradox of Social Cost'. *Journal of Business Ethics*, 15: 321–57.

Peattie, K. 1998. 'Golden Goose or Wild Goose? The Hunt for the Green Consumer'. *Business Strategy and the Environment*, 10: 187–99.

Perrow, C. 2002. *Organizing America: Wealth, Power, and the Origins of Corporate Captialism*. Princeton: Princeton University Press.

Petrick, J. and Quinn, J. 2001. 'The Challenge of Leadership Accountability for Integrity Capacity as a Strategic Asset'. *Journal of Business Ethics*, 34: 331–43.

Pfeffer, J. 1985. 'Organizations and Organization Theory', in G. L. E. Aronson (ed.), *Handbook of Social Psychology*. New York: Random House, vol. 1: 379–440.

Porter, M. E. and Kramer, M. R. 1999. 'Philanthropy's New Agenda: Creating Value'. *Harvard Business Review*, Nov.–Dec.: 121–30.

———— 2002. 'The Competitive Advantage of Corporate Philanthropy'. *Harvard Business Review*, Dec.: 56–68.

—— and Van der Linde, C. 1995. 'Green and Competitive: Ending the Stalemate'. *Harvard Business Review*, 73(5): 120–33.

Posner, B., and Schmidt, W. 1992. 'Values and the American Manager'. *California Management Review*, 25(2): 80–94.

Prahalad, C. K. 2004. *The Fortune at the Bottom of the Pyramid: Eradicating Poverty through Profits*. Upper Saddle River, NJ: Wharton School Publishing.

—— and Hammond, A. 2002. 'Serving the World's Poor, Profitably'. *Harvard Business Review*, 80(9): 48–58.

—— and Hart, S. L. 2002. 'The Fortune at the Bottom of the Pyramid'. *Strategy+Business*, 26: 54–67.

PRESTON, L. E., and O'BANNON, D. P. 1997. 'The Corporate Social-Financial Performance Relationship: A Typology and Analysis'. *Business and Society*, 35(4): 419–29.

QUINN, D., and JONES, T. 1995. 'An Agent Morality View of Business Policy'. *Academy of Management Review*, 20(1): 22–42.

RIORDAN, C. M., GATEWOOD, R. D., and BILL, J. B. 1997. 'Corporate Image: Employee Reactions and Implications for Managing Corporate Social Performance'. *Journal of Business Ethics*, 16(4): 401–12.

ROMAN, R. M., HAYIBOR, S., and AGLE, B. 1999. 'The Relationship between Social and Financial Performance: Repainting a Portrait'. *Business in Society*, 38(1): 109–25.

ROWLEY, T., and BERMAN, S. 2000. 'A Brand New Brand of Corporate Social Performance'. *Business & Society*, 39(4): 397–418.

RUSSO, M. V., and FOUTS, P. A. 1997. 'A Resource-Based Perspective on Corporate Environmental Performance and Profitability'. *Academy of Management Journal*, 40: 534–59.

SALZMANN, O., IONESCU-SOMERS, A., and STEGER, U. 2005. 'The Business Case for Corporate Sustainability: Literature Review and Options'. *European Management Journal*, 23(1): 27–36.

SCHMIDT ALBINGER, H., and FREEMAN, S. J. 2000. 'Corporate Social Performance and Attractiveness as an Employer to Different Job Seeking Populations'. *Journal of Business Ethics*, 28(3): 243–53.

SEN, S., and BHATTACHARYA, C. B. 2001. 'Does Doing Good Always Lead to Doing Better? Consumer Reactions to Corporate Social Responsibility'. *Journal of Marketing Research*, 38(2): 225–44.

SETHI, S. P. 1979. 'A Conceptual Framework for Environmental Analysis of Social Issues and Evaluation of Business Response Patterns'. *Academy of Management Review*, 4: 63–74.

SMITH, N. C. 1990. *Morality and the Market: Consumer Pressure for Corporate Accountability*. London: Routledge.

—— 1994. 'The New Corporate Philanthropy'. *Harvard Business Review*, 72(3), May–June: 105–16.

—— 2003. 'Corporate Social Responsibility: Whether or How?' *California Management Review*, 45(4): 52–76.

SOLOMON, R. C. 1997. *It's Good Business*. Lanham, Md. Rowman & Littlefield Publishers, Inc.

—— 2004. 'Aristotle, Ethics and Business Organizations'. *Organization Studies*, 25(6): 1021–43.

STANWICK, P. A., and STANWICK, S. D. 1998. 'The Relationship between Corporate Social Performance and Organizational Size, Financial Performance, and Environmental Performance: An Empirical Examination'. *Journal of Business Ethics*, 17: 195–204.

STIGLER, G. J. 1962. 'Information in the Labor Market'. *Journal of Political Economy*, 70: 49–73.

STORMER, F. 2003. 'Making the Shift: Moving from "Ethics Pays" to an Inter-Systems Model of Business'. *Journal of Business Ethics*, 44(4): 279–88.

STORY, D., and PRICE, T. J. 2006. 'Corporate Social Responsibility and Risk Management?' *The Journal of Corporate Citizenship*, 22: 39–51.

SWANSON, C. 1995. 'Addressing a Theoretical Problem by Reorienting the Corporate Social Performance Model'. *Academy of Management Review*, 20(1): 43–64.

—— 1999. 'Towards an Integrative Theory of Business and Society: A Research Strategy for Corporate Social Performance'. *Academy of Management Review*, 24(3): 506–21.

TREVINO, L. K., and WEAVER, G. R. 1994. 'Normative and Empirical Business Ethics: Separation, Marriage of Convenience, or Marriage of Necessity?' *Business Ethics Quarterly*, 4: 129–43.

TURBAN, D. B. and GREENING, D. W. 1997. 'Corporate Social Performance and Organizational Attractiveness to Prospective Employees'. *Academy of Managment Journal*, 40: 658–72.

VAN MARREWIJK, M. 2003. 'Concepts and Defintions of CSR and Corporate, Sustainability'. *Journal of Business Ethics*, 44: 95–105.

VARADARAJAN, P. R., and MENON, A. 1988. 'Cause-Related Marketing—A Coalignment of Marketing Strategy and Corporate Philanthropy'. *Journal of Marketing*, 52(3): 58–74.

VOGEL, D. J. 2005. 'Is There a Market for Virtue? The Business Case for Corporate Social Responsibility'. *California Management Review*, 47(4): 19–45.

WADDELL, S. J. 2002. 'Six Societal Learning Concepts for a New Era of Engagement'. *Reflections*, 3(4): 18–26.

WADDOCK, S., BODWELL, C., and GRAVES, S. 2002. 'Responsibility: The New Business Imperative'. *Academy of Management Executive*, 16(2): 132–48.

—— and GRAVES, S. B. (1997a). 'The Corporate Social Peformance-Financial Performance Link'. *Strategic Management Journal*, 18(4): 303–19.

—— —— (1997b). 'Quality of Management and Quality of Stakeholder Relationships: Are They Synonymous?' *Business & Society*, 36(3): 250–79.

WHEELER, D., COLBERT, B. A., and FREEMAN, R. E. 2003. 'Focusing on Value: Reconciling Corporate Social Responsibility, Sustainability and a Stakeholder Approach in a Network World'. *Journal of General Management*, 28(3): 1–28.

—— and GRAYSON, D. 2001. 'Business and its Stakeholders'. *Journal of Business Ethics*, 32: 101–6.

—— McKAGUE, K., THOMSON, J., DAVIES, R., MEDALYE, J., and PRADA, M. 2005. 'Creating Sustainable Local Enterprise Networks'. *MIT Sloan Management Review*, Fall: 33–40.

—— and SILLANPAA, M. 1997. *The Stakeholder Corporation: A Blueprint for Maximising Stakeholder Value*. London: Pitman.

—— —— 1998. 'Including the Stakeholders: The Business Case'. *Long Range Planning*, 31(2): 201–10.

WICKS, A. C., BERMAN, S. L., and JONES, T. M. 1999. 'The Structure of Optimal Trust: Moral and Strategic Implications'. *Academy of Management Review*, 24(1): 99–116.

—— and FREEMAN, R. E. 1998. 'Organization Studies and the New Pragmatism: Positivism, Anti-positivism, and the Search for Ethics'. *Organization Science*, 9: 123–40.

WILBER, K. 1998. *The Essential Ken Wilber: An Introductory Reader*. Boston: Shambhala.

—— 2000. *A Theory of Everything: An Integral Vision for Business, Politics, Science and Spirtuality*. Boston: Shambhala.

WOOD, D. 1991. 'Corporate Social Performance Revisited'. *Academy of Management Review*, 16: 691–718.

CHAPTER 5

CORPORATE SOCIAL PERFORMANCE AND FINANCIAL PERFORMANCE

A RESEARCH SYNTHESIS

MARC ORLITZKY

INTRODUCTION

WHAT is the relationship between corporate social performance (CSP) and corporate financial performance (CFP)? The community of Business and Society scholars has been investigating this question for over 30 years. The typical conclusion, based on narrative reviews of this literature, is that the empirical evidence is too mixed to allow for any firm conclusions (e.g. Ullmann, 1985). In these reviews, poor measures and weak theory construction are often mentioned as causes of this apparent variability in findings (see e.g. Griffin and Mahon, 1997; Wood and Jones, 1995). The assumption that this research stream is inconclusive has persisted until after the turn of the millennium (Godfrey, 2005; McWilliams and Siegel, 2001; Schuler and Cording, 2006).

So, what may be required at this point is a critical examination of the evidence that seems to have motivated these (inconclusive) conclusions. In this chapter I will argue that certain types of literature review should be treated with caution. I will propose an alternative and use this more rigorous methodology of literature reviews in order to assess the cumulative evidence on the two core constructs which are defined at the beginning of this chapter. Then I will present the general conclusions from this research program. The next three sections will describe possible mediators, moderators, and confounds in greater depth. The chapter will conclude with some suggestions of future research needs in the corporate social-financial performance domain.

Superficially, a literature review looks like an easy task. A researcher tabulates the empirical evidence pro and con a particular research hypothesis. In this type of research review, the real difficulty, it is assumed, lies in including all relevant studies, not so much in the actual technique of reviewing the literature. In the end, it is argued, all we need to do is count the vote tally that supports, or fails to support, the research question that motivated the review. This classic solution of vote counting of statistically significant and non-significant results sounds reasonable, but comes with a host of pitfalls and weaknesses (Chalmers and Lau, 1994; Hedges and Olkin, 1980; Hunt, 1997). In psychology and medicine, such simplistic literature reviews are now held in disdain (Hunt, 1997). In contrast, certain communities of researchers within Organizational Behavior and Organization Theory continue to rely on vote counting, or what is labeled the 'box-score method' (Schwab, 1999: 301), although statisticians, psychologists, and at least one prominent economist have long argued that a rigorous literature review requires a quantitatively more sophisticated underpinning than that afforded by the typical narrative literature review (e.g. Cohen, 1994; Hedges and Olkin, 1985; Hunter and Schmidt, 2004; McCloskey, 1998). Because the errors can be grave (Orlitzky, 2002), such reliance on classic types of literature review ought to become as much of a taboo in this research stream as it is in other disciplines and research programs. Meta-analysis avoids these methodological and logical mistakes and, thus, will be the type of research synthesis on which this literature review is based.

Meta-analysis is a type of literature review that goes beyond the outcomes of statistical significance tests (Schmidt, 1992). Instead, it focuses on effect sizes, such as the correlation coefficient r or effect size d (Rosenthal, 1984; Rosenthal and DiMatteo, 2001). One particular method of meta-analysis, called 'psychometric meta-analysis', not only takes into account sample size differences, but also corrects for measurement error (unreliability in measures), dichotomization of variables, and several other study artifacts that typically affect primary studies (Hunter et al., 2004). Because of their ability to correct for these study artifacts, meta-analytic research syntheses have become very influential in the social sciences

(Cooper and Hedges, 1994; Hunt, 1997). For this reason it makes good sense in this review to rely primarily on two award-winning meta-analyses (Orlitzky and Benjamin, 2001; Orlitzky *et al.*, 2003),[1] which problematized and relativized the aforementioned typical conclusions about the seemingly 'equivocal' relationship between CSP and CFP.

THE TWO CORE CONSTRUCTS

Corporate Citizenship and Corporate Financial Performance

The first core concept at the heart of this literature review is *corporate social performance* (CSP). Wood (1991: 693) defined CSP as a 'business organization's configuration of principles of social responsibility, processes of social responsiveness, and policies, programs, and observable outcomes as they relate to the firm's societal relationships'. This comprehensive definition assumes that CSP is broader than corporate social responsibility (CSR), which consists of three norms at different levels of analysis: institutional, organizational, and individual (Wood, 1991). In addition, CSP includes organizational processes of environmental assessment, stakeholder management, and issues management, but also, and perhaps most important, various measures of its external manifestations and societal effects, such as social impacts. The apparent complexity of the definition of CSP can be untangled conceptually by visualizing Wood's model as a relatively straightforward systems model of inputs, throughputs, and outputs. In retrospect, because the construct conceptually and operationally includes considerations of company performance vis-à-vis the natural environment, a better term for it may be *corporate citizenship* (Davenport, 2000). At best it is awkward, at worst false, to include the caveat that corporate *social* performance also refers to corporate *environmental* performance (cf. also Holliday *et al.*, 2002). There are many other good reasons to prefer the term 'corporate citizenship' (CC), or regard CC as slightly different from CSP (Gunther, 2004; Matten and Crane, 2005), but for the purpose of this chapter I will

---

[1] Orlitzky and Benjamin (2001) won the 2001 Best Article Award given by the International Association for Business and Society (IABS) in association with *California Management Review*. Orlitzky, *et al.* (2003) won the 2004 Moskowitz award for outstanding quantitative research relevant to the social investment field. The sponsors of the Moskowitz Prize are Calvert Group, First Affirmative Financial Network, KLD Research & Analytics Inc., Nelson Capital Management, Rockefeller & Co., and Trillium Asset Management Corporation. The Moskowitz Prize is awarded each year to the research paper that best meets the following criteria: (1) practical significance to practitioners of socially responsible investing; (2) appropriateness and rigor of quantitative methods; and (3) novelty of results. Both award-winning papers were based on my doctoral dissertation, which was completed in July 1998.

consistently use CC as a (conceptually equivalent, yet rhetorically superior) synonym of CSP.

In contrast, *corporate financial performance* (CFP), the other core construct of this review, is usually considered less ambiguous and, thus, less contentious, than CC. The view of CFP as the 'financial viability of an organization' (Price and Mueller, 1986: 128) seems clear enough. So, CFP is the degree to which a firm is able to achieve its economic, or financial, goals (Venkatraman and Ramanujam, 1986). However, different measures of financial performance seem to diverge rather than converge (Meyer and Gupta, 1994). Therefore, although we can distinguish between two main CFP operationalizations, namely market and accounting measures, we cannot a priori assume that CC has questionable measurement properties, while CFP is clear-cut and uncontroversial. In fact, a closer measurement examination has generally shown that the construct validity of both core constructs is far from perfect, but still useful for research synthesis (Orlitzky, 1999). Construct validity refers to the degree of correspondence between a variable's operationalization and the conceptual definition, or mental image, of the construct that such a measure is designed to represent (Schwab, 1980). While measurement error is caused by random errors, lack of construct validity is produced by systematic errors (Hunter *et al.*, 2004; Nunnally and Bernstein, 1994). Both types of error can render a research literature uninterpretable. In this case, we deal with constructs which are imperfect (as is typical in all social science research domains; cf. Hunter and Schmidt, 2004), but their measurement properties can be judged good enough to allow for meta-analysis (Orlitzky, 1999).

THE GENERAL CONCLUSIONS

Overall, the meta-analysis by Orlitzky, Schmidt, and Rynes (2003) supports a positive relationship between CC and CFP. Specifically, the meta-analytically determined true score correlation ρ was +0.36. Sampling and measurement errors alone accounted, on average, for 24% of the variance in observed correlations across studies. In general, reputation measures of CC were better predictors of CFP than social-audit disclosures, and the economic impact of CC was stronger on accounting measures than market measures of a firm's economic performance. Orlitzky and his colleagues also addressed concerns about availability bias—the possibility that studies which fail to show a relationship between CC and CFP were unlikely to get published. File drawer analysis is a technique useful for assessing this concern. The file drawer analysis indicated that over 1,000 such unpublished studies excluded from the meta-analysis would be needed to change the overall conclusions of the meta-analysis.

CC also seems to reduce business risk (Orlitzky and Benjamin, 2001). Again, these effects are most likely mediated by organizational reputation. By balancing a multitude of stakeholder interests, a firm may increase various stakeholder groups' confidence that the firm will be understanding and non-adversarial in resolving future stakeholder conflicts (Jones, 1995). In turn, this may reduce the variability of accounting rates of return and share prices because the investment community will not respond to temporary company set-backs by panic-selling of its shares, for example. Conversely, less business risk may lead to higher CC because discretionary spending on CC is facilitated by greater predictability of future cash-flows and slack resources. A corresponding causal model is depicted in Orlitzky and Benjamin's (2001) article.

In addition, the meta-analysis suggests that the organizational activities entailed by CC and CFP can be considered mutually reinforcing. Through the use of time lags, Orlitzky and his colleagues found that CFP is a positive predictor of future CC, and that CC also predicts CFP. In other words, the meta-analytic findings suggest that a business can develop mutually beneficial relations with stakeholder groups, which might pay off surprisingly fast for the socially responsible firm. In turn, these positive economic effects of CC might translate into more slack resources available for future investments in CC. Over time, these dynamics might constitute a virtuous cycle for the socially responsible firm (Waddock and Graves, 1997a).

MEDIATORS: THE CAUSAL MECHANISMS THAT LINK CC AND CFP

In conjunction with primary studies, the meta-analytic evidence can also shed more light on the possible mediators or causal linkages between the two core constructs. The empirical evidence accumulated to date indicates that CC and CFP are most likely positively correlated because CC helps improve managerial knowledge and skills and enhance corporate reputation (Logsdon and Wood, 2002; Orlitzky et al., 2003). When stakeholders are engaged constructively (rather than treated as adversarial forces or 'side constraints') they may look more favorably upon a socially responsible company. For example, firms high in CC may attract better and more committed employees (Backhaus et al., 2002; Greening and Turban, 2000; Turban and Cable, 2003; Turban and Greening, 1996). Also, external stakeholders, such as customers, may become more willing to buy the company's products or pay a premium for the goods from socially responsible firms (Auger et al., 2003). Although the meta-analysis suggested that internal competency-building was a less important factor than external reputation in the economic performance-enhancing effects of CC, socially responsible organizations can develop learning mechanisms and other internal resources which will facilitate adaptation to various environmental uncertainties (Russo and Fouts, 1997).

In short, there seem to be a variety of causal mechanisms responsible for the observed positive relationship between CC and CFP. In the following section I will only describe the most likely and important mediators. Orlitzky (2006) elaborates on many of these theoretical links and introduces several others. Frank (1996) provides another interesting overview of possible theoretical linkages.

Enhancing Organizational Reputation

From theoretical and practical perspectives, organizational reputation ranks as one of the most important mediating variables linking CC to CFP (e.g. Fombrun and Shanley, 1990; Read, 2004). Because of their own moral convictions and value systems, customers and suppliers may be, or become, more willing to deal with companies with a good CC track record. 'Ethical investors' may be willing to pay a premium for stocks of companies with high CC disclosures (Anderson and Frankle, 1980; Simon *et al.*, 1972). Thus, when studying external reputation effects, it may be important to consider information intensity and consumer decision processes (Schuler and Cording 2006).

Not all reputation effects are external, though. Employees may show more goodwill toward their high-CC employer and, because of increased organizational commitment and task motivation, produce better results and demonstrate more organizational citizenship behaviors (Davis, 1973; Hodson, 2001; McGuire *et al.*, 1988). The external and internal effects, in aggregate, could explain an increase in CFP as a consequence of increasing CC, mediated by organizational reputation.

The empirical research accumulated over 30 years lends strong support to reputation as a mediator (Orlitzky *et al.*, 2003). The true score correlation (ρ) between CC *reputation* measures and CFP (0.49) was 36% larger than the overall true score correlation (of 0.36; see previous discussion). However, the variance of this meta-analytic, corrected correlation was also much larger (0.32), which suggests that the way in which organizational reputation is manifested and managed by top management serves as an important moderator. For example, a further subdivision of the reputation CC data shows that company disclosures of CSR in annual reports or shareholder letters tend to contribute to organizational reputation only to a minor extent (Orlitzky *et al.*, 2003: 417–19).

From a slightly different angle, the fact that environmental performance is related to financial performance to a negligible (but still positive) extent might be seen as evidence corroborating the importance of organizational reputation as a mediator (Orlitzky *et al.*, 2003: 414–15). Anecdotal evidence suggests that *at present* many consumers, especially US consumers, are not particularly concerned about a company's environmental track record (Gunther, 2004; Read, 2004).[2] At the moment, environmental performance is typically either just a small blip on an organization's radar screen or treated as a cost only (not as an investment). That is, many organizations treat the natural environment as a legal (i.e. regulatory compliance) issue rather than an essential aspect of organizational reputation that needs to be managed proactively. Some observers claim that only when environmental activists institutionalize environmental concerns in the form of influential social movements do organizations respond (Gunther, 2004; cf. also McVeigh *et al.*, 2003).[3] But by that time, it may be too late to derive strategic benefits from reactionary adherence to already widely institutionalized norms of environmental responsibility.

Improving Internal Resources and Skills (Efficiency)

Another quite influential variant of the pro-CSR paradigm implicates organization-internal resources and skills as an important mediator between CC and CFP. Advocates of the internal-resources view of CC predict that CC enhances managerial competencies with respect to the efficient use and allocation of resources (e.g. accounting return measures such as return on assets or return on equity). Increased internal efficiencies may directly translate into savings from higher CC (Holliday *et al.*, 2002: 83–102). Also, CC may help top management develop better scanning skills, processes, and information systems which increase the organization's anticipation of, and preparedness for, external changes or turbulences. Know-how with respect to corporate environmental performance has been argued to be especially important in growing industries (Russo *et al.*, 1997). According to this view, whether CC measures are disclosed or not is largely irrelevant because organizational learning and the development of internal capabilities do not depend on the communication of the corporation's commitment to CSR to various stakeholders.

The integration of prior CC-CFP research shows that, although the internal-skills perspective is substantiated empirically to some extent, the internal learning effects of CC tend to be 33% smaller than the reputation effects emanating from high CC. As tabulated in Orlitzky *et al.* (2003: 418), the effect sizes pertaining to the internal-efficiency versus external-reputation explanations were 0.33 and 0.49, respectively. However, 0.33 is still a quite sizeable mean true score correlation (ρ). In addition,

[2] In the future consumers may exhibit greater environmental awareness, for example, because of sharp increases in energy prices or catastrophic climate shifts. These possible attitudinal changes may, in the future, result in the emergence of a company's concern for the natural environment as the most important dimension of CC reputation.

[3] Of course, there are industry- and firm-specific exceptions to this rule (e.g. Interface and Patagonia). These exceptions illustrate the importance of executive values in managing company reputation for high CSR (cf. also Orlitzky and Swanson, 2002).

the empirical analyses (Orlitzky *et al.*, 2003: 418) point to the greater generalizability of the internal-skills effects relative to the CSR reputation effects (which may be industry- or firm-specific). In sum, this meta-analytic evidence reaffirms CC as an important, but not essential, *internal* resource.

Increasing Rivals' Costs

A company may become relatively more efficient not only by decreasing its own costs but also by raising competitors' costs. Thus, a related resource-based argument focuses on the effects of CC as a political strategy to increase rivals' costs (McWilliams *et al.*, 2002). High-CC firms can try to make their new technology an industry standard through which they effectively restrict access to substitute resources. It can be shown that companies, especially large ones, can use occupational safety and health as well as environmental regulations strategically to raise rivals' costs. Some organizations may concentrate on those social or environmental criteria that they already find relatively easy to meet or exceed, and then push their various stakeholder coalitions for broader adoption of those policies in their organizational fields. McWilliams and her colleagues (2002) presented various examples of CC as indirect rent-seeking strategy. Ultimately, strategic actors will adopt those CC practices that make the firm-specific resources valuable, rare, and costly to imitate in order to render the company's competitive advantage more sustainable. This explanation is not only consistent with the resource-based view of the firm, but also the view of CC as a signal to government about expected compliance costs with future costly and rigid government regulation (Heyes, 2005).

Attracting a More Productive Workforce

Firms with high CC may also attract better employees. There is some empirical support for this explanation (Backhaus *et al.*, 2002; Greening *et al.*, 2000; Turban and Greening, 1997). CC may serve as a signal to potential applicants that the organization is a socially responsible employer and upholds ethical values. Because, as a result of these signals, applicants may experience positive affects, such as an enhanced self-concept (Greening *et al.*, 2000), they will be more attracted to high- rather than low-CC firms. This association between CC and company attractiveness as an employer has been found at the organizational level (Turban and Greening, 1997) as well as the individual level of analysis (Backhaus *et al.*, 2002; Greening *et al.*, 2000). When competitive advantage increasingly depends on a quality workforce (Huselid, 1995; Pfeffer, 1994, 1998), a large labor pool from which to select employees is usually beneficial to companies. Companies with low CC inadvertently restrict the labor pool from which they can recruit by appearing unattractive to potential job applicants and, thus, are at a human resource and economic disadvantage relative to companies with high CC (cf. also Orlitzky, 2007*c*).

Boosting Sales Revenues

Probably the most direct explanation of a positive effect of CC on CFP is the view of CC as a revenue generator—especially in the long run. Firms that enjoy favorable reputations for their CC may be able to charge premiums for their products and services (Auger *et al.*, 2003). Consumers may value social responsibility so highly that they are willing to pay more for products and services from socially responsible companies. In addition, by conveying important information about how products have been manufactured in a socially or environmentally responsible manner, companies may increase market share relative to competitors that are poor corporate citizens (Miller, 1997). Whether the effect is through increased prices or a larger customer base, CC may help the business generate more sales revenues. Authors in the popular business press adhere to this revenue-generating view of CC to some extent (e.g. Read, 2004), although the academic experimental research evidence is more tenuous (Elliott and Freeman, 2001; Folkes and Kamins, 1999; Roberts, 1996). Certain customer segments (e.g. members of Amnesty International, older women, or Generation Y) have been found to be willing to pay premium prices for products from high-CC firms, but these purchasing decisions may not be generalizable to the whole population of consumers (Auger *et al.*, 2003; Read, 2004). However, the currently weak corroboration of this mediator does not strike a fatal blow to the positive view of CC-CFP linkages because, as I argue in this chapter and elsewhere (Orlitzky, 2006), there are so many other mediating variables that have received strong empirical support.

Reducing Business Risk

Firms may also financially benefit from CC because it tends to reduce business risk (Orlitzky and Benjamin, 2001). CC can decrease business risk by allowing firms to anticipate environmental upheavals more effectively (King, 1995). Good CC is typically characterized by effective environmental assessment (Wood, 1991), which helps companies address stakeholder concerns proactively or interactively (Waddock, 2002). By balancing a multitude of stakeholder concerns, firms can potentially lower their legal costs because it is precisely the unaddressed stakeholder concerns that usually turn into lawsuits against neglectful companies.

There is strong evidence that the higher a firm's reputation for its CC, the lower the business risk (Orlitzky and Benjamin, 2001). That is, CC and business risk have been found to be inversely correlated. However, the negative CC-risk associations also exhibited relatively large variabilities around the meta-analytic means (Orlitzky and Benjamin, 2001: 385). This implies that such study artifacts as sampling error and measurement error explained only modest amounts of cross-study variability in findings. The only notable exception was the relationship between CC and total market risk, which was not only the largest correlation found (true score correlation coefficient ρ of -0.57), but also had the smallest true score variance around it (Orlitzky and Benjamin, 2001: 385). Of all CC measures, reputation tended to reduce risk to the greatest extent (ρ of -0.32), followed by social audits, processes, and outcomes (-0.13), CC disclosures (-0.10), and management social responsibility values (-0.07). The order of these corrected correlation coefficients was generally consistent with theoretical expectations (Orlitzky and Benjamin, 2001). Interestingly, and contrary to expectations, corporate environmental performance was related to risk to only a negligible degree (-0.02). However, a major caveat applies to this last finding because the number of quantitative studies that were integrated in the meta-analysis was small (only eight).

Reverse Causation?

So far, the discussion has implied that CC was the causal determinant, and thus temporal antecedent, of CFP. However, there are also strong theoretical arguments for reverse causation, with CFP as the precursor of CC. The arguments about reverse causation may generally be subdivided into two broad categories: the slack resources view and the (normative) '*noblesse oblige*' view.

First, previously high levels of CFP may provide the slack resources necessary for a company to engage in corporate social responsibility and responsiveness (Cyert and March, 1963; Ullmann, 1985). CC often represents an area of relatively high managerial discretion (Carroll, 1979), so that the initiation and maintenance of voluntary social and environmental policies may depend on the availability of excess funds (McGuire et al., 1988). While executive leadership (cf. also Orlitzky and Swanson, 2002, 2006; Orlitzky et al., 2006) and organizational culture (cf. also Swanson, 1999) must be supportive of CC, profits and thus slack resources represent the necessary conditions for high CC. In other words, a firm's prior profit level, if it is low, may act as a factor inhibiting CC activities and investments.

Second, a consistent track record of organizational success may create a sense of obligation among executives to give back to the community (*Economist*, 2006). This normative obligation may not only be felt by top managers on an individual level, but these communitarian values may also be expressed in the organizational activities initiated by those leaders. In his seminal institutional theorizing, Selznick (1949) demonstrated how normative commitments affected organizational behavior at the Tennessee Valley Authority. Internalized and legitimized shared norms can explain the persistence of organizational activities at the macro level as well (e.g. Kilduff, 1993). Above and beyond regulative pressures, network embeddedness and consequent network dependencies may stabilize and maintain organizational practices (Powell, 1991), such as industry-wide voluntary product standards (Hemenway, 1975; Scott, 1995: 79). In short, the slack resources argument, an instrumental explanation, may be insufficient by itself to explain the diffusion and maintenance of CC in organizational fields. Institutional theory (Powell and DiMaggio, 1991; Scott, 1995) can provide important additional insights focusing on normative pressures, which are likely to increase with increasing CFP.

The meta-analytic evidence accumulated by Orlitzky, Schmidt, and Rynes (2003) supports this view of reverse causality (CFP $\rightarrow$ CC) to about the same degree as a CC $\rightarrow$ CFP link. Regardless of the temporal order of the two core constructs, the true score correlation ρ was 0.29. Interestingly, the strongest meta-analytic correlation was found when both constructs were measured concurrently (ρ of 0.44)—i.e., in the same quarter or year. This meta-analytic evidence supports Waddock and Graves's (1997a, 1997b) good management argument. CC and CFP may reinforce each other in a virtuous cycle because good managers are capable of taking positive strategic action in both economic and social domains. Astute managers are able to identify and implement specific CSR activities through which their organization's reputation can be enhanced in social or environmental domains—and they also ensure that slack resources are invested wisely to promote and exploit these opportunities. Furthermore, skillful executives can sidestep the perception that the socially responsible activities by their companies are merely marketing ploys. They are able to convey to internal and external stakeholders that their company's CC is in fact rooted in top managers' deeply felt commitments to social and environmental causes.

MODERATORS: THE CONTINGENCY FACTORS ON WHICH THE CC-CFP RELATIONSHIP DEPENDS

The main moderators that Orlitzky, Schmidt, and Rynes (2003) and Orlitzky and Benjamin (2001) proposed were the measurement strategies associated with CC and CFP, respectively. Unlike a narrative literature review, a meta-analysis can empirically examine the strength of moderator (or interaction) effects by disaggregating the overall meta-analytic data set into relatively homogeneous subgroups (which are categorized by the postulated moderator). When (a) the mean correlations differ in those subgroups and (b) the study artifacts explain more cross-study variability in these subgroups compared to the overall meta-analytic data set, a meta-analysis can demonstrate the existence of contingencies. Both meta-analyses by Orlitzky and his colleagues showed that the way CC and CFP were operationalized exerted a great impact on the study effects found. Thus, any new primary study that attempts to measure only one specific dimension of CC may not capture the full economic impact of CC.

Because Orlitzky *et al.*, found only a few instances in which study artifacts explained between 75% and 100% of cross-study variability in the CC-CFP effect sizes, several other contingency factors are likely to affect this relationship as well. One of them, already confirmed in a primary study of one dimension of CC, is industry growth. Russo and Fouts (1997) found that industry growth, as a moderator, strengthened the relationship between corporate environmental performance and profitability. That is, CC was a more important internal resource when an industry was growing relative to when it was stable. Most likely, this moderator effect exists because a firm operating in a growing industry requires the kind of environmental assessment and management for which CSR provides the normative (rather than instrumental) foundation and benefits more from the resource-based, internal benefits of CC under those growth conditions. Generally, though, a lot more research is required to examine the moderator effects that have been proposed in the literature. The theoretically most compelling argument for moderator effects is presented by McWilliams and Siegel (2001) in their supply and demand model of CSR. Their proposed moderators included an organization's size, level of diversification, research and development, advertising, government sales, consumer income, labor market conditions, and stage in the industry life cycle. All of them require empirical follow-up research.

CONFOUNDING VARIABLES

The empirical impact of confounding variables must be distinguished from these postulated moderator effects. Moderators interact with exogenous variables to affect the dependent variable under consideration. That is, moderators are modeled mathematically as multiplicative effects. Confounding variables act differently. Confounding variables may create spurious relationships if the study design or data analysis does not control for their impact. Their impact is (usually) additive. The importance of these potential confounds explains the fact that potential confounds are typically entered first in multiple regression models. Variance explained (R^2) is often considered a pretty good indicator of the impact of potential unmeasured confounds, but not of the magnitude of contingency effects. The higher R^2, the lower the probability that important confounds have been ignored. However, R^2 may also be deceptive because any effect size between CC and CFP may be artificially inflated because the conceptual model is incomplete or misspecified. Such

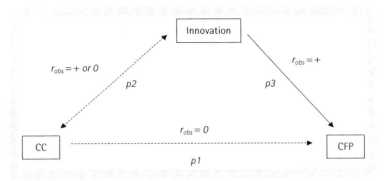

Fig. 5.1 Innovation as confounding variable

misspecifications are sometimes labeled 'errors of the third type' (cf. also Leamer, 1983).

Innovation

Innovation, often operationalized as a firm's level of investments in research and development, can be considered a potential confound of the CC–CFP relationship. McWilliams and Siegel (2000, 2001) emphasize that the association between CC and CFP cannot properly be understood without consideration of organizational innovation. McWilliams and Siegel (2000) argued that if studies statistically controlled for firms' investments in research and development (R&D), the positive association between CC and CFP would vanish. Such a postulated confounding effect is shown in Figure 5.1. However, the direct association between CC and CFP might also be zero or statistically non-significant if innovative activities were *mediating* the relationship between CC and CFP, as shown in Figure 5.2. In my view, Figure 5.2 is as plausible as Figure 5.1 (cf. Geroski, 1994 on the

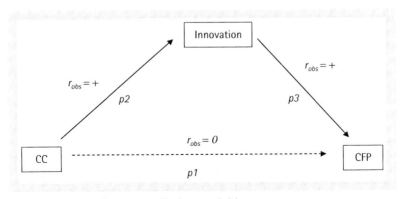

Fig. 5.2 Innovation as mediating variable

innovation–financial performance relationship; Waddock *et al.*, 2002 on the CSP–innovation relationship). Moreover, from the methodological literature (Schwab, 1999), we can infer that innovation tends to inflate the zero-order correlation between CC and CFP if the association between CC and innovation ($p2$) is positive rather than zero, or statistically nonsignificant. Hence, because the main difference between Figures 5.1 and 5.2 tends to boil down to the causal arrow of $p2$ (i.e. Is CC a causal predictor of innovation or is innovation a causal predictor of CC?), this particular facet of the CC–CFP research program certainly represents an area in need of future empirical study. From a theoretical viewpoint, it will be important to go beyond the consideration of R&D expenditures as a control variable—and study designs will have to reflect that.[4]

Organization Size

Another variable which may confound the CC–CFP relationship is organizational size. Large firms may both exhibit greater financial performance and engage in more socially responsible activities as they tend to have more slack resources (which are needed not only for CSR investments but also for other investments that may allow a given firm to stay ahead of its competitors). If this argument, which Orlitzky (2001) presented in greater depth, were true, the CC–CFP relationship may, in fact, be spurious.

The meta-analytic data do not support this view. When size is added as a variable influencing both CC and CFP (in a similar way as 'Innovation' in Fig. 5.1), the path-analytic model shows that the 'true score' correlation ρ between CC and CFP remains high ($\rho = 0.37$) despite this statistical control (Orlitzky, 2001). Importantly, this meta-analytic finding suggests that large *and* small firms can financially benefit from being or becoming good corporate citizens, albeit (most likely) due to different causal mechanisms. Why this is the case awaits future research.

CONCLUSIONS: RESEARCH POLITICS AND FUTURE DIRECTIONS

In conjunction with a meta-analysis of event studies (Frooman, 1997), this research program has generated some generalizable knowledge:

---

[4] Though interesting in theory, the direction of the causal arrow of $p2$ (CSP $\rightarrow$ innovation or innovation $\rightarrow$ CSP?) may not be so important in practice.

- Overall, there is a positive, but also highly variable, relationship between CC and CFP.
- CC and CFP tend to be mutually reinforcing organizational activities.
- CC and CFP are positively correlated, most likely because social performance helps enhance corporate reputations, and, to a lesser extent, improve managerial learning and internal efficiencies.
- The large variability of findings in studies is partly due to primary-study artifacts.
- CC may also reduce business risk.
- Organization size does not confound the relationship between CC and CFP.
- The large variability of the CC–CFP relationships suggests several moderators (e.g. measurement strategies, industry growth, etc.) which should be examined in future research.

Because of this variability, scholars in this area should probably reformulate the question that introduced and motivated this research synthesis as follows: How can we characterize the relationship between corporate citizenship (CC) and corporate financial performance (CFP)? Rephrasing the question this way is sensible for two main reasons. First, it acknowledges that a company can become a responsible corporate citizen through more routes than only high *social* performance (see also Holliday *et al.*, 2002). Second, and more important, the reformulation puts the researcher and the community of researchers at center stage (Orlitzky, 2007*a*). This is vital in any research domain in which construct validity is a key problem. For example, what some people regard as the epitome of CSR (e.g. affirmative action) is denounced by others as morally questionable organizational conduct. Value relativism demands a balanced attention to the normative foundation of every single dimension of CC. We cannot assume that the manifestations of CC in a particular domain are self-evident. At the same time, though, an 'anything-goes' definition of CSR (e.g. 'CSR is whatever market participants consider CSR') may, in fact, be as damaging to future refinement as an absolutist insistence on certain ideologies. Conceptually, we need to come to a consensus about the types of activities that have a net positive impact on business environments. To 'better society' is hardly a sufficient guide for a scientifically useful definition of CSR. I agree with Rowley and Berman (2000) that, at present, CSP as a construct probably raises more questions than it answers. At the same time, I think the correct research strategy is not a moratorium on the CC–CFP research stream, but instead an intensified, politically aware examination of the philosophical underpinnings of CC, so that it becomes useful for social scientists of all political persuasions.

As a case in point, some writers (e.g. Entine, 2003) argue that CSR represents advocacy of an inherently Liberal or even irrational conception of business activity. To some extent, these criticisms are a call to arms for CC researchers to demonstrate that their actual operationalizations of CC do not give priority to a particular political view of societal governance. Instead, our objective measures must reflect societal values which every reasonable person would deem 'positive'. This research may lead to a more limited view of CC because it would imply that we shift our focus from the motivations of CC to the actual social and environmental impact of CC. In this effort, our measurement of CC must become more sophisticated and ask the actual stakeholders about their satisfaction with an organization's CC activities (Orlitzky, 2007b). Consistent with the advocacy of more verifiable measures of the 'triple bottom line' (Elkington, 1998), we must demonstrate the validity (see e.g. Sharfman, 1996) and reliability of our chosen measures—without succumbing to the illusion that our measures will ever be perfect.

Better measures will enable us to answer the moderator and mediator questions with greater confidence, but we also need to make sure that our study designs and data analyses are in line with the theoretical complexity of these questions. For example, the postulation of CC as a causal determinant of CFP requires much more than the concurrent measurement of both constructs in the same time period. In turn, for the investigation of lagged effects, it will be important to use theory as a guide for possible lead-lag times and mediating variables (Orlitzky, 2006; Orlitzky et al., 2003; Schuler and Cording, 2006).

This being said, the meta-analytic evidence does *not* point to the overall equivocality and inconclusiveness of this research stream. Researchers of corporate social and financial performance must not repeat the same mistakes that have been made in so many other social science research literatures which, until the introduction of meta-analysis, were littered with the false appearance of conflicting results (Hunt, 1997; Schmidt, 1992). When, based on narrative reviews, many different moderators effects were postulated, social scientists would conduct contingency studies, which only resulted in a more complex variability of findings. Ultimately, researchers would conclude that the variable under consideration actually had no 'generalizable' effects, and the research community ultimately turns to more 'tractable' problems. Over time, history shows that the same social science research pattern seems to repeat itself in many different areas of research (Schmidt, 1992). Taking the method of meta-analysis more seriously prevents this pattern because, based on meta-analytic findings, social science studies are, in fact, about as generalizable as studies in the natural sciences (Hedges, 1987). But overcoming this pattern will not be easy because, at first at least, the proposition of contingencies generally leads to the funding of more primary studies because the previous 'flawed' literature has only produced 'ambiguous' evidence and, therefore, additional new research should be supported (according to the typical argument). In this context it is no surprise that other academics emphasize the variability of findings reported by Orlitzky, Schmidt, and Rynes (2003) much more than practitioners and journalists, who focus on the means (e.g. Kelly, 2004).

We must confront the research politics not only of 'inconclusive' findings, but also of positive relationships. Researchers that believe in a positive relationship between CC and CFP are really caught between a rock and a hard place. On the one hand, they will be attacked by conservatives who believe that the 'business of business is business' (e.g. Friedman, 1970; Levitt, 1958). On the other hand, they will have to defend their findings against attacks from the Left. Social democrats and believers in big government may dislike the implications of positive CC–CFP correlations. Based on non-negative CC–CFP correlations, researchers can in fact argue that business will not always be reluctant to embrace CSR. Market forces may signal where the business opportunities for discretionary spending on CSR lie and in turn these market signals may turn out to be more reliable indicators of genuine social responsibility than government regulations emerging from interest-group politics. Those on the political Left know the case for governmental regulation would be much stronger if CC–CFP relationships were negative.[5] Occupying a middle ground between these views on the political right and left, the advocates of a generally positive CC–CFP association will be in a much better position to justify their views if they develop more defensible measures and study designs in illuminating these empirical relationships.

In the corporate social-financial performance research domain there is no short-age of rich theory (e.g. McWilliams and Siegel, 2001; Orlitzky *et al.*, 2003; Schuler and Cording, 2006). Before turning to the development of even more complex theory, though, we must be clear about two questions. First, are the findings really as equivocal as they appear? I hope this chapter has contributed to answering this question. The second question, though, is of a different, more philosophical nature: What is CSR? One important element of better conceptualization will have to heed Friedman's (1970) caveat about the socialist overtones of the doctrine of 'social re-sponsibility'. But is CSR necessarily a collectivist doctrine? When we recognize (and can convincingly demonstrate) that 'socially responsible' behavior can *also* serve a firm's enlightened self-interest, we may be able to abandon the common-sense notion of 'social responsibility' as synonymous with 'altruism' or 'self-sacrifice' (see also Dalai Lama and Cutler, 1998; Rand, 1964). The second question requires an in-depth normative analysis by business ethicists. In fact, a comprehensive conceptual clarification of corporate responsibility is a necessary precondition for more valid and reliable measurement of CSP, CSR, and/or CC—and for better theory.

REFERENCES

ANDERSON, J. C., and FRANKLE, A. W. 1980. 'Voluntary Social Reporting: An Iso-beta Prot-folio Analysis'. *Accounting Review*, 55: 467–79.

[5] A negative relationship implies an economic disincentive emerging from CC. In turn, those businesses that show the greatest profits and steepest share price increases would be least likely to engage in CC. This means that, according to this view, market forces work at cross-purposes with non-market issues and interests—and only government intervention, it is argued, can correct this market–non-market discrepancy.

AUGER, P., BURKE, P., DEVINNEY, T. M., and LOUVIERE, J. J. 2003. 'What will Consumers Pay for Social Product Features?' *Journal of Business Ethics*, 42(3): 281–304.

BACKHAUS, K. B., STONE, B. A., and HEINER, K. 2002. 'Exploring the Relationship between Corporate Social Performance and Employer Attractiveness'. *Business & Society*, 41: 292–318.

CARROLL, A. B. 1979. 'A Three-dimensional Conceptual Model of Corporate Social Performance'. *Academy of Management Review*, 4: 497–506.

CHALMERS, T. C., and LAU, J. 1994. 'What is Meta-analysis'? *Emergency Care Research Institute*, 12: 1–5.

COHEN, J. 1994. 'The Earth is round (p < .05)'. *American Psychologist*, 49: 997–1003.

COOPER, H. M., and HEDGES, L. V. 1994. *The Handbook of Research Synthesis*. New York: Russell Sage Foundation.

CYERT, R. M., and MARCH, J. G. 1963. *A Behavioral Theory of the Firm*. Englewood Cliffs, NJ: Prentice Hall.

DALAI LAMA, H. H., and CUTLER, H. C. 1998. *The Art of Happiness: A Handbook for the Living*. New York: Riverhead Books.

DAVENPORT, K. 2000. 'Corporate Citizenship: A Stakeholder Approach for Defining Corporate Social Performance and Identifying Measures for Assessing it (Dissertation Abstract)'. *Business & Society*, 39(2): 210–19.

DAVIS, K. 1973. 'The Case for and against Business Assumptions of Social Responsibilities'. *Academy of Management Journal*, 16: 312–17.

Economist. 2006. 'Billanthropy', *The Economist*, 380: 11.

ELKINGTON, J. 1998. *Cannibals with Forks: The Triple Bottom Line of the 21st Century*. Oxford: Capstone.

ELLIOTT, K. A., and FREEMAN, R. B. 2001. 'White Hats or Don Quixotes? Human Rights Vigilantes in the Global Economy'. Cambridge, Mass: National Bureau of Economic Research.

ENTINE, J. 2003. 'The Myth of Social Investing: A Critique of its Practices and Consequences for Corporate Social Performance Research'. *Organization & Environment*, 16: 352–68.

FOLKES, V. S., and KAMINS, M. A. 1999. 'Effects of Information about Firms' Ethical and Unethical Actions on Consumers' Attitudes'. *Journal of Consumer Psychology*, 8(3): 243–59.

FOMBRUN, C., and SHANLEY, M. 1990. 'What's in a Name? Reputation Building and Corporate Strategy'. *Academy of Management Journal*, 33: 233–58.

FRANK, R. H. 1996. 'Can Socially Responsible Firms Survive in a Competitive Environment?' in D. M. Messick and A. E. Tenbrunsel (eds.), *Codes of Conduct: Behavioral Research into Business Ethics*. New York: Russell Sage Foundation, 86–103.

FRIEDMAN, M. 1970. 'The Social Responsibility of Business is to Increase its Profits'. *New York Times Magazine*, 33 ff.

FROOMAN, J. 1997. 'Socially Irresponsible and Illegal Behavior and Shareholder Wealth: A Meta-analysis of Event Studies'. *Business & Society*, 36(3): 221–49.

GEROSKI, P. A. 1994. *Market Structure, Corporate Performance and Innovative Activity*. Oxford: Oxford University Press.

GODFREY, P. C. 2005. 'The Relationship between Corporate Philanthropy and Shareholder Wealth: A Risk Management Perspective'. *Academy of Management Review*, 30(4): 777–98.

GREENING, D. W., and TURBAN, D. B. 2000. 'Corporate Social Performance as a Competitive Advantage in Attracting a Quality Workforce'. *Business & Society*, 39: 254–80.

GRIFFIN, J. J., and MAHON, J. F. 1997. 'The Corporate Social Performance and Corporate Financial Performance Debate: Twenty-five Years of Incomparable Research'. *Business & Society*, 36: 5–31.

GUNTHER, M. 2004. 'The Mosquito in the Tent'. *Fortune*, 149(9): 68–73.

HEDGES, L. V. 1987. 'How Hard is Hard Science, How Soft is Soft Science? The Empirical Cumulativeness of Research'. *American Psychologist*, 42(2): 443–55.

——and OLKIN, I. 1980. 'Vote Counting Methods in Research Synthesis'. *Psychological Bulletin*, 88: 359–69.

————1985. *Statistical Methods for Meta-analysis*. Orlando, Fla.: Academic Press.

HEMENWAY, D. 1975. *Industrywide Voluntary Product Standards*. Cambridge, Mass.: Ballinger.

HEYES, A. G. 2005. 'A Signaling Motive for Self-regulation in the Shadow of Coercion'. *Journal of Economics and Business*, 57(3): 238–46.

HODSON, R. 2001. *Dignity at Work*. Cambridge: Cambridge University Press.

HOLLIDAY, C. O., SCHMIDHEINY, S., and WATTS, P. 2002. *Walking the Talk: The Business Case for Sustainable Development*. San Francisco: Greenleaf.

HUNT, M. 1997. *How Science takes Stock: The Story of Meta-analysis*. New York: Russell Sage Foundation.

HUNTER, J. E., and SCHMIDT, F. L. 2004. *Methods of Meta-analysis: Correcting Error and Bias in Research Findings*, 2nd edn. Thousand Oaks, Calif.: Sage.

HUSELID, M. A. 1995. 'The Impact of Human Resource Management Practices on Turnover, Productivity, and Corporate Financial Performance'. *Academy of Management Journal*, 38: 635–72.

JONES, T. M. 1995. 'Instrumental Stakeholder Theory: A Synthesis of Ethics and Economics'. *Academy of Management Review*, 20(2): 404–37.

KELLY, M. 2004. 'Holy Grail Found'. *Business Ethics Magazine online*, 3.

KILDUFF, M. 1993. 'The Reproduction of Inertia in Multinational Corporations', in S. Ghoshal and D. E. Westney (eds.), *Organization Theory and the Multinational Corporation*. New York: St Martin's, 259–74.

KING, A. 1995. 'Avoiding Ecological Surprise: Lessons from Long-standing Communities.' *Academy of Management Review*, 20: 961–85.

LEAMER, E. 1983. 'Let's Take the Con out of Econometrics'. *American Economic Review*, 73: 31–43.

LEVITT, T. 1958. 'The Dangers of Social Responsibility'. *Harvard Business Review*, 36(5): 38–44.

LOGSDON, J. M., and WOOD, D. J. 2002. 'Reputation as an Emerging Construct in the Business and Society field: An Introduction'. *Business & Society*, 41(4): 365–70.

MATTEN, D., and CRANE, A. 2005. 'Corporate Citizenship: Toward an Extended Theoretical Conceptualization'. *Academy of Management Review*, 30(1): 166–79.

McCLOSKEY, D. N. 1998. *The Rhetoric of Economics*, 2nd edn. Madison: University of Wisconsin Press.

McGUIRE, J. B., SUNDGREN, A., and SCHNEEWEIS, T. 1988. 'Corporate Social Responsibility and Firm Financial Performance'. *Academy of Management Journal*, 31: 854–72.

McVEIGH, R., BJARNASON, T., and WELCH, M. R. 2003. 'Hate Crime Reporting as a Successful Social Movement Outcome'. *American Sociological Review*, 68(3): 843–67.

McWILLIAMS, A., and SIEGEL, D. 2000. 'Corporate Social Responsibility and Financial Performance: Correlation or Misspecification?' *Strategic Management Journal*, 21: 603–9.

McWILLIAMS, A., and SIEGEL, D. 2001. 'Corporate Social Responsibility: A Theory of the Firm Perspective'. *Academy of Management Review*, 26: 117–27.

——VAN FLEET, D. D., and CORY, K. D. 2002. 'Raising Rivals' Costs through Political Strategy: An Extension of Resource-Based Theory'. *Journal of Management Studies*, 39(5): 707–24.

MEYER, M. W., and GUPTA, V. 1994. 'The Performance Paradox'. *Research in Organizational Behavior*, 16: 309–69.

MILLER, C. 1997. 'Marketers Weigh the Effects of Sweatshop Crackdown'. *Marketing News*, 31(10): 1, 19.

NUNNALLY, J. C., and BERNSTEIN, I. H. 1994. *Psychometric Theory*, 3rd edn. New York: McGraw-Hill.

ORLITZKY, M. 1999. '*A Meta-analysis of the Relationship between Corporate Social Performance and Firm Financial Performance*'. Unpublished doctoral dissertation thesis, The University of Iowa, Iowa City, IA.

——2001. 'Does Organizational Size Confound the Relationship between Corporate Social Performance and Firm Financial Performance?' *Journal of Business Ethics*, 33(2): 167–80.

——2002. *People and Profits? The Search for a Link between a Company's Social and Financial Performance* by J. D. Margolis and J. P. Walsh [book review]. *The International Journal for Organizational Analysis*, 10(2): 191–4.

——2006. 'Links between Corporate Social Responsibility and Corporate Financial Performance: Theoretical and Empirical Determinants', in J. Allouche (ed.), *Corporate Social Responsibility, Vol. 2: Performances and Stakeholders*. London: Palgrave Macmillan, 41–64.

——2007a. 'Doing Well by Doing Good: Objective Findings, Subjective Assumptions, or Selective Amplification.' Best Paper Proceedings, Academy of Management Conference, Philadelphia.

——2007b. 'The Meaning and Measurement of "Doing Good" at the Company Level of Analysis'. Paper presented at the Academy of Management Conference, Philadelphia.

——2007c. 'Recruitment Strategy', in P. Boxall, J. Purcell, and P. M. Wright (eds.), *The Oxford Handbook of Human Resources Management*. Oxford: Oxford University Press, 273–99.

——and BENJAMIN, J. D. 2001. 'Corporate Social Performance and Firm Risk: A Meta-analytic Review'. *Business & Society*, 40(4): 369–96.

——SCHMIDT, F. L., and RYNES, S. L. 2003. 'Corporate Social and Financial Performance: A Meta-analysis'. *Organization Studies*, 24(3): 403–41.

——and SWANSON, D. L. 2002. 'Value Attunement: Toward a Theory of Socially Responsible Executive Decision Making'. *Australian Journal of Management*, 27, Special Issue: 119–28.

————2006. 'Socially Responsible Human Resource Management: Charting New Territory', in J. R. Deckop (ed.), *Human Resource Management Ethics*. Greenwich, Conn.: Information Age Publishing, 3–25.

————and QUARTERMAINE, L.-K. 2006. 'Normative Myopia, Executives' Personality, and Preference for Pay Dispersion: Toward Implications for Corporate Social Performance'. *Business & Society*, 45(2): 149–77.

PFEFFER, J. 1994. *Competitive Advantage through People: Unleashing the Power of the Workforce*. Boston: Harvard Business School Press.

——1998. *The Human Equation: Building Profits by Putting People First*. Boston: Harvard Business School Press.

POWELL, W. W. 1991. 'Expanding the Scope of Institutional Analysis', in Powell and DiMaggio (1991).

——and DiMAGGIO, P. J. 1991. *The New Institutionalism in Organizational Analysis*. Chicago: University of Chicago Press.

PRICE, J. L., and MUELLER, C. W. 1986. *Handbook of Organizational Measurement*, 2nd edn. Marshfield, Mass.: Pitman.

RAND, A. 1964. *The Virtue of Selfishness: A New Concept of Egoism*. New York: New American Library.

READ, E. 2004. 'Green Means go for Picky Buyers'. *The New Zealand Herald*: C4.

ROBERTS, J. A. 1996. 'Will the Real Socially Responsible Consumer Please Step Forward?' *Business Horizons*, 39(1): 79–83.

ROSENTHAL, R. 1984. *Meta-analysis Procedures for Social Research*. Beverly Hills, Calif.: Sage.

——and DiMATTEO, M. R. 2001. 'Meta-analysis: Recent Developments in Quantitative Methods for Literature Reviews'. *Annual Review of Psychology*, 52: 59–82.

ROWLEY, T. J., and BERMAN, S. 2000. 'A Brand New Brand of Corporate Social Performance'. *Business & Society*, 39: 397–418.

RUSSO, M. V., and FOUTS, P. A. 1997. 'A Resource-Based Perspective on Corporate Environmental Performance and Profitability'. *Academy of Management Journal*, 40: 534–59.

SCHMIDT, F. L. 1992. 'What do Data really Mean? Research Findings, Meta-analysis, and Cumulative Knowledge in Psychology'. *American Psychologist*, 47: 1173–81.

SCHULER, D. A., and CORDING, M. 2006. 'A Corporate Social Performance-Corporate Financial Performance Behavioral Model for Consumers'. *Academy of Management Review*, 31(3): 540–58.

SCHWAB, D. P. 1980. 'Construct Validity in Organizational Behavior', in B. M. Staw and L. L. Cummings (eds.), *Research in Organizational Behavior*, vol. 2. Greenwich, CT: JAI Press, 3–43.

——1999. *Research Methods for Organizational Studies*. Mahwah, NJ: Lawrence Erlbaum.

SCOTT, W. R. 1995. *Institutions and organizations*. Thousand Oaks, Calif.: Sage.

SELZNICK, P. 1949. *TVA and the Grass Roots*. Berkeley, Calif.: University of California Press.

SHARFMAN, M. 1996. 'A Concurrent Validity Study of the KLD Social Performance Ratings Data'. *Journal of Business Ethics*, 15: 287–96.

SIMON, J. G., POWERS, C. W., and GUNNEMANN, J. P. 1972. *The Ethical Investor: Universities and Corporate Responsibility*. New Haven, Conn.: Yale University Press.

SWANSON, D. L. 1999. 'Toward an Integrative Theory of Business and Society: A Research Strategy for Corporate Social Performance'. *Academy of Management Review*, 24: 506–21.

TURBAN, D. B., and CABLE, D. M. 2003. 'Firm Reputation and Applicant Pool Characteristics'. *Journal of Organizational Behavior*, 24(6): 733–51.

——and GREENING, D. W. 1996. 'Corporate Social Performance and Organizational Attractiveness to Prospective Employees'. *Academy of Management Journal*, 40(3): 658–72.

————1997. 'Corporate Social performance and Organizational Attractiveness to Prospective Employees'. *Academy of Management Journal*, 40: 658–72.

ULLMANN, A. 1985. 'Data in Search of a Theory: A Critical Examination of the Relationship among Social Performance, Social Disclosure, and Economic Performance'. *Academy of*

Management Review, 10: 540–77.

VENKATRAMAN, N., and RAMANUJAM, V. 1986. 'Measurement of Business Performance in Strategy Research: A Comparison of Approaches'. *Academy of Management Review*, 11: 801–14.

WADDOCK, S. A. 2002. *Leading Corporate Citizens: Vision, Values, Value Added*. Boston: McGraw-Hill.

—— BODWELL, C., and GRAVES, S. B. 2002. 'Responsibility: The New Business Imperative'. *Academy of Management Executive*, 16(2): 132–48.

—— and GRAVES, S. B. 1997a. 'The Corporate Social Performance-Financial Performance Link'. *Strategic Management Journal*, 18: 303–19.

—— —— 1997b. 'Quality of Management and Quality of Stakeholder Relations: Are they Synonymous?' *Business & Society*, 36(3): 250–79.

WOOD, D. J. 1991. 'Corporate Social Performance Revisited'. *Academy of Management Review*, 16: 691–718.

—— and JONES, R. E. 1995. 'Stakeholder Mismatching: A Theoretical Problem in Empirical Research on Corporate Social Performance'. *International Journal of Organizational Analysis*, 3: 229–67.

PART III

CRITIQUES OF CORPORATE SOCIAL RESPONSIBILITY

CHAPTER 6

PRINCIPALS AND AGENTS

FURTHER THOUGHTS ON THE FRIEDMANITE CRITIQUE OF CORPORATE SOCIAL RESPONSIBILITY

JOSÉ SALAZAR

BRYAN W. HUSTED

SINCE Milton Friedman's well-known essay, 'The Social Responsibility of Business is to Increase its Profits', was published in the *New York Times Magazine* over thirty-five years ago, the 1976 winner of the Bank of Sweden Prize in Economic Sciences in Memory of Alfred Nobel has become the unwitting center of debate in the field of Business and Society. That essay is now often featured as required reading in many introductory courses in the field because of its polemical nature. Undoubtedly, the title of the essay was more provocative than its actual content, given that Friedman's argument specifies important boundary conditions for profit maximization—specifically, that such behavior should occur within the limits set by the law and ethical custom. Although his argument includes several different strands, we focus on that strand related to agency relationships between the corporation and its managers.

Friedman (1962) originally framed the issue of socially responsible versus profit-maximizing behavior in terms of whether business managers should be what he called 'civil servants' or alternatively agents of their stockholders. In that respect, Friedman's argument is an ethical one. Basically, he argues that managers as agents owe the owners of the corporation, the stockholders, a duty to pursue their interests. In other words, managers should spend the corporation's money as its owners would want. To the extent that expenditures in favor of corporate social responsibilities (CSR) do not accord with the desires of stockholders, the agent violates that duty.

Curiously, the agency argument within the essay does not entirely eliminate the possibility of CSR expenditures. Although Friedman goes on to find other reasons for arguing against CSR, they are not related to the agency argument. Since the 1970 essay was published, many stockholders have in fact decided that they do want corporations to make expenditures on social programs. Sometimes they have made this decision based on the so-called 'business case' for CSR. This business case argues that CSR is good for business. The search for a positive link between CSR or related concepts like social performance and financial performance has spawned an abundant literature, the results of which remain somewhat inconclusive, with some authors discovering a positive relationship between social performance and financial performance, others encountering a negative relationship, and still others finding no relationship (Griffin and Mahon, 1997; Margolis and Walsh, 2001; Orlitzky et al., 2003). Still, there appears to be a growing consensus in the business community that CSR is good for business (Davis, 2005). The business case has re-emerged more recently as a discussion of strategic CSR (Burke and Logsdon, 1996; McWilliams et al., 2006)—a concept that Friedman himself would have called 'hypocritical window-dressing,' but consistent with profit-maximizing behavior of the firm.

Given the possibility that owners may want the firm to engage in social initiatives, then the fundamental question that agency theory asks is: What should be the appropriate compensation for the managers of companies that seek to be socially responsible? Since Friedman's original critique ended with the conclusion that firms should only seek to maximize profits within the bounds of the law and ethical custom, the question of compensation for agents was moot. In this chapter, we extend Friedman's original argument by attempting one possible answer to the compensation question. We take up this issue using the perspective of information economics as it elucidates our understanding of principal–agent relationships (Arrow, 1985).

The compensation question depends upon agency costs, which are the costs involved in ensuring that the agent (the informed actor) acts in the interests of the principal (the uninformed actor) (Rasmussen, 1989). We examine the kinds of agency costs that would occur for different motivations on the part of the principal. We can identify three basic motivations for investment in CSR projects: altruism, coercion, and strategy (Baron, 2001; Husted and Salazar, 2006). Altruistic projects are undertaken without regard to the economic benefits of the project for the firm. Strategic projects seek to maximize economic benefits for the firm, while coerced projects seek to minimize costs of implementation. In addition, we examine the difference in agency costs that occurs for different kinds of principals (stockholders vs. non-shareholding stakeholders). Although principal-agent models have typically focused on the stockholder as the principal, Kenneth Arrow (1985) has argued that the principal may encompass other stakeholders. The main distinction between stockholders and non-shareholding stakeholders is that stockholders are generally risk-neutral, while other stakeholders are risk-adverse (Sundaram and Inkpen, 2004).

These combinations (altruistic, coercive, strategic motivation of agents and principals; stockholder principals vs. other stakeholder principals) give rise to eighteen different ways in which agency costs are generated. The possible avenues of inquiry are many, but we will focus on three cases where the agent is assumed to act strategically, but the motivation of the stockholder principal varies. Table 6.1 indicates the possible avenues of research and those that are taken up in this chapter. The focus of Table 6.1 is on the stockholder principal. However, we will also keep in mind the potential agency costs that may exist with respect to other principals.

In each case, agency costs are minimized to the extent that the motivation of the principal and the agent are aligned. Given the desire to spend as little as possible in order to comply with these pressures, external controls (i.e. compensation) serve to reduce agency costs. Friedman's essay largely dealt with the case of the altruistic agents of non-altruistic principals. As mentioned earlier, Friedman himself admitted that agency theory was not violated in cases where the principal wanted agents to make CSR expenditures for strategic reasons. Similarly, no problem would exist in the case of altruistic principals encouraging CSR expenditures by their agents. In this chapter, we focus on the strategic agent in cases where the motivation of the principal for CSR expenditures varies.

Before continuing further, we need to define corporate social responsibility (CSR). CSR research is hampered by the many definitions and approaches that have

Table 6.1 Relationship of chapter to prior and future research

	Stockholder Principal		
	Altruist	Coercive	Strategic
Agent			
Altruist	No Problem	Friedman	Friedman
Coercive	Future work	No Problem	Future work
Strategic	This chapter	This chapter	This chapter, but no problem

been developed in the literature (Garriga and Melé, 2004). Rather than revisiting the myriad of issues behind the definition of CSR, we follow the approach taken by Husted and Allen (2006), based on Sethi (1978), which defines CSR as 'the firm's obligation to respond to the externalities created by market action.' This definition, based on welfare economics, is compatible with the approach taken in this chapter, although other definitions may be appropriate.

We begin by reviewing agency theory as developed in Friedman's argument and as used in further research since his 1970 article. We examine some of the implications of this work. In order to demonstrate some of the conclusions in a more analytic way, we slightly modify the Laffont and Martimort (2002) principal-agent model to include CSR projects and derive conclusions about the incentives that may most effectively align managerial behavior with corporate value maximization through CSR projects. We discuss how these results may change as the principal's motivation varies. This exercise highlights the limitations inherent in CSR as presently conceived and given current methods of measurement. But these limitations also point the way to the opportunities that CSR offers when employed wisely.

Agency Theory in Friedman's Argument

Agency models employ two actors: the principal and the agent. The principal delegates authority to the agent to act on his or her behalf. The principal's problem is to motivate the agent to do what he or she was asked to do (Jensen and Meckling, 1976; Fama, 1980). Unfortunately, agents sometimes exercise discretion to maximize their own utility rather than that of the principal. Agency theorists generally assume that agents seek their own interests, rather than those of the principal. In addition, agency problems only exist where the agent has more information than the principal. The costs associated with motivating the agent to act on behalf of the principal are referred to as agency costs.

As mentioned earlier, agency theory plays a key role in Milton Friedman's critique of CSR. He states quite clearly: '[T]he manager is an agent of the individuals who own the corporation or establish the eleemosynary institution, and his primary responsibility is to them' (Friedman, 1970: 255). His argument is a moral one—it is unethical for the corporate manager or agent to engage in CSR activities because the agent violates his or her duty to act in the interest of the principal. 'What does it mean to say that the corporate executive has a "social responsibility" in his capacity as businessman? If this statement is not pure rhetoric, it must mean that he is to act in some way that is not in the interest of his employers' (Friedman, 1970: 255).

In the case of CSR projects, the manager would be spending someone else's money for a general social interest—a kind of moral hazard problem. '[T]he great virtue of private competitive enterprise [is that] it forces people to be responsible for their own actions and makes it difficult for them to "exploit" other people for either selfish or unselfish purposes. They can do good—but only at their own expense' (Friedman, 1970: 257). However, the owners or principals may establish objectives other than profit maximization, even in the case of the corporation. Nevertheless, for Friedman the same argument applies if some stockholders agree to CSR investment, thereby taking away money from other stockholders, employees, or customers. In each case, someone suffers the consequences of another's responsible actions. Embedded within his argument are relevant ideas about information in relationships between the principal and agent.

Friedman's critique of CSR has been the subject of much empirical study. If Friedman is correct, then CSR activities will reduce the firm's financial performance and value. The 'business case' literature has developed to examine the relationship between CSR and firm financial performance. Some of these studies base their study on agency theory, while many use other theoretical perspectives. Let us review some of the studies that incorporate agency theory explicitly into their analysis.

Atkinson and Galaskiewicz (1988) examined the charitable giving behavior of firms according to ownership structure of firms in the Twin Cities. CEO stock ownership should reduce agency conflicts and thus costs by aligning the CEO's interests with those of the stockholders. Consistent with the predictions of agency theory, they found that firms with high levels of CEO ownership gave less generously to charity than firms with low levels of CEO ownership.

In contrast, Navarro (1988) found that charitable giving is profit maximizing. He found evidence that charitable contribution acts as a kind of advertising expense and a kind of 'quasi-fringe benefit' for employees. Here the findings support the idea that CSR expenditures are consistent with stockholders' interests, supporting the strategic form of CSR that Friedman finds to be hypocritical.

Wright and Ferris (1997) examine the effect of divestment of South African subsidiaries on the value of multinational enterprises. Using agency theory, they demonstrate that managers are susceptible to political pressures in making the divestment decision, rather than to pressures for value maximization from stockholders. They found that the announcement of the divestment decision was accompanied by significant, negative returns. Such a finding is consistent with the existence of an agency problem in which managers do not seek to maximize shareholder wealth.

In a follow-up study of corporate contributions in the Twin Cities, Galaskiewicz (1997) found mixed support for agency theory. Consistent with agency theory, corporate philanthropy was negatively influenced by CEO stock ownership. However, having a large outside stockholder who owned more than 10% of the shares had no effect on contributions. Under agency theory, one would have expected the existence of a large outside stockholder to act as a control on managerial discretion.

EXTENDING FRIEDMAN'S WORK

The initial analysis by Friedman and ensuing work leave open numerous questions that need to be answered. Given that there does seem to exist empirical support for the creation of agency costs due to CSR projects, one needs to examine the kinds of incentives that will align the interests of agents with those of the principal. One could answer quite simply that the principal should simply prohibit CSR expenditures. Such a simplistic solution ignores the fact that CSR is now taken for granted as part and parcel of the business enterprise. It becomes necessary to move beyond Friedman's original critique to analyze the different kinds of agency costs that are generated and how agents may be compensated so as to minimize the agency problem.

There are two relationships that are relevant in this analysis. The first relationship to be analyzed is the one between the person who implements the decision to invest in social responsibility (the agent) and the stockholder who benefits or suffers from such investment (the principal). The second relationship exists between the same agent as in the first case and another principal—the non-shareholding stakeholder (Arrow, 1985). In the second case, the effects of CSR expenditures are designed to go beyond the stockholder to encompass diverse non-shareholding stakeholders. This framework allows us to study the relevant agency relations inherent in corporate social responsibility activities. In Table 6.2, we present the expected principals and agents, according to the type of motivation that predominates in CSR expenditures for the principals. We focus on varying motivations of the principal precisely because Friedman allows the principal to set the objectives.

In the altruistic case, the firm's owners (principal) make a decision to contribute to a social cause due to the personal commitments and values of the principal, rather than to help the firm's profit objectives. Those social problems that are targeted may include social groups with little or no relationship to the firm's business mission. Such a case is not as outlandish as it may first sound. Arguably, firms like the Body Shop, Ben & Jerry's, and others were originally established for purposes other than profit maximization. Often, the shares of this kind of firm may be privately held.

In the case of coercion, the stockholders may see a decrease in their expected profits in the short run and possibly the long run. In this way, the stockholders are directly affected by the CSR expenditure. However, it may be possible that the firm

Table 6.2 Impact of CSR expenditures for principals by type of motivation

Motivation	Explanation
	a. Principal (Stockholders)
Altruism	This type of CSR project usually means a net cost and decrease in the financial performance of the firm. It may possibly involve some improvement in the image of the owners and managers with some stakeholders.
Coercion	The potential social benefit derived from this action does not normally go with an increase in the competitive position and/or firm profitability. Rather, it represents an operating cost, where in some cases, benefits are generated for the industry, which are not easily appropriated.
Strategy	There is a positive relationship between CSR expenditures and the competitive and financial performance of the firm. CSR activity is part of the management strategy to create wealth for stockholders.
	b. Principal (Non-shareholding Stakeholders)
Altruism	Benefits for some non-shareholding stakeholders.
Coercion	Societal benefits are generated by compliance with legal and social norms.
Strategy	Benefits for non-shareholding stakeholders may be difficult to identify.

and its stockholders receive benefits in terms of an improved image and reputation. The principals may also include legally protected groups or other stakeholders who exert pressure on the firm. Competitors may also receive benefits derived from the reduced social pressure produced by CSR expenditures of other firms.

Finally, a strategic motivation has to do with expenditures that not only contribute to social causes, but also allow the firm to improve its competitive performance. Although the primary beneficiaries of social expenditures would be the non-shareholding stakeholders, firm profits may improve and thereby increase stockholder wealth.

The objective of expenditures that are directly related to the business activity of the firm generally is to create value for the stockholders. In the case of CSR, this objective is not so clear because such expenditures are also intended to affect other stakeholders. This additional purpose creates ambiguity in the relationship between expenditures and earnings. Due to the lack of a functional link between profits and CSR expenditures, our objective in studying agency relations in this area is to minimize agency costs that arise from the potential divergence in objectives between the principal and the agent. Two factors are especially relevant in the estimation of agency costs: motivation and information asymmetry. First, given the different motivations for CSR expenditures already discussed, one can make different conjectures about what determines greater or lower agency costs. In other words, does strategic CSR result in lower agency costs than CSR made for reasons of altruism or coercion? Considering the two kinds of principals, we can say, on the one hand, that agency costs affect the profit that the firm can expect from CSR projects, and on the other, that there are agency costs that affect the expected social benefit that non-shareholding stakeholders may obtain from such projects.

Second, the estimation of agency costs is also complicated by problems of information asymmetry in CSR processes: moral hazard (promise keeping) and adverse selection (truth telling). How should one design incentives so that agents will act in the interests of principals with respect to CSR activities? We can then study to what extent the actions of the agent are observable or not by the principals and whether there exists sufficient information to have a clear idea of the results of these actions. In Table 6.3, we summarize the nature of information asymmetry according to the stockholder's different motivations for engaging in CSR. Although our work in this chapter focuses on moral hazard, we have included in the table some ideas about what adverse selection in CSR might look like.

In the case of altruism, moral hazard may exist because the agent seeks only to maximize his financial well-being rather than the altruistic objectives of the stockholder principal. Agency cost could be incurred by the non-shareholding, community stakeholder who does not receive the intended benefits from the stockholder's altruism. In the coercive and strategic cases, moral hazard also exists since the lack of commitment on the part of the agent for this type of investment may put the firm at risk for either not complying with community demands or for not taking advantage of competitive niches that could be exploited by competitors.

If we examine non-shareholding stakeholders as the principal, the specific beneficiary may not accurately reflect the interests of the group they supposedly represent. The worst risk occurs when the firm fulfills the CSR demands of the stakeholder representatives, but does not comply exactly with the needs of their supposed 'constituents' and thus remains subject to social boycotts or reduced competitiveness.

Generally speaking, we expect the severity of agency costs to differ in the context of CSR activities compared to business activities for two reasons. First, given our still limited knowledge and the lack of consensus about what constitutes best CSR practice and its impact on society and the firm, one might argue initially that managers (agents) do not have a greater level of knowledge than stockholders (principals) in this area. If this statement is correct, the problem of asymmetric information would be less severe in CSR investments than in those associated with the traditional business activities of the firm where the managers have a greater knowledge than the stockholders. However, to the extent that there are differences in the efficacy of CSR strategies to increase social welfare and maximize profits, and managers know these strategies and gain experience while executing them, then the relationship between managers and stockholders is more likely to generate agency costs. Also, if the principal does not know the agent's knowledge is inadequate, then agency costs will increase.

Table 6.3 Expected elements of moral hazard and adverse selection by CSR motivation

Motivation of Principal (Stockholder)	Moral Hazard		Adverse Selection	
	Agent	Principal (Non-shareholding Stakeholder)	Agent	Principal (Non-shareholding Stakeholder)
Altruistic	Commitment may be very low on the part of the manager.	The requests of the stakeholders may not represent social interests but rather the interests of particular groups.	• It is difficult to know social interests or to know the size of need. • It is difficult to anticipate the effects of CSR expenditure on profits or competitive advantage.	Does the information or capacity of the principal differ from that of the agent in terms of CSR projects?
Coercive	Failure to comply with standards set by law or by stakeholder groups.	Laws are biased in favor of stakeholder groups.	The manager is hired to pursue firm goals, subject to legal and social obligations. Legal goals generally will be more clearly defined than social goals.	It would be difficult for the principal to know what to do in terms of social projects beyond what the law requires and thus what to ask the agent to do.
Strategic	The agent uses the CSR expenditure for the purpose of achieving personal benefits and not for pursuing firm profits and objectives.	Breach of commitments in exchange for receiving support.	• It's difficult to know social interests or to measure the size of the need. • It is difficult to anticipate the effects of CSR expenditure on profits or competitive advantage.	Dispersed, unsystematic information with variables that are often difficult to operationalize.

Second, the difficulty of measuring the effects of CSR activities makes this type of expenditure more subject to moral hazard than those core business activities traditionally developed by the firm which are generally characterized by well-developed measures. Moral hazard occurs when the objective function of the agent differs from that of the principal. If the stockholder principal, due to social commitments or personal values, believes the firm should contribute to social causes due to altruism, then the agent may undertake actions with a zero or negative rate of return for the firm. At the same time, if the contract between the principal and agent includes an incentive mechanism that depends only on the financial returns obtained, then the objective functions of the principal and agent will differ and moral hazard will arise.

Since the relationship between the CSR activity of the agent and its consequences may not be observable, it is difficult to write a contract that specifies clearly the activities to be undertaken by the agent and the corresponding incentive mechanism. Given these limitations, CSR expenditures can be made for almost any social need without really knowing whether society benefits. This difficulty is key to understanding the contract design problem between the agent and principal that arises under moral hazard.

If the agent (manager) is risk neutral, the problem of not observing the results of CSR activity has no impact on efficiency and moral hazard does not create any agency cost. A risk-neutral agent would be indifferent to the choice between traditional business projects and riskier CSR projects. Thus, the risk-neutral agent is more likely to fulfill the principal's objectives through participation in CSR projects. Consequently, the contract between the principal and the agent will only specify rewards and punishments related to the financial performance of the firm and the risk of investing in social responsibility will be assumed by the agent. Even in this case, if the agent possesses relatively little wealth in comparison to the operating levels of the firm, the possibility of punishments is limited given that the agent's wealth could not possibly compensate for losses due to a failure to seek the principal's objectives. Thus the contract needs to be designed on the sole basis of rewards for reaching the planned objective.

However, in the more likely case that the agent is risk adverse, a fixed salary is needed to eliminate his or her insecurity. Unfortunately, a fixed salary does not necessarily induce a high level of effort. Thus, the incentive leading to greater effort would also include paying a certain risk premium over the fixed salary. In other words, in order to accept this risk, the agent will demand a premium, which leads to a trade-off between security and efficiency.

In the case of CSR, incentives for the agent tied only to firm financial performance would tend to eliminate any expenditure for CSR of the altruistic type and minimize those expenditures that correspond to a coercive type. Strategic CSR projects would have to compete with other business projects in terms of their rates of return, which, given the difficulty of measuring the expected results, would require a certain premium over the normal rate of return.

In order to demonstrate the foregoing conclusions, we develop a model based on the general model of moral hazard of Laffont and Martimort (2002) in which they consider two levels of effort by the agent and two corresponding levels of performance and describe the set of incentive contracts that induce a greater level of effort. We modify the Laffont and Martimort model only slightly by distinguishing the agent's actions that are traditionally related to the firm's business and those that are related to CSR. This general model begins with the standard relationship between the principal and agent, where the agent is the manager and the principal is the sole shareholder. Given the technical nature of the model, we include it as an appendix.

CHANGING CSR MOTIVATIONS

In this section, we examine the model in light of the assumption that there are different motivations behind CSR expenditures and that these motivations have different impacts on the financial performance of the firm. Although motivation could be considered either from the perspective of the principal stockholder or the agent, here we will observe what happens when the motivation differs for the principal. However, we will continue to trace how the agent's action affects two principals: the stockholder and a non-shareholding stakeholder. Agency costs will vary according to the different motivations for the principal. The results are summarized in Table 6.4.

Table 6.4 Agency costs according to type of principal and motivation

Motivation	Type of Principal	
	Stockholder	Community Stakeholder
Altruist	High	Low
Coercion (assuming no governmental failure)	Low	High
Coercion (assuming governmental failure)	High	High
Strategic	High	Low

In the altruistic case, the stockholder wants to contribute to the community's well-being,[1] and instructs the agent (manager) to allocate some firm resources for this purpose. The stockholder has no expectation of recovering any part of this expenditure and largely considers it to be a unilateral transfer from the firm to society. From the agent's perspective, if the agent were given a contract in which incentives were tied to the financial performance of the firm, and if he were completely indifferent to any community cause, one would expect that he would minimize any CSR expenditure or even eliminate it. The actions of the agent affect at least two principals: the stockholder and the non-shareholding stakeholder—in this case a community stakeholder. The main agency cost would be greater with respect to the agent-stockholder relation than with respect to the agent-community relation. On the one hand, the stockholder has manifested an interest in the community expenditure. However, the 'community' may not expect anything from the firm. This case is quite common in developing economies where there are usually few civil society organizations that defend social interests. In such a situation, the community will tend to look to the government, rather than the firm, for social improvements. Thus, the conclusion of the prior model expressed in equation (A-15) (see Appendix) would not vary when the motivation of the stockholder for making CSR investments is altruistic. If the stockholder wants to eliminate the risk that the agent will reduce CSR expenditures, she should authorize a transfer T greater than t, the incentive for normal business activities, so that T includes a premium for the greater risk implicit in not producing profits as a result of the CSR expenditure.

In the case of coercion, we begin with a stockholder who recognizes the existence of common benefits that accrue by submitting to mutual restrictions with non-shareholding stakeholders. In addition, she is willing to allocate firm resources to CSR activities up to the level needed to avoid legal sanction and/or the reduction of business activities because of actions by community stakeholders (e.g. boycotts) or its competitors (e.g. lower-cost compliance or participation in strategic CSR), without seeking some positive impact on the financial performance of the firm. In this case and given a contract with incentives tied exclusively to the financial performance of the firm, the agent will undertake effort $E = 1$ in order to avoid legal and/or community sanctions when the expected value of the cost of fines

---

[1] Both pure altruism and egoism have been presented by some philosophers as impossible behaviors and inconsistent, contradictory concepts (Moore, 1997; Gauthier, 1998; and Grant, 2001). The conceptual orientation behind the idea of egoism and altruism in this chapter coincides with that offered on the one hand by Stark (1999), given that we see the altruist as an agent who tends to transfer goods in order to increase the welfare of others, and on the other hand by Gauthier (1998), who starts with the assumption of the non-existence of a purely egoistic being, and introduces the idea of an incomplete egoist, who recognizes the existence of common benefits upon submitting to mutual restrictions. This incomplete egoist is set forth in this chapter as the business person whose CSR activity is due to either some type of coercion or strategic considerations, which derive from improving the competitive position of the firm through the practice of CSR.

(f), closure due to temporary work stoppage (c), or reduction in competitiveness given CSR expenditures of other industry participants (d) is greater than the minimum necessary investment in CSR, I^{CSR}. Defining p as the probability of being fined, s as the probability of being stopped by some community group, and r as the possibility of losing competitive advantage given the CSR strategy of other participants, we have:

$$E = 1 \text{ if } I^{CSR} \le p(f) + s(c) + r(d) \tag{1}$$

$$E = 0 \text{ in any other case.}$$

It is not in the interest of either the stockholder or the agent for the firm to be fined or closed. The stockholder in this case expects that the agent will make the least expenditure possible in order to fulfill legal and social norms as well as industry expectations. However, since a community stakeholder may seek greater CSR expenditures, the agency cost would be greater in the agent–community relationship, given that the agent would resist fulfilling maximal stakeholder expectations. In the agent–stockholder relationship, agency costs would be lower, given that their objectives would be the same. However, if coercion creates costs only for the firm and not for the agent, their interests would diverge. Consequently, CSR expenditures in poorly regulated countries and countries where civil society is poorly organized will tend to be lower and the moral hazard between the stockholder and the agent would tend to increase. Such a situation might occur where firm policy requires it to comply with local regulations, regardless of the likelihood of enforcement. However, if coercion implies a sanction for the agent, this sanction reinforces the similarity in the objectives of the agent and stockholder and therefore lowers agency costs in their relationship.

In the case of coercion, the probability of a public or social intervention in the case of regulatory non-compliance will determine the agent's level of effort. If the probability is very high, T could be non-existent, given that obtaining payments t for the agent and not incurring fines or stoppage would also be determined by CSR expenditures, which become an additional input in the production functions for q. If the probability is very low, then we revert to the results obtained in equation (A-15) as the principal will need to motivate any CSR activity not likely to incur sanctions, even if only to comply with legal and/or social norms.

When the stockholder's dominant motivation is strategic and thus CSR is undertaken as a means to generate value for the firm as well as the community, although the actions of the agent affect both the stockholder and the community, it is to the former that he is accountable, rather than the latter. Thus again, as in the altruistic case, one can speak of a greater agency cost between the agent and the stockholder than between the agent and the community stakeholder. One could say that equations (A-1) to (A-15) represent this case.

Although we have tried to imagine two principals, in reality the interests of the community would be determined to the extent that the stockholder understands those interests and pursues them. If the stockholder considers that community objectives are achieved, then the stockholder could make some payment (transfer) to the agent. However, it is not the community that directly determines the transfers to the agent. Thus, the condition in equation (A-15) would not vary in the strategic case.

CONCLUSION

Friedman's original critique of corporate social responsibility remains one of the most important in the CSR literature. Perhaps it would be more accurate to say that Friedman provides an outline of a critique as he does not fully develop his arguments. In any case, in this chapter, we have read Friedman as defining the requirements for a CSR which is ethical because it does not renounce obligations to shareholding principals, as well as specifying the challenges of CSR given the nature of the principal-agent relationship. By following the logic inherent in Friedman's argument, we can highlight some of the very practical problems that need to be resolved in order to move the CSR agenda forward.

Our results indicate that there appears to be a dependence between the agency costs that are present in social responsibility expenditures in specific projects and the type of motivation upon which the expenditure is based. The identity of the principal and the difficulty of measuring the impacts of CSR expenditures on the firm as well as on society also influence these agency costs.

The task of designing adequate incentives for CSR activity thus requires defining the motivation behind such investment and identifying the principal. The available evidence about CSR and its impact on firm financial performance is ambiguous and the literature has largely ignored the motivations behind CSR. As CSR is less subject to efficient incentives, the work of designing contracts also implies the task of arriving at methodologies that permit a degree of measurement of objectives similar to that which exists in other branches of corporate activity. The lack of these methods clearly leaves CSR expenditure at a disadvantage with respect to traditional business projects because the determination of incentives is a more difficult task.

Curiously, agency costs appear to be lowest in the case where governments oblig-ate CSR activity by the firm. This result might be used to support CSR legislation as it is being proposed in different countries, such as in Spain. To the extent that legislation reflects societal needs, the gap between what the stockholder believes are needs and what these needs really are can be reduced. If the legislation is

accompanied by appropriate sanctions and/or incentives, it provides tools for measuring performance. With such tools, there is a lower probability of moral hazard
and a greater probability of writing contracts *ex ante* with appropriate incentives.

The chapter identifies many of the challenges that CSR faces if it is to move
beyond symbol to substance. First, agents may not act in the interests of either the
stakeholders or the stockholders. Second, stakeholder-principals may not represent
social interests accurately. Third, countries with weak regulatory environments may
not provide an appropriate institutional framework for CSR expenditure. Fourth,
agents will require higher incentives for CSR activities than for traditional business
activities in order to exert effort in favour of CSR. Finally, more accurate measurement methodologies for CSR need to be developed. By working within the logic
of principal-agent theory, the weaknesses of CSR management can be identified in
order to provide a clear path ahead for future research and development.

APPENDIX—A MODEL OF COMPENSATION
FOR THE AGENT

Following Laffont and Martimort (2002), let's consider two levels of effort $e_0 = 0$ and $e_1 = 1$,
that the agent undertakes in order to obtain certain transfers (t) for activities and tasks
related to the firm's traditional business mission. Such efforts cause a reduction in the agent's
utility equal to $\eta(e)$, which takes values corresponding to 0 and 1, depending on the two
levels of effort. We will also consider the levels of effort, $E_0 = 0$ and $E_1 = 1$, that the agents
undertake in order to receive certain transfers (T) for a set of CSR activities, which cause it
to lose utility $\eta(E)$. Thus the net utility of the agent who undertakes both business-related
and CSR activities would be given by:

$$U = u(t) + u(T) - \eta(e) - \eta(E) \tag{A-1}$$

The agent's stochastic level of output q can take the values of q_0 or q_1 for traditional business
activities and Q_0 and Q_1 for CSR activities, where $q_0 < q_1$ and $Q_0 < Q_1$. The influence
of effort on output is characterized by the following probabilities for traditional business
activities:

$$\Pr(q = q_1 | e = 0) = \pi_0 \tag{A-2}$$

which represents the probability of obtaining a high output given no effort;

$$\Pr(q = q_1 | e = 1) = \pi_1 \tag{A-3}$$

which represents the probability of obtaining high output given high efforts;
and for CSR activities:

$$\Pr(Q = Q_1 | E = 0) = \Pi_0 \tag{A-4}$$

which similarly represents the probability of obtaining high CSR output given no effort; and

$$\Pr(Q = Q_1|E = 1) = \Pi_1 \tag{A-5}$$

which represents the probability of obtaining high CSR output given high effort;

where $\pi_0 < \pi_1$, since we assume that it is more likely to reach a production level q when effort is 1 than when it is 0. On the other hand, Π_0 may be different from or equal to Π_1 given that we do not know *a priori* whether the CSR activities lead to a certain level of output Q. Also, we can say that $\pi_0 = \Pi_0$, while $\pi_1 \neq \Pi_1$.

$\Pr(q \leq q^*|e)$, where q^*, the optimal level of output, is decreasing in e for any given level of output q^*, but the behavior of $\Pr(Q \leq Q^*|E)$ is uncertain in the case of E, where the verification of output is more difficult.

So, $\Pr(q \leq q_0|e = 1) = 1 - \pi_1 < 1 - \pi_0 = \Pr(q \leq q_0|e = 0)$; in other words, the probability of not reaching q_1 given high effort ($e = 1$) is less than the probability of not reaching q_0 given no effort ($e = 0$). Stated slightly differently, the probability of obtaining no output given a high effort is less than the probability of obtaining no output given no effort.

If the principal desires to offer a contract with incentives, she should base it on that behavior which is observable and verifiable at a given moment. Let's suppose that at the moment of designing the contract for traditional business activities, we can use measurements of the output of these activities, which are observable and verifiable. In the case of CSR activities, such measurements are less common and in some cases almost impossible to conceive.

Given this situation, the principal can offer incentives in the amount of $t(q)$ based on the output for business activities and $T(Q)$ for CSR activities. Business and CSR output can achieve levels of (q_0, q_1) and (Q_0, Q_1) respectively. If the agent produces q_0, he obtains a transfer t_0, and if he produces q_1, he obtains a transfer t_1. Similarly, with respect to CSR activities, for outputs Q_0 and Q_1 the agent would obtain transfers T_0 and T_1.

The expected utility of the principal when the agent's effort is e_1 and E_1, is:

$$V = (1 - \pi_1)[S(q_0) - t_0] + \pi_1[S(q_1) - t_1] + (1 - \Pi_1)[S(Q_0) - T_0] + \Pi_1[S(Q_1) - T_1] \tag{A-6}$$

where S represents the benefits received by the principal for each level of output or type of activity (q_0, q_1, Q_0, Q_1).

The incentive contract is feasible if it motivates a positive effort and assures the participation of the agent, who demands a certain level of compensation for his effort. Thus, the following expression indicates the incentive constraint to be satisfied in the contract.

$$(1 - \pi_1)u(t_0) + \pi_1 u(t_1) + (1 - \Pi_1)u(T_0) + \Pi_1 u(T_1) - \eta$$
$$\geq (1 - \pi_0)u(t_0) + \pi_0 u(t_1) + (1 - \Pi_0)u(T_0) + \Pi_0 u(T_1) \tag{A-7}$$

which means that the agent will undertake the effort only in the case that the expected utility of this effort is greater than the expected utility of not undertaking such effort. If the agent makes the effort with any non-negative incentive, the participation constraint:

$$(1 - \pi_1)u(t_0) + \pi_1 u(t_1) + (1 - \Pi_1)u(T_0) + \Pi_1 u(T_1) - \eta \geq 0 \tag{A-8}$$

and the size of the adequate incentives would be obtained by maximizing the expected utility of the principal subject to the constraint on the agent's effort. Using a Lagrange multiplier

λ, the linear program would be:

$$V = (1 - \pi_1)[S(q_0) - t_0] + \pi_1[S(q_1) - t_1] + (1 - \Pi_1)[S(Q_0) - T_0] + \Pi_1[S(Q_1) - T_1]$$
$$+ \lambda[(1 - \pi_1)u(t_0) + \pi_1 u(t_1) + (1 - \Pi_1)u(T_0) + \Pi_1 u(T_1) - \eta] \tag{A-9}$$

Upon deriving the first order conditions, we obtain:

$$\partial V/\partial t_0 = -(1 - \pi_1) + \lambda(1 - \pi_1)u'(t_0^*) = 0 \tag{A-10}$$

$$\partial V/\partial t_1 = -\pi_1 + \lambda\pi_1 u'(t_1^*) = 0 \tag{A-11}$$

$$\partial V/\partial T_0 = -(1 - \Pi_1) + \lambda(1 - \Pi_1)u'(T_0^*) = 0 \tag{A-12}$$

$$\partial V/\partial T_1 = -\Pi_1 + \lambda\Pi_1 u'(T_1^*) = 0 \tag{A-13}$$

From equations (A-10), (A-11), (A-12), and (A-13), we obtain:

$$\lambda = 1/u'(t_0^*)$$
$$\lambda = 1/u'(t_1^*)$$
$$\lambda = 1/u'(T_0^*)$$
$$\lambda = 1/u'(T_1^*)$$

so that we can conclude:

$$t_0^* = t_1^* = T_0^* = T_1^* \tag{A-14}$$

Thus, when the effort is verifiable, either based on variables stipulated at the moment of signing the contract or afterwards, through tools that can be adopted to measure the results of these variables when the stipulated events have taken place, the agent would receive with certainty the same transfer, independent of the level of output or type of activity. In addition, given the constraint in equation (A-8), the transfer will be only that which would be necessary to cover the disutility η.

If the standards of measurement in the case of CSR activities are subject to greater error than those employed in traditional business activities, it should be recognized a priori that we expect the same probability for either underestimating or overestimating the output. If the agent is risk-adverse, this would bias his preferences toward undertaking more traditional business activities rather than CSR activities, which would imply that even given the result expressed in (A-14), the consideration of possible measurement error, being greater in CSR activities than in traditional business activities, would make it necessary to add to the payment for traditional business activities, t, some proportion $k > 0$, where k is a disincentive related to the uncertainty associated with CSR measurement, leading us to the result that:

$$t_0^* = t_1^* = T_0^*(1 - k) = T_1^*(1 - k) \tag{A-15}$$

In this case, the principal can negotiate contracts in which the transfer would be determined in time 2 after the effort has been exerted in time 0 and the output is known at time 1. This transfer will depend on the expectation regarding the bargaining power that the principal may think she has at time 0 rather than at time 2. If her bargaining power is greater at time 0, she will prefer to write a contract before the effort is exerted (*ex ante*), and in the contrary case, she will prefer to write the contract after the effort is exerted (*ex post*).

REFERENCES

ARROW, K. J. 1985. 'The Economics of Agency', in J. W. Pratt and R. J. Zeckhauser (eds.), *Principals and Agents: The Structure of Business*. Boston: Harvard Business School Press, 37–51.

ATKINSON, L., and GALASKIEWICZ, J. 1988. 'Stock Ownership and Company Contributions to Charity'. *Administrative Science Quarterly*, 33: 82–100.

BARON, D. P. 2001. 'Private Politics, Corporate Social Responsibility, and Integrated Strategy'. *Journal of Economics and Management Strategy*, 10(1): 7–45.

BURKE, L., and LOGSDON, J. M. 1996. 'How Corporate Social Responsibility Pays off'. *Long Range Planning*, 29: 495–502.

DAVIS, I. 2005. 'The Biggest Contract'. *The Economist*, 26 May 2005.

FAMA, E. F. 1980. 'Agency Problems and the Theory of the Firm'. *Journal of Political Economy*, 88/2: 288–307.

FRIEDMAN, M. 1962. *Capitalism and Freedom*. Chicago: University of Chicago Press.

——1970. 'The Social Responsibility of Business is to Increase its Profits'. *New York Times Magazine*, 13, Sept. reprinted in C.S. McCoy (1985), *Management of Values: The Ethical Difference in Corporate Policy and Performance*. Boston: Pitman, 253–60.

GALASKIEWICZ, J. 1997. 'An Urban Grants Economy Revisited: Corporate Charitable Contributions in the Twin Cities, 1979–81, 1987–89', *Administrative Science Quarterly*, 42: 445–71.

GARRIGA, E., and MELÉ, D. 2004. 'Corporate Social Responsibility Theories: Mapping the Territory', *Journal of Business Ethics*, 53: 51–71.

GAUTHIER, D. 1998. *Egoismo, moralidad, y sociedad liberal*. Barcelona: Paidós.

GRANT, C. 2001. *Altruism and Christian Ethics*. Cambridge: Cambridge University Press.

GRIFFIN, J. J., and MAHON, J. F. 1997. 'The Corporate Social Performance and Corporate Financial Performance Debate: Twenty-Five Years of Incomparable Research'. *Business and Society*, 36(1): 5–31.

HUSTED, B. W., and ALLEN, D. B. 2006. 'Corporate Social Responsibility in the Multinational Enterprise: Strategic and Institutional Approaches'. *Journal of International Business Studies*, 37(6): 838–49.

——and SALAZAR, J. 2006. 'Taking Friedman Seriously: Maximizing Profits and Social Performance'. *Journal of Management Studies*, 43(1): 75–91.

JENSEN, M., and MECKLING, W. 1976. 'Theory of the Firm: Managerial Behavior, Agency Costs, and Capital Structure'. *Journal of Financial Economics*, 3: 305–60.

LAFFONT, J.-J., and MARTIMORT, D. 2002. *The Theory of Incentives*. Princeton: Princeton University Press.

McWILLIAMS, A., SIEGEL, D. S., and WRIGHT, P. M. 2006. Guest editors' introduction. *Journal of Management Studies*, 43(1): 1–18.

MARGOLIS, J., and WALSH, J. 2001. *People and Profits: The Search for a Link between a Company's Social and Financial Performance*. Rahway, NJ: Erlbaum Associates.

MOORE, G. E. 1997/1903. *Principia ethica*, trans. A. Diaz and A. Stellino. Mexico: UNAM; Ist pub. 1903.

NAVARRO, P. 1988. 'Why do Corporations Give to Charity'? *Journal of Business*, 61(1): 65–93.

ORLITZKY, M. O., SCHMIDT, F. L., and RYNES, S. L. 2003. 'Corporate Social and Financial Performance: A Meta-analysis'. *Organization Studies*, 24: 403–42.

Rasmussen, E. 1989. *Games and Information: An Introduction to Game Theory*. Cambridge, Mass.: Blackwell.

Sethi, S. P. 1978. 'An Analytical Framework for Making Cross-cultural Comparisons of Business Responses to Social Pressures: The Case of the United States and Japan', in L. Preston (ed.), *Research in Corporate Social Performance and Policy*, vol. 1. Greenwich, Conn.: JAI Press.

Stark, O. 1999. *Altruism and Beyond: An Economic Analysis of Transfers and Exchanges within Families and Groups*. Cambridge: Cambridge University Press.

Sundaram, A. K., and Inkpen, A. C. 2004. 'The Corporate Objective Revisited', *Organization Science*, 15(3): 350–63.

Wright, P., and Ferris, S. P. 1997. 'Agency Conflict and Corporate Strategy: The Effect of Divestment on Corporate Value'. *Strategic Management Journal*, 18: 77–83.

CHAPTER 7

....

RETHINKING CORPORATE SOCIAL RESPONSIBILITY AND THE ROLE OF THE FIRM—ON THE DENIAL OF POLITICS

....

GERARD HANLON

CORPORATE Social Responsibility (CSR) is an increasingly important area of study, comment, and strategy in the 'new economy' of the early twenty-first century. It is growing in the university, corporations are spending more time and resources

This chapter forms part of the work from the ESRC-funded project entitled 'Shaping Knowledge through Dialogue' (ESRC grant no. Res-334-25-0011). This is one project in a series of projects from the Evolution of Business Knowledge Program.

The author would like to express his gratitude to Stefano Harney at the School of Business and Management, Queen Mary for his comments on an earlier draft of this chapter.

on it, *The Economist* recently ran a special section on CSR (22 January 2005), and ever more scholarly manuscripts are written about it. All of this activity could lead one to assume that CSR is expanding both as an area of interest and perhaps as a challenge to 'traditional' business practice—that in some sense CSR is of the left. Eminent thinkers such as Milton Friedman (1962) have argued as much. However, we should be cautious about rushing to such an assessment because concepts often hold contradictory meanings to those that appear on the surface. For example, the seeming nineteenth century emancipation of the French peasant from the feudal ties of the land often impoverished people and locked them further into a wage society and another form of servitude (Marx, 1973: 240–4). In sympathy with such readings, this chapter will argue that CSR does not represent a challenge to business. On the contrary, the chapter suggests that CSR represents a further embedding of capitalist social relations and a deeper opening up of social life to the dictates of the marketplace. Furthermore, it protests that CSR is not a driving force of change but rather an outcome of changes brought on by other forces. Most particularly, it is the result of a shift from a fordist to a post-fordist regime of accumulation at the heart of which is both an expansion and a deepening of wage relations.

In the (Second) Beginning

It is arguable that in the Anglo-American world CSR has come into sharp focus since the mid-1990s. In contrast to the seemingly more abrasive capitalism of the Thatcherite and Reaganite 1980s, the 1990s were characterized by a series of events that appeared to herald the transition to a softer capitalism (Blowfield and Frynas, 2005). For example, Royal Dutch Shell entered into a long period of self-analysis after Greenpeace attacked it over its disposal plans for the oil rig, the 'Brent Spar' and after the negative publicity it received in the wake of Ken Saro-Wiwa's execution at the hands of the then Nigerian dictatorship. The execution of the Nobel Prize winner was prompted by his involvement in the Ogoni people's hostility to the oil industry. These reputational attacks led Shell to undergo a global review of its activities with the intention of (1), analysing society's expectations of it and (2), attempting to become the 'world's most admired company' via a process of transparency (Fombrun and Rindova, 2000: 82). This chapter will somewhat conveniently trace the (re) emergence of CSR as an issue beyond the academy from the 1990s whilst acknowledging the academic work on CSR carried out earlier (Carroll, 1979 or Owen, 2003 on the democratic push in CSR during the 1970s). CSR in the 1990s became an area of increasing strategic importance as global corporations, the World Bank, the IMF, governments, and the globalization project more generally were subject to attack from an increasingly large and diverse set of protestors involved in anti-corporate and anti-globalization protests (see Lloyd, 2001; Crossley, 2003; Townsend *et al.*, 2004; North and Huber, 2004; Holzer and Sørensen, 2003). How then should we understand this recent (re) emergence of CSR?

WAYS OF SEEING

CSR is normally understood from one of two conflicting views (see Blowfield and Frynas, 2005, who highlight four positions but emphasize the importance of these two)—the ethico-political case and the business case (for the sake of simplicity let us pretend the business case does not entail an 'ethical' perspective although many would argue the opposite—see Kurucz *et al.*, Chapter 4 this volume). The ethico-political way of seeing CSR is to view it from an ethical standpoint. Jones *et al.* (2005) examine the case for CSR and business ethics in some detail. They suggest that the bulk of current scholarship on these things comes from three perspectives—consequentialism (and utilitarianism in particular), deontology, and virtue ethics. They argue that each has its own problems and highlight the further limitation that these works tend to foreclose a politics and a wider societal view. They also stress that as it stands today this work ignores much of the thinking of modern European philosophers such as Derrida or Levinas. Indeed, they argue that what should be celebrated here is not a solution but rather ongoing problems. In particular, they highlight the problems of accommodating difference and 'the other'—a problem which can never be definitively resolved. They suggest that oftentimes what happens in the ethics literature is an analysis of case studies to prove the ethical/unethical basis of action from a particular viewpoint. Assessing the vast literature outlining the different ethical positions corporations do and should take is not the remit of this chapter nor indeed the expertise of the author. Rather, what is suggested is that although ethics is one way of examining CSR, on its own it is insufficient because it usually closes down the social and political nature of organizations which are embedded in practice (Althusser, 2005: 219–47)—i.e. practice shapes the ethical not vice versa (for a further elaboration of this point regarding CSR see Tinker and Gray, 2003). By not linking the ethical to practice and the material in this way, business ethics decouples the ethical from issues of power, interest, etc. (see Owen, 2005 for an example). In light of this foreclosure, I wish to argue for examining CSR from a production regime perspective.

The business case generally suggests that CSR is good provided it does not damage profitability and that the corporation's primary obligation remains its shareholders (see Chapter 4 for a fuller elaboration). Thus, at a minimum, the corporation must adhere to the law whilst beyond that socially responsible behaviour is to be wished for provided it does not harm profitability. Friedman (1962) is the most obvious example; however, he is not alone. One could also suggest that stakeholder models of the corporation which stress that increased profits will result from CSR are also of this view (see Donaldson and Preston, 1995). Although real differences exist between many of these groups, ultimately an appeal to the bottom line unites them. Protagonists argue that CSR is or is not good for profitability and it is this profitability that will ultimately decide the issue. To summarize Matten and Crane (2005), these corporate citizens engage for self-interested reasons and hence their ethical contribution is perhaps somewhat tarnished.[1]

There are difficulties with the business case approach. The most obvious issue is that it treats CSR as a commodity and a factor of production and hence like all commodities it is developed for its exchange not its use value. Exchange value means that the object is not generated for the qualities it has in and of itself, rather it is manufactured only if its exchange value is higher than the cost of its production. But this is true for all commodities—in such a world CSR could be pornography or some other product produced as the market dictates (Marx, 1976: 125–77). For example, when a phone company introduces a new mobile phone service for blind people it subjects the new service to a full market evaluation process and decides that the introduction of this service is or is not financially viable. Hence this phone service is intended to be a profit maker. Is this responsibility via the business case or simply business as usual?

In this instance business is delivering what we can reasonably claim to be a 'positive'. However, the key here is not the positive but the market. The market does not discriminate where profit is concerned; hence the phone is produced but the flip side of this lack of discrimination is that unless a profit is generated no product services for the blind would be endorsed in the long term. Again what is key here is not the product but its exchange value, not its intrinsic benefits and characteristics but how much it can be sold for. Such an analysis takes us close to the perils of the commodity fetishism described in Marx wherein human responsibilities to one another are mediated through commodities and profit (Marx, 1976: 125–77). Services for the blind and, say, pornography down the phone, undergo the same financial analysis—the product itself is irrelevant. In reality, the business case denies the social relations actually involved in such a process because these relations are determined by the profitability filter of those with the power to control resources and to consume. The problems of social relations are denied via the business case and the politics of the business case are put aside through this fetishism. This elision means business case-driven CSR can never get to the heart of social relations (Christian Aid, 2004; Jones, 2003; Roberts, 2003; Jones et al., 2005).

[1] Equating self-interest with the unethical downplays the perspective of Adam Smith for example, who argued that self-interested acts could be ethical and that by not accepting this possibility social cohesion was oftentimes hampered (Muller, 1993).

This is not to say, however, that CSR is a sham or that business is not interested in CSR—it is. It is interested for two reasons. First, as Nichols (1969) highlighted so admirably, tales of profitability are often genuinely and deeply entrenched in business people's accounts of social responsibility. Ideologically, managers see the drive to profit as the socially responsible thing to do. Capitalism's search for profit is hailed as the deliverer of social progress. Individual managers may be mendacious about particular acts but it seems plausible that collectively managers and owners believe that from profit good things flow—firms stay open, workers are paid, government derives taxes for welfare provision, shareholders are rewarded, etc. Profit is the orthodoxy that cannot be questioned (see e.g. Carroll, 1998 but elements of this are also found in the work of more critical thinkers such as David Owen, 2003). Because of these entrenched views, CSR is always neutralized and pulled back from imaginary possibilities to the actually possible. If CSR ever had any potential radicalism within this managerial context it is always stillborn (see Banerjee 2003 for the impact of this view of society on the developing world).

Second, CSR is important to businesses because it is one of the keys to opening up the future. Cogman and Oppenheim (2002) and Davis (2005) have both suggested that commoditization and CSR are not enemies but bedfellows. Writing for the *McKinsey Quarterly* they believe that the big future markets are in areas where the two meet and intertwine. Companies will increasingly need to develop and invest in their CSR as they would in any other area of strategic importance—'this spending may well be a source of growth, since many of today's most exciting opportunities lie in controversial areas such as gene therapy, the private provision of pensions, and products and services targeted at low income consumers in poor countries. These opportunities are large and mostly untapped, and many companies want to open them up' (Cogman and Oppenheim, 2002: 1). Those firms in the best position to open these opportunities up will be the ones perceived as socially responsible, thereby making CSR important (Blowfield and Frynas, 2005). This then begs the question why CSR is a key to the future but not the recent past? What follows attempts to map the answer to this question via a historical materialist analysis.

REGIMES OF ACCUMULATION—FROM FORDISM TO POST-FORDISM

The contention of this chapter is that CSR emerges strongly in the 1990s because of the shift from a fordist to a post-fordist regime of accumulation. A regime of accumulation centers around three interrelated features: (1) the allocation of net production, by which is meant the distribution between accumulation and consumption, (2) the type of production process based upon this allocation, for example an allocation based on mass consumption requires mass production techniques, and (3) the nature of the social reproduction of labour via consumption, working conditions, career paths, occupational structures, and so on (Aglietta, 2000; Lipietz, 1987: 16–41). When synchronized these three features lend a regime a sustained period of stability before the internal contradictions emerge to undermine it.

At the center of these contradictions is capital's reactivity not its proactivity. For example, the demand from skilled workers to manage the production process during the late nineteenth and early twentieth centuries (the era of liberal capitalism) encouraged capital to react via new technology, new production techniques, deskilling, etc. and hence it created a massified semiskilled labor force. This both generated huge productivity gains which led to an over-supply of goods and also created the labor movement as an autonomous force. This labor movement simultaneously became the key to the future via demand and a subversive threat which needed to be controlled (Hardt and Negri, 1994: 26.7) so that annulling of this threat placed an emphasis on productivity increases from labor, state intervention and rising living standards for the working class, which stimulated demand in return for granting management the 'right' to manage. To simplify, these struggles led to the New Deal, similar compromises in Europe, and to the long boom that ended in the mid-1970s. Central to all of this was the state as economic planner *par excellence*. However, although fordism led to increased welfare and living standards for the working class, it should not simply be viewed as a victory for the left. On the contrary, it further embedded the working class into wage society and led to a large rise in the profitability of capital; it represented a radical shift in the allocation of net production away from labor as the rise in capital investment outstripped wages; it also re-organized the production process and the social reproduction of labor (Aglietta, 2000: 151–208, Lipietz, 1987; Hardt and Negri, 1994) so that for example, 1960s Britain looks radically different to Britain of the 1930s.

How, if at all, do these changes impact on CSR? Debates about CSR are largely noticeable by their absence during fordism's heyday. CSR-related debates about the organization and role of the corporation are prevalent during the time of crisis in the 1920s and 1930s. For example, Keynes (1926) and Berle and Means (1932) pose serious questions about the responsibility of managers and businesses, Roosevelt specifically questions the behaviour of business,[2] European states enter a period of crisis and social strife in the 1920s and 1930s culminating in the Second World War, etc. All of these things suggest a crisis of capitalism and hence raise questions about the role of business and, importantly, the state (Hardt and Negri, 1994). The fordist solution is to incorporate a (hopefully) de-radicalized labor movement into

[2] In 1936 he commented 'We had to struggle with the old enemies of peace—business and financial monopoly, speculations, reckless banking, class antagonism, sectionalism, war profiteering'.

governance alongside corporations and the state. Part of the payoff is that the state and corporations guarantee increasing living standards and the social reproduction of labor in return for productivity increases and support for capitalism. In such a world CSR beyond this tripartite structure is not needed—there is only room for a small 'civil society' because the state is increasingly the key organizing institution (Hardt and Negri, 1994).

However, because of the necessary antagonism between labor and capital inherent within capitalism, this regime of accumulation eventually succumbed to its own contradictions. When this happens CSR re-enters the fray. The breakdown of fordism emerges in the 1960s and becomes a crisis in the 1970s—at the time that Owen (2003) links the emergence of CSR in accounting with demands for greater accountability and democracy. The undermining of fordism emerges for a variety of reasons. First, international competition begins to weaken the dominance of the USA, markets for the consumer durables and white goods associated with fordism's mass production begin to saturate, labor becomes expensive, and the subsequent rise in capital goods resulting from this is also increasingly expensive. Furthermore, significant elements of wage society are challenged as non-work via education, retirement, opting out, etc. becomes more prevalent and the welfare state makes the necessity of work recede somewhat (see Butler, 1998; Tronti, 1972; Lipietz, 1987; Aglietta, 2000 for a perspective from the left and Bacon and Eltis, 1976 from the right) and global capitalism is challenged in the developing world.

FORDISM: BREEDING CULTURAL CHALLENGES TO HEGEMONY?

Fordism's success allowed people to demand new ways of being and new subjectivities and freedoms within which the centrality of work was increasingly challenged (Butler, 1998). Thus the rise of the feminist movement (with, for example, demands for payment for housework), the civil rights movement in the USA (with, for example, demands for an end to discrimination in the labor market), the gay movement, the rise of challenges in the 1950s and 1960s to colonialism and the exploitation of the developing world's resources by Western capitalism and the desire to break from dependency and neo-colonialism whilst refusing Western take-off models of development (Fanon, 1963; Young, 2001: 200–5), the Vietnam War, etc. all challenged the way in which people saw themselves, the societies they lived in, and how they themselves should live. In the West, one of the key challenges concerned the role of work, the role of the state, and the right of the citizen to a guaranteed level of consumption, that is, the questioning of property rights and the market. For example, from a conservative position, Bell (1974, 1976) argued that society was shifting in a technocratic direction wherein expertise rather than profit would dominate and that individuals were increasingly losing their work ethic and demanding a guaranteed optimizing lifestyle. In the developing world, many leaders began to openly challenge the international status quo, the role of Western capital and Western governments. These difficulties have given rise to a new crisis of profitability as the stability between labor, capital, and the state begins to unravel nationally and the global order is more unstable internationally (Young, 2001). For example, between 1965 and 1973 wages in the USA grew whilst profits fell (Harrison and Bluestone, 1988) and in the European Union (EU) profitability fell by 40 % between 1967 and 1975 (Commission of the European Communities, 1989, table 42). All of this led to O'Connor's (1973) fiscal crisis as governments continued to spend on welfare in response to the demands of their populations and labor continued to demand wage increases and to resist linking them to productivity rises. These processes undermine profitability.

In response to this crisis capital made a number of moves. First, it shifted overseas in search of new markets and new supplies of labor in order to weaken the power of labor in its heartlands. Second, it undermined the social consensus of fordism via an attack on the bureaucratic rights built up by labor in the previous 40 years (for an analysis of these rights see Edwards, 1979). Third, capital began to experiment with the re-organization of the production process (Elam, 1994). Fourth, and perhaps most importantly, the state, especially in the Anglo-American world, has shifted to the right, begun to reform welfare (Jordan, 1998) and is a key player in dismantling fordism's tripartite arrangements (Gamble, 1994). Finally, at the international level, Western governments and organizations have become deeply involved in defending the economic and political status quo in Latin America, Africa, Asia, and the Middle East using economic, political, and military means (Young, 2001). A combination of these features leads to a new regime because combined they alter net production or the allocation between accumulation and consumption; they change the production process from a mass production system to a globalized system of flexible specialization, and lastly, they significantly alter the ways in which labor is socially reproduced in terms of working and consumption patterns. None of this was inevitable (Lipietz, 1987: 19) nor is it fully worked out today (Aglietta, 2000: 388–445).

REGIMES OF ACCUMULATION: FROM THE STATE-LED TRIPARTITE TO CSR

As suggested, this transition reintroduces the need for CSR because this new economy requires new forms of regulation. If the old consensus of labor, capital, and the state could no longer regulate a profitable regime of accumulation, new techniques needed to be found. But this new regulatory form would also proceed on a new scale. One of the impacts of the shift to post-fordism has been the huge global increase in wage society as capitalism grows through the extensive commoditization of swathes of social life in China, India, etc. and second, this new regime is reaching newly intensive levels of commoditization in the historic powerhouses of capitalism—namely the EU, USA, and Japan. These two factors mean that post-fordism represents a growth of capitalism, not an undermining of it, despite the supposed challenges of CSR.

A number of traits shape this new regime. The most important again reflect an alteration in the allocation of net production as accumulation levels and the nature of consumption shift, a change in the nature of the production process as it is newly globalized and made more flexible and finally, the changed way in which labour is reproduced, i.e. the lifestyles of people have altered. Certain characteristics of this emerging regime are perhaps obvious today—globalization, the increased dominance of finance, the rise of the institutional investor, the decline of collective bargaining, the increasing growth of the non-standard working 'career', the retrenchment and commoditization of large parts of the welfare state, increased polarization of income inequality, etc. (Aglietta, 2000: 412–45). Many of these changes have empowered corporations, enabled a return to profitability, and placed the burden of social reproduction onto the individual via calls for individuals to be responsible for their own health, education, old age, employability, etc. (Sennett, 1998: 32–64; Beck, 2000; Stiglitz, 2002).

In the West, the outlook of this new economy is perhaps best seen in global cities, such as New York, London, Tokyo, Paris, etc. Sassen (1991, 1994) has demonstrated how these cities are being radically transformed by globalization. A number of features pertain—the decline of traditional manufacturing, the rise of services, and the re-emergence of sweatshop labor (on sweatshop labor, see Ross, 1997). A combination of these three features has led Sassen to suggest that globalization leads to a peripheralization of the core as immigrants enter these cities to take up work in illegal sweatshops and in the low skilled service areas of growth entailed in gentrification.[3] Gentrification is umbilically linked to these processes because it is fuelled by the increased need for high skilled labor necessary for controlling the new economy and hence capable of consuming large supplies of personal services, etc. The new service employment is highly polarized between those with low skills engaged in cleaning, serving, etc. and high skilled work such as management consultancy, legal work, financial services, etc. who help organize the global system (Sklair, 2001). This polarization is reflected in emerging consumption patterns; witness—housing booms, increased commuting times for the poor, a newly emerging super-rich, the

---

[3] Although coming from a different theoretical perspective to Sassen, Ulrich Beck (2000) echoes these sentiments with his view that we may see the increasing 'Brazilianization' of the West.

decline of living standards for many,[4] the growth of eating out, the growth of travel, the intensification of educational apartheid between the classes, the massive rise in the employment of domestic labor based on gender and racial lines, the slowdown or reversal of social mobility rates, etc. (see Sassen, 1994; Beck, 2000; Ehrenreich, 2001; Bott, 2005). All of this reflects a regime change.

In what is called the South the outlook of this new economy is also emerging. It is an economy of increasing disparity and tension as non-state regulatory institutions such as the International Monetary Fund (IMF) and the World Bank and certain state bodies such as the US Treasury enforce the neo-liberal 'Washington Consensus'. This consensus emerged in the 1980s and stressed liberalization, privatization, and fiscal austerity to a point where a non-radical ex-Chief Economist of the World Bank and Nobel Prize winner suggests it 'is unnecessarily corroding the very fabric of society' (Stiglitz, 2002: 76). Here we have a new regime wherein the market takes precedence over the state and trickle-down economics will supposedly bring improvement for all. However, this world is one dominated by multinationals such as Exxon, Shell, Nike, Cargill, Nestlé, etc. and finance capital against which much of the South has little leverage (Stiglitz, 2002). Thus the assertion by Western corporations for property rights in bio-technology, tribal land rights, mineral use, and so on are increasingly to the fore in what has been called the 'new enclosures' (Shiva, 2000; O'Neill, 1998). Furthermore, policies forced on developing nation states often encouraged them to open up their natural resources, manufacturing, and banking sectors to Western companies whilst leaving agricultural products in the West protected (Stiglitz, 2002: 53–88). Capital has also moved manufacturing overseas, raising questions of job losses and corporate responsibility at home (e.g. Pat Buchanan's various campaigns to win the Republican nomination and Presidency in the USA) and raising issues of sweatshops and the searching out of cheap, vulnerable labor overseas (Klein, 2000), which again raised issues of corporate responsibility. Within all of this, corporate profitability and human inequality grew (Stiglitz, 2002: 18).

Combined, these developments in the South and in the North represent a major shift in social organization. Yet social systems need legitimacy to reproduce themselves and provide stability and this is found in the idea that they promote social progress (Aglietta, 2000: 403). In light of this, how is progress defined in this emerging regime? One way is through claims that corporations are socially responsible, trustworthy, and indeed better than the state at delivering progress and the social good. In the new regime the state is portrayed as inefficient, partisan, based on producer interests, etc., whereas the market and corporations are portrayed as efficient, neutral, meritocratic, and consumer led. Indeed, such a view is the credo of the New Right, which came to dominate Anglo-American societies

---

[4] In the USA, per capita GNP rose by 75% between 1974 and 2004 while in constant dollars the wages per hour of the average male rose from $15.24 to $15.26 (Supiot, 2006).

from the late 1970s onwards (Gamble, 1994; Gray, 1986; Hayek, 1944; Stiglitz, 2002). This is a dramatic role reversal in comparison with fordism where the state (not the market or the corporation) was 'no longer merely a source of economic support and incentive, of stabilization and innovation. It has become the prime mover of economic activity' (Hardt and Negri, 1994: 42.3).[5]

To be sure, today civil society needs to be involved in governing this new regime, but because it was so unimportant to fordism, this civil society is being created presently; it is not extant. Hence civil society too is subject to these forces and is a result of rather than a creator of this emerging form—civil society is the end point not the beginning of this process. Indeed, it is part of the problem because it is subject to shaping by multinational corporations, often highly sympathetic Western states, and international civil society bodies such as the World Trade Organization (WTO) who are a part of the shift to the right (Martin, 1993; Sklair, 2001; Stiglitz, 2002).[6] CSR is seen as 'a bridge connecting arenas of business and development, and increasingly [policy-makers] discuss CSR programmes in terms of their contribution to development' (Blowfield and Frynas, 2005: 499). Implicitly Cogman and Oppenheim (2002), for example, realize that through CSR and engagement with civil society, corporations can claim legitimacy for the newly emerging regime and hence open up markets that were previously denied to them, such as the welfare state, the developing world, new bio-technologies, etc. In short, through CSR the world can be further commoditized, wage society expanded, and legitimacy for corporate dominance solidified. CSR engagement with seeming opposites like Oxfam or Greenpeace is actually a victory in this process not a defeat. It further lends credibility to the marketization of social life by acknowledging corporations as legitimate actors in new technologies, welfare state reform, environmental issues, globalization of governance, etc.

CREATING CIVIL SOCIETY: DIALOGUE, PLURALISM, AND LEGITIMACY

At the tactical heart of the corporate embracing of CSR in the pursuit of legitimacy is a sense of dialogue (Davis, 2005; Bennett, 2004; Roberts, 2003). Thus the assumption is that compromise and pluralism rather than conflict are the building blocks of legitimacy and the new civil society (see also Kuhn and Deetz, Chapter 8).

---

[5] This is not to say that the state has withered away with post-fordism. Far from it, one could argue that the state is more powerful and disciplining than before (Hardt and Negri, 2000).

[6] Indeed, today international civil society and non-state-led institutions such as the IMF are deeply involved in the micro-regulating of states and the setting of their policy priorities (Stiglitz, 2002).

This is different to fordism which emerged from a history of workplace and social conflict based on opposing visions of possible social orders (Hardt and Negri, 1994; Polanyi, 1957; Hayek, 1944). Hence today the leading firms on the FTSE or the Dow Jones write CSR reports, tobacco companies attempt to engage with public health officials and campaigners, all organizations claim to be environmentally friendly, and so on. Crucial to dialogue is the concept of compromise, a willingness to see the other point of view. In this world, dialogue is everything. Depending on the organization, it can be simply putting your CSR Report on the web, posting it to a set of 'stakeholders', engaging in roundtable discussions with NGOs, it can be about exchanging knowledge and experience with other corporations, etc.

However, there are limitations to dialogue. Essentially, dialogue is agreeing there are inter-subjective understandings about what responsibility is (on the creation of inter-subjective meaning see Apel, 1977). In short, a pluralist viewpoint is seen as a positive. Yet Žižek (1997: 27–9) suggests one of the difficulties with pluralism is that the other viewpoint or the 'other' that we acknowledge is a tamed other, a folklorist other. Hence we appear to be open but when the other is really herself we reject it as being too different, as fundamentalist, extreme, traditional, behind the times, etc. For example when the German SDP Chairman, Franz Müntefering, accused private equity firms of being socially irresponsible companies and the 'locusts' of the emerging economic structure, *The Economist* (7 May 2005) dismissed him as being something of a dinosaur,[7] as unreasonable. For post-fordism, the tenets of the Washington Consensus, the privileging of market, commoditization of more and more areas of social life are the basis of this reasonableness. The property rights of capital and profitability as social responsibility are key. CSR here ensures that subversive alternatives suffer the fate of utopias—they are dismissed as impossible however attractive we find them (see Osborne, 2006). Furthermore, this process is based on a form of knowledge that is inherently 'limited'. Nietzsche (1994) argues that knowledge or thought loses its critiquing edge when it is subject to reason. It becomes a pale imitation of critique. Thought then begins to dissuade and set limits to possibility because things are beyond a boundary. In a setting where 'real' thinking was carried out it would, to quote Deleuze (1983: 101), 'then mean *discovering, inventing new possibilities of life*' (emphasis in the original). This type of thinking would give 'responsibility' its positive sense (Deleuze 1983: 21). But pluralism cuts off this thinking and hence it is better to think of CSR as the limiting of possibility.

Such a view of CSR is held by Žižek's (2006) 'liberal communists'—the owners and managers of large-scale capitalist enterprises and state officials. This elite believes capitalism, unbounded by the state and seemingly devoid of the ideological vestiges of the past, will deliver social progress. For liberal communists there is

---

[7]   It is also worth noting that although a leading member of government in the third largest economy on the planet, Müntefering felt the need to call on consumers not the state to intervene and halt the buying up of German assets by these firms.

no dichotomy in post-industrial capitalism between owner-worker, profit-social responsibility, etc. He comments (2006):

Liberal communists are top executives reviving the spirit of contest or, to put it the other way round, countercultural geeks who have taken over big corporations. Their dogma is a new, postmodernised version of Adam Smith's invisible hand: the market and social responsibility are not opposites, but can be reunited for mutual benefit. As Friedman (Thomas) puts it, nobody has to be vile in order to do business these days; collaboration with employees, dialogue with customers, respect for the environment, transparency of deals—these are the keys to success.

These capitalists believe they are at the forefront of at new capitalism—they are smart and

Being smart means being dynamic and nomadic, and against centralised bureaucracy; believing in dialogue and co-operation as against central authority; in flexibility as against routine; culture and knowledge as against industrial production; in spontaneous interaction and autopoiesis as against fixed hierarchy.

Their way of being will deliver progress and they engage in dialogue and CSR to be inclusive and legitimate. They use CSR to represent their 'interests as the common interest of all the members of society, that is, expressed in ideal form; it has to give its ideas the form of universality, and represent them as the only rational universally valid ones' (Marx and Engels, 1970: 65). In short, although they deny it or are unaware of it, their CSR and their new capitalism are inevitably ideological.

CONCLUSION—THE OLD CAPITALISM

The new economy is not so novel. Just as Nichols's (1969) managers were locked into a world where profitability was the base upon which all good things were built, so too are the liberal communists. They are also not new in another sense. As Žižek (2006) notes, they deny the contradictions of their position. Hence at the same time as they have embraced collaboration with employees, are against bureaucracy, believe in dialogue and cooperation, etc., they are also at the forefront of the push towards a new regime of accumulation. At the center of this push is the desire to weaken labor's attachment to the gains it made in the postwar boom, and a desire to globalize and intensify wage society. As such, they appear to share much in common with the likes of Henry Ford and Andrew Carnegie, who donated massive amounts to charity whilst also violently attacking organized labor. Thus we return to Marx and the limits within which capitalists find themselves. No matter how much they try, these capitalists are locked within the contradictions of capitalism and the search for profit is paramount over and above all else, thereby eradicating the possibility for a 'caring capitalism'.

There is also a very real material point to this embracing of CSR. The new regime needs legitimacy because it has systematically been criticized by labor unions, environmentalists, anti-globalization protestors, etc. In order to counteract these critiques businesses must be aware of social issues. Davis (2005) in the *McKinsey Quarterly* expresses it in the following manner: 'From a defensive point of view, companies that ignore public sentiment make themselves vulnerable to attack.' But Davis goes further, he sees this unease with capitalism not as a threat but a market opportunity. He comments 'Social pressures often indicate the existence of unmet social needs or consumer preferences. Businesses can gain advantage by spotting and supplying these before their competitors do.' We are thus back to the beginning—CSR is a commodity that can advantage corporations by allowing them to be perceived as legitimate and hence open up new markets. Furthermore, this view of threat as opportunity is redolent of fordism. Fordism was a response to labor's new-found power. This created a situation wherein 'Capitalism now faced a working class that had been socially levelled by the repression brought against it, that had become massified to the point where its autonomy had to be recognized, and that simultaneously had to be both recognized in its subversive potential and grasped as the decisive element and motive power behind any future model of development' (Hardt and Negri, 1994: 26.7). Today the subversion of the environmentalists, labor unions, anti-globalization protestors, etc. is also simultaneously a threat to be recognized and a market opportunity upon which to build post-fordism.[8] These dissenting subjectivities and the alternatives they raise provide capital its key to the future (Negri, 2005).

Thus for Davis (2005), the Milton Friedman argument is flawed because it allows corporations to be portrayed as illegitimate and thereby allow other actors take up the social activity that businesses could pull into a marketized space. He goes on to recommend that firms study state activity, consumer groups, the media, etc. to see and head off the next big problem areas for businesses. However, CSR is more than this. Although it seems Davis is unaware of it, CSR is not simply a rough guide to unmet social needs which the corporation can then provide for us. It is actually a glimpse at how our sociality—our humanness—is developing. This 'thing' is beyond the corporation, beyond its control, and yet without it the corporation has no function and no innovative potential—after all, how else does it know of need? In short, CSR will help to make money from the problems businesses have helped create, thereby improving shareholder value. And, as with the other *McKinsey Quarterly* writers, the big markets that will follow are based around

---

[8] Ford has just launched £1 bn in investment in R&D in the UK alone to develop green technologies (Milne, 2006)—something that is hard to imagine without the environmental movement.

the developing world, marketization of welfare services, and so on. CSR here is acting as a legitimating ideology for a 'new capitalism' and in this sense it shares a common heritage with the debates about the role of the organization that heralded the birth of 'the old capitalism'. But it is also a way into our material future and, for corporations, the innovative road map they need for production, yet it is always outside the corporation.

REFERENCES

AGLIETTA, M. 2000. *A Theory of Capitalists' Accumulation: The US Experience*. London: Verso.

ALTHUSSER, L. 2005. *For Marx*. London: Verso.

APEL, K. O. 1997. 'The A Priori of Communication and the Foundation of the Humanities', reprinted in F. R. Dallmayr and T. A. McCarthy (eds.), *Understanding and Social Inquiry*. London: University of Notre Dame Press.

BACON, R., and ELTIS, W. 1976. *Britian's Economic Problems—Too Few Producers*. London: Macmillan.

BANERJEE, S. B. 2003. 'Who Sustains Whose Development? Sustainable Development and the Revolution of Nature'. *Organization Studies*, 24(1): 143–80.

BECK, U. 2000. *The Brave New World of Work*. London: Polity Press.

BELL, D. 1974. *The Coming of Post-industrial Society*. London: Heinemann.

—— 1976. *The Cultural Contradictions of Capitalism*. London: Heinemann.

BENNETT, C. 2004. 'A Little Less Conversation, a Little More Action'. *Elements*, 21 Feb.

BERLE, A., and MEANS, G. C. 1932. *The Modern Corporation and Private Property*. New York: Macmillan.

BLOWFIELD, M., and FRYNAS, J. G. 2005. 'Setting New Agendas: Critical Perspectives on Corporate Social Responsibility in the Developing World'. *International Affairs*, 81(3): 499–513.

BOTT, E. 2005. 'Too Close for Comfort? "Race" and the Management of Proximity, Guilt and Other Anxieties in Paid Domestic Labour'. *Sociological Research Online* <http://www.socresonline.org.uk/10/3/bott.html>.

BUTLER, J. 1998. 'Merely Cultural'. *New Left Review*, 227: 33–44.

CARROLL, A. B. 1979. 'The Three Dimensional Conceptual Model of Corporate Performance'. *Academy of Management Review*, 4(4): 497–505.

—— 1998. 'The Four Faces of Corporate Citizenship'. *Business and Society Review*, 100–1: 1–7.

CHRISTIAN AID. 2004. *Behind the Mask*. London: Christian Aid.

COGMAN, D., and OPPENHEIM, J. M. 2002. 'Controversy Incorporated'. *The McKinsey Quarterly*, No 4.

Commission of the European Communities. 1989. *Employment in Europe*. Brussels: European Commission.

CROSSLEY, N. 2003. 'Even Newer Social Movement? Anti-corporate Protests, Capitalist Crises and the Remoralization of Society'. *Organization*, 10(2): 287–305.

DAVIS, I. 2005. 'What is the Business of Business?' *McKinsey Quarterly*, No. 3.

DELEUZE, G. 1983. *Nietzsche and Philosophy*. London: The Athlone Press.

DONALDSON, T., and PRESTON, L. E. 1995. 'The Stakeholder Theory of the Corporation: Concepts, Evidence and implications'. *Academy of Management Review*, 20(1): 65–91.

EDWARDS, R. 1979. *Contested Terrain: The Transformation of the Workplace in the Twentieth Century*. New York: Basic Books.

EHRENREICH, B. 2001. *Nickel and Dimed: On (Not) Getting By in America*. New York: Henry Holt & Company.

ELAM, M. 1994. 'Puzzling Out the Post-fordist debate; Technology, Markets and Institutions', in A. Amin (ed.) *Post-Fordism: A Reader*. Oxford: Blackwell.

FANON, F. 1963. *The Wretched of the Earth*. New York: Grove Press.

FOMBRUN, C. J., and RINDOVA, V. P. 2000. 'The Road to Transparency: Reputation Management at Royal Dutch Shell', in M. Schutz, Harch, M. J., and Larsen, M. H. (eds.), *The Expressive Organization*. Oxford: Oxford University Press.

FRIEDMAN, M. 1962. *Capitalism and Freedom*. Chicago: University of Chicago Press.

GAMBLE, A. 1994. *The Strong State and the Free Market*. Basingstoke: Macmillan.

GRAY, J. 1986. *Liberalism*. Milton Keynes: Open University Press.

HARDT, M., and NEGRI, A. 1994. *Labour of Dionysus: A Critique of the State Form*. Minneapolis: University of Minnesota Press.

——— 2000. *Empire*. Harvard: Harvard University Press.

HARRISON, B., and BLUESTONE, B. 1988. *The Great U-Turn: Corporate Restructuring and the Polarising of America*. New York: Basic Books.

HAYEK, F. 1944. *The Road to Serfdom*. London: Routledge.

HOLZER, B., and SØRENSEN, M. P. 2003. 'Rethinking Subpolitics beyond the "Iron Cage" of Modern Politics'. *Theory, Culture & Society*, 20(2): 79–102.

JAMES, C. L. R. 1963. *Beyond a Boundary*. Durham, NC: Duke University Press, reprinted 1993.

JONES, C. 2003. 'As if Business Ethics Were Possible, "Within Such Limits."' *Organization*, 10(2): 223–48.

—— PARKER, M., and TEN BOS, R. 2005. *For Business Ethics*, London: Routledge.

JORDAN, B. 1998. *The New Politics of Welfare*. London: Sage Publications Ltd.

KEYNES, J. M. 1926. *The End of Laissez-Faire*, available at <http://www.panarchy.org/Keynes/laissez-faire.1926.html>.

KLEIN, N. 2000. *No Logo*. London: Flamingo.

LIPIETZ, A. 1987. *Mirages and Miracles—The Crisis of Global Fordism*. London: Verso.

LLOYD, J. 2001. *The Protest Ethic*. London: Demos.

MARTIN, B. 1993. *In the Public Interest: Privatization and Public Sector Reform*. London: Zed Books.

MARX, K. 1973. *Surveys from Exile*. Harmondsworth: Penguin.

—— 1976. *Capital: A Critique of Political Economy Volume One*. Harmondsworth: Penguin.

—— and ENGELS, F. 1970. *The German Ideology*, edited by C. J. Arthur. London: Lawrence and Wishart.

MATTEN, D., and CRANE, A. 2005. 'Corporate Citizenship: Toward an Extended Theoretical Conceptualization'. *Academy of Management Review*, 30(1): 166–79.

MILNE, M. 2006. 'Ford puts £1 bn behind UK Research in Drive to Cut Carbon Emissions'. *Guardian*, available at <http://www.guardian.co.uk/environment/2006/jnl/18/travelsenvironmentalimpact.motoring>.

MULLER, J. Z. 1993. *Adam Smith: In His Time and Ours*, Princeton: Princeton University Press.

NEGRI, A. 2005. *The Politics of Subversion: A Manifesto for the Twenty-First Century.* London: Polity Press.

NICHOLS, T. 1969. *Ownership, Control & Ideology: An Enquiry into Certain Aspects of Modern Business Ideology.* London: George Allen & Unwin.

NIETZCHE, F. 1994. *On the Genealogy of Morality.* Cambridge: Cambridge University Press.

NORTH, P., and HUBER, U. 2004. 'Alternative Spaces of the "Argentinazo".' *Antipode,* 965–84.

O'CONNOR, J. 1973. *The Fiscal Crisis of the State.* Basingstoke: Macmillan.

O'NEILL, J. 1998. *The Market: Ethics, Knowledge and Politics.* London: Routledge.

OSBORNE, P. 2006. 'The Dreambird of Experience: Utopia, Possibility, Boredom'. *Radical Philosophy,* 137, May–June: 36–44.

OWEN, D. 2003. 'Recent Developments in European Social and Environmental Reporting and Auditing Practice—A Critical Evaluation and Tentative Prognosis'. *Research Paper Series, International Centre for Corporate Social Responsibility,* No. 03-2003.

—— 2005. 'CSR after Enron: A Role for the Academic Accounting Profession?' *European Accounting Review,* 14(2): 395–404.

POLANYI, K. 1957. *The Great Transformation.* Boston: Beacon Press.

ROBERTS, J. 2003. 'The Manufacture of Corporate Social Responsibility: Constructing Corporate Sensibility'. *Organization,* 10(2): 249–65.

ROSS, A. 1997. *No Sweat: Fashion, Free Trade and the Rights of garment Workers.* New York: Verso Press.

SASSEN, S. 1991. *The Global City—New York, London, Tokyo.* Princeton: Princeton University Press.

—— 1994. *Cities in a World Economy.* Thousand Oaks, Calif.: Pine Forge Press.

SENNETT, R. 1998. *The Corrosion of Character.* New York: W. W. Norton & Co.

SHIVA, V. 2000. 'Poverty and Globalisation', BBC Reith Lectures, available at <http://www.news.bbc.co.uk/hi/english/static/events/reith_2000/lecture5.stm>.

SKLAIR, L. 2001. *The Transnational Capitalist Class.* Oxford: Blackwell.

STIGLITZ, J. 2002. *Globalization and its Discontents.* New York: W. W. Norton & Co.

SUPIOT, A. 2006. 'The Condition of France'. *London Review of Books,* 28(11).

TINKER, T., and GRAY, R. 2003. 'Beyond a Critique of Pure Reason: From Policy to Politics to Praxis in Environmental and Social Research'. *Accounting, Auditing and Accountability Journal,* 16(5): 727–61.

TOWNSEND, J. G., PORTER, G., and MAWDSLEY, E. 2004. 'Creating Spaces of Resistance: Development NGOs and their Clients in Ghana, India and Mexico'. *Antipode,* 871–89.

TRONTI, M. 1972. 'Workers and Capital'. *Telos,* No. 14, winter: 25–62.

YOUNG, ROBERT. 2001. *Post-Colonialism—An Historical Introduction.* Oxford: Blackwell Publishers.

ŽIŽEK, S. 1997. *The Abyss of Freedom.* Ann Arbor: University of Michigan Press.

—— 2006. 'Nobody Needs to be Vile'. *London Review of Books,* 28(7). London.

....

CRITICAL THEORY AND CORPORATE SOCIAL RESPONSIBILITY

CAN/SHOULD WE GET BEYOND CYNICAL REASONING?

TIMOTHY KUHN

STANLEY DEETZ

....

THOSE who approach corporate social responsibility (CSR) from a perspective informed by critical theory tend to be deeply skeptical about the motivations and effects of corporate action. Critical theorists, in general, see corporations as political entities, sites characterized by power struggles in which some groups dominate others by creating meanings that draw upon resources from both the firm and the broader society that favor particular interests. Although CSR initiatives are often presented as efforts to respond to businesses' obligations to their communities,

We thank John McClellan and Cynthia Stohl for helpful comments on an earlier draft of this chapter.

as recompense for past transgressions, or to demonstrate that contemporary corporations are not the exploitative and profit-hungry monsters of 19th-century industrial capitalism, critical theorists distrust such portrayals. Operating from a 'discourse of suspicion' (Ricoeur, 1970), critical scholars contend that things are not what they seem: that so-called 'socially responsible' activities can obscure the deeper contradictions and systems of valuation that enable corporate socio-economic domination and, in turn, that such activities actually prevent the creation of a democratic society because they mollify citizens who might otherwise demand systemic change. Critical theorists seek to expose and interrogate CSR's unarticulated logics or examine the implications of the increased role of the corporate citizen in contemporary globalized capitalism, usually with attention to the underlying institutional/legal order (e.g. Banerjee, 2003, 2006; Freeman and Liedtka, 1991; Moon *et al.*, Matten, 2005; Parker, 2003; Scherer and Palazzo 2007). Consequently, scholars usually advance normative claims regarding the content and outcomes of CSR initiatives, questioning whether corporate activities actually promote community interests. Such claims are valuable and necessary in our understanding of CSR, but they tend to overlook corporate decisional *processes*. We suggest that an investigation of *whose* values become represented in corporate decision-making and *how* those representations influence reasoning can provide two valuable contributions to CSR thinking: It conceptually connects CSR activities and routine corporate action rather than rendering them separate domains, and provides an epistemological location for new models of collaboration in corporate decision-making. This is based on the view that organizational decisions are not simply economically rational, but are inevitably interested and value-laden; thus, our concern is to examine how the various conflicting values and social interests are (or are not) given an equal opportunity to influence decision-making. Significant public decisions are made in the corporate site, creating systematic distortions in social and economic developments, and posing important moral and political questions. The ultimate hope of critical theory is the inclusion of more diverse values within decision practices to benefit the wider public and specific disadvantaged groups, and we aim to provide an account of how that might occur.

We begin the chapter by arguing that values shape corporate decisions in three general ways: managerial choices, routines, and reasoning processes; governmental regulation, incentives, tax structures, and oversight; and consumption choices within market systems. We show that, alone and jointly, these 'sites' are fundamentally weak in their capacity to produce greater CSR in the sense of more diverse values and reasoning processes. Institutionalized power relations, various forms of systematically distorted communication, and ideology provide insight into different weaknesses and pitfalls. Work regarding each of these issues provides much space for critical theorists' skepticism. Here we will explore critical theory's engagement with these issues to provide an understanding of the cynicism and look for places of hope.

Ideology is core to much of the critical work of the last several years. We will treat ideology as the presence of values embedded in language, routines, practices, and positions that privilege dominant groups which are difficult to identify, discuss, and assess owing to various covering mechanisms. Ideological critique inspired by critical theory will then be discussed as a way to understand and talk about value preference and domination across organizational actions. We show how ideology critique evaluates CSR activities, demonstrating that this approach inevitably generates cynicism and carries a tone of value elitism, neither of which stimulates trust in a democratic populace's ability to create the society it wishes. Following this, we turn to exploring communication systems and practices that can provide for a more sustainable, and democratic, CSR.

How Values Enter Decisions

Most CSR discussions suggest that social concerns primarily impact business decisions through (1) managerial goodwill and stewardship (often supported through hopes of economic gain or diminished regulation); (2) governmental regulation and oversight; or (3) consumer choices. Most CSR promotion agendas rely on some combination of these. Critical theorists generally see weaknesses in each as an approach.

First, stewardship is often seen as a value-based add-on to value-free economic rationality. At least since Chandler's (1962) work we have known that 'managerial capitalism' is disconnected from idealized models of capitalism. Managerial self-interest and managerial dominance have a major impact on corporate decisions. Discussing CSR and value representation as a contrast to an economic-only view of organizations is misleading. Organizational decisions are inevitably value-laden, and beliefs and values fill the gaps between what can be known and the need to act. Managers' assumptions about people, fairness, and business practices endlessly direct their choices. Values are embedded within, for instance, standard accounting practices and knowledge production activities (Lyon, 2005; Power, 1997), but we tend to talk about them as values only when they arise from non-managerial groups, and then mostly only when there is some specific harm to the larger society. From a critical standpoint, as mentioned above, CSR and value representation concerns are not about *whether* values influence choices, but *whose* values get represented, and *how* the representation occurs in business decisions.

Some of the non-critical discussion of CSR has focused on the morality or ethical principles of corporate leaders, including their qualities as citizens of national, regional, and world communities, as well as how these become embedded in the culture and practices of organizations (e.g. MacIntyre, 1984; Treviño and

Weaver, 2003). This orientation treats CSR problems as arising from individual defects rather than governance and decisional structures and the solution as policies and standards rather than better decision-making processes. Furthermore, the growth of executive salaries, especially in the USA, has been startling to say the least. Upper-level executives, aided by friendly boards of directors and compensation consultants, have acted less like citizens and have deployed a somewhat rawer economic logic with less consideration of the consequences for the organization, other employees, and host societies (Khurana, 2002). Personal agendas and 'identity needs' have more greatly influenced product development and merger and acquisition strategies. Consequently, relying on managerial goodwill and character to motivate CSR is highly questionable.

Second, governmental intervention in corporate decisions, while important, can only be part of the solution. Even though regulation and incentives can influence system choices, most significant decisions remain within corporations themselves. Even if they wanted to, governments can not micro-manage companies. Further, the effects of their enticements are uneven at best (see special forum, *Academy of Management Review*, April 2005) and 'monitoring of compliance is in general underdeveloped' (OECD, 2004: p. 11) or weak (pp. 52–3). Governments lack both the popular legitimacy and capacity to make or require more proactive corporate choices. Governmental policy is often influenced by corporate leaders and lobbyists, and rarely do public agencies have enough information soon enough to actively participate in corporate processes and foster public accountability. Additionally, regulation inevitably leads to a costly double bureaucracy—a public one to establish guidelines and monitor compliance, and a private one that struggles to find loopholes and avoid regulation. The application of endless bureaucratic rules constantly runs counter to good situational judgments and common sense. With the rise of globalization, a larger set of potentially competing values are introduced, yet the ability of governmental powers to support the inclusion of these diverse values is weak (Scherer and Palazzo, chapter 18 this volume; Stohl *et al.*, 2007); and, further, international trade agreements often outlaw social value representation (OECD, 2001: 31). Thus, CSR dependent upon government intervention is unpredictable at best.

Finally, the prospect of consumer choices leading to more responsible businesses and wider value representation is not convincing either, though the concept is clear enough. Multiple value systems could be integrated into business choices through strategic consumption, the argument goes, since stakeholders unhappy with managerial decisions could eventually 'vote' with their feet or their money. Unfortunately, in this formulation, social and political relations are reduced to economic dealings, democracy is reduced to capitalism, citizens to consumers, and discussion to buying and selling. These transformations have costs. Translating values into the economic code constrains people's capacity to make decisions together and reduces human potential to choices already available in the system, as controlled by others. In short, the marketplace does not work well as a way of representing social values. The pervasiveness of marketing and advertising, the ability to exclude and/or externalize social and environmental costs, the complexity and length of decision chains, the difficulty of translating some values into economic terms, and inequitable distribution of money all weaken the ability of consumption to represent values. And those who endeavor to resist such forces often find counter-cultural movements co-opted into market capitalism (Heath and Potter, 2004). As many have shown, free-market capitalism was never intended to represent the public well; it was intended to describe how to make a return on financial invest-ment (Kelly, 2001). The idea that market choices accomplish representation, and money measures it, is a misleading fiction. Markets are value-laden rather than neu-tral representation processes, but the values are rarely explored (see Schmookler, 1992).

Corporate goodwill, government regulation, and consumer choice offer very weak mechanisms for value representation and virtually no support for commu-nication processes that create situations where multiple stakeholders—including shareholders—can successfully pursue their mutual interests (Deetz, 1995). Perhaps more importantly, they neither enable nor stimulate creative decisions whereby cor-porate economic objectives and social good are synergetic rather than competing interests. Acknowledging the shortcomings of these mechanisms, CSR advocates often urge corporations to take more explicit or programmatic action. These ini-tiatives, however, generate cynicism among critical scholars for what seem to be attempts to mask a corporatist ideology that allows 'business as usual' to continue unabated. In the next section, we discuss the theoretical basis for such a claim and review arguments against three common forms of CSR activity.

IDEOLOGY CRITIQUE AND CORPORATE SOCIAL RESPONSIBILITY

Critical theory plays a central role in thinking more deeply about values and aids our understanding of CSR practices and effects. 'Critical Theory' names a loosely coupled body of thought most commonly drawing on theorists following a Marxist tradition, such as Althusser, Marcuse, Horkheimer, Adorno, and Habermas (Alvesson and Willmott, 1992; Deetz, 2001). Much of this thought is associated with the Frankfurt School's Institute for Social Research and is concerned primarily with the relationships between power, discourse, and social forms such as large-scale corporations. In organization studies, critical scholars are a conceptually diverse lot (Fournier and Grey, 2000), yet contemporary research inspired by critical theory is united by an adoption of some version of a social constructionist stance in assuming that social structures produce systems that afford corporations heretofore unprecedented influence, but that these systems could have followed very different trajectories had different choices been made. Given this contingency, critical scholars cannot be content with describing or explaining social phenomena, but must additionally evaluate the social value of organizational practices and seek emancipation from obscured or illegitimate forms of internal and external coercion.

One key tenet of much critical theorizing is that the activity and knowledge of corporations and individual social actors are shaped by *ideologies*. Existing at both the societal and organization-specific levels, ideologies create chains of signification and shape actors' interpretive schemata. Ideologies are implicated in ongoing social practice as well as in the meanings created through those practices and provide the framework by which some meanings and interests are privileged over others (Hall, 1985; Mumby, 1988). To examine ideology, therefore, 'is to study the ways in which meaning (or signification) serves to sustain relations of domination' (Thompson, 1984: 4).

Examinations of social arrangements based on ideology thus investigate how dominant powers communicatively depict a particular vision of reality as legitimate and reproduce it across space and time. There are three main strategies of legitimation and reproduction, the investigation of which we call 'ideology critique' (see Deetz, 1992; Deetz and Mumby, 1990). A first route is when social formations are *reified*: when the historical struggles involved in creating social structures become forgotten and the formations are considered natural. Portraying a given organization, or organizational practice, as a concrete object that offers responses to (equally concrete) social needs ignores the communicative processes and power relations characterizing the formation of both organizations and social needs. As Boatright (1996) noted, the corporate goal of profit maximization was originally an assumption introduced by economic theories of the firm to explain firm behavior, but—as an unintended consequence—it has gradually become a normative goal of corporate governance so firmly entrenched that we rarely think otherwise. Indeed, 'the market' itself is a modern invention (Polanyi, 1944). In other words, reification makes it difficult to see firms and their 'imperatives' as anything but natural and normal elements of the social scene and, in turn, to see their social influence as legitimate.

A second path to legitimation and reproduction occurs when sectional interests are portrayed as universal, as when managerial concerns—which are often equated with both the 'bottom line' and the 'long term'—are advanced as those shared by all. Managers become seen as the conscientious stewards of the shareholders (Alchian and Demsetz, 1972), whose decisions are given preference over all others who might legitimately be considered 'owners'. In the process, managerial interests *define* those of the firm and, in turn, the interests of those whose efforts create and support it.

A third method is through the marshaling of *consent*. Instead of overtly forcing conformity to the sectional interests represented by a corporatist agenda, ideologies shape actors' knowledge, identities, and social relations in ways that make routine self-interested activity unwittingly benefit dominant groups (Burawoy, 1979; Deetz, 1998). It is not merely that social formations are perceived as natural (as in reification), but that actors contribute to dominant groups' desires even when their action is demonstrably antagonistic to their own interests. Thus, when consent is produced, individuals and communities see no need to examine corporate activity because no divergence in interests appears (Giddens, 1979; Lukács, 1971). Individuals implicated in corporate activity (both within and outside the firm) frequently act in ways contrary to their own interests due to their subjection to these pervasive corporatist ideologies.

In these ways, corporations, their practices, and their supporting institutions express *values*—they form, and are formed by, ideologies—but these values are rendered undiscussable when practices that depict the firm, its authority structure, its performance measures, and its orientation to stakeholder groups are believed to be natural and neutral. Ideology critique proposes that corporate ideologies are antithetical to the interests of the vast majority of the globe, yet because ideologies remain hidden, ideology critique argues that we must first *expose* ideologies if we are to create radical changes in both corporate practices and social structures more generally. Contemporary CSR interventions are attractive targets.

Ideology Critique and CSR Interventions

Critical theorists see contemporary corporate capitalism as tremendously adaptive in its ability to appropriate and re-configure challenges in ways that ultimately strengthen or insulate the system. Although CSR practices are sometimes shaped by civil society organizations and social critics whose sensibilities are informed by ideology critique, many critical scholars remain suspicious of corporate action and call for an inclusion of *stakeholders*. For instance, Bowie (1991) argued that decision-makers in corporations have a moral obligation to obtain the input of all affected stakeholders, refrain from giving the interests of a single stakeholder priority, and develop procedures to ensure that relations among stakeholders are governed by principles of justice. In this literature, there is debate about which 'stakes' managers should consider legitimate (Donaldson and Preston, 1995; Mitchell *et al.*, 1997) and whether performance, as traditionally measured, aligns with a stakeholder orientation (Berman *et al.*, 1999; Margolis and Walsh, 2001; Orlitzky *et al.*, 2003; Post *et al.*, 2002). The underlying claim is that the interests of groups implicated in corporate activity have intrinsic value beyond the firm's profit motivation and, therefore, should be taken into account by management, countering libertarian economists' claims that CSR activities amount to an unjustified seizure of stockholder wealth (e.g. Friedman, 1962; Lantos, 2001).

CSR initiatives commonly draw on some version of stakeholder thinking. Here, we examine three interventions: ecological sustainability, social accounting/socially responsible investing, and awards for CSR activity. Based on ideology critique, we show why critical theorists are skeptical about these programs while additionally showing the limitations of such critiques.

Ecological Sustainability

One approach to CSR involves mitigating the environmental impacts of business. Well-known examples of environmentally devastating events abound: Royal Dutch-Shell's Brent Spar platform, Exxon's Valdez oil spill, and Union Carbide's Bhopal disaster. Calls to not only avoid catastrophe but to treat the environment as a legitimate stakeholder are becoming increasingly common across industries. Often referred to as organizational 'greening,' these initiatives assert that social pressure from environmentalists can encourage managers to recognize the detrimental effects of corporate practices and, in time, can generate large-scale changes that can also be advantageous for business (Gladwin *et al.*, 1995; Hawken, 1994). Corporations incorporate this drive for sustainability in ways that range from a rarely seen 'total quality' approach pervading the entire organizational system to trading expensive ecologically benign technologies for rights to develop a region's natural resources (Jermier and Forbes, 2003; Shrivastava, 1995). Corporations can thus be viewed as potential agents of beneficial community and environmental development, not merely as egocentric exploiters of resources.

Critical theory's ideology critique leads to substantial doubt and cynicism regarding ecological sustainability initiatives. Based on Marcuse's (1964) argument that our relationship to the environment is a product of our means of organization within capitalism, many argue that a *holistic*, rather than selective, approach to greening is required. This would be an approach 'that elicits deep caring through a well-resourced environmental mission' (Jermier and Forbes, 2003: 168), shaping not only corporate practices but also individuals' identities. Critics argue that most corporate sustainability initiatives do not come from this sort of commitment, but instead are occasioned by regulations, an opportunity for competitive advantage, or a quest for a virtuous public image. Such motivations are often captured under the label 'greenwashing' to derogate corporate public relations/issues management efforts that are likely to be insincere, piecemeal, temporary, and of limited benefit to interests beyond the corporation's profitability objective (Greer and Bruno, 1996; Munshi and Kurian, 2005; Saravanamuthu, 2004). Critical theorists contend that the ideologically structured discourses around 'practical' and 'reasonable' business–environment trade-offs enable environmentalism to be palatable to managers, but end up hegemonically portraying ecological claims as irrational or naïve (Prasad and Elmes, 2005). They show that the discourses of sustainability view the environment as a controllable entity, one that can only be managed according to a logic of the marketplace and in the interests of capitalist 'development' (Banerjee, 2003).

In other words, critical theorists hold that when ecological sustainability interests are transformed into concern for how the public perceives and influences the corporation and its business pursuits, environmentalists retain little hope of transforming dominant managerial ideologies or corporate governance (Freeman and Liedtka, 1991; Roberts, 2003); environmentalism of this sort merely reifies and reproduces corporatist ideologies.

Social Auditing and Socially Responsible Investing

A second approach to CSR includes broad-based efforts to establish standards for action and, in turn, evaluate corporate actors against these standards. For instance, efforts such as the Global Reporting Initiative, the Organization for Economic Co-operation and Development's Guidelines for Multinational Enterprises, the Ethical Trading Initiative, and the Social Accountability 8000 standard (Gordon, 2001; Karapetrovic and Jonker, 2003; Shäfer, 2005) propose guidelines based on the Core Conventions of the International Labour Office. These frameworks generally have a threefold goal: to operationalize the claims on corporate activity produced by stakeholder or environmental concerns, to provide a vehicle by which individuals and NGOs may exert pressure for change, and to demonstrate a 'business case' for CSR activities (Jonker, 2003). Such guidelines then become standards for environmental, social, and economic performance.

Critical theorists assert that such reporting guidelines are likely to have little effect on corporate practice without mechanisms for oversight that compel reform (Bhimani and Soonawalla, 2005). Consequently, such standards are sometimes coupled with calls for modifying firms' internal accounting systems or for investors to exert influence. Projects such as 'triple bottom line' accounting (Elkington, 1998) attempt to establish principles and benchmarks that give CSR activities a status equal to profitability concerns on the corporate agenda by rendering them the responsibility of line (rather than staff) managers. Another example is socially responsible investing (SRI) initiatives, which attempt to promote corporate reform by leveraging stockholder ownership. The SRI camp believes that the real agents of change are the managers of mutual and pension funds rather than individual investors. The logic is that fund managers—who often hold substantial proportions of a company's stock—could wield considerable influence by voting (or refusing to vote) their proxies on a host of governance issues at company shareholders' meetings.

Critical theorists are, however, wary of these programs. One key concern is that non-compliance with social issues, unlike more easily quantified or objectively verifiable factors, is not easily assessed through audits, and is particularly challenging when the audit considers only a single point in time (O'Rourke, 2002). A second concern is the degree to which such changes alter the nature of the firm's actual business activities. Many companies have introduced 'ethics officers' and codes of ethical conduct, but these are often pushed to the periphery or appropriated in ironic fashion because they are perceived as out of touch with traditional measures of performance (Kuhn, 2005; Kuhn and Ashcraft, 2003). The content of decisions includes ethical concerns only when executives both perceive pressure and believe they will enjoy a positive external image (Stevens *et al.*, 2005). This suggests that ideologies of managerialism and instrumentalism likely trump these voluntary codes. Ideology critique, then, suggests that managerialism co-opts other interests despite audit-based efforts to monitor and modify corporations.

CSR Awards

Burgeoning popular interest in CSR prompted many civic organizations, consulting firms, and chambers of commerce to develop rating criteria designed to audit and publicize particular versions of 'responsible' practice. One example is *Business Ethics* magazine's yearly list of '100 Best Corporate Citizens'. The ranking, conducted by an independent research firm, requires most nominees to apply for consideration. The measure averages scores across eight criteria, including returns to stockholders, 'community' (i.e. philanthropic giving and volunteer programs), 'environment' (i.e. pollution prevention and use of clean energy), and 'governance' (i.e. transparency in political contributions and effective social reporting) (Raths, 2006). The 'best corporate citizen' label is attained by claiming an orientation that speaks to the inclusion of stakeholder values in company practice, though the production of the rating involves no examination of managerial choice-making, organizational routines, or reasoning processes.

Although awards such as this purport to measure and celebrate CSR accomplishments, they can be misleading and may direct attention away from serious exploration of the presence, or lack thereof, of wider social values embedded in corporate practices and decisions. An unintended consequence is that they may close off discussion on potentially troublesome practices, enabling companies to proclaim virtuous corporate governance while generating confusing or invisible standards that fail to expose *un*ethical practices (Hopkins, 2003). Moreover, CSR awards are often presented by seemingly neutral arbiters of corporate responsibility that assess and proclaim success but which are actually established and supported by the very firms they evaluate. Shamir (2004) calls these groups 'MaNGOs' (Market-oriented Non-Governmental Organizations), and argues that they 'are established in order to disseminate and actualize corporate-inspired versions of 'social responsibility' while enjoying the aura of disinterestedness often bestowed on non-profit 'civil society' entities' (pp. 680–1). Such organizations insert CSR issues into corporate conversations but can actually *prevent* the sort of fundamental changes many critics desire. Given increasing attention to CSR in the broad marketplace and a widespread need to cultivate a positive corporate image, supporting and competing for these awards is logical for firms. But we would also expect companies to perform rituals of redemption after unethical activities are encountered, rather than rely on awards that provide only a thin veneer of cover until scrutiny subsides and competition intensifies (Knight and Greenberg, 2002). Thus, we must examine the values embedded in these awards in more detail.

CSR awards generally focus on formal programs, official policies, and disbursements of corporate funds—activities managed by those in positions of authority. The distribution of these awards thus simultaneously renders management as a benign and neutral steward of community interests while endorsing the values of authority. Informal business practices, decision-making processes, and the consequences of actual conduct are outside the measures' scope. This helps explain how companies such as Enron could make *Fortune's* list of 'Most Admired Companies' from 1996 to 2000 (Fox, 2003) but implode shortly thereafter. In short, the unarticulated values built into CSR awards both reinforce managerial control and absolve management of the responsibility for interrogating whose values are included—and how they are included—in corporate decisions.

Summary

Ideology critique can produce insight into initiatives such as ecological sustainability, social auditing/socially responsible investing, and CSR awards, but suffers from two unarticulated conceptual shortcomings. The first is a tendency to assume a simplistic model of social relations in which (powerful) corporations dominate (powerless) stakeholders. The second is an underlying liberal version of democracy (see Deetz, 1992, 1995; Scherer and Palazzo, Chapter 18 this volume), in which decision-making assumes the unproblematic representation of one's own and others' interests, moral concerns are relegated to the private domain (Bauman, 2001), and participation in decisions is restricted in terms of both the conception of 'stakes' and the assessment of organizational success. A consequence of these shortcomings is that substantive change can be undermined since there is no positive or productive model beyond either a utopian vision of a post-capitalist world or a mild tempering of corporations' profit pursuit. Consequently, what counts as 'doing good' or being a 'responsible corporate citizen' is vague, depends on the pronouncements of 'interested' parties like the aforementioned MaNGOs, and may shift based on the standards of conflicting communities. And all of this makes managers' tasks even more challenging (Matten and Crane, 2005).

At base, the critical question must be about the degree of change generated by these CSR initiatives. Doane (2005) suggests that CSR scholars 'should be asking ourselves whether or not we've in fact been spending our efforts promoting a strategy that is more likely to lead to business as usual, rather than attacking the more fundamental problems' (p. 28). Although ideological critiques are important and informative, they are likely to fail to attack the fundamental problems because they can be perceived as disconnected from, and unconcerned with, routine activity in corporations. They tend to operate from an elite position (Deetz, 2001) in which the content and outcomes of CSR activities are considered further evidence of an ideologically created corporate hegemony, while they rarely offer plausible alternatives.

We argue, in contrast, that critical theorists must problematize the 'nature' of the corporation and its governance *processes* if their critiques are to occasion substantive change. An alternative critical perspective, based on a communicative vision of organizing and decisional process, offers not only novel insight on intervention, but one that it is better suited to the needs of a democratic society. Our claim is that CSR might be better advanced by new forms of inclusion and discussion rather than ideological critique of standards, audits, sustainability programs, and awards.

A Space for Hope or the Need for a Process-Oriented Critical Perspective

Despite the skepticism, some critical theorists believe CSR can be improved and can offer guidance to organizing practices. Habermas, in his development of a theory of communicative action, provided a way to think of a normative ideal based on processes of interaction rather than a priori theories of domination and the privileging of specific value preference held by specific groups. While Habermas retained a relatively linear model of communication and system of argumentation—and, hence, could not provide for creativity and productivity in interaction—he did give us a new way to frame and think through the problem.

The gradual development of critical communication theory, when attached to a reformed conception of stakeholder governance, opens new possibilities for the CSR discussion. A significant problem with the more traditional understanding of stakeholder participation in decision-making is that it is based in liberal democratic communication conceptions where interests are treated as fixed and conflicts are resolved by trade-offs. These forms of participation are insufficient for engendering creativity. This conception of critical communication theory differs from ideology critique in that it offers the opportunity to overcome ideology (as possessed by all stakeholders) through genuine encounter and interrogation by difference rather than critical reflection and compromise. The task is to look outward, inventing futures, rather than resolving the present.

The Non-inevitability of Contradictions between Social and Business Concerns

Many business leaders, as well as some critical theorists and left-leaning activists, share an assumption that a basic contradiction exists between doing good and doing well. Business leaders feel that the inclusion of social concerns is costly, while activists believe that profits inevitably equal exploitation. Such a contradiction forestalls many potentially interesting approaches to CSR.

We wish to assess the validity of this assumption. Available evidence across specific firms and industries indicates that the causal direction between 'doing good' and 'doing well' is ambiguous. Further, plenty of support suggests that there is no necessary contradiction (OECD, 2004: 77–8; de Jong and Witteloostuijn, 2004; Lawler, 1999; Clarkson, 1995; McLagan and Nel, 1995). Instead, the differences in relationships appear to be linked to external conditions and the manner of value inclusion. If CSR is about incorporating diverse social and business values in decisional processes, then finding a system of inclusion is central.

Value inclusion, however, does not appear to come from managerial goodwill, reduced litigation and regulation, or proactive consumer choice alone. Rather, the principal source may come from within the organization through the breaking of standard managerial decision routines. The economic viability of inclusion was detailed in the outcomes of various decisional impasses in the co-management process in the early days at Saturn before they returned to a more standard GM model (Rubinstein *et al.*, 1993). Other well-accepted claims advance the position that diversity can enable greater creativity. In these cases, opposition and difference become essential for assessing existing decision routines and inventing new ones. As Kerr (2004) showed in his analysis of the value of diverse inputs at HP and Southwest Airlines, participation 'will contribute positively to an organization's performance where . . . the organization's output must be diverse and original' (p. 91). Further, the use of distributed expertise can lead to faster, higher quality decisions, because members at the point of business activity are often in a better position to innovate and improve processes. Overall, evidence on decisional quality, effectiveness, and efficiency consistently favors participatory decisional forms over traditional hierarchical alternatives (Seibold and Shea, 2001; Cheney *et al.*, 1998; Lawler, 1999; McLagan and Nel, 1995). And where participation programs have been less successful, the lack of managerial acceptance and inadequate participation processes appear to have been largely responsible (Cotton *et al.*, 1988). CSR efforts might, thus, be more effective if driven from within organizations sponsoring particular processes of participation and value inclusion.

Ultimately, new corporate governance conceptions and practices can reduce the opportunity for scandals, encourage growth and long-term thinking, balance managerial self-interest, and make decisions more responsive to wider social values while at the same time encourage greater creativity in product development and decision-making, increase employee commitment, enhance coordination, and enable greater product customization. Organizations, in fact, could be the necessary social institutions providing the appropriate forums for the articulation, and creative resolution, of important social conflicts; particularly regarding the use of natural resources, the production of desirable goods and services, the development of personal qualities, distribution of income, and the future direction of society. In some ways, the workplace could be a better site for public decision-making than the traditional political process given the close connection between organizational decisions, their public consequences, and the speed of adjustment. Steering from the inside may be more effective for CSR than some of the carrot and stick motivations used today. The corporation might be the right place to concentrate on developing the decisional processes needed for CSR to incorporate and foster the necessary variety of social values.

Critical Models of Stakeholder Participation

From a critical theory standpoint, meeting both economic and social goals requires a transformation of organizational governance and decision-making processes to include more decisional voices representing diverse business and community values and generating explicit value contestation. Such representation and contestation can enhance creativity, productivity, economic performance, and greater fulfillment of social good. Accomplishing this requires both new models of corporate governance, focusing on stakeholders rather than shareholders, and new models of communication enabling more productive discussions and decision processes (see also Scherer and Palazzo, 2007). Such a stakeholder model has to include a critical model of inclusion absent from most existing stakeholder thinking.

Implementing stakeholder models that include wider social values within decisional processes has proven challenging. Labor unions, supplier cartels, and consumer groups are some ways stakeholders have attempted to acquire the size and clout necessary to be represented in corporate decisions. But, as we know from other collaborative decision-making contexts, creativity and mutual satisfaction are based on commitment to a co-determinative process rather than just having a place to argue out self-interests (e.g. Gray, 1989). Most stakeholder models place management in an oppositional role to other stakeholders rather than generate a group committed to mutual accomplishment. In a more robust stakeholder model, management's function would become the coordination of the conflicting stakeholder interests rather than the managing or controlling of them. The logic is not one of *containing* stakeholder interests, but trying to accomplish them *through* corporate activity.

Thus far the stronger versions of this stakeholder model have mostly been developed in quasi-public enterprises and in environmental collaborations. While some of these efforts have been reduced to 'venting', 'buy-in' mechanisms, or greenwashing ploys, others have offered creative and beneficial solutions. For example, building on insights from bona fide group theory (Putnam and Stohl, 1990), Lange (2003) detailed the successful functioning of 'ecosystem management' following the Clinton Forest Plan beginning in 1994. Some for-profit companies have also incorporated stakeholder inclusion opportunities. While partly restricted to works councils, de Jong and van Witteloostuijn (2004) showed how the Dutch Breman Group's structures and processes of participation helped to 'develop and sustain organizational adaptation and learning' (p. 54). In addition, many successful companies currently practice various forms of employee participation. The willingness to embrace employee involvement may be instructive in looking to the potential of including other stakeholders. Stakeholder inclusion is essential for the processes of creativity that can advance both social and economic interests rather than trade them off against each other. Such a juxtaposition of goals is a critical feature of any attempt to move to creativity and innovation. Yet many questions remain to be answered in the development of advanced stakeholder governance, particularly as they relate to CSR.

Basic questions for approaching CSR from this perspective are little different from those for participation more generally: Which stakeholders should be involved? Where and how should they be involved? Who should speak on behalf of a stakeholder group? Will stakeholders, when involved, understand and effectively articulate their own interests? How do we keep potential costs of participation down? Finally, and most importantly, what is to be the nature of the stakeholder interaction in the decision-making process? Even fairly complete reviews of participation processes overlook this crucial communicative issue. Unlike many traditional critical theory discussions, the biggest task may not be overcoming the autocratic tendencies of many managers and the communication structures, principles and practices fostered by this, but in providing new ways to think about and 'do' communication in places where participation is genuinely favored. Consequently, if CSR is to be motivated by difference and foster creative possibilities, an appropriate model of stakeholder communication is needed.

MODELS OF STAKEHOLDER COMMUNICATION

The—what might appear to be benign—communication conceptions and practices in stakeholder interventions have tremendous impact on the success and viability of diverse value inclusion. Communication is an integral part of any form of participation; indeed, communication *constitutes* participation. Thus, the form and practices of participation, not just their existence, matter. Having a right and place to say something and having a process to positively impact decisions are often very different. This will be developed below in looking at alternative understandings of communication, democracy, conflict, and dialogue.

Native communication concepts and practices have been largely treated as unproblematic, thus leading to a focus on developing participation *forums* and higher levels of involvement with uneven consequences for decision processes. Even in countries with strong co-determination models and structures like Germany, Sweden, and Denmark, the communication models and practices may be fairly traditional and greatly reduce the impact and benefits of participation. Much of this results from dominant 'enlightenment' conceptions of communication that overlook critical aspects of interaction processes whereby meanings and interests are produced. In other words, traditional models of communication give priority to the expression of meaning rather than the production of personal meanings.

Managerially driven forms of participation based in these older conceptions often involve strategic attempts to increase loyalty and commitment or decrease resistance rather than seeking genuine decisional input. The lack of *voice*, even with appropriate *forums*, results from constrained decisional contexts, inadequate or distorted information, socialization and colonization activities, and the solicitation of 'consent' where stakeholders 'choose' to suppress their own needs and internal value conflicts (see Deetz, 1998). Even team-based decision-making is often filled with self-generated limits to open participation (Barker, 1999). Overcoming these problems requires a collaborative constitutive view of communication based in conflict rather than consensus models.

However, managers are often ill-prepared to engage in alternative forms of democratic communication. Not only are managers hesitant to include employees, let along other stakeholders, in crucial decisions by disclosing information, sharing power, or granting autonomy, they lack the concepts and skills necessary to do so even if they liked. Clearly managers lack the critical skills of democratic communication necessary for coordinating divergent interests, let alone the ability to facilitate interaction that can lead to creative mutually satisfying outcomes.

But what models would they need? Several models have emerged from the increased use and talk about team decisions, dialogue, and forms of participation generally. Often, however, these alternatives have not been theoretically or empirically investigated and have been presented in a vague unproblematic way as simply 'democratic' communication or 'dialogue' (see Isaacs, 1993). And, frequently, these communication practices have been seen as requiring little training or development. Rather than facilitating a complex process interaction that engages multiple values and perspectives, they seem to operate on the premise that if we build a trusting team, members will communicate well; or if we develop participatory attitudes, appropriate skills will spontaneously arise. If critical theory is to motivate CSR, then a more appropriate model of participatory stakeholder communication is necessary.

Critical theories of communication originating primarily from Habermas (1979, 1984, 1990) have revived discussion of communication in public decision-making and may also provide guidance for corporate processes of stakeholder participation. The description of an ideal speech situation provides a heuristic for determining the minimal conditions for stakeholder involvement in decision-making discussions. Most of these are familiar. At the minimum we might expect reciprocity of opportunity for expression; some equality in expression skills; the setting aside of authority relations, organizational positions, and other external sources of power; the open investigations of stakeholder positions and 'wants' to more freely ascertain their interests; open sharing of information and transparency of decision processes; and the opening of fact and knowledge claims to re-determinization based on con-testation of claims and advantaged modes of knowledge creation (e.g. accounting processes etc.; see Deetz, 1992, for development).

This heuristic is directly applicable to stakeholder decision-making processes. For instance, such concepts have been developed by Forester (1989, 1999) regarding public planning processes. Much of this shows how organizational talk can be analyzed to discover the retention and protection of hidden values and ideology (e.g. Fairclough, 1992) and the presence of various forms of discursive closure (see Deetz, 1992; Thackaberry, 2004). Pearce and Littlejohn (1999), from a somewhat different perspective, show how to develop communication processes for engaging even moral conflicts where deep cultural differences produce what would appear to be intractable conflict. Similarly, Barge and Little (2002) illustrate how a Bakhtinian conception of dialogic communication can help develop contingent and situated practices that enhance responsiveness to conflicting stakeholder values.

These efforts help develop an understanding that social responsibility and in-creased economic health is found in fostering particular communicative micro-practices in everyday work contexts. Communication difficulties arise from com-munication practices which preclude value debate and conflict, which substitute images and imaginary relations for self-presentation and truth claims, which arbi-trarily limit access to communication channels and forums, and which then lead to decisions based on arbitrary authority relations. Critical theories are useful because they identify the key problem as the nature of the discussion itself rather than the profiles of the participants. However, Habermasian concepts of communication, like theories of dialogue advanced by Senge, Isaacs, and others, are based more on finding common ground and obtaining consensus rather than in producing a future beyond current cultural constraints (Isaacs, 1993; Deetz and Simpson, 2004; Senge, 1990). Furthermore, most of these theories are aimed at participants understanding each other rather than the need to make decisions together. (See this developed in Benhabib's (1992) critique of Habermas's ideal speech situation.) Critical the-ory alone does not offer a theory or practice of dialogue embracing difference and facilitating decision-making on the part of stakeholders (Wolin, 1996; Young, 1996).

If stakeholder models, and CSR more specifically, require communicative processes of value inclusion, then appropriate concepts and practices of commu-nication are required to move beyond mere mutual understanding toward making quality decisions together. Our research group's investigations across several sites (e.g. MacDonald, 2004; Heath, 2005), along with studies summarized by Lange (2003) regarding environmental collaborations, suggest a few basic insights. First, programs that focus on stakeholders jointly making decisions are of much greater value than those that simply give stakeholders a 'say.' Second, membership based on the diversity of interests of those at the table and discussion processes that encourage emergent solutions are of greater value than those whose members represent external groups and are committed to maintaining positions held by those not at the table. Third, as shown for years by people working with conflict, focusing on outcomes and interests in the interaction is of greater value than focusing on problems or wants and bargaining over preferred solutions. This is especially the case when stakeholder problems are defined as the absence of their preferred solutions. Finally, maintaining conflicts and differences as a positive energy toward creativity is of greater value than seeking common ground and value consensus.

Thus, while critical theory provides focus on the internal micro-practices of decisional processes, any development and actualization of these concepts and practices requires an enriched theory of communication. Such a theory focuses on understanding the cultural politics of experience and processes of domination in interaction, has a strong conception of 'other' and 'otherness', and is grounded in conflict theories. This helps turn the insights of critical theory into positive practices. A stronger conception of communication shows how difference or 'distanciation' enables exploring of alternatives and producing creative decisions. Such a theory works against native views focused on similarity, consensus, and finding common ground in showing how requisite diversity and contestation coupled with the ability to invent creative options can sustain mutual commitment and mutual accomplishment of interests, thus including diverse social values (Kuhn and Poole, 2000; Maclagan, 1999).

Workplaces can be enhanced by the application of a conflict-based communication theory for the sake of greater responsibility and more effective production. Such an application can: (1) provide a communication-based understanding of the complex processes of organizational life; (2) direct the evaluation of existing organizational forms and activities, including the possibility that the development of CSR standards (as discussed above) can draw upon multiple voices and may foster meaningful stakeholder dialogue; and (3) provide guidance for the education of members and redesign of organizational structures and practices. Effective moves toward CSR cannot rely only on managerial goodwill, government regulation, or consumer choice alone. Rather, the efficacy of CSR must be based upon a critical theory and motivated by enriched processes of communication that engender authentic stakeholder participation, incorporate various social values, and operate within a process that constructively engages in conflict to inspire creative solutions. In sum, CSR can be enhanced by the inclusion of multiple social values into the decisional premises, processes, and routines and the development of communication processes that utilize the situations of conflict and difference to generate creative 'win-win' responses.

CONCLUSION

This chapter is based on a simple premise: A conception of CSR based in a rich vision of communication has the potential to both expose and incorporate the myriad values present in organizational decision-making. We discussed why many critical theorists are skeptical of common CSR interventions and corporations' claims of virtue. We then advanced an alternative critical view, one committed to both surfacing the values embedded in CSR initiatives and to making those values a key element of stakeholder dialogues oriented toward decisional creativity rather than to false consensus.

Initiatives promoting environmental sustainability, efforts at social auditing/socially responsible investing, and awarding companies for pro-social activities are standard elements of CSR practice and are often designed with 'stakeholders' in mind, but can be anathema to the sort of reformed stakeholder dialogue outlined here. Not only can such conventional practices direct attention away from the *processes* of community engagement and corporate decision-making, they can also create the belief among members of both the company and the community that managers have addressed (and should be entrusted to handle) issues that affect corporations' multiple constituencies. Our call for an enriched critical version of stakeholder communication represents a radical departure from typical CSR practice, as well as from versions of critical theory rooted in ideology critique. But there is reason to believe that such a re-orientation can produce novel and positive outcomes for the array of firms and communities that currently see CSR as a necessity for addressing complex social problems. We agree with Banerjee's (2006) contention that corporations, given their present practices, are inappropriate agents for social change; we argue that a richer version of communication than conventionally employed in CSR interventions can address critical theorists' cynicism and generate productive problem-solving.

REFERENCES

ALCHIAN, A. A., and DEMSETZ, H. 1972. 'Production, Information Costs, and Economic Organization.' *American Economic Review*, 62: 777–95.

ALVESSON, M., and WILLMOTT, H. 1992. 'Critical Theory and Management Studies: An Introduction', in M. Alvesson and H. Willmott (eds.), *Critical Management Studies*. Newbury Park, Calif.: Sage, 1–20.

BANERJEE, S. B. 2003. 'Who Sustains whose Development?: Sustainable Development and the Reinvention of Nature.' *Organization Studies*, 24: 143–80.

——— 2006. 'The Problem with Corporations as Social Change Agents: A Critical Perspective.' Paper presented at the Annual Meetings of the Academy of Management, Atlanta, Ga., Aug.

BARGE, J. K. and LITTLE, M. 2002. 'Dialogical Wisdom, Communicative Practice, and Organizational Life'. *Communication Theory*, 12: 375–97.

BARKER, J. R. 1999. *The Discipline of Teamwork: Participation and Concertive Control.* Thousand Oaks, Calif.: Sage.

BAUMAN, Z. 2001. *The Individualized Society.* London: Polity Press.

BENHABIB, S. 1992. *Situating the Self: Gender, Community, and Postmodernism in Contemporary Ethics.* New York: Routledge.

BERMAN, S. L., WICKS, A. C., KOTHA, S., and JONES, T. M. 1999. 'Does Stakeholder Orientation Matter? The Relationship between Stakeholder Management Models and Firm Financial Performance.' *Academy of Management Journal*, 42: 488–506.

BHIMANI, A., and SOONAWALLA, K. 2005. 'From Conformance to Performance: The Corporate Responsibilities Continuum.' *Journal of Accounting and Public Policy*, 24, 165–74.

BOATRIGHT, J. R. 1996. 'Business Ethics and the Theory of the Firm.' *American Business Law Journal*, 34: 217–38.

BOWIE, N. E. 1991. 'The Firm as a Moral Community', in R. M. Coughlin (ed.), *Morality, Rationality, and Efficiency: New Perspectives on Socio-economics.* Armonk, NY: M. E. Sharp, 169–83.

BURAWOY, M. 1979. *Manufacturing Consent: Changes in the Labor Process under Monopoly Capitalism.* Chicago: University of Chicago Press.

CHANDLER, A. D. 1962. *Strategy and Structure: Chapters in the History of the Industrial Enterprise.* Cambridge, Mass: MIT Press.

CHENEY, G., STRAUB, J., SPEIRS-GLEBE, L., STOHL, C., DEGOOYER, D. WHALEN, S., GARVIN-DOXAS, K. and CARLONE, D. 1998. 'Democracy, Participation and Communication at Work: A Multidisciplinary Review', in M. E. Roloff (ed.), *Communication Yearbook 21*, 35–91. Thousand Oaks, Calif.: Sage, 35–91.

CLARKSON, M. 1995. 'A Stakeholder Framework for Analyzing Corporate Social Performance'. *Academy of Management Review*, 20: 92–117.

COTTON, J. L., VOLLATH, D. A., FROGGATT, K. L., LENGRICK-HALL, M. L., and JENNINGS, K. R. 1988. 'Employement Participation: Diverse Forms and Different Outcomes', *Academy of Management Review*, 13: 8–22.

DEETZ, S. A. 1992. *Democracy in an Age of Corporate Colonization: Developments in Communication and the Politics of Everyday Life.* Albany, NY: State University of New York Press.

——1995. *Transforming Communication, Transforming Business: Building Responsive and Responsible Workplaces.* Cresskill, NJ: Hampton Press, Inc.

——1998. 'Discursive Formations, Strategized Subordination and Self-Surveillance', in A. McKinlay and K. Starkey (eds.), *Foucault, Management, and Organization Theory.* Thousand Oaks, Calif.: Sage, 151–72.

——2001. 'Conceptual Foundations', in F. M. Jablin and L. L. Putnam (eds.), *The New Handbook of Organizational Communication.* Thousand Oaks, Calif.: Sage, 3–46.

——and MUMBY, D. K. 1990. 'Power, Discourse, and the Workplace: Reclaiming the Critical Tradition', in J. A. Anderson (ed.), *Communication Yearbook 13.* Newbury Park, Calif.: Sage, 18–47.

——and SIMPSON. J. 2004. 'Critical Organizational Dialogue: Open Formation and the Demand of "otherness" ', in R. Anderson, L. Baxter, and K. Cissna (eds.), *Dialogic Approaches to Communication.* New York: Lawrence Erlbaum, 141–58.

DE JONG, G. and VAN WITTELOOSTUIJN, A. 2004. 'Successful Corporate Democracy'. *Academic of Management Executive*, 18: 54–66.

DOANE, D. 2005. 'The Myth of CSR.' *Stanford Social Innovation Review*, 3, fall: 22–9.

DONALDSON, T., and PRESTON, L. 1995. 'The Stakeholder Theory of the Corporation: Concepts, Evidence, Implications.' *Academy of Management Review*, 20: 65–91.

ELKINGTON, J. 1998. *Cannibals with Forks: The Triple Bottom Line of 21st Century Business*. Stony Creek, Conn.: New Society Publishers.

FAIRCLOUGH, N. 1992. *Discourse and Social Change*. Cambridge: Polity Press.

FORESTER, J. 1989. *Planning in the Face of Power*. Berkeley: University of California Press.

——1999. *The Deliberative Practitioner: Encouraging Participatory Planning Processes*. Cambridge, Mass: MIT Press.

FOURNIER, V., and GREY, C. 2000. 'At the Critical Moment: Conditions and Prospects for Critical Management Studies.' *Human Relations*, 53: 7–32.

FOX, L. 2003. *Enron: The Rise and Fall*. Hoboken, NJ: John Wiley & Sons.

FREEMAN, R. E., and LIEDTKA, J. 1991. 'Corporate Social Responsibility: A Critical Approach.' *Business Horizons*, 34(4): 92–8.

FRIEDMAN, M. 1962. *Capitalism and Freedom*. Chicago: University of Chicago Press.

GIDDENS, A. 1979. *Central Problems in Social Theory*. Berkeley: University of California Press.

GLADWIN, T. N., KENNELLY, J. J., and KRAUSE, T.-S. 1995. 'Shifting Paradigms for Sustainable Development: Implications for Theory and Research.' *Academy of Management Review*, 20: 874–907.

GORDON, K. 2001. 'The OECD Guidelines and other Corporate Responsibility Instruments: A Comparison.' *OECD Working Papers on International Investment*. Paris.

GRAY, B. 1989. *Collaborating: Finding Common Ground for Multi-party Problems*. San Francisco: Jossey-Bass.

GREER, J., and BRUNO, K. 1996. *Greenwash: The Reality behind Corporate Environmentalism*. New York: Apex Press.

HABERMAS, J. 1979. *Communication and the Evolution of Society*, trans. T. McCarthy. Boston: Beacon.

——1984. *The Theory of Communicative Action, Volume 1: Reason and the Rationalization of Society*. trans. T. McCarthy. Boston: Beacon.

——1990. *Moral Consciousness and Communicative Action*, trans. C. Lenhardt and S. W. Nicholsen. Cambridge, Mass: MIT Press.

HALL, S. 1985. 'Signification, Representation, Ideology: Althusser and the Post-structuralist Debates.' *Critical Studies in Mass Communication*, 2: 91–114.

HAWKEN, P. 1994. *The Ecology of Commerce: A Declaration of Sustainability*. New York: Harper Business.

HEATH, J., and POTTER, A. 2004. *Nation of Rebels: Why Counterculture became Consumer Culture*. New York: Harper Business.

HEATH, R. 2005. 'Interorganizational Collaboration: Implications for Democracy in Community Models of Communication and Problem Solving'. Unpublished doctoral dissertation, University of Colorado.

HOPKINS, M. 2003. *The Planetary Bargain: Corporate Social Responsibility Matters*. London: Earthscan.

ISAACS, W. 1993. 'Taking Flight: Dialogue, Collective Thinking, and Organizational Learning.' *Organizational Dynamics*, 22: 24–39.

JERMIER, J. M., and FORBES, L. C. 2003. 'Greening Organizations: Critical Issues', in M. Alvesson and H. Willmott (eds.), *Studying Management Critically*. London: Sage, 157–176.

JONKER, J. 2003. 'In Search of Society: Redefining Corporate Social Responsibility, Organi-sational Theory and Business Strategies', in J. A. Batten and T. A. Fetherson (eds.), *Social Responsibility: Corporate Governance Issues*, vol. 17. Amsterdam: JA, 423–39.

KARAPETROVIC, S., and JONKER, J. 2003. 'Integration of Standardized Management Systems: Searching for a Recipe and Ingredients'. *Total Quality Management*, 14: 451–9.

KELLY, M. 2001. *The Divine Right of Capital: Dethroning the Corporate Aristocracy*. San Francisco: Berrett-Koehler.

KERR, J. 2004. 'The Limits of Organizational Democracy'. *Academic of Management Execu-tive*, 18: 81–95.

KHURANA, R. 2002. *Searching for a Corporate Savior: The Irrational Quest for Charismatic CEOs*. Princeton: Princeton University Press.

KNIGHT, G., and GREENBERG, J. 2002. 'Promotionalism and Subpolitics: Nike and its Labor Critics'. *Management Communication Quarterly*, 15: 541–70.

KUHN, T. 2005. 'Engaging Networks of Practice through a Communicative Theory of the Firm', in J. Simpson and P. Shockley-Zalabak (eds.), *Engaging Communication, Transform-ing Organizations: Scholarship of Engagement in Action*. Cresskill, NJ: Hampton, 45–66.

——and ASHCRAFT, K. L. 2003. 'Corporate Scandal and the Theory of the Firm: For-mulating the Contributions of Organizational Communication Studies'. *Management Communication Quarterly*, 17: 20–57.

——and POOLE, M. S. 2000. 'Do Conflict Management Styles Affect Group Decision-Making?: Evidence from a Longitudinal Field Study'. *Human Communication Research*, 26: 558–90.

LANGE, J. 2003. 'Environmental Collaboration and Constituency Communication', in L. Frey (ed.), *Group Communication in Context*. Hillsdale, NJ: Erlbaum, 209–34.

LANTOS, G. P. 2001. 'The Boundaries of Strategic Corporate Social Responsibility'. *Journal of Consumer Marketing*, 18: 595–630.

LAWLER, E. 1999. 'Employee Involvement Makes a Difference'. *Journal for Quality and Par-ticipation*, 22: 18–20.

LUKÁCS, G. 1971. *History and Class Consciousness*, trans. R. Livingstone. Cambridge, Mass: MIT Press.

LYON, A. 2005. ' "Intellectual Capital" and Struggles over the Perceived Value of Members' Expert Knowledge in a Knowledge-Intensive Organization'. *Western Journal of Communi-cation*, 69: 251–71.

MACDONALD, J. 2004. 'Public Involvement in Dispersing Public Funds: Values, Native Com-munication Theories and Collaboration'. Unpublished doctoral dissertation, University of Colorado.

MACINTYRE, A. 1984. *After Virtue: A Study in Moral Theory*, 2nd edn. Notre Dame, Ind.: University of Notre Dame Press.

MACLAGAN, P. 1999. 'Corporate Social Responsibility as a Participative Process'. *Business Ethics: A European Review*, 8, 43–9.

MCLAGAN, P., and NEL, C. 1995. *The Age of Participation: New Governance for the Workplace and the World*. San Francisco: Berrett-Koehler Publishers.

MARCUSE, H. 1964. *One-Dimensional Man: Studies in the Ideology of Advanced Industrial Society*. Boston: Beacon Press.

MARGOLIS, J. D., and WALSH, J. P. 2001. *People and Profits?: The Search for a Link between a Company's Social and Financial Performance*. Mahwah, NJ: Lawrence Erlbaum.

MATTEN, D., and CRANE, A. 2005. 'Corporate Citizenship: Toward an Extended Theoretical Conceptualization'. *Academy of Management Review*, 30: 166–79.

MITCHELL, R. K., AGLE, B. R., and WOOD, D. J. 1997. 'Toward a Theory of Stakeholder Identification and Salience: Defining the Principle of Who and What Really Counts'. *Academy of Management Review*, 22: 853–86.

MOON, J., CRANE, A., and MATTEN, D. 2005. 'Can Corporations be Citizens?: Corporate Citizenship as a Metaphor for Business Participation in Society'. *Business Ethics Quarterly*, 15: 429–53.

MUMBY, D. K. 1988. *Communication and Power in Organizations: Discourse, Ideology, and Domination*. Norwood, NJ: Ablex.

MUNSHI, D., and KURIAN, P. 2005. 'Imperializing Spin Cycles: A Postcolonial Look at Public Relations, Greenwashing, and Separation of Publics'. *Public Relations Review*, 31: 513–20.

OECD 2001. *Corporate Responsibility: Private Initiatives and Public Goals*. Organization for Economic Co-operation and Development, <http://www.SourceOECD.org>.

—— 2004. *Corporate Governance: A Survey of OECD Countries*. Organization for Economic Co-operation and Development, <http://www.SourceOECD.org>.

ORLITZKY, M., SCHMIDT, F. L., and RYNES, S. 2003. 'Corporate Social and Financial Performance: A Meta-analysis'. *Organization Studies*, 24: 403–41.

O'ROURKE, D. 2002. 'Monitoring the Monitors: A Critique of Third-Party Labour Monitoring', in R. Jenkins, R. Pearson and G. Seyfang (eds.), *Corporate Responsibility and Labour Rights: Codes of Conduct in the Global Economy*. London: Earthscan, 196–208.

PARKER, M. 2003. 'Business, Ethics, and Business Ethics: Critical Theory and Negative Dialectics', in M. Alvesson and H. Willmott (eds.), *Studying Management Critically*. London: Sage, 197–219.

PEARCE, W. B. and LITTLEJOHN, S. 1999. *Moral Conflicts*. Thousand Oaks, Calif.: Sage.

POLANYI, K. 1944. *The Great Transformation*. New York: Rinehart.

POST, J. E., PRESTON, L. E., and SACHS, S. 2002. *Redefining the Corporation: Stakeholder Management and Organizational Wealth*. Stanford, Calif: Stanford University Press.

POWER, M. 1997. *The Audit Society: Rituals of Verification*. Oxford: Oxford University Press.

PRASAD, P., and ELMES, M. 2005. 'In the Name of the Practical: Unearthing the Hegemony of Pragmatics in the Discourse of Environmental Management'. *Journal of Management Studies*, 42: 845–67.

PUTNAM, L. and STOHL, C. 1990. 'Bona Fide Groups: A Reconceptualization of Groups in Context'. *Communication Studies*, 41: 248–65.

RATHS, D. 2006, '100 Best Corporate Citizens for 2006'. *Business Ethics*, 20, spring: available at <http://www.business-ethics.com/whats_new/100best.html>.

RICOEUR, P. 1970. *Freud and Philosophy: An Essay on Interpretation*, trans., D. Savage, New Haven, Conn.: Yale University Press.

ROBERTS, J. 2003. 'The Manufacture of Corporate Social Responsibility: Constructing Corporate Sensibility'. *Organization*, 10: 249–65.

RUBINSTEIN, S., BENNETT, M., and KOCHAN, T. 1993. 'The Saturn Partnership: Co-management and the Reinvention of the Local Union', in B. Kaufman and M. Kleiner (eds.), *Employee Representation: Alternatives and Future Directions*. Madison: The Industrial Relations Research Association, 339–70.

SARAVANAMUTHU, K. 2004. 'What is Measured Counts: Harmonized Corporate Reporting and Sustainable Economic Development'. *Critical Perspectives on Accounting*, 15: 295–302.

SCHERER, A. G., and PALAZZO, E. T. (2007). 'Towards a Political Conception of Corporate Responsibility: Business and Society Seen from a Habermasian Perspective.' *Academy of Management Review* 32: 1096–120.

SCHMOOKLER, A. 1992. *The Illusion of Choice: How the Market Economy Shapes our Destiny.* Albany, NY: SUNY Press.

SEIBOLD, D. R., and SHEA, B. C. 2001. 'Participation and Decision Making', in F. Jablin and L. Putnam (eds.), *The New Handbook of Organizational Communication*. Thousand Oaks, Calif.: Sage, 664–703.

SENGE, P. M. 1990. *The Fifth Discipline: The Art and Practice of the Learning Organization.* New York: Currency Doubleday.

SHÄFER, H. 2005. 'International Corporate Responsibility Rating Systems'. *Journal of Corporate Citizenship*, 20, winter: 107–20.

SHAMIR, R. 2004. 'The De-radicalization of Corporate Social Responsibility'. *Critical Sociology*, 30: 669–89.

SHRIVASTAVA, P. 1995. 'The Role of Corporations in Achieving Ecological Sustainability'. *Academy of Management Review*, 20: 936–60.

STEVENS, J. M., STEENSMA, H. K., HARRISON, D. A., and COCHRAN, P. L. 2005. 'Symbolic or Substantive Document? The Influence of Ethics Codes on Financial Executives' Decisions'. *Strategic Management Journal*, 26: 181–95.

STOHL, M., STOHL, C., and TOWNSLEY, N. C. 2007. 'A New Generation of Corporate Social Responsibility', in S. May, G. Cheney, and J. Roper (eds.), *The Debate Over Corporate Social Responsibility*. New York: Oxford University Press, 30–56.

THACKABERRY, J. A. 2004. 'Discursive Opening and Closing in Organizational Self Study: Culture as the Culprit for Safety Problems in Wildland Firefighting'. *Management Communication Quarterly*, 17: 319–59.

THOMPSON, J. 1984. *Studies in the Theory of Ideology*. Berkeley: University of California Press.

TREVIÑO, L. K., and WEAVER, G. 2003. *Managing Ethics in Business Organizations: Social Scientific Perspectives*. Stanford, Calif.: Stanford University Press.

WOLIN, S. 1996. 'Fugitive Democracy', in S. Benhabib (ed.), *Democracy and Difference: Contesting the Boundaries of the Political*. Princeton: Princeton University Press.

YOUNG, I. 1996. 'Communication and the Other: Beyond Deliberative Democracy', in S. Benhabib (ed.), *Democracy and Difference: Contesting the Boundaries of the Political*. Princeton: Princeton University Press, 120–36.

CHAPTER 9

MUCH ADO ABOUT NOTHING

A CONCEPTUAL CRITIQUE OF CORPORATE SOCIAL RESPONSIBILITY

J. (HANS) VAN OOSTERHOUT*

PURSEY P. M. A. R. HEUGENS

INTRODUCTION

CORPORATE Social Responsibility (CSR) is arguably the most established notion in business and society research (de Bakker *et al.*, 2005). Dating back to the 1950s, it has the longest track record in the field and is often seen as a kind of primitive to other business and society concepts (Carroll, 1999), such as stakeholder theory (Donaldson and Preston, 1995; Freeman, 1984) and corporate citizenship (Gardberg and Fombrun, 2006; Matten and Crane, 2005). Moreover, CSR is a popular managerial notion, with many companies having some form of CSR policy in place or making explicit CSR communications (Maignan and Ralston, 2002). Yet, the case for CSR as a theoretical concept in social science and the humanities is weak if

*Corresponding author.

not outright fatal. The problem is that it is not clear what CSR is, that we do not understand its causes and consequences, and that the notion is not very helpful in understanding what is desirable or required at the business–society interface. We conclude, therefore, that the notion of CSR is better dispensed with altogether in favor of more established conceptual frameworks in the field of management and organization. In particular, we highlight the conceptual and empirical superiority of economizing (Williamson, 1991) and legitimizing (Suchman, 1995) perspectives for business and society theorizing.

Our conceptual critique of the CSR concept is structured as follows. First, we introduce some distinctions for evaluating CSR as an academic concept. We then sketch a short history of CSR concept formation, and elaborate on definitions and operationalizations of the CSR concept. Finding that CSR is problematic both theoretically and empirically, we proceed to explore what—if any—role remains for the notion of CSR in business and society research. We conclude that it would be prudent for the field to dispense with the notion of CSR altogether.

SOME DISTINCTIONS RELEVANT TO CONCEPT FORMATION AND EVALUATION

Although evaluating social science concepts is a complex matter, a number of relatively uncontroversial distinctions can be made (cf. van Oosterhout, 2005). A first distinction deals with how to define a concept, which can be done in two ways. It can be *extensionally* defined, first, by pointing out the set of real-life phenomena the concept refers to. Alternatively, it can be *intensionally* defined by specifying the conjunction of general attributes that make up the concept.[1] Thus an extensional definition of CSR would involve pointing out those phenomena in business and management that instantiate this concept in real life, whereas an intensional definition would involve specifying those general attributes that each are necessary, and conjunctively are sufficient conditions for the concept to apply. It is obvious that developing an intensional definition is the primary objective of CSR theory building, whereas producing an extensional definition is necessary for empirical research and CSR measurement. It should be clear, however, that the intension and extension of a concept are two sides of the same coin and

---

[1] The distinction between intensional and extensional definitions of a concept is also referred to as the distinction between 'meaning' (or 'sense') and 'reference', or between 'connotation' and 'denotation'. The distinction comes from (philosophical) logic and is commonly attributed to Gottlob Frege (1892). Through logical positivism, the distinction found its way into the social sciences. Sartori (1970) gives an informative and accessible account for the social sciences.

that good academic use of any concept requires that we capitalize on both simultaneously. Kant observed over two centuries ago that measurements without theoretical guidance are blind (because they lump together things that are not systematically related) while purely theoretical concepts—regardless of their analytical sophistication—are empty (because they do not refer to anything in real life).[2] We return to the relationship between intensional and extensional definitions of CSR below.

A second distinction that is relevant for concept evaluation in social science pertains to the ambition of the theory in which the scrutinized concept figures. Positive theory aims to describe and explain the world as we find it, whereas normative theory is ultimately justificatory in that it strives to provide reasons that would justify a way of looking at the world in terms of what it ought to be like. The distinction can be understood in terms of the 'direction of fit' (Searle, 1983). Positive theory has a 'theory-to-world' direction of fit, such that if the world as we find it does not accord with how we conceptually understand it, it is our conceptual understanding that should be revised. Normative theory, in contrast, has a 'world-to-theory' direction of fit, implying that if the world conflicts with our normative conceptualizations, it is the world, rather than our conceptualizations, that ought to give way (Searle, 1983). Although the CSR literature contains both positive and normative research (de Bakker *et al.*, 2005), the ambitions of individual publications are often confounded or left implicit. We return to the ambitions of CSR theorizing below.

A final distinction pertains to the explanatory aspirations of CSR research. Although explanation is often seen exclusively as part of positive theorizing, it figures prominently in normative theorizing too. In more or less the same way that we do not expect our positive theories to be independent of matters of fact, we should not expect our normative theories to be self-evident without further explanation. Explanation, in our view, is best seen as an argumentative relationship between premises on the one hand, and a conclusion on the other. Whether the explanation has a positive or normative ambition depends not only on the kind of conclusion to be drawn, but also on the nature of the premises, as one cannot validly draw a normative conclusion from exclusively positive premises (Moore, 1983). Regardless of the ultimate ambition of explanatory arguments, however, the CSR concept can figure within explanations in two different ways (Hempel and Oppenheim, 1948). It can figure as an *explanandum*, in which case CSR is explained by other premises, or it can function as *explanans*, meaning that it is used to explain something else. Although both kinds of arguments can be found in the CSR literature, the latter kind has dominated empirical research (Rowley and Berman, 2000). This fact alone is telling and we shall attend to it below.

---

[2] Of course Kant was not primarily concerned with questions of measurement and operationalization. He literally said: 'Thoughts without content are empty; intuitions without concepts are blind' (1965/1787: 75).

A SHORT BIOGRAPHY OF THE CSR CONCEPT

Conceptual analysis is often facilitated by an awareness of the intellectual history of the concept, if only to grasp how present understandings result from historical contingencies and path-dependencies. Both literature review (Carroll, 1999) and bibliometrical analysis (de Bakker *et al.*, 2005) support the conclusion that the notion of CSR originated in the 1950s and that it pioneered the emergence of the business and society field. Although the societal dimension of economic organization was already on the academic agenda before World War II (e.g. Barnard, 1968), Carroll takes Howard R. Bowen to be the 'father of Corporate Responsibility' (1999: 270). His book *The Social Responsibilities of the Businessman* (*sic*) was pioneering in exploring the responsibilities of executives to pursue actions and policies that 'are desirable in terms of the objectives and values of our society' (Bowen, 1953: 6). Others soon followed suit, and by the 1970s the intuition that business had some form of social responsibility over and above its responsibility to perform economically had already been cashed out in a number of publications (Frederick, 1960; Davis and Blomstrom, 1966; Walton, 1967). Although these publications often provided crude definitions of CSR, the predominant concern was to drive home the argument that CSR is desirable, either in its own right (cf. Frederick, 1960; McGuire, 1963) or because it is in the long-term economic interest of corporations to engage in it (cf. Davis, 1960; Johnson, 1971). As we shall see, this—mostly implicit— 'justificatory' stance of early CSR research has had a major impact on the way the CSR framework evolved.

The following decades witnessed many attempts to conceptually come to grips with the notion of CSR. But as Carroll (1999) observes, this resulted in a 'proliferation' of definitions rather than the construction of a systematic conceptual framework. The only common element in these diverse conceptualizations remained the rather unsophisticated intuition that business ought to be concerned with 'issues beyond the narrow economic, technical, and legal requirements of the firm' (Davis, 1973: 312). That CSR became a popular topic for empirical research from the 1980s onward did not remedy the conceptual confusion, due to serious measurement problems and a self-justificatory bias in research questions (Rowley and Berman, 2000). By the turn of the century, competing conceptualizations, such as stakeholder theory and the notion of corporate citizenship, had emerged and were claiming ground in the business and society field (Carroll, 1999; de Bakker *et al.*, 2005). In addition to the familiar confusion over what CSR means, this created puzzles as to how these different—and at least partially overlapping—concepts relate to each other.

The upshot is that the business and society field presently lacks both solid conceptual foundations and a systematic research tradition (van Oosterhout and Heugens, forthcoming). The most popular concepts are typically used in a very loose manner. There is hardly any systematic—let alone cumulative—relationship between empirical research and theory building efforts, as novel frameworks appear to be introduced at will. As Matten and Crane (2005) observe, even the brightest minds succumb to the temptation to introduce new notions (e.g. corporate citizenship) that cover substantially the same ground as the old ones (e.g. CSR) without adding any insight that would justify conceptual innovation (e.g. Carroll, 1998).

CSR Theory and the Intension of the CSR Concept

One observation about the evolution of the notion of CSR is of particular interest from the perspective of a more systematic conceptual analysis. This is the fact that the CSR concept evolved from predominantly *normative* origins (Matten *et al.*, 2003). Rather than resulting from an attempt to explain actual business behavior, it was the normative debate about whether corporations had social responsibilities over and above their economic self-interest that sparked CSR research (cf. Davis, 1973). This normative origin is more than an interesting historical idiosyncrasy, as it is indicative of a normative bias in CSR theorizing (see also: Matten *et al.*, 2003). It accounts for the way in which the concept has evolved and for the present state of the business and society field. Yet contrary to some authors (Matten and Crane, 2005; Rowley and Berman, 2000), we do not believe that the notion of CSR can be saved when this bias is corrected for, as it is inherent in the conceptual structure of CSR.

A casual inspection of the terminology used to denote CSR already suggests that there is a normative dimension to our conceptual understanding of the concept. Most scholars agree that *Corporate Social Responsibility* is about (*a*) the *social*, hence not specifically or particularly addressed, (*b*) *responsibility*, which is commonly understood in this context as the consequentialist equivalent of the deontological notion of 'duty' (Goodin, 1986), of (*c*) *corporations*, which typically refers not only to corporate *legal* entities but to business organizations in general. In this typical yet unsophisticated account, the answer to the *positive* question of what CSR is, will be a function of the answer to the *normative* question of which responsibilities business organizations owe to society to begin with. And this is not just the case with unsophisticated understandings of CSR. Even the most refined conceptualizations are ultimately premised on some normative background argument establishing what it ought to be.

Carroll's (1979: 500) well-known definition of CSR as encompassing 'the economic, legal, ethical and discretionary expectations that society has of organizations at any point in time' is a case in point. For how could these expectations constitute corporate responsibilities if one does not assume that they are justified and that business organizations therefore ought to contribute in some way to their realization? In general: your expectations towards A will only lead to A's responsibility to meet them if they are justified. Without justification your expectations are just that. They would have no logical connection to any responsibility that A has. That there is a normative dimension to the CSR concept, however, is not just because of talk about (justified) expectations. The general issue is that the notion of CSR can only have a discernible meaning against a background of normative premises that tell us what is desirable, and that business organizations have a responsibility to (help) bring about that desirable state of affairs. Without these normative premises, it could not be clear what CSR is and what it is not.

Tellingly, CSR researchers typically assume rather than elaborate on these premises, even though their veracity and acceptability are far from obvious. Even Carroll's widely accepted 'domains approach' to CSR, which has been refined and revised over the years (Carroll, 1991; Pinkston and Carroll, 1996; Schwartz and Carroll, 2003), is subject to debate. The issue does not concern the economic and legal responsibilities of business. Even a one-eyed neoclassical economist like Milton Friedman agrees that business has the responsibility 'to use its resources and engage in activities designed to increase its profits so long as it stays within the rules of the game' (Friedman and Friedman, 1962: 133). Instead, the disagreement is about the ethical and discretionary responsibilities of business, and therefore about what distinguishes CSR from everyday business. That precisely the features that distinguish CSR from ordinary business responsibilities are disputed, makes it a contested rather than an established concept.

CSR is not alone, however, in that there are many concepts in the social sciences that are all but beyond dispute. Examples include the notions of efficiency in economics, power and legitimacy in political science, integration in sociology, and freedom in political theory (cf. Connolly, 1974). Gallie (1956) uses the term 'essentially contested concepts' to denote such inherently unclear and disputable concepts. Conceptual disputes typically arise because there is an irreducibly normative dimension to the meaning of these concepts (Taylor, 1985). Yet in spite of their contested status, many of these concepts are firmly embedded within the disciplines in which they figure. To delete them from the disciplinary vocabularies would come down to dispensing with these disciplines altogether. This is not the case with the notion of CSR, as we can well imagine there being a field of business and society without it. So what makes the notion of CSR different?

In our view, the main point is that CSR is hardly doing any explanatory work. There are only a few studies that attempt to explain why business organizations engage in CSR activities or what CSR means in the first place (e.g. Aguilera *et al.*,

2007; McWilliams and Siegel, 2001).[3] Yet in spite of it being highly ambiguous what CSR is, the notion has been used extensively as an explanans to explain corporate financial performance (or CFP)—with mixed conclusions (Rowley and Berman, 2000). While Orlitzky et al. (2003) find an overall positive relationship through a meta-analysis of the many studies that have been published on the CSR–CFP relationship, Griffin and Mahon (1997) report mixed results due to the wide variety of measures and methodologies used. It should be emphasized here that it is highly ambiguous what is explained in CFP by CSR if we really do not know what CSR is, other than a mostly implicit assumption that business organizations owe something to society.

CSR's explanatory track record is therefore rather poor. Insofar as it has played any explanatory role in normative or positive theories in business and society it has figured mostly as an explanans, and even then almost exclusively to explain CFP rather than anything else (Rowley and Berman, 2000). This unidirectional focus of CSR research reveals an implicitly normative, self-justificatory concern, as the explanatory relationship in which CSR is used to explain CFP is typically used as a justification of CSR itself. This not only makes much of CSR theory blatantly circular, but it also confounds normative and positive claims. It is clear that both are highly undesirable. Proper theorizing ought to be concerned with explaining propositions from other premises and with a clear separation of positive and normative arguments (see van Oosterhout et al., 2006: 533–4). If we are to do things right in the field of business and society, we need to doubly unpack the theoretical relations that now constitute much of CSR research. Not only do we need to explain CSR itself before we attempt to explain anything from it, but we also need to carefully separate normative and positive arguments in a way that enables both better positive and normative theorizing. Yet we believe that if we do precisely that, the notion of CSR can be deleted without loss. This will become clear after discussing the problems pertaining to the extension of the CSR concept.

CSR MEASUREMENT AND THE EXTENSION OF THE NOTION OF CSR

An alternative way of defining a concept is to assess its extension (or denotation): the 'class of things to which the word applies' (Salmon, 1963: 90) or the 'totality of objects indicated by that word' (Sartori, 1970: 1041). When business and society

[3] In spite of the fact that these two studies attempt to explain CSR from other premises, both take the meaning of CSR more or less for granted.

researchers explore an organization's manifest social responsibilities, they typically do not study CSR but its *Corporate Social Performance* or CSP. This is because responsibilities—like duties—are located in normative space and can therefore neither be observed directly, nor have an unambiguous domain of observable phenomena to which they refer. Observables only result when an actor accepts (or denies) a certain duty, and follows up by endorsing (or challenging) that duty with corresponding behaviors. In the case of CSR, we can only observe manifest corporate extra-legal and extra-economical behaviors, and infer that these behaviors simultaneously signal (*a*) the corporate actor's recognition of a given social responsibility, and (*b*) its attempts to meet that responsibility. Neither assertion is likely to be wholly unproblematic. For now, it suffices to acknowledge that corporate responsibilities and corporate actions are not simply two of a kind.

There is no lack of CSP studies. In a comprehensive bibliometrical analysis, de Bakker *et al.* (2005) identified 155 CSP papers, all published between 1972 and 2002. Many scholars apparently try to avoid the philosophically challenged concept of CSR by studying more readily observable corporate actions. The abundance of CSP research evidences an unarticulated desire by business and society scholars to leave the difficult task of intensionally defining CSR behind and focus their efforts on staking out what companies actually do to meet their social responsibilities. This 'flight forward' does not resolve their problems, however, because at least two issues remain.

First, by studying actual corporate behaviors, business and society researchers loosen the ties between their empirical work and the concept of CSR. This seems like an attractive move, as one can do meaningful descriptive scientific work on corporate extra-legal and extra-economical behaviors while the underlying conceptual issues are still pending. But by creating a wedge between concept formation and empirical research, these researchers disregard the epistemic insight that operationalizations of CSR (its extension) only make sense when they are closely related to theoretical definitions of CSR (its intension). By ignoring the conceptual issues, they are creating a body of empirical results that is vulnerable to the imperialistic ambitions of other social science disciplines, which seek to explain the same results by other conceptual means. If a field presents itself as little more than a collection of 'data looking for a theory' (cf. Wood, 1991; Zenisek, 1979), one should not be surprised if sooner or later some 'extra-disciplinary' theory will appear on the scene capable of explaining previously 'intra-disciplinary' phenomena.[4] Second, even if we take CSP as the empirical manifestation of a firm's self-accepted social

---

[4] A case in point is provided by the concept of non-market strategy (Baron, 1995). Here an outsider to the business-and society field lays claim to a number of concepts that were previously intra-disciplinary, and explains them with tools borrowed from strategic management. Other examples include Hill and Jones (1992) using agency theory, Rowley (1997) using network theory, Frooman (1999) using resource dependence theory, and Coff (1999) using the resource-based view of the firm—all explaining important CSP-related findings with the powerful aid of extra-disciplinary theories.

responsibilities, the issue of how to operationalize and measure this construct remains. Scholars agree that CSP is a 'multidimensional construct' (Rowley and Berman, 2000; Waddock and Graves, 1997) or a 'composite term' (Bendheim *et al.*, 1995) that simultaneously refers to organizational inputs, transformation processes, and outputs, as well as the development of more holistic programs concerning corporate values or ethics. There is no uncontestable way of measuring such a complex construct, and this is not simply because researchers are unlikely to agree upon a clearly demarcated empirical domain for it. Prior attempts to identify the extension of CSP have all fallen victim to one of four interrelated problems: (1) negative extension; (2) under-inclusiveness; (3) category lumping; and (4) outcome fetishism.

Negative Extension

Many researchers define their core concept by stating what CSP is *not*. Telling in this respect is the use of so-called CSP screens, which are often used in empirical research to separate the sheep from the goats. A CSP screen is a straightforward (and usually quite crude) filter that prevents firms involved with certain types of business activities from being classified as 'socially responsible'. The screening approach is popular amongst CSP researchers, largely because the indexing firm KLD Research & Analytics, Inc. (<http://www.kld.com>) has a tradition of making screening-based data sets available to the academic community. Numerous prior studies have used the KLD data (e.g. Berman *et al.*, 1999; Deckop *et al.*, 2006; Graves and Waddock, 1994; Johnson and Greening, 1999; McWilliams and Siegel, 2001; Turban and Greening, 1997; Waddock and Graves, 1997). We focus on KLD's most important social investment index—the Domini 400 Social Index or DSI—to illustrate how screens work, and why a reliance on screens is a bad way of extensionally defining CSP.

The DSI consists of a dynamic set of 400 publicly listed US firms, roughly composed of 250 Standard & Poor (S&P) 500 companies, 100 other companies chosen for sector diversification, and 50 additional companies with 'exemplary' social and environmental records. To become eligible for inclusion, companies must have a demonstrated potential for high financial performance.[5] From this

---

[5] For many academic studies on the relationship between CSP and corporate financial performance (CFP), this raises the issue of sampling on the dependent variable. As an investment analyst, it is KLD's deliberate intention to select firms that generate better-than-average financial returns. If a researcher subsequently tries to assess the differential performance of firms that have been screened into one of the KLD indexes and firms that have been screened out, he or she may well find a performance effect for KLD membership. Moreover, the effect is likely to be positive, as poorly performing firms are likely to have been dropped from the KLD basket. The point is, of course, that even if there is a positive performance effect of being screened into one of the KLD indexes, it is empirically impossible to determine whether this effect should be attributed to the potentially positive performance implications

larger set of high-performing firms, KLD then weeds out all companies involved with alcohol, tobacco, firearms, gambling, nuclear power, and military weapons. KLD subsequently adds a number of refinements, such as individual company assessments on criteria like diversity, employee relations, and human rights, but at its core the KLD index construal approach relies on the categorical exclusion of certain industries to separate 'responsible' from 'irresponsible' companies. This is not an adequate way of extensionally defining CSP for two reasons.

First, with respect to the denotation of allegedly irresponsible corporate behavior, it is not clear on which grounds certain industries are excluded. Entine (2003) traces the origin of so-called 'sin screens' condemning the use of alcohol, tobacco, and gambling to 18th century religious beliefs held by minority factions in the United States, noting that the Quakers were the first to withdraw their business from organizations involved with such 'sinful' behaviors. It is probably fair to say that the categorical exclusion of companies involved with the production of alcoholic beverages is overly moralistic in many contemporary Western societies, in which (moderate) alcohol consumption is a generally accepted part of social life.

Second, the screening approach remains silent with respect to the denotation of responsible corporate behavior. It defines responsibility *negatively* by stating that responsible firms are those that abstain from the production of alcohol, cigarettes, etc. Yet, firms operating in sectors that are eligible for inclusion in the DSI are not all angels. Companies in uncontested industries can still do very bad things, and there are clearly more and less responsible ways of operating in contested industries. In sum, the screening approach is flawed because of the ambiguous grounds on which the screens are defined and applied.

Under-Inclusiveness

As stated, CSP is a complex, multidimensional construct that refers to many aspects of corporate behavior. According to established views in the field, CSP ought to reference various stakeholder groups (Clarkson, 1995), address multiple societal issues (Wartick and Cochran, 1985), and span multiple dimensions of corporate behavior (Wood, 1991). Yet many authors rely on singular operationalizations of CSP (Rowley and Berman, 2000). Some authors have operationalized CSP strictly as environmental pollution control (Chen and Metcalf, 1980; Judge and Douglas, 1998; Spicer, 1978), measures to prevent corporate illegal behaviors (Baucus, 1989; Davidson and Worrell, 1988), and efforts to recall bogus products (Davidson and Worrell, 1992; Bromiley and Marcus, 1989). As others have pointed out (Griffin and

of CSP, or to the exceptional quality of the KLD analysts for picking 'winners' in the stock market. Thus, prudent researchers should avoid using KLD membership as a proxy for above-par CSP, especially if their ambition is to use CSP as an explanatory variable for CFP.

Mahon, 1997; Rowley and Berman, 2000), such singular operationalizations raise issues of validity and reliability.

A measure is valid when it evidences a satisfactory correspondence between the measurement scores and the 'true' properties of a phenomenon under investigation (Cronbach and Meehl, 1955). Single-item measures are unlikely to be valid proxies for CSP because they 'inadequately reflect the breadth of the construct' (Griffin and Mahon, 1997: 25). Seen through the multiple-issue interpretation of CSP (Wartick and Cochran, 1985), measuring a company's performance on the issue of environmental pollution is unlikely to yield a valid estimate of that company's CSP profile, as it reveals no information on its performance on other issues like human rights, racial diversity, child labor, and employee safety. Similarly, seen through the stakeholder lens (Freeman, 1984), a company's social policies with respect to consumers are not informative about its performance towards financiers, suppliers, and regulators.

A measure is reliable when it yields a satisfactory consistency across various measurement scores obtained from a phenomenon under investigation (Cronbach, 1951). Note that reliability has to do with the relationships amongst the test scores themselves rather than their relationship with the phenomenon. Strictly speaking, it is impossible to assess the reliability of single-item measures in a cross-sectional research design, because there are no other measures available for systematic comparison. Thus, the single-item approach to CSP measurement is flawed because of the limited validity and reliability of the measurement scores it yields.

Category Lumping

A third way of operationalizing CSP is by using multiple-item measures that do more justice to the multidimensional nature of CSP (cf. Rowley and Berman, 2000; Griffin and Mahon, 1997). The simplest way of treating this type of data is to collect firm scores on a number of items related to its social performance, and to subsequently add these scores up into a single aggregate measure. KLD's company-specific CSP scores are a case in point (see Waddock and Graves, 1997: 317–19). In the early 1990s, KLD used to assess a given company's CSP on eight different dimensions,[6] notably: (1) community involvement, (2) treatment of women and minorities, (3) employee relations, (4) environmental stewardship, (5) product quality and safety, (6) business involvement in South Africa before Apartheid was abolished, (7) military weapons-related contracting, and (8) involvement with the production of nuclear power. Companies could obtain scores ranging from −2 (very poor performance) to +2 (excellent performance) on the first five dimensions, and scores ranging from −2 to 0 on the last three (as these latter dimensions were

---

[6] The dimensions have been altered since, but not the rating procedure, so the illustrative potential of this example remains intact.

only seen as areas for concern, not as areas in which a company could excel). Common practice has long been to aggregate these scores into a single variable without weighting or controlling for measurement error, which would in this case result in a single CSP variable with a spread from −16 to +10. Studies in which CSP is treated as a simple aggregate of multiple dimensions include (but are certainly not limited to): Deckop *et al.* (2006); Igalens and Gond (2005); Ruf *et al.* (1998, 2001); and Waddock and Graves (1997). Aggregate measures, however, come with a number of problems.

First, aggregation destroys information. It is not that aggregation is a bad technique *per se*, as adding items that share a lot of variance does not destroy all that much information and may allow for the use of simple statistical techniques that are not hampered too much by unrealistic or overly restrictive assumptions (such as OLS regressions). The problem with CSP data is that the various items typically share very little variance. Various studies have demonstrated that the KLD dimensions, for example, are only weakly correlated (Berman *et al.*, 1999; Johnson and Greening, 1999). By aggregating such orthogonal factors, we lose precisely the information that is strategically most relevant: is a firm with an average score 'stuck in the middle' because it pays moderate attention to all its stakeholders (Porter, 1980), or is it instead pursuing an aggressive differentiation strategy whereby it squeezes certain stakeholders in order to please others (Carter and Deephouse, 1999)? With aggregate measures, we will never know. As Griffin and Mahon have put it: 'Collapsing [CSP's] multiple dimensions into a unidimensional index may mask the individual dimensions that are equally important and relevant' (1997: 25).

It is not just that we lose valuable information through aggregation. Aggregation only makes sense when it is based on reasons that both explain *how* we should aggregate—as there are endless ways in which even a small number of variables can be aggregated—and provide some *justification* for aggregation to begin with. Without such reasons, it is impossible to tell what a composite measure is a measure of, let alone put this measure to work in explaining something else. The logic that should underlie any aggregation exercise can consist either of empirical, theoretical, or normative reasons, or of a combination of these. Empirical reasons exist when scores on different variables are actually related in some observable manner. Theoretical reasons may explain why there exist correlations between these variables to begin with, or provide a rationale for aggregation even in the absence of obvious empirical correlations, as relationships between variables are sometimes more complex (e.g. non-linear, non-additive; see Fiss, 2007) than straightforward statistical techniques are able to handle. Think of the many different ways in which we can conceive and operationalize corporate performance. It is widely accepted that corporate performance has a financial, an ecological, and a social dimension, but there is no obvious way in which these three dimensions can be reduced to a single variable. Yet each dimension is important to an overall evaluation of corporate performance and it may therefore be necessary to aggregate all of them in some systematic manner in order to explore determinants and consequences of overall corporate performance. The example illustrates that there may also be normative reasons to aggregate scores on different variables, as different kinds of performance may serve different interests and ultimate values that each merit some consideration. The upshot is that in the absence of a rationale, aggregation of different variables into a single measure will be just about as sensible as adding the phone numbers in a telephone directory.

An alternative to aggregation that meets most of these concerns is to use *multiple* operationalizations for CSR/CSP. In order to do meaningful empirical work, one then has to resort to more sophisticated statistical techniques that use some kind of factorial analysis that preserves the unique information enclosed in all dimensions of the CSR/CSP construct by keeping them separate, such as correspondence analysis (see Lamertz *et al.*, 2005, for an application) or structural equations modeling (see Johnson and Greening, 1999; Judge and Douglas, 1998; Maignan and Ferrell, 2000; and Rehbein and Schuler, 1999, for applications). But even though these techniques are gaining popularity, they are not yet commonly used and accepted by all CSP scholars. In sum, many multiple-item CSP measures are flawed because they use simple aggregation techniques that not only destroy essential information concerning firms' CSP profile, but may also result in non-sensible measures that are of little explanatory use.

Outcome Fetishism

When scholars extensionally define CSP, they must choose between measuring organizational inputs, core transformation processes, or outcomes (or some combination of the above). Most scholars tend to operationalize CSP as an outcome variable. Jones (1980) has long argued against an output orientation, mostly on grounds that it is difficult to reach consensus as to what constitutes an appropriate level of CSP. Interestingly, the discussion as to whether scholars should be measuring outputs or processes has recently emerged in the field of corporate strategy too (cf. Henderson and Cockburn, 1994; Ray *et al.*, 2004; Schroeder *et al.*, 2002). This may come as a surprise to some, since the entire raison d'être of the strategy field lies in its potential to explain a single outcome variable, i.e. sustainably superior firm performance (cf. Rumelt *et al.*, 1994). Yet, according to Ray and his colleagues (2004), it may not always be wise to focus on firm performance in case one wants to understand the behavior of business organizations. Their arguments against an exclusive outcome orientation are highly relevant to the CSP debate.

First, both CFP and CSP are aggregated dependent variables. Mediocre CFP or CSP may obscure a firm's outstanding performance on key transformation processes when these peaks are leveled in the aggregate by poor performance on other processes. By aggregating data in the form of CSP or CFP one therefore loses sight of the drivers of that performance, which makes purposive intervention in ongoing systems difficult. Second, there is no reason to assume that CFP or CSP will neatly materialize within the boundaries of the firm. As Coff (1999) notes, the fact that we do not see a firm realizing high levels of CFP does not imply that high performance is not taking place. If, for example, a firm's stakeholders experience an increase in their bargaining power over the firm—either because they gain control over critical resources (Frooman, 1999) or learn how to operate social influencing mechanisms (Mahon *et al.*, 2004; Rowley, 1997)—they may be able to appropriate a larger piece of the residual than if they lacked such power. Yet a different distribution of the residual says little about the efficiency of the firm's transformation processes.[7] Especially if a firm operates under a weak appropriability regime (Teece, 1986), exceptional CFP may be redistributed over various stakeholders as a result of *ex post* bargaining (cf. Williamson, 1985; Zingales, 1998).

Of course, few companies are likely to voluntarily surrender profits to outsiders, but when it comes to CSP, redistributive effects may even be a part of the firm's deliberate CSR policies. The CSR policies of many firms are not intended to improve their own social performance, but instead the well-being of actors outside the firm's boundaries. Improving the working conditions in suppliers' plants or demanding that business partners in emerging markets apply certain standards with respect to child labor and pollution are cases in point. Policies aimed at creating such extra-organizational effects may not be visible as a higher CSP for the focal firm, but this does not imply that the firm's CSP does not increase. Hence, the positive effects of a firm's CSR policies may well—and often are intended to—materialize beyond the boundaries of the focal firm. In sum, many output-focused CSP measures are flawed because they are blind to the fundamental transformation processes behind good or bad CSP outcomes.

Is CSR Conceptually Epiphenomenal?

The question remains what role is left for the concept of CSR in the field of business and society. Our answer is that CSR is at best conceptually epiphenomenal in both normative and positive theorizing. An epiphenomenon is something that, although caused by some clearly delineated set of conditions, has no *significant* reciprocal relation to these conditions, nor to any other theoretically or empirically relevant factor. It is, in short, a kind of by-product. This somewhat pejorative connotation captures the message we want to convey here: although we do not—and

---

[7] That is, at least in the short run. In the longer run, a weak appropriability regime will of course affect the incentives to invest as it will influence expected returns.

cannot—deny that CSR research is about something, we hold that what the notion of CSR typically means to capture is best seen as a by-product of the work of other, more powerful conceptual schemes. We submit that CSR theorizing can be reduced without loss to economizing and legitimizing perspectives on business and society (cf. van Oosterhout and Heugens, forthcoming). It is beyond the scope of this contribution to argue this thesis extensively. We will, however, demonstrate how this thesis plays out with respect to *positive* CSR theorizing, as this is presently the most popular approach in business and society research.

Legitimizing and Economizing Perspectives on Business and Society

The legitimizing and economizing conceptual frameworks arguably present the two main theoretical pillars in the field of management and organization (Baum and Dobbin, 2000). The economizing framework is premised on methodological individualism and an understanding of human action that is motivated by self-interest and the rational maximization of whatever it is that one prefers (e.g. Blaug, 1992; Mueller, 2004). The framework has proven extraordinarily powerful both within (cf. Barney and Hesterly, 1996) and outside (cf. Becker, 1978; Mäki, 2001) the field of economic organization. In this chapter we take a deliberately broad view of the economizing perspective. It not only includes rational choice theory narrowly conceived, such as organizational economics (e.g. Milgrom and Roberts, 1992), agency theory (e.g. Jensen and Meckling, 1976), property rights theory (Grossman and Hart, 1986), and transaction cost theory (Williamson, 1985), but all theories that in some way rely on a self-interested and rational pursuit of superior outcomes. This perspective therefore also includes: structural contingency theory (e.g. Donaldson, 1995), resource dependence theory (e.g. Pfeffer and Salancik, 1978; Thompson, 1967), and strategic management theory (Rumelt *et al.*, 1994). The economizing conceptual framework is used to pursue not only positive but also normative theoretical ambitions. Classical welfare economics in general (Feldman, 1980; Mishan, 1981), and law and economics more specifically (Coase, 1988; Posner, 1977) both instantiate highly successful theories that aim to understand what an ideal institutional order would look like, rather than to explain the world as we find it. The latter is presently even a dominant perspective in normative institutional analysis (e.g. Kaplow and Shavell, 2001).

In contrast to the rational, individualist, and self-regarding stance of the economizing perspective, the legitimizing conceptual framework proceeds from the assumption that social reality contains 'chunks of irreducible social matter' (van Oosterhout, 2002: 125) that, through rule-like generalized expectations, provide the interpretative and legitimizing schemes that guide human and organizational action (e.g. Meyer *et al.*, 1997). This institutional perspective has developed across the boundaries of different disciplines (Goodin, 1996), with a focus on different levels of analysis (cf. Scott, 2001). At the current level of focus, gaining legitimacy means reaching a state in which an organization is seen as proper or appropriate 'within some socially constructed system of norms, values, beliefs, and definitions' (Suchman, 1995: 574). In order to become seen as legitimate, organizations must adopt certain structural, strategic, or symbolic features which signal their dedication to the 'rationalized myths' of the larger social system in which they operate (Meyer and Rowan, 1977).

The pressures that support adoption of those features range from (DiMaggio and Powell, 1983) (a) coercion, which occurs when actors upon whom these organizations depend for support favor adoption of certain policies; through (b) uncertainty, which makes firms 'mimic' powerful exemplary organizations in order not to be left behind when the future consequences of behavior are unknown; to (c) prescription, which takes place when the environment exercises normative pressures on the focal organization (cf. Etzioni, 1975). Although organizations can defy or resist these isomorphic pressures (cf. Oliver, 1991), they do so only at the risk of delegitimation and deinstitutionalization. Like the economizing perspective, the legitimizing perspective has both positive and normative ambitions. But although normative institutional considerations have been used as explanans in many positive institutional explanations (Scott, 2001; Suchman, 1995), it is currently theoretically underdeveloped for justificatory purposes (cf. van Oosterhout and Heugens, forthcoming). We now turn to demonstrating how the positive explanatory work of the economizing and legitimizing frameworks makes the concept of CSR theoretically redundant in explaining phenomena that exemplify CSR theorizing.

CSR in Positive Research and Theorizing

Positive theorizing involves the development of theories that aim to predict and explain empirical facts ('what is') without any ambition to approve or disapprove of these facts ('what ought to be'). Even though 'much of the seminal work on CSR was largely normative' (Matten et al., 2003: 110), positive theorizing is immensely popular in the business and society field. A recent bibliometric analysis of 549 published CSR/CSP papers shows that only 2.9% of this work is explicitly normative (de Bakker et al., 2005). In other words, the vast majority of work in CSR/CSP has predominantly positive ambitions. To support our claim that the notion of CSR is largely redundant in the field of business and society, we demonstrate that an explanatory story can be told about phenomena that are typically taken to instantiate the notion of CSR without any reference to the concept of CSR itself. The phenomena we investigate involve (1) the appointment of stakeholder directors and (2) the adoption of formal ethics programs.

The Appointment of Stakeholder Directors

Many corporations choose to appoint stakeholder directors on their corporate boards as a way of acknowledging and anchoring stakeholder interests. As Mitchel *et al.* have voiced it, appointing directors on behalf of stakeholders is a way of putting a 'formal mechanism in place that acknowledges the importance of their relationship with the firm' (1997: 876). Empirical evidence supports the observation that stakeholder representation on boards is a salient feature of the contemporary business landscape. Luoma and Goodstein (1999), for example, studied 224 NYSE-listed firms over the 1984–94 period, and found that on average some 14% of these firms had appointed one or several stakeholder directors. Similarly, Hillman *et al.* (2001) studied 250 S&P firms in 1995, and found that these firms on average had appointed 2.4 stakeholder directors who were primarily affiliated with parties like customers, suppliers, or local communities.

We can make sense of the appointment of stakeholder directors, however, without reference to the concept of CSR, either as (part of) the explanans, or as a concept denoting the explanandum, that is, by understanding the appointment of stakeholder directors as an instantiation—and therefore operationalization— of CSR. For one thing, the appointment of stakeholder directors may very well be understood as a potentially efficient remedy against agency problems that may burden the relationship between the firm and its most important stakeholders (e.g. Hill and Jones, 1992). Suppliers and customers are specifically vulnerable to such agency problems, because problems of adverse selection and moral hazard (Akerlof, 1970; Arrow, 1985) may stand in the way of conducting efficient transactions between the firm and these parties (Hansmann, 1996). The joint realization of quality and product safety is a case in point. Similarly, the appointment of stakeholder directors can be seen as an act of co-optation that is motivated by the goal to internalize crucial external dependencies of the focal organization. Such co-optation of external directors is well known in the case of representatives of non-equity capital suppliers (Pfeffer and Salancik, 1978), but the same logic can be extended to any external party that may critically affect corporate flourishing (Jones, 1995). The appointment of stakeholder directors, in short, can be accounted for from an economizing perspective without any reference to the notion of CSR, or without taking it to be an instantiation of what CSR is about.

Alternatively, the appointment of stakeholder directors can be explained by appealing to the legitimizing logic of institutional theory (Suchman, 1995). That is, corporations may not actually appoint stakeholder directors because they hope to gain from it directly and instrumentally, but rather because of coercive, mimetic, and normative pressures they may experience through the organizational field (DiMaggio and Powell, 1983). Such pressures may drive them to adopt—cognitively or normatively—legitimized organizational features. Typically, there is a significant symbolic dimension to the adoption and diffusion of such features, which distinguishes legitimizing accounts from straightforward economizing explanations. Thus Staw and Epstein (2000), as well as Zbaracki (1998), for example, found that organizations typically devote considerable resources to external communication about the implementation of popular management techniques like TQM, even if their actual implementation lags behind the rhetoric. Similarly, Westphal and Zajac (1994) and Fiss and Zajac (2004) found that symbolic management is an important element in firms' corporate governance strategies, in that firms' public testimonies on the adoption of corporate governance reforms are often more important for appeasing shareholders than their actual adoption. As it happens, even exclusively symbolic adoptions of corporate governance reforms can have a significant positive effect on total shareholder value (Zajac and Westphal, 2004), which potentially brings symbolic action into the realm of economizing explanations. The gist of the issue, however, is that the notion of CSR figures nowhere in these legitimizing accounts of the appointment of stakeholder directors.

The Adoption of Formal Ethics Programs

Organizations increasingly try to influence organizational ethics through formal ethics programs (Weaver et al., 1999). Such programs include training activities, the adoption of ethical codes to set organizational norms and guide concrete behavior, formalized procedures for auditing and evaluating ethical standards, disciplinary processes set up to sanction those who fail to live up to ethical expectations, and formal ethics management departments. Weaver et al. (1999), for example, drawing on a sample of 254 large US companies, found that these businesses had on average implemented 2.7 elements of a formal ethics program, such as appointing an official ethics policy or an ethics officer. Similarly, Stevens et al. (2005) found that out of a paired sample of 407 Fortune 1,000 and non-Fortune 1,000 companies, 302 had adopted a formal code of ethics (74%).

It is tempting to see firms' adoption of formal ethics programs as an instance of CSR, but again it is possible to give an account of the prevalence of such programs that does not involve any reference to the notion of CSR. The economizing perspective offers one viable alternative. It can be maintained, for example, that a formal ethics program can be adopted as some kind of risk management tool (Godfrey, 2005). By improving the ethical climate of the organization, managers may seek to avoid excessive costs associated with risks like employee theft, fraud, and bribery. Furthermore, ethics programs may serve as legal insurance premiums, that is, as small investments in preventive measures which are deliberately made in order to avoid much greater liabilities in *ex post* litigation (Treviño et al., 1999).[8] Finally, organizations may adopt an ethics program when powerful stakeholders,

[8] In the United States, for example, corporations can significantly reduce their fine once they have been found guilty in criminal procedures by showing that an effective ethics program was in place. See on this the 2005 Federal Sentencing Guidelines, specifically Chapter 8 on organizational defendants at: <http://www.ussc.gov/orgguide.htm>.

like financiers or suppliers of critical production factors, threaten to discontinue their support of the organization if it does not do so (Frooman, 1999). In short, the economizing perspective is fully capable of providing a satisfactory account of the adoption of formal ethics programs. This account is wholly grounded in the—enlightened—self-interested behavior of economic agents and does not involve any reference to CSR, either as an explanans, or as a concept describing the explanandum.

The legitimizing perspective provides another plausible account of the adoption of formal ethics programs. According to legitimacy theorists, pressures favoring the adoption of legitimizing structures or strategies may result from the explicit normative or coercive demands of institutional actors like the state or the professions (DiMaggio and Powell, 1983; Meyer and Rowan, 1977), or from more implicit exemplary behavior of high-status peers in the field (Haveman, 1993). The United States Sentencing Commission (USSC) provides one illustration of a more explicit isomorphism-generating mechanism, as this organization 'softly' coerces business firms into adopting corporate ethics programs (see also note 8). The USSC guidelines not only offer reduced fines and penalties to organizations convicted of violating federal laws if they can offer proof of having taken (potentially) effective steps to guide their behavior (Weaver *et al.*, 1999), but also provide a standard of appropriate behavior. Similarly, the Conference Board—a high profile Washington-based business association—illustrates the more implicit mimicking mechanisms alluded to earlier. At its annual ethics meeting, it usually presents 'best practice' cases of how high-status organizations have successfully implemented ethics programs. Attending companies without such programs, who are uncertain about their impact on future business performance, are likely to minimize future regret by imitating successful peers (Weaver *et al.*, 1999). Again, especially in the case of coercive institutional pressures, the boundaries between the economizing and legitimizing perspectives begin to blur. More significant, however, is the fact that the CSR notion again proves unnecessary to explain the proliferation of formal ethics programs.

SUMMARY AND CONCLUSION

It is hard to deny that there is something appealing about the notion of CSR. First, it has a strong mobilizing quality. Under its banner, generations of scholars have investigated the impact of managerial decisions on the social environment of business as well as the reciprocal influence of such decisions on corporate performance (Carroll, 1999). Second, it operates as a real-world focal point for managerial initiatives at the business–society interface. A broad range of activities that were previously known under diffuse labels like corporate philanthropy, corporate community involvement, issues-, ethics-, and sustainability management, as well as stakeholder integration, -management, and -dialogue, are now conveniently rubricated under the more encompassing heading of CSR, and presented as if they were an integrated and coherent set of policies and outcomes. Unfortunately, these mobilizing and organizing qualities alone constitute an insufficient basis for the concept of CSR to make sound academic sense.

Our evaluation of the notion of CSR in the field of management and organization began with an assessment of the concept's intensional and extensional definitions. Sadly, we found that no satisfactory intensional definition of CSR—one that specifies with precision and clarity which conjunction of attributes makes up the concept—is available or to be expected. Equally pitiful is that each of the available extensive definitions of CSR—which are supposed to point out the real-life phenomena to which the concept refers—is troubled by one or several of four operationalization problems that we discussed at length. Even more serious, however, is the fact more than 50 years of CSR research and theory building has not resulted in a systematic relationship between the notion's intension or theoretical conceptualizations, on the one hand, and its extension or empirical operationalizations, on the other. In the absence of such a systematic relationship one can take neither CSR theory building, nor empirical research on CSR, very seriously.

CSR scholars have responded to the resulting conceptual confusion with a number of conceptual revisions (Waddock, 2004). The general tendency of these revisions has been to complement the notion of CSR with conceptual annexes that were meant to include domains of meaning allegedly left out by the original understanding of CSR. The latter, which is now referred to as CSR1 ('corporations' obligation to work for social betterment'; Frederick, 1994: 150), has been expanded to include CSR2 or 'corporate social responsiveness' ('the capacity of a corporation to respond to social pressures'; Frederick, 1994: 150). Although some welcomed the strategic, action-oriented connotations of this addition, cynical observers saw CSR2 merely as a managerial toolbox full of tricks and ploys that served to *avoid* the acceptance of more far-reaching social obligations. Things got considerably worse when the notion was stretched further to CSR3, or 'corporate social rectitude' (Frederick, 1986), and CSR4 or 'corporate social religiosity' (Frederick, 1998), which apparently serves to capture some corporate 'obligation' to recognize and respect members' need for spirituality.

The upshot of these revisions, however, has only been to strengthen the case against CSR. Not only have they stretched the notion beyond meaningful confines (Sartori, 1970), but the propagation of CSR3 and CSR4 has sought to include in our understanding of CSR areas of life that both academe and liberal democracy prefer to see banishe to the private domain. The incorporation of religion and spirituality into conceptualizations of CSR, in particular, threatens to inflate CSR to totalitarian proportions, bringing with it the non-trivial risk that the organizations that adopt it turn into total institutions of Stalinesque proportions. But what seals CSR's fate, in our view, is the simple fact of the notion's redundancy in both positive and normative theorizing in business and society.

We have demonstrated only its redundancy in positive theorizing in the present contribution, but there is no reason to assume that it will fare better in normative theory (cf. van Oosterhout and Heugens, forthcoming). For decades, CSR researchers have labored to collect exemplars of corporate extra-legal and extra-economical behaviors, but due to weak conceptualizations and operationalizations they have merely crafted a significant pool of 'data in search of a theory' (Ullman, 1985: 540). We have shown that there are alternate theoretical frameworks available that have laid imperialistic eyes on CSR's alleged domain of empirical content. We have labeled these broad conceptual schemes as economizing and legitimizing theories. The former see CSR activities as rational means to corporate ends under specified conditions, the latter focus on the ceremonial qualities of such activities and their legitimizing potential in the eyes of critical constituencies. It is not just that these alternate frameworks score demonstrably better than the CSR perspective on general criteria for theory evaluation like parsimony, generalizability, and falsifiability (cf. Bacharach, 1989), but they also draw on more established disciplinary origins (i.e. economics and sociology; cf. Baum and Dobbin, 2000), while being able to generate more coherent and robust explanations for the type of phenomena CSR researchers claim as their object. Our final judgment, therefore, is that the notion of CSR is at best a conceptual epiphenomenon: a largely insignificant by-product of other conceptual schemes that can safely be removed from all future theorizing in management and organization. We propose that business and society scholars do so without further ado.

REFERENCES

Aguilera, R., Rupp, D., Williams, C., and Ganapathi, J. 2007. 'Putting the S Back in Corporate Social Responsibility: A Multi-level Theory of Social Change in Organizations'. *Academy of Management Review*, 32(3): 836–63.

Akerlof, G. 1970. 'The Market for Lemons: Qualitative Uncertainty and the Market Mechanism'. *Quarterly Journal of Economics*, 84: 488–500.

Arrow, K. J. 1985. 'The Economics of Agency', in J. W. Pratt and R. J. Zeckhauser (eds.), *Principals and Agents: The Structure of Business*. Boston: Harvard Business School Press.

Bacharach, S. B. 1989. 'Organizational Theories: Some Criteria for Evaluation'. *Academy of Management Review*, 14(4): 496–515.

Barnard, C. 1968. *The Functions of the Executive*. Cambridge, Mass.: Harvard University Press; 1st pub. 1938.

Barney, J., and Hesterly, W. 1996. 'Organizational Economics: Understanding the Relationship between Organizations and Economic Analysis'. *Handbook of Organization Studies*: 115–47.

BARON, D. 1995. 'Integrated Strategy: Market and Nonmarket Components'. *California Management Review*, 37(2): 47–65.

BAUCUS, M. S. 1989. 'Why Firms Do It and What Happens to Them: A Reexamination of the Theory of Illegal Corporate Behavior'. *Research in Corporate Social Performance and Policy*, 11: 93–118.

BAUM, J., and DOBBIN, F. 2000. *Economics Meets Sociology in Strategic Management.* Stamford, Conn.: JAI Press.

BECKER, G. 1978. *The Economic Approach to Human Behavior.* Chicago: University of Chicago Press.

BENDHEIM, C., WADDOCK, S., and GRAVES, S. 1998. 'Determining Best Practice in Corporate-Stakeholder Relations using Data Envelopment Analysis: An Industry-Level Study'. *Business & Society*, 37(3): 306–38.

BERMAN, S., WICKS, A., KOTHA, S., and JONES, T. 1999. 'Does Stakeholder Orientation Matter? The Relationship between Stakeholder Management Models and Firm Financial Performance'. *Academy of Management Journal*, 42(5): 488–506.

BLAUG, M. 1992. *The Methodology of Economics: Or How Economists Explain.* New York: Cambridge University Press.

BOWEN, H. R. 1953. *Social Responsibilities of the Businessman.* New York: Harper & Row.

BROMILEY, P., and MARCUS, A. 1989. 'The Deterrent to Dubious Corporate Behavior: Profitability, Probability and Safety Recalls'. *Strategic Management Journal*, 10(3): 233–50.

CARROLL, A. 1979. 'A Three-Dimensional Conceptual Model of Corporate Performance'. *Academy of Management Review*, 4(4): 497–505.

CARROLL, A. 1991. 'The Pyramid of Corporate Social Responsibility: Toward the Moral Management of Organizational Stakeholders'. *Business Horizons*, 34(4): 39–48.

——1998. 'The Four Faces of Corporate Citizenship'. *Business & Society Review*, 100(1): 1–7.

——1999. 'Corporate Social Responsibility: Evolution of a Definitional Construct'. *Business & Society*, 38(3): 268–95.

CARTER, S. M., and DEEPHOUSE, D. L. 1999. ' "Tough Talk" and "Soothing Speech:" A Comparison of Reputations for Being Tough and Being Good'. *Corporate Reputation Review*, 2: 308–32.

CHEN, K., and METCALF, R. 1980. 'The Relationship between Pollution Control Record and Financial Indicators Revisited'. *Accounting Review*, 55(1): 168–77.

CLARKSON, M. B. E. 1995. 'A Stakeholder Framework for Analyzing and Evaluating Corporate Social Performance'. *Academy of Management Review*, 20: 92–117.

COASE, R. 1988. *The Firm, the Market, and the Law.* Chicago: University of Chicago Press.

COFF, R. 1999. 'When Competitive Advantage Doesn't Lead to Performance: The Resource-Based View and Stakeholder Bargaining Power'. *Organization Science*, 10(2): 119–33.

CONNOLLY, W. E. 1974. *The Terms of Political Discourse.* Lexington, Mass.: Heath.

CRONBACH, L. J. 1951. 'Coefficient Alpha and the Internal Structure of Tests'. *Psychometrika*, 6: 297–334.

——and MEEHL, P. 1955. 'Construct Validity in Psychological Tests'. *Psychological Bulletin*, 52(4): 281–302.

DAVIDSON, W., and WORRELL, D. 1988. 'The Impact of Announcements of Corporate Illegalities on Shareholder Returns'. *Academy of Management Journal*, 31(1): 195–200.

————1992. 'The Effect of Product Recall Announcements on Shareholder Wealth'. *Strategic Management Journal*, 13(6): 467–73.

DAVIS, K. 1960. 'Can Business Afford to Ignore Social Responsibilities'. *California Management Review*, 2, spring: 70–6.

——1973. 'The Case for and against Business Assumption of Social Responsibilities'. *Academy of Management Journal*, 16(2): 312–22.

——and BLOMSTROM, R. L. 1966. *Business and its Environment*. New York: McGraw-Hill.

DE BAKKER, F. G. A., GROENEWEGEN, P., and DEN HOND, F. 2005. 'A Bibliometrical Analysis of 30 Years of Research and Theory on Corporate Social Responsibility and Corporate Social Performance'. *Business & Society*, 44(3): 283–317.

DECKOP, J., MERRIMAN, K., and GUPTA, S. 2006. 'The Effects of CEO Pay Structure on Corporate Social Performance'. *Journal of Management*, 32(3): 329–42.

DIMAGGIO, P. J., and POWELL, W. W. 1983. 'The Iron Cage Revisited: Institutional Isomorphism and Collective Rationality in Organizational Fields'. *American Sociological Review*, 48: 147–60.

DONALDSON, L. 1995. *American Anti-management Theories of Organization: A Critique of Paradigm Proliferation*. Cambridge: Cambridge University Press.

DONALDSON, T., and PRESTON, L. 1995. 'The Stakeholder Theory of the Corporation: Concepts, Evidence, and Implications'. *Academy of Management Review*, 20(1): 65–91.

ENTINE, J. 2003. 'The Myth of Social Investing'. *Organization & Environment*, 16(3): 352–68.

ETZIONI, A. 1975. *A Comparative Analysis of Complex Organizations: On Power, Involvement, and their Correlates*, 2nd edn. New York: The Free Press.

FELDMAN, A. M. 1980. *Welfare Economics and Social Choice Theory*. Boston and London: Nijhoff.

FISS, P. C. 2007. 'A Set-Theoretic Approach to Organizational Configurations', *Academy of Management Review* 32(4) 1180–98.

——and ZAJAC, E. 2004. 'The Diffusion of Ideas over Contested Terrain: The (Non) Adoption of a Shareholder Value Orientation among German Firms'. *Administrative Science Quarterly*, 49: 501–34.

FREDERICK, W. C. 1960. 'The Growing Concern over Business Responsibility'. *California Management Review*, 2(4): 54–6.

——1986. 'Toward CSR 3: Why Ethical Analysis is Indispensable and Unavoidable in Corporate Affaires'. *California Management Review*, 28(2): 126–41.

——1994. 'From CSR1 to CSR2: The Maturing of Business and Society Thought'. *Business & Society*, 33(2): 150–64.

——1998. 'Moving to CSR4: What to Pack for the Trip. *Business & Society*, 37(1): 40–9.

FREEMAN, R. E. 1984. *Strategic Management: A Stakeholder Approach*. Boston: Pitman.

FREGE, G. 1892. 'Über Sinn und Bedeutung'. *Zeitschrift für Philosophie und philosophische Kritik*, 100: 25–50.

FRIEDMAN, M., and FRIEDMAN, R. D. 1962. *Capitalism and Freedom*. Chicago: University of Chicago Press.

FROOMAN, J. 1999. 'Stakeholder Influence Strategies'. *Academy of Management Review*, 24(2): 191–205.

GALLIE, W. 1956. 'Essentially Contested Concepts'. *Proceedings of the Aristotelian Society*, 56: 167–98.

GARDBERG, N., and FOMBRUN, C. 2006. 'Corporate Citizenship: Creating Intangible Assets Across Institutional Environments'. *Academy of Management Review*, 31(2): 329–46.

GODFREY, P. 2005. 'The Relationship between Corporate Philanthropy and Shareholder Wealth: A Risk Management Perspective'. *Academy of Management Review*, 30(4): 777–98.

GOODIN, R. 1986. 'Responsibilities'. *Philosophical Quarterly*, 36(142): 50–6.

——1996. 'Institutions and their Design', in R. E. Goodin (ed.), *The Theory of Institutional Design*. Cambridge: Cambridge University Press, 1–53.

GRAVES, S., and WADDOCK, S. 1994. 'Institutional Owners and Corporate Social Performance'. *Academy of Management Journal*, 37(4): 1034–46.

GRIFFIN, J., and MAHON, J. 1997. 'The Corporate Social Performance and Corporate Financial Performance Debate: Twenty-Five years of Incomparable Research'. *Business & Society*, 36(1): 5–31.

GROSSMAN, S., and HART, O. 1986. 'The Costs and Benefits of Ownership: A Theory of Vertical and Lateral Integration'. *Journal of Political Economy*, 94(4): 691–719.

HANSMANN, H. 1996. *The Ownership of Enterprise*. Boston: Harvard University Press.

HAVEMAN, H. A. 1993. 'Follow the Leader: Mimetic Isomorphism and Entry into New Markets'. *Administrative Science Quarterly*, 38: 593–627.

HEMPEL, C. G., and OPPENHEIM, P. 1948. 'Studies in the Logic of Explanation'. *Philosophy of Science*, 15(2): 135–75.

HENDERSON, R., and COCKBURN, I. 1994. 'Measuring Competence? Exploring Firm Effects in Pharmaceutical Research'. *Strategic Management Journal*, 15 (Winter Special Issue): 63–84.

HILL, C., and JONES, T. 1992. 'Stakeholder-Agency Theory'. *Journal of Management Studies*, 29(2): 131–54.

HILLMAN, A. J., KEIM, G. D., and LUCE, R. A. 2001. 'Board Composition and Stakeholder Performance: Do Stakeholder Directors make a Difference? *Business & Society*, 40(3): 295–314.

IGALENS, J., and GOND, J. 2005. 'Measuring Corporate Social Performance in France: A Critical and Empirical Analysis of ARESE Data'. *Journal of Business Ethics*, 56(2): 131–48.

JENSEN, M. C., and MECKLING, W. H. 1976. 'The Theory of the Firm: Managerial Behavior, Agency Costs and Ownership Structure'. *Journal of Financial Economics*, 3: 305–60.

JOHNSON, H. 1971. *Business in Contemporary Society: Framework and Issues*. Belmont, Calif.: Wadsworth Publishing Co.

JOHNSON, R., and GREENING, D. 1999. 'The Effects of Corporate Governance and Institutional Ownership Types on Corporate Social Performance'. *Academy of Management Journal*, 42(5): 564–76.

JONES, T. 1980. 'Corporate Social Responsibility Revisited, Redefined'. *California Management Review*, 22(3): 59–67.

——1995. 'Instrumental Stakeholder Theory: A Synthesis of Ethics and Economics'. *Academy of Management Review*, 20(2): 404–37.

JUDGE, W., and DOUGLAS, T. 1998. 'Performance Implications of Incorporating Natural Environmental Issues into the Strategic Planning Process: An Empirical Assessment'. *Journal of Management Studies*, 35(2): 241–62.

KANT, I. 1965/1787. *Critique of Pure Reason*, trans. N. K. Smith. New York: St Martin's Press, 1st pub. 1787.

KAPLOW, L., and SHAVELL, S. 2001. 'Fairness versus Welfare'. *Harvard Law Review*, 114(4): 961–1388.

LAMERTZ, K., HEUGENS, P. P. M. A. R., and CALMET, L. 2005. 'The Configuration of Public Organizational Identities among Firms in the Canadian Beer Brewing Industry'. *Journal of Management Studies*, 42(4): 817–43.

LUOMA, P., and GOODSTEIN, J. 1999. 'Stakeholders and Corporate Boards: Institutional Influences on Board Composition and Structure'. *Academy of Management Journal*, 42(5): 553–63.

MCGUIRE, J. 1963. *Business and Society*. New York: McGraw-Hill.

MCWILLIAMS, A., and SIEGEL, D. 2001. 'Corporate Social Responsibility: A Theory of the Firm Perspective'. *Academy of Management Review*, 26(1): 117–27.

MAHON, J. F., HEUGENS, P. P. M. A. R., and LAMERTZ, K. 2004. 'Social Networks and Nonmarket Strategy'. *Journal of Public Affairs*, 4(2): 170–89.

MAIGNAN, I., and FERRELL, O. 2000. 'Measuring Corporate Citizenship in Two Countries: The Case of the United States and France'. *Journal of Business Ethics*, 23(3): 283–97.

—— and RALSTON, D. 2002. 'Corporate Social Responsibility in Europe and the US: Insights from Businesses' Self-Presentations'. *Journal of International Business Studies*, 33(3): 497–515.

MÄKI, U. 2001. *The Economic World View: Studies in the Ontology of Economics*. New York: Cambridge University Press.

MANNE, H. 1973. *The Modern Corporation and Social Responsibility*. American Enterprise Institute for Public Policy Research.

MATTEN, D., and CRANE, A. 2005. 'Corporate Citizenship: Toward an Extended Theoretical Conceptualization'. *Academy of Management Review*, 30(1): 166–79.

—— —— and CHAPPLE, W. 2003. 'Behind the Mask: Revealing the True Face of Corporate Citizenship'. *Journal of Business Ethics*, 45(1): 109–20.

MEYER, J. W., BOLI, J., THOMAS, G. M., and RAMIREZ, F. O. 1997. 'World Society and the Nation-State'. *American Journal of Sociology*, 103(1): 144–81.

—— and ROWAN, B. 1977. 'Institutionalized Organizations: Formal Structure as Myth and Ceremony'. *American Journal of Sociology*, 83(2): 340–63.

MILGROM, P. R., and ROBERTS, J. 1992. *Economics, Organization and Management*. Englewood Cliffs, NJ: Prentice Hall.

MISHAN, E. 1981. *Introduction to Normative Economics*. New York: Oxford University Press.

MITCHELL, R. K., AGLE, B. R., and WOOD, D. J. 1997. 'Toward a Theory of Stakeholder Identification and Salience: Defining the Principle of Who and What Really Counts. *Academy of Management Review*, 22(4): 853–86.

MOORE, G. 1993. *Principia Ethica*. Cambridge: Cambridge University Press.

MUELLER, D. 2004. 'Models of Man: Neoclassical, Behavioural and Evolutionary'. *Politics, Philosophy & Economics*, 3(1): 59–76.

OLIVER, C. 1991. 'Strategic Responses to Institutional Processes'. *Academy of Management Review*, 16: 145–79.

ORLITZKY, M., SCHMIDT, F. L., and RYNES, S. L. 2003. 'Corporate Social and Financial Performance: A Meta-analysis'. *Organization Studies*, 24(3): 403–41.

PFEFFER, J., and SALANCIK, G. 1978. *The External Control of Organizations: A Resource Dependence Perspective*. New York: Harper & Row.

PINKSTON, T. S., and CARROLL, A. B. 1996. 'Retrospective Examination of CSR Orientations: Have they Changed?' *Journal of Business Ethics*, 15(2): 199–206.

PORTER, M. E. 1980. *Competitive Strategy*. New York: Free Press.

Posner, R. 1977. *Economic Analysis of Law*. Boston: Little, Brown.

Ray, G., Barney, J. B., and Muhanna, W. A. 2004. 'Capabilities, Business Processes, and Competitive Advantage: Choosing the Dependent Variable in Empirical Tests of the Resource-Based View'. *Strategic Management Journal*, 25: 23–37.

Rehbein, K., and Schuler, D. 1999. 'Testing the Firm as a Filter of Corporate Political Action'. *Business & Society*, 38(2): 144–66.

Rowley, T. 1997. 'Moving beyond Dyadic Ties: A Network Theory of Stakeholder Influences'. *Academy of Management Review*, 22(4): 887–910.

——and Berman, S. 2000. 'A Brand New Brand of Corporate Social Performance'. *Business & Society*, 39(4): 397–418.

Ruf, B., Muralidhar, K., and Paul, K. 1998. 'The Development of a Systematic, Aggregate Measure of Corporate Social Performance'. *Journal of Management*, 24(1): 119–33.

————Brown, R., Janney, J., and Paul, K. 2001. 'An Empirical Investigation of the Relationship between Change in Corporate Social Performance and Financial Performance: A Stakeholder Theory Perspective'. *Journal of Business Ethics*, 32(2): 143–56.

Rumelt, R., Schendel, D., and Teece, D. 1994. *Fundamental Issues in Strategy*: Boston: Harvard Business School Press.

Salmon, W. C. 1963. *Logic*. Englewood Cliffs, NJ: Prentice Hall.

Sartori, G. 1970. 'Concept Misformation in Comparative Politics'. *American Political Science Review*, 64(4): 1033–53.

Schroeder, R., Bates, K., and Junttila, M. 2002. 'A Resource-Based View of Manufacturing Strategy and the Relationship to Manufacturing Performance'. *Strategic Management Journal*, 23(2): 105–17.

Schwartz, M. S., and Carroll, A. B. 2003. 'Corporate Social Responsibility: A Three-Domain Approach'. *Business Ethics Quarterly*, 13(4): 503–30.

Scott, W. R. 2001. *Institutions and Organizations*, 2nd edn. Thousand Oaks, Calif.: Sage.

Searle, J. 1983. *Intentionality: An Essay in the Philosophy of Mind*. Cambridge: Cambridge University Press.

Spicer, B. 1978. 'Investors, Corporate Social Performance and Information Disclosure: An Empirical Study'. *Accounting Review*, 53(1): 94–111.

Staw, B. M., and Epstein, L. D. 2000. 'What Bandwagons Bring: Effects of Popular Management Techniques on Corporate Performance, Reputation, and CEO Pay'. *Administrative Science Quarterly*, 45(3): 523–56.

Stevens, J., Steensma, K. H., Harrison, D., and Cochran, P. 2005. 'Symbolic or Substantive Document? The Influence of Ethics Codes on Financial Executives' Decisions'. *Strategic Management Journal*, 26(2): 181–95.

Suchman, M. 1995. 'Managing Legitimacy: Strategic and Institutional Approaches'. *Academy of Management Review*, 20(3): 571–610.

Taylor, C. 1985. *Philosophy and the Human Sciences*. Cambridge: Cambridge University Press.

Teece, D. 1986. 'Profiting from Technological Innovation: Implications for Integration, Collaboration, Licensing and Public Policy'. *Research Policy*, 15(6): 285–305.

Thompson, J. D. 1967. *Organizations in Action: Social Science Bases of Administrative Theory*. New York: McGraw-Hill.

Trevino, L., Weaver, G., Gibson, D., and Toffler, B. 1999. 'Managing Ethics and Legal Compliance: What Works and What Hurts'. *California Management Review*, 41(2): 131–51.

TURBAN, D., and GREENING, D. 1997. 'Corporate Social Performance and Organizational Attractiveness to Prospective Employees'. *Academy of Management Journal*, 40(3): 658–72.

ULLMAN, A. H. 1985. 'Data in Search of a Theory: A Critical Examination of the Relationships among Social Performance, Social Disclosure, and Economic Performance of US Firms'. *Academy of Management Review*, 10(3): 540–57.

VAN OOSTERHOUT, J. 2002. *The Quest for Legitimacy: On Authority and Responsibility in Governance*. Rotterdam: Erasmus Research Institute of Management.

—— 2005. 'Corporate Citizenship: An Idea whose Time has Not Yet Come'. *Academy of Management Review*, 30(4): 677–81.

—— and HEUGENS, P. P. M. A. R. Forthcoming. 'Cleaning out the Imperial Wardrobe: Conceptual Sense and Nonsense in the Business and Society Interface'. *RSM Erasmus University working paper*.

—— —— and KAPTEIN, M. 2006. 'The Internal Morality of Contracting: Advancing the Contractualist Endeavor in Business Ethics'. *Academy of Management Review*, 31(3): 521–39.

WADDOCK, S. 2004. 'Parallel Universes: Companies, Academics, and the Progress of Corporate Citizenship'. *Business Society Review*, 109(1): 5–42

—— and GRAVES, S. 1997. 'The Corporate Social Performance-Financial Performance Link'. *Strategic Management Journal*, 18(4): 303–19.

WALTON, C. 1967. *Corporate Social Responsibilities*. Belmont, Calif.: Wadsworth.

WARTICK, S. L., and COCHRAN, P. L. 1985. 'The Evolution of the Corporate Social Performance Model'. *Academy of Management Review*, 10(4): 758–69.

WEAVER, G., TREVINO, L., and COCHRAN, P. 1999. 'Integrated and Decoupled Corporate Social Performance: Management Commitments, External Pressures, and Corporate Ethics Practices'. *Academy of Management Journal*, 42(5): 539–52.

WESTPHAL, J. D., and ZAJAC, E. J. 1994. 'Substance and Symbolism in CEOs' Long-Term Incentive Plans'. *Administrative Science Quarterly*, 39(3): 367–90.

WILLIAMSON, O. E. 1985. *The Economic Institutions of Capitalism: Firms, Markets, Relational Contracting*. New York: Free Press.

—— 1991. 'Strategizing, Economizing, and Economic Organization'. *Strategic Management Journal*, 12: 75–94.

WOOD, D. 1991. 'Corporate Social Performance Revisited'. *Academy of Management Review*, 16(4): 691–718.

ZAJAC, E., and WESTPHAL, J. 2004. 'The Social Construction of Market Value: Institutionalization and Learning Perspectives on Stock Market Reactions'. *American Sociological Review*, 69(3): 433–57.

ZBARACKI, M. 1998. 'The Rhetoric and Reality of Total Quality Management'. *Administrative Science Quarterly*, 43(3): 602–5.

ZENISEK, T. 1979. 'Corporate Social Responsibility: A Conceptualization Based on Organizational Literature'. *Academy of Management Review*, 4(3): 359–68.

ZINGALES, L. 1998. 'Corporate Governance', in P. Newman (ed.), *The New Palgruve Dictionary of Economics and the Law*. London: Macmillan, 497–503.

PART IV

ACTORS AND DRIVERS

....

CHAPTER 10

TOP MANAGERS AS DRIVERS FOR CORPORATE SOCIAL RESPONSIBILITY

....

DIANE L. SWANSON

THE idea that top managers can be drivers for corporate social responsibility came from the business sector itself. Specifically, the roots to this literature can be traced to the 1950s when corporate leaders in the United States, followed by academics at pedigree universities, called for business to act as a trustee of social well-being. According to Frederick (2006), one of the first such calls came in 1951 from Frank Abrams (Abrams, 1951), chairman of the board of directors of Standard Oil of Jersey and the author of a seminal statement about the duties executives have to society. Later, in 1971, the Committee for Economic Development (CED, 1971), composed mainly of top-level corporate executives, encouraged business to adopt a broader, more humane view of its function in society. The fact that Joseph Wharton founded the first business school in the United States as a vehicle for social enterprise knowledge reflected these early calls for business responsibility. Hence, the popularly held myth in some circles that corporate social responsibility advocates and business representatives are in opposing camps is not well founded, given that business practitioners helped shape ideas about the social role of business. Furthermore, in many cases corporations have adopted tenets of social responsibility as standard practices for responding to public interests (Carroll and Buchholtz, 2006; Frederick, 2006). When such standards are adopted, top managers are pivotal to ensuring their implementation.

This chapter addresses top managers as drivers for corporate social responsibility in three main sections. First I will summarize the responsibility roles implied by or assigned to managers in selected models of corporate social performance. Second, given this backdrop for business and society research, I will focus on the importance of moral leadership in directing the formal and informal organization toward socially responsible goals. In other words, the emphasis will be on the focal role of top executive managers in driving social responsibility. This focus is not meant to convey that middle or lower managers are irrelevant to corporate social responsibility. It is simply that their decision-making discretion is largely circumscribed by top managers (Schein, 1992; Simon, 1957), which is why middle and lower managers often face uncomfortable moral dilemmas when their values are incompatible with those established at a higher level of command (Jackall, 1989; Perrow, 1986). Finally, I will point to some contextual factors that impact socially responsible leadership in terms of external and internal controls.

The Role of Managers in Business and Society Research

Early on in business and society inquiry, Davis (1960) hinted at the role of managers in the social enterprise of business by suggesting that corporate responsibility involves decisions in the business sector that go beyond the firm's direct economic interests. That this responsibility involves managerial discretion was an underlying theme of Jones's (1983) proposal that social control of business is central to business and society research and his contention that the voluntary adoption of social responsibility and ethics by corporate decision-makers constitutes an important mechanism of self-control. Epstein (1987) added that business ethics literature emphasizes that such self-regulation in decision-making involves value-based moral reflection and choice pertaining to critical issues and problems confronting organizations. This interest in the voluntary adoption of social responsibility by organizational decision-makers stems quite naturally from a concern for the immense power wielded by business and claims that corporations will lack legitimacy if they are not held accountable to the norms and expectations of appropriate conduct established by society (ibid.; Berg and Zald, 1978; Davis, 1960, 1973; Zeitlin, 1978). This view implies both negative and positive motivations for assuming social responsibilities, negative when decision-makers act out of fear of adverse legal ramifications or pending legislation and positive when they voluntarily and affirmatively enact caring attitudes regarding their obligations to society. Although motivation is a slippery subject, difficult to ascertain, it will be addressed later in the section on possible attributes of moral leadership. For now, an examination of select corporate social performance models demonstrates that a concern for business legitimacy has been a recurring motif in business and society research and a rallying point for positing that corporations should fulfill certain obligations to society. Discussed next, this concern ultimately points to how managers handle ethical and social issues (Windsor, 2006).

Select Models of Corporate Social Performance

The notion that managers, due to their decision-making discretion, can be drivers of social responsibility has long been conveyed by corporate social performance models. As background, these models have played a critical role in reflecting the evolution of business and society thought and influencing ideas about corporate social responsibility. Although these models do not embody all relevant literature, they are nevertheless critical to theory development because as consolidations of research topics, they serve as major markers of understandings derived from compilations of research and point the way to future inquiry (Jones, 1983). Taking a longitudinal view of this research, Frederick (1978, 1987, 2006) observed that corporate social responsibility was fueled in the 1950s by the belief that business should fulfill obligations to society by acting as a trustee for a wide range of social claimants. This idea, somewhat vague at the time, was followed in the 1970s by a related but distinct strain of thought. Influenced by the work of Ackerman and Bauer (1976) and others, this next vein of thought, dubbed 'corporate social responsiveness', focused on the behavioral patterns that help firms respond to social demands and needs. Managerial in tone and quintessentially pragmatic, inquiry into responsiveness looks to institutionalized company policies, such as social auditing and social scanning techniques, as means by which organizations can carry out their reactions to social expectations, many of which are embodied in public policy processes that serve as cues for substantive goals of responsiveness (Preston and Post, 1975). While responsibility is marked by the moral overtones of obligations or duty to others, responsiveness developed out of a 'how to' mentality. As will become evident, it is the latter that provides a toolkit for the former. In fact, the idea that managers can be drivers of social responsibility may have never taken root, if not for the development of responsiveness techniques (Frederick, 1978, 1987, 2006).

While the longitudinal view of responsibility and responsiveness has been very influential, most corporate social performance models are static classifications of these topics at a point in time. In one such early taxonomy Sethi (1975) framed responsibility and responsiveness with legitimacy as a standard for evaluating corporate social performance, classifying three categories of business behavior as proscriptive, prescriptive, or anticipatory and preventative. The criteria for proscriptive legitimacy are that firms meet economic and legal obligations only. In the second case of prescriptive responsibility, business aligns its behavior with prevailing social norms, values, and expectations. Finally, if a firm practices social responsiveness it anticipates social changes and takes the lead in preventing adverse impacts of corporate activity even before external social actors are aware of problems or public policy is formulated to address them. This practical tone is also reflected in Carroll's (1979) three part model of corporate social performance in terms of social responsibility, modes of responsiveness, and the social or stakeholder issues involved.

In Carroll's model corporate social responsibility is sequentially four-fold, with economic responsibilities seen by society as the basic building block of business, followed by the expectation that corporations obey the law. The third component of responsibility is that business be ethical and conform to society's expectations of right conduct not yet embodied in law. Finally, some social constituents expect business to be a good citizen and voluntarily fulfill philanthropic responsibilities to community. This model also conveys that modes of responsiveness can be expressed as proaction, accommodation, defense, or reaction in response to social or stakeholder issues such as consumerism, the environment, product safety, occupational safety, and shareholder interests, thereby highlighting the role of managers in getting a fix on what social issues should be of interest to the firm and what responsibilities are entailed. As a classification of research topics, Carroll's framework underscores an historical development in the field of business and society: its scholars have affixed more specificity to responsibility and responsiveness over time, ultimately refining the role of managers in both.

In one such refinement, Wartick and Cochran (1985) extended Carroll's model by proposing that one of its dimensions had matured into a new field called 'social issues management' which focuses on issues identification, issues analysis, and response development, and features the business sector as a moral agent while emphasizing that responsiveness involves managerial approaches (Carroll and Buchholtz, 2006). Wood (1991) subsequently highlighted the role of managerial discretion as a driver of corporate social responsibility, processes of corporate social responsiveness, and outcomes of corporate behavior. In the process she demarcated the potential managers have to affect social performance by determining a firm's responses to society vis-à-vis environmental assessment and stakeholder and issues management, which, in turn, lead to various outcomes for society that can either reinforce or conflict with public expectations of social responsibility.

Responsibility and Responsiveness as a Means-End Continuum

To recap, corporate social performance research encapsulates business responsibility, responsiveness, and outcomes. Whereas corporate social responsiveness refers to how business organizations and their agents actively interact with and manage their environments, corporate social responsibility accentuates the moral obligations that business has to society. Hence, responsiveness and responsibility are interrelated in that responsiveness can be shaped or triggered by public expectations of business responsibilities. Generally speaking, these responsibilities are implied by the terms of the social contract, which legitimizes business as an institution with the expectation that it serve the greater good by generating commerce while adhering to society's laws and ethical norms (Donaldson, 1989). From this perspective, corporations are in a dynamic relationship with society in which responsiveness is a means to responsible social outcomes. Compared to responsibility, responsiveness is more forward looking, action-oriented, and malleable, since it is based on the premise that corporations have the capacity to anticipate and adapt to environmental factors. It is this quality that makes decision-making among managers germane to driving corporate social responsibility (Swanson, 1995).

Wood's model suggests the possibility of placing responsiveness and outcomes on a means–end continuum and highlighting the responsibilities of managers in the process. Swanson (1999)[1] employed this method in her model of corporate social performance which takes up where Wood's leaves off by placing managerial discretion squarely at the top of corporate structure and modeling the organizational dynamics involved in directing firms to enact the type of responsiveness that can bring about socially responsible outcomes (see Swanson, 1995, for an earlier version of this model). That is, building on previous corporate social performance models, Swanson highlighted the potential of moral leadership to drive organizational processes toward responsible social goals or ends. She also modeled the type of leadership that neglects to do so. Both types of leadership will be outlined after a discussion of the importance of moral leadership to the formal and informal organization.

THE PIVOTAL ROLE OF MORAL LEADERSHIP

The rationale for the type of leadership that seeks to direct corporate activities toward socially responsible goals is that corporations are granted power and status in

---

[1] Swanson's (1999) article was awarded 'The Best Article in Business and Society' in 2001, given by the International Association for Business and Society (IABS) in association with *California Management Review*.

society because of their ability to serve the greater good. Frederick (1995, 2006) conceives of this ability broadly as economizing and ecologizing, the former referring to the ability to efficiently convert inputs into outputs, mostly through competitive behaviors, and the latter to forging cooperative, collaborative linkages with society that function adaptively to sustain life. Because the economizing function of the firm is widely recognized, executive managers are sometimes referred to as stewards of transforming scarce resources into goods and services. This function harkens to the first level of Carroll's (1979) model, discussed earlier, which indicates that firms should first and foremost fulfill their economic obligations to society. Since ecologizing refers to cooperative, collaborative linkages with society that function adaptively to sustain life, it encapsulates the other three responsibilities in Carroll's model in that attending to legal obligations and various stakeholder expectations of ethical conduct over and above the letter of the law can help sustain the social good, as does giving back to society in the form of philanthropy or programs targeted at the betterment of community.

The enactment of all these forms of corporate social responsibility, sometimes referred to as 'corporate citizenship', and the balancing of their tensions and trade-offs is largely under the influence of the executive manager or chief executive officer who sets the moral tone for an organization's conduct in society through his or her span of control over the formal and informal organization (Drucker, 1968; Schein, 1992; Selznick, 1957; Simon, 1957; Swanson, 1999). In both equally important realms, and in keeping with a means–end continuum of responsiveness described previously, the executive has access to several mechanisms for directing organizational conduct toward constructive social ends, beginning with the formal or structural organization.

Leading the Formal Organization

The importance of top executives driving corporate social responsibility is reinforced by research indicating that mid and lower level managers and other employees often feel squeezed by pressure from above (Jackall, 1989; Joseph, 2000; Perrow, 1986). This is not surprising, given that socialization in the work environment involves the inculcation of respect for authority structure, loyalty to bosses, conformity to organizational practices, and, above all else, performance goals (Carroll and Buchholtz, 2006). When this pressure poses a moral dilemma for employees, they may have to choose between going along with questionable directives and blowing the whistle. For the employee of conscience, either choice will be difficult, especially since whistle blowers typically face harsh retaliation or excommunication (Grover, 2003). In fact, the most recent corporate scandals and subsequent indictments and convictions of top executives along with the establishment of new regulatory rules meant to hold board members and top managers more accountable are emblematic of what can happen when moral leadership does not come from the top of organizational structure. Clearly, massive harmful impacts to society and new forms of social control can result.

The view taken here, based on Swanson's (1999) corporate social performance model, is that the chief executive officer can help guide a firm toward responsible corporate conduct vis-à-vis the formal organization by directing other managers and employees along the chain of command structure to attend responsibly to concerns expressed by internal and external stakeholders, the former including employees and investors and the latter consumers, suppliers, the media, government agencies, and other groups in society that can affect or are affected by the firm's activities (see Freeman, 1984). The issues raised by these groups are often articulated in terms of moral expectations, as when employees claim the right to fair treatment, investors expect honest and transparent financial statements, consumers assert entitlements to safe products, and social activists exert pressure for sustainable business practices. If the executive manager establishes formal policies that direct managers and other employees—especially boundary spanners in the office of external affairs—to listen to, document, and attend to these concerns in a timely way, then it is possible for the firm to develop collaborative relationships with stakeholders instead of adversarial or avoidance postures (see Ackerman and Bauer, 1976; Waddock, 2002). From this vantage point, moral leaders should use their formal organizational authority to seek to ensure that firms perform their economic function in society while also ecologizing or addressing stakeholder issues efficiently, effectively, and collaboratively so that the social benefits of corporate impacts are maximized while harmful outcomes are prevented or minimized.

The formal mechanisms available to executives for doing so include not only establishing and overseeing an attentive office of external affairs but also initiating oversight from an ethics committee made up of board members and other senior managers as well as the services of an ethics officer and his or her staff in formulating and implementing legal and ethics compliance programs, ethics codes of conduct, hiring procedures that screen potential employees for ethical standards, and ethics orientation and training sessions. Another formal mechanism for encouraging desirable employee conduct is the implementation of an anonymous reporting system or ethics hotline by which workers can disclose their concerns—such as suspicions of unsafe products, dangerous work conditions, sexual harassment, or questionable financial accounting—with anonymity or due protection. If the top executive follows through by making sure questionable practices or situations are rectified in a timely manner, then it is possible that some legal and ethical problems can be avoided or ameliorated while employee commitment to high moral standards is strengthened. Employing the services of an ombudsperson is yet another formal mechanism by which executives can signal that employee concerns will be dealt with objectively before ethical issues escalate into legal problems (Swanson and Paul, 2002–3). Moral leadership might also involve participating in industry-wide 'best practices forums' aimed at establishing and maintaining collective ethical self-governance among peer firms. In terms of evaluation and control, executives may institute an ethics audit as a means of assessing the effectiveness of ethics programs, policies, and procedures and identifying deviations from established standards. Finally, establishing and implementing a formal policy of rewarding employees who adhere to established ethics standards is critical if the goals of socially responsible conduct are to be taken seriously (Orlitzky and Swanson, 2006).

Leading the Informal Organization

Formal programs can be viewed as ineffective or mere 'window dressing' if employees are not convinced of upper management's commitment to moral leadership (Jackall, 1989), especially since employees look outside themselves to significant others for ethical guidance (Brown et al., 2005). Such commitment or lack of it can be evident in a firm's informal organizational culture. In fact, Schein (1992) asserts that the most important thing a leader does is to create and manage organizational culture, which he defines as a system of shared assumptions and beliefs, often taken-for-granted, and based on learned products of group experience which ultimately reflect values or beliefs about what employees 'ought to do.' According to Schein, the organization's founder can significantly impact these beliefs by embedding certain values in the culture early on. Moreover, he identifies five primary mechanisms that the executive manager has access to for shaping and reinforcing culture on an ongoing basis: (1) what he or she pays attention to, measures, and controls, (2) how he or she reacts to critical incidents and crises, (3) his or her deliberate role modeling, teaching, and coaching, (4) his or her criteria for allocation of rewards and status, and (5) his or her criteria for recruitment, selection, promotion, retirement, and excommunication. While these mechanisms are often expressed formally, they can be more powerful informally in that employees ultimately learn what behavior is expected of them by what leaders *do*, not simply by what they say or endorse as formal statements, policies, programs, and procedures.

For example, if the formal corporate code of conduct stresses honesty, but the chief executive officer models unethical behavior or attends to, mentors, promotes, and rewards employees known for shady or non-transparent dealings, then the unspoken message to employees is that honesty is not really valued in the culture. Accordingly, formally espoused programs, policies, and procedures advocating honesty will likely be 'decoupled' from actual behavior, meaning that the executive will actually encourage the development of a culture marked by dishonesty and a lack of transparency. The exemplary scenario in terms of moral leadership is for executives to use mechanisms for shaping and reinforcing cultures that establish and maintain an organization's ability to respond affirmatively to stakeholder expectations of social responsibility while directing employees to enact conduct befitting such an organization, all the while providing them with a personal model or example of such behavior. In terms of ethical climates, the resulting organization ideally embodies benevolence or concern for others and integrity or adherence to principled rules and procedures (see Victor and Cullen, 1988).

TYPIFYING EXECUTIVE LEADERSHIP OF CORPORATE SOCIAL PERFORMANCE

The idea that corporate social responsibility starts at the top harkens to Abrams (1951) early call for executives to accept their responsibilities to society, referred to in the introduction. For Abrams, this meant that executives should adopt a professional attitude toward their duties to a wide range of interested groups, including shareholders, customers, employees, and the public at large, a vision that eventually became the basic tenet of stakeholder theory (Frederick, 2006). Davis (1964) echoed a similar sentiment by observing that the managerial role in more advanced and productive cultures is differentiated to reflect expectations that managers imbibe professional norms that help them achieve constructive social aims. What followed in corporate social performance literature was an elaboration of these responsibilities and mechanisms of responsiveness, several of which were described previously. Combining this research with insights from the sociology of organizations, Swanson's (1999) more recent model elaborates on role differentiation at the top, linking it with decision-making processes in the formal and informal organization that culminate in two different types of responsiveness to society. Specifically, she conceptualized executive *normative myopia* and organizational *value neglect* on the one hand and executive *normative receptivity* and organizational *value attunement* on the other as contrasting points of reference for inquiry into the relationship between executive decision making and corporate social performance.

Before describing these two models of corporate social performance and defining their terms, it is important to emphasize that they are *ideal types* or systems of logical implications drawn from extant research on business and society and organizational theory. In using this method, Swanson relied on Weber's (1922/1947) construction of an ideal type as a simplified model that focuses attention on a subject's distinctive features in order to highlight their logical implications systematically across levels of analysis. Since this method accentuates a one-sided view that emphasizes a phenomenon's distinctive features, it is a particularly useful method for generating logical implications from existing classification systems (Bailey, 1994),

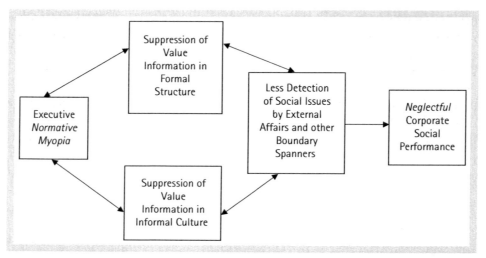

Fig. 10.1 Value neglect: executive *normative myopia* and *neglectful* Corporate Social Performance

Source: Adapted from Swanson (1999), as published in Orlitzky and Swanson (2006).

in this case corporate social performance models. To be clear, the two heuristics of value neglect and value attunement do not represent actual organizations nor do they constitute full fledged theories. Rather, they are typifications designed to be contrasting points of reference for theory development that incorporates the executive mindset as a driver of corporate social responsibility. Moreover, since neglect and attunement are based on ideal types or systems of logical implications across the individual, organizational, and societal levels of analysis, they lend themselves to research that seeks to understand corporate social performance holistically on the means–end continuum, introduced earlier.

Normative Myopia and Corporate Neglect

Swanson's overarching proposition for value neglect is that when executive managers exhibit normative myopia by ignoring, suppressing, or denying the role of values in their decisions, then whole organizations can eventually lose touch with stakeholder expectations of social responsibility. These expectations, which are value-based, include calls for product safety, respect for human rights, fair employment standards, and sustainable business practices. Figure 10.1 represents a simplification of Swanson's model which indicates that normative myopia and an organizational tendency to neglect social values go hand in hand.

Its logic is as follows. Executives who exhibit normative myopia use formal and informal mechanisms (either consciously or unconsciously) to encourage other employees to follow suit and suppress value awareness and analysis in their decision-making. Formally, executives can do so by using their authority to set a narrow range for employee decision-making along chain of command structures. Practically speaking, this means that executives can discourage employees from including information about stakeholder expectations in official reports, statements, and other feedback mechanisms. In this way, the range of discretion for subordinate decision-making gets aligned with the narrow value premises set on a higher level of administration (see Simon, 1957). Borrowing terminology from Weick's (1969) perspective, the variety of information in the environment gets reduced as subordinates select, retain, and enact the narrow mindset of the top decision maker. Informally, executives can also signal their approval of myopia by using certain cultural mechanisms. For instance, they can mentor and promote sycophants who convey only desired information to decision-makers and excommunicate or ignore employees who give fuller accountings (Schein, 1992).

The upshot of these formal and informal signals is that myopic decision-making gets replicated among employees, a dynamic Chikudate (2002) refers to as 'collective myopia.' When boundary-spanning employees, such as public affairs specialists, align with this shortsightedness, they fail to communicate important information about the social environment to senior managers and others in the organization (Swanson, 1999), which undermines the very task they are supposed to carry out (Ackerman and Bauer, 1976). The situation tends to be self-perpetuating in that employees develop a reluctance to convey stakeholder expectations of corporate social responsibility to the executive who signaled disinterest in the first place. Executive and organizational myopia eventually align as the executive proclivity to ignore or downplay values gets played out as a chronic tendency for the organization to neglect social concerns (see Scott and Hart, 1979).

As illustrated in Figure 10.1, normative myopia and poor corporate social performance are inextricably linked in the model of value neglect. In terms of a business and society perspective, neglect represents a violation of the social contract that imputes legitimacy to corporations because they enhance the greater good (Donaldson, 1989). Under the terms of this social contract, corporate responsibilities include not only economizing behaviors but also the ability to forge cooperative, symbiotic linkages or relationships with the external environment that function adaptively to sustain life (Frederick, 1995, 2006). A firm that manifests value neglect fails to forge such linkages. Since these relationships also facilitate a firm's ability to function economically, value neglect ultimately represents a dual failure to economize and ecologize. In this way, the corporations that lost substantial economic value and public confidence in the most recent wave of business scandals not only exemplify value neglect, they also reinforce those studies indicating a significant positive correlation between sound financial performance and responsible social performance (e.g. Orlitzky and Benjamin, 2001; Orlitzky et al., 2003) as well as data that suggests that the latter contributes to the former vis-à-vis the enhancement of corporate reputations (e.g. Fombrun, 1996; Turban

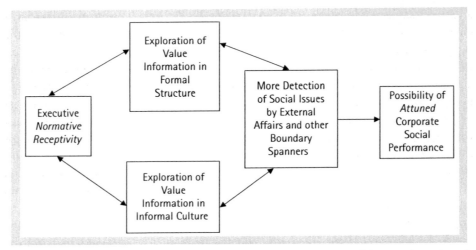

Fig. 10.2 Value attunement: executive *normative receptivity* and *attuned* Corporate Social Performance

Source: Adapted from Swanson (1999), as published in Orlitzky and Swanson (2006).

and Greening, 1997). That corporate social responsibility correlates with economic benefits simply underscores its salience to top managers.

Normative Receptivity and Corporate Attunement

Since it is the task of the executive leader to anticipate social problems and work toward their solution (Drucker, 1968), value neglect can be seen as a benchmark or frame of reference for understanding what can happen when executives exhibit a blind spot in the realm of social responsibility. More specifically, it typifies an organization's overall posture toward society when the chief executive consistently fails to acknowledge and examine the values implicated in his or her decisions and those of other employees (see also Logsdon and Corzine, 1999). In contrast, Swanson modeled normative receptivity as executive decision-making that consciously strives to incorporate values or normative information as a precursor to the organization's potential to do so. Receptivity (see Fig. 10.2) is the converse of the logic embodied in Figure 10.1 in that it represents an enhanced awareness and appreciation of values in the executive mindset that gets transmitted throughout the informal and formal organization and acted upon by boundary-spanners and other employees.

Accordingly, when executives use formal and informal mechanisms to signal that employees should also attend to normative information, then the possibility of value attunement exists. Put differently, when decision-makers throughout the organization are directed by formal creed and informal signals to recognize and attend to stakeholder concerns, then the organization's posture toward the host environment can undergo a change for the better. In terms of ecologizing, the executive ideally directs employee behavior toward constructive social purposes, notably compliance with the law and important ethical norms that go beyond the law, so that cooperatively adaptive symbiotic linkages with the social environment become possible. Along these lines, some advocates of social responsibility hold that executives who seek to maximize the benefits of corporate actions will also give back to community in the form of corporate philanthropy whenever possible, perhaps in collaboration with not-for profit organizations (Saiia et al., 2003). Increasingly, such philanthropy is deemed strategic if it contributes not only to social goals but also to a firm's long-run economic performance by enhancing its reputation and increasing community goodwill (Porter and Kramer, 2002). In short, it can be an opportunity both to economize and ecologize.

In terms of business and society, value attunement implies that a corporation has the potential to carry out its part of the social contract by seeking to anticipate stakeholder concerns and accommodate them whenever possible. The point is for the executive to direct his or her firm to learn about the stakeholder environment and be attuned to it, informed by long-term strategic planning that starts with an assessment of the firm's external environment. For instance, this kind of assessment might reveal a trend that society has increased expectations that firms will enhance the quality of life in communities. A more fine-tuned analysis would identify the stakeholders who hold this expectation and the issues of importance to them. This information in turn might prompt a bank to make a commitment to invest in community development projects aligned with the goals of local residents and aimed at generating goodwill befitting public expectations of corporate citizenship. In terms of strategic management, these projects would necessarily reflect the bank's formal policy toward community development carried out by employees in departmental programs guided by specific procedures, such as the criteria for approving loan applications aimed at a measure of profitability. In this way, an awareness of environmental factors can prompt concrete changes in corporate social responsiveness or the ways firms interact with and manage their social relationships as they quest for an attuned balance between economizing and ecologizing.

Neglect and Attunement in Perspective

As a theoretical perspective, value attunement is more tentative than value neglect (Swanson, 1999). For one thing, it does not specify the exact value enactments that can lead to socially responsible outcomes, although Frederick's value processes of economizing and ecologizing provide general performance goals. Moreover, although attunement hinges on a robust consideration of normative information, the exact nature of this information, which may include competing value trade-offs (e.g. the rights of some stakeholders may clash with claims of justice for others), is not specified. This reflects the overall state of business and society research in that despite rising demand for and recognition of the theoretical and practical importance of corporate social responsibility, there has been little consensus on the substantive content of decision-making processes (Windsor, 2006). While more research in this area is needed, attunement represents a step in the direction of understanding the general nature of socially responsible decision-making processes in that normative receptivity on the part of the top executive can be thought of as a necessary but perhaps not sufficient condition for it. Moreover, it is important to stress that attunement typifies a pattern of organizational behavior that is open-ended and dynamic instead of an objective reached at a point in time. Indeed, this is the case both for neglect and attunement in that they represent pure forms or ideal types of decision-making processes that drive organizations away from or toward socially responsible goals. In reality, however, organizations manifest tendencies toward neglect or attunement instead of perfect alignments. Similarly, empirical research suggests that executives exhibit degrees of normative myopia or receptivity instead of pure forms of these decision processes (Orlitzky and Swanson, 2006).

Two Illustrative Examples

To illustrate how neglect and attunement can be used as points of reference for corporate social responsibility, consider the longstanding controversy surrounding Nestlé's sales of infant formula. For decades Nestlé Corporation faced social opposition to its marketing of infant formula in developing countries. Critics, including the World Health Organization, claimed that insanitary water and low rates of literacy rendered the sale of the product unsafe in those countries (Sethi, 1994). Eventually Nestlé was the target of intense pressure from stakeholders aimed at forcing the firm to comply with an international code aimed at restricting such sales. This controversy can be seen as a clash between narrow profit seeking and broader social values in that it appears that Nestlé executives adopted a myopic mindset, referencing narrow company objectives to the detriment of broader community values, particularly a respect for infant life (Swanson, 1999).

In other words, Nestlé exhibited neglect instead of striving for attunement and engaging critics in a timely, constructive dialogue. By adhering rigidly to original plans, it appears that top executives failed to consider other options. For example, the controversy might have been averted in its early stages if Nestlé executives had decided to treat the infant formula not as a food product but as a health care product, dispensing it by prescription through pharmacies (Husted, 2000). A precedent for this kind of re-evaluation already existed in that pharmaceutical companies such as Abbott Labs had successfully responded to stakeholder concerns by making the switch (Austin and Kohn, 1990). That Nestlé was unable to re-envision its identity as a food company can be seen as a failure of executive managers to exhibit normative receptivity and factor compelling social values into their decisions, an ability that would seem to be particularly important when corporations operate internationally in host environments with cultures different from those of the home country.

While attuned responsiveness ideally results from long-term strategic planning, it can also take the form of a more immediate reaction to a crisis. Whether a crisis results from an oil spill, product tampering, or another unexpected event, the conventional wisdom is that corporations should develop the capacity to anticipate emergencies and respond swiftly to the needs of adversely affected stakeholders. The case of Johnson & Johnson Tylenol poisonings has become a classic study of executive-led responsible crisis management. Briefly, seven people died in 1982 after cyanide was added to Tylenol capsules while they were on store shelves, prompting Johnson & Johnson, the maker of the product, to incur hefty expenses by voluntarily recalling and destroying remaining capsules. During this process, James Burke, the chief executive officer, made aggressive use of the media to apprise consumers of the steps that were being taken to address the crisis and protect the public. Shortly thereafter, Johnson & Johnson introduced tamper-resistant packaging as a preventative measure, demonstrating that attuned crisis management involves not only swift responsiveness and effective communication with stakeholders, but also the kind of organizational learning that can help minimize or prevent future crises. Along these lines, receptivity and attunement can serve as points of reference for understanding how important it is for top managers to keep the public good in mind while attending to stakeholder needs adaptively. Conversely, the logic embodied in myopia and neglect help explain why social control of business, such as the pressure exerted on Nestlé, becomes necessary in the first place.

Possible Attributes of Morally Attuned Leadership

As mentioned earlier, motivations for assuming social responsibilities may be either negative or positive. Negative motivation may be prompted by social control, including the law and stakeholder pressure, whereas positive motivation may stem from a regard for obligations to others that has been internalized by the decision-maker. Although there is no one generally accepted theory of moral leadership, there is a preponderance of research suggesting that moral leaders are capable of positive motivation. Not surprisingly, much of this literature emphasizes the importance of other-regarding behavior in lieu of self-aggrandizement (Swanson, forthcoming). For instance, decision-making based on the felt sentiment of helping others first is the basis for servant leadership (Greenleaf, 1977), which would seem to be a particularly fitting motivation for attuned executives who strive to lead corporations to serve the social good by economizing and ecologizing. A similar perspective based on Kohlberg's (1981) model of moral development suggests that managers capable of articulating and defending their decisions in terms of what is good for society as a whole while applying principles of justice, rights, and social welfare universally to others exhibit the highest level of moral reasoning and, by extension, are capable of moral leadership in action (Weber and Green, 1993). Virtue ethics implies that moral managers are those who have imbibed certain character traits, such as fairness, honesty, and benevolence (Moberg, 1997), while the literature on integrity suggests that they are able to utilize such characteristics coherently to establish publicly their trustworthiness and ability to make balanced judgments in the face of moral complexity (Petrick and Quinn, 2000). According to a dialogic perspective, it is important that this ability translate into respecting, listening to, and giving voice to various stakeholder concerns (Calton and Payne, 2003). Particularly consistent with attunement theorizing is other research positing that a necessary condition for moral leadership is the cognitive ability to factor values and ethics consciously into decision-making (Trevino et al., 2000; Waddock, 2002) and use moral imagination in doing so (Werhane, 1999). A social learning perspective to moral leadership stresses the ability to model such traits to others (Brown et al., 2005) while a more naturalistic vein of research suggests that the capacity for such abilities may be hard-wired or built into the neural circuits or algorithmic brain patterns of decision-makers (Frederick, 2006). These perspectives, taken as a whole, point to the importance of screening executive job candidates for moral decision-making capacities, discussed further in the last section on internal control.

SOME CONTEXTUAL FACTORS FOR MORALLY ATTUNED LEADERSHIP

Moral leadership as a driving force for corporate social responsibility does not occur in a vacuum. Rather, certain circumstances or contextual factors may temper, enhance, or help define this form of leadership in the form of external and internal controls.

External Control

The extent to which society seeks external control over business is reflected in the standards embodied in the law, public policy, and government regulation (Preston and Post, 1975). Moreover, if the legitimacy of business is challenged because corporations ignore social expectations of responsibility, then government regulation tends to follow (Davis, 1960). The US Sarbanes–Oxley (SOX) Act of 2002 was such a reaction to corporate neglect of social responsibilities (Windsor, 2006). That SOX requires the chief executive officers of public firms to sign off on financial statements while dictating stronger board audit committees and protections for whistle blowers underscores society's expectation that some level of external control over corporate governance is necessary. More broadly, public policy has long been used to mitigate the negative spillover effects of business, as when economic expansion or cost-cutting leads to unsafe working conditions for employees or pollution jeopardizes the health and well-being of the community at large. In other words, while society expects corporations to economize and ecologize, these value processes can be subject to trade-offs that challenge even the most normatively receptive executive.

For instance, the executive who voluntarily decides to use expensive pollution control equipment could place his or her firm at a competitive disadvantage whereas this dilemma may be obviated if government regulation mandates such equipment for all firms in the industry. In this way, public policy in the form of external control can protect community interests while leveling the playing field for executives facing unavoidable trade-offs between economic and other social interests. A cautionary note is that corporations are increasingly exerting influence on the government in the form of political advocacy, which includes lobbying policy-makers and contributing financially to their election campaigns (Carroll and Buchholtz, 2006). As a result, the connection between responsiveness and responsibility can be compromised to the extent that this influence results in legislation that favors business interests at the expense of the greater good. After all, corporate social responsibility does not equate simply to corporations creating their own rules to which they then respond (Frederick, 1987, 2006).

External control can also take the form of stakeholder pressure toward firms perceived as neglectful of social concerns. As the case of Nestlé demonstrates, such perception can lead to unfavorable media coverage, tarnished reputations, and stakeholder pressure tactics such as public protests and consumer boycotts. In short, corporate neglect invites social control. On the other hand, executives can seek to forge an attuned posture toward society by scanning the stakeholder environment proactively for potential concerns and engaging critics constructively before their concerns escalate into intractable problems. This type of managerial discretion is even more salient in global environments where multinational corporations face legal and ethical dilemmas due to disparate cultural and economic conditions (DeGeorge, 1993; Windsor, 2006). Faced with such dilemmas, executives seeking attunement may voluntarily work with public interest groups and other firms in the industry to establish norms or codes of conduct such as those crafted by the Fair Labor Association and Council on Economic Priorities which seek to target working conditions in developing countries (Carroll and Buchholtz, 2006). Indeed, as of the time of this writing the Academy of Management is collaborating with

United Nations Global Compact to explore the use of management knowledge to lead positive change worldwide (AoM, 2006; see also Shinn, 2006), which underscores the role top managers can have in driving corporate social responsibility in global markets where uniform standards of external control are often lacking (DeGeorge, 1993; Donaldson, 1989; Windsor, 2006).

Internal Control

In 1978 the chairman of the American Bar Association's Section of Corporation, Bank and Business Law reiterated a frequent allegation that management, primarily through the chief executive officer, runs the corporation without accountability to the board of directors (Epstein, 1979). In light of recent corporate scandals, this concern for internal control is all the more relevant (Ray, 2005). While some board controls are mandated by law, such as those required by SOX, there are also discretionary areas that boards aiming for attuned social responsibility may consider, including executive hiring practices, the make-up of board committees, and organizational design.

In terms of hiring practices, boards can try to screen executive candidates for normative receptivity, bearing in mind that one survey designed to tap such receptivity found that those executives who reported a favorable attitude toward values also scored high on a personality trait that denotes an individual's inclination to be cooperative, friendly, altruistic, tender-minded, and trusting (Orlitzky et al., 2006). Boards may also consider the educational background of these candidates, since some evidence suggests that normative myopia increases with the amount of business coursework taken (ISIB, 2003; ibid.). By implication, it may be wise to screen executive candidates for coursework in ethics and corporate social responsibility. Because such courses are in the minority in the business school curriculum (Willen, 2004), those executives with strong educational training in these subjects might possess a distinct advantage for helping their firms develop an attuned posture toward society (see Adler, 2002; Cohen and Holder-Webb, 2006; Ghoshal, 2005; ISIB, 2003; Frederick, 2006; Mitroff, 2004; Swanson, 2004; Waddock, 2006; Windsor, 2002).

Boards aiming for social responsibility may also consider establishing committees that reflect a focus on social responsibility, such as issues and crisis management, public affairs, and employee relations. As part of this effort, a permanent ombudsperson attached to the board could be established so that the interests of stakeholders have a legitimate and fair hearing in the absence of direct representation (Ray, 2005). Finally, flattening organizational structure could be another board-level initiative in support of corporate social responsibility (see Gerde, 2001), since large bureaucratic organizations with tall chain-of-command structures tend to produce hierarchical decision-making that is slow to react to novel information

(Frederick, 1995; Jackall, 1989; Perrow, 1986; Schein, 1992). The corollary is that attuned responsiveness to stakeholder concerns would be more likely in organizations with flatter structures (Swanson, 1999; see also Halal, 1994).

CONCLUSION

This chapter has outlined the role of executive managers in driving their firms toward irresponsible or responsible corporate social performance. Essentially, executives can direct their corporations to tune into or neglect social concerns, depending upon whether or not they engage in and encourage value-inclusive organizational decision-making processes. Factors that influence the potential for responsible leadership include external control in the form of public policy and stakeholder pressure and internal control exerted by boards of directors.

REFERENCES

ABRAMS, F. 1951. 'Management's responsibilities in a complex world'. *Harvard Business Review*, May: 29–34.

Academy of Management (AoM). 2006. 'Call for Papers. United Nations Collaboration: Business as an Agent of World Benefit Forum'. <http://www.aomonline.org>.

ACKERMAN, R. W. 1975. *The Social Challenge to Business*. Cambridge, Mass.: Harvard University Press.

——and BAUER, R. 1976. *Corporate Social Responsiveness: The Modern Dilemma*. Cambridge, Mass.: Harvard University Press.

ADLER, P. S. 2002. 'Corporate scandals: It's Time for Reflection in Business Schools'. *Academy of Management Executive*, 16: 148–9.

Aspen Initiative for Social Innovation through Business (ISIB). 2003. 'Where Will they Lead? MBA Student Attitudes about Business & Society' (New York, NY: Aspen ISIB). (<http://www.aspeninstitute.org/aff/cf/%7BDEB6F227-659-4EC8-8F84-8DF23CA704F5%FD/ASPEN%20EXEX%20SUM%20FINALPDF>).

AUSTIN, J. E., and KOHN, T. O. 1990. *Strategic Management in Developing Countries: Case Studies*. New York: Free Press.

BAILEY, K. D. 1994. *Typologies and Taxonomies*. Belmont, Calif.: Sage.

BERG, I., and ZALD, M. N. 1978. 'Business and Society'. *Annual Review of Sociology*, 4: 115–43.

BROWN, M. E., TREVINO, L. K., and HARRISON, D. A. 2005. 'Ethical Leadership: A Social Learning Perspective for Construct Development and Testing'. *Organizational Behavior and Human Decision Processes*, 97: 117–34.

CALTON, J. M., and PAYNE, S. L. 2003. 'Coping with Paradox: Multistakeholder Learning Dialogue as a Pluralist Sensemaking Process for Addressing Messy Problems'. *Business & Society*, 42: 7–42.

CARROLL, A. B. 1979. 'A Three Dimensional Model of Corporate Social Performance'. *Academy of Management Review*, 4: 497–505.

—— and BUCHHOLTZ, A. K. 2006. *Business & Society: Ethics and Stakeholder Management*. Mason, Ohi.: Thomson South-Western.

CHIKUDATE, N. 2002. 'Collective Myopia and Disciplinary Power behind the Scenes of Unethical Practices: A Diagnostic Theory on Japanese Organization'. *Journal of Management Studies*, 39: 289–307.

COHEN, J. R., and HOLDER-WEBB, L. L. 2006. 'Rethinking the Influence of Agency Theory in the Accounting Academy'. *Issues in Accounting Education*, 21: 17–30.

Committee for Economic Development (CED), Research and Policy Committee. 1971. *Social Responsibilities of Business Corporations: A Statement on National Policy*. New York: Committee for Economic Development.

DAVIS, K. 1960. 'Can Business Afford to Ignore Social Responsibilities'? *California Management Review*, 2(3): 70–6.

—— 1964. 'The Public Role of Management: Evolving Concepts in Management'. *Proceedings of the 24th Annual Academy of Management*, Chicago.

—— 1973. 'The Case For and Against Business Assumption of Social Responsibilities'. *Academy of Management Journal*, 16: 312–22.

DEGEORGE, R. T. 1993. *Competing with Integrity in International Business*. New York: Oxford University Press.

DONALDSON, T. 1989. *The Ethics of International Business*. New York: Oxford University Press.

DRUCKER, P. F. 1968. *The Age of Discontinuity: Guidelines to our Changing Society*. New York: Harper & Row.

EPSTEIN, E. M. 1979. 'Societal, Managerial, and Legal Perspectives on Corporate Social Responsibility—Product and Process'. *Hastings Law Journal*, 30: 1287–320.

—— 1987. 'The Corporate Social Policy Process: Beyond Business Ethics, Corporate Social Responsibility, and Corporate Social Responsiveness'. *California Management Review*, 29: 99–114.

FOMBRUN, C. J. 1996. *Reputation: Realizing Value from the Corporate Image*. Boston: Harvard Business School Press.

FREDERICK, W. C. 1978. 'From CSR to CSR2: The Maturing of Business-and-Society Thought'. Working Paper No. 279. Graduate School of Business, University of Pittsburgh.

—— 1987. 'Theories of Corporate Social Performance', in S. P. Sethi and C. Falbe (eds.), *Business and Society: Dimensions of Conflict and Cooperation*. New York: Lexington Books, 142–61.

—— 1995. *Values, Nature, and Culture in the American Corporation*. New York: Oxford University Press.

—— 2006. *Corporation, be Good! The Story of Corporate Social Responsibility*. Indianapolis: Dog Ear Publishing.

FREEMAN, R. E. 1984. *Strategic Management: A Stakeholder Approach*. Marshfield, Mass. Pitman.

GERDE, V. W. 2001. 'The Design Dimensions of the Just Organization: An Empirical Test of the Relation between Organization Design and Corporate Social Performance'. *Business & Society*, 40: 472–77.

GHOSHAL, S. 2005. 'Bad Management Theories are Destroying Good Management Practices'. *Academy of Management Learning & Education*, 4: 75–91.

GREENLEAF, R. K. 1977. *Servant Leadership.* New York: Paulist Press.

GROVER, L. P. 2003. 'Whistleblowers: A Rare Breed'. *Strategic Finance*, Aug.: 51–3.

HALAL, W. H. 1994. 'From Hierarchy to Enterprise: Internal Markets are the New Foundation of Management'. *Academy of Management Executive*, 8: 559–65.

HUSTED, B. 2000. 'A Contingency Theory of Corporate Social Performance'. *Business & Society*, 39: 24–48.

JACKALL, R. 1989. *Moral Mazes: The World of Corporate Managers.* New York: Oxford University Press.

JONES, T. M. 1983. 'An Integrative Framework for Research in Business and Society: A Step toward the Elusive Paradigm?' *Academy of Management Review*, 8: 559–64.

JOSEPH, J. 2000. 'National Business Ethics Survey'. Web page of the Ethics Resource Center: <http://www.ethics.org>.

KOHLBERG, L. 1981. *Essays in Moral Development, Volume I: The Philosophy of Moral Development.* New York: Harper & Row.

LOGSDON, J. M., and CORZINE, J. B. 1999. 'The CEO's Psychological Characteristics and Ethical Culture'. *Current Topics in Management*, 4: 63–79.

MITROFF, I. 2004. 'An Open Letter to the Deans and Faculties of American Business Schools', copyright.

MOBERG, D. 1997. 'Virtuous Peers in Work Organizations'. *Business Ethics Quarterly*, 7: 67–85.

ORLITZKY, M., and BENJAMIN, J. D. 2001. 'Corporate Social Performance and Firm Risk: A Meta-analytic Review'. *Business & Society*, 40: 369–96.

—— SCHMIDT, F. L., and RYNES, S. L. 2003. 'Corporate Social and Financial Performance: A Meta-analysis'. *Organization Studies*, 24: 403–41.

—— and SWANSON, D. L. 2006. 'Socially Responsible Human Resource Management: Charting New Territory', in J. R. Deckop (ed.), *Human Resource Management Ethics.* Greenwich, Conn.: Information Age, 13–31.

—— —— and QUARTERMAINE, L. K. 2006. 'Normative Myopia, Executives' Personality, and Preference for Pay Dispersion: Toward Implications for Corporate Social Performance'. *Business & Society*, 45: 149–77.

PERROW, C. 1986. *Complex Organizations: A Critical Essay*, 3rd edn. New York: Random House.

PETRICK, J. A., and QUINN, J. R. 2000. 'The Integrity Capacity Construct and Moral Progress in Business'. *Journal of Business Ethics*, 32: 3–18.

PORTER, M. E., and KRAMER, M. R. 2002. 'The Competitive Advantage of Corporate Philanthropy'. *Harvard Business Review*, Dec.: 57–68.

PRESTON, L. E., and POST, J. E. 1975. *Private Management and Public Policy.* Englewood Cliffs, NJ: Prentice Hall.

RAY, D. M. 2005. 'Corporate Boards and Corporate Democracy'. *Journal of Corporate Citizenship*, 20 winter: 93–105.

SAIIA, D. H., CARROLL, A. B., and BUCHHOLTZ, A. K. 2003. 'Philanthropy as Strategy: When Corporate Charity "begins at home."' *Business & Society*, 42: 169–201.

SCHEIN, E. H. 1992. *Organizational culture and leadership*, 2nd edn. San Francisco: Jossey-Bass.

SCOTT, W. G., and HART, D. K. 1979. *Organizational America.* Boston: Houghton Mifflin.

SELZNICK, P. 1957. *Leadership in Administration.* New York: Harper & Row.

SETHI, S. P. 1975. 'Dimensions of Corporate Social Performance: An Analytical Framework'. *California Management Review*, 17(3): 58–64.

SETHI, S. P. 1994. *Multinational Corporations and the Impact of Public Advocacy on Corporate Strategy: Nestle and the Infant Formula Controversy.* Norwell, Mass.: Kluwer.

SHINN, S. 2006. 'Dimensions of Peace'. *BizEd*, May/June.

SIMON, H. 1957. *Administrative Behavior.* New York: Macmillan.

SWANSON, D. L. 1995. 'Addressing a Theoretical Problem by Reorienting the Corporate Social Performance Model'. *Academy of Management Review*, 20: 43–64.

—— 1999. 'Toward an Integrative Theory of Business and Society: A Research Strategy for Corporate Social Performance'. *Academy of Management Review*, 24: 506–21.

—— 2004. 'The Buck Stops Here: Why Universities must Reclaim Business Ethics Education', in D. Reed and R. Wellen (eds.), 'Special Issue on Universities and Corporate Responsibility', *Journal of Academic Ethics*, 2(1): 43–61.

—— Forthcoming. 'Moral leadership', in B. Kolb (ed.), *Encyclopedia of Ethics in Business and Society*, Thousand Oaks, Calif: Sage.

—— and PAUL, R. J. 2002–3. 'Violations of Ethical Expectations: The Toxicity of Organizational Pain and Some Remedies'. *Journal of Individual Employment Rights*, 10: 25–39.

TREVINO, L. K., HARTMAN, L. P., and BROWN, M. 2000. 'Moral Person and Moral Manager: How Executives Develop a Reputation for Ethical Leadership'. *California Management Review*, 42: 128–42.

TURBAN, D. B. and GREENING, D. W. 1997. 'Corporate Social Performance and Organizational Attractiveness to Prospective Employees'. *Academy of Management Journal*, 40: 658–73.

VICTOR, B. and CULLEN, J. B. 1988. 'The Organizational Bases of Ethical Work Climates'. *Administrative Science Quarterly*, 33: 101–25.

WADDOCK, S. 2002. *Leading Corporate Citizens: Vision, Values, Value Added.* New York: McGraw Hill.

—— 2006. 'Hollow Men and Women at the Helm . . . Hollow Accounting Ethics'. *Issues in Accounting Education*, 20: 125–50.

WARTICK, S. L. and COCHRAN, P. L. 1985. 'The Evolution of the Corporate Social Performance Model'. *Academy of Management Review*, 10: 758–69.

WEBER, J. and GREEN, S. 1993. 'Principled Moral Reasoning: Is it a Viable Approach to Promote Ethical Integrity'? *Journal of Business Ethics*, 10, 325–33.

WEBER, M. 1922/1947. *The Theory of Social and Economic Organization* trans. A. H. Henderson and T. Parsons. New York: Oxford University Press.

WEICK, K. E. 1969. *The Social Psychology of Organizing.* Reading, Mass: Addison-Wesley.

WERHANE, P. 1999. *Moral Imagination and Management Decision Making.* New York: Oxford University Press.

WILLEN, L. 2004. 'Kellogg Denies Guilt as B-Schools evade Alumni Lapses'. Bloomberg, 8 Mar. <http://www.cba.k-state.edu/departments/ethics/docs/bloombergpress.htm>.

WINDSOR, D. 2002. 'An Open Letter on Business School Responsibility', 8 Oct.

—— 2006. 'Corporate Social Responsibility: Three Key Approaches'. *Journal of Management Studies*, 43: 93–114.

WOOD, D. 1991. 'Corporate Social Performance Revisited'. *Academy of Management Review*, 16: 691–718.

ZEITLIN, M. 1978. 'Managerial Theory vs. Class Theory of Corporate Capitalism', in L. E. Preston (ed.), *Research in Corporate Social Performance and Policy*, 1. Greenwich, Conn.: JAI Press, 255–63.

SOCIALLY RESPONSIBLE INVESTMENT AND SHAREHOLDER ACTIVISM

LLOYD KURTZ

INTRODUCTION

SOCIALLY responsible investment is a broad field with many points of connection and disconnection with corporate social responsibility (CSR). It would be natural to assume that socially responsible investment represents an implementation of CSR in financial markets, but many social investors have motivations very different from what we might call the academic view of CSR. Socially responsible investment has a long history, and many of its practices pre-date modern conceptions of social responsibility.

I thank Stephen Fowler of the University of San Francisco, James Hoopes of Babson College, Steven Lydenberg of Domini Social Investments, Kellie McElhaney of the University of California at Berkeley, Erica Plambeck of Stanford University, Donald Siegal of the University of California at Riverside and Meir Statman of Santa Clara University, for comments on material included in this chapter. I also acknowledge the support of Nelson Capital Management and the Wells Fargo Corporation. All errors are my own.

Since studies of socially responsible investment are often cited in discussions of CSR, it is important to understand what is, and what isn't, being said. We therefore begin by reviewing some basic definitional issues.

Some Brief Definitions

Like CSR, *socially responsible investment* is a broad and sometimes controversial term. The third section of this chapter is devoted to bringing greater clarity to its definition.[1] But there are a few illustrative statements we can make at the outset:

- All social investors include in their investment decision processes, over and above considerations of financial risk and return, some combination of ethical, religious, social, and environmental concerns. This is the broadest possible definition, and, unless otherwise indicated, this is the meaning we intend in this chapter.
- Many social investors construct portfolios using a process known as *screening*. This is a systematic method of excluding objectionable investments according to decision rules established beforehand. One common decision rule is to exclude companies involved in tobacco, alcohol, or gambling—the so-called *sin stocks*.
- Many social investors seek to change corporate behavior via proxy resolutions and negotiation with management, a process known as *shareholder activism*. Shareholder activism may or may not be combined with screening, depending on the objectives of the investor.
- Some social investors seek to include companies with notably positive social records in their portfolios, a process oxymoronically known as *positive screening*.
- Finally, socially responsible investment may also refer to investments that by-pass traditional financial channels and are viewed as having high social impact. This area is often termed *community investment*. It might take the form of *microfinance* (small loans to entrepreneurs, usually in developing countries), *social venture capital*, or *community lending* (bank lending focused on low- and moderate-income communities).[2]

---

[1] Other phrases used to describe the same activities include 'guideline investing', 'sustainability investing', 'social investing', and 'ethical investing'.

[2] A full discussion of community investment is beyond the scope of this chapter. For further information on social venture, see the Global Social Venture Competition sponsored by the Haas School at the University of California, Berkeley. Leading practitioners of microfinance and community lending include the Grameen Bank in Bangladesh and Shorebank Corporation in the United States.

Types of Social Investors

In the United States socially responsible investment has its roots in religious movements of various types, along with the Nuclear Freeze movement and South Africa boycott of the 1970s and 1980s. In recent years new approaches have emerged, particularly in Europe, placing greater emphasis on environmental issues and sustainable business practices. Kinder (2005) offers the following taxonomy of social investors today:

- *Value-based investors*: These social investors act in accordance with deeply held religious or ethical views. Their decision to include non-financial variables in their portfolio policy is driven primarily by their desire to have investments that are consistent with their moral beliefs. Most religious institutions that practice socially responsible investment fall into this category, as do many secular organizations focused on causes such as the environment or human rights.
- *Value-seeking investors*: Value-seeking investors use social and environmental data to enhance portfolio performance. There is some evidence that value can be captured in this way. Derwall *et al.* (2005) find that stocks with high environmental ratings markedly outperformed poorly rated ones for the 1995–2003 time period. Jean Frijns, Chief Investment Officer of the Dutch pension fund ABP Netherlands, believes that 'there is a growing body of evidence that companies which manage environmental, social, and governance risks most effectively tend to deliver better risk-adjusted financial performance than their industry peers'.[3]
- *Value-enhancing investors*: This group uses shareholder activism techniques to enhance investment value, and focuses primarily on corporate governance. The California pension fund CalPERS, discussed below, is an example of a value-enhancing investor.

Beyond these core groups are many other funds targeting a wide range of specific concerns (see examples in Table 11.1). These focused funds have not succeeded in attracting substantial investor interest, however, accounting for less than 1% of socially responsible investment assets in the United States.

The Prevalence and Significance of Social Investing

We believe both proponents and opponents of socially responsible investment tend to overstate its significance in financial markets—proponents do so because they wish to emphasize their influence, opponents because they wish to emphasize the threat. It appears socially responsible investment is an important niche in the

---

[3] Source: Kiernan (2005).

Table 11.1 Examples of special-purpose social investment mutual funds in the USA

- Amana Fund—Invests according to Islamic principles.
- Ave Maria Fund—Seeks to invest in 'companies that do not violate the core teachings of the Catholic Church'.
- New Alternatives—Invests primarily in companies involved in alternative energy and activities supportive of the environment.
- The Timothy Plan—Invests according to conservative Christian principles.
- Vice Fund—Invests *primarily* in alcohol, tobacco, gambling, and defense stocks.
- Women's Equity Fund—Invests primarily in companies judged to be helpful to the 'advancement of women in the workplace'.

financial marketplace, but recent data from the United States and Europe show it is not particularly large in the context of broader financial markets.

The Social Investment Forum (2006) reports that approximately one dollar in ten of assets under management in the United States ($2.3 trillion) is invested according to some type of social constraint. This figure is based on a broad definition of socially responsible investment which includes shareholder activism and investors employing a single social screen. Narrowing the focus further, we find that investors who employ more than one social screen (the image most of us have of a social investor) account for $954 billion, or 4% of all US assets under management.[4]

Estimates for Europe indicate roughly the same level of involvement, but with more involvement by institutions. Eurosif, a European socially responsible investment organization representing institutional investors, states that its membership accounts for about €600 billion in assets. Bartolomeo and Familiari (2005) estimate assets in European social investment mutual funds at €24 billion, relatively small compared to institutional commitments, but double the level of two years before.

The importance of socially responsible investment transcends its size, however. Social investors stand—some deliberately, others unwittingly—at the center of an important debate in the Western intellectual tradition. The question is whether ethics should play a role in capital allocation decisions, or not.[5]

Social investors take the view that ethics should matter, and that they should be incorporated directly into the investment decision-making process. It is, of course, a minority view. But that does not mean that they are wrong.

In the sections that follow we will:

- Review and discuss the rationale for socially responsible investment,
- Provide examples of the strategies social investors use to define and quantify corporate social responsibility,

[4] This consists of $120 bn in mutual funds and $834 bn in separately managed accounts.
[5] We use the term 'ethics' here in its most basic philosophical sense—pertaining to questions of what is right or wrong.

- Review performance of socially responsible investment strategies, and
- Comment on two recent critiques of CSR and socially responsible investment.

THE RATIONALE FOR SOCIALLY
RESPONSIBLE INVESTMENT

Socially responsible investment stands at the intersection of two powerful streams of western thought—on the one hand, religious and moral reasoning; on the other, economic and financial theory. One tradition insists on the relevance of ethics to all realms of human activity, the other argues for a narrow focus on risk and return in capital allocation decisions. Social investors have set themselves the daunting task of crafting portfolios that meet the requirements of both traditions.

The theoretical financial arguments against socially responsible investment are well-rehearsed, although they have often been mischaracterized or oversimplified.[6] But social investors can draw substantial support from other areas of the Western intellectual tradition, including economics, ethics, and theology.

In our specialized age, these arguments do not contend with one another across academic boundaries. MBA candidates often experience severe dissonance as they encounter significantly different world views from their ethics and finance professors, with no formal attempt to reconcile them. There is a good reason for this—reconciling them is very difficult. But socially responsible investment is based on the premise that both world views matter. Making sense of their interaction is a challenge we must take up.

John Wesley and the Uses of Money

As we mentioned at the beginning of this chapter, socially responsible investment has a great deal in common with CSR, but there are significant differences as well. One of the most important of these is the role of religion. Religious belief was the first rationale for socially responsible investment, and remains an important force today, especially in the United States.

Christian investors find abundant support for social investment in the scriptures.[7] Burkholder (2002) writes in a Mennonite publication that:

---

[6] For a discussion of how socially responsible investment is viewed under various financial theories, see Kurtz (1998, 2005).

[7] The Koran also provides extensive guidance on the use of money, particularly on the charging of interest.

In the New Testament, Jesus had more to say about money matters than any other single subject, be it worship, sexual behavior, violence and peace, or even eternal life. From his parables (the rich fool, the rich man and Lazarus) and his encounters with people (Zacchaeus, the rich ruler), a basic assumption emerges: for those who would follow Jesus, economic questions are really spiritual questions.

As a result, the proper use of money has been an important topic in Christian discourse for hundreds of years. Mackenzie (1997), in his instructive thesis on socially responsible investment, points out that John Wesley, the founder of Methodism,

> ...emphasised in the 1700s that the use of money was the second most important subject of New Testament teaching. He gave four consecutive addresses entitled: 'Earn all you can'; 'But not at the expense of conscience'; 'Not at the expense of our neighbours' wealth'; 'Not at the expense of our neighbours' health'.

Wesley's sermons may be read as the first blueprint for socially responsible investment, and many of the restrictions he recommended are still widely observed today. He believed that a Christian should never engage in a business that harmed another person's health, citing particularly the sale of alcoholic spirits. And he warned 'we cannot, if we love everyone as ourselves, hurt anyone in his *substance*', citing as examples the exploitation of others through gambling, overcharging for services, or charging excessive rates of interest.

Not coincidentally, Methodist organizations have had significant influence on the development of modern socially responsible investment. Pax World, recognized as the first socially responsible mutual fund in the United States, was founded in 1971 by United Methodist ministers Jack Corbett and Luther Tyson, and Methodist pension plans are major institutional practitioners of socially responsible investment in the United States.[8]

As compelling as arguments from religious conviction are for the converted, they are bound to be insufficient in a broader investment context. In a proxy fight, more is needed to persuade the majority to vote in favor of a social or environmental proposal.

Religious investors have created institutions to specifically address this challenge. Today the Interfaith Center on Corporate Responsibility (ICCR) advocates on behalf of 275 faith-based institutions in the United States, including Roman Catholic, Protestant, and Jewish organizations. This organization has been successful in forging alliances beyond the religious community: affiliated organizations include Amnesty International and New York City's Office of the Comptroller.

[8] For Tyson's detailed account of the founding of Pax World, see Brick (2005–6).

ICCR Core Values[9]

Faith-Based   Faith guides and shapes our priorities for action.

Justice   We challenge ourselves and corporations to accountability for right relationships with all of creation.

Integrity   We are striving to be credible practitioners of the values we set forth.

Inclusive   We welcome diversity as we covenant to work together.

'Das Adam Smith Problem'

A more secular rationale for socially responsible investment might appeal to economic self-interest, a secular ethical framework, or both. Social investors pursuing this type of rationale find themselves in the garden Adam Smith grew up in.

Social investors have typically heard about Adam Smith from their critics. Smith famously showed in *The Wealth of Nations* that markets allocate resources efficiently, and believed they work best when participants act primarily in their own self-interest:

> ... every individual necessarily labours to render the annual revenue of the society as great as he can. He generally, indeed, neither intends to promote the public interest, nor knows how much he is promoting it ... he intends only his own gain, and he is in this, as in many other cases, led by an invisible hand to promote an end which was no part of his intention. Nor is it always the worse for the society that it was no part of it. By pursuing his own interest he frequently promotes that of the society more effectually than when he really intends to promote it.

Smith then appears to explicitly deny the concept of moral capitalism:

> I have never known much good done by those who affected to trade for the public good. It is an affectation, indeed, not very common among merchants, and very few words need be employed in dissuading them from it.

These passages are so well-known and widely cited that it may come as a surprise that Smith was a moral philosopher as well. In his *Theory of Moral Sentiments* he placed great emphasis on the ethical responsibilities of individuals in society, and particularly on a person's capacity for empathy and restraint of self-regard. Muller (1993), in his *Adam Smith in His Time and Ours*, describes Smithian ethics this way:

> Our desire for the sympathy of others leads by steps to the restraint of our self-love ... Our natural egoism is partially restrained by our awareness of an external standard, the standard we would use to judge our actions if we were a spectator who was biased neither toward ourselves nor toward those affected by our actions.

[9] Source: Interfaith Center for Corporate Responsibility (2006).

Although Smith was religious, this moral view is based on observation as much as revelation and one does not need to be of a particular faith to subscribe to it.

Smith's economic and moral views therefore appear to be highly dissonant. Should we be selfish or not? Economist Joseph Schumpeter referred to this apparent contradiction as 'Das Adam Smith Problem', and it has long been a subject of debate among economists.[10]

Smith must have been aware of this tension in his thought—indeed, he was immersed in it from the start of his education. Muller explains that:

At the age of fourteen, Smith was sent to the University of Glasgow [where he] first confronted the great issues which were to drive Scottish moral philosophy in the eighteenth century. The first of those issues was how to reconcile classical and Christian demands for altruism and benevolence in human relations with recent arguments by Thomas Hobbes and Bernard Mandeville that egoism and self-interest were the driving force in society, and how to do so without resorting to the disputed authority of revelation.

Yet Smith never fully resolved the contradiction. Perhaps he thought it intractable, perhaps he thought it sufficient to acknowledge that ethics and markets are both important, or perhaps he just ran out of time.

Steven Lydenberg (2005), the Chief Investment Officer of Domini Social Investments and a longtime social investor, believes that Smith's world view is consistent with socially responsible investment, and even provides clues as to how to better harness the power of markets to improve society. His ambitious *Corporations and the Public Interest* refers to Smith extensively, and in the process broadens the argument for socially responsible investment from a religious to a secular basis.

Lydenberg observes that Smith's formulation of the invisible hand concept does not mean that he supported *laissez-faire* economics. On the contrary, he believed business affairs should be regulated. He wrote disparagingly of the 'overgrown standing army' of business interests that sought to influence Parliament in his own time.

The question, from Lydenberg's perspective, is how to use the power of markets to encourage corporations to behave in ways that are beneficial to society. This implies a major change in the nature of business regulation, one where capital markets would play a central enforcement role. Markets have been very successful in getting corporations to employ labor efficiently and invent new technologies, Lydenberg argues. Why not bring markets to bear on corporate social and environmental behavior as well?

There's been a secular shift in our society to corporations since at least the 1980s. The pendulum has been swinging away from government, and now governments feel maybe it's swung too far...Even the Wall Street Journal editorial page says 'markets need adult supervision.'

---

[10] See Heilbroner (1982).

And that creates a dilemma—how do you do that? How do you direct corporations to the public interest? We need new vocabulary to do that, new data. And I think [socially responsible investment] can bring great value to that. We can bring fresh perspectives to risk, intangible assets, and wealth creation.[11]

In Lydenberg's vision, all investors could become social investors, as companies make better disclosures about their social and environmental practices and markets evaluate and react to this information. But to realize this vision, important changes must be made in our investment culture. In particular, Lydenberg argues that the social/environmental characteristics of investment products should be reported to the customer 'at the point of purchase. Only then can people make good judgments about investment product attributes beyond return.'

Social investors today fill this function to some degree. By disseminating information about the conduct of corporations they offer data that individuals can ignore or incorporate into their investment decisions. So, even if there is no general solution to 'Das Adam Smith Problem', people can work toward a personal balance that works for them. Some people may be totally motivated by economic interests, while others may be totally motivated by ethical ones. The availability of good social data makes it possible for the latter group to act on their beliefs, and for people who wish to refer to both ethics and economics to strike the appropriate balance.

Exit, Voice, and Loyalty

Adam Smith tells us that both economics and ethics are important, but not how they interact. When should we employ economic reasoning, and when should we adopt ethical reasoning? Economists and ethicists will both say 'all the time!' but that is not much help. Pietra Rivoli of Georgetown University was the first to note the importance of the economist Albert Hirschman's (1970) *Exit, Voice, and Loyalty* in this analysis. Although Hirschman, a noted liberal economist, did not address social investment specifically, his work is a valuable resource for understanding the options available to social investors, and the choices they make.

Hirschman contends that conventional economic reasoning is incomplete and that in some situations its basic assumptions do not hold. And, like social investors, he is interested in the question of how to deal with the 'failure of some actors to live up to the behavior which [society expects] of them'. He sees two possible options for a stakeholder concerned about an organization's behavior—one closely connected to Smith's invisible hand, the other more related to the social sciences:

Exit is the classical economic response to dissatisfaction with organizational behavior. A firm that provides an unpalatable investment opportunity will lose shareholders, just as a company selling an inferior product will lose customers. Indeed,

---

[11] Author's interview with Steven Lydenberg, 23 Mar. 2005.

the most common advice social investors hear from Wall Street is: if you don't like the company, sell the stock. Most social investment funds do exactly that, providing elaborate descriptions of the types of stocks they choose *not* to own.[12]

Exit is an excellent choice for investors who want to form portfolios consistent with their moral beliefs, but do not aspire to change corporate behavior. For more activist investors, however, it is bound to be insufficient. Hirschman explains that the problem with Exit is that it abandons the opportunity to change things for the better.

This problem is not unique to social investors. In April 2005, SEC Chairman Harvey Goldschmid told the Council of Institutional Investors

> If shareholders don't like what is going on, they can simply sell their shares in a public market. If, however, because of a management's disastrous course, my shares have fallen from $40 to $20, selling them before they fall to $10 will be beneficial (though painful) for me, but will not improve the corporation's governance or performance. Wouldn't a rational economic system permit shareholders to bring about mid-course corrections? Is waiting for bankruptcy the ideal way to deal with wrongheaded, economically destructive boards and senior managers?[13]

Voice There is another option, Hirschman explains. The alternative to exit is *voice*. Customers of a company producing an inferior product may complain before they defect. And investors, confronted with objectionable corporate behavior, may raise their concerns with management before choosing to sell the stock.

But when should we sell and when should we stay? In Hirschman's framework, the choice of voice or exit is mediated by *loyalty*. Loyalty is not a leap of faith—it is a rational assessment of the likelihood that the organization will do the right thing over time. In a social investment context, this means companies with remediable problems might remain in portfolios as long as they appear willing to address them.

As an example, Wal-Mart was a member of the Domini 400 Social Index, a broad-based socially responsible benchmark in the United States, until 2001. Its continued inclusion, despite many controversies, was at least partly attributable to the company's willingness to engage in dialogue with concerned parties about these issues. In April 2001, however, Wal-Mart was removed from the index. Kyle Johnson, project manager for the index, cited concerns that the company's statements about its involvement in controversial manufacturing operations abroad had not been accurate, and that the company, instead of making itself more transparent, 'did the opposite by trying to cover up'.[14] In Hirschman's framework, the managers of the Domini index decided that the possibility of change was too low to justify their continued loyalty.

[12] See, for example, 'Domini Social Equity Fund Standards' at <http://www.domini.com> or 'Social Analysis Criteria' at <http://www.calvert.com>.

[13] Goldschmid, Harvey J. 'Critical SEC Issues for 2005–2006'. Remarks before the Council of Institutional Investors, 11 Apr. 2005.

[14] 'Wal-Mart Booted Out of the Domini 400'. Socialfunds.com (social investment news service), 17 Apr. 2001.

Hirschman's work offers a playbook for investors who hope to influence corporate behavior, and strongly suggests that both screening and shareholder activism techniques should be employed.

The Universal Owner

For many large institutional investors, exit is difficult or even impossible. Operating under legal requirements that they fully diversify their assets, they must own a broad range of companies, even those that engage in behavior that is objectionable or harmful to the institutions' beneficiaries. It follows from Hirschman's analysis that voice is the only strategy by which these organizations can address objectionable behavior by the companies in their portfolios. Graeme Davies (2005), Chairman of the Universities Superannuation Scheme in the UK, characterizes this as seeking 'to change the direction of the ship rather than jumping ship'.

Corporate governance activist Robert Monks (1994) coined the term 'universal owner' to describe these large institutional investors. In their outstanding book, *The Rise of Fiduciary Capitalism*, James Hawley and Andrew Williams (2002a) deeply examine the role of universal owners in society. They report that institutional ownership of equities in the United States has been on the rise for a generation. In the 1970s individuals owned approximately 75% of the US stock market. By 2000, institutions owned 60% of the top 1,000 US companies.[15] This, they argue, has had profound effects on governance:

[O]wnership, and indeed private property in the corporate form, is rapidly being transformed into an institution in which agents represent agents in what can be quite long and complex chains between the firm at one end and the ultimate beneficial 'owner' or claimant at the other. Property and ownership increasingly have become bureaucratic and organizational while the rights and responsibilities of operational ownership (that is, investment decisions, proxy voting, etc.) increasingly reside in the hands of professionalized management teams operating as fiduciary intermediaries.

Institutional investors have become an important player in addressing externalities created by corporations, because 'they own a broad cross section of the economy and ... therefore internalize externalities'. With the top 25 institutional investors in the United States controlling 60% of the financial assets, institutional investors must be more cognizant of their potential influence on corporations, particularly in areas that could impact the health and welfare of their beneficiaries.

Financial practitioners have not welcomed this argument with open arms. Portfolio management is a complex exercise. The universal owner concept comes uncomfortably close to political activity, and threatens to compromise the integrity of an already-challenging decision-making process. It also raises a host of slippery

---

[15] Sullivan and Mackenzie (2006) report that the situation is the same in the UK, where about half of the stock market is controlled by institutional investors such as insurance companies and pension funds.

slope problems—if political considerations are introduced into the investment process, what prevents them from dominating it?

But Hirschman demonstrates that this politicization is an inevitable consequence of institutions' relationships with corporations. The exercise of influence, he argues, is always a political process, although his definition of 'political' is broader than the image we might have of campaign buttons and television ads.

Hawley and Williams acknowledge that we are moving into territory that resembles political activity in important ways. In Hawley's words, 'universal owners must confront the messy fact that they have quasi-political responsibilities'.[16] Global climate change, he says, is 'a good example of a policy that could be addressed by governments, but absent that you have this public policy role [for institutions]'.

Hawley and Williams see a hierarchy of potential actions an institutional investor can take in response to this challenge:

- Develop policy guidelines on a particular issue.
- Survey portfolio firms on particular policies.
- Monitor the lobbying efforts of portfolio companies.
- Grade portfolio firms on a particular issue.
- Target specific portfolio companies on specific issues.
- Do nothing.

Today, most large institutional investors choose the last option. With a few exceptions, large institutions have not made serious attempts to change corporate social or environmental behavior.

Hawley and Williams comment that inaction can be a constructive policy 'when it is taken in full consideration of the facts. [But] it is not a constructive policy when an institution fails to take a position because it has failed to inform itself on the issues involved.'

One institution that *has* taken an activist role, primarily on the corporate governance side, has been CalPERS, the California Public Employees' Retirement System. Since 1992 CalPERS has published an annual 'Focus List' of companies it views as having inadequate corporate governance practices. While Hawley and Williams view this program as a natural outgrowth of CalPERS' responsibility as a universal owner, some critics argue that it has been an inappropriate use of resources.

We believe there is good evidence that the CalPERS program has been a successful one. Nesbitt (1994) argued that CalPERS' corporate governance initiatives had added significant value up to that time. Barber (2006) analyzes the performance of the CalPERS Focus List from 1992 to 2005 and finds 'small, but reliably positive, market reactions of 23 basis points on the date focus list firms are publicly announced'. Although this effect may not appear dramatic, it translates into $3.1 billion in added value over the 14-year period.

---

[16] Author's interview with James Hawley, 5 May 2006.

Barber notes, however, that that most of this gain came from initiatives that could be tangibly linked to shareholder value, not those with primarily social objectives. He expresses concern that individual agents might use the pension fund's influence to advance their own political interests. Hawley and Williams would certainly agree with his view that: 'when activism cannot be justified as a mechanism to improve shareholder value, the moral or political objectives of investors, not fund managers, should be considered paramount'.

Barber raises two important questions faced by universal owners.

- What do we do when correcting objectionable behavior would be costly to shareholders? From a universal owner's perspective the economic cost should be balanced against the benefits of ending the behavior, but this type of analysis is rarely done.
- Whose opinion counts in deciding what corporate behavior is objectionable? In theory, the beneficiaries' wishes should be an important factor, but in most cases there is no established mechanism to provide a reliable gauge of their views.

How Social Investors Define and Quantify Social Responsibility

Definition and Quantification

In this section we will provide examples of strategies social investors use to define and quantify corporate social responsibility. One of the most common criticisms of social investment is that the central concept is ill-defined. Unfortunately for social investors, there is an element of truth to this.

There need be no ambiguity at the client level. Most institutional clients provide written policy statements detailing exactly which investments advisors should avoid or include. Leading social investment funds offer carefully written explanations of how they identify socially responsible companies. The Calvert mutual fund group in the United States publishes the names of stocks in their Calvert Social Index, so anyone who cares to inspect their work can do so.[17] Several social investment research firms, notably KLD, clearly specify their research topics and make historical data available for academic research. Definitions of social responsibility may vary, but we would argue the concept is well-specified in these cases.

The ambiguity arises when we aggregate many social investors and try to generalize about their behavior. Then 'socially responsible investment' becomes a very

---

[17] As of June 2007, this material was available on the Calvert website at <http://www.calvert.com/sri_calvertindex.html>.

general term. Can we really speak meaningfully about the common experiences of a Catholic institution, an environmental foundation, and a mutual fund focused on diversity issues? Paul Hawken (2004), a progressive critic of the socially responsible investment industry, argues that 'the term "socially responsible investing" is so broad it is meaningless'.

This may seem like semantics. Certainly, insisting on rigorous definition of terms is a proven method of diverting attention away from other issues. And we live with ambiguity in terms all the time, even in disciplines that are viewed as quantitative.

But in studies of social responsibility the whole enterprise rides on the validity of the definition. Supporting empirical work can only have meaning if the independent variable is clearly defined. If that first step is wrong, all the regressions, analysis, and verbiage that follow can simply be discarded.

In the sections that follow we will discuss approaches social investors take to defining and quantifying social responsibility, and propose some new techniques. Although none of these approaches gives results that agree exactly with academic views of CSR, all have potential value to CSR researchers. Social investors have considerable experience with some of the tough measurement questions: Should ratings be absolute or relative? If relative, should we compare companies to the broad universe of stocks, or only to their own industry? And how do we combine data from different issue areas into a single rating?

Stepwise Screening

One way to define something is to say what it is not. Social investors are good at this. Most have a list of investments that must be avoided, developed through the use of a stepwise screening procedure. The majority of social investors in the United States have the simplest possible one-step screening procedure: they don't buy tobacco stocks.[18]

Of course, many investors employ more detailed criteria. An Islamic client might specify:

- No investment in companies with revenues from alcohol, tobacco, gambling, or pornography.
- No investment in manufacturers of pork-related products.
- No investment in financial companies lending money at interest, or otherwise having the trade of interest-bearing assets as a primary business activity.
- No investment in businesses with more than one-third of their capital derived from debt-related instruments.[19]

[18] The Social Investment Forum (2005) reports that the tobacco screen is the most prevalent among both institutions and mutual funds. It estimates that $800 bn in institutional money is screened for tobacco, as opposed to $300 bn for the MacBride Principles, the next most-common screen.
[19] I have provided a simplistic example here for illustrative purposes. For a detailed explanation of Islamic screening practices, see the Dow Jones Islamic Index (2006).

A list of companies fitting these criteria can then be compiled and presented to the investment manager as a 'don't buy' list. As an example, a stepwise screening procedure was the first step in the development of the Domini 400 Social Index.[20]

This approach has many virtues:

- The inputs can be clearly specified.
- The output is unambiguous—an investment is either prohibited or it is not.
- It can be structured to make efficient use of scarce research resources, a very important consideration in the early days of socially responsible investment. In the initial construction of the Domini Social Index, a large pharmaceutical company was excluded because it did business in South Africa. By evaluating the relatively clear South Africa issue first, the researchers saved themselves the trouble of evaluating the company's complex environmental record at that time.

But this kind of restriction-driven investing has important shortcomings. For one thing, there is no mechanism to recognize positive social characteristics. Some companies that are excluded are also generous donors to charity, or have a strong record of promoting diversity in their organizations. Under stepwise screening they are removed because of involvement with a particular issue and cannot be recovered, regardless of how many positive characteristics are present. Many clients prefer a more nuanced view of corporate responsibility.

Another problem with stepwise screening is that the portfolio may be overconstrained. It is not hard to develop a reasonable-sounding list of restrictions that eliminates almost the entire investment universe from consideration.[21]

Despite its shortcomings, stepwise screening remains the most common method of constructing social investment portfolios, and allows precise definition of the term 'social responsibility' in studies of risk and return.

Relative Weighting

Under relative weighting, companies are not automatically excluded. Instead, an assessment is made of both strengths and weaknesses for each company. This information is then incorporated into the investment manager's portfolio construction policies. This approach is widely-practiced in Europe, and interest from US investors is growing.

---

[20] See Kurtz and Lydenberg (1992) for a description of the construction of this index. A list of portfolio holdings for the Domini 400 Social Index is available at <http://www.domini.com>.

[21] The most-constrained fund of which we are aware is the Sierra Club Mutual Fund in the United States. According to Garvin Jabusch, Director of the Sierra Mutual Fund Complex, its rigorous environmental screens exclude 70–75% of the S&P 500. For further information on the financial characteristics of this fund see Edelen (2004).

■ Ratings Indicators	■ Controversial Issues
❑ Community	❑ Adult Entertainment
❑ Corporate Governance	❑ Alcohol
❑ Diversity	❑ Firearms
❑ Employee Relations	❑ Gambling
❑ Environment	❑ Military Weapons
❑ Human Rights	❑ Nuclear Power
❑ Product	❑ Tobacco

Fig. 11.1 KLD research categories

In 2005 KLD Research & Analytics launched the KLD Select Social Index which provides a good example of the relative weighting approach. Using its social database, KLD summarizes the social record of each company in the Russell 1000 stock index into a numerical score (see Figures 11.1 and 11.2 for examples of the data used in this analysis).

This social score is then entered into a portfolio management system as a return expectation, and the software is instructed to match the risk level of the portfolio to that of a market benchmark. Almost any company may qualify for inclusion in the portfolio if its positive characteristics sufficiently offset its negatives.[22] The resulting portfolio has market-like risk and return characteristics, but maximizes exposure to overall social and environmental performance.

While the KLD Select Social Index compares each company to others in the benchmark, not all relatively weighting systems do so. The research firm Innovest, for example, ranks companies within industries. The benefit of doing this is that comparisons are easier to make among peer companies, and companies within an industry typically face the same constellation of social and environmental challenges.

Whether comparisons are made across the universe or within industries, relative weighting offers several advantages over stepwise screening. It is better from an advisor's standpoint because it confers superior financial flexibility. A relative weights approach may allow investors to include the 'best of the worst' in certain categories, giving the manager better opportunities to diversify the portfolio. This is an important risk management tool in eras when industries excluded under stepwise screening performed strongly, such as in the late 1980s when pharmaceutical stocks outperformed the market in anticipation of the recession, but were excluded wholesale from social portfolios because of their South African involvement. A more recent example is the underweighting of the energy sector by some social investors sector in the mid-2000s due to environmental constraints, leading to underperformance in some cases.

Portfolios formed using the relative weighting approach may also be useful in quantitative studies of CSR. The definition of CSR is transformed under relative

---

[22] The one exception is tobacco companies, which are automatically excluded.

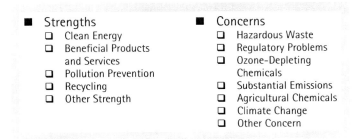

Fig. 11.2 KLD subcategory example: the environment

weighting from a binary one (in the portfolio or out) to a scaled variable, which may be better suited to quantitative analysis.

But relative weighting also has disadvantages. It recognizes companies that perform well across a broad spectrum of social or environmental criteria, but may not appropriately recognize those with exceptional records on just one or two dimensions of the analysis. Often these are the companies that clients most want to include.

Finally, the 'best of the worst' philosophy inherent in relative weighting may make it impractical for investors who do not wish to compromise their values. For these investors, if a whole industry is behaving badly, it is not acceptable to own the stock of a company behaving slightly *less* badly. Wesley said 'we cannot, if we love everyone as ourselves, hurt anyone in his *substance*'. He did not say '...we cannot hurt anyone in his *substance* unless, relatively speaking, we are the least harmful of the participants in our industry'.

It is a paradox of socially responsible investment that clients are idealists, but practitioners must be relativists. Whether they use stepwise screening or relative weights, practitioners must rank companies on the social and environmental dimensions, and then consult with the client about where to draw the line. Under both systems this process can create an uncomfortable sensation of appeasement or compromise. Why, clients ask, can't they own only the very best social and environmental performers?

Focusing on Excellence

Some social investors wish to create portfolios focusing primarily on the positive aspects of corporate behavior. Instead of merely excluding bad companies or preferring companies with a preponderance of positive attributes, they want to hold only stocks that exemplify their values.

There have been many attempts to create portfolios of this type in the United States. Notable examples include the Women's Equity Fund, which focuses on firms that have positive records on women's issues; the Meyers Pride fund, which sought to invest in companies with strong records on gay/lesbian issues, and the PowerShares Wilder Hill Clean Energy Portfolio, an exchange-traded fund which focuses on companies involved in clean energy.

Although most of these products have had limited commercial success, they may be of particular interest to CSR researchers because they represent independently compiled lists of firms judged to be excellent in specific issues areas. As researchers strive to understand the financial effects of CSR, they can use the holdings of these portfolios as a resource for empirical research.

It would be helpful to bring this focus on excellence to the broader concept of social responsibility. As noted above, we can define something by exclusion—but we can also define something by citing exceptional examples. We could do this if we had a credible list of the very best social performers. We propose here a methodology to identify those positive outliers, along with a preliminary finding for the US market.

In 2005 we conducted a poll of the membership of SIRAN, the professional association of social investment research analysts in the United States, asking them to name a few companies they thought had exceptional social responsibility records. The resulting list of 20 publicly traded US companies was then compared with the top 20 companies on social performance from a database maintained by KLD Research & Analytics.[23] Eight firms appeared on both lists. They were:

- Dell
- Gap
- General Mills
- Hewlett-Packard
- Intel
- Southwest Airlines
- Starbucks
- Timberland

These stocks are widely held in social portfolios, and we believe there is strong evidence that they are viewed as top CSR performers both inside and outside the socially responsible investment industry. They have several other points of resemblance:

- All have strong brand names. This is consistent with the claims of CSR advocates that a record of social responsibility has reputational value.
- All are consumer-facing. Four of the companies operate in consumer sectors, three in high-tech, and one in transportation. The energy, materials, healthcare, finance, capital goods, telecommunications, and utilities sectors are not represented.

---

[23] This database is used in the construction of the KLD Select Social Index, discussed above.

- For virtually all of these companies, historical growth rates, reinvestment rates, and market expectations for future growth were above market averages at the time of the poll. Angel and Rivoli (1997) predict that companies with higher growth rates will have a greater incentive to maintain a reputation for social responsibility, as their share prices would be more vulnerable in the event of a boycott of their stock.
- These are big companies. This again accords with the predictions of Angel and Rivoli.
- Of this group, unionized employees are in the majority only at Southwest Airlines.[24]

For researchers interested in studying the characteristics of companies with exemplary social records, we believe this list would be a good place to start.

CSR and Socially Responsible Investment Performance

From CSR to Socially Responsible Investment

Some social investors believe their research methods can help them beat the market. Indeed, an entire book, Camejo's (2002) *The SRI Advantage: Why Socially Responsible Investing has Outperformed Financially*, has been dedicated to the topic. Unfortunately, empirical evidence for such an effect is minimal.

The most obvious argument against a stock performance benefit is that most investors just don't care. Milton Moskowitz, long a champion of corporate social responsibility, comments that 'I have rarely seen a company's share price move up as a result of a new social initiative taken by the company. For most of Wall Street, it's irrelevant.'[25]

But Wall Street *is* interested in results, and there is some evidence that social responsibility has a positive effect on earnings. Waddock and Graves (1997) show that CSR is positively associated with accounting measures of financial performance, a finding replicated by Tsoutsoura (2004) over a different time period. But McWilliams and Siegel (2000) question whether these studies can be taken at face value, given that adjustments are not made for R&D intensity. They show that when R&D is included in the analysis, CSR loses its statistical significance.

---

[24] Source: KLD Research & Analytics, 'SOCRATES: The Corporate Social Ratings Monitor', accessed 30 June 2006.
[25] Correspondence with the author, 20 Sept. 2006.

Waldman *et al.* (2004) find a strong correlation between CSR and R&D, again raising the question of what we are really measuring.

This debate also raises difficult questions of causality. Laffer *et al.* (2004) argue that social responsibility is likely to be an effect, not a cause, since only profitable companies can invest in CSR initiatives. Consider Amgen, one of the most profitable firms in the world, a significant R&D spender, and also a strong CSR performer. McWilliams and Siegel might argue that the first cause of Amgen's success was its intensive R&D investment, not its charitable giving program or highly regarded daycare center. Their account of the firm's success might look like this:

$$\text{Intensive R\&D} \rightarrow \text{Superior Profitability} \rightarrow \text{Heavy CSR Investment}$$

CSR advocates might paint a different picture, arguing that the successful R&D program might not have been possible without investments to retain skilled employees and attract the best talent in a knowledge-intensive industry:

$$\text{Heavy CSR Investment} \rightarrow \text{Intensive R\&D} \rightarrow \text{Superior Profitability}$$

Orlitzky *et al.* (2003) address some of these issues in a careful statistical review of the CSR literature. Like Waddock and Graves and Tsoutsoura, they find a positive association between CSR and financial performance. And they confirms Laffer *et al.*'s intuition that good financial performance precedes good social performance. But they also provide evidence that CSR investments tend to pay off in the form of superior corporate earnings. Once the ball is rolling, CSR and superior profitability appear to be self-reinforcing.

Marjorie Kelly, editor of the US magazine *Business Ethics*, sees Orlitzky *et al.*'s study as the end of history for social investors:

Holy Grail Found:

Absolute, definitive proof that responsible companies perform better financially ... I'm here to announce the search is over. The evidence is in. And even the statisticians are saying it's conclusive. Social and environmental responsibility does go hand in hand with superior financial performance ... [26]

But even if these studies are exactly right about the earnings impact of CSR, superior stock performance is *not* assured. Social investors will only earn superior returns over time *if the market consistently underestimates the impact of CSR initiatives.* We can illustrate this with a stylized example:

Suppose a company pays out half its earnings as dividends, and is expected to grow 5% a year in the future. Given a return expectation of 8%, the market would award this company a Price/Earnings (P/E) ratio of about 17.[27] Now let's assume that the company plans to adopt a CSR program that will raise its sustainable growth

---

[26] Marjorie Kelly, 'Holy Grail Found', *Business Ethics*, winter 2004.

[27] We use a transformation of the model introduced by Gordon (1962)—see the Appendix for details of this calculation and those that follow.

rate by 1%. Then a much higher P/E ratio would be appropriate—the standard formula suggests a level of 25.

Investment performance therefore depends on the valuation *prior* to the implementation of the CSR program. If the stock trades at a P/E of 17 before the program is announced, results should be good as the higher future growth rate is recognized and the P/E expands to 25. But if the P/E is already 25, the market will have already discounted the positive effects of the program, and returns will be just average. And if the stock is purchased at a P/E above 25, performance will be poor even if the 6% growth target is met.

Social investors who seek superior performance therefore face a daunting triple hurdle. For them to consistently beat the market:

(1) CSR policies must add economic value to the firm over time, *and*
(2) This effect must be large enough to matter to the intrinsic value of the firm, *and*
(3) Financial markets must fail to anticipate the financial benefits of CSR.[28]

The last hurdle is perhaps the toughest one. Studies of socially responsible investment portfolios have consistently shown that they have a growth bias—that is, the market already expects above-average growth from socially responsible companies. It follows that socially responsible companies must beat elevated expectations before social investors can beat the market.

Socially Responsible Investment Performance

This is an important disconnect between financial academics and social investment practitioners. Few financial academics think social responsibility has a major impact on stock returns. There is a robust body of academic literature on the historical determinants of stock returns—and social responsibility is not one of them. In their canonical study of returns, Fama and French (1992) present strong evidence that differences in returns among equity portfolios can be primarily attributed to:

- Risk, as measured by beta,
- Valuation, as measured by price/book ratio, and
- Size, as measured by market capitalization.

This finding has been replicated, extended to time periods both before and after the initial study, and institutionalized.[29] Today there are commercial performance analysis systems that explain portfolio returns using these and dozens of other variables. These tools can explain 90% or more of the difference in returns between portfolios.[30]

---

[28] See Boatright (1999) for further discussion of this aspect of the debate.
[29] For an excellent introduction to this literature, see Davis (2001).
[30] BARRA and Northfield Information Systems are leading vendors of this software.

Research into social investment returns falls into two categories—studies conducted with an awareness of this body of knowledge, and everything else. Most studies using modern risk models and covering long time periods show that socially responsible investments have performed as well as their unscreened peers, but not better.

Particularly strong studies of social investment returns include:

- Bauer *et al.* (2002), which analyzes 103 German, UK, and US screened mutual funds for the 1990–2001 time period, and finds risk-adjusted returns of screened funds were about the same as those of unscreened funds.
- Geczy *et al.* (2003) focus on the 35 US funds with three-year track records through 12/01. The retrospective analysis in this paper fits with the findings of Bauer *et al.*, although the authors introduce an important technical critique of socially responsible investment.
- Bollen and Cohen (2004) examine US funds for the 1980–2002 time period and conclude that risk-adjusted returns were slightly better than those of unscreened funds.
- On the fixed income side, Derwall and Koedijk (2006) examine screened bond fund returns for the 1987–2003 time period and conclude that their returns were competitive with, or even a little better than, those of unscreened funds.

For a full review of the recent literature of social investment performance, see Kurtz (2005).[31]

Some social investors argue that the real benefits of CSR are likely to show up in the risk dimension. This is intuitively appealing. Equity markets have a decidedly short-term outlook. The turnover of shares on the New York Stock Exchange runs at about 100%, suggesting the average share is held for approximately one year.[32] Social investors, by contrast, often focus on issues of long-term concern. There is a rational economic case for avoiding tobacco stocks, for example, if one believes there may be significant additional financial liabilities associated with the negative health effects of tobacco. But an investor who wishes to bet on this belief may have to wait many years before these liabilities become visible to market. As Hong and Kacperczyk (2006) demonstrate, it has not been a rewarding wait so far—tobacco stocks have done well, even better than a Fama and French model would project. But if social investors are, in fact, adept at identifying and avoiding these long-term problems, one would expect their portfolios to exhibit less risk over time.

Unfortunately, there is little evidence that social investment portfolios are less risky than market averages. The Domini and Calvert social indexes both exhibit risk (as measured by beta) that is higher than that of the Standard & Poor (S&P) 500,

---

[31] The best study we have seen of the performance of Islamic accounts is Warrick and Yacksick (2004).

[32] Source: 'NYSE Monthly Turnover Rates', NYSE Group website, as of 30 June 2006. Accessed at: <http://www.nyse.com/marketinfo/datalib/1091545087955.html>.

although this appears to be due to industry effects rather than social factors. Lucas-Leclin *et al.* (2006) studied the relationship between company betas and Innovest environmental ratings, and found that the highly rated companies actually had *higher* betas than poorly rated ones:

> The fact that the non-adjusted SRI ratings [Innovest] have an inverse effect on the level of risk to that expected poses a genuine, conceptual difficulty. If SRI best practices are implemented, with results in line with them, there ought to be an improvement in the risk profile and not this clear deterioration.

This preliminary finding is not conclusive, but the fact that the observed effect runs in the wrong direction should give social investors pause.

The Case for a Performance Benefit

Despite all we have said so far, there are some reasons to maintain an open mind about the possibility of superior social investment performance.

Some analysts find evidence of unexplained outperformance by social investors. On the 15th anniversary of the Domini 400 Social Index, KLD Research & Analytics (2005) published an analysis of the index's performance from inception, including a set of industry-standard risk adjustment calculations. This showed superior performance on both a nominal and risk-adjusted basis, a result few would have predicted when the index launched. Attribution work on this index by Luck (1998) using the BARRA risk model found that conventional investment factors did not fully account for its outperformance during the 1990s, although DiBartolomeo and Kurtz (1999) were unable to replicate this finding using a different risk model.

If markets don't fully understand the financial benefits of CSR, what might they be missing? We would single out governance, the environment, and employee relations as three areas where some data suggest the market does not fully appreciate the economic impact of CSR policies. For each of these issues, the conceptual links between social responsibility and economic performance are reasonably clear, making the positive empirical findings more plausible:

1. Governance Of the variables listed here, the empirical case for a 'governance effect' is the strongest—but it is also the issue on which social investors have historically placed the least emphasis. Gompers *et al.* (2001) demonstrate that stocks of US companies with governance policies favoring management over shareholders performed poorly in the 1990s. Brown and Caylor (2004) find that companies awarded high governance scores by Institutional Shareholder Services outperformed those with low scores over three-, five-, and ten-year periods. And, as noted above, Barber (2006) provides evidence that CalPERS' governance initiatives have positively impacted firm valuations. For a fuller review of the recent governance literature, see Eisenhofer and Levin (2005).

2. *The Environment* Many studies claim positive valuation or performance impacts from environmental variables. The most recent and compelling of these is the sophisticated review by Derwall *et al.* (2005), which finds that stocks with high environmental ratings markedly outperformed poorly rated ones for the 1995–2003 time period. In a related study, Guenster *et al.* (2005) provide evidence of a positive association between environmental performance and both firm valuation (Tobin's Q) and earning power (ROA).

3. *Employee Relations* We believe this variable has significant investment potential, simply because the workforce obviously matters to business performance, and detailed information about companies' human resource practices are not widely available, creating the opportunity for value-added research. Human resource academics and consultants share this view—Becker and Huselid (1997) and Pfau (2001) present empirical work suggesting HR policies matter for stock returns. Bassi *et al.* (2004) develops this work further, demonstrating a positive relationship between investments in human capital and returns.[33] Edmans (2007) presents evidence showing that, even after adjusting for size, style, and momentum effects, a portfolio of *Fortune* magazine's 'Best Companies to Work For in America' would have outperformed the market for the 1998–2005 time period.

These results show that some things social investors care about may influence returns. But most social investors include with these a host of other factors that most likely have a neutral impact overall. There may also be issues associated with *inferior* investment returns, offsetting the potential positive impact from these variables.

Socially responsible investment returns should be examined through the lens of a modern risk model, and should be evaluated over long time periods, ideally ten years or more. When this is done, performance is usually found to be competitive, but not superior. There are some data supporting the *possibility* of a performance advantage for social investors, but claims that socially responsible investment can systematically outperform other investment styles over time strike us as unsupported and ill-advised.

TWO RECENT CRITIQUES

Social investors have attracted critical attention from across the intellectual spectrum. They have been criticized for both excessive ambition and insufficient effort, for being too performance-oriented and for not being performance-oriented enough, for being too true to their principles and for not being true enough. To

[33] For a different view see Gorton and Schmid (2000), who finds that greater employee involvement in German firms (union representation at the board level) was associated with lower earning power and lower valuations.

conclude our chapter we review two critiques we believe to be both representative and thoughtful.

Peter Brabeck—CSR can Create Risks to Shareholder Wealth

In March 2005, Nestlé CEO Peter Brabeck gave a brief talk at Boston College in which he challenged key premises of both CSR and socially responsible investment. Although he did not mention socially responsible investment specifically, his comments bear directly on it. The speech attracted the attention of social investors, several of whom penned rebuttals.[34]

Mr Brabeck is notable here because, of all the commentators we have cited, he alone runs a large corporation. Balancing competing opinions about what Nestlé should do is his full time job. He is also noteworthy because, unlike most CEOs, he has shown a sustained interest in both social responsibility and governance issues.[35] He has been willing to engage with and debate CSR advocates and has promoted academic research into how CSR policies can be better integrated into Nestlés business structures.[36]

We focus here on two elements of his talk—his observation that management preoccupation with social or governance concerns raises agency issues, and his claim that there are instances when such policies can be harmful to shareholder wealth.

[A]s managers, we have to be careful with what we give back, we are handing out money that belongs to shareholders, and we should only do it if it works out as a good investment.

The agency issue is often overlooked. The firm's money, Brabeck points out, belongs to all shareholders, not just those who hold a particular view. And it is a fact that social investors represent a minority of the shareholder base of most firms. This minority status is something they sometimes forget, and it underscores the importance of framing proposals in a way that appeals to the interests of the broader shareholder base.

Brabeck's second point is that there are some projects that offer CSR benefits, but have negative economic returns. We may illustrate this in Figure 11.3, which classifies investment opportunities for a firm into four categories. These illustrate

---

[34] See Peter Kinder, 'Investors and Public Want Corporate Accountability More than Ever. So Why is It Under Attack?' KLD Newsline, June 2005.

[35] The interest in governance was not entirely voluntary. In April 2005, Mr Brabeck was at the center of a controversy over whether it was appropriate for him to hold both the CEO and Chairman titles at Nestlé. The American governance research firm, Institutional Shareholder Services, was among the organizations opposing the plan. Nestlé shareholders affirmed his dual role, however, at the firm's annual meeting. See 'Discomfort Food', *The Economist*, 14 Apr. 2005.

[36] In March 2006 Nestlé held an 'SRI Forum' involving social investors from both the United States and Europe. This Forum presented the results of a case study analysis by Mark Kramer of Foundation Strategy Group and Michael Porter of the Harvard Business School, and invited investor feedback.

Low CSR/High Profit ?	High CSR/High Profit Always Invest
Low CSR/Low Profit Never Invest	High CSR/Low Profit ?

Fig. 11.3 Classifying investment opportunities for a firm

the CEO's dual mission—he must deliver on the bottom line while simultaneously focusing on the reputational and other effects of CSR.[37]

From a CEO's perspective, decisions in the upper-right and lower-left quadrants are straightforward. But decisions in the other two are difficult and risky.

Brabeck raises the concern that an uncritical view of CSR may lead managers to overinvest in the High CSR/Low Profit quadrant. But there is little evidence that this has occurred, despite the heightened focus on CSR in recent years. US corporations are more profitable today than they have been in decades—the net profit margin for the S&P 500 reached a 20-year high in 2005, as did corporate profits as a percentage of GDP.[38, 39] Corporate America does not appear to be overinvesting in much of anything, much less CSR projects.

But there are two situations in which we believe opportunities in the lower-right quadrant should be considered:

1. *When the projected cost is minimal* If a company can do something highly beneficial by spending a trivial sum, why not do it? Companies have many opportunities to make a difference through small expenditures because of their unique resources, specialized personnel, and systems. Companies that occasionally make small, financially suboptimal investments in CSR will grow closer to their communities and have significant positive social impact. From any perspective other than a narrow bottom-line focus, that is a good thing.

[37] Jack Welch, then CEO of General Electric, presented a similar classification of corporate managers in his 1991 *Letter to Shareholders*. Of the problematic high profit/low ethics group he wrote: 'Then there's the fourth type [of manager]—the most difficult for many of us to deal with. That leader delivers on commitments, makes all the numbers, but doesn't share the values we must have. This is the individual who typically forces performance out of people rather than inspires it: the autocrat, the big shot, the tyrant. Too often all of us have looked the other way—tolerated these "Type 4" managers because "they always deliver"—at least in the short term.' He concluded that, because of the importance of innovation to GE, 'we cannot afford management styles that suppress and intimidate'.

[38] Source: Baseline database.

[39] Source: Analysis by Vitaliy N. Katsenelson, Investment Management Associates, Denver Colorado. Accessed at 'Vitaliy's Contrarian Edge', <http://investmentinsight.blogspot.com/>.

2. To manage risk Some unattractive-looking investments may greatly reduce the likelihood of an unpleasant negative event. An extra compliance training program not required by law might be viewed as an expense by the accounting department. But a smart CEO sees it as insurance, even if the price paid does not appear 'economically rational'. This type of analysis can never be done precisely, but the high-profile corporate disasters at Arthur Andersen, Enron, Worldcom, Adelphia, and many other companies this decade suggest overpaying is better than underpaying.

This leaves the final and most problematic category of capital allocation opportunities—profitable investments that pose CSR challenges. CEOs are hired by shareholders and are charged with enriching them. So their natural bias is to pursue projects if they are legal and will enhance profits. For a pragmatic manager, it is tempting to set ethical conceptions aside, capture the profits, and defend unpopular behavior by pointing out that the firm is in compliance with all applicable laws and regulations. This is a disaster from the perspective of social investors, but it happens all the time.

Lynn Paine, an ethicist at the Harvard Business School, argues that this is where a company's ethical risk is greatest:

[I]n virtually every case of misconduct that I've studied, the perpetrators justified their actions by reference to the anticipated financial gains.

[T]oday's companies are being held to a higher standard. Financial results are a must, but in addition, leading companies are expected to achieve those results by acting in an ethically acceptable manner. This represents a dramatic departure from centuries of tradition holding that corporations are by nature amoral and thus incapable of assuming responsibility, adhering to ethical standards, or exercising moral judgment. But abundant evidence shows that companies today are expected to do all these things.[40]

In situations where the profit opportunity is high but significant harm may be done to the environment or society, it is the CEO and the board who must be ready to say 'no'. We do not pretend that this is simple—these decisions must balance tangible financial returns against considerations that cannot be fully quantified.[41] Brabeck deserves credit for noting the difficulty of the challenge and taking concrete steps to better understand it.

Frank Dixon—Socially Responsible Investment should Promote System Change

In contrast to Brabeck, Frank Dixon (2003), formerly of the research firm Innovest and now an executive with Wal-Mart, says traditional social investors are not

[40] Carla Tishler. 'Where Morals and Profits Meet: The Corporate Value Shift'. Interview with Lynn S. Paine, *Working Knowledge* newsletter. Harvard Business School. 18 Nov. 2002.

[41] Reputational risk is an important consideration here and can have meaningful impacts on shareholder value—see Karpoff *et al.* (2005) for an excellent discussion of the academic work on this topic.

doing enough to promote change. 'Our most pressing problem,' he warns, 'is the fact that we are killing ourselves...every life support system on the planet is in decline'.

Dixon argues that traditional social investment approaches should be discarded in favor of a more proactive, systems-oriented strategy. 'The traditional CSR movement has been focused on improving corporate environmental and social performance....This has prompted great improvement, but much more is needed to achieve sustainability. The missing element...is system change.'

Dixon introduces the term 'Total Corporate Responsibility' (TCR) to capture the type of corporate behavior he believes should be supported, explaining that it 'encourages firms to continue traditional CSR activities. However, the emphasis is placed on working proactively with others to promote system changes that hold firms fully responsible.' Dixon wants social investors to invest only in companies that lead in promoting system change.

Dixon's critique targets a problem inherent in traditional social investment methods—their focus on individual issue areas at the expense of the bigger picture. Under the stepwise screening approach, a company with extensive efforts in the development of clean energy products could be excluded for owning a small brewery. In his view, such an exclusion would be myopic.

We might take issue with Dixon's recommendation to own only the best companies, however. If the goal is system change, then adopting a policy of exit cannot be the right way to achieve it. Borrowing from Hirschman, we would argue that voice should be the preferred strategy. This affords the opportunity for influence, and also makes it possible to enlist large shareholders who cannot exit as allies.

Moreover, investing *only* in the most exemplary companies is bound to introduce uncompensated risk into portfolios. It is one thing to exclude, say, 30–40% of the companies in the S&P 500 (a figure we believe to be typical of social investors in the United States and UK). But to exclude 80% or 90% would lead to unacceptable volatility for many clients.

But one need not agree with all of Dixon's views to appreciate his deeper point. Certainly it is possible that our global preoccupation with short-term economic returns could lead to the destruction of assets that are of great value to all of us, such as fisheries and rainforests. Surely private enterprise has generated significant externalities in the past, and may be doing so now. If that is happening, what mechanisms could operate to slow or reverse the process? Who could act to prevent further harm?

The answer lies, as it always has, with the people who write the checks. Nothing happens in our global society without the deployment of capital. Most social investors believe that a narrow focus on risk and return is not enough to ensure the best outcomes for society or the planet. It is, of course, a minority view. But that does not mean that they are wrong.

APPENDIX—DETAILS OF PRAGMATIC MULTIPLIER CALCULATION

The Pragmatic Multiplier model is a modified form of the dividend discount model known as the Gordon Growth Model.[42] It may be specified as:

$$P / E = [(D / E)/(k - g)]$$

where

P = the price of the stock
E = the forecasted earnings per share of the stock over the next year
D = the forecasted dividends from the stock over the next year
k = the required rate of return
g = the forecasted growth rate of dividends to perpetuity

In our first example, the P/E ratio of 17 is computed as follows:

$$P / E = [(D / E)/(k - g)]$$

$$P / E = [(50\%)/(8\% - 5\%)]$$

$$P / E = 16.7 \approx 17$$

In our second example, the P/E ratio of 25 is computed as follows:

$$P / E = [(D / E)/(k - g)]$$

$$P / E = [(50\%)/(8\% - 6\%)]$$

$$P / E = 25$$

REFERENCES

ANGEL, JAMES, and RIVOLI, PIETRA. 1997. 'Does Ethical Investing Impose a Cost Upon the Firm? A Theoretical Examination.' *Journal of Investing*, winter.

BARBER, BRAD. 2006. 'Monitoring the Monitor: Evaluating CalPERS' Shareholder Activism'. Working Paper, University of California, Davis, Mar.

BARTOLOMEO, MATTEO, and FAMILIARI, GIOVANNI. 2005. *Green, Social, and Ethical Funds in Europe 2005*. Milan: Sustainable Investment Research International (SiRi) Company, Nov.

BASSI, LAURIE, HARRISON, PAUL, LUDWIG, JENS, and McMURRER, DANIEL. 2004. 'The Impact of U.S. Firms' Investments in Human Capital on Stock Prices'. Working Paper, Bassi Asset Management, June.

---

[42] The Gordon Growth Model was introduced by Gordon (1962) and is discussed in most investment textbooks. In order to solve for P/E rather than price, we have divided both sides of the model by E. For further information on the Gordon Growth Model, see Bodie *et al.* (2004).

BAUER, ROB, KOEDIJK, KEES, and OTTEN, ROGER. 2002. 'International Evidence on Ethical Mutual Fund Performance and Investment Style'. Working Paper, Erasmus University, Jan.

BECKER, BRIAN E., and HUSELID, MARK A. 1997. 'Human Resources Strategies, Complementarities, and Firm Performance'. Presentation to the Academy of Management Annual Meeting.

BOATRIGHT, JOHN R. 1999. *Ethics in Finance*. Oxford: Blackwell Publishers.

BODIE, ZVI, KANE, ALEX, and MARCUS, ALAN J. 2004. *Investments*. New York: McGraw-Hill.

BOLLEN, NICOLAS P. B., and COHEN, MARK A. 2004. 'Mutual Fund Attributes and Investor Behavior'. Working Paper, Vanderbilt University, 24 May.

BRICK, TRICIA. 2005–6. 'Investing in Social Change: A Conversation with Luther Tyson, founder of Pax World Fund'. *Focus*, online magazine of Boston University School of Theology, winter.

BROWN, LAWRENCE D., and CAYLOR, MARCUS L. 2004. 'The Correlation between Corporate Governance and Company Performance'. Institutional Shareholder Services.

BURKHOLDER, J. R. 2002. 'Biblical Faith and Investment: Toward a Theology for "Making Money"'. Mennonite Mutual Aid. Accessed at: <http://www.mmapraxis.com/features/columns/feature_burkholder.html>.

CAMEJO, PETER (ed.). 2002. *The SRI Advantage: Why Socially Responsible Investing has Outperformed Financially*. Gabriola Island, BC: New Society Publishers.

DAVIS, JAMES L. 2001. 'Explaining Stock Returns: A Literature Survey'. Dimensional Fund Advisors, Dec. Accessed at: <http://library.dfaus.com/articles/>.

DERWALL, JEROEN, GUNSTER, NADJA, BAUER, ROB, and KOEDIJK, KEES. 2005. 'The Eco-Efficiency Premium Puzzle'. *Financial Analysts Journal*, Mar.–Apr.

——— and KOEDIJK, KEES. 2006. 'Socially Responsible Fixed-Income Funds'. Working Paper, Erasmus University, May.

DIBARTOLOMEO, DAN, AND KURTZ, LLOYD. 1999. 'Managing Risk Exposures of Socially Screened Accounts'. Northfield Working Paper.

DIXON, FRANK. 2003. 'Total Corporate Responsibility: Achieving Sustainability and Real Prosperity'. *Ethical Corporation Magazine,* Dec.

——— 2006. 'CSR, Wal-Mart, and System Change'. Presentation to American Enterprise Institute, 3 Mar.

EDELEN, ROGER. 2004. 'Benchmarking an Environmentally Responsible Investment (ERI) Portfolio'. Sierra Club Funds presentation at SRI in the Rockies conference, Oct.

EDMANS, ALEX. 2007. 'Does the Stock Market Fully Value Intangibles? Employee Satisfaction and Equity Prices.' Working Paper, Massachusetts Institute of Technology.

EISENHOFER, JAY W., and LEVIN, GREGG S. 2005. 'Does Corporate Governance Matter to Investment Returns?' *Corporate Accountability Report*, 23 Sept.

FAMA, EUGENE, and FRENCH, KEN. 1992. 'The Cross-Section of Expected Stock Returns'. *Journal of Finance* (47).

GECZY, CHRISTOPHER C., STAMBAUGH, ROBERT F., and LEVIN, DAVID. 2003. 'Investing in Socially Responsible Mutual Funds'. Wharton School, Working Paper, May.

GOMPERS, PAUL, ISHII, JOY L. and METRICK, ANDREW. 2001. 'Corporate Governance and Equity Prices'. National Bureau of Economic Research, Working Paper 8449.

GORDON, MYRON J. 1962. *The Investment, Financing, and Valuation of the Corporation*. Homewood, Ill.: R. D. Irwin.

GORTON, GARY, and SCHMID, FRANK. 2000. 'Class Struggle Inside the Firm: A Study of German Codetermination'. Working Paper, Wharton School Center for Financial Institutions, University of Pennsylvania, Aug.

GUENSTER, NADJA, DERWALL, JEROEN, BAUER, ROB, and KOEDIJK, KEES. 2005. 'The Economic Value of Corporate Eco-Efficiency'. Working Paper, Erasmus University, 25 July.

HAWKEN, PAUL. 2004. 'Is Your Money Where Your Heart Is? The Truth about SRI Mutual Funds'. Conscious Enlightenment Publishing, at <http://www.dragonflymedia.com/portal/2004/10/hawken_paul.html>.

HAWLEY, JAMES, and WILLIAMS, ANDREW. 2000a. *The Rise of Fiduciary Capitalism—How Institutional Investors Can Make Corporate America More Democratic.* Philadelphia: University of Pennsylvania Press.

———— 2000b. 'The Emergence of Universal Owners: Some Implications of Institutional Equity Ownership.' *Challenge: The Magazine of Economic Affairs,* July.

———— 2005. 'Universal Owners, Fiduciary Duty, and Materiality'. *o.618,* publication of the UNEP Financial Initiative, Jan.

HEILBRONER, ROBERT. 1982. 'The Socialization of the Individual in Adam Smith'. *History of Political Economy.*

HIRSCHMAN, ALBERT O. 1970. *Exit, Voice, and Loyalty: Responses to Decline in Firms, Organizations, and States.* Cambridge, Mass.: Harvard University Press.

HONG, HARRISON, and KACPERCZYK, MARCIN. 2006. 'The Price of Sin: The Effects on Social Norms on Markets'. Working Paper, Princeton University, Apr.

Interfaith Center for Corporate Responsibility. 2006. 'Working Together for Peace, Economic Justice, and Stewardship of the Earth.' *About ICCR.* <http://www.iccr.org>.

KARPOFF, JONATHON M., LOTT, JOHN R., JR., and WEHRLY, ERIC W. 2005. 'The Reputational Penalties for Environmental Violations: Empirical Evidence'. *Journal of Law and Economics,* Oct.

KIERNAN, MATTHEW. 2005. ' "Sustainability"—Enhanced Investing—Combining Financial Out-Performance with Fiduciary Leadership'. Presentation to the Business and Sustainability Conference, Tuck School of Business. 25 Feb.

KINDER, PETER. 2005. 'Socially Responsible Investing: An Evolving Concept in a Changing World'. KLD Research & Analytics, Sept.

KLD Research & Analytics. 2005. 'KLD's Domini 400 Social Index at 15: A Risk and Return Analysis'. Sept.

KURTZ, LLOYD. 1998. ' "Mr. Markowitz, Meet Mr. Moskowitz"—A Review of Studies on Socially Responsible Investing'. *The Investment Research Guide to Socially Responsible Investing.* The Colloquium on Socially Responsible Investing.

———— 2005. 'Answers to Four Questions'. *Journal of Investing,* fall.

———— and LYDENBERG, STEVEN. 1992. 'The Domini Social Index', in Peter Kinder (ed.), *The Social Investment Almanac.* New York: Henry Holt.

LAFFER, ARTHUR B., COORS, ANDREW, and WINEGARDEN, WAYNE. 2004. 'Does Corporate Social Responsibility Enhance Business Profitability?' Laffer Associates.

LUCAS-LECLIN, VALERY, NAHAL, SARBJIT, DANIEL, YANNICK, and JACOLIN, MATHIEU. 2006. 'SRI and Valuation: the Missing Link?' Société Générale Equity Research, Apr.

LUCK, CHRISTOPHER. 1998. 'Domini Social Index Performance'. *The Investment Research Guide to Socially Responsible Investing.* The Colloquium on Socially Responsible Investing.

LYDENBERG, STEVEN. 2005. *Corporations and the Public Interest: Guiding the Invisible Hand.* San Francisco: Berrett-Koehler.

MACKENZIE, CRAIG. 1997. 'Ethical Investment and the Challenge of Corporate Reform'. Submitted by Craig Mackenzie for the degree of Ph.D. of the University of Bath. Accessed at: <http://staff.bath.ac.uk/hssal/crm/phd/crm-phd.pdf>.

McWILLIAMS, ABAGAIL, and SIEGEL, DONALD. 2000. 'Corporate Social Responsibility and Financial Performance: Correlation or Misspecification?' *Strategic Management Journal,* 21.

MONKS, ROBERT. 1994. 'Corporate Governance in the Twenty-First Century: A Preliminary Outline'. Draft. The Corporate Library. Accessed at <http://www.lens-library.com>.

MULLER, JERRY Z. 1993. *Adam Smith in His Time and Ours.* Princeton: Princeton University Press.

NESBITT, STEPHEN L. 1994. 'Long-Term Rewards from Shareholder Activism: A Study of the "CalPERS Effect" '. *Journal of Applied Corporate Finance,* 6.

ORLITZKY, MARC, SCHMIDT, FRANK L., and RYNES, SARA L. 2003. 'Corporate Social and Financial Performance: A Meta-analysis'. *Organization Studies,* 24.

PFAU, BRUCE. 2001. 'Watson Wyatt's Human Capital Index: Human Capital as a Lead Indicator of Shareholder Value'. Watson Wyatt Worldwide.

RIVOLI, PIETRA. 2003. 'Making a Difference or Making a Statement? Finance Research and Socially Responsible Investment'. *Business Ethics Quarterly,* July.

SMITH, ADAM. 1994. *The Wealth of Nations.* Modern Library edn. New York: Random House.

Social Investment Forum. 2006. '2005 Report on Socially Responsible Investing Trends in the United States—10 Year Review'. Social Investment Forum Industry Research Program, 24 Jan.

SULLIVAN, RORY, and MACKENZIE, CRAIG. 2006. *Responsible Investment.* Sheffield: Greenleaf Publishing.

TSOUTSOURA, MARGARITA. 2004. 'Corporate Social Responsibility and Financial Performance'. University of California, Berkeley, Working Paper, Mar.

WADDOCK, SANDRA A., and GRAVES, SAMUEL B. 1997. 'The Corporate Social Performance-Financial Performance Link'. *Strategic Management Journal.*

WALDMAN, DAVID A., SIEGEL, DONALD, and JAVIDIAN, MANSOUR. 2004. 'Transformational Leadership and Corporate Social Responsibility'. Working Paper, Jan.

WARRICK, ALEXANDER, and YACKSICK, RUDY. 2004. 'Developing a Global Islamic Index Fund with Minimum Tracking Error to a Broad Market Index'. Mystic, Connecticut Eastern Finance Association Annual Meeting, Apr.

WESLEY, JOHN. 2000. 'The Uses of Money', edited by Jennette Descalzo, student at Northwest Nazarene College (Nampa, Ida.), with corrections by George Lyons for the Wesley Center for Applied Theology. General Board of Global Ministries, The United Methodist Church. Accessed at: <http://gbgm-umc.org/umhistory/wesley/sermons/serm-050.stm>.

....

CHAPTER 12

CONSUMERS AS DRIVERS OF CORPORATE SOCIAL RESPONSIBILITY

....

N. CRAIG SMITH

LEGEND has it that King Arthur's Knights of the Round Table embarked on various quests for the Holy Grail, the cup from which Christ is said to have drunk at the Last Supper and a symbol of mystical union with God. These quests and their more prosaic modern day counterparts are often an elusive search for perfection. Many scholars and business practitioners are on a search for a 'holy grail' in trying to identify the business case for corporate responsibility (CR). If there is not a business case for corporate responsibility then reliance must be placed on the normative (moral) case—that is, simply put, doing the right thing because it is the right thing to do. However, this poses a major if not insurmountable problem, at least for managers of publicly held companies when their desire to make responsible business decisions appears to be at odds with fiduciary duties to shareholders (Smith, 2003). On the other hand, if there is a business case for corporate responsibility then we have a 'win-win' where everybody gains, including shareholders.

The business case is often grounded in three key drivers: that consumers, employees, and investors care in ways that create economic incentives for companies to give attention to corporate responsibility. As Starbucks explains in its 2001 *Corporate Social Responsibility Annual Report* (p. 3):

Consumers are demanding more than 'product' from their favorite brands. Employees are choosing to work for companies with strong values. Shareholders are more inclined to invest in businesses with outstanding corporate reputations. Quite simply, being socially responsible is not only the right thing to do; it can distinguish a company from its industry peers.

Much has been written on the business case for corporate responsibility. It is evident in the reports of many of the large companies that today extol the virtues of their CR activities to shareholders and other stakeholders. British American Tobacco, for example, in its 2003/4 *Social Report*, says: 'Accepting corporate social and environmental responsibilities, and contributing in the ways that a business can, makes good business sense.' Presumably, this explains BAT's role in establishing the Elimination of Child Labour in Tobacco Growing Foundation and its claim that it does not employ children in its operations. A survey of CR reporting by KPMG found that 74% of company CR reports identified 'economic considerations' as a driver for corporate responsibility (reputation or brand, and market position/market share improvement specifically were identified by 27% and 21% respectively).[1]

Various associations produce reports on the business case for corporate responsibility, such as Business for Social Responsibility (see <http://www.bsr.org>), the World Business Council for Sustainable Development (<http://www.wbcsd.org>), and the International Business Leaders Forum (<http://www.iblf.org>) which, in its report *Profits With Principles*, shows 'the quantifiable and enduring business advantage to "doing the right thing"'. Even governments are producing guides to the business case, with the UK's Department of Trade and Industry supporting projects that explore the business case because the government sees CSR 'as good for society and good for business' (see <http://www.csr.gov.uk>)—the UK government even has a minister responsible for CSR.

However, attention to *the* business case for corporate responsibility can be misguided in two respects. First, there is no one business case other than at the most basic level ('corporate responsibility can provide an enduring economic advantage for a company'). Second, because the business case is idiosyncratic, it varies markedly in both form and strength across companies, industries, and other situational

---

[1] KPMG produces a regular and comprehensive survey of corporate responsibility reporting. CR reporting has been steadily increasing since 1993, with more than 1,600 company reports covered in KPMG's 2005 survey; 64% of the G250 (top 250 companies of the Fortune 500) report on CR with 52% of the G250 producing separate reports and 41% and 33% respectively of the N100 reporting (the N100 are the top 100 companies in each of 16 countries). At the national level, the top two countries in terms of separate CR reporting are Japan (80%) and the UK (71%). See KPMG, *International Survey of Corporate Responsibility Reporting 2005*, at: <http://www.kpmg.com/hr/rdonlyres/66422f7f-35ad-4256-96f8-f36facca9164/0/kpmg intlcrsurvey2005.pdf>, accessed 15 Aug. 2007. Context (2005) found that 87% of the top 100 European companies and 45% of the top US companies (by market capitalization) produced CR reports.

considerations. Without doubt, there are circumstances, and increasingly so, under which corporate responsibility is in the best economic interests of a particular company. However, because the business case for corporate responsibility is contingent upon a variety of circumstantial factors, it is difficult to find a justification for many of the generalizations—and much of the hyperbole—about the business case, beyond wishful thinking. Vogel (2005: 45) has observed:

> Unfortunately, a review of the evidence…finds little support for the claim that more responsible firms are more profitable. But this does not mean that there is no business case for virtue. It is rather to suggest that any such claim must be more nuanced. CSR does make business sense for some firms in specific circumstances.

With these caveats in mind, this chapter takes a critical look at the role of consumers in corporate attention to CR. The emphasis is in looking at what research and more anecdotal evidence suggests are the conditions under which consumers might serve as drivers of corporate responsibility.

In the next two sections, we turn to illustrative examples of 'ethical consumerism', survey data, and a theoretical rationale that support the general idea that consumers care about issues of corporate responsibility and that this can influence their behavior as consumers and potentially, therefore, that of the companies from which they buy. We also examine various marketer initiatives that reflect a belief in ethical consumerism, from cause-related marketing to ethical branding. We then turn to more theoretical treatments and empirical research findings on, first, consumer support for pro-social corporate conduct ('positive ethical consumerism') and, second, consumer punishment of CR failings, most notably in consumer boycotts ('negative ethical consumerism'). We conclude with observations on when and how we might expect consumers to be a factor in the business case for corporate responsibility.

Consumer boycotts as ethical consumerism

In *Morality and the Market: Consumer Pressure for Corporate Accountability*, Smith (1990: 7) wrote of ethical influences on consumer behavior ('ethical purchase behavior') and how they might serve as a form of social control of business, with consumers exercising 'purchase votes on social responsibility issues'. Novel then, this idea is taken for granted today. It goes by a variety of names—'conscience consumerism,' 'ethical consumerism,' the 'green consumer'—but the idea is essentially the same, that consumers care about issues of corporate responsibility and this will influence their purchase and consumption behaviors and this, in turn, provides incentives for companies to be socially and environmentally responsible.

Smith's thesis (1990: 184–96) relied theoretically on consumer sovereignty as the rationale for capitalism. Although the concept is often ideologically laden (e.g. 'the consumer is king'), there is certainly some measure of consumer authority in highly competitive consumer markets. Smith suggested that the domain of consumer sovereignty could extend beyond the more immediate characteristics of the product to include corporate responsibility practices of the producer. In support, he drew on the most clearly identifiable and deliberate form of ethical consumerism (at that time): pressure group-organized consumer boycotts. Smith cited evidence of consumers in relatively large numbers boycotting companies over social responsibility issues; for example, as many as one in four UK consumers were said to be boycotting South African produce over apartheid and the pressure on Barclays Bank in its home market (coupled with its North American aspirations) was ultimately a key factor in the bank's decision to withdraw from South Africa (it was the largest bank there). Vogel's (1978) *Lobbying the Corporation* offered similar evidence in its account of boycotts in the United States over civil rights and the Vietnam War.

Historically, the boycott is attributed with some spectacular successes. The American colonialists' boycott of British goods led to the repeal of the Stamp Act by the British government in 1766 (Friedman, 1999). Wolman (1916) and Laidler (1963) described how the consumer boycott was the key to unionization in the United States at the turn of the twentieth century. Gandhi organized boycotts of British salt and cloth, as part of a strategy of non-violent direct action that ultimately gave rise to Indian independence in 1947 (Bondurant, 1965). Rosa Parks's refusal to give up her seat on a city bus to a white man triggered the Montgomery bus boycott of 1955, a boycott that nearly bankrupted the bus company and was supported by more than 90% of blacks until bus segregation was ended in the city. Friedman (1999) describes this as the most influential consumer boycott in American history, having marked the beginning of the modern civil rights movement in the United States and launched Rev. Martin Luther King, Jr., as its leader.

The late 1960s boycott of Dow Chemical's Saran Wrap because of Dow's manufacture of napalm didn't end the Vietnam War, but Dow did discontinue napalm production (after allegedly having submitted a deliberately uncompetitive tender) and the boycott tainted the firm's reputation for years (Vogel, 1978). Around the same time, public support for the California grape boycott enabled the formation of a union for American farm workers and forced substantial concessions from the growers (Brown, 1972). As these examples show, the boycott often has been used by the relatively powerless to assert their rights (Sharp, 1973).

More recent evidence of large-scale support for boycotts, if not boycott successes, include the Greenpeace-inspired boycott of Shell over its attempt to dispose of the Brent Spar oil platform in the Atlantic Ocean, a boycott that reportedly led to a

50% decline in sales at some German Shell stations during the height of the protests (Moldoveanu and Paine, 1999). Commenting on the boycott after Shell abandoned sea disposal of the platform, *The Economist* (1995: 15) suggested that 'it may be no bad thing ... for consumers to ask for a higher standard of behavior from the firms they buy from'. Shell's problems were compounded by public reactions to reports of environmental harm as a result of its operations in Ogoniland, Nigeria and the company's apparent failure to use its influence to prevent the execution by Nigerian authorities of Ken Saro-Wiwa, who had been protesting Ogoni rights. Criticism of Shell by environmentalists and human rights activists and the associated boycotts were said to be major contributors to a fundamental transformation in how the company strives to live up to its social and ethical responsibilities (Cowe, 1999; Shell, 1998). Environmentalists subsequently turned their attention to ExxonMobil, with a global boycott organized over its opposition to climate change theories. Over one million UK motorists were said to have participated in the boycott, according to research by MORI.[2]

Although boycotts often are associated with liberal causes, they can come from the right as well as the left and are not unique to Western democracies. Middle East sales of Danish dairy giant Arla ($430 m. annually) vanished almost overnight as a result of a boycott in early 2006, following the publication of cartoons that carica-tured the Prophet Muhammad in the Danish newspaper *Jyllands-Posten* (Ettenson *et al.*, 2006).

Ethical consumerism is clearly demonstrated in these examples of consumer boy-cotts. However, while they confirm the existence of ethical consumerism and its po-tential effects on corporate responsibility, in many respects they are extreme cases. What of more everyday examples? Broadly defined, 'ethical purchasers ... have political, religious, spiritual, environmental, social or other motives for choosing one product over another ... The one thing they have in common is that they are concerned with the effects that a purchasing choice has, not only on themselves, but also on the external world around them' (Harrison *et al.*, 2005: 2). How pervasive are such considerations in consumer purchase and consumption behavior? To what extent can they be a driver of corporate responsibility?

ETHICAL CONSUMERISM MORE GENERALLY

Survey data suggest that up to 90% of consumers consider corporate responsibility in their purchase and consumption behaviors (Vogel, 2005). For example, MORI (and others) reported high levels of consumer interest in corporate responsibility

<hr />

[2] Source: <http://www.stopesso.com/campaign/00000066.php>. Accessed 16 Jan. 2007.

in the Millennium Poll, administered to 25,000 consumers in 23 countries (Environics, 1999):

Around the world, 40% of the 25,000 respondents have thought in the past year about punishing a specific company perceived as not socially responsible; half of them—1 in 5 worldwide—have avoided the product of a company or spoken out to others against the company. Meanwhile, consumers were just as likely to 'reward' a company perceived as socially responsible.

Vogel (2005) cited this study and a half-dozen more. Bhattacharya and Sen (2004: 9) report a 2002 Cone Communications study that found '84% of Americans say they would be likely to switch brands to one associated with a good cause, if price and quality are similar'. Survey numbers in these studies vary according to where the survey was conducted and whether respondents were asked if corporate responsibility was a factor in purchase, or if they had avoided products/companies with a social responsibility failing, or if they would pay more for products/companies associated with good CR practices. Nonetheless, survey findings are suggestive of widespread ethical consumerism.

However, for all these expressions of good intentions, the evidence for extensive practice of ethical consumerism is less readily available. Vogel (2005: 48) observed: 'there is little evidence to support these assertions. There is a major gap between what consumers say they would do and their actual behavior.' The problem is the well-known demand effect in social science research of social desirability bias—respondents providing a socially desirable response that they believe the questioner wishes or expects to hear. Consumers may well say in surveys that they do 'the right thing' (why wouldn't they?) but their 'revealed preferences' (as economists put it) suggest they are more self-interested when it comes to purchase and consumption behaviors.

Thus, studies of ethical consumerism *behavior* suggest it is far less prevalent than surveys of attitudes and intentions—perhaps engaged in by only 10% or less of the population. Vogel (2005) referred to a 2004 European study that found 75% of respondents indicating that they would modify purchase because of social and environmental criteria, but only 3% having done so and US data suggesting only 10–12% of consumers making any effort to purchase more environmentally sound products, despite more than two decades of green marketing. Schwartz and Gibb (1999: 11) write that 'green and socially oriented consumers may amount to only an average 10 percent of the market'. However, they add that 'many more people make at least some of their purchasing and shareholding decisions on the basis of company reputation'. Thus surveys appear to overstate the influence of ethical consumerism, but data on sales directly attributable to social and environmental concerns understate the influence. Social and environmental factors may well be a consideration in purchase for many more than 10%

of consumers, though this may not be evident from purchase behavior. As we discuss further below in relation to the academic literature, attention to sales (only) provides an incomplete account of how and why consumers respond to corporate responsibility.

Recent data and examples from the UK are also suggestive of growing support for ethical consumerism. For example, Fairtrade sales doubled in the UK between 2003 and 2005, from £92.3 m. to £195 m., with Fairtrade coffee comprising £65.8 m.[3] A five-country study of 5,000 consumers by GfK NOP, comprising the United States, UK, Germany, France, and Spain, found that UK shoppers emerged as the most aware of ethical consumerism and the most critical of ethical claims. A third of respondents overall told researchers they would pay a 5–10% price premium for 'ethical products' (Grande, 2007).

The Ethical Consumerism Report 2005, a UK survey produced by the Co-operative Bank, reported that 54% of people surveyed in 2004 agreed with the statement, 'As a consumer, I can make a difference to how responsibly a company behaves'. Only 17% disagreed with the statement (figures were 51% and 26% respectively, in 1999). Ethical consumerism is defined as 'personal consumption where choice has been informed by a particular ethical issue—be it human rights, social justice, the environment or animal welfare' (p. 7). The report identifies nearly £26 bn. of 'ethical spending' in 2004 (up 15.4% on 2003), comprising £4 bn. on food (including organic and vegetarian products), £2.6 bn. on the 'green home' (e.g. energy-efficient electrical appliances), £1.6 bn. on travel and transport, £7 bn. on personal items (e.g. clothing), and £10.6 bn. on ethical finance (e.g. ethical investments). Its calculations include boycotts (with an allowance made for double counting where somebody bought a Fairtrade alternative, say, instead of the boycotted product) and charitable contributions. However, even at £26 bn., this is reported to be still less than 2% of UK consumer spending.[4] In some categories, the proportion is much greater, with expenditure on free-range eggs (£215 m. in 2004) one of the largest categories with a 41% share, leading Simon Williams of the Co-operative Bank to dismiss the idea of targeting ethical consumers as niche marketing: 'Four in ten eggs bought in the UK are now free range, despite the higher price…That is not a niche' (quoted in Edwards, 2005: 28).

[3] Source: <http://www.fairtrade.org.uk/about_sales.htm>. Accessed 15 Sept. 2006. For an assessment of fair trade marketing in Europe and the United States see Witkowski (2005).

[4] The *Ethical Consumerism Report 2005* (p. 6) notes that 'the role of the ethical consumer is to support and pioneer the early development of ethical products and services. Subsequently, with the help of Government intervention, they can make the next step. Typically, the "goods" are incentivised (such as lead-free petrol), and ultimately "bads" restricted/banned (leaded petrol). At this point, datasets "fall out" of the Ethical Consumerism Report as they have become the market norm.'

MARKETER RESPONSES

Sales of free-range eggs in the UK may speak to the potential of ethical consumerism to extend to a relatively large proportion of a given market, however, historically, niche marketing has been the norm, with marketers targeting a relatively small segment of ethical consumers. Classic examples of companies founded on ethical consumerism are Ben and Jerry's (ice cream), Stonyfield Farm (dairy products), and the Body Shop (cosmetics). While all three are highly successful companies, they are still relatively small and Ben and Jerry's and the Body Shop have recently been acquired by much larger competitors. For example, Body Shop profits in the year ending February 2006 were £29 m. ($54 m.) on sales of £772 m. ($1.42 bn.), just prior to its acquisition by L'Oréal, the largest cosmetics company in the world with sales 20 times those of the Body Shop. Nonetheless, ethical branding is a growing activity with companies either developing brands where ethical values are central to brand meaning or differentiating existing brands by emphasizing ethical values as an important but not necessarily central part of brand meaning. In the latter case, ethical branding can provide a critical point of differentiation where the consumer sees little difference between competing brands.

Ethical branding where ethical values are central to brand meaning includes, for example, Innocent, the Toyota Prius, and The Co-operative Bank. Innocent drinks, market leader with over 60% of the £100 m. rapidly growing smoothie market in the UK (2005), says somewhat modestly, 'we want to leave things a little better than we find them'. It claims to do this through '100% natural products that are 100% good for people' (its smoothies are not made from concentrate), ethical procurement, ecologically sound packaging, reduced/offset carbon emissions, and 10% of profits to countries where the fruit is sourced.[5]

The Toyota Prius, the world's first mass-produced gas (petrol) and electric hybrid vehicle, was introduced in Japan in 1997 and entered the US market in 2000, soon gaining a loyal following among environmentally conscious consumers. It offered the appeal of 'driving a car as well as a revolution.'[6] However, it can hardly be described as a niche product. In 2005, with US sales exceeding 100,000 units, it was Toyota's third best-selling vehicle, behind the Camry (the best-selling vehicle in the United States) and the Corolla. Sales of the Prius worldwide exceeded half a million vehicles in April 2006.[7]

The Co-operative Bank is part of the Co-operative Group, the UK's largest consumer cooperative (with origins in Robert Owen's Co-operative Movement).

[5] Source: <http://www.innocentdrinks.co.uk/>. Accessed 18 Jan. 2007.
[6] Source: <http://www.toyota.com>. Accessed 19 Jan. 2007.
[7] Source: <http://www.prnewswire.com>. Accessed 19 Jan. 2007.

It has an advertising campaign theme of 'we're good with money' and a strap-line that says it is 'customer led, ethically guided'. Its website claims 'your money will never be invested in unethical organisations' and reports that it turned away £10 m. worth of business in 2005, saying: 'This analysis demonstrates that through thick and thin we are prepared to turn away business for ethical reasons in line with our customers' concerns. Despite this scrutiny, the Bank's corporate business goes from strength to strength with a growing proportion of business customers coming to the Bank because of our ethical positioning.' A quarter of the bank's corporate customers join the bank because it is prepared to turn away business inconsistent with its ethical policy.[8]

Simon Williams of The Co-operative Bank says 'there are many respects in which The Co-operative Bank is just like other banks. There is one important difference; we are the only high street bank that gives our customers a say in how their money is managed—most importantly, by encouraging their input into the ongoing development of our ethical policy.' The original ethical policy was formulated in 1992 on the basis of survey research with target customers (identifying concerns with issues such as human rights, animal exploitation, and environmental damage) and the decision that the bank would 'focus on the responsible sourcing and distribution of funds as its distinctive ethical message'. The current policy precludes, for example, providing financial services to tobacco companies, companies involved in animal experimentation, or speculating against the pound (sterling).[9] Consumer deposits grew from £1 billion to £6 billion in the ten years following (Edwards, 2005). It was named the most responsible company in the UK by Business in the Community, coming top of its Corporate Responsibility Index 2006.[10]

Ethical branding where existing brands are differentiated by emphasizing ethical values as an important but not necessarily central part of brand meaning includes, for example, leading retailers such as Marks and Spencer, Tesco, and Wal-Mart. Co-op Food, a grocery retailer that is part of the Co-operative Group, has for many years positioned itself as a 'responsible retailer', carrying Fairtrade products in all its stores as early as 1999 and its own brand fair trade range. Today, however, it is facing increasing competition as the big retailers begin to emulate the strategy. Commenting on this trend, the *Financial Times* observed that the evidence suggests that ethical consumption 'has hit the mainstream and is here to stay' (Rigby, 2006). It reported that Marks and Spencer switched all its tea and coffee to Fairtrade and started selling Fairtrade T-shirts, socks, and jeans in 2006.

[8] Source: <http://www.co-operativebank.co.uk>. Accessed 18 Jan. 2007.
[9] Source: <http://www.co-operativebankcasestudy.org.uk/>. Accessed 18 Jan. 2007.
[10] Source: <http://www.bitc.org.uk/what_we_do/cr_index/past_index_results.html>.   Accessed 18 Jan. 2007.

In January 2007, Marks and Spencer announced a £200 m. five-year program to become the UK's greenest retailer, pledging to make the group carbon neutral and eliminate all waste to landfill by 2012 (Rigby and Harvey, 2007). Tesco, the UK's largest retailer, swiftly followed by announcing that it would 'carbon label' all its products, with labels recording the amount of carbon dioxide emitted during the production, transport, and consumption of the 70,000 products it sells. Commenting on the move, chief executive Terry Leahy said: 'The market is ready. Customers tell us they want our help to do more in the fight against climate change...We have to make sustainability a significant, mainstream driver of consumption' (Rigby *et al.*, 2007). It is interesting to note that, unlike the Marks and Spencer decision to carry only tea and coffee that is Fairtrade, the carbon labelling by Tesco will leave the decision to buy products with high, medium, or low carbon emissions, in part at least, to the consumer. Wal-Mart, the world's largest retailer, no doubt with similar thoughts in mind to Tesco, as well as broader reputational concerns to address, has also announced that it is taking its 'first steps towards sustainability' by reducing the energy needs of all existing stores by 20% by 2009 and cutting total carbon dioxide emissions by 25% by 2012.[11]

An interesting development of ethical branding is the '(RED)' brand, launched at the World Economic Forum meeting by rock star Bono in February 2006. This is a combination of what we might term 'umbrella social-cause branding' with the more familiar idea of ingredient branding (think 'Intel Inside'). It extends the long-standing idea of cause-related marketing to a family of brands under the (RED) umbrella, including American Express, the Gap, Motorola, Converse, Armani, and Apple. A proportion of profits from sales of the (RED) branded products offered by these companies goes towards the Global Fund to Fight AIDS, Tuberculosis and Malaria—over $10 m. by September 2006 (see the Red Manifesto in Table 12.1).[12]

An early pioneer of cause-related marketing was American Express with its 1983 program in support of restoration of the US Statue of Liberty, where a penny was donated to the renovation for each use of the card and a dollar for each new card issued. Essentially, it is 'a marketing program that strives to achieve two objectives—improve corporate performance and help worthy causes—by linking fund raising for the benefit of a cause to the purchase of the firm's products and/or services' (Varadarajan and Menon 1988: 59). Clearly it reflects a belief by marketers that social causes will influence consumer behavior. While this is not necessarily consumers as drivers of corporate responsibility, it is illustrative of consumer preference influenced by social concerns and, at least, as a potential driver of corporate philanthropy.

---

[11] Source: <http://*walmartstores.com/microsite/walmart_sustainability.html*>. Accessed 19 Jan. 2007.
[12] Source: <http://www.joinred.com/>. Accessed 19 Jan. 2007.

Table 12.1 The (RED)™ Manifesto

All things being equal, they are not.

As first world consumers, we have tremendous power. What we collectively choose to buy, or not to buy, can change the course of life and history on this planet.

(RED) is that simple an idea. And that powerful. Now, you have a choice. There are (RED) credit cards, (RED) phones, (RED) shoes, (RED) fashion brands. And no, this does not mean they are all red in color, although some are.

If you buy a (RED) product or sign up for a (RED) service, at no cost to you, a (RED) company will give some of its profits to buy and distribute anti-retroviral medicine to our brothers and sisters dying of AIDS in Africa.

We believe that when consumers are offered this choice, and the products meet their needs, they will choose (RED). And when they choose (RED) over non-(RED), then more brands will choose to become (RED) because it will make good business sense to do so. And more lives will be saved.

(RED) is not a charity, it is simply a business model. You buy (RED) stuff, we get the money, buy the pills and distribute them. They take the pills, stay alive and continue to take care of their families and contribute socially and economically in their communities.

If they don't get the pills, they die. We don't want them to die. We want to give them the pills. And we can. And you can. And it's easy.

All you have to do is upgrade your choice.

Source: <http://www.joinred.com/manifesto.asp>.

RESEARCH ON POSITIVE ETHICAL CONSUMERISM

Consumer support for pro-social corporate conduct can be described as 'positive ethical consumerism'. In some contexts, this has been referred to as a 'buycott' where historically, for example, unions have used 'fair' lists to identify companies friendly to the union and to be patronized in contrast to companies subject to boycott by the union (Friedman, 1999). Consumer preference is influenced favorably by the perception that the company or brand is engaged in socially responsible behavior or the product itself is socially responsible. 'Negative ethical consumerism', by contrast, includes where consumers punish a company for perceived social responsibility failings, including boycotts. Thus a consumer preference for Fairtrade products or 'dolphin-friendly' tuna reflects positive ethical consumerism and results directly from the practices of the producer/marketer (see Fig. 12.1). Positive ethical consumerism also might result from societal causes, such as a belief in the importance of buying domestically produced goods (perhaps encouraged by 'Buy British' or 'Buy American' advertising campaigns) or, more recently, anti-Western

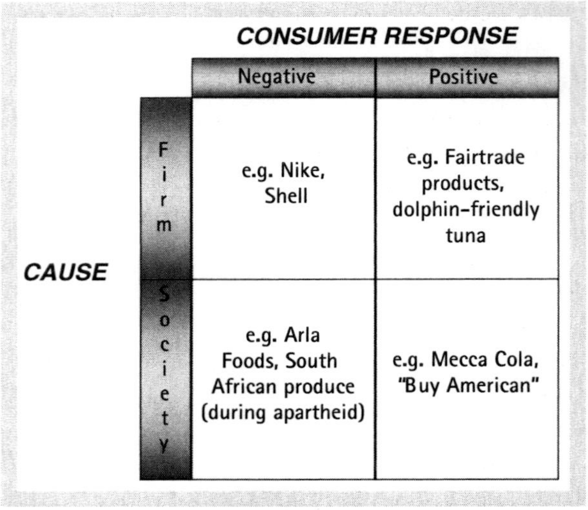

Fig. 12.1 Types of ethical consumerism

Source: Adapted from Ettenson, Smith, Klein and John (2006).

sentiment among Muslim consumers manifest in support for non-Western colas such as Mecca Cola or Quibla Cola (Ettenson *et al.*, 2006).

Among academic research of ethical consumerism, the studies by Brown and Dacin (1997) and Sen and Bhattacharya (2001) are particularly noteworthy. They build on an extensive literature conceptualizing ethical consumerism or examining it in exploratory studies or field research (e.g. Creyer and Ross, 1996; Drumwright, 1994; Kassarjian, 1972; Roberts, 1996; Smith, 1990, 1999; Strong, 1996; Webster, 1974). Brown and Dacin (1997) and Sen and Bhattacharya (2001) utilized the high degree of control possible in laboratory studies to go beyond demonstrating that ethical consumerism exists to examine when, why, and how consumers respond to corporate social initiatives and corporate responsibility more generally. This provides a much more nuanced perspective on ethical consumerism than studies that look at sales alone.

Brown and Dacin (1997: 68) established that what a person knows about a company or 'corporate associations' (e.g. corporate image) influences product evaluations and that there are two types, corporate ability associations and corporate social responsibility associations. They found that corporate ability associations appear to be more influential on product attribute perceptions and the overall corporate evaluation than a reputation for social responsibility (largely operationalized in their studies, however, by corporate philanthropy rather than by core CR activities). Nonetheless, they found (1997: 80) that 'CSR associations have a significant influence on consumer response to new products ... negative CSR associations ultimately can have a detrimental effect on overall product evaluations, whereas positive CSR associations can enhance the product evaluations.' This was through their effect on corporate evaluation rather than an influence on specific product attributes.

Sen and Bhattacharya (2001) also looked at the relationship between a company's CSR actions and consumers' attitudes toward that company and its products. Their focus, however, was on key moderators of consumers' CSR responses and the mechanisms underlying these responses. Their studies go some way toward explaining the heterogeneity in consumer responses to CR (operationalized in their empirical work by corporate record on diversity and on sweatshop labor issues). In this sense, they help explain some of the apparent disconnect between surveys reporting attitudes and behavioral intentions on ethical consumerism and actual behaviors, which can be markedly different (as discussed above).

More specifically, Sen and Bhattacharya (2001) found that positive and negative CSR information had an effect on company evaluations and on purchase intentions, with consumers' company evaluations more sensitive to negative than positive information. However, this effect of CSR information on company evaluations is mediated by consumer perceptions of self-company congruence (i.e. overlap consumers perceive between the company's character, as revealed by its CSR efforts, and their own) and moderated by their support of the CSR domain (the issue itself). So, for example, information on the Body Shop not testing products on animals is likely to have a greater effect on consumers who more readily identify with the Body Shop because of its CR-related activities and who care about the issue of animal testing.

They found a more complex effect of CSR information on purchase intentions, with a direct effect and indirect effects, including the possibility of positive effects on company evaluations been counteracted by negative effects on purchase intentions. This can occur where consumers believe CSR is at the expense of product quality. Consumers' CSR–CA (CSR–corporate ability) beliefs can view what the company does as a trade-off (especially among consumers with low levels of support for the CSR issue) or, alternatively, as a win-win, with CSR enhancing corporate ability. The win-win view is possibly illustrated by Nike's decision to introduce monitoring of factories manufacturing its sneakers following reports of abusive labor practices. Phil Knight observed: 'Good shoes are made in good factories; good factories basically have good labor relations.'[13] Quite conceivably, consumers could agree with this statement and believe that Nike shoes are of better quality as a result of this CR initiative.

Nonetheless, Bhattacharya and Sen (2004), consistent with Vogel (2005), are skeptical of surveys suggesting a high proportion of consumers have purchase intentions influenced by corporate responsibility. Their research suggests (2004: 18) that 'if CSR plays a role at all in purchase, it matters at the margin and they are unwilling, even if they view the CSR initiatives positively, to trade-off CSR for

[13] Remarks by Phil Knight, founder and chief executive officer, Nike Inc., at the Annual Shareholder's Meeting, Oregon Convention Center, Portland, Oregon, 22 Sept. 1997.

product quality and/or price'. Devinney *et al.* (2006: 35) also report a consumer resistance to sacrificing product quality (functional attributes of the product) in a six-country study: 'although some consumers will pay more for products with positive social attributes, they will invariably only do so when functional attributes of those products meet their needs . . . consumers almost always choose the product with poor social but good functional attributes.' Bhattacharya and Sen (2004) do acknowledge that some consumers are willing to pay more for CR (also supported in research by Auger *et al.*, 2003 and Kimeldorf *et al.*, 2006), but research suggests this is likely to be a minority of consumers, if not a small niche (the Toyota Prius and free-range egg sales in the UK, as discussed earlier, would appear to be exceptions).

Overall, Bhattacharya and Sen (2004) argue for a more sophisticated appreciation of how corporate responsibility influences consumers, noting in particular that a focus on behavioral outcomes (i.e. purchase) is myopic. In this sense it is useful to differentiate between direct effects (on sales) and the more indirect effects that still ultimately are of economic consequence for the company, such as positive word-of-mouth, increased loyalty, or greater 'resilience' (a willingness to give a company the benefit of the doubt or forgive an apparent lapse in behavior; see Klein and Dawar, 2004). This is aside from the effects on other parties, such as the consumers themselves or the social issues that benefit from corporate responsibility.

As important, these studies highlight the need for CSR influences on consumers to be understood as highly contingent upon company, consumer, and issue-related factors in particular. Company factors include the CR issue/domain (and whether it is perceived to be relevant to corporate ability), the valence (positive or negative company performance) and level of CR-related activity, product quality, and price. Consumer factors include support for the CR issue/domain, consumer-company congruence, and CR-related beliefs, especially in relation to the effects of CR on corporate ability (also see Ellen *et al.*, 2006 for consumer attributions regarding CR programs and their effects on purchase intentions). These factors, of course, assume that consumers are sufficiently knowledgeable about the company CR activities—often this will not be the case (Elliott, 2005; Smith, 1990).

RESEARCH ON NEGATIVE ETHICAL CONSUMERISM

Negative ethical consumerism involves a refusal to purchase, often in the form of consumer punishment for perceived corporate responsibility failings, though it can extend to consumer preferences only indirectly reflecting corporate responsibility failings, if at all (e.g. vegetarians who avoid meat for ethical reasons). It can be part of organized protest, with a boycott called by a campaign group, consistent with Friedman's (1999: 4) definition of a consumer boycott as: 'an attempt by one or more parties to achieve certain objectives by urging individual consumers to refrain from making selected purchases in the marketplace'. Equally, if not more typically, there may be an informal boycott (perhaps suggested in media coverage of questionable business activities) or individual consumers deciding for themselves to refuse to buy certain brands and products because of ethical or corporate responsibility concerns (e.g. consumers who refuse to buy automobiles for environmental reasons). As with positive ethical consumerism, refusal to purchase may stem from the activities of an individual company (e.g. boycott of Nike over alleged labor abuses in its supply chain or Esso over its position on global warming) or from societal causes (e.g. Muslim boycott of Danish companies, including Arla Foods, because of cartoons of Muhammad in a Danish newspaper). (See Fig. 12.1.)

Boycotts are relatively exceptional cases of negative ethical consumerism. However, because they are organized and deliberate, they do provide a good opportunity for researchers to better understand consumer refusal to purchase and ethical consumerism more generally (Klein *et al.*, 2004). Thus in looking at research on negative ethical consumerism, we will focus on boycotts and particularly consumer motivations for boycott participation and the factors in boycott success.

Various researchers have examined boycotts and attempted to offer explanations for their success or failure. Friedman's (1999) comprehensive study, drawing on more than 100 boycotts, employed instrumentality theory to develop an explanation for boycott success. He suggested that before initiating a boycott, campaign groups should ask themselves if: (1) consumers care about the boycott issues and objectives, (2) the boycott task is likely to be successfully executed, and (3) its execution is likely to lead to the desired consequences specified by the boycott objectives. Meanwhile, Garrett (1987) identified six factors in boycott participation: awareness of consumers, the values of potential participants, the consistency of boycott goals with participant attitudes, the cost of participation, social pressure, and the credibility of the boycott leadership. He proposed a theory of boycott success based on research of 30 boycotts between 1981 and 1984, suggesting that the determinants are economic pressure (due to lost sales), corporate image pressure (due to adverse publicity), and policy commitment (target's determination not to change the policy in question).

Smith's (1990) field research identified several factors that influence boycott effectiveness (defined as a significant reduction in sales) and boycott success (achieving the aims of the boycott organizers), including: the choice of target, the organization and strategy of the campaign group, and responses from consumers and others to the boycott call. More broadly, consumers must be concerned, willing, and able to act in support of the boycott. Boycotts need not substantially reduce sales to be successful. Firms may comply with boycott demands in response to the moral pressure and concern for the firm's reputation, even absent any impact on sales. Similarly,

Vogel (2005: 46) suggested that while a company's degree of social responsibility or irresponsibility has rarely affected sales, 'many companies have changed their social or environmental practices in response to "civil regulation" ... pressures from social activists, socially oriented consumers, shareholders, and employees'. Thus the risk or a mere threat of a consumer boycott can be a driver of corporate responsibility (also see Friedman, 1999; Garrett, 1987).

Kozinets and Handelman's (1998) ethnographic web-based study suggested that boycott participation represents a complex emotional expression of individuality and a vehicle for moral self-realization, findings that surely extend to other types of ethical consumerism. Sen *et al.*'s (2001) social dilemma perspective on boycotts was the first attempt to empirically test a theoretical framework that explains an individual's decision to participate in a boycott. They suggested that there is a fundamental question underlying a consumer's boycott decision: is this boycott going to be successful? They found in laboratory studies that an individual's participation in a boycott is influenced by his or her perception of the likelihood of the boycott's success and, in addition, the individual's susceptibility to normative social influences (social pressure) and the costs associated with boycotting.

Drawing upon the helping behavior and boycott literatures, Klein *et al.* (2004) took a cost–benefit approach to the decision to boycott and presented a conceptualization of motivations for boycott participation that was tested during a high profile boycott of a multinational firm (over factory closure). The perceived egregiousness of the firm's actions was a powerful predictor of boycott participation. The more seriously wrong a consumer perceived the firm's behavior to be, the more likely was that consumer to boycott. However, while consumers who viewed the factory closures as egregious were more likely to boycott the firm, only a minority did so. Egregiousness notwithstanding, most of the nationally representative sample (N = 1216) was *not* participating in the boycott: 95% of respondents were aware of the boycott, 81% disapproved of the factory closures (with 60% of the sample rating three or higher on a four-point egregiousness scale), but only 19% of the disapprovers were boycotting and only 16% of all respondents were boycotting. This shows, again, that high levels of concern about a social issue don't necessarily translate into ethical consumerism.

In addition to perceived egregiousness, the Klein *et al.* (2004) framework also incorporated four cost-benefit factors. They found that consumers need to believe that boycotting can 'make a difference' (i.e. the extrinsic rewards from participating in an appropriate and effective response, such as potentially changing the firm's decision). Consumers were also motivated by 'self-enhancement' (the benefit from intrinsic rewards of boycott participation, such as boosting self-esteem by responding to social pressure). This had a direct effect and also moderated the effect of egregiousness on boycott participation. Further, consumers also took account of 'constrained consumption' (the cost of a preferred product foregone), as well as various 'counter-arguments' (the costs of boycott-induced harms and doubts about whether participation is really necessary). Many of these costs also moderated the effect of egregiousness on boycotting.

Thus the level of consumer support for a boycott is a function of consumers weighing up the various costs and benefits of participation as well as the perceived egregiousness of the target company's behavior. Klein *et al.* (2004; also see Ettenson *et al.*, 2006) suggest that boycott participation and impact are typically overestimated, though boycott targets may not realize the harm to brand image in the eyes of non-boycotters if managers focus only on sales effects of boycotts. However, they also suggest that long-term harm from boycotts may be underestimated, drawing on anecdotal evidence (e.g. longevity of the Barclays boycott—effects reported to be still evident with UK consumers 20 years later) as well as their studies.

In sum, boycott participation is shown by these studies to be complex and involve a heterogeneity of response, with multiple motives at work, not all of which reflect the issue at hand (e.g. self-enhancement versus a desire to stop the target company engaging in behaviors not perceived to be socially responsible). It seems likely that the mixed motives in boycotts are evident in other forms of negative ethical consumerism and, perhaps, in positive ethical consumerism. For example, purchasing a Toyota Prius helps the environment but is also a highly visible symbol of its driver's green credentials (and research suggests that boycotts of products involving conspicuous consumption are more likely to be effective). Also likely to be common to other types of ethical consumerism are counter-arguments (e.g. my reduced emissions from driving a Prius are too small to make a difference to climate change) and constrained consumption, the sacrifice inherent in denying oneself a product one would otherwise choose to have (e.g. the sports car performance I forsake to drive a Prius).

CONCLUSIONS

Corporate responsibility has never been more prominent on the corporate agenda and primarily because the business case is perceived to be much stronger. However, it is important that business not simply accept the generalizations of the generic business case, nor dismiss it as flawed, but look to when, where, and how greater attention to corporate responsibility is demanded.[14] Consumers are an important

[14] As I have argued elsewhere (Ward and Smith, 2006), companies should do more than passively wait for the business case to emerge—on more pressing social issues like climate change, they should proactively build the business case.

potential driver of attention to CR for many companies, along with employees, investors, and others (e.g. regulators are particularly important drivers for
pharmaceutical companies). However, they are likely to be more important for
some companies than others. For instance, B2B (business-to-business) companies that do not serve consumers directly may be less influenced by consumers,
though consumer pressure can transmit up the value chain, as suppliers of wood
products to DIY retail chains have learnt (Smith, 2003) and CR concerns can be
a factor in organizational buying regardless of consumer concerns (Drumwright,
1994).

Consumer surveys typically overstate the influence of ethical concerns on consumer behavior. Nonetheless, the evidence is clear that some consumers are influenced in purchase and consumption decisions by ethical and corporate responsibility considerations and sometimes this is a sizable minority (e.g. free-
range eggs, Toyota Prius), if not a majority (e.g. major consumer boycotts, such
as Montgomery bus boycott, Shell Brent Spar boycott). This may take the form
of purchase refusal—what we are calling negative ethical consumerism—with
boycotts being the most obvious example. Increasingly, however, it appears to
be taking the form of purchase preference or positive ethical consumerism. Often, of course, the two forms are the opposite sides of the same coin, with
the positive ethical consumerism a preference for a more socially responsible
product resulting from a boycott of a competitor's product (assuming the consumer doesn't choose to deny himself or herself a product from the category
altogether).

For any given company—or any given issue, to take the campaign group
perspective—the likelihood of corporate responsibility affecting consumer behavior can vary tremendously. Academic research findings of positive and negative
ethical consumerism highlight the heterogeneity and complexity of consumer response. As yet we do not fully understand consumer choice behavior in this context.
Marketers often refer to the famous saying of Lord Leverhulme (William Hesketh
Lever): 'I know that half of my advertising budget is wasted, but I don't know which
half.' While we know that advertising works, we (still) struggle to know whether
particular advertising campaigns will work (or why). In many respects, it is a similar
scenario with ethical consumerism. Sustainability and CR-related considerations
do influence consumer behavior, but our understanding is limited of when, how,
and why.

Ethical consumerism as a purchase preference or a refusal to purchase appears to
be highly contingent. Research and more anecdotal evidence suggest it is dependent
in particular upon the following:

- Company action on the corporate responsibility issue—how much it is doing
  in support of, or conversely, how egregious its conduct is on the issue (both in
  absolute terms and relative to competitor activity);

- Company-issue fit—salience relative to core activities of the company and reputation (e.g. action on carbon emissions is an obvious priority for energy companies but less relevant to professional services firms, for example, their impacts are likely to be much greater in other areas);
- Company communications of corporate social performance—quantity, quality, and credibility of information provided, whether it is endorsed by third parties (e.g. media, campaign groups, auditors of social reports) and recognizing the potential for backlash against companies that overstate their performance (i.e. greenwash);
- Consumer concern for the CR issue—do they know and care sufficiently about the issue? (and possibly sufficient to act contrary to their more immediate self-interest);
- Consumer perceived effectiveness—can they make a difference? (will ethical consumerism help tackle the issue? are there enough other like-minded consumers?);
- Consumer sacrifice involved (higher price, lower quality, greater inconvenience, denial of product the consumer would otherwise choose to have);
- Consumer scope for self-enhancement—does the ethical consumption behavior make consumers feel better about themselves? (e.g. via conspicuous consumption, because of social pressure);
- Consumer recourse to counter-arguments (e.g. possibility of free-riding on ethical consumerism of others; sense of being too small to make a difference).

For all these reasons, consumer concern about or support for a CR practice may not translate into an effect on purchase behavior. However, this does not mean that there are not other less immediate or less tangible effects that companies need to consider, relative to reputation, brand image, willingness to pay a price premium, word-of-mouth, loyalty, or resilience. In this sense, sales are only the tip of the iceberg.

It is also important to consider the effects of ethical consumerism on consumers and the issue itself. For example, if sales are affected, conceivably the company would continue with a good CR practice or stop a bad one. However, even where there isn't any response by the company, awareness is raised which might benefit a campaign group and consumers have become better informed (there may even be a form of consciousness-raising). These potential benefits for consumers and the issue could exist even if sales are not affected.

Increasingly it seems that consumers see themselves as citizens in their consumer role, especially through positive ethical consumerism (Fitzgerald and Cormack, 2006). But there are multiple potential drivers of corporate responsibility and other stakeholders to which companies must attend, including employees, who may also be concerned citizens in that role too.

REFERENCES

AUGER, PAT, BURKE, PAUL, DEVINNEY, TIMOTHY M., and LOUVIERE, JORDAN. 2003. 'What Will Consumers Pay for Social Product Features?' *Journal of Business Ethics*, 42, Feb.: 281–304.

BHATTACHARYA, C. B., and SEN, SANKAR. 2004. 'Doing Better at Doing Good: When, Why and How Consumers Respond to Corporate Social Initiatives'. *California Management Review*, 47, fall: 9–24.

BONDURANT, JOAN V. 1965. *The Conquest of Violence: The Gandhian Philosophy of Conflict*, Berkeley: University of California Press; 1st pub. 1958.

BROWN, JERALD BARRY. 1972. 'The United Farm Workers Grape Strike and Boycott, 1965–1970: An Evaluation of the Culture of Poverty Theory'. Doctoral Dissertation: Cornell University.

BROWN, TOM J., and DACIN, PETER A. 1997. 'The Company and the Product: Corporate Associations and Consumer Product Responses'. *Journal of Marketing*, 61, Jan.: 68–84.

CONTEXT. 2005. *Corporate Responsibility: A United State?* London: Context Group.

COWE, ROGER. 1999. 'Boardrooms Discover Corporate Ethics'. *Guardian Weekly*, 28, Mar.: 27.

CREYER, ELIZABETH H., and ROSS, JR., WILLIAM T. 1996. 'The Influence of Firm Behavior on Purchase Intention: Do Consumers Really Care about Business Ethics?' *Journal of Consumer Marketing*, 14(6): 421–32.

DEVINNEY, TIMOTHY, AUGER, PATRICE, ECKHARDT, GIANA, and BIRTCHNELL, THOMAS. 2006. 'The Other CSR'. *Stanford Social Innovation Review*, fall: 30–7.

DRUMWRIGHT, MINETTE E. 1994. 'Socially Responsible Organizational Buying: Environmental Concern as a Noneconomic Buying Criterion'. *Journal of Marketing*, 58 July: 1–19.

The Economist. 1995. 'Saints and Sinners'. *The Economist*, 24 June: 15–16.

EDWARDS, HELEN. 2005. 'Moral Minority'. *Marketing*, 8 March: 28–30.

ELLEN, PAM SCHOLDER, WEBB, DEBORAH J., and MOHR, LOIS A. 2006. 'Building Corporate Associations: Consumer Attributions for Corporate Socially Responsible Programs'. *Journal of Academy of Marketing Science*, 34, spring: 147–57.

ELLIOTT, DAVID J. 2005. 'Can Sustainable Consumption Become an Effective Brand Attribute?' Paper presented at XVI Basque Studies Congress, 'Sustainable Development', Bilbao, Nov.

Environics. 1999. 'The Millennium Poll on Corporate Social Responsibility: Executive Briefing'. <http://www.ipsos-mori.com/polls/1999/millpoll.shtml>.

ETTENSON, RICHARD, SMITH, CRAIG N., KLEIN, JILL G., and JOHN, ANDREW. 2006. 'Rethinking Consumer Boycotts'. *Sloan Management Review*, 47, summer: 6–7.

FITZGERALD, NIALL, and CORMACK, MANDY. 2006. 'The Role of Business in Society: An Agenda for Action'. A report as part of the Clinton Global Initiative. Jointly published by The Conference Board, Harvard University CSR Initiative and the International Business Leaders Forum. Available at: <http://www.iblf.org/resources/general.jsp?id=123831>. Accessed: 16 Mar. 2007.

FRIEDMAN, MONROE. 1999. *Consumer Boycotts*. New York: Routledge.

GARRETT, DENNIS E. 1987. 'The Effectiveness of Marketing Policy Boycotts: Environmental Opposition to Marketing'. *Journal of Marketing*, 51 Apr: 46–57.

GRANDE, CARLOS. 2007. 'Businesses Behaving Badly, Say Consumers'. *Financial Times*, 20 Feb.

HARRISON, ROB, NEWHOLM, TERRY, and SHAW, DEIDRE. 2005. *The Ethical Consumer*. London: Sage.

KASSARJIAN, HAROLD H. 1972. 'Incorporating Ecology into Marketing Strategy: The Case of Air Pollution'. *Journal of Marketing*, 35, July.

KIMELDORF, HOWARD, MEYER, RACHEL, PRASAD, MONICA, and ROBINSON, IAN. 2006. 'Consumers with a Conscience: Will They Pay More?' *Contexts*, 5, winter: 24–9.

KLEIN, JILL, and DAWAR, NIRAJ. 2004. 'Corporate Social Responsibility and Consumers' Attributions and Brand Evaluations in a Product-Harm Crisis'. *International Journal of Research in Marketing*, 21, Sept.: 203–17.

—— SMITH, N. CRAIG, and JOHN, ANDREW. 2004. 'Why We Boycott: Consumer Motivations for Boycott Participation'. *Journal of Marketing*, 68, July: 92–109.

KOZINETS, ROBERT V., and HANDELMAN, JAY M. 1998. 'Ensouling Consumption: A Netnographic Exploration of Boycotting Behavior', in J. Alba and W. Hutchinson (eds.), *Advances in Consumer Research*. Provo, Ut.: Association for Consumer Research, 475–80.

LAIDLER, HARRY W. 1963. *Boycotts and the Labor Struggle: Economic and Legal Aspects*. New York: Russell & Russell, 1st pub. 1913.

MOLDOVEANU, MIHNEA, and PAINE, LYNN SHARP. 1999. 'Royal Dutch/Shell in Nigeria (A)'. Harvard Business School case study 9-399-126. Boston: Harvard Business School Publishing.

RIGBY, ELIZABETH. 2006. 'Ethical Consumers: Supermarkets and Clothes Chains Alike have Realised that Shoppers View the Ethics of Sustainability and Ecological Responsibility as Core to their Buying Decisions'. *Financial Times*, 12 June: 4.

—— and HARVEY, FIONA. 2007. 'M&S Vows to Spend £200 m Going Green'. *Financial Times*, 15 Jan.

—— —— and CROOKS, ED. 2007. 'Tesco to 'Carbon Label' its Products'. *Financial Times*, 19 Jan.: 1.

ROBERTS, JAMES A. 1996. 'Will the Real Socially Responsible Consumer Please Step Forward?' *Business Horizons*, Jan.–Feb.: 79–83.

SCHWARTZ, PETER., and GIBB, BLAIR. 1999. *When Good Companies Do Bad Things: Responsibility and Risk in Age of Globalization*. New York: Wiley.

SEN, SANKAR, and BHATTACHARYA, C. B. 2001. 'Does Doing Good Always Lead to Doing Better? Consumer Reactions to Corporate Social Responsibility'. *Journal of Marketing Research*, 38(2): 225–44.

—— GURHAN-CANLI, ZEYNEP, and MORWITZ, VICKI. 2001. 'Withholding Consumption: A Social Dilemma Perspective on Consumer Boycotts'. *Journal of Consumer Research*, 28, Dec.: 399–417.

SHARP, GENE. 1973. *The Politics of Nonviolent Action*. Boston: Porter Sargent.

SHELL. 1998. *Profits and Principles—Does There Have to be a Choice?* London: Shell International.

SMITH, N. CRAIG. 1990. *Morality and the Market Consumer Pressure for Corporate Accountability*. London: Routledge.

—— 1999. 'Ethics and the Typology of Consumer Value', in Morris B. Holbrook (ed.), *Consumer Value: A Framework for Analysis and Research*. New York: Routledge, 147–58.

—— 2003. 'Corporate Social Responsibility: Whether or How?' *California Management Review*, 45, summer: 52–76.

STRONG, CAROLYN. 1996. 'Features Contributing to the Growth of Ethical Consumerism: A Preliminary Investigation'. *Marketing Intelligence and Planning*, 14(5).

VARADARAJAN, P. RAJAN, and MENON, ANIL. 1988. 'Cause-Related Marketing: A Coalignment of Marketing Strategy and Corporate Philanthropy'. *Journal of Marketing*, 52, July: 58–75.

VOGEL, DAVID. 1978. *Lobbying the Corporation: Citizen Challenges to Business Authority*. New York: Basic Books.

—— 2005. *The Market for Virtue: The Potential and Limits of Corporate Social Responsibility*. Washington: Brookings Institution Press.

WARD, HALINA, and SMITH, N. CRAIG. 2006. 'Business as Usual is Not the Answer to Society's Problems'. *Financial Times*, 20 Oct.: 17.

WEBSTER, FREDERICK E. 1974. *Social Aspects of Marketing*. Englewood Cliffs, NJ: Prentice-Hall.

WITKOWSKI, TERRENCE H. 2005. 'Fair Trade Marketing: An Alternative System for Globalization and Development'. *Journal of Marketing Theory and Practice*, 13, fall: 22–33.

WOLMAN, LEO. 1916. *The Boycott in American Trade Unions*. Baltimore: Johns Hopkins Press.

CORPORATE SOCIAL RESPONSIBILITY, GOVERNMENT, AND CIVIL SOCIETY

JEREMY MOON

DAVID VOGEL

INTRODUCTION

THE last decade has witnessed new roles and relationships between governments and corporations. The UK government has created a ministerial portfolio of Corporate Social Responsibility (CSR); corporations have created forms of self-reporting (e.g. the Global Reporting Initiative), as well as self-regulation (company-specific supply chain assurance systems); non-governmental organizations (NGOs) such as the World Wildlife Fund and Amnesty International have entered partnerships with corporations in order to help them improve various social and environmental practices. There has also been substantial growth in the number of ethical or social mutual funds as well as in the market share of various ethical or social brands (Vogel, 2005).

The purpose of this chapter is to contextualize, illustrate, explain, and evaluate these developments. It begins by exploring the relationship between CSR and particular patterns of business–government–civil society relations. It then examines the patterns of business–government relations (BGR) that are associated with CSR. We explore two basic models. One is the dichotomous view that posits that CSR and government are, by definition, mutually exclusive; accordingly, the scope of CSR is defined by the absence of regulation and public policy. The second posits that CSR is the relationship between market actors and governments.

This essay also investigates changes in business–government–civil society relations which explain the recent growth and development of CSR. Business social responsibilities have ebbed and flowed in certain societies as governmental powers have waxed and waned. In addition, perceived and actual governance deficits at both the national and international levels have played a critical role in the growth of CSR. Finally, we examine the ways in which governments have promoted CSR and the relationship between responsible public and private policies.

CSR, Government, and Civil Society

Howard Bowen, often regarded as the father of CSR, defined the social responsibilities of 'businessmen' as their obligations to 'pursue those policies, to make those decisions, or to follow those lines of action which are desirable in terms of the objectives and values of our society' (1953: 6). Allied concepts such as corporate social responsiveness (Sethi, 1979) and corporate social performance (Wartick and Cochran, 1985) also link the responsiveness and performance of firms to society in general. Stakeholder models of strategic management typically include 'government' and 'society' as among those constituencies to whom firms should be accountable. (Freeman, 1984). Such definitions beg the question of the relationship between these business responsibilities and those of government either to represent or to meet the interests and values of society.

The Dichotomous View of Business and Government Responsibilities

In his oft-quoted essay, 'The Social Responsibility of Business is to Increase its Profits', Friedman distinguishes the responsibilities of business managers from those of government (1970). This perspective is shared by many skeptics of CSR who are concerned that acceptance of its legitimacy by firms may compromise effective functioning of markets (e.g. Crook, 2005). Friedman's distinction was premised on utilitarian and accountability grounds. His utilitarian case is that political representatives and public officials are trained for and experienced with addressing public policy issues whereas business managers are trained for and experienced in managing business organizations. The accountability case is both that business managers' prime responsibility should be to company shareholders who, he presumes, generally expect profits, while in democratic systems the accountability of government officials to the electorates is secured through elected political representatives. However, arguments which imply autonomous and dichotomous roles to business and government on the basis of democratic accountability are not the sole preserve of the libertarian right. For example, critics on the left have criticized the 'silent take-over' of government by corporations and excessive dependency of governments upon big business (Hertz, 2002; Monbiot, 2001).

This dichotomy has not, however, been reflective of public policy nor of business practice. Governments structure the behavior of private actors to serve public ends through both regulations and incentives. Moreover, public policy is influenced by the articulation and aggregation of business (and other societal) interests and their respective lobbying activities (Finer, 1958; Lowi, 1964). Governments typically partner with business (and other organized interests) to formulate and implement public policy. This occurs not only in 'neo-corporatist' systems in which bargaining among sectional interests and with government is institutionalized (Schmitter and Lehmbruch, 1979) but also in systems such as the USA and the UK where government officials informally engage business and other interests in defining policy objectives and in assisting in their implementation (Heclo, 1979; Richardson and Jordan, 1979). In Britain, Ayres and Braithewaite distinguish among command regulation with non-discretionary punishment; command regulation with discretionary punishment; enforced self-regulation; and self-regulation. They conclude that much UK regulation consists of complementary rather than dichotomous frameworks (1992).

The Embedded View of Business and Government Responsibilities

Although all markets necessarily consist of individuals and companies, they pursue their economic interests in the context of specific social and political environments. As Polanyi (2001) notes, markets are embedded in human societies and are created and maintained by specific state actions, specifically through the design of legal frameworks that protect property rights and assure the integrity of market transactions. According to Granovetter (1985), economic action is embedded in the structures of social relations as well as in hierarchies that shape market incentive structures and economic choices.

By definition, CSR presumes an autonomous corporation, free to exercise discretion in how it deploys its resources. Yet the concept also entails conformance with laws which are primarily national in character, scope, and application, as well as with 'customary ethics' (Carroll, 1991), which again may reflect different ethical systems rooted in distinct patterns of business–government–society (BSG) relations. The significance of this point is underscored by the fact that one of the primary reasons why companies engage in CSR is in order to be trusted by society. The importance of trust is reflected in such terms as 'the social licence to trade', 'legitimacy', and 'corporate citizenship'. Thus, CSR often involves the development of 'network relations' among corporations, as both private and government actors invest in and draw upon social capital (Habisch and Moon, 2006).

There is considerable variety in the structure and regulation of markets; in the accountability of governments and the operation of the justice system; and in the freedom and flourishing of civil society. This is particularly the case with respect to differences among advanced capitalist democracies, stable, authoritarian developed societies, and failed states. In the latter two cases, governments, either by oppressive practices that restrict the functioning of civil society, and/or widespread corruption and incompetence, may make it extremely difficult for corporations to act responsibly.

Even relatively similar systems with strong commitment to liberal democracy and welfare capitalism, such as the USA and Western Europe, can produce important differences in BSG relationships which can in turn produce rather different forms and kinds of CSR. Thus, the relatively more explicit emphasis on CSR found in the USA throughout the twentieth century compared to that in Western Europe can be understood in terms of differences in the role of and social attitudes toward government (this section draws upon Matten and Moon, 2008).

Although the USA has strong local governments that provide primary and secondary public education, tertiary or higher education is in significant measure private, dependent for much of its financing on student tuition and contributions. Not surprisingly, support for higher education has been a long-standing and more important feature of individual and business philanthropy in the USA than in Western Europe, where it is more likely to be publicly financed. Similarly, Western European governments have historically played a central role in labor market regulation, often due to trade union pressure. Their influence is reflected in neo-corporatist relations between organized labour and capital (Schmitter and Lehmbruch, 1979). Accordingly, there was comparatively less scope for companies in Europe to make pensions, wages, and health insurance a component of their corporate responsibilities, as these were either supplied by government or determined through negotiations with unions. By contrast, the American government has played a less important role in supplying welfare benefits to employees and has rarely been involved in wage negotiations. Accordingly, labor relations in the USA have been more closely associated with CSR. For example, at the beginning of the twentieth century, the President of Studebaker Motor Company stated:

The first duty of an employer is to labor…It is the duty of capital and management to compensate liberally, paying at least the current wage and probably a little more, and to give workers decent and healthful surroundings and treat them with utmost consideration. If management cannot do this, then it is incompetent. (Quoted in Heald, 1970: 36)

Thus, the USA and Western Europe have been characterized by different patterns of business, society, and government relations. These differences include: the relative capacity of Americans for participation (De Tocqueville, 1835/1956), their relative capacity for philanthropy (Bremner, 1988), and, in particular, the relative capacity of business people for philanthropy (Dowie, 2001); their relative skepticism about big government (King, 1973); and their relative confidence in the moral worth of capitalism (Vogel, 1992). Pasquero (2004) has argued that American CSR is embedded in American institutions and culture, particularly in the traditions of individualism, democratic pluralism, moralism, and utilitarianism.

The American government has often not used its regulatory and fiscal capacities as extensively as their Westen European counterparts in such areas as employment law, the provision of social services, and the establishment and financing of cultural institutions. Hence, these represent important dimensions of CSR in America. By contrast, the more collectivist cultural and political traditions of Western Europe explain why many dimensions of CSR that have been historically important in the USA were slower to emerge in Europe (Maignon and Ralston, 2002).

In the light of the embedded view of CSR in business–government–society relations, the question then arises as to why and how CSR norms and practices have changed? This question is especially pertinent as CSR has clearly evolved in important ways in the last decade or so. In the next section, we consider how broad changes in public governance have contributed to the development of CSR.

CSR and Governance

Governance systems have witnessed important changes in the last few decades and these have in turn expanded the scope and importance of CSR.

CSR and Domestic Governance Deficits

In the late 1970s and early 1980s a variety of theoretical perspectives, including neo-liberalism (e.g. Brittan, 1975), and neo-Marxism (e.g. Habermas, 1975), identified a governance crisis in democratic capitalism. Terms like 'ungovernability', the 'legitimation crisis', 'government overload', 'governing under pressure', and 'fiscal bankruptcy' appeared in numerous political analyses.

Concern with the impacts of racial discrimination and disadvantage in the USA prompted corporations in the 1960s and early 1970s to develop CSR policies, particularly in the areas of inner-city development and education. The United Kingdom, a country which had been regarded as comparatively consensual, not only saw a very sharp rise in unemployment in the late 1970s and early 1980s but also urban riots and other manifestations of urban alienation. These had a marked impact on business and the role and importance of CSR. Most obviously, it created general anxiety about the social license to trade which was captured in *The Economist* magazine's description of Marks and Spencer's expenditure on community work and charity as 'making a sensible investment in its market place. If urban disorders become a regular fact of life, many of its 260 stores would not survive.' It added the maxim that 'wealthy high streets require healthy back streets' (20 Feb. 1982).

Another motivation for CSR in this context was to offset the threat of regulation:

> ... companies fear that if they make no attempt to find solutions to community problems, the government may increasingly take on the responsibility itself. This might prove costly to employers both in terms of new obligations and greater intervention in the labour market. Many companies prefer to be one step ahead of government legislation or intervention, to anticipate social pressures themselves and hence be able to develop their own policies in response to them. (CBI, 1981, quoted in Moon and Richardson, 1985: 137)

These developments led to many new manifestations of CSR. Among the most significant and enduring was the creation of the leading British business association for CSR, Business in the Community, which now has over 700 corporate members and a regional support structure.

In other democratic capitalist countries, challenges to postwar systems of governance were less dramatic but nonetheless important. Many governments have followed the UK in privatizing former publicly owned industries, thereby making corporations more autonomous, and in reforming the welfare state, which has often resulted in reductions in state provision. Changes in the responsibilities of corporations in Europe have also been influenced by changes in the state-sponsored systems of political representation, mediation, and exchange among organized interests, particularly of industrial labor and capital, often referred to as corporatism or neo-corporatism. Whereas for the first thirty or forty years of the postwar period these relationships were often relatively hierarchical, broad in scope, and consensual, they have subsequently changed. These changes are related to the emergence of new 'post-industrial'/'post-Fordist' issues (e.g. education, health care, the environment), the proliferation of actors and networks, decentralization of decision-making, and the increase in business self-regulation (Molina and Rhodes,

2002). All these developments have contributed to the recent growth of CSR in Europe.

As a result, the growth of CSR must be understood in relation to the changes in public sector governance that have occurred during the last two decades. The nature and timing of these changes have varied among national systems. They have been particularly marked in Australia, New Zealand, and the UK, most notably though privatization and reforms of the welfare state. Moreover these governments have increasingly turned to governance arrangements that do not involve the deployment of organizational and fiscal resources underpinned by the authority of government. These changes are reflected in titles such as 'Governing without Government' (Rhodes, 1996), 'What's a Government to Do?' (Peters, 1996), and 'The Enabling State' (Deakin and Walsh, 1996).

Initially, much of the business participation in new forms of governance represented an extension of a relatively long-standing tradition of corporate social involvement in the community through philanthropy, with a particular focus on education, training, and local economic development (Moon, 2004a; Moon and Sochacki, 1996, 1998). These efforts were often institutionalized both within corporations and in public organizations. More recently, governments have encouraged network and partnership approaches to governance, and drawn in community organizations, NGOs, as well as corporations.

Thus, corporations have assumed a greater role in societal governance not only through markets, but also via networks—many of which also involve the non-profit sector. This in turn has created a policy space for CSR. Beck (1997) argues that corporations have increasingly stepped into a 'subpolitical' role, particularly in ecological issues as governments have blatantly failed to avert or handle the undesired side-effects of an energy-intensive form of production and consumption (e.g. global warming, nuclear power), new technologies (e.g. GM food), or scandals (e.g. mad cow disease), etc.

CSR, Globalization, and Governance Deficits

The growth of CSR also has an important global dimension, again reflecting perceived governance shortcomings. A central theme of much scholarship on the growth of private, market-based, non-state regulation that has emerged to govern a number of sectors, most notably forestry, energy, minerals and mining, and textiles, is that global CSR standards represent a response to the failures of national and international business regulation. According to this analysis, economic globalization, as measured by the growth of international trade and the expansion of international investment, has created a 'governance deficit' (Newell, 2002: 908). Much of the growth of global civil regulation is rooted in the perception that economic globalization has created a structural imbalance between the size and power of global firms and markets, and the capacity, willingness, and ability of governments to regulate them. 'Transnational corporations appear to wield power without responsibility. They are often as powerful as states and yet unaccountable' (Newell, 2000: 121).

NGOs have sought to step into the regulatory vacuum created by the inadequacies of both national governments and international institutions to regulate MNCs by 'forging alliances with consumers, institutional investors and companies themselves' (Newell, 2000: 117–18). While they cannot replace the role of the state, these social movements have created new mechanisms of global business regulation. Moreover, 'targeting companies directly offers the prospect of higher "returns" given that the investment decisions of major TNCs now dwarf those of many states' (Newell, 2000: 120).

Other scholars echo Newell's analysis. According to Knill and Lehmkuhl, global corporate responsibility is intended to 'compensate for the decreasing capacities of national governments for providing public goods [as] ... internationalization yields an increasing gap between territorially bound regulatory competences at the national level and emerging problems of global scope' (2002: 42–4). Lipschutz (2005) argues that CSR represents an effort to counter or challenge the increasing reluctance or unwillingness of national governments to impose regulations on global firms due to their fear that such regulations will discourage domestic investment and make their economies less competitive.

Accounts of the origins of various mechanisms of global private governance often specifically situate them in the context of the shortcomings of international business regulation. For example, in the late 1980s, the British chapter of the environmental NGO, Friends of the Earth, proposed the creation of an international forest certification regime under the auspices of the International Tropical Timber Organization (ITTO). When the British government made such a suggestion at a meeting of the ITTO in 1989, it was bitterly attacked by timber-exporting countries. They argued that since such similar certification mechanisms did not exist for non-tropical forests, such a certification scheme represented both a non-tariff barrier to trade and an assault on their sovereignty. Accordingly, the British proposal was effectively taken off the agenda: As one NGO activist put it, 'the Forest Certification Council [a private forest certification scheme] was a response to the failure of international organizations that ought to have had the remit to enforce, to implement and develop good forestry standards—ITTO in particular ...' (Bartley, 2003: 452).

Subsequently, at the 1992 Rio 'Earth Summit', many environmental NGOs actively lobbied for a binding international agreement on forestry management. However, no such agreement was reached, largely due to the opposition of developing countries. Environmental groups regarded the Rio Summit as close to a complete failure on forestry issues and accordingly concluded that 'private rather than intergovernmental initiatives were the place to focus their energies' (Bartley, 2003: 453).

According to Newell (2002), the growth of interest in the private regulation of global firms is a direct outgrowth of the lack of effective regulation of global firms at the international level. Thus, the regulation of transnational firms was dropped from the agenda of the UN Commission on Environment and Development, while another UN-related initiative—Agenda 21—refused to recommend the creation of global codes of conduct for multinational corporation (MNCs). Likewise, the Commission on International Investment and Transnational Corporations was unable to agree on a code of conduct for global firms due to conflicts between developed and developing nations. While the organization for Economic Co-operation and Developments (OECD) has issued guidelines for MNCs, they are entirely voluntary. 'It is against this background of weak instruments and failed initiatives at the international level that NGOs have begun to target TNCs with increasing frequency and vigor in recent years' (Newell, 2002: 910).

Private labor standards have emerged from a similar dynamic. While the International Labor Organization (ILO) has established minimum standards for working conditions—and these have been agreed to by numerous governments—they are entirely voluntary; the ILO has no enforcement capacity. During the mid-1990s, in response to growing public concern about the treatment of workers by firms in developing countries making products for western companies, American Secretary of Labor Robert Reich asked the ILO to develop a 'global social label' that would certify to consumers that products carrying it were made in compliance with ILO labor standards. His proposal was strongly denounced by representatives from developing countries as a form of protectionism and it was abandoned. This setback in turn encouraged the formation of private labor certification standards that now represent a critical dimension of contemporary global corporate responsibility (Vogel, 2005: chapter 4).

The growth of global CSR can also be viewed in the context of developments in international trade law. The World Trade Organization (WTO) has restricted the ability of governments—even if they were willing to do so—from restricting imports on the basis of the environmental or labor standards prevailing in the exporting country. More specifically, WTO rules generally prohibit a country from requiring product labelling that describes how a product was produced outside of its borders. Many NGOs have actively campaigned for the inclusion of labor, human rights and environmental standards in trade agreements. But while a number of bilateral and regional trade agreements entered into by both the USA and the European Union (EU) do contain such provisions, they tend to be vague and are rarely enforced. Accordingly, private product labelling and certification represents a way to provide consumers and firms with such information without running afoul of WTO rules on non-tariff trade barriers, since the WTO only governs— and restricts—the decisions of governments. Indeed, such measures are entirely consistent with both the spirit and letter of WTO rules, which emphasize the use of market mechanisms.

Government as a Driver for CSR

While CSR is generally viewed as an alternative to government regulation, this does not mean that it is has evolved separately from public policy. In fact, many governments have played an active role in encouraging corporations to voluntarily assume greater responsibility for the social and environmental impacts of their business policies. These initiatives can be distinguished from command and control regulations in that they do not involve legally binding or enforceable substantive standards for corporate behavior. Rather they seek to harness various market mechanisms to promote CSR. They have been promoted by national governments, the European Union and various inter-governmental organizations, most notably the United Nations and OECD. We turn first to examine policies introduced by national governments.

Government Policies for CSR

Governments have often encouraged CSR in order to manage an array of governance issues. Again, there is variety here, reflecting both the ways in which CSR had previously been embedded in business–government–society relations, as well as the ways in which more recent changes in systems of governance have shaped opportunities and imperatives for new forms of business responsibility. Many governments, such as those of Australia and Denmark in the 1990s, shared the UK 1980s government concern with the effects of the unemployment crisis. More recently the UK has been more concerned with the governance of sustainability and new competitiveness strategies. In the case of South Africa, concern has focused on the governance implications of the shift from apartheid to democracy.

Many governments have chosen to draw business further into governance issues without actually mandating behavior and specifying penalties for non-compliance, the more traditional command regulatory model. Thus the UK government's Society and Business website states that:

The Government can also provide a policy and institutional framework that stimulates companies to raise their performance beyond minimum legal standards. Our approach is to encourage and incentivise the adoption of CSR, through best practice guidance, and, where appropriate, intelligent (i.e. soft) regulation and fiscal incentives.

We can distinguish three main means by which governments can promote or encourage CSR: endorsement and exhortation; facilitation, and partnering (Fox *et al.*, 2002).

First, governments can use their imprimatur to exhort and encourage business responsibility. In the 1980s the UK Secretary of State for the Environment even went so far as to articulate governmental incapacity and dependency:

...we (government) do not have the money. We do not have the expertise. We need the private sector again to play a role which, in Britain, it played more conspicuously a century ago than it does now. (Michael Heseltine, quoted in Moon, 2004a: 55)

Similarly, in the context of high levels of unemployment and social exclusion in Denmark, the Minister of Social Affairs, Karen Jesperson (2003) initiated the 'It Concerns Us All' campaign to draw attention to the ways in which CSR could assist in addressing public policy problems and formed the National Network of Company Leaders to provide advice to the government with respect to groups at risk of social exclusion due to long-term unemployment, lack of training, mental illness, and alcoholism (Rosdahl, 2001). In Australia, Prime Minister John Howard formed the Business Leaders' Roundtable as a means of encouraging business leaders to think about how they could assist in solving social problems. The Swedish government's CSR initiative invites companies to sign up to a commitment to uphold relevant international standards.

More recently in the UK, the Blair Labour government has given considerable encouragement to CSR. In his first address to the Labour Party as its leader, the Prime Minister announced his support for expanding public–private partnerships in schools. According to the former Minister of Education, David Miliband:

... we cannot do this on our own. Education is a joint enterprise—between teachers and students but also between schools and the wider community. Business can sponsor Specialist schools and Academies. Business can contribute to curriculum enhancement. Business can offer work placements and work experience. Business can offer mentoring and governor support. (quoted in Moon 2004a: 15)

The creation of the position of Minister for CSR within the UK Department of Trade and Industry perhaps represents one of the strongest endorsements of CSR by a government.

Second, governments can facilitate CSR by setting clear frameworks to guide business behavior, establishing non-binding codes and systems, and providing information about CSR to firms and industries. Those governments which encouraged CSR as a response to mass unemployment (e.g. the UK, Australia) created public policies which encouraged companies to participate by providing work experience and training opportunities through trainee subsidies, and support for the processing of trainees and design and support for qualification systems which companies could use in their own employment decisions (Moon and Richardson, 1985; Moon and Sochacki, 1996).

Governments can also facilitate CSR by providing guidance on best practice. This occurred in Japan where close relationships between government ministries and corporations have developed, reminiscent of the historic roles of the Japanese government in working with major corporations on various dimensions of industrial policy. Thus, the CSR reporting practices of the Japanese closely follow the suggested framework of the Ministry of Environment (Fukukawa and Moon, 2004).

Third, governments can bring their organizational, fiscal, and authoritative resources to form partnerships for CSR. The precise roles can vary but include government acting as a catalyst, convenor, or equal participant. In the UK, the government operates numerous partnerships with business organizations to encourage CSR. For example, it partners Business in the Community through (BITC) sponsorship of the BITC Awards, the Impact on Society Report, and the BITC Corporate Responsibility Index, and through website links. It also partners a network to provide a CSR competency framework, known as CSR Academy. This partnership also includes the business college, Ashridge and the Corporate Responsibility Group (CSR professionals) at the design stage, and the Chartered Institute of Personnel Development, British Chambers of Commerce, the Association of Business Schools, supported by BITC and Accountability, at the implementation stage.

In sum, there has been a broadening of the scope of policies for CSR. Originally mainly oriented at community involvement, they now address a much wider range of public problems. This has been accompanied by a shift in motivation from concern with governance shortcomings to a concern with government enhancement and responsiveness to society and business itself. In addition, there has been an expansion in the means deployed to encourage CSR from endorsing and facilitating to include partnering and mandating through soft regulation.

Government Policies for Global CSR

With respect to government policies for global CSR, we can distinguish those which consist of the development of codes for international business, particularly in foreign direct investment and international supply chains; those which seek to encourage socially responsible international investment; those which require reporting or labelling of social, environmental, and ethical impacts of global business; and those which seek to encourage overall increases in responsibility standards. We illustrate these developments with reference to national government policies designed to shape the international behavior of 'home-based' multinational companies and to policies introduced by inter-governmental organizations such as the OECD, the UN, and the EU.

An early example of international codes of conduct was inspired by the US government. The Clinton Administration encouraged representatives of the apparel industry, labor unions, and NGOs to join the Apparel Industry Partnership in order to improve overseas working conditions. This organization subsequently developed into the Fair Labor Association, which is one of the most important industry labor codes. The British government played a critical role in developing another voluntary code, the Extractive Industries Transparency Initiative (EITE). Its purpose is to increase the transparency of payments made by corporations to governments in the extractive industry sector with the goal of reducing corruption and promoting public sector fiscal responsibility. The government not only participates in the EITE multi-stakeholder conferences but also facilitated it through a £1 million subsidy of the first phase of the EITI's implementation.

It also was instrumental in establishing the Ethical Trading Initiative—an alliance of retail companies, non-government organizations, and trade unions to improve conditions in member company supply chains, with special reference to ensuring that they maintain the international employment standards enshrined in the International Labor Organisation conventions. Similarly, the UK government is a partner in the Fair Trade system designed to help producers raise their incomes though better management and skills and better-managed retail supply chains. It has endorsed the Fair Trade system through supporting media campaigns and facilitated it through assistance in technical aspects creating systems across a range of product types and in representing the scheme at the inter-governmental level.

Both the American and British governments together established the Voluntary Principles on Security and Human Rights. It establishes standards to govern the conduct of security forces responsible for protecting investments by natural resource firms in developing countries. For its part, the German government has established a 'Round Table on Corporate Codes of Conduct' in order to improve labor and social standards in developing countries through codes of conduct. The German government specifically helped organize a code of conduct for global coffee production. The government of Italy has developed a voluntary CSR standard.

At the inter-governmental level, the OECD has issued a set of guidelines to govern the social and environmental conduct of multinational firms. Following a speech in 1999 by UN Secretary General Kofi Annan, the United Nations worked with the International Labor Organization, NGOs, and leading MNCs to form the UN Global Compact. This agreement defined initially nine and later ten standards for responsible global corporate conduct which signatory firms are expected to meet. These standards address human rights, labor standards, the environment, and corruption. These principles were drawn up by companies, NGOs, labor organizations, and UN agencies. The UN assists firms in operationalizing their commitments through Policy Dialogues, Learning, Country/Regional Networks, and Projects (McIntosh *et al.*, 2004). More than 3,000 firms have endorsed the UN Global Compact. Finally, the private investment arm of the World Bank has promoted the adoption of the Equator Principles by global banks. Signatory banks have agreed to develop procedures to assess and monitor the social and environmental impact of project development financing in developing countries. To date, they have been endorsed by forty-one global banks.

Another way in which governments have sought to promote CSR is by encouraging investment funds to consider various social or ethical criteria in allocating the capital under their control. The governments of Belgium, Germany, Sweden, and the United Kingdom require administrators of pension funds to report whether they use social, ethical, or environmental criteria in making their investment decisions, while the French government requires that administrators of pension funds define the criteria they are employing in their stock selection and specifically requires public pension funds to take account of social, environmental, and ethical criteria (Aaronson and Reeves, 2002; Perrini *et al.*, 2006)

Several governments have sought to promote global CSR by requiring firms to report on their social and environmental policies and practices. Various kinds of corporate disclosure requirements have been adopted by Denmark, Germany, Finland, France, and Sweden, while the British have issued voluntary guidelines on corporate social reporting. Other mechanisms that various governments have adopted include giving permission for companies to use social labels if their global production meets various social criteria, providing preferential procurement policies for socially responsible firms and linking trade policies to environmental, human rights, and labor standards (Buckland *et al.*, 2006).

In addition, several regional and bilateral trade agreements include labor provisions whose purpose is to encourage developing country governments to enforce either their own labor standards or those of international organizations such as the International Labor Organization. One of the most important, and successful, of such initiatives involves an agreement between the USA and the government of Cambodia. In exchange for working with foreign investors and local firms to bring Cambodian labor standards in line with those of the ILO, Cambodia textile exports to the USA have received preferential treatment (Polaski, 2004).

These government policies, however, represent only one dimension of the efforts of various governments to promote CSR. Of at least equal importance have been a wide range of informal efforts to encourage firms to engage with stakeholders, learn best practices, and more generally, to persuade firms of the business benefits of acting more responsibly. While many of these efforts have taken place at the national level within Europe, a particularly critical educational role has been played by the EU. On numerous occasions since the late 1990s, the EU has issued statements and reports that emphasize the importance of CSR. For the EU, CSR represents an integral part of its multifaceted efforts to promote European competitiveness: it represents both a strategy for companies to improve their long-term financial viability—and a way for Europe to become more innovative, dynamic, and competitive. To encourage firms to improve their CSR practices and recognize its business benefits, the EU has organized a series of conferences and workshops that bring together employees, trade unions, NGOs, and academics.

In its influential Green Paper of 2001, the European Commission provided a comprehensive inventory of the various ways in which governments could promote CSR as well as an overview of the various dimensions of best CSR practices (Commission of the European Communities, 2001).

The Commission of the EU has issued various reports on the subject of CSR, one of the most important of which is 'Implementing the Partnership for Growth and Jobs'. In this report, the Commission identifies its roles in awareness raising and best-practice exchange, support of stakeholder initiatives, cooperation with member states, consumer information and transparency, research, education, SMEs and the international dimension. (<http://euv-lex.europa.eu/LexUriServ/site/en/com/2006/can 2006_0136en01.pdf>). In 2006, the European Commission (EC), along with several business leaders established the European Alliance for Corporate Responsibility. 'Its ambition is to make Europe a pole of excellence on corporate social responsibility', by promoting cultural change within business (Spidla, 2006: 14). However, the formation of the Alliance disappointed European NGOs, who had hoped that the European Multi-stakeholder Forum on CSR, which had ended in 2004, would result in a policy document that reaffirmed the EC's commitment to involve non-business constituencies in shaping the EC's CSR policies, and would develop a European CSR framework based on internationally agreed standards, such as those of the OECD and the ILO, along with credible provisions for monitoring and verification (Oldenziel, 2000). Nonetheless, the EU, along with the British government, has played a critical role in promoting awareness of CSR among European-based firms.

REDRESSING THE GOVERNMENT–CSR BALANCE

We have suggested that while CSR is primarily associated with corporate social and environmental initiatives that are voluntary in the literal sense, they are not legally required, in fact, CSR cannot be viewed in isolation from government. This is true in a number of respects. First, the specific national content of CSR reflects the role of the state: areas in which the state has assumed a central role are less likely to be the focus of voluntary corporate initiatives. This in part explains why historically CSR emerged first in the USA, the capitalist polity in which the state has played a much smaller social role than in other capitalist democracies.

Second, CSR has emerged at both the national and international levels as a response to the perceived failures, shortcomings, or limitations of government regulation: its emergence in large measure reflects a perceived government deficit. This in part explains why CSR has recently become much more salient in Europe, where on some dimensions the role of government has diminished and the importance of business and markets has increased. Governance failures also help us understand the increasing importance of global CSR: corporate codes governing global firms and global markets in large measure reflect the perceived shortcomings of existing national and international laws to govern the recent expansion of global business.

Third, somewhat paradoxically, many national governments, along with international governmental organizations such as the UN, World Bank, and OECD, have themselves played an important role in promoting CSR. Such initiatives can be usefully seen as a form of soft or market-based regulation: they typically do not mandate specific kinds of corporate conduct or behavior, but rather seek to encourage firms to act more responsibly, through measures such as reporting requirements for firms and financial institutions, reports on business practices, support for research and working with firms and industries to establish voluntary codes, etc. Their motives vary. In the case of international organizations, CSR initiatives represent an effort to enlist the support of the private sector to further their broad policy goals. For its part, the EU regards CSR largely as a way to enhance the global competitiveness of European firms, while many national governments are responding to public pressures to reconcile economic globalization with various social and environmental objectives.

In the final analysis, corporate and governmental responsibility are invariably related. This in turn raises two additional, critical issues. The first has to do with the role of business in affecting public policy; the second has to do with linkages between corporate voluntary initiatives and public policy. The first primarily involves business–government relations in developed countries; the second addresses business–government relations in developing ones.

The boundaries between business and government do not take place in a vacuum; they are strongly influenced by corporate political preferences and their lobbying activities. For all the increasing importance of CSR, public policy remains the most important vehicle by which private business purposes and broader social objectives can be reconciled. Accordingly, one of the critical dimensions of CSR involves not what firms do voluntarily, but the role they play in affecting government regulation of business. While CSR is often viewed as an alternative to regulation, in many areas, corporations cannot afford to engage in more responsible behavior unless public policy requires that all firms act in a similar manner. This suggests that the definition of CSR should be expanded to encompass how, to what extent, and for what purposes corporations participate in the policy process. In other words, corporate lobbying also needs to be responsible. (For an extended discussion of this dimension of CSR see 'Towards Responsible Lobbying: Leadership and Public Policy', 2005.)

One important example that illustrates the interdependency of CSR and public policy involves global climate change. On one hand, according to one study, 74 companies from 28 industries have adopted policies to reduce their greenhouse gas emissions, and these policies have produced cost savings of more than $11 billion (*The Economist*, 10 June 2006: 59–60) Yet on the other hand, many capital-intensive firms are reluctant to make long-term investment decisions until they know the future scope and extent of government regulation of carbon. Consequently, several business leaders in the UK, organized into an association called Corporate Leaders on Climate Change, have indicated their interest in working with the British government to support sound, long-term responsible public policies that will enable them to address the business challenges of global climate change without incurring a competitive disadvantage. In early 2007, a similar pro-regulation business coalition with respect to climate change also emerged in the USA.

The limitations of CSR—and the need for it to be complemented by responsible public policies—emerges even more starkly in the case of developing countries. In the case of labor standards, western firms lack the capacity to adequately inspect all their suppliers; host country government regulation also needs to be strengthened if labor practices are to be improved. 'Although codes of conduct are a force for positive change ... current approaches are far likelier to bring sustainable improvements when implemented within comprehensive, public sector-governed frameworks. Governments have good reasons to invest in developing such frameworks ... that contribute positively to national competitiveness' (Cramer and Pruzan-Jergensen, 2006: 76).

In the case of failed states plagued by violence, civil war, and ethnic strife, corporate community building programs are likely to be ineffective. Perhaps most importantly, private sector efforts to reduce corruption are likely to fail unless developing country governments improve their own governance. In short, as a World Bank study concludes, for CSR in developing countries to be effective in improving social, labor, and environmental practices, the public sector has a critical role to play. Strengthening local governmental capacity represents an essential condition for improving the impact of CSR. To accomplish this requires the coordinated efforts of firms, developed country governments, and international institutions (Ward, 2004).

CONCLUSIONS

We have seen a range of ways in which CSR is located in business–government–society relations. CSR is thus highly contextual, depending particularly on the country and the general state of governance at any one time. The nature of CSR is therefore unlikely to be stable as respective actor responsibilities undergo continuing reappraisal and redefinition.

Looking to the future it is worth noting that there is some evidence of a shift in the motivations of governments for encouraging CSR. Twenty or thirty years ago, this tended to be associated with addressing various governance deficits. More recently there has been greater attention to the more positive impact of improving policies with respect to issues such as social cohesion, national competitiveness, and social and environmental sustainability. This is complemented by the interest of government not simply in encouraging CSR but also in developing CSR capacity, suggesting that governments see CSR as a long-term feature of societal governance and business regulation.

Second, there is evidence of a shift from simply endorsing and facilitating CSR to include partnering and even mandating CSR through soft legislation. Again, this speaks of a greater desire to institutionalize CSR in the government's own work and its relations with business. Partnerships tend to entail ongoing relationships and commitments and soft legislation gives rise to searches for benchmarking and best practice.

Governments have not used CSR as a vehicle for simple privatization, in the sense of a wholesale shift of responsibility from the public to the private sectors, but rather to complement government policies. This development reflects new forms of governance in which governments employ a much richer and subtler array of mechanisms to affect business behavior, rather than simply employing rule making and enforcement. Rather than imposing legal compliance, the use of policies that endorse, facilitate, and partner with firms is further characteristic of the new governance paradigm which emphasizes norms, networks, incentives, and voluntarism. Thus, CSR constitutes part of a change in the mix of governance roles and in the balance of government's own tools and resources with those of other actors; in effect, creating a shift towards 'the enabling state' (Deakin and Walsh, 1996: 33–48). Moreover, government involvement in CSR can assist business in addressing some collective action problems by, for example, initiating and providing resources and legitimacy for new CSR initiatives.

The new roles of business in these new forms of governance pose a number of challenges for managers. First, managers will need to be attentive to the responsibilities that participation in government CSR policies will entail. In the new forms of governance, which have fewer rules and clear boundaries, some managers are expressing concern that expectations are being made of business which are outside of their proper sphere of responsibility. Relatedly, the network and partnership aspects of new governance do risk a certain clouding of accountability that managers would do well to clarify. The conjunction of CSR as a mechanism for corporate social investment and societal governance blurs two different types of accountability system—the corporate and the governmental as adumbrated by Friedman. One does not need to agree with the dichotomizers of business and government activities to share an interest in the question of where accountability lies if CSR is inspired or legitimated by government.

In conclusion, not only is CSR an idea that has blossomed but so too has government's interest in encouraging it. What once would have seemed paradoxical or even a contradiction in terms can be understand in the context of the emergence of new forms of governance at both the national and international levels.

REFERENCES

AARONSON, S., and REEVES, J. 2002. *Corporate Responsibility in the Global Village: The Role of Public Policy.* Washington: National Policy Association.

AYRES, I. and BRAITHEWAITE, J. 1992. *Transcending the Deregulation Debate.* New York: Oxford University Press.

BARTLEY, T. 2003. 'Certifying Forests and Factories: States, Social Movements, and the Rise of Private Regulation in the Apparel and Forest Product Field'. *Politics and Society,* 31(3), Sept.

BECK, U. 1997. *The Reinvention of Politics: Rethinking Modernity in the Global Social Order,* trans. M. Ritter. Cambridge, Mass.: Polity Press.

BOWEN, H. 1953. *Social Responsibilities of the Businessman.* New York: Harper & Row.

BREMNER, R. H. 1988. *American Philanthropy.* Chicago: Chicago University Press.

BRITTAN, S. 1975. 'The Economic Contradictions of Democracy'. *British Journal of Political Science,* 55(1): 109–129.

BUCKLAND, HELOISE, ALBAREDA, L., LOZANO, J. M., TENCATI, A., PERRINI, F., and MIDTTUN, A. 2006. 'The Changing Role of Government in Corporate Responsibility: A Report for Practitioners.' Escade, Bocconi, BI, 21 Mar. Unpublished paper.

CARROLL, A. B. 1991. 'The Pyramid of Corporate Social Responsibility: Toward the Moral Management of Organizational Stakeholders'. *Business Horizons,* 34 (4): 39–48.

Commission of the European Commission. 2001. 'Promoting a European Framework for Corporate Social Responsibility'. Green Paper Brussels. com (2001) 366 final.

CRAMER, A., and PRUZAN-JERGENSEN, P. M. 2006. 'Engaging Governments in Support of Corporate Social Responsibility in Global Supply Chains', in Marc Epstein and Kirk Hanson (eds.) *The Accountable Corporation, vol. 4—Business-Government Relations.* Westport, Conn.: Praeger, 75–119.

CROOK, C. 2005. 'The Good Company'. *The Economist,* 22 Jan.

DEAKIN, N., and WALSH, K. 1996. 'The Enabling State: The Role of Markets and Contracts'. *Public Administration,* 74(1): 33–48.

DE TOCQUEVILLE, A. 1835/1956. *Democracy in America.* New York: Mentor.

DOWIE, M. 2001. *American Foundations: An Investigative History.* Cambridge, Mass.: The MIT Press.

FINER, S. 1958. *Anonymous Empire: A Study of the Lobby in Great Britain.* London: Pall Mall.

FREEMAN, R. E. 1984. *Strategic Management: A Stakeholder Approach.* Boston: Pitman. 1984

FRIEDMAN, M. 1970. 'The Social Responsibility of Business is to Increase its Profits'. *New York Times Magazine,* 13 Sept.: 32–3 and 122–6.

FUKUKAWA, K., and MOON, J. 2004. 'A Japanese Model of Corporate Social Responsibility? A Study of Website Reporting'. *Journal of Corporate Citizenship,* 16: 45–59.

GRANOVETTER, M. 1985. 'Economic Action and Social Structure: The Problem of Embeddedness'. *American Journal of Sociology,* 91(3): 481–510.

HABERMAS, J. 1975. *Legitimation Crisis* Boston: Beacon Press

HABISCH, A., and MOON, J. 2006. 'Social Capital and Corporate Social Responsibility', in J. Jonker and M. de Witte (eds.) *The Challenge of Organising and Implementing CSR.* Basingstoke: Palgrave.

HEALD, M. 1970. *The Social Responsibilities of Business: Company and Community, 1900–1960.* Cleveland: The Press of Case Western Reserve University.

HECLO, H. 1979. 'Issue Networks and the Executive Establishment', in A. King (ed.), *The New American Political System*. Washington: American Enterprise Institute.

HERTZ, N. 2002. *The Silent Takeover*. London: Arrow.

JESPERSON, K. 2003. 'Social Partnerships: The Role of Government in Denmark', in M. Morsing and C. Thyssen (eds.), *Corporate Values and Responsibility: The Case of Denmark*. Frederiksberg C.: Samfundslitteratur.

KING, A. 1973. 'Ideas, Institutions and the Policies of Governments: A Comparative Analysis'. *British Journal of Political Science*, 3: 291–314.

KNILL, C., and LEHMKUHL, D. 2002. 'Private Actors and the State: Internationalization and Changing Patterns of Governance'. *Governance*, 15(1), Jan.: 41–63.

LIPSCHUTZ, R., with ROWE, J. 2005. *Globalization, Governmentality and Global Politics: Regulation for the Rest of Us?* London: Routledge.

LOWI, T. 1964. 'American Business, Public Policy, Case Studies and Political Theory'. *World Politics*, 16(4): 677–715.

MCINTOSH, M., WADDOCK, S., and KELL, G. (eds). 2004. *Learning to Talk: Corporate Citizenship and the Development of the UN Global Compact*. Sheffield: Greenleaf.

MAIGNON, I., and RALSTON, D. 2002. 'Corporate Social Responsibility in Europe and the U.S.: Insights from Businesses' Self-Presentations'. *Journal of International Business Studies*, 33(3): 497–515.

MATTEN, D., and MOON, J. 2008. '"Implicit" and "Explicit" CSR: A Conceptual Framework for a Comparative Understanding of Corporate Social Responsibility'. *Academy of Management Review* April 33(2).

MOLINA, O., and RHODES, M. 2002. 'Corporatism: The Past, Present and Future of a Concept'. *Annual Review of Political Science*, 5: 305–31.

MONBIOT, G. 2001. *Captive State: The Corporate Takeover of Britain*. London: Pan Books.

MOON, J. 2004a. 'CSR in the UK: An Explicit Model of Business–Society Relations', in A. Habisch, J. Jonker, M. Wegner, and R. Schmidpeter (eds.), *Corporate Social Responsibility across Europe*. Berlin: Springer-Verlag.

—— 2004b. 'Government as a Driver of Corporate Social Responsibility: The UK in Comparative Perspective'. *ICCSR Working Papers*, No. 20, Nottingham.

—— and RICHARDSON, J. J. 1985. *Unemployment in the UK: Politics and Policies*. Aldershot: Gower.

—— and SOCHACKI, R. 1996. 'The Social Responsibility of Business in Job and Enterprise Creation: Motives, Means and Implications'. *Australian Quarterly*, 68: 21–30.

———— 1998. 'New Governance in Australian Schools: A Place for Business Social Responsibility?' *Australian Journal of Public Administration*, 55: 55–67.

NEWELL, P. 2000. 'Environmental NGOs and Globalization: The Governance of TNCs', in R. Cohen and S. Rai (eds.), *Global Social Movements*. London: Athlone Press.

—— 2002. 'Managing Multinationals: The Governance of Investment for the Environment'. *Journal of International Development*, 13: 907–19.

OLDENZIEL, JORIS. 2000. 'European Commission Abandons Multi-stakeholder Approach in CSR'. Ethical Corporation, Apr.: 15.

PASQUERO, J. 2004. 'Résponsibilité sociale de l'enterprise: les approches nord-americaines', in J. Igalens (ed.), *Tous Responsables*. Paris: Editions d'Organisation.

PERRINI, F., POGUTZ, S., and TENCATI, A. 2006. *Developing Corporate Social Responsibility: A European Perspective*. Cheltenham: Edward Elgar.

PETERS, B. G. 1996. 'Shouldn't Row, Can't Steer: What's a Government to Do?' *Public Policy and Administration*, 12(1): 51–2.

POLANYI, K. 2001. *The Great Transformation: The Political and Economic Origins of Our Time*. Boston: Beacon Press; 1st pub. 1944.

POLASKI, S. 2004. 'Protecting Labor Rights through Trade Agreements: An Analytical Guide'. *Journal of International Law and Policy*, 14. July.

RHODES, R. 1996. 'New Governance: Governing without Government'. *Political Studies*, 44(4): 652–67.

RICHARDSON, J. J., and JORDAN, A. G. 1979. *Governing under Pressure: The Policy Process in a Post-parliamentary Democracy*. Oxford: Robertson.

ROSDAHL, A. 2001. 'The Policy to Promote Social Responsibility of Enterprises in Denmark'. Paper prepared for the European Commission DG Employment Peer Review Program 2000. Copenhagen: The Danish National Institute of Social Research, Aug.

SCHMITTER, P., and LEHMBRUCH, G. 1979. *Trends towards Corporatist Intermediation*. Beverly Hills, Calif.: Sage.

SETHI, P. 1979. 'Dimensions of Corporate Social Responsibility'. *Californian Management Review*, 17(3): 58–64.

SPIDLA, V. 2006. 'Corporate Social Responsibility: The European Perspective'. *Ethical Corporation*, Apr.

'Towards Responsible Lobbying: Leadership and Public Policy'. 2005. London: Accountability.

VOGEL, D. 1992. 'The Globalization of Business Ethics: Why America Remains Different'. *California Management Review*, 35(1): 30–49.

—— 2005. *The Market for Virtue: The Potential and Limits of Corporate Social Responsibility*. Washington: Brookings.

WARD, H. 2004. *Public Sector Roles in Strengthening Corporate Social Responsibility: Taking Stock*. Washington: The World Bank.

WARTICK, S. L., and COCHRAN, P. L. 1985. 'The Evolution of the Corporate Social Performance Model'. *Academy of Management Review*, 10: 758–69.

PART V

MANAGING CORPORATE SOCIAL RESPONSIBILITY

....

CHAPTER 14

CORPORATE GOVERNANCE AND CORPORATE SOCIAL RESPONSIBILITY

....

ANN K. BUCHHOLTZ

JILL A. BROWN

KAREEM M. SHABANA

Corporate Governance is concerned with holding the balance between economic and social goals and between individual and communal goals. The corporate governance framework is there to encourage the efficient use of resources and equally to require accountability for the stewardship of those resources. The aim is to align as nearly as possible the interests of individuals, corporations and society.

> (Sir Adrian Cadbury in the foreword to 'Global Corporate Governance Forum', World Bank, 2003)

THE wave of corporate scandals that ushered in the twenty-first century represented a complete failure of the checks and balances that good corporate governance is intended to provide. This failure of corporate governance affected more than the shareholders of the companies involved; the shockwaves affected a range of other stakeholders. Employees, not only of the firms involved but of others in the value chain, found that their work was either curtailed or disappeared. Charities that relied on corporate philanthropy had their budgets reduced dramatically and local governments found their tax bases eroded, leading to deep cuts in the services upon which community residents depend. The resultant distrust of financial markets led William McDonough, Chairman of the United States Securities and Exchange Commission (SEC), to declare that the 'whole American system of life' was in jeopardy (Toedtman, 2003: 1). The pervasive societal impacts these corporate governance failures wrought underscore the responsibility that corporate governance has not only to economic and individual goals but, as Sir Cadbury articulates, to social and communal goals as well.

In Whose Interests should Corporations be Governed?

A properly designed corporate governance structure asks the right questions and has the right controls in place to make sure the answers lead to long-term, sustainable value (Monks and Minow, 2004). For whom that value is created, however, is a source of some controversy; should shareholders be accorded primacy or should a firm's other stakeholders be of equal concern in corporate governance? As Phillips et al. (2003) note, stakeholders' costs, risks, and contributions should be factored into any decisions regarding the benefits they receive. Using those criteria, one could argue that shareholders achieve primacy through the moral force of their property rights, the contribution of their equity capital, and the risks that investment can mean for their personal wealth. Certainly, the shareholder is a dominant stakeholder, possessing the attributes of power and legitimacy (Mitchell et al., 1997), who will often develop into a definitive stakeholder when issues become urgent.

Corporate governance systems throughout the world are converging on a shareholder-centric ideology (Engelen, 2002; Hansmann and Kraakman, 2001). However, shareholders are not a homogeneous group with a sole interest in wealth maximization. They vary in their investment horizons (Gaspara et al., 2005), their trust levels and risk preferences (Ryan and Buchholtz, 2001), and their goals (Ryan and Schneider, 2003). Institutional investors may embrace concepts of corporate social responsibility and value stakeholder welfare maximization (Ryan and Schneider, 2002, 2003). As evidence, Neubaum and Zahra (2006) found that long-term institutional ownership was positively correlated with corporate social performance. Johnson and Greening (1999) found that pension fund groups were more likely to invest in firms that had good social performance relative to people (women and minorities, community, and employee relations) and a solid record of product quality (relative to both the product and the environment). Thus shareholders and stakeholders are not always opposing forces. As Ryan and Schneider (2003) note, the heterogeneity of their financial and performance expectations may make institutional investors more sympathetic to the corporate social performance demands of stakeholders than current theory suggests. In fact, as share ownership becomes more accessible to a wider range of people, the concerns of stakeholders may be addressed as diverse shareholders assert their ownership rights (Ryan and Schneider, 2003). Furthermore, stakeholders often purchase shares of a company's stock to achieve the rights and privileges that share ownership accords.

We will begin our discussion by examining the role of corporate governance in creating value for shareholders. The issues of shareholder property rights and stakeholder theory are covered in earlier chapters so we will delve no further into that debate. Shareholder activism and social investing are also covered elsewhere in this volume and so we will not be discussing the actions of shareholders. Instead, we will focus on the actions of the corporation and the board toward its shareholders and other stakeholders, i.e. how corporate governance serves or fails to serve their interests. We will cover the assumptions that underlie theories of corporate governance and the expected outcomes of various board structures and compositions. Then we will examine the state of corporate democracy, the issue of accountability, and key legislation relative to corporate governance.

UNDERLYING ASSUMPTIONS ABOUT MANAGERS

Much of the literature on corporate governance reflects an underlying assumption that managers will operate with self-serving motivation; this stems from agency theory. Agency theory, with its origins in information economics (Eisenhardt, 1989), provides the predominant framework for understanding governance of the publicly traded corporation. An agency relationship may be defined as a contract in which a principal engages an agent to perform a service on their behalf; this necessitates the delegating of some level of decision-making authority to the agent (Jensen and Meckling, 1976). Shareholders are the principals in corporate governance. They delegate decision-making authority to managers with the expectation that those managers will make decisions and take actions that are in the shareholders' best interests. Agency problems arise when the interests of managers and shareholders diverge and managers opt to act in their own self-interest as opposed to the interests of shareholders. The expectation inherent in agency theory is that managers will pursue self-interest whenever possible.

Managerial hegemony carries with it many of the assumptions of agency theory. It is a theory that sees managers as self-interest maximizing and in need of strong controls. While agency theory focuses on the actions managers will take that are not in the shareholder's interests, managerial hegemony theory focuses upon the control managers can have over the board and how that can enable managers to maximize their own self-interest (Kosnik, 1987). Boards of directors hire and fire managers and so they should not be controlled by them; however, boards are dependent on managers for information about the corporation and managers can exert significant control over the board election process (Dallas, 1996). When managers are able to control boards of directors, the opportunity for them to pursue their own self-interest over that of shareholders and stakeholders is rife.

Stewardship theory offers an alternative depiction of the nature of managers to that proposed by agency and managerial hegemony theories (Davis *et al.*, 1997). Agency and managerial hegemony theories adopt the model of man, prevalent in economics research, that depicts managers as individualistic, opportunistic, and self-serving. In contrast, stewardship theory draws on research from psychology and sociology to adopt a different model of man that argues they can be collectivists, pro-organizational, and trustworthy. Using this alternative model of man, stewardship theory presents another view of the manager–shareholder relationship based on contingencies of individual's psychological attitudes and organizational situational characteristics. Stewardship theory is set forth as a complement to agency theory. The argument is not that agency theory is wrong, only that it is incomplete and assumptions about the manager as self-interest maximizing will not always hold (Davis *et al.*, 1997).

BOARD COMPOSITION AND STRUCTURE

The board of directors is charged with the ultimate responsibility for corporate governance: they are tasked with designing mechanisms that protect shareholder interests and putting those mechanisms into place (Walsh and Seward, 1990). Board composition is an area of corporate governance that receives attention for the role of composition in providing governance guidelines, as well for its role in firm financial and social performance. Theoretically, the agency issues of corporate governance continue to run as a theme through board composition studies that review the role of board members as representatives of shareholder interests, but with potential conflicts of interests in the battle for control between management and the board (see Mizruchi, 1983; Sundaramurthy and Lewis, 2003; and Walsh and Seward 1990 for further discussion of the paradox of control and collaboration for board members). Other theories that have been investigated in the context of board composition include stewardship theory as a contrast to agency theory whereby the board is collaborative with management (Davis *et al.*, 1997); circulation of power theory regarding CEO–board relationships that change over time due to political and technical contestations (Ocasio, 1994); social network theory discussing the impact of CEO–board social ties (McPherson *et al.*, 1992; Wade *et al.*, 1990; Westphal 1999) as well as the role of social ties between board members and members of interlocked directorate (Davis and Greve, 1997; Granovetter, 1973; Hillman, 2005; Ibarra and Andrews, 1993; Koenig and Gogel, 1981; Mizruchi, 1996). With these theory approaches to understanding the role of board composition and structure, it becomes clear that board composition and structure have considerable potential for impact on the social responsibility and responsiveness of the firm. We begin this section with a definition of what board composition entails, and then discuss some of the studies that highlight antecedents and outcomes of board composition as they relate to CSR.

According to Monks and Minow (2004), board composition consists of director qualifications and membership criteria, the director nomination process, and board leadership and independence. Board structure is usually mentioned in reference to composition, and encompasses the size of the board and the division of labor between the board and CEO (Finkelstein and Hambrick, 1996). Typically, board structure is measured as a ratio of outside to inside directors (e.g. Westphal, 1998; Pearce and Zahra, 1989). Demographic and relational characteristics of board members are the measures for qualifications and membership criteria, including occupation, tenure, gender, race, functional background, educational background and type of director, and committee membership (e.g. Weirsema and Bantel, 1992; Westphal and Zajac, 1995).

Perhaps the most researched outcome variable associated with board composition is firm financial performance, the foundation of corporate social responsibility. Performance implications of board composition and structure have been the subjects of an extensive body of research; however, a meta-analytic review of the relationship between board composition, leadership structure, and financial performance concluded that there is little evidence of a relationship between board composition and financial performance (Dalton *et al.*, 1998). Although the results of this meta-analysis do not obviate any relationships between aspects of board composition and the financial performance aspect of corporate social responsibility, it does mean that any relationships found in individual studies should be approached with caution.

Other related outcomes of board composition have been studied. These include the effects of board composition on: executive compensation (Kerr and Kren, 1992;

Main *et al.*, 1995; Zajac and Westphal, 1994), CEO turnover (Cannella and Lubatkin, 1993; Ward *et al.*, 1999), corporate strategy (Goodstein and Boeker, 1991; Hillman *et al.*, 2000; Pearce and Zahra, 1989, 1992), market for corporate control provisions (Buchholtz and Ribbens, 1994; Davis and Greve, 1997; Kosnik, 1987), and corporate R&D structure (Baysinger *et al.*, 1991).

CEO duality (when the CEO is also the board chair) is another issue that has received attention from corporate governance researchers. To have the CEO chair the board represents the worst fear of managerial hegemony, that the CEO will have undue power over the board thus robbing the board of its monitoring function. From an agency theory standpoint, CEO duality increases the likelihood that agency problems will arise because the board is not likely to restrain its chair from pursuing self-interest. In spite of these concerns, CEO duality has its positive aspects. Finkelstein and D'Aveni (1994) acknowledge that duality presents the potential problem of entrenchment that agency theory predicts, but they note too that duality provides a unity of command that can enable CEOs to act quickly and decisively. Empirical studies have not led to any consistent conclusions about the impact of duality (Baliga *et al.*, 1996; Dalton *et al.*, 1998). This may mean that there is evidence for both agency and stewardship arguments and that the integration of the two perspectives would provide a deeper understanding of CEO duality and the issues it presents (Boyd, 1995). That argument is consistent with stewardship theory's contention that managers are not necessarily self-interest-maximizing agents nor are they always stewards; people vary in their situations and motivations depending on the contingencies involved (Davis *et al.*, 1997).

Beyond financial performance, researchers have conducted studies to determine if there are any links between the characteristics of the board and the firm's other forms of social responsibility. Johnson and Greening (1999) found that that the people dimension of corporate social responsibility, which incorporates women and minorities, community, and employee relations issues, was positively associated with outside director representation. Similarly, they found that the product quality dimension, which includes the environment, was associated positively with outside directors. Kesner and colleagues approached the question of board composition and social performance from the opposite direction, asking whether board composition would lessen the likelihood of negative social outcomes. In a study of board composition and stockholder suits, Kesner and Johnson (1990) found that boards dominated by insiders were more likely to be the subject of suits, with the effect being even stronger when the CEO also held the position of board chair. However, they found no relationship between board composition and the outcome of the actual rulings. In an earlier study with a consistent finding, Kesner *et al.* (1986) found that outsiders on the board had no discernible relationship with the illegal acts conducted by a firm.

Corporate philanthropy, the discretionary aspect of corporate social responsibility, provides an opportunity to directly examine the relationship between the board and the firm's level of giving. The extent to which the board is dominated by insiders or outsiders has varied in its relationship with corporate philanthropy. Using agency theory logic, Wang and Coffey (1992) found a positive relationship between inside directors and corporate philanthropy: they also found corporate philanthropy to be positively related to women and minority representation on the board. In contrast, Ibrahim *et al.* (2003) found that outside directors in the service industry exhibited greater concern for the discretionary component of social responsibility; however, they found no difference between insiders and outsiders on the ethical and legal components. Williams (2003) found a relationship between the proportion of women on the board and the firm's corporate philanthropy: The relationship held in the areas of community service and the arts but not in education or public policy issues. Buchholtz *et al.* (1999) directly tested the board processes that are inferred from board composition and structure. They found that the extent to which the board allowed managers decision-making discretion mediated the relationship between managerial values and corporate philanthropy.

Stock ownership has also been shown to link corporate governance and corporate social responsibility. Neubaum and Zahra (2006) found long-term institutional ownership to be associated positively with corporate social performance. Similarly, Graves and Waddock (1994) examined the relationship between institutional ownership and corporate social performance and found a positive relationship between social performance and the number of institutions holding company shares. Atkinson and Galaskiewicz (1988) found that if the CEO or another individual owned a significant amount of stock in the company, the firm contributed less to corporate philanthropy. Similarly, Galaskiewicz (1997) found that CEO ownership had a negative relationship with corporate philanthropy throughout the 1980s in St Paul, Minnesota, and Bartkus *et al.* (2002) found that blockholders and institutional owners were negatively associated with a firm's level of philanthropy.

Board diversity is an issue particularly relevant to the relationship between corporate governance and corporate social responsibility. Board composition is shifting to include more women and minority representation, however progress is slow (Hillman *et al.*, 2002). Joo (2003) argues that a board must be diverse to understand and accommodate the diverse needs of a firm's many stakeholders. He acknowledges the strides that have been made in employee diversity but warns 'Celebrating employee diversity while ignoring director and executive diversity, however, is not only hypocritical but ominous' (p. 739). Homogeneous boards run the risk of falling prey to groupthink and failing to challenge the assumptions underlying their decisions (Ramirez, 2003). In theory, diverse boards should have the range of experiences necessary to understand the needs of a diverse group of stakeholders, helping them to manage their diversity more effectively (Joo, 2003). Although a consistent empirical link has yet to be established between stakeholders on the board and the firm's capacity for stakeholder management, research on that topic has just begun and more work in the area is needed (Hillman *et al.*, 2001). Of course, with boards of directors still being relatively homogeneous in composition, it is difficult to find opportunities to test the impact of board diversity. Some scholars argue that substantive change will have to occur before the goal of board diversity is realized because the current design of board elections results in a self-perpetuating homogeneous board (Joo, 2003). Only when new corporate governance procedures are enacted and shareholders are able to elect board members will boards achieve the level of diversity already present in their stakeholders (Ray, 2005). In the next section, we discuss the problem of corporate democracy—an idea that is strongly supported by theory but sorely lacking in practice.

CORPORATE DEMOCRACY

Despite their heterogeneity in expectations, shareholders have much in common. They are owners of the company and, as such, they have ultimate control over the corporation. This control carries with it the right to select the board of directors and to voice concerns over corporate governance. The board then is charged with the responsibility for ascertaining that managers act in the best interests of the shareholders. Given that many nations' systems of corporate governance are isomorphing toward the shareholder-centric Anglo-American model (Engelen, 2002), it is important to examine how that model is working in practice.

Mintzberg (1983) argues that a country cannot consider itself to be free if its major institutions do not subscribe to democratic principles. Ironically, those countries that hold a strong belief in the democratic tradition do not necessarily extend shareholders an actual right to participation. For example, boards in the United States can ignore shareholder resolutions about executive pay and votes against board candidates are not counted (*Economist*, 2006). Only a majority of the votes *actually cast* for board members are counted and so withholding a vote has no consequence (Joo, 2003). In Europe, many of the largest firms do not have a one-share one-vote rule (*Economist*, 2005). The process of proxy voting is supposed to guarantee that shareholder preferences are respected because the agent designated to vote the proxies is required to follow the wishes of the shareholders (Schwartz, 1983). However, the process of soliciting proxy votes is expensive and those expenses are covered by the corporation; this leaves shareholders with a slate chosen by the board and a board that is, in effect, electing itself (Blair and Stout, 1999). The result of this skewed election process is a 'self-perpetuating oligarchic board' (Ray, 2005: 93) because whoever controls board selection controls the governance of the corporation (Directorship, 2004). The annual meeting is supposed to be an opportunity for institutional and individual investors to choose their representatives and to have their concerns heard but in the current system it is often an exercise in futility (Augustine, 2004).

Boards are charged with being accountable to shareholders. Accountability is *answerability* for one's actions or behaviors (Dicke and Ott, 1999: 504) and it involves both process and outcome accountability (Simonson and Staw, 1992). While accountability has been shown to both increase individual information processing and decrease social loafing (Karau and Williams, 1993; Tetlock, 1985), the impact of accountability depends on whether individuals are 'aware or unaware of the preferences of their audience' (Stewart *et al.*, 1998: 19). Therefore, it is difficult for a board to answer a stakeholder who has no forum for asking questions or expressing preferences. Self-perpetuating homogeneous boards do not provide stakeholders with representation. Without that representation, firms do not achieve the accountability criterion necessary for a democracy (Jones and Goldberg, 1982). Thus it should come as no surprise that the recent rash of corporate scandals involved not only a lack of transparency, which would be bad enough, but also a conscious decision to deceive.

Another obstacle on the road to corporate democracy is the issue of classified boards (boards with members that serve staggered terms). With a classified board, only a fraction of board members are elected in any given year. For example, a twelve-person board might have elections of four members each year. Each member would be elected for a three-year term and it would take three years to vote out the entire slate of directors. Shareholder advocates have called increasingly for the declassification of classified boards. From this perspective, unitary boards (wherein each board member is up for election each year and members are elected to one-year terms) provide shareholders with greater redress of grievances that arise. By being able to vote on each board member each year, shareholders are better able to express their views in decisions that impact their own wealth. Advocates of declassification believe that the tide of corporate wrongdoing would be stemmed by providing a more independent eye with which to judge managerial actions (Bebchuk *et al.*, 2004) In contrast, advocates of classified boards contend that directors need a certain level of autonomy to exercise sound business judgment on the many difficult issues that boards face. They claim that giving shareholders the option of replacing each board member each year will only slow down decisions that must be made quickly to maintain competitiveness. They argue that shareholders are not infallible and the shareholder push for short-term returns has been part of the problem (Wilcox, 2002). From this perspective, declassification will promote a short-term perspective and break the continuity important for success in today's competitive environment.

The market for corporate control is another area in which shareholder wishes are not always respected. Tender offers occur when a potential acquirer makes an offer to buying outstanding shares of stock at a premium. This creates a divergence of interests between shareholders and managers. Shareholders are likely to want to accept this wealth-maximizing offer, while managers are inclined to resist an offer that may well mean the loss of a job for them. The more an employee has invested in firm-specific human capital, the more that employee will seek to have protections (Williamson, 1985) and so managers often try to institute poison pills of various kinds that make it more difficult for an acquirer to take a firm over without management's approval. Golden parachutes are often offered to managers to minimize the likelihood that they will resist a shareholder wealth-maximizing tender offer but there is no evidence that these efforts to align manager and shareholder incentives in the market for corporate control make any difference in subsequent resistance (Buchholtz and Ribbens, 1994). Takeover contests are a mixed bag of outcomes with stakeholders and shareholders often in conflict, but the implications for corporate democracy are clear. This is another venue where the concerns of shareholders are often not heard and the board is not held accountable.

Given the difficulty that shareholders as owners of the firm face in being accorded democratic rights and privileges, it is not surprising that non-owner stakeholders fare even worse. Their option for making their voices heard is through the mechanism of shareholder resolutions and so many interest groups will invest in a corporation to be afforded access to the election process, becoming shareholders in the hope that they can use ownership power to get the corporation to hear their concerns. However, shareholder access to corporate decision makers is a concept that works better in theory than in practice.

How then can the corporation implement democratic principles and offer shareholders and stakeholders true access to its workings? The first step is to increase board diversity. As Joo (2003) explains, homogeneous boards when left to their own devices will perpetuate their homogeneity. Some countries have dealt with this issue by imposing quotas for board composition. For example, countries such as Israel and Norway require a minimum number of women on their board to address the gender imbalance that has occurred (Joo, 2003). Ray agrees that the key is to make boards more representative and he offers recommendations that, in his words, are 'somewhere between the German model of co-determination which guarantees that corporations of a certain size have direct employee representation on the board and the American model that guarantees that boards are self-perpetuating oligarchies' (Ray, 2005: 100). His recommendations include an ombudsperson who would be available to hear stakeholder concerns, a minimum of two candidates for each board seat, ratification of board elections by a majority of firm employees, and nominations from shareholders and employees, as well as the board.

Relevant Legislation

As a result of corporate governance scandals, we see significant legal policy changes designed to force the hand of businesses not only to engage in good governance practice and avoid economic pitfalls, but also to encourage increased disclosure and transparency as part of good business ethics (Trevino and Nelson, 1999). Clark (2005) notes that these reforms are part of a 'new reform movement' that includes the federal Sarbanes–Oxley Act of 2002 (SOX), the new listing requirements for publicly traded companies governed by the New York Stock Exchange (NYSE) CG Rules, the increasing influence of private governance rating agencies and proxy advisers, and the changing tone of judicial opinions (especially in the courts of Delaware, where over half of American public companies are incorporated). We add to this the SEC mandates which enforce Sarbanes–Oxley and NYSE rules, and recent SEC rules that amend disclosure requirements for executive and director compensation, related party transactions, director independence, and security ownership of officers and directors. For the most part, these reforms concentrate on audit-related changes, board-related changes, and changes in disclosure and accounting rules (Clark, 2005: 5). Audit-related changes include limits on multiple roles by auditors, reduction of conflicts of interest between auditors and companies, increased internal control processes, certifications of financial reports, financial literacy, and required financial expertise on audit, compensation, and nominating committees. The NYSE and SOX requirements that key committees like the nominating, audit, and compensation committees can have only independent directors play a tremendous role in these reforms that seem to indicate a trend towards a 'supermajority' of independent directors (Clark, 2005: 13). There are additional requirements for regularly scheduled director sessions, codes of ethics, board self-assessments, and limits on 'over-boarding' by directors, although most of these are dictated by private rating agencies. Recent Delaware court system rulings have indicated that as a result of mistrust of boards due to recent corporate scandals, many court rulings are overriding the practice of 'business judgment rule' whereby the court does not challenge the decision of a director when it appears that the director acted with loyalty and exercised all possible care.

International corporate governance reflects the fact that the there has been substantial growth in global corporations, unusually enhanced by emerging international markets and growing privatizations in the world economy. The general reduction of import tariffs and trade restrictions globally has also contributed to this, and therefore the demand for capital for these companies has grown. In one respect then, international governance reflects the fact that investors of global corporations are demanding transparency and accountability in return for capital (Monks and Minow, 2004). This shareholder approach to international governance is particularly true of the United States and the UK, as reflected in the US Sarbanes-Oxley legislation noted above and in the original UK 1992 Cadbury Committee list of 'best practice' governance standards to which companies were encouraged to aspire.

Recent international governance scandals have encouraged further global regulation. Most of the scandals involve failure of disclosure, including the Asian financial crisis of 1997, the 2000 Belgium Lernout and Hauspie accounting scandal, and the 2003 Italian Parmalat scandal, which created the largest bankruptcy in European history, representing 1.5% of Italian GNP in 2003. As a result of such governance failures, there is a continued call for global general guidelines for corporate governance. International governance, especially continental European governance, is generally characterized as more multi-stakeholder oriented, as opposed to American and British, corporate governance, which is characterized as emphasizing the pursuit of shareholder value (Barnard and Deakin, 2002). However, guidelines issued in 1999 by the Paris-based Organization for Economic Co-operation and Development (OECD) to offer a global set of principles for governance still emphasize the rights and responsibilities of shareholders separate from the rights of stakeholders, the need for disclosure and transparency, as well as the need to address the role and structure of boards. The International Corporate Governance Network (ICGN), a group of major institutional investors and global activists, also issued support of the OECD principles in 1999 and has subsequently supported initiatives for more global accounting standards and more equitable shareholder voting procedures, among other initiatives. Together, the ICGN and the OECD formed the Global Corporate Governance Forum in 1999 to bring international organizations into compliance with a set of prescriptive standards of governance. Other international governance groups include the World Bank, which responded to 1997's world financial market collapse by demanding tough rules of disclosure in return for financial assistance and is responsible for assessing the OECD Principles. Additionally, the United Nations, in 2006, announced a set of UN Principles of Responsible Investment to address issues of transparency and disclosure in global investment.

Many of the international governance dictums remain shareholder-oriented in areas of board composition and equity ownership, and for the most part, voluntary (for a review of literature, see Denis and McConnell, 2003). Updates in the UK to the original Cadbury Committee standards include the Higgs Report update and the 2003 version of the Combined Code encouraging independent board directors and separate CEO/chair board membership among other standards for management best practice. The European Union and its European Commission have perhaps made the most progress towards balancing stakeholder interests beyond shareholder disclosure requirements to issue a number of directives on corporate social responsibility including health and safety, the social aspects of corporate restructuring, executive remuneration, and employee involvement at board level (Barnard and Deakin, 2002). Additionally, the EU adopted International

Accounting Standards in 2002 to complement EU rules of best management practice. Other notable governance mechanisms, by country, include: (1) France's New Economic Regulations Act, which permitted more companies to split the chairman and CEO jobs, and the Bouton code for tougher governance benchmarks; (2) Portugal's Comissao do Mercadeo de Valores Mobiliarios (CMVM) which monitors compliance to a best practice code modeled after the OECD guidelines, and (3) Germany's voluntary Cromme Commission's 'Kodex' of best practices that, while voluntary, requires companies to explain non-compliance.

While progress has been made in international governance, developing global standards for governance remains a challenge. OECD disclosure requirements, while good in theory, are difficult to enforce across countries. For example, companies in Eastern Asia, like Korea, Thailand, and Indonesia involve conglomerates controlled by families, where close relationships exist between these conglomerates and banks (Arsalidou and Wang, 2005). The OECD principles therefore require much more disclosure than is reinforced by the securities and exchange commissions in those countries. Similarly, the Japanese system was inherently non-transparent just a decade ago, but they now publish more information on CSR activities (Fukukawa and Moon, 2004). The Corporate Governance Forum of Japan was established in 1998 to issue guidelines for corporate governance, such as a call for more outside directors, and they asked the Tokyo Stock Exchange to incorporate these guidelines in practice. Companies in France are also heavily controlled by the state and cross-shareholding is common practice, which poses governance challenges. German companies, also state-controlled, have only recently been required to disclose supervisory board members' names, and boards remain heavily union represented. While global standards are increasing, they are often criticized for their unenforceability in light of disparate corporate structures, market differences, and overly simplistic mechanistic prescriptions without the involvement of policy makers (Norburn *et al.*, 2000).

WHERE DO WE GO FROM HERE?

Despite the considerable effort that has been expended in studying boards of directors and how they can be constructed to be more effective, the issues are far from settled. From a board structure standpoint, past and current research in this area stresses the need for some optimal mix of outside, inside, and independent board of directors. For a while there was 'near consensus' (Dalton *et al.*, 1998: 270) on the idea that effective boards would be comprised of a greater proportion of outside directors. By 2000, pressure from institutional investors and public opinion resulted in boards that had more outside directors and more stock ownership by directors (Byrne, 2000). This was to have led to greater assurance that shareholders' best interests would be represented. However, one year later the Enron and World-Com débâcles unfolded, followed by a wave of restatements that indicated boards were not running as tight a ship as their performance on governance checklists would indicate. The emphasis on director independence as a means of insuring that boards would monitor the CEO effectively had been a disappointment. The 'usual suspects' of percentage of outside directors, board stock ownership, board size, and CEO duality (holding the board chair as well as the CEO position), which already lacked robust research support, now failed to come through in practice (Finkelstein and Mooney, 2003: 101). One point is certain—simple governance checklists are not enough to insure that boards are functioning effectively. It is necessary to delve more deeply into board processes (Finkelstein and Mooney, 2003). This is true for designing boards that more effectively maximize shareholder wealth and it is true for designing boards that more effectively protect stakeholder interests.

While examining processes as opposed to indicators is important, it still is not enough. We need to examine the assumptions that underlie our corporate governance prescriptions. Both agency and managerial hegemony theories presume that monitoring is the most important board function and that it must be done from arm's length: In doing so, they fail to factor in the important relational roles that boards perform (Dallas, 1996). When Pearce and Zahra (1989) conducted their study of boards and firm performance, they found that the boards associated with the strongest firm performance were the participative boards, where the board was very powerful but the CEO was too. These boards and CEOs worked together to bring about a high level of performance. Perhaps it is time to acknowledge that we live in a complex world. As stewardship theory argues, some managers may pursue their self-interest when the opportunity arises, but not all will. Boards are responsible for more than monitoring the CEO's behavior—they must share in the leadership of the firm to insure that the firm fulfills its economic, legal, ethical, and discretionary social responsibility to the firm.

Much of the concern regarding corporate social responsibility and corporate governance is addressed toward the ways in which corporate governance is failing a range of stakeholders. However, as the above discussion on corporate democracy shows, the owner of the corporation, the shareholder, is not faring much better. The Enron and WorldCom débâcles, coupled with the spate of accounting restatements that followed, are indications that shareholders are not getting the information they need to make informed investment decisions. Furthermore, even if shareholders were given the full range of information available, they would not have a meaningful opportunity to express and act upon their concerns. Corporate democracy is an ideal whose time is overdue. Boards will not be truly independent until they are elected by shareholders not only in rhetoric but also in reality.

Economic responsibility is the foundation of corporate social responsibility (Carroll, 1991). Until a firm meets its economic responsibility to shareholders, little else is likely to occur. Shareholders must be given accurate and timely information about the corporation's activities and they must have a forum from which they can express their concerns. Fulfilling responsibilities to shareholders is the keystone of good corporate governance—and it's only from that foundation that effective stakeholder management can occur. Providing shareholders with the information they need and a democratic platform from which to act also is the beginning of providing other stakeholders with a say in how the firm operates. Share ownership is no longer the exclusive province of the wealthy and privileged: Through mutual funds, worker pensions, and a general increase in personal wealth, a wider spectrum of society throughout the world is now able to own stock (Hansmann and Kraakman, 2001). As a result, the interests of the modern investor are heterogeneous, a mixture of both financial and social goals. Shareholders and stakeholders are not at opposing ends of a continuum; instead they are in a position to be allies in the fight for corporate democracy (Ryan and Schneider, 2003). As such, a system that makes managers responsible to shareholder interests, first and foremost, may well be the most effective way to ascertain that corporations will behave responsibly and protect the best interests of society at large (Hansmann and Kraakman, 2001).

References

Arsalidou, D., and Wang, M. 2005. 'The Challenges with Imposing the OECD Disclosure Requirements in East Asia'. *European Business Law Review*, 16(6): 1477–99.

Atkinson, L., and Galaskiewicz, J. 1988. 'Stock Ownership and Company Contributions to Charity'. *Administrative Science Quarterly*. 33(1): 82–100.

Augustine, N. R. 2004. 'The Annual Meeting: An Exercise in Corporate Democracy or Corporate Futility?' *Directors & Boards*, 29: 6–38.

Baliga, B. R., Moyer, R. C., and Rao, R. S. 1996. 'CEO Duality and Firm Performance: What's the Fuss?' *Strategic Management Journal*, 17(1): 41–53.

Barnard, C., and Deakin, S. 2002. 'Reinventing the European Corporation? Corporate Governance, Social Policy and the Single Market.' *Industrial Relations Journal*, 33(5): 484–99.

Bartkus, B. R., Morris, S. A., and Seifert, B. 2002. 'Governance and Corporate Philanthropy: Restraining Robin Hood?' *Business Society*, 41(3): 319–44.

Baysinger, B. D., Kosnik, R. D., and Turk, T. A. 1991. 'Effects of Board and Ownership Structure on Corporate R&D Strategy'. *Academy of Management Journal*, 34(1): 205–14.

Bebchuk, L. A., Cohen, A., and Ferrell, A. 2004. 'What Matters in Corporate Governance?' Harvard Law and Economics Discussion Paper No. 491, <http://ssrn.com/abstract=593423>.

Blair, M. M., and Stout, L. A. 1999. 'A Team Production Theory of Corporate Law'. *Virginia Law Review*, 85(2): 247–328.

BOYD, B. K. 1995. 'CEO Duality and Firm Performance: A Contingency Model'. *Strategic Management Journal*, 16(4): 301–12.

BUCHHOLTZ, A. K., AMASON, A. C., and RUTHERFORD, M. A. 1999. 'Beyond Resources: The Mediating Effect of Top Management Discretion and Values on Corporate Philanthropy'. *Business Society*, 38(2): 167–87.

—— and RIBBENS, B. A. 1994. 'Role of Chief Executive Officers in Takeover Resistance: Effects of CEO incentives and Individual Characteristics'. *Academy of Management Journal*, 37(3): 554–79.

BYRNE, J. A. 2000. 'The Best and Worst Boards'. *Business Week* 142.

CANNELLA, A. A., and LUBATKIN, M. 1993. 'Succession as a Sociopolitical Process: Internal Impediments to Outsider Selection'. *Academy of Management Journal*, 36(4): 763–93.

CARROLL, A. B. 1991. 'The Pyramid of Corporate Social Responsibility: Toward the Moral Management of Organizational Stakeholders'. *Business Horizons*, 34(4): 39–48.

—— and BUCHHOLTZ, A. K. 2006. *Business and Society: Ethics and Stakeholder Management*. Mason, Oh.: Thomson Southwestern.

CLARK, R. C. 2005. 'Corporate Governance Changes in the Wake of the Sarbanes–Oxley Act: A Morality Tale for Policymakers Too'. Harvard Law and Economics Discussion Paper No. 525, available at <http//ssrn.com/abstract=808244>.

DALLAS, L. L. 1996. 'The Relational Board: Three Theories of Corporate Boards of Directors'. *Journal of Corporation Law*, 22(1): 1.

DALTON, D. R., DAILY, C. M., ELLSTRAND, A. E., and JOHNSON, J. L. 1998. 'Meta-analytic Reviews of Board Composition, Leadership Structure, and Financial Performance'. *Strategic Management Journal*, 19: 269–90.

DAVIS, G. F., and GREVE, H. R. 1997. 'Corporate Elite Networks and Governance Changes in the 1980s'. *American Journal of Sociology*, 103(1): 1.

DAVIS, J. H., SCHOORMAN, F. D., and DONALDSON, L. 1997. 'Toward a Stewardship Theory of Management'. *Academy of Management Review*, 22: 20–47.

DENIS, D. K., and MCCONNELL, J. J. 2003. 'International Corporate Governance'. *Journal of Financial and Quantitative Analysis*, 38(1): 1–36.

DICKE, L. A., and OTT, J. S. 1999. 'Public Agency Accountability in Human Services Contracting'. *Public Productivity and Management Review*, 22(4): 502–16.

Directorship. 2004. 'Who Selects, Governs'. 30(5): 6.

Economist. 2005. 'What Shareholder Democracy?' 26 Mar.: 62.

—— 2006. 'Ownership Matters'. 11 Mar.: 10.

EISENHARDT, K. M. 1989. 'Agency Theory: An Assessment and Review'. *Academy of Management Review*, 14: 57–74.

ENGELEN, E. 2002. 'Corporate Governance, Property and Democracy: A Conceptual Critique of Shareholder Ideology'. *Economy and Society*, 31(3): 391–413.

FINKELSTEIN, S., and D'AVENI, R. A. 1994. 'CEO Duality as a Double-Edged Sword: How Boards of Directors Balance Entrenchment Avoidance and Unity of Command'. *Academy of Management Journal*, 37(5): 1079–108.

—— and HAMBRICK, D. C. 1996. *Strategic Leadership: Top Executives and their Effects on Organizations*. St Paul, Minn.: West Publishing Company.

—— and MOONEY, A. C. 2003. 'Not the Usual Suspects: How to Use Board Process to Make Boards Better'. *Academy of Management Executive*, 17(2): 101–13.

FUKUKAWA, K., and MOON, J. 2004. 'A Japanese Model of Corporate Social Responsibility?' *Journal of Corporate Citizenship* (16): 45–59.

GALASKIEWICZ, J. 1997. 'An Urban Grants Economy Revisited: Corporate Charitable Contributions in the Twin Cities, 1979–81, 1987–89'. *Administrative Science Quarterly*, 42(3): 445–71.

GASPARA, J.-M., MASSA, M., and MATOS, P. 2005. 'Shareholder Investment Horizons and the Market for Corporate Control'. *Journal of Financial Economics*, 76(1): 135–65.

GOODSTEIN, J., and BOEKER, W. 1991. 'Turbulence at the Top: A New Perspective on Governance Structure Changes and Strategic Change'. *Academy of Management Journal*, 34(2): 306–30.

GRANOVETTER, M. 1973. 'The Strength of Weak Ties'. *American Journal of Sociology*, 78: 1360–80.

GRAVES, S. B., and WADDOCK, S. A. 1994. 'Institutional Owners and Corporate Social Performance'. *Academy of Management Journal*, 37(4): 1034–46.

HANSMANN, H., and KRAAKMAN, R. 2001. 'The End of History for Corporate Law'. *Georgetown Law Journal*, 89(2): 439–68.

HILLMAN, A. J. 2005. 'Politicians on the Board of Directors: Do Connections Affect the Bottom Line?' *Journal of Management*, 31(3): 464–81.

——CANNELLA, A. A., and HARRIS, I. C. 2002. 'Women and Racial Minorities in the Boardroom: How do Directors Differ?' *Journal of Management*, 28(6): 747–63.

——and PAETZOLD, R. L. 2000. 'The Resource Dependence Role of Corporate Directors: Strategic Adaptation of Board Composition in Response to Environmental Change'. *Journal of Management Studies*, 37(2): 235–55.

——KEIM, G. D., and LUCE, R. A. 2001. 'Board Composition and Stakeholder Performance: Do Stakeholder Directors Make a Difference?' *Business Society*, 40(3): 295–314.

IBARRA, H., and ANDREWS, S. B. 1993. 'Power, Social Influence, and Sense Making: Effects of Network Centrality and Proximity on Employee Perceptions'. *Administrative Science Quarterly*, 38(2): 277–303.

IBRAHIM, N. I. A., HOWARD, D. P., and ANGELIDIS, J. P. 2003. 'Board Members in the Service Industry: An Empirical Examination of the Relationship between Corporate Social Responsibility Orientation and Directorial Type'. *Journal of Business Ethics*, 47(4): 393–401.

JENSEN, M. C., and MECKLING, W. H. 1976. 'Theory of the Firm: Managerial Behavior, Agency Costs and Ownership Structure'. *Journal of Financial Economics*, 3(4): 305–60.

JOHNSON, R. A., and GREENING, D. W. 1999. 'The Effects of Corporate Governance and Institutional Ownership Types of Corporate Social Performance'. *Academy of Management Journal*, 42(5): 564–76.

JONES, T. M., and GOLDBERG, L. D. 1982. 'Governing the Large Corporation: More Arguments for Public Directors'. *Academy of Management Review*, 7(4): 603–11.

JOO, T. W. 2003. 'A Trip through the Maze of "Corporate Democracy": Shareholder Voice and Management Composition'. *St John's Law Review*, 77(4): 735–67.

KARAU, S. J., and WILLIAMS, K. D. 1993. 'Social Loafing: A Meta-analytic Review and Theoretical Integration'. *Journal of Personality and Social Psychology*, 65(4): 681–706.

KERR, J. L., and KREN, L. 1992. 'Effect of Relative Decision Monitoring on Chief Executive Compensation'. *Academy of Management Journal*, 35(2): 370–97.

KESNER, I. F., and JOHNSON, R. B. 1990. 'An Investigation of the Relationship between Board Composition and Stockholder Suits'. *Strategic Management Journal*, 11(4): 327–36.

——VICTOR, B., and LAMONT, B. T. 1986. 'Board Composition and the Commission of Illegal Acts: An Investigation of Fortune 500 Companies'. *Academy of Management Journal*, 29(4): 789–99.

KOENIG, T., and GOGEL, R. 1981. 'Interlocking Corporate Directorships as a Social Network'. *American Journal of Economics and Sociology*, 40(1): 37–50.

KOSNIK, R. D. 1987. 'Greenmail: A Study of Board Performance in Corporate Governance'. *Administrative Science Quarterly*, 32(2): 163–85.

McPHERSON, J. M., POPIELARZ, P., and DROBNIC, S. 1992. 'Social Networks and Organizational Dynamics'. *American Sociological Review*, 57: 153–70.

MAIN, B. G., O'REILLY, C. A., and WADE, J. 1995. 'The CEO, the Board of Directors and Executive Compensation: Economic and Psychological Perspectives'. *Industrial and Corporate Change*, 4(2): 293–332.

MINTZBERG, H. 1983. 'Why America Needs, but Cannot Have, Corporate Democracy'. *Organizational Dynamics*, 11(4): 5–20.

MITCHELL, R. K., AGLE, B. R., and WOOD, D. J. 1997. 'Toward a Theory of Stakeholder Identification and Salience: Defining the Principle of Who and What Really Counts'. *Academy of Management Review*, 22(4): 853–86.

MIZRUCHI, M. S. 1983. 'Who Controls Whom? An Examination of the Relation between Management and Boards of Directors in Large American Corporations'. *Academy of Management Review*, 8(3): 426–35.

——1996. 'What Do Interlocks Do? An Analysis, Critique, and Assessment of Research on Interlocking Directories'. *Annual Review of Sociology*, 22(1): 271–98.

MONKS, R. A. G., and MINOW, N. 2004. *Corporate Governance* 3rd edn. Malden, Mass: Blackwell Publishing.

NEUBAUM, D. O., and ZAHRA, S. A. 2006. 'Institutional Ownership and Corporate Social Performance: The Moderating Effects of Investment Horizon, Activism, and Coordination'. *Journal of Management*, 32(1): 108–31.

NORBURN, D., BOYD, B., FOX, M., and MUTH, M. 2000. 'International corporate governance reform'. *European Business Journal*: 116–33.

OCASIO, W. 1994. 'Political Dynamics and the Circulation of Power: CEO Succession in U.S. Industrial Corporations'. *Administrative Science Quarterly*, 39(2): 285–312.

PEARCE, J. A., and ZAHRA, S. A. 1989. 'The Relative Power of CEOs and Boards of Directors: Associations with Corporate Performance'. *Strategic Management Journal*, 12: 135–53.

————1992. 'Board Composition from a Strategic Contingency Perspective'. *Journal of Management Studies*, 29(4): 411–38.

PHILLIPS, R., FREEMAN, R. E., and WICKS, A. C. 2003. 'What Stakeholder Theory Is Not'. *Business Ethics Quarterly*, 13(4): 479–502.

RAMIREZ, S. A. 2003. 'A Flaw in the Sarbanes–Oxley Reform: Can Diversity in the Boardroom Quell Corporate Corruption?' *St John's Law Review*, 77(4): 837–66.

RAY, D. M. 2005. 'Corporate Boards and Corporate Democracy'. *Journal of Corporate Citizenship* (20): 93–105.

RYAN, L. V., and BUCHHOLTZ, A. K. 2001. 'Trust, Risk, and Shareholder Decision Making: An Investor Perspective on Corporate Governance'. *Business Ethics Quarterly*, 11(1): 177–93.

——and SCHNEIDER, M. 2002. 'The Antecedents of Institutional Investor Activism'. *Academy of Management Review*, 27(4): 554–73.

————2003. 'Institutional Investor Power and Heterogeneity: Implications for Agency and Stakeholder Theories'. *Business and Society*, 42(4): 398–429.

SCHWARTZ, D. E. 1983. 'Shareholder Democracy: Reality or Chimera'. *California Management Review*, 25(3): 53–67.

SIMONSON, I., and STAW, B. M. 1992. 'Deescalation Strategies: A Comparison of Techniques for Reducing Commitment to Losing Courses of Action'. *Journal of Applied Psychology*, 77(4): 419–26.

STEWART, D. D., BILLINGS, R. S., and STASSER, G. 1998. 'Accountability and the Discussion of Unshared, Critical Information in Decision-Making Groups'. *Group Dynamics: Theory, Research, and Practice*, 2(1): 18–23.

SUNDARAMURTHY, C., and LEWIS, M. 2003. 'Control and Collaboration: Paradoxes of Governance. *Academy of Management Review*, 28(3): 397–415.

TETLOCK, P. E. 1985. 'Accountability: The Neglected Social Context of Judgment and Choice'. *Research in Organizational Behavior*, 7: 297–332.

TOEDTMAN, J. 2003. 'Lawmakers Commemorate One-Year Anniversary of Corporate Governance Legislation'. *Knight-Ridder Tribune Business News*, July: 31, 1.

TREVINO, L. K., and NELSON, K. A. 1999. *Managing Business Ethics: Straight Talk about How to Do It Right*. New York: J. Wiley & Sons.

WADE, J., O'REILLY, C. A., and CHANDRATAT, I. 1990. 'Golden Parachutes: CEOs and the Exercise of Social Influence'. *Administrative Science Quarterly*, 35(4): 587–603.

WALSH, J. P., and SEWARD, J. K. 1990. 'On the Efficiency of Internal and External Corporate Control Mechanisms'. *Academy of Management Review*, 15(3): 421–56.

WANG, J., and COFFEY, B. S. 1992. 'Board Composition and Corporate Philanthropy. *Journal of Business Ethics*, 11(10): 771–8.

WARD, A., BISHOP, K., and SONNENFELD, J. A. 1999. 'Pyrrhic Victories: The Cost to the Board of Ousting the CEO'. *Journal of Organizational Behavior*, 20(5): 765–8.

WESTPHAL, J. D. 1998. 'Board games: How CEOs Adapt to Increases in Structural Board Independence from Management'. *Administrative Science Quarterly*, 43(3): 511–38.

—— 1999. 'Collaboration in the Boardroom: Behavioral and Performance Consequences of CEO-Board Social Ties'. *Academy of Management Journal*, 42(1): 7–24.

—— and ZAJAC, E. J. 1995. 'Who Shall Govern? CEO/Board Power, Demographic Similarity, and New Director Selection'. *Administrative Science Quarterly*, 40(1): 60–83.

WIERSEMA, M. F., and BANTEL, K. A. 1992. 'Top Management Team Demography and Corporate Strategic Change'. *Academy of Management Journal*, 35(1): 91–121.

WILCOX, J. C. 2002. 'Two Cheers for Staggered Boards'. *Corporate Governance Advisor*, 10 (Nov./Dec.): 1–5.

WILLIAMS, R. J. 2003. 'Women on Corporate Boards of Directors and their Influence on Corporate Philanthropy'. *Journal of Business Ethics*, 42(1): 1–10.

WILLIAMSON, O. E. 1985. *The Economic Institutions of Capitalism: Firms, Markets, Relational Contracting*. New York and London: Free Press, Collier Macmillan.

ZAJAC, E. J., and WESTPHAL, J. D. 1994. 'The Costs and Benefits of Managerial Incentives and Monitoring in Large U.S. Corporations: When is More Not Better?' *Strategic Management Journal*, 15(8): 121–42.

CHAPTER 15

··

STAKEHOLDER THEORY

MANAGING CORPORATE SOCIAL RESPONSIBILITY IN A MULTIPLE ACTOR CONTEXT

··

THOMAS W. DUNFEE

DISCRETIONARY socially responsible actions by corporations benefit needy stakeholders around the globe. These actions have a total value in the billions of dollars on an annual basis. One may envision a market-like phenomenon in which there are many possible corporate suppliers of discretionary socially responsible actions and many potential recipients of corporate largesse. In some cases no other supplier can match the social good resulting from a particular corporate intervention. Some recipients receive benefits from a multitude of providers while others look only to a single source based on a close relationship. Remarkably, this market-like phenomenon in the provision of social goods by corporations has been little studied. (See Baron, 2001; Aguilera *et al.*, 2007, as exceptions.) Little is known about how managers allocate discretionary social resources and even less has been written as to how managers should make such decisions.

The constraints that managers face are intuitive and obvious. They have limited discretionary resources that need to be triaged in the face of extensive demand for social goods. There are many competing demands for corporate help from potential recipients who present a daunting array of characteristics. Some are powerful and can affect the ability of the corporation to achieve its goals. Others have little power. Some have direct ties to the organization through contracts or other legal devices. Some operate internally within the organization. Others are remote. Some are at great risk if they don't receive help. Others have many other potential suppliers for their needs.

Managers face considerable opaqueness in trying to evaluate the needs of alternative claimants. They can't always tell whether the needs are as urgent as presented or whether the requested assistance will be effective. In many cases the resources available can only make a small dent in the needs of the claimants (AIDS victims in Africa) and the corporate intervention will not be able to fully satisfy the need. In some unique situations corporations may converge in supplying social goods to the same set of recipients creating a wasteful surplus of resources available to the favored beneficiaries (victims of an earthquake, tsunami, or hurricane where positive media coverage creates a stampede of visible support), leaving other deserving recipients without succor. This chapter considers the role of the stakeholder concept in helping managers make decisions allocating spending on discretionary social responsibility. As a first step, it will be necessary to sort out the various definitions of corporate social responsibility so that we may be clear as to what is meant by the term in this chapter.

DEFINING CORPORATE SOCIAL RESPONSIBILITY

McWilliams *et al.* (2006) rightly note that the current state of CSR theory and analysis is embryonic. Baron (2001: 9) describes it as 'an ill- and incompletely defined concept.' This is reflected in the wildly varying definitions of the core idea of CSR itself. Windsor broadly defines CSR as 'any concept concerning how managers should handle public policy and social issues' (2006: 93). McWilliams and Siegel more narrowly 'define CSR as actions that appear to further some social good, beyond the interests of the firm and that which is required by law' (2001: 117). Definitions diverge over several core questions. I will briefly highlight two.

First is the question of motive. Is it necessary to have a social motive underlying apparent CSR where corporate activities and/or resources provide a social good? Should it be considered genuine CSR if in reality the apparent CSR is a disguised business strategy designed to increase earnings, market share, or competitive position? From a normative perspective the answer depends on the ethical theory that is applied.

Duty-based normative theorists emphasize intention. The worthiness of a particular action will depend on the motive behind it. John and Jim both give the same amount of money to a homeless person. John does it because he feels a sense of duty to help the homeless person and thinks that giving money will be a benefit. Jim does it because he wants to impress Judy who is watching him even though he feels no sense of duty to the homeless person. In the view of the duty-based ethicist, John's act counts as an act of charity while Jim's does not. A utilitarian on the other hand would say that the outcomes are the same and therefore the acts count equally. So it depends on the normative definition used.

Corporations may act in a manner similar to that of John and Jim in the example. ABC Corporation may initiate a program of philanthropy as a matter of competitive strategy (Porter and Kramer, 2002) while XYZ has an identical philanthropic program based on what is primarily a social motive. ABC's program counts as CSR when CSR is defined in outcomes rather than motives, and does not count if CSR is defined to require a social motive.

Motive is tricky as a component of a definition of CSR. Motive is opaque to corporate outsiders. For a variety of reasons, a firm may not wish to reveal its true motivations. Depending on the context, firms may have incentives to softly conceal the real purpose behind what appears to be CSR. If a firm is facing demanding, powerful stakeholders it may wish to represent that its actions are based on a social motive, even though in fact the CSR program was undertaken purely for business reasons as in the case of social cause marketing or strategic philanthropy. But the opposite may also be true. There may be a reverse social desirability phenomenon[1] at work. The standard social desirability effect is when a respondent to a survey gives what she assumes is the socially expected answer rather than a fully honest answer. A social undesirability effect would involve a firm refusing to reveal a genuine social motive because of a fear of a negative reaction. For example, a firm facing aggressive hedge funds or other critics may want to present a CSR program that was undertaken based on social motives as having been part of a sensible business strategy.

Baron (2001) includes motivation in his definition of CSR, noting that corporate social expenditures may be motivated by profit maximization, altruism, and threats. Social spending motivated by profit maximization is not CSR for his purposes. Aguilera et al. (2007) analyze motive across four different levels of interaction: individual, organization, nation, and transnational. They consider instrumental, relational, and moral motives. Most significantly, Aguilera et al. recognize that motives may exist concurrently and their framework is designed to allow for simultaneous consideration of the relationships among the three types of motives. It seems plausible that a significant number of corporate social initiatives are based upon mixed motives.

---

[1] A social undesirability effect?

A second area of divergence in CSR definitions involves the question of whether CSR should encompass actions mandated by regulators. That is, does CSR have to be voluntary? Note that a definition requiring that CSR be voluntary and a definition requiring a social motive are not quite the same thing. A firm may implement a legally required smokestack scrubber because senior management thinks limiting air pollution is the right thing to do. The legal requirement was not the reason for the implementation.

As with motive, it will not always be possible to determine whether a firm is acting voluntarily when it provides a social good. Sometimes there will even be a question as to whether something has been actually 'required' by law. Lawmakers may provide positive tax incentives to encourage investments in a social good, such as the use of designated smokestack scrubbers. Although the tax provision signals a public policy preference that firms make use of scrubbers, and further indicates that the public sector will share the cost, it is not fully compulsory. On the other hand, regulators may use a range of negative sanctions such as escalating fines for non-compliance or enhanced liability for private causes of action.

On the other side of the coin, firms may react to regulation quite differently. Some may be very adversarial, pushing back wherever possible and only reluctantly going along with what is required. Others may proactively support regulation and comply with its spirit as well as the letter of the law. Again, Baron (2001: 12) eliminates compulsory actions by stating that 'CSR thus involves going beyond what the letter and spirit of the law require or the market demands'. Baron, however, is defining CSR for purposes of his model of private politics and is not seeking to develop a definitive definition of CSR.

Broader definitions of CSR allow for making a distinction between the different types of corporate responses and motivations. Husted and Salazar (2006) make a useful distinction between strategic, altruistic, and coerced CSR. Strategic is implemented as a business strategy à la Porter; an altruist is concerned with social benefits which they define in terms of returns to the firm; and a 'coerced' firm is influenced by taxes or subsidies.

In this chapter, the focus will be on CSR defined as 'discretionary spending in furtherance of an explicit measurable social objective consistent with relevant social norms and laws.' I will use the acronym dCSR to make clear the particular definition I am using. The focus in dCSR is most closely related to the top tier of Archie Carroll's famous Pyramid of Corporate Social Responsibility (Carroll and Buchholtz, 2000). His pyramid has four tiers as follows, starting from the bottom: economic responsibilities, legal responsibilities, ethical responsibilities and philanthropic responsibilities. The top tier is justified as desired by society (p. 36). Under dCSR the emphasis is on voluntary rather than required or coerced social investment. A motive is assumed in that firms are expected to have a measurable social objective as a basis for their investment. The investment must be consistent with relevant norms and laws. This latter element requires a brief considera-tion of the arguments of those who claim that CSR as herein defined is never appropriate.

JUSTIFICATION FOR DISCRETIONARY CSR BASED ON SOCIAL OBJECTIVES

Jensen (2002) famously argues in the business ethics literature that it is impossible for managers to seek to maximize more than one objective function. He argues that the single meaningful objective function is for managers to seek to maximize the long-term market value of the firm. This is in contrast to seeking, for example, to maximize accounting profits or market share. Jensen then connects this principle to stakeholder theory in what he calls Enlightened Stakeholder Theory. Jenson states '(E)nlightened stakeholder theory adds the simple specification that the objective function of the firm is to maximize total long-term firm value.' (2002: 246). Al-though Jensen is cleverly appearing to endorse many of the concepts of stakeholder theory, what he is actually doing is reframing it so that only the market value of the firm is used as a measure. Shareholders' interests track most closely with the overall market cap value, which is presumably the most relevant measure of firm value over time.

Windsor (2006) emphasizes that all forms of discretionary CSR represent a wealth transfer away from investors to society. He argues that ethical responsibility and economic responsibility are antithetical concepts which cannot be synthe-sized by the concept of corporate citizenship. Husted and Salazar (2006) try to take the arguments of Milton Friedman (1970) seriously by recognizing that CSR, particularly as defined in this chapter, should be seen as a wealth transfer from the shareholders to society. Further, as they and McWilliams and Siegel (2001) view it, firms that provide CSR will likely have higher costs, putting them at a competitive disadvantage vis-à-vis firms that eschew such expenditures. Both pairs of authors come up with similar solutions. McWilliams and Siegel advocate that '(t)o maximize profit, the firm should offer precisely that level of CSR for which the increased revenue (from increased demand) equals the higher cost (of using resources to provide CSR)' (2001: 124.) Husted and Salazar advocate that firms provide CSR resources up to the point that the social cost curve intersects the social benefit curve. Both thereby use stakeholder returns to the firm as a proxy for overall social benefit. So if a firm attracts more sales, or more committed and competent employees, or a lower cost of capital as a result of the reputation effects of their CSR expenditure, then that is seen as a justification for the social investment.

Complex measurement problems are associated with these approaches. How can one attribute increased financial benefits to particular CSR expenditures? McWilliams and Siegel recognize this constraint by noting that it hasn't been clearly established that Merck achieved any significant long-term financial value by its investment in Mectizan (2006: 4) in response to the prevalence of river blindness disease in developing countries. The point is often made that reputation tends to be ethereal and is capable of changing quickly and dramatically. The positive reputation so carefully cultivated by Merck during the Roy Vagelos years has not seemed to offer Merck protection against the fallout from the Vioxx controversy. The difficulties in measuring benefits pose problems for advocates of social investments. The monies required for a particular social investment are generally immediate and can be measured with relative precision. The social returns are in the future, and are inherently more speculative. So even though it may be the case that the tests proposed by McWilliams and Siegel and Husted and Salazar can be satisfied, it may be difficult to convince the CFO of that ex ante.

Mahoney (2006: 2) argues persuasively that '... viewing shareholders as the sole residual claimants is an increasingly tenuous description of the actual relationships among a corporation's various stakeholders.' In some ways the Friedman argument against social responsibility has always been odd. Billions of dollars are spent each year on social interventions by public corporations. *Business Week* provides an annual report on the level of cash and in-kind philanthropy. In 2005, the total philanthropy listed for the top ten firms was nearly $6 billion and even this large number likely falls far short of capturing the value of all forms of dCSR. Tax laws support most dCSR. If this is all illegal or inappropriate activity, then the relevant authorities must be asleep at the switch. So a better way to view the Friedman-Jensen arguments is that they are just that, arguments about a way they would prefer to see the world structured. But that is not the world that we live in. Nor is it likely a world that most citizens would prefer to live in. True there are some agency abuses by executives, and yes, much philanthropy is incoherent and unfocused. But that does not mean that society would prefer that all firms cancel their programs of social investment.

Under the definition used in this chapter, CSR is not compulsory. It is purely a voluntary activity. Management of a firm should make social investment decisions based on the core values and objectives of the organization. A Freidmanite firm could and should state that it is not going to engage in any philanthropy or social initiatives because it is inconsistent with its core values. Such a firm could announce after incidents such as Hurricane Katrina or the 9/11 attacks that, although they have resources and competencies that could help the victims of the disasters, they will not provide help because it is inconsistent with their view of the proper social role for firms. Transparency is critically important for firms whatever their position on CSR. Friedmanite firms should disclose their policies, as should firms committed to dCSR. The reaction of markets and the public will be an important test of whether or not the disclosing firms are acting consistently with social expectations.

Donaldson and Dunfee (1999) describe the relationship between a social contracts based approach to corporate responsibility and stakeholder obligations. They offer as a core principle the following: 'Relevant sociopolitical communities are a primary source of guidance concerning the stakeholder obligations of organizations formed or operating within their boundaries.' (p. 250). They emphasize that through a 'process of reference to community authentic norms, organizational managers can obtain useful guidance concerning the resolution of difficult stakeholder questions.' (p. 252). Community norms will be reflected in public reactions to corporate dCSR policies and announcements.

Full transparency concerning corporate social policies, actions, and motives is an essential prerequisite for community norms to be able to properly influence corporate behavior. The strong public reaction in recent years to corporate opaqueness reflected in off-the-books partnerships, bogus accounting, and concealed wrong-doing reflects general public recognition of the vital importance of transparency.

In each community context, managers should consult local laws and be aware of local norms pertaining to the scope of their discretionary authority to make social investments. Tax deductibility of the investment is a key signal, as are general public reactions to decisions to allocate, or not to allocate, corporate resources for public purposes. Additional sources of guidance come from the overall reaction in the media and from the actions of broad-based NGOs. Scherer and Palazzo (forthcoming) propose a deliberative concept of CSR embedded in a neo-Habermasian concept of legitimate links between civil society and the state. Although they criticize Integrative Social Contracts Theory (Donaldson and Dunfee, 1999) as problematic because of its focus on a single actor's reasoning, the norms that could be generated under their approach would be important action-guiding microsocial norms under ISCT. The author believes that in most of the developed countries, it is possible to identify sociopolitical norms that support extensive discretionary authority for corporate social investment.[2]

STAKEHOLDER THEORY AND THE dCSR ALLOCATION PROBLEM

The mere fact that managers have discretionary authority to invest corporate assets for social purposes does not provide guidance concerning how they should allocate such resources. Managers with the responsibility to allocate social investment

---

[2] Agency theorists are correct that there are many instances in which managers seek their own advantage by the allocation of corporate resources for social proposes. That is a major topic that the author is exploring in other writings. It is impossible to do justice to this important issue here.

invariably face the problem of relatively few resources to allocate across a wide range of theoretically possible investments. The question then becomes whether Stakeholder Theory[3] can play an important role in resolving this allocation problem.

Stakeholder Theory turns on the definition of 'stakeholder'. One might assume that after all of these years there is fundamental agreement regarding such a critical term and concept. It turns out that assumption is entirely unfounded. In fact, it appears that there is more consensus concerning the meaning of 'corporate social responsibility' than for 'stakeholder'. Mitchell *et al.* (1997), in a tour de force, provide a table listing 27 different definitions of the term. They sort the definitions into two extreme categories: broad and narrow. Broad approaches focus on the power that the putative stakeholder has to influence the ability of the firm to achieve its objectives. The power can be used in either direction: positively to help the firm achieve objectives or negatively to prevent the firm from achieving its goals. In contrast, narrow approaches focus on the legitimacy of the stakeholders' claims. All definitions contain an explicit or implied proviso that the stakeholder has some interest in the corporation's decisions in that the corporation can have an effect, positive or negative, on the putative stakeholder.

In their classic article, Donaldson and Preston (1995) point out that stakeholder interests are of intrinsic value. Even though that is true, it does not resolve the allocation problem because it is impossible for corporations to respond to all of the needs of all of their stakeholders. Triage is required.

The focus in much of the stakeholder literature on defining stakeholders and discussing how they fit into various legal and economic models of the corporation has resulted in a neglect of what is probably the most challenging aspect of stakeholder management. As Mahoney (2006: 4) notes '[T]he...question of how the economic surplus generated by the firm is, or should be, allocated among the various *stakeholders* has been given little research attention.' In fact, surprisingly little progress has been made in the 14 years since Hosseini and Brenner's (1992) creative attempt to apply Saaty's Analytic Hierarchy Process to weighing competing stakeholder interests.

Even under relatively narrow definitions of the term 'stakeholder', the set includes those who have inherently competing interests. Better terms for creditors and higher wages for employees often mean lower returns for shareholders. Better terms for suppliers or distributors may mean higher prices for consumers. When one considers the large number of stakeholders who could be potential beneficiaries

---

[3] Of course there is a serious question concerning whether the current state of the literature about stakeholders has risen to the level of constituting a theory. The better answer is that it is not. See Rowley (1997). It is more a set of definitions and some general ideas rather an analytically rigorous, empirically testable construct. However, the phrase is being used throughout this volume and was in the title assigned for this chapter. I realize that I could have easily changed the title, but, instead, I have chosen to go along with the 'local norm' in this context and make reluctant, and limited, reference to Stakeholder Theory.

of discretionary social investment, the problem becomes extreme. If a global pharmaceutical reprices drugs to help AIDS victims in Botswana, it thereby reduces its ability to reprice drugs to help equally deserving victims in other Sub-Saharan countries. Viewing this allocation problem as a market-like phenomenon in which those in need compete for resources from a limited set of potential suppliers provides a revealing, realistic frame for the dimensions and nature of the phenomenon.

The definition of stakeholder used for the purposes of this chapter is consistent with the approach taken by Donaldson and Dunfee (1999). Community norms and laws provide guidance concerning who may be considered a stakeholder of a firm, and may even mandate that certain parties be treated as stakeholders. No one can be considered a stakeholder if doing so would violate a hypernorm.[4] No stakeholder interest can be considered if doing so would violate a hypernorm. In between mandatory and prohibited stakeholder considerations is a domain of discretion in which managers are free to treat someone as a stakeholder, even though remote from the organization. Thus, Avon may identify breast cancer victims as stakeholders even though they are not customers of the firm and have no other connection to the firm. Similarly, GSK can identify young AIDS victims in Africa as stakeholders even though they lack the capacity to be paying customers or employees.

Although there is a large zone of discretion, it does not follow that an organization should identify anyone randomly as a stakeholder. Instead, a firm should act on the basis of its own core values, coupled with an assessment of its core competencies. Only firms that are non-Friedmanite in their basic operating philosophy will be identifying discretionary stakeholders who may benefit from social investments. Presumably, as non-Friedmanite firms they have some set of values or beliefs that guide their social activities. Firms should be transparent about these values and publish them in social reports, on their websites, and in other appropriate fora. So if, for example, a firm has as its core fundamental value to improve and extend human health, then its social investments should correlate to those values. They should be investing in improving health, not in art or theater.

Once the firm's core values have been considered, managers should then evaluate the core competencies of the organization to determine which stakeholders they should support by dCSR investments. Because this chapter focuses on corporate social investments, core competencies take on an atypical meaning. The standard approach is to define core competencies in terms of attributes that can give a firm a comparative advantage vis-à-vis competitors (Prahalad and Hamel, 1990). The

---

[4] Hypernorms are manifest, universal norms that represent 'principles so fundamental to human existence that...we would expect them to be reflected in a convergence of religious, philosophical, and cultural beliefs' (Donaldson and Dunfee, 1994: 265). In general, hypernorms are similar to the idea expressed by Michael Walzer (1992: 9) that there exists a thin 'set of standards to which all societies can be held—negative injunctions, most likely, rules against murder, deceit, torture, oppression, and tyranny.' Donaldson and Dunfee (1999: chapters 3 and 5) identify a process by which hypernorms relevant to business ethics may be identified.

traditional focus is on some unique, effective asset that cannot be easily duplicated by a competitor and thus provides a sustainable marketplace advantage. Here there is a different focus. The question instead is whether the firm has some unique capability that allows it to respond to a social need more effectively than other potential providers. Thus, core competency is defined in terms of a particular social need. Competencies may lie in intellectual property, or proximity, or ability to distribute, or in the special knowledge of employees. Thus, drug companies have core competencies relevant to mitigating the effect of AIDS. They hold patents for retroviral drugs and are experienced, efficient distributors. They have employees who are knowledgeable about treatment regimes and who know how to educate local health providers. Similarly, a wireless company may have a unique capacity to restore communications to an area hit by a natural disaster. A bottling company may have supplies of fresh bottled water in warehouses adjacent to an area hit by a tsunami or a hurricane. The examples are limitless.

Thus, the definition of a stakeholder in this context is (1) anyone whom relevant laws and norms require be recognized as a stakeholder, (2) anyone whom hypernorms require be recognized as a stakeholder, and (3) anyone whom the managers of the organization determine, acting consistently with organizational values, to have a legitimate need which can be ameliorated through the use of the core competencies of the corporation. Assuming that many people and groups will fit these definitions, managers are still left with the triage issue of whom to select as a beneficiary of the organization's social investment. We now consider whether stakeholder theory can go beyond its role of helping identify appropriate stakeholders and provide direction concerning choosing among worthy stakeholders.

Using Stakeholder Theory to Determine Allocation Strategy

As noted, there have been few attempts to specifically apply Stakeholder Theory to situations involving competing stakeholder claims. One very specific attempt was by Hosseini and Brenner (1992) using a particular multi-attribute decision-making tool, the Analytic Hierarchy Process (AHP), to give weights to various value concerns and influence factors. They envisioned collecting information from stakeholders and also having managers rank the interests of stakeholders. These rankings are then to be compared and synthesized through use of the AHP technique. A major problem with their approach was generating the initial data. Weak or invalid data would render the sophisticated analysis meaningless.

More recently, Reynolds *et al.* (2006) conducted an empirical study to determine the impact of resource divisibility on stakeholder allocation decisions. Some resources are easily divided (anti-retroviral drugs) while others are not (availability of a stadium owned by a firm on a particular date). Although divisibility has an expected influence on allocation decisions, that finding was not particularly relevant to the task at hand. Reynolds *et al.* (2006) also compared two different types of allocation strategies. One, which they called 'within decision' involves treating each allocation as a discrete, isolated case. Similar to act utilitarianism, every judgment is assessed on its own merits. In contrast is the 'across-decision' approach, in which decisions are considered as a composite across time and stakeholder groups. In that way, stakeholders who are not favored in one allocation can be subject to a make-up or balancing allocation at a future point in time. Their research was based upon a convenience sample of students. Their subjects found the across-decision approach to be more instrumentally useful .The subjects viewed the across-decision approach as more ethical than the within-decision alternative.

Rowley (1997) applied network theory to get beyond the tendency to focus on the merits of a single stakeholder. Rowley looks at 'the interaction of multiple influences from the entire stakeholder set' (p. 890). He proposes that density (relative number of ties in a network for the focal firm) and centrality (relative position of the firm within the network) will have an impact on the ability of a firm to resist stakeholder pressure for allocation of organizational resources.

Mitchell *et al.*'s (1997) (hereinafter referred to as MAW) analysis of stakeholder identification and salience is the most detailed attempt to provide a relevant sorting among stakeholders. Unfortunately, they stop short of providing specific guidance for weighing competing stakeholder claims in specific decision contexts. Nonetheless their discussion and analysis provides helpful guideposts.

After reviewing the stakeholder literature, particularly that pertaining to stakeholder definition or identity, MAW (1997) parse out three key attributes that may pertain to particular stakeholders. First, there is power, or the power to carry out one's own will despite resistance. This may be exercised by coercive, utilitarian, or normative means. Second is legitimacy, which they describe as 'loosely referring to socially accepted and expected structures and behaviors' (p. 866). This principle correlates most closely to the definition used in this chapter which incorporates references to law and social norms. Third is urgency where the claim is time sensitive and important to the holder.

Based upon these attributes, MAW (1997) classify stakeholders into three different categories: low salience, moderate salience and high salience. Their analysis can be represented in Table 15.1.[5]

In their analysis, MAW (1997) emphasize that the position of specific stakeholders can change over time. They recognize a continuing dynamism in stakeholder

---

[5] To emphasize, this is the author's table not theirs. They may be appalled by this attempt.

Table 15.1 MAW's (1997) categorization of stakeholder salience

Salience	Category	Attributes
High Salience	Definitive	Power + Legitimacy + Urgency
Moderate Salience	Dominant	Power + Legitimacy
"	Dependent	Urgency + Legitimacy
"	Dangerous	Urgency + Power
Low Salience	Dormant	Power only
"	Discretionary	Legitimacy only
"	Demanding	Urgency only

Source: Based on MAW (1997). The table is developed by the author and should not be attributed to the authors of MAW.

attributes. For the purposes of allocating discretionary social investment, the attribute of power becomes much less important. Legitimacy in the sense that the investment is supported by social norms, organizational values and applicable laws takes on much greater importance. Similarly, in the allocation of scarce resources, the attribute of urgency becomes critical.

The assumption is that managers will first pay attention to the high salience Definitive Stakeholders who not only have legitimate urgent claims but who also have the power to reward or punish the firm based on its response. The tendency may be to ignore any of the other stakeholder groups, or at the least to give them very low priority. In contrast, the dCSR approach justifies considering the interests of certain moderate and low salience stakeholders. Dependent Stakeholders have legitimate claims, supported by social norms, and their claims are serious and urgent. They should be included among the candidates to be benefited by corporate social investment. Similarly, Discretionary Stakeholders should be considered as potential beneficiaries.

The MAW classification scheme, similar to most of the writings focusing primarily on the nature and status of stakeholder claims, is essentially mute concerning fit with the competencies of the corporation. While the MAW authors recognize that managerial characteristics can be a moderator of the relationships upon which the stakeholder attributes are based (p. 871), they do not go on to provide specific guidance as to how that might work. As it is, the MAW approach, while helpful in a general sense, is nonetheless very coarse-grained.

The stakeholder literature described here does not provide sufficient guidance for managers facing allocation issues. Is such guidance possible from Stakeholder Theory? It is possible that future extensions of Stakeholder Theory may be helpful in resolving allocation issues, but that doesn't seem likely in the near term. The hopes that do exist in this domain will probably come from academic recognition of rapidly evolving corporate experience. The thriving practice of stakeholder management may provide new insights concerning allocation dilemmas. Stakeholder practice, influenced by social auditing standards and increasing attention to corporate social reporting, is developing ever better ways of engaging stakeholders and of determining the real preferences of stakeholders. Practice may ultimately influence theory and enable theorists to identify effective ways of resolving the allocation problem.

But perhaps a better question is whether fine-grained guidance from stakeholder theory is necessary? The surprising answer may be no, it isn't. Managers need to connect their assessment of the core competencies of the firm relevant to social investment to their decisions concerning which stakeholders to benefit through social investment strategies. Each firm needs to act at the basis of its own relationships with stakeholders built over time. Firms need to act consistently with their core values in making such decisions. None of those factors can be adequately considered looking solely at the stakeholder side of the equation. Nor can relatively precise generic formulas be developed that would apply across the board to all types of firms. Each firm is to an important extent sui generis when it comes to dCSR allocations.

Stakeholder theory, as it exists today, is more a general orientation than a theory capable of predicting or proscribing specific types of dCSR investments. The theory has served as a focal point for critics of CSR and in that context, stakeholder theory has become a bulwark against the Friedmanites. It also provides general schemes for assessing the relative merits of general categories of stakeholders. Beyond that, stakeholder theory does not appear to offer definitive solutions to the allocation problem.

MARKET-BASED AND OTHER POTENTIAL SOLUTIONS TO THE MULTI-ACTOR ALLOCATION PROBLEM

The management literature offers other ways of thinking about the allocation problem when viewed from the firm perspective. Hart (1995) attempts to take the resource-based view of the firm ('valuable, costly-to-copy firm resources and capabilities provide the key sources of sustainable competitive advantage' (p. 986)) and reframe it into a *natural* resource-based view. Hart focuses on pollution prevention, product stewardship, and ultimately, sustainable development. His approach to product stewardship entails integrating the voice of the environment, including external stakeholder perspectives. In so doing, Hart attempts to integrate a perspective of the firm as a social goods provider with putative stakeholders as potential social beneficiaries. Unfortunately, Hart's model does not deal specifically with resource allocation issues.

Resource dependency theorists look at the relationship between firms and those who provide resources on which the firms depend for survival and success. A condition of high resource dependency may give external stakeholders the power to influence corporate decisions, including those involving traditional CSR (Frooman, 1999). In the area of dCSR these ideas may connect most closely with those of Michael Porter and his advocacy of the use of philanthropy as a means of capturing sustainable competitive advantage. To the extent that the primary focus of a manager is on competitive advantage or the sustaining of resources critical to the firm, it does not fall within the domain of dCSR as defined in this chapter.

A more promising line of thinking lies in the potential for framing the allocation problem as a marketplace-like decision. Baron (2001) provides an elaborate model of a game-theoretic interaction between an activist seeking a favorable allocation of dCSR and a firm responding to the activist. The firm can respond to pressure from an activist by going along with the demand, contesting it, or by reaching some sort of middle-ground settlement. Most of the model focuses on a single dyadic relationship, although there is some consideration of industry-level implications.

As noted above, McWilliams and Siegel (2001) and Husted and Salazar (2006) both use broad market concepts in analyzing standard CSR. Both sets of authors use profit as a basis for market judgments. That certainly represents familiar ground and provides a seemingly[6] hard measure of whether actions taken are appropriate. On the other hand their approaches fail to capture inputs based on social norms and laws in any direct sense. Is it possible to think more broadly concerning how a marketplace analogy might work in this context?

Assume that the market looks something like this. There is a great demand for social services and interventions. These needs are the result of the substantial shortfalls in the provision of nutrition, education, health services, etc. for the global population. Potential suppliers include governmental agencies, NGOs, private citizens, and to a small extent, corporations. Various intermediaries facilitate the exchange between those in need and the suppliers of social goods.

True there is no simple demand and supply mechanism. Instead, this market is vaguely similar to the idea of a marketplace of morality (Dunfee, 1998), in which individuals with different interests and moral perspectives attempt to influence decisions. Here the stakeholders themselves and their representatives attempt to influence potential providers of necessary social goods. They may do this through media placements, boycotts, public requests, demonstrations, lawsuits, negotiations,

---

[6] See earlier discussion of how hard it is to measure the types of returns that McWilliams and Siegel value.

and conversations, etc. On the other side are the potential providers who make decisions based on their assessment of value, competencies, and needs. There are many potential suppliers who may act jointly through public–private partnerships and other devices. In many cases, suppliers just act on the basis of their own goals and rules. Aguilera *et al.* (2007) consider in some detail the motives that might induce firms to seek to bring about positive social change through investments in CSR initiatives.

This 'market' has many inefficiencies evidenced in the oversupply of goods in response to popular causes, such as providing help after the Southeast Asian tsunami, the 9/11 attack, and Hurricane Katrina. If one looks just at the relatively small part of this market which involves corporations as potential suppliers, there are several strategies which, if followed, could help make this 'market' more 'efficient'.

First, as stressed throughout this chapter, managers should always make sure that their firms have some comparative advantage justifying a dCSR strategy. The comparative advantage will generally be found in a core competency relevant to the provision of social goods.

Second, social investments should be treated as seriously as financial investments. Therefore, managers should specify their social objectives and have a plan for measuring whether the social objections are being obtained.

Third, and most importantly, firms should be completely transparent concerning dCSR initiatives. They should disclose the motives for their social investments. They should also disclose their objectives and the measurement tools they plan to use. That way, outsiders, including relevant stakeholders and their representatives, can render independent judgments concerning whether the firm is achieving its goals. Concurrently, other potential corporate suppliers can use the information to better inform their own decisions as to how they should allocate resources.

Firms acting consistently with social expectations, norms, and laws should be happy to disclose their strategies because this should enhance their reputations. At the same time, the sunshine let in by full transparency provides strong incentives to make sure that dCSR programs are coherent, focused, and effective.

Conclusion

How should managers allocate discretionary social resources in the face of limited information and competing demands? This chapter introduces the concept of discretionary corporate social responsibility, dCSR, which involves voluntary spending on explicit social objectives consistent with societal expectations. dCSR is justified as a proper and legitimate business investment based on supportive social political norms and supportive laws in most developed countries.

Managers are seen as having a large zone of discretion in designating stakeholders as beneficiaries of social investment. Ironically, stakeholder theory, at least in its current state of development, fails to provide fine-grained help concerning how managers should cope with the allocation problem when making social investments. It does provide some general help in determining overall stakeholder salience. This chapter suggests that a useful way to think of the problem is to frame it as a market-like phenomenon involving needy stakeholders competing for assistance from potential suppliers of social goods, including corporations. For corporations to enhance their role in this market-like phenomenon, they should (1) align their social investments with their comparative advantages in providing social goods, (2) treat social investments in a manner similar to their financial investments by specifying social goals and objectives and then evaluating their investments to make sure that the goals and objectives are realized, and (3) be completely transparent in all dimensions of dCSR.

REFERENCES

AGUILERA, R. V., RUPP, D. E., WILLIAMS, C. A., and GANAPATHI, J. 2007. 'Putting the S back in Corporate Social Responsibility: A Multi-level Theory of Social Change in Organizations'. *Academy of Management Review*, 32(3): 836–63.

BARON, D. P. 2001. 'Private Politics, Corporate Social Responsibility and Integrated Strategy'. *Journal of Economics and Management Strategy*, 10(1): 7–45.

CARROLL, A. B., and BUCHHOLTZ, A. K. 2000. 'Business and Society: Ethics and Stakeholder Management', 4th edn. Cincinnati: South-Western Publishing Company.

DONALDSON, T., and DUNFEE, T. W. 1994. 'Towards a Unified Conception of Business Ethics: Integrative Social Contracts Theory'. *Academy of Management Review*, 19(2): 252–84.

————1999. 'Ties that Bind: A Social Contracts Approach to Business Ethics'. Cambridge, Mass.: Harvard Business School Press.

——and PRESTON, L. E. 1995. 'The Stakeholder Theory for the Corporation: Concepts, Evidence, Implications'. *Academy of Management Review*, 20(1): 65–91.

DUNFEE, T. W. 1998. 'The Marketplace of Morality: First Steps Toward a Theory of Moral Choice'. *Business Ethics Quarterly*, 8(1): 127–45.

FRIEDMAN, M. 1970. 'The Social Responsibility of Business is to Increase its Profits'. *New York Times Magazine*, Sept.: 32–3, 122, 124, 126.

FROOMAN, J. 1999. 'Stakeholder Influence Strategies'. *Academy of Management Review*, 24(2): 191–205.

HART, S. L. 1995. 'A Natural Resource-Based View of the Firm', *Academy of Management Review*, 20(4): 986–1014.

HOSSEINI, J. C., and BRENNER, S. N. 1992. 'The Stakeholder Theory of the Firm: A Methodology to Generate Value Matrix Weights'. *Business Ethics Quarterly* 2(2): 99–119.

HUSTED, B. W., and SALAZAR, J. 2006. 'Taking Friedman Seriously: Maximizing Profits and Social Performance'. *Journal of Management Studies*, 43(1): 75–91.

Jensen, M. C. 2002. 'Value Maximization, Stakeholder Theory, and the Corporate Objective Function'. *Business Ethics Quarterly*, 12(2): 235–56.

Mahoney, J. T. 2006. 'Towards a Stakeholder Theory of Strategic Management'. Working Paper. (Copy available from author.)

McWilliams, A., and Siegel, D. 2001. 'Corporate Social Responsibility: A Theory of the Firm Perspective'. *Academy of Management Review*, 26(1): 117–27.

—————— and Wright, P. M. 2006. 'Corporate Social Responsibility: Strategic Implications'. *Journal of Management Studies*, 43(1): 1–18.

Mitchell, R. K., Agle, B. R., and Wood, D. J. 1997. 'Toward a Theory of Stakeholder Identification and Salience: Defining the Principle of Whom and What Really Counts. *Academy of Management Review*, 22(4): 853–86. (Cited as MAW, 1997.)

Porter, M. E., and Kramer, M. R. 2002. 'The Competitive Advantage of Corporate Philanthropy'. *Harvard Business Review*, Dec.: 57–68.

Prahalad, C. K., and Hamel, G. 1990. 'The Core Competence of the Corporation'. *Harvard Business Review*, May–June: 79–91.

Reynolds, S. J., Schultz, F. C., and Heckman, D. R. 2006. 'Stakeholder Theory and Managerial Decision-Making: Constraints and Implications of Balancing Stakeholder Interests'. *Journal of Business Ethics*, 64(3): 285–301.

Rowley, T. J. 1997. 'Moving beyond Dyadic Ties: A Network Theory of Stakeholder Influences'. *Academy of Management Review*, 22(4): 887–910.

Scherer, A., and Palazzo, G. Forthcoming. 'Towards a Political Conception of Corporate Responsibility: Business and Society Seen from a Habermasian Perspective.' *Academy of Management Review*, 32(4).

Walzer, M. 1992. 'Moral Minimalism'. in W. R. Shea and G. A. Spadafora (eds.), The Twilight of Probability: Ethics and Politics. Cantono, Mass.: Science History Publications.

Windsor, D. 2006. 'Corporate Social Responsibility: Three Key Approaches'. *Journal of Management Studies*, 43(1): 93–114.

CHAPTER 16

RESPONSIBILITY IN THE SUPPLY CHAIN

ANDREW MILLINGTON

INTRODUCTION

DURING the concluding decades of the twentieth century business has been subject to developments which have fundamentally changed both the extent and nature of purchasing behavior. Firms have consistently sought to reduce costs and increase strategic flexibility by outsourcing non-core activities replacing hierarchies with networks. At the same time supply networks have been substituted for markets as much of the world trade in labour-intensive products (e.g. clothes, shoes, and fresh vegetables) has come to be organized by lead firms who may be retailers, or manufacturers (Gerrefi, 1999; Dolan and Humphrey, 2000; Schmitz and Knorrega, 2000; Humphrey and Schmitz, 2001). These developments have been exacerbated by the movement of production to the developing and transitional economies and in particular Asia. Corporate social responsibility (CSR) is increasingly concerned therefore with supply chain management and in particular with global supply chain management.

The substitution of supply networks for markets and hierarchies has profound implications for CSR. While companies are able to maintain and extend their economic control over supply chains, outsourcing devolves the legal obligation for social and environmental impacts from the lead company to suppliers (Sobszak, 2006). On the other hand the substitution of supply networks for markets provides lead companies with opportunities for control and influence which would not have been present within market-based relationships; such governance structures may become essential as buyers become increasingly involved in product specification in the supplier (Gerrefi, 1999).

Both developments raise questions about the boundaries of CSR and the extent to which buyers can be held responsible for the activities of their suppliers (Roberts, 2003). As Hall comments within the context of environmental impacts, 'the responsibility for regulations rests on the firm engaged in the polluting activity. Firms therefore have a limited responsibility toward the environmental activities of their suppliers. Customer firms may be liable for purchased products or services, but they are not legally responsible for their supplier's other activities' (Hall, 2000: 457). It remains true however that while the legal obligation of buyers for the activities of suppliers are limited, inappropriate environmental or social activities have been widely reported and associated with lead companies (e.g. Frenkel and Kim, 2004). The competitive advantage of many of these companies, particularly in the footwear and garment markets, is based on brand and while many of these companies have no production facilities, poor social and environmental performance in the supply chain may have damaging implications for the brand and corporate reputation (Humphrey and Schmitz, 2001). The supply chain and in particular the environmental and social performance of suppliers may therefore be seen as a source of risk to the parent company (Rao, 2004).

The management of international supply networks poses particular problems since suppliers in different countries are subject to different regulatory regimes which may or may not be enforced. In these circumstances lead companies in developed countries must seek to manage supply relationships where the legal obligation for environmental and social conduct lies with the supplier and the supplier is subject to a different institutional, cultural, and regulatory environment. In addition the focus on low cost production in many international sourcing decisions may reduce the priority given to social and environmental initiatives in the supply chain (Preuss, 2001). Recent estimates suggest that Asia may account for over half of global production by 2025 (Zhu and Sarkis, 2004). This movement has been motivated by both the development of emerging markets and the development of export platforms in low cost countries (Zhu and Sarkis, 2004). In labour-intensive industries price competition has led to a continuous search for lower labor costs (Humphrey and Schmitz, 2001). Multinational companies (MNCs) have been described as exploiters of third world labour, taking advantage of weak labor laws and low wages (Grieder, 1997). This suggestion is supported by recent studies of sports good manufacturers which imply that location decisions have been driven by a demand for lower costs and in particular lower labor costs. Low wages and poor working conditions at Nike and Reebok suppliers have been widely publicized (Frenkel, 2001) and recent evidence suggests that poor working conditions remain endemic in local suppliers in developing countries including China, Indonesia, and Vietnam (Cavanagh, 1997; Chan, 1998).

The nature of supply relations has also been subject to fundamental change. There has been a shift in the activities of purchasing departments away from 'merely' buying towards the proactive management of supply chains. In these cases long-term commitments and close, cooperative relationships with a smaller number of suppliers can improve the prospects for the adoption of just-in-time (JIT) supply arrangements and total quality control (TQC) (Imrie and Morris, 1992; Womack and Jones, 1996). The development of partnership sourcing has encouraged greater involvement by buyers in the operation of suppliers and this may enhance the ability of buyers to influence the behavior of suppliers and in particular their approach to social and environmental responsibility (Geffen and Rothenberg, 2000; Bowen et al., 2001). In the Western developed countries emphasis has been placed on supplier certification through environmental management systems such as EMAC (the Eco-Management and Audit Scheme) and ISO 14001, whilst in the developing world lead firms not only emphasize environmental management systems but have also encouraged the adoption of international codes of conduct such as the Global Reporting Initiative and ILO labor standards (Doh, 2005). Some MNCs have also sought to implement corporate codes of conduct across their suppliers which stipulate minimum wages and working conditions (Frenkel, 2001). It has been suggested that corporate codes may fill a regulatory vacuum, improving working conditions in developing countries. According to Frenkel these codes offer significant advantages to MNCs since they 'enable firms to tailor labour relations to their own needs, they also motivate employees by improving wages and conditions and by introducing uniform rules they confer legitimacy on the global firms products' (Frenkel, 2001: 533).

The preceding discussion emphasizes the increasing importance of effective supply chain management for corporate social performance (CSP) in the 21st century. Although the legal obligations for social and environmental issues are increasingly devolved to suppliers, as supply networks replace hierarchies and markets, the role of lead firms in the development of ethical supply chain management (ESCM) has been the subject of considerable debate. In the following discussion we focus on two questions which are central to the development of ESCM. First, we look at stakeholder pressure for ESCM and its implications for the involvement of lead firms in ESCM. Second, the conditions under which lead firms will be able to influence suppliers and implement ESCM are considered. The impact of ESCM on social and environmental performance is then reviewed and the implications for the development of effective ESCM are outlined in the concluding section.

STAKEHOLDER PREFERENCES AND ESCM

Although the efficiency and performance benefits of environmental supply chain policies (Green *et al.*, 1996; Carter and Carter, 1998; Lippmann, 1999; Drumwright, 1994; Coeck, 1993) and to a lesser extent social supply chain policies (Frenkel, 2001) have been explored, earlier literature suggests that the primary motivation for ESCM lies in external stakeholder pressure (Theyal, 2001; Zhu and Sarkis, 2004).

Stakeholder theory places the firm within a constellation of interests which may lie inside or outside the company and have conflicting or competing demands. Freeman (1984) defines a 'stakeholder as any group or individual who can affect or is affected by the achievement of the organisations objectives' (Freeman, 1984: 46). It has been suggested that the ethical and social performance of supply chains has been subject to significant attention by legislative and political stakeholders, consumers, and financial stakeholders (e.g. Frenkel and Scott, 2002; Frenkel and Kim, 2004; Theyal, 2001). Although much of this literature focuses on Western countries, stakeholders in different countries may be expected to exhibit different preferences for environmental and social responsibility. Recent studies suggest that environmental issues have higher salience in Western Europe and North America than in Asian countries (Murphy and Bendall, 1997; Hall, 2000) and that Chinese consumers are less likely than American consumers to translate environmental preferences into purchasing behavior (Chan and Lau, 2001). For lead firms which are located in West European and North American markets the challenge is, however, to meet stakeholder demands in their home markets even though these requirements may exceed those in overseas and particularly Asian markets. Indeed recent results suggest that environmental policies in Japanese firms have been motivated by international rather than domestic stakeholders (Elkington, 1994). Since environmental and social performance is predominantly a concern of Western European and North American stakeholders, the following discussion places particular emphasis on stakeholder preferences in the Western World and their implications for environmental and social performance in supply chains.

LEGISLATIVE AND REGULATORY STAKEHOLDERS

Legislative and political stakeholders constrain the activities of firms and managers, restraining the anti-competitive activities of firms and restricting socially and environmentally damaging behavior. Companies may invest in ESCM in order to improve external perceptions of the company, influence external decision-makers, and reduce the risk of regulatory activity that may limit management discretion, or reduce the value of the firm (Watts and Zimmermann, 1978; Roberts, 2003). The last decade has seen a significant increase in government action to encourage socially responsible behavior by companies (HMSO, 2001; European Commission, 2001). This has included environmental regulation (HMSO, 1999a, 1990) and closer controls over the activities of some industries with socially damaging externalities (European Commission, 2001). Government encouragement of socially responsible behavior has been reinforced by legislative action to encourage ethical investment practices (HMSO, 1999b). Relationships between buyers and their suppliers are subject to influence from national and international regulation. Most of this pressure is essentially voluntary or applied indirectly through government pressure on other stakeholders such as financial institutions and quasi-governmental organizations. In the UK both the National Health Service and Local Authorities have stringent purchasing requirements which increasingly require 'green certification' such as ISO 14001 (Brammer and Millington, 2006). UK and EU policy encompasses the environment, community investment, the workplace, and supports international instruments and initiatives such as the OECD Guidelines for Multinationals, the UN Global Compact and Global Reporting Initiative, and the ILO declaration on fundamental rights and principles of work. These internationally agreed core standards are concerned with the freedom to work and the right to collective bargaining; the elimination of forced and child labour; and the elimination of discrimination in employment (ILO, 1997). It is important to note however that while both the UK and the EU support such initiatives, corporate involvement is voluntary and not legally enforceable. It has been suggested that by emphasizing the voluntary nature of involvement in CSR the European 'Commission is giving businesses carte blanche to operate as they want with scant regard for environmental or social concerns' (Lambert, 2007). Extension of these voluntary codes of conduct to suppliers remains problematic. Since legal responsibility for the operation of the supplier lies with the supplier rather than the purchasing company and buyers may have limited influence over suppliers, it would appear unreasonable to hold Western firms responsible for the social and environmental consequences of their supplier's operations (Humphrey and Schmitz, 2001). The OECD Guidelines suggest that MNCs should encourage CSR in their business partners, but recognizes that the ability of lead companies to influence suppliers is limited by 'the numbers of suppliers or other business partners, the structure and complexity of the supply chain and the market position of the enterprise vis-à-vis suppliers' (OECD, 2002: 4).

CONSUMER STAKEHOLDERS

Consumers and community stakeholders may seek to modify corporate behavior directly, through negative publicity or discriminatory purchasing behavior, and indirectly through the encouragement of government action, or changes in shareholder behavior. Stakeholder groups, such as Greenpeace, target and publicize individual companies (*Financial Times*, 2001) seeking to influence corporate behavior and consumer perceptions. Consumers can be seen to pursue both positive and negative strategies towards social and environmental issues in the supply chain. Positive strategies are concerned with the growth of green markets and socially responsible consumption and this is reflected in the development of the 'organic market' and social labels such as 'Fair Trade', which provides a commitment to decent working conditions and a fair price. Negative strategies are concerned with the withdrawal of consumer support for particular products. Consumers use negative strategies to express concern over socially or environmentally irresponsible practices by choosing not to purchase particular brands or products or through participation in consumer boycotts. These campaigns are largely motivated and led by NGOs and focus on large companies with a strong brand image. In the UK the Clean Clothes Campaign and Oxfam put particular pressure on leading retailers such as Marks and Spencer during the mid-1990s while the largest DIY retailers were the subject of campaigns led by NGOs with a particular interest in deforestation (Roberts, 2003). In the United States organizations such as the United Students against Sweatshops (US) and the Workers Rights Consortium (WRC) raised the profile of core labor standards in universities while public criticism of working standards in their overseas contractors, largely managed by NGOs, led Nike to tighten its control over working conditions in the supply chain, illustrating the reputational damage that such campaigns can inflict on high profile-branded products (Frenkel, 2001).

While consumer pressure on lead firms which are close to consumers and have a strong brand image is well attested by case study evidence, the depth of the consumer movement is less clear. Recent studies on the importance of the consumer movement and its influence on the supply chain provide mixed results (Elkington, 1994; Williams *et al.*, 1993; Steger, 1993; Schwepker and Cornwell, 1991). Within Europe this is reflected in a clear distinction between consumer perceptions of the importance of CSR (what they say) and the extent to which this is reflected in consumption decisions (what they do). According to a MORI poll carried out in 1998, 45% of British adults had boycotted a product on ethical grounds and 47% had selected a product /service because of a company's ethical reputation (Business in the Community, 2001). Seventy percent of consumers stated that MNCs should ensure good working conditions and fair treatment for employees in developing and transitional economies (Cowe and Williams, 2001). Comparative cross-country studies appear to support this position. A recent survey of 25,000 individuals in 26 countries suggested that consumers placed greater weight on CSR than brand or financial reputation when assessing companies (Environics, 1999). It remains true however that the total market share for ethical goods and services is less than 3% in the UK (Ethical Consumerism Report, 2004) and this encompasses a broad range of products and underlying interest groups which include: organic products, animal testing, the environment, ethical investment, labor standards, and Fair Trade goods. Recent estimates suggest that the most important sectors were finance, personal products, food, and climate change, with evidence of substantial increases in the importance of Fair Trade products and organic food sales. Although labor standards in developing countries are of significant concern and have been highlighted in a number of recent cases, evidence for significant pressure is restricted. Ethical clothing sales accounted for only £43 m. in the UK in 2004 while ethical boycotts of particular brands accounted for £296 m. (Ethical Consumerism Report, 2005). In the UK boycotts focused on high street food and clothing brands and were particularly concerned with animal welfare, environmental impacts, and labor standards (Ethical Consumerism Report, 2005). In practice consumers will consider social environmental issues when making purchase choices but only if price and quality considerations are met; yet within these choices consumers in the UK appear to place the greatest weight on employee working conditions emphasizing the importance of labor standards for lead companies (Cowe and Williams, 2001).

FINANCIAL STAKEHOLDERS

Financial stakeholders are recognized as a potential influence on supply chains in much of the recent literature (e.g. Theyal, 2001). Their impact on ethical supply chain management will depend on their preferences and influence within the company. Recent evidence emphasizes the growing importance of ethical investment. Corporate social performance is coming under increasing scrutiny from both ethical investment research services and fund managers. These developments reflect continuing legislative pressure during the study period. UK pension funds were required to state their investment principles in 1995 (HMSO, 1996b) and to identify the role of social, environmental, and ethical considerations in investment planning (HMSO, 2001). There was significant public interest in socially responsible investment (SRI), with NOP survey results suggesting that 73% of respondents supported ethical pensions (Denham, 1998). Between 1990 and 1999 the amount invested in retail SRI funds increased from £321 m. to £3,197 m. doubling approximately every three years (Sparkes, 2000).[1] The growing importance of socially responsible investment may be expected to have significant implications for ethical supply chain management as institutional shareholders and shareholder activists use company AGMs to pursue CSR issues (Roberts, 2003) and legislative pressure encourages social disclosure (Sobszak, 2006). The growing importance of socially and environmentally responsible supply management is reflected in the inclusion of supply chain metrics in the EIRIS indices of corporate social performance. There is however little or no systematic evidence on the relationship between institutional investment patterns and ethical supply chain management.

IMPLICATIONS

The preceding discussion suggests that stakeholder pressure for ethical supply chain management is both limited and focused on a subset of companies. Although national and supranational bodies are concerned with ESCM, their prescriptions for national and multinational companies are largely voluntary and while supply chain issues have achieved a significant salience in the minds of consumers, this is only partially reflected in their purchasing decisions. In practice consumer pressure for ESCM is focused on large companies whose competitive advantage is associated with brand image. Since proximity to customers is important, firms in intermediate and capital goods industries appear to come under little pressure to implement ESCM (Hall, 2000). The key role played by NGOs in mobilizing and organizing consumer support for ESCM may be contrasted with the relatively minor role played by NGOs in the motivation of generic environmental initiatives (Florida, 1996; Green et al., 1996).

The central role of consumers in the process may also have implications for the composition of ESCM. The preceding discussion emphasized the broad range of issues which concern consumers; these include animal rights, and organic produce, as well as environmental impacts and labor rights. To the extent that ESCM is motivated by consumer demands we might expect firms to respond directly to consumer requirements restricting the range of issues that ESCM focuses on and emphasizing those aspects which have an emotional resonance with consumers (ILO, 1997). According to Sobszak, firms are pleased to emphasize children's rights but are 'strikingly less involved regarding the protection of other fundamental social rights such as the freedom of association or the right to collective bargaining' (Sobszak, 2006: 180).

---

[1] This figure provides an underestimate of the true influence of ethical investment since it excludes wholesale investments.

The likelihood and significance of stakeholder intervention is however likely to be mediated by the characteristics of the individual firm and the industry in which it operates. This reflects the visibility of the firm to stakeholder groups, which depends on both the size of the firm and the social and environmental footprint of the industry in which it operates. Since the preceding discussion suggests that ESCM is predominantly driven by the risk of media and public exposure of poor supply chain management, the onus for developing and implementing ESCM falls disproportionately on large lead companies who are characterized by strong brand images and close proximity to key stakeholder groups such as consumers (retailers and branded goods) and government (hospitals, local government). In contrast suppliers are usually distant from key stakeholder groups and since the economic gains from ESCM are often unclear or unproven, suppliers may only be willing to implement ESCM within the context of strong supply management processes initiated by lead firms (Hall, 2000).

WHAT DETERMINES SUCCESSFUL IMPLEMENTATION OF ESCM?

Having discussed the conditions under which firms may be motivated to implement ESCM, we now consider the factors which determine successful implementation of ESCM. Much of the discussion of ESCM has been placed within the context of relational or obligational contracting (Sako, 1992). Such systems are characterized by long-term cooperative relationships between buyers and suppliers, which are based on trust and the relatively free exchange of information. These systems enable buyers to develop JIT supply arrangements and TQC in suppliers through a close working partnership. Such systems and the evolution of acceptable performance levels in local suppliers may involve significant investment by the supplier in dedicated quality control procedures and the acceptance of increased levels of control and monitoring by the buyer (Womack and Jones, 1996). Earlier studies of the relationship between supply chain management and the implementation of environmentally sound processes in suppliers suggest both that they are more likely to develop within a partnership approach (Green et al., 1996) and that collaborative approaches enable buyers to obtain a clearer understanding of the environmental consequences of production (Lamming and Hampson, 1996). It is important to note however that partnership and obligational contracts rarely extend below tier 1 or immediate suppliers. The dispersion of ESCM is therefore limited by the very nature of supply chain management.

The success of such systems and *inter alia* local supplier adaptation to buyer requirements may be expected to depend on both power-dependency relationships between the partners and institutional and cultural factors within the supplier which may encourage or discourage the implementation of such activities. Recent studies suggest that significant cultural and institutional differences exist both between local and foreign invested enterprises and between forms of local enterprise (Peng *et al.*, 2004) which may significantly effect supplier adaptation to buyer requirements (Millington *et al.*, 2005). Although the supply chain literature emphasizes the partnership and collaborative aspects of supply chain management (Lamming and Hampson, 1996), supply relationships range from market transactions at one extreme to partnership and obligational contacting at the other. Even within collaborative relationships 'there remain considerable adversarial features in these relationships most importantly that it was the buyers who are primarily responsible for...changes' (Hall, 2000: 460). Frenkel and Scott (2002) distinguishes between compliance where the global firm has domination over suppliers and 'develops and introduces the code, communicates its importance to the contractors and is responsible for its enforcement' (Frenkel and Scott, 2002: p. xx) and collaboration where supply chain management is characterized by partnership but not necessarily by power equality (Frenkel and Scott, 2002).

Since external pressure for ESCM is felt by lead firms rather than suppliers, buyer power over the supplier may be a necessary precondition for the implementation of ESCM (Hall, 2000). In the subsequent section the conditions under which ESCM may evolve are analyzed within the context of a power-dependency model.

POWER-DEPENDENCY THEORY AND THE IMPLEMENTATION OF ESCM

Power-dependency theory argues that power resides in the ability of one party to make another do what they otherwise might not have done. Such power may derive from the degree of sales and profits that one party contributes to the other (Frazier *et al.*, 1989), the availability of alternatives, the costs of switching to alternatives (Porter, 1980), and the extent to which an organization is dependent on an external source for a large proportion of input or output (Pfeffer and Salancik, 1978: 271). Power-dependency theory, then, makes the simple argument that the power to control or influence another resides in the extent of the other's dependence on one for the things they value (Emerson, 1962). Recent

	LOW	HIGH
	Buyer dependency	
LOW *Supplier dependency*	Balanced power Buyer–supplier independence **Market**	Power imbalance **Supplier power**
HIGH *Supplier dependency*	Power imbalance **Buyer power**	Balanced power Buyer–supplier interdependence **Mutual dependence**

Fig. 16.1 Power–dependence relationships

work suggests that we can distinguish between two dimensions of resource dependence: power imbalance and mutual interdependence (Casciaro and Piskorski, 2004). Power imbalance is present when one organization is dependent on another but this is not reciprocated. Interdependence is characterized by mutual dependence. Casciaro and Piskorski (2004) suggest that the 'most likely result of this power imbalance is the appropriation by the powerful partner of a larger part of the overall benefits accruing from the exchange' (2004: 9), while interdependence is likely to encourage the use of long-term contracts or permanent inter-organizational linkages as tactics for both organizations to ensure the stable flows of resources.

The implications of the power-dependency distribution for bargaining behavior are summarized in Figure 16.1 where buyer dependency is plotted against supplier dependency. Four quadrants are identified: quadrant 1 corresponds to the 'market', buyer and supplier dependence are both low and the participants have little power over each other; quadrants 3 and 3 are characterized by power imbalance and either the buyer (quadrant 2) or the supplier (quadrant 3) is seen to have power in a situation where the trading partner is dependent; the fourth quadrant corresponds to the case where buyer and supplier are mutually dependent.

In the context of supplier adaptation to buyer demands for ESCM, the relative power of the participants is likely to reflect the number of buyers, and sellers of the product or service, the relative importance of the supplier to the buyer, and the ability of the supplier/buyer to switch to alternative suppliers/buyers. The provision of customized and specialized products and services characterizes relational contracting and reduces the ability of the participants to substitute alternative suppliers and sources of supply or demand and encourages clear governance procedures between the participants (Gereffi, 1999). Both power imbalance and interdependence may be expected to contribute to the willingness of the supplier to adapt to buyer requirements.

The preceding analysis suggests that the supplier is least likely to acquiesce to buyer demands for supplier adaptation to ESCM in quadrant 1 where neither partner has the power to impose its requirements on the other. This quadrant corresponds to a competitive market and is characterized by large numbers of buyers and sellers, standardized products and/or commodities, and freely available price and product information. Typical industries include standardized electrical products and basic chemicals. Quadrant 2 (Supplier power) is characterized by supplier power and buyer dependency. Typical examples include state-owned organizations (SOEs) in China which continue to control significant sectors of the economy within protected markets. Under these conditions the buyer lacks the power to enforce adaptation to ESCM. Although buyer dependency reduces the risks inherent in supplier investments in adaptation, investments in ESCM in the supplier are likely to be restricted unless economic benefits can be generated. In quadrant 3 (Buyer power), the buyer has power over a dependent supplier and the supplier is therefore more likely to acquiesce to buyer demands for supplier adaptation. This situation is consistent with supplier compliance where the global firm has domination over suppliers (Frenkel, 2001). Under these conditions buyers may be able to ensure that suppliers adopt ESCM as a condition for recognition. Typical examples include elements of the sports goods and clothing industries where lead companies choose between a large numbers of competing suppliers located in developing countries. Quadrant 4 (Mutual dependence) is characterized by interdependence. This case most closely corresponds to the conditions under which relational or obligational contracting is likely to be found and is associated with the oligopsonistic characteristics which define buyer–supplier relationships in the automotive industry (Millington et al., 1998). These industries are characterized by small numbers of buyers and sellers and products or services which are specific to the customer. We might expect to see both supplier adaptation and a deeper relationship as both partners seek to protect their position within a more integrated organizational structure. Since relational or obligational contracting is associated with process development and higher levels of supplier monitoring, this provides the ideal circumstances in which to implement ESCM.

From the preceding discussion it is clear that ESCM may only be possible within a subset of relationships. While lead firms may wish to implement ESCM, their ability to do so is restricted by the relative power of buyers and sellers. This is consistent with recent evidence that suggests that the increasing salience of environmental issues is not reflected in the incidence of ESCM within the West or China (Zhu et al., 2005). It is interesting to note that while Florida (1996) suggests that 49% of buyers identify the role of suppliers in pollution control, almost 70% of buyers in a recent UK survey stated that they applied little or no pressure to their suppliers to reveal information concerning the management of their environmental impacts or to improve on particular impacts (Brammer and Millington, 2006).

ESCM and Environmental and Social Performance

While the motivation for ESCM forms the basis of a growing literature, the relationship between ESCM and the economic performance of lead companies or the social and environmental performance of suppliers remains largely unexplored (Rao and Holt, 2005). The environmental and social consequences of supply chain management may arise from ESCM processes or reflect the underlying processes and characteristics of supply chain management. Supply chain management is usually associated with the implementation of JIT processes which include lean production and total quality management. JIT is designed to reduce inventories (Millington *et al.*, 1998) and it has been suggested that both lean production and TQM reduce waste and pollution (King and Lennox, 2001), while the reductions in the number of suppliers increase production runs and enable suppliers to benefit from economies of scale and learning (Millington *et al.*, 1998). The implementation of these processes through the supply chain should therefore be expected to have beneficial effects on resource utilization and the environment. The implications of JIT for the environment are however ambiguous. The minimization of stock is underpinned by small and frequent deliveries from suppliers, which may act to increase congestion and pollution (Rothenberg *et al.*, 2001; Cusumano, 1994) and while the frequency of this transport pattern has been reduced in the car assembly industry through the implementation of the 'milk round', it remains prevalent in other industries. At the same time other authors have suggested that reductions in inventory at lead companies have been substituted by increased levels of inventory across the supply chain (Matthews *et al.*, 2002) as suppliers have insured against 'stock outs' and the imposition of penalty clauses (Millington *et al.*, 1998). Improvements in environmental and economic performance in lead companies may, therefore, reflect an increase in environmental and economic costs outside the lead company (Zhu *et al.*, 2005).

In practice many of the generic processes which are associated with supply chain management have been linked to ESCM (e.g. continuous improvement, TQM) (Florida, 1996) and used to underpin the argument for a relationship between ESCM and environmental performance. However, justification for a link between ESCM and performance must lie in the link between distinctive ESCM processes and performance rather than environmental and social gains which would have arisen under supply chain management and independent of ESCM. Zsidisin and Hendrick (1998) suggest that environmental supply chain management is associated with a range of processes which encompass the inclusion of environmental considerations in design specifications, environmental audits, and ISO 14001 certification.

Although Green *et al.* (1996) found no conclusive evidence of a relationship between organizational performance and the green supply chain, recent work by Rao (2004) suggests that lead firms believe that greening the supply chain has resulted in environmental benefits. This supports earlier evidence of a positive relationship between supplier relationships and environmental performance (Geffen and Rothenberg, 2000). Later work within a restricted sample of large MNCs with facilities in South East Asia and ISO 14001 accreditation found evidence of a positive relationship between green supply policies, competitiveness, and performance (Rao and Holt, 2005).Within the remit of ESCM great emphasis has been placed on the adoption of codes of conduct such as ISO 14001 and EMAC as minimum requirements for suppliers. However, recent work suggests that these systems may be viewed by buyer and supplier as a routine bureaucratic response to external pressure rather than a meaningful engagement with environmental impacts; with evidence that participating firms felt that environmental performance would not affect purchasing decisions (Brammer and Millington, 2006).

Within the context of social supply chain management the implementation of corporate codes of conduct is central to ESCM. Although the incidence and content of corporate codes of conduct forms the basis of an extensive literature (e.g. Nijhof *et al.*, 2003; Schlegelmilch and Houston, 1989; Murphy and Mathew, 2001; Kaptein, 2004; Carasco and Singh, 2003), relatively little work has been done on the application of such codes to suppliers or the compliance of suppliers with such codes after their adoption. Most of this work is based on case studies and focuses on a limited group of companies within the clothing (Graafland, 2002) and athletic footwear markets (Murphy and Mathew, 2001; Frenkel, 2001; Frenkel and Scott, 2002; Frenkel and Kim, 2004; O'Rourke and Brown, 1999). Within this restricted sample the studies provide evidence of increasing action by leading firms with highly visible brands developing and implementing codes of conduct in their suppliers (e.g. Frenkel, 2001; Frenkel and Scott, 2002; Frenkel and Kim, 2004). However, both the dispersion of appropriate labour practices through the supply chain and the level of supplier compliance with adopted codes of conduct may be questioned. Almost nothing is known about the incidence or application of corporate codes of conduct in suppliers to lead companies outside the clothing and footwear industries and even within these industries the analysis is largely restricted to brand leaders. Supplier compliance with the codes of conduct of lead companies has been questioned, with emerging evidence that suppliers falsify documentation in order to meet the requirements of lead firms and satisfy external monitoring (Graafland, 2002; O'Rourke, 2002). Such behavior is consistent with reports that 'efforts by the UN [ILO] and other international bodies, such as the World Bank, and even the governments of industrialized countries, have failed to make a noticeable progress in the face of resistance from countries which have an abysmal record of protecting workers' human rights, health and safety' (Sethi, 2006: 273).

Managerial Constraints on ESCM

The relative failure of ESCM initiatives may reflect managerial deficiencies within the purchasing function. The purchasing function rarely has a presence at board level and most purchasing managers occupy middle management positions. As such they implement senior management decisions rather than set them (Preuss, 2001). Recent evidence suggests that these goals are strongly related to the efficiency of supply relationships and their governance rather than the social or environmental responsibility of suppliers (Maignan *et al.*, 2002). The JIT culture within which they work is a high pressure environment in which managers must respond rapidly to changes in corporate supply requirements while managing supplier failures and their development (Drumwright, 1994); it can be described as both a reactive and a firefighting culture (Preuss, 2001). Although it can be questioned whether purchasing managers have the requisite skills to deal with the ethical aspects of ESCM, the JIT culture within which they work may therefore leave little room for the social and environmental aspects of supply chain management since the 'moral content of the discourse about environmental protection is largely filtered out and only amoral technical parameters are left for purchasing to react to' (Preuss, 2001: 356). Since small firms have been identified with relatively low levels of environmental innovation, due to resource and information constraints (Kempe and Soete, 1992; Hunt and Auster, 1990; Walley and Whitehead, 1994) and relatively low response rates to environmental supply chains pressure (Hill, 1997), shortages in mentoring skills and trained personnel in the lead company may have particular implications for the development of ESCM in small firms (Rao and Holt, 2005).

CONCLUSIONS

During the past decade outsourcing and globalization have resulted in the development of complex supply networks which are often led by large Western MNCs. These developments have resulted in the devolution of legal obligations for environmental and social impacts to suppliers who are often located in countries with weak or weakly enforced regulation (Sobszak, 2006) and has raised questions about the boundaries of CSR in the supply chain (Roberts, 2003). Supply chain management and the evolution of partnership or relational contracting between buyers and sellers have been seen as an opportunity to develop and diffuse environmental and social initiatives through ESCM; the implementation and monitoring of corporate codes of conduct and/or the requirement for institutional codes (e.g. 14001, EMAC) is argued to play a central role in this process.

Although national and international authorities have emphasized the role of supply chain management in the diffusion of environmentally and socially responsible behavior from lead companies to suppliers in domestic and international markets, national and international codes of conduct are largely voluntary (e.g. OECD Guidelines for Multinationals). The preceding discussion suggests that the voluntary nature of such policies has severe limitations. The implementation of ESCM imposes costs on the participating companies but the relationship between ESCM and financial performance in the supplier and the buyer remains unclear and may significantly reduce competitiveness in low cost industries, where significant concerns have been expressed about labor standards. Analysis of stakeholder demands for ESCM implies that the market for ethical products is relatively small and suggests that relatively few companies and sectors are targeted by NGOs or affected by consumer boycotts. The reputational risks of non-participation are therefore restricted to a relatively small group of companies who are close to consumers with strong brand images. Even within lead companies with a commitment to ESCM, their ability to implement and monitor appropriate policies will be constrained by power-dependency relationships between the partners and cultural and institutional constraints in developing and transitional economies. A significant proportion of components and services are sourced within markets rather than partnerships where the buyer has little power to implement ESCM; other buyer–supplier relationships are characterized by supplier power where buyers have little control. This emphasizes the limitations of ESCM as a mechanism for diffusing appropriate social and environmental behavior in suppliers and highlights the importance of appropriate national and international social and environmental regulation. Lead companies may play an important role in developing and diffusing good practice in developing and transitional economies but cannot act as a substitute for actively implemented environmental and social regulation.

Within those companies who do undertake ESCM, corporate and institutional codes of conduct are central to the development of environmental and social responsibility in suppliers. However, earlier evidence suggests that corporate codes are partial and substantially reflect a subset of issues which have high stakeholder salience. Although the implementation of codes of conduct which seek to control environmental and social issues through the supply chain may have beneficial effects for the environment and employees, the requirement for such codes may also have significant implications for supplier participation in the supply chain. Within the UK context the requirement for ISO 14001 certification and the significant fixed costs involved in this process has effectively excluded some small firms from participation (Brammer and Millington, 2006) while Humphrey and Schmitz (2001) emphasize the potentially damaging consequences of such initiatives for small firms in the third world. The evidence does not in any case support the widespread implementation of such codes through ESCM. Although ESCM forms the basis of some relatively high-profile case studies, there is little evidence to suggest that ESCM is widely embedded through the supply chain either in Western countries or more particularly in the developing world. Even in those cases where it is observed, for example the increasingly widespread adoption of standards such as ISO 14001, it appears to be primarily process driven, with limited engagement by supply managers and little evidence of implementation beyond tier 1 suppliers. To some extent this appears to reflect managerial practices within supply departments and the incentive structures within which these operate.

Although ESCM forms the basis of an emerging literature, much remains to be done. The existing literature is firmly located within the developed world and analysis of ESCM in developing and transitional markets is largely restricted to a limited range of case studies. The movement of services and manufacturing to developing and transitional economies and the substitution of markets and hierarchies by networks have highlighted the need for systematic cross-section analysis of ESCM in these markets. Such analysis should move beyond the socially sensitive industries which are at the forefront of consumer and NGO concerns (e.g. footwear and clothing, mineral extraction) and extend beyond tier 1 suppliers. Much of the existing literature is concerned with the content of codes and the ethical and moral justification for ESCM rather than the implementation of such processes in suppliers. The implementation of such processes in transitional and developing economies where training and expertise may not be present and such initiatives may be subject to substantial cultural and institutional barriers poses significant managerial problems. Greater emphasis needs to be placed on effective implementation of ESCM in developing and transitional economies and the managerial processes which underpin such developments in suppliers. The movement of production to the transitional economies has highlighted the need for research in countries where training and expertise may not be present and such initiatives may be subject to substantial cultural and institutional barriers. Finally most studies of ESCM focus on policy and practice in the lead company. Greater emphasis should be placed on supplier compliance with such policies, particularly in third world countries where compliance could be hindered by institutional and cultural differences.

REFERENCES

BOWEN, F. E., COUSINS, P. D., LAMMING, R. C., and FARUK, A. C. 2001. 'The Role of Supply Management Capabilities in Green Supply'. *Production and Operations Management*, 10: 174–89.

BRAMMER, S., and MILLINGTON, A. 2006. *Environmental Management: Strategy, Capacity, and Incentives in the United Kingdom*. Unpublished Report for Envirowise, CBOS, University of Bath.

Business in the Community. 2001. 'The Business Case'. <http://www.bitc.org.uk>.

CARASCO, E., and SINGH, J. 2003. 'The Content and Focus of the Codes of Ethics of the World's Largest Transnational Corporations'. *Business and Society Review*, 108: 71–94.

CARTER, C. R., and CARTER, J. R. 1998. 'Interorganizational Determinants of Environmental Purchasing: Initial Evidence from the Consumer Products Industry'. *Decision Sciences*, 29: 28–38.

CASCIARO, T., and PISKORSKI, M. J. 2004. 'Power Imbalance and Interorganizational Relations: Resource Dependence Theory Revisited'. Paper presented at the Academy of Management, New Orleans.

CAVANAGH, J. 1997. 'The Global Resistance to Sweat-Shops', in Andrew Ross (ed.), *No Sweat: Fashion, Free Trade and the Rights of Garment Workers*. New York: Verso, 39–50.

CHAN, A. 1998. 'Labor Standards and Human Rights: The Case of Chinese Workers under Market Socialism'. *Human Rights Quarterly*, 20: 886–904.

CHAN, R. Y. K., and LAU, L. B. Y. 2001. 'Explaining Green Purchasing Behavior: A Cross-Cultural Study on American and Chinese Consumers'. *Journal of International Consumer Marketing*, 14: 9–41.

COECK, P. 1993. 'The Integration of Environmental Considerations into Corporate Strategy'. *Competitiveness Review*, 3: 16–21.

COWE, R., and WILLIAMS, S. 2001. '*Who are the Ethical Consumers?* UK: Co-operative Bank.

CUSUMANO, M. A. 1994. 'The Limits of Lean'. *Sloan Management Review*, Summer: 27–32.

DENHAM, J. 1998. 'Speech to the UK Investment Forum (UKSIF) AGM in July 1998.

DOH, J. P. 2005. 'Offshore Outsourcing: Implications for International Business and Strategic Management Theory and Practice'. *Journal of Management Studies*, 42: 695–704.

DOLAN, C., and HUMPHREY, J. 2000. 'Governance and Trade in Fresh Vegetables the Impact of UK Supermarkets on the African Horticulture Industry'. *Journal of Development Studies*, 37: 147–76.

DRUMWRIGHT, M. E. 1994. 'Socially Responsible Organizational Buying: Environmental Concern as a Noneconomic Buying Criteria'. *Journal of Marketing*, 58: 1–19.

ELKINGTON, J. 1994. 'Towards the Sustainable Corporation: Win-Win-Win Business Strategies for Sustainable Development'. *California Management Review*, 36: 90–100.

EMERSON, R. 1962. 'Power-Dependence Relations'. *American Sociological Review*, 27: 31–41.

Environics. 1999. '*The Millennium Poll on Corporate Social Responsibility*'. Executive Briefing, Environics.

Ethical Consumerism Report. 2005. UK: Co-operative Bank.

European Commission. 2001. '*Promoting a European Framework for Corporate Social Responsibility*'. Luxembourg: Directorate-General for Employment and Social Affairs, CEC.

Financial Times. 2001. 'Greenpeace takes Carrot and Stick to Multinationals'. 17 Nov.

FLORIDA, R. 1996. 'Lean and Green: The Move to Environmentally Conscious Manufacturing', *California Management Review*, 39: 80–102.

FRAZIER, G., GILL, J., and KALE, S. 1989. 'Dealer Dependence Levels and Reciprocal Actions in a Channel of Distribution in a Developing Country'. *Journal of Marketing*, 53: 50–69.

FREEMAN, R. E. 1984. '*Strategic Management: A Stakeholder Approach*. Englewood. Cliffs, NJ: Prentice-Hall.

FRENKEL, S. J. 2001. 'Globalization, Athletic Footwear Chains and Employment Relations in China'. *Organization Studies*, 22: 531–62.

—— and KIM, S. 2004. 'Corporate Codes of Labour Practice and Employment Relations in Sports Shoe Contractor Factories in South Korea'. *Asia Pacific Journal of Human Resources*, 42: 6–31.

——and SCOTT, D. 2002. 'Compliance, Collaboration, and Codes of Labor Practice: The Adidas Connection'. *California Management Review*, 45: 29–49.

GEFFEN, C., and ROTHENBERG, S. 2000. 'Suppliers and Environmental Innovation: The Automotive Paint Process'. *Reference*, 20: 166–86.

GEREFFI, G. 1999. 'International Trade and Industrial Upgrading in the Apparel Commodity Chain'. *Journal of International Economics*, 48: 37–70.

GRAAFLAND, J. J. 2002. 'Sourcing Ethics in the Textile Sector: The Case of C&A'. *Business Ethics: A European Review*, 11: 282–94.

GREEN, K., MORTON, B., and NEW, S. 1996. 'Purchasing and Environmental Management: Interactions Policies and Opportunities'. *Business Strategy and the Environment*, 5: 188–97.

GRIEDER, W. 1997. '*One World, Ready or Not: The Manic Logic of Global Capitalism.* New York: Simon & Schuster.

HALL, J. 2000. 'Environmental Supply Chain Dynamics'. *Cleaner Production*, 8: 455–71.

HILL, K. 1997. 'Supply Chain Dynamics, Environmental Issues and Manufacturing Firms'. *Environment and Planning A*, 29: 1257–74.

HMSO. 1990. '*This Common Inheritance: White Paper on the Environment.* London.

——1999*a*. *A Better Quality of Life in the UK: A Strategy for Sustainable Development for the UK*. CM4345. London.

——1999*b*. *The Occupational Pension Scheme (Investment, and Assignment, Forfeiture, Bankruptcy etc) Amendment Regulations*. London.

——2001. '*Business and Society: Developing Corporate Social Responsibility in the UK.* London: Department of Trade and Industry.

HUMPHREY, J., and SCHMITZ, H. 2001. 'Governance in Global Supply Chains'. *IDS Bulletin*, 32: 19–29.

HUNT, C., and AUSTER, E. 1990. 'Proactive Environmental Management: Avoiding the Toxic Trap'. *Sloan Management Review*, winter: 69–75.

IMRIE, R., and MORRIS, J. 1992. 'A Review of Recent Changes in Buyer-Supplier Relations'. *International Journal of Management Science*, 20: 641–52.

International Labour Office. 1997. *The ILO, Standard Setting and Globalisation*. Report of the Director-General. Geneva: International Labour Office.

KAPTEIN, M. 2004. 'Business Codes of Multinational Firms: What Do They Say?' *Journal of Business Ethics*, 50: 13–31.

KEMPE, R., and SOETE, L. 1992. 'The Greening of Technological Progress, an Evolutionary Perspective'. *Futures*, 26: 1047–59.

KING, A. A., and LENNOX, M. J. 2001. 'Lean and Green? An Empirical Examination of the Relationship between Lean Production and Environmental Performance'. *Production and Operations Management*, 10: 244–56.

LAMBERT, J. 2007. <http://www.euractive.com/en/socialeurope/csr-corporate-social-responsibility/article-153315>.

LAMMING, R., and HAMPSON, J. 1996. 'The Environment as a Supply Chain Management Issue'. *British Journal of Management* 7: 45–62.

LIPPMANN. 1999. 'Supply Chain Environmental Management: Elements for Success'. *Corporate Environmental Strategy*, 6(2): 175–82.

MAIGNAN, I., HILLEBRAND, B., and MCALISTER, D. 2002. 'Managing Socially-Responsible Buying: How to Integrate Non-economic Criteria into the Purchasing Process'. *European Management Journal*, 20: 641–48.

MATTHEWS, M. E., HENDRICKSON, C., and LAVE, L. 2002. 'The Economic and Environmental Implications of Centralized Stock Keeping'. *Journal of Industrial Ecology*, 6: 71–83.

MILLINGTON, A. I., EBERHARDT, M., and WILKINSON, B. 2005. 'Supplier Performance and Selection in China'. *International Journal of Operations and Production Management*, 26: 185–201.

——MILLINGTON, C. E. S., and COWBURN, M. 1998. 'Local Assembly Units in the Motor Components Industry: A Case Study of Exhaust Manufacture'. *International Journal of Operations and Production Management*, 18: 180–94.

MURPHY, D., and BENDALL, J. 1997. *In the Company of Partners*. Cambridge Mass.: Harvard University Press.

——and MATHEW, D. 2001. *Nike and Global Labour Practices: A Case Study Prepared for the New Academy of Business Innovation Network for Socially Responsible Business*. Bristol: New Academy of Business.

NIJHOF, A., CLUDTS, S., FISSCHER, O., and LAAN, A. 2003. 'Measuring the Implementation of Codes of Conduct: An Assessment Method Based on a Process Approach of the Responsible Organization'. *Journal of Business Ethics*, 45: 65–78.

Organisation for Economic Co-Operation and Development. 2001. 'Codes of Corporate Conduct: Expanded Review of their Contents'. *Working Papers on International Investment*, No. 2001/6. Paris: OECD.

——2002. *Roundtable on Corporate Responsibility: Supply Chains and the OECD Guidelines for Multinational Enterprise*. Paris: OECD.

O'ROURKE, D. 2002. 'Monitoring the Monitors: A Critique of Third Party Labor Monitoring', in R. Jenkins, R. Pearson, and G. Seyfang (eds.), *Corporate Responsibility and Labour Rights: Codes of Conduct in the Global Economy*. London: Earthscan, 196–208.

——and BROWN, G. 1999. *Beginning to Just Do It: Current Workplace and Environmental Conditions at the Tae Kwang Vina Nike Shoe Factory in Vietnam*. Boston, Mass.: Massachusetts Institute of Technology.

PENG, M. W., TAN, J., and TONG, T. W. 2004. 'Ownership Types and Strategic Groups in an Emerging Economy'. *Journal of Management Studies*, 41: 1105–29.

PFEFFER, J., and SALANCIK, G. 1978. *The External Control of Organizations: A Resource-Dependence Perspective*. New York: Harper & Row.

PORTER, M. 1980. *Competitive Strategy*. New York: Free Press.

PREUSS, L. 2001. 'In Dirty Chains? Purchasing and Greener Manufacturing'. *Journal of Business Ethics*, 34: 345–59.

RAO, P. 2004. 'Greening Production: A South-East Asia Experience'. *International Journal of Operations and Production Management*, 24: 289–320.

——and HOLT, D. 2005. 'Do Green Supply Chains Lead to Competitiveness and Economic Performance?' *International Journal of Operations and Production Management*, 25: 898–916.

ROBERTS, S. 2003. 'Supply Chain Specific? Understanding the Patchy Success of Ethical Sourcing Initiatives'. *Journal of Business Ethics*, 44: 159–70.

ROTHENBERG, S., PIL, F. K. and MAXWELL, J. 2001. 'Lean, Green and the Quest for Superior Environmental Performance'. *Production and Operations Management*, 10: 228–43.

SAKO, M. 1992. *Prices, Quality and Trust: Inter-firm Relations in Britain and Japan*. Cambridge: Cambridge University Press.

SCHLEGELMILCH, B., and HOUSTON, J. 1989. 'Corporate Codes of Ethics in Large UK Companies: An Empirical Investigation of Use, Content and Attitudes'. *European Journal of Marketing*, 23: 7–24.

SCHMITZ, H., and KNORREGA, P. 2000. 'Learning from Global Buyers'. *Journal of Development Studies*, 37: 177–205.

SCHWEPKER, C., and CORNWELL, T. 1991. 'An Examination of Ecologically Concerned Consumers and their Intentions to Purchase Ecologically Packaged Products'. *Journal of Public Policy and Marketing*, 10: 77–101.

SETHI, S. P. 2006. 'A Search for Standards to Monitor Labour Conditions Worldwide'. *Business Ethics Quarterly*, 16: 271–87.

SOBCZAK, A. 2006. 'Are Codes of Conduct in Global Supply Chains Really Voluntary? From Soft Law Regulation of Labour Relations to Consumer Law'. *Business Ethics Quarterly*, 16: 167–84.

SPARKES, R. 2000. 'Social Responsible Investment Comes of Age'. *Professional Investor*, June. Reproduced by UKSIF, <www.uksif.org/publications/article-2000-06>.

STEGER, U. 1993. 'The Greening of the Board Room: How German Companies are Dealing with Environmental Issues', in K. Fischer and J. Schot (eds.), *Environmental Strategies for Industry*. Washington: Island Press.

THEYAL, G. 2001. 'Customer and Supplier Relations for Environmental Performance'. *Greener Management International*, 35: 61–9.

WALLEY, N., and WHITEHEAD, B. 1994. 'It's Not Easy being Green'. *Harvard Business Review*, May–June: 46–53.

WATTS, R. L., and ZIMMERMANN, J. L. 1978. 'Towards a Positive Theory of the Determination of Accounting Standards'. *The Accounting Review*, 53: 112–34.

WILLIAMS, H., MEDHURST, J., and DREW, K. 1993. 'Corporate Strategies for a Sustainable Future', in K. Fischer and J. Schot (eds.), *Environmental Strategies for Industry*. Washington: Island Press.

WOMACK, J. P., and JONES, D. T. 1996. *Lean Thinking*. New York: Simon & Schuster.

ZHU, Q., and SARKIS, J. 2004. 'Relationships between Operational Practices and Performance among Early Adopters of Green Supply Chain Management Practices in Chinese Manufacturing Enterprises'. *Journal of Operations Management*, 22: 265–89.

———— and GENG, Y. 2005. 'Green Supply Chain Management in China: Pressures, Practices and Performance'. *International Journal of Operations and Production Management*, 25: 449–68.

ZSIDISIN, G. A., and HENDRICK, T. E. 1998. 'Purchasing's Involvement in Environmental Issues: A Multi-country Perspective'. *Industrial Management and Data Systems*, 7: 313–20.

....

CHAPTER 17

CORPORATE SOCIAL RESPONSIBILITY

THE REPORTING AND ASSURANCE DIMENSION

....

DAVID L. OWEN

BRENDAN O'DWYER

INTRODUCTION

....

RECENT years have witnessed a remarkable growth in the number of companies in industrialized nations across the globe reporting publicly on various aspects of their social and environmental performance. Whilst for many this has simply entailed providing rudimentary, and generally qualitative, information on policies and performance within the annual financial report, an increasing number of 'leading edge' reporters have gone much further. For this latter group, predominantly, but not exclusively, large companies operating in 'sensitive' industrial sectors, the preferred means of dissemination has become the production on an annual basis of a substantial 'stand-alone' report, either paper and/or (increasingly) web-based, featuring copious quantitative, as well as qualitative, data. Additionally, the reliability of the data presented is increasingly likely to be attested to by an independent assurance provider.

KPMG's latest (2005) triennial international survey of corporate responsibility reporting practice on the part of the world's largest corporations, namely the top 250 of the Fortune 500 together with the top 100 companies in 16 leading industrialized countries, bears witness to this rising reporting trend.[1] For the former group, 52% issued separate reports in 2005, compared with 45% in the previous survey in 2002, whereas for the latter the respective figures are 33% and 23%. Whilst Japan (80%) and the United Kingdom (71%) are, by some margin, the leading reporting nations, most countries have experienced significant increases, with Italy, Spain, Canada, France, and South Africa leading the way. A further survey (Context, 2006) draws attention to another significant contrast in international reporting practice, in indicating that whereas 90 of the largest 100 European companies publish substantial information on their social and environmental impacts, only 59 of their US counterparts do so. Whereas this latter figure represents a significant improvement from the previous year, when less than half of the US companies reported, Context's analysis also points to the fact that there are still more reporters in Japan, Brazil, Australia, and the rest of the non-transatlantic world than in the United States. KPMG's survey also draws attention to clear sectoral differences in reporting volume. Perhaps not surprisingly, industries with a prominent environmental profile, notably utilities, mining, chemicals, oil and gas, and forestry, pulp, and paper, exhibit the highest reporting rates, although the most marked increase in reporting activity is in the financial sector, which has traditionally lagged behind the others.

The purpose of this chapter is to provide a brief overview of the development of corporate social and environmental reporting practice since it first began to achieve some degree of prominence on an international scale in the 1970s, before offering a critical evaluation of the state of current practice.[2] Our evaluation focuses particularly upon the contribution present day reporting, and associated assurance, initiatives make towards enhancing the transparency of corporate social and environmental impact, together with delivering enhanced levels of accountability to organizational stakeholders. A large part of the chapter draws on research in social and environmental accounting within the field of interdisciplinary accounting research. This research field has a 35-year history and has developed in parallel with certain streams of corporate social responsibility research in the management literature. For example, social and environmental accounting research embraces both normative concerns with fulfilling obligations and duties to the wider society

---

[1] It should be noted that reporting is overwhelmingly a large company phenomenon. Outside of the top 100 samples, amongst 'second tier' companies and small and medium-sized enterprises (SMEs) it is largely conspicuous by its absence.

[2] Due to the space constraints inherent in a short chapter such as this, our focus is predominantly placed upon developments in Europe and, to a somewhat lesser extent, the United States.

(embedded in Frederick's (1994) conception of corporate social responsibility (CSR1)) and pragmatic concerns aimed at enabling corporations to become more socially responsive (Frederick's (1994) corporate social responsiveness (CSR2)). A key aim of the work of many social and environmental accounting scholars is to fuse the conceptual emphasis of CSR1 with the operational focus of CSR2 in order to describe, theorize, and enable greater organizational accountability (see O'Dwyer, 2006).

The Development of Social and Environmental Reporting

Early Reporting Initiatives and Subsequent Decline

Social disclosure within the medium of corporate reports is far from being a recent phenomenon, and can indeed be traced back to the beginning of the twentieth century (see, for example, Guthrie and Parker, 1989). However, the issue first achieved real prominence in the 1970s, largely as a consequence of the debate then raging concerning the role of the corporation in society at a time of rising social expectations and emerging environmental awareness. More perceptive managements speedily grasped the public relations benefits of producing, at least rudimentary, social reports which attempted to convey a picture of corporate responsiveness to key societal concerns.

Reporting initiatives in Western Europe in the 1970s placed an overriding emphasis on the enterprise–employee relationship, reflecting a continuing debate at that time over the status of labor and its position within the enterprise. The most highly developed manifestation of such reporting appeared in France, where a legislative requirement to produce an annual *bilan social* was introduced in 1977. This particular document, mandatory initially for companies having more than 750 employees, and later extended to those employing more than 300, is exclusively concerned with employee matters and provides detailed quantitative information ranging across such issues as numbers employed and associated fringe benefits, health and safety conditions, education and training, and industrial relations.

A notable exception to the general reporting pattern observed in Europe in the 1970s is provided by the activities of a number of larger German companies, particularly those operating in the chemical and oil industries, whose published *socialbilanz* attempted to present the organization's performance as it affected the total societal environment. Particularly prominent amongst these companies was Deutsche Shell whose 'goal directed' reporting employed quantitative indicators to describe the attainment of a wide range of social objectives and attempted to integrate such data with traditional financial reporting. This approach to reporting social and environmental impact has interestingly, but probably largely unwittingly, been resurrected in the wave of more recent corporate environmental, and subsequently sustainability, reporting initiatives.

A similar more rounded approach to reporting practice is observable in the United States throughout the 1970s, as the annual monitoring by the accounting firm Ernst & Ernst of social and environmental disclosure within the annual financial reports of the Fortune 500 companies makes clear. The widespread prevalence of such practice is evident from the finding in the 1978 survey, the last one produced by Ernst & Ernst, that 89.2% of sample companies were making some form of social disclosures, with information on pollution control, energy conservation, and equal employment opportunity being particularly to the fore. Turning to voluntary disclosure practice outside the confines of the annual report, emphasis tended to be placed on community and consumer issues, together with some notable attempts to address environmental issues, as opposed to the employment focus of European reporting initiatives.

Throughout the 1970s, the United States indeed provided a fertile breeding ground for debate and experimentation concerning social and environmental reporting issues. In the former context, the link between social (and environmental) responsibility and accounting was thoroughly probed in influential reports emanating from both academic (see, e.g., American Accounting Association, 1973a, 1973b, 1975) and professional (see, e.g., American Institute of Certified Public Accountants, 1977) accounting bodies. In the latter context, particularly noteworthy were a number of ambitious attempts at developing reporting models, at both a theoretical (e.g. Linowes, 1972; Estes, 1976) and practical (e.g. Abt and Associates, 1972 ff.) level which sought to arrive at a (highly subjective) financially quantified 'bottom line' measure of corporate social and environmental performance.

Whereas business experimentation with social and environmental reporting in the 1970s was certainly innovative, particularly in the United States as indicated above, the prevailing climate of voluntarism generally produced reports that were largely public relations driven and sought to portray the organization in a favorable light. A notable exception to this general pattern was, however, provided by the activities of the UK-based independent research and lobbying organization Social Audit Ltd. Adopting an uncompromising stance of holding to public account the activities of powerful economic entities, Social Audit Ltd. conducted a number of critical exposes ('audits') of major commercial organizations, publishing the results in its journal *Social Audit Quarterly* (1973–6). In stark contrast to self-serving corporate reporting initiatives, these detailed, lengthy reports, typically ranging from upwards of 50 pages in length, were centrally informed by the ideals of transparency and accountability (Medawar, 1976). As such, they not only provide an ongoing fund of ideas for researchers (and indeed, reporters) today, but also offer a yardstick by which modern reporting practice may be judged.

The dawn of the 1980s heralded a sharp decline in voluntary corporate social and environmental reporting activity, apparently reflecting fading public interest as the 'New Right' policies of the Thatcher–Reagan era appeared to increasingly hold sway. Additionally, as Roberts (1990) notes, macroeconomic factors, notably rising unemployment consequent upon a slow-down in economic growth, were arguably instrumental in focusing attention on economic priorities and away from matters of corporate social performance. Admittedly, the employment dimension continued to figure in European reporting practice, notably in France where publication of a *bilan social* remained a legislative requirement. Additionally, in the United Kingdom employee consultation issues received fairly widespread, if somewhat cursory, attention, reflecting largely government-initiated moves to weaken trade union influence. Similarly, community issues began to figure in a rudimentary fashion in UK corporate reports as the private sector gradually took over responsibilities abdicated by central government for regional economic and social development.

In sum, as the 1980s progressed, social and environmental issues in general became increasingly peripheral as far as much corporate reporting practice was concerned. There was, however, the odd exception to this general rule. For example, the public accountability preoccupations of Social Audit Ltd. were carried forward by a number of UK Local Authorities which undertook plant closure social audits seeking to highlight the human and public financial cost of the run-down of much traditional manufacturing activity in the early to mid-1980s (see Harte and Owen, 1987). Perhaps of far more significance, in the light of subsequent developments, was the fact that environmental issues remained very much on the public policy agenda as far as the United States was concerned. This is most significantly exemplified by the passing of the Comprehensive Environmental Response Compensation and Liability Act (CERCLA), now better known as 'Superfund', in 1980. This particular piece of legislation was designed to identify and force 'responsible parties' to clean up land contaminated by industrial activity. The potential costs here are enormous and, amongst other things, raise significant accounting issues concerning the reporting of actual, and potential, environmental liabilities.

The Rise of Environmental Reporting

The Superfund legislation heralded the development of an approach to environmental reporting in the United States based on mandatory and financial disclosure. In the latter context, the Securities and Exchange Commission (SEC) has been particularly proactive in developing specific environmental pollution disclosures to be included in the annual report and accounts. In addition to providing guidance on the reporting of environmental liabilities in line with Superfund requirements, the SEC, through Regulation S-K, also requires 'appropriate disclosure ... as to the material effects that compliance with Federal, State and local [environmental] provisions...may have upon the capital expenditures, earnings and competitive position of the registrant and its subsidiaries'. In addition, disclosure is required of estimated current and future capital environmental expenditures, together with information on any significant legal proceedings on environmental matters. Further guidance on how to apply the SEC reporting requirements has been provided by the Financial Accounting Standards Board and the American Institute of Certified Public Accountants. The US focus on the mandatory disclosure route, in this case comprising non-financial disclosure, is further evidenced by the provisions of the Toxic Release Inventory (TRI), which requires businesses in 20 industrial categories to report annually releases and transfers of prescribed listed chemicals from each US facility to local communities and the general public. From its introduction in the late 1980s, the amount of information required to be collected for TRI reporting purposes, and industry sectors required to report, has been steadily expanded despite considerable business-led opposition (see Gerde and Logsdon, 2001).

Despite the strides made in mandatory environmental reporting, developments in both the quantity, and quality, of 'stand-alone' voluntary reporting initiatives by US companies have tended to lag behind those of their European counterparts. Traditionally leading the way here have been companies from Germany, the Netherlands, and Scandinavia, with UK companies coming very much to the forefront in recent times.

Corporate environmental reports first appeared on the scene in Europe in significant numbers in the early 1990s. This was probably largely as a response to the heightened critical scrutiny to which the corporate world was subjected following a number of prominent environmental catastrophes, such as Bhopal, the Sandoz Rhine spill, and Exxon Valdez, and the consequent rise in public awareness of the potential negative impacts of corporate economic activity on the overall quality of life. Whilst early reporting efforts, the 'green glossies', were generally sketchy documents, amounting to little more than crude public relations exercises, reporting quality rapidly increased. Indeed, despite the general lack of any definitive regulatory guidance for reporting at a corporate level, a coherent and comprehensive reporting framework soon emerged. One can now expect the typical stand-alone report to feature the following key elements: an organizational profile; evidence of board-level commitment; an environmental policy statement; disclosure of quantified targets; detailed performance and compliance data; a description of the environmental management systems in place; and site-level data for organizations operating from multiple sites. Additionally, in order to enhance the confidence of users in the reliability of the reported information, increasingly reports are accompanied by some form of externally prepared, independent assurance statement.

An alternative, more holistic, approach to the above target-setting approach is that of eco (or mass) balance reporting which is largely confined to Austrian,

German, and Swiss companies.[3] Whilst scoring highly on the completeness criterion, in their identification of physical quantities of inputs and energy use, outputs (products and waste), and emissions from the production process, these reports do pose distinct problems in terms of comprehension. A similar reservation can be made concerning the highly sophisticated approach adopted by the Dutch consulting and electrical engineering company, BSO Origin, in a series of annual reports appearing in the 1990s which aimed to financially quantify the organization's total environmental impact. This latter figure was then deducted from that of the company's financial value-added in order to arrive at a net measure of societal value-added. Some similarity to the 'bottom line' orientated reporting experiments from the United States in the 1970s that we referred to earlier is evident here, with, of course, similar inherent subjectivity problems encountered.

Underpinning corporate reporting initiatives has been a plethora of advice and published guidelines emanating from supranational bodies, such as the United Nations Environment Programme (UNEP), national governments, and business and industry associations. In the latter context, the work of the World Business Council for Sustainable Development has been particularly noteworthy, whilst on a specifically European level the European Chemical Industry Council's (CEFIC) Responsible Care Programme's reporting guidelines have achieved a high take-up level. Finally, the accounting profession has been heavily involved in promoting the cause of environmental reporting. Particularly notable has been the work of the Federation des Experts Comptables Européens (FEE), the umbrella organization for the European accountancy profession, in developing both guidelines for providing assurance on environmental reports together with a conceptual framework to underpin such reporting. Additionally, international accounting firms have been heavily involved in verification and consultancy work, whilst national professional bodies have actively promoted research in the area. Prominent amongst the latter has been the UK's Association of Chartered certified Accountants (ACCA), which, amongst many initiatives, launched an Environmental Reporting Awards scheme in 1991. The scheme has grown over the years to encompass the social and sustainability reporting dimensions in addition to the environmental one, and also gave rise to a European Awards Scheme (EERA) in 1996.

ACADEMIC DEBATE IN THE 1980S AND 1990S

The aforementioned rise in CSR in the 1980s and 1990s was accompanied by expanded academic debate and research on CSR in the interdisciplinary accounting

---

[3] An interesting exception here, which has received much attention in the literature, is the 1993 annual report of Danish Steel Works Ltd., which included six pages of 'Green Accounts', the centrepiece of which was a summarized mass balance statement (reproduced in Gray et al., 1996: 180–1).

literature. Some researchers, while skeptical of certain company disclosure practices, advocated forms of CSR involving specified content in stand-alone reports aimed at enhancing organizational accountability. Prominent among these were Gray, Owen, and Maunders (1987, 1988), who proposed a minimalistic compliance with standard (CWS) report to enable stakeholders to assess the extent to which organizations followed their legal responsibilities (see also, Gray et al., 1996; Owen, 1992). These authors, along with others, argued that greater and more robust levels of reporting had the potential, given a supportive regulatory environment, to enhance stakeholder accountability (see Bebbington, 1997; Boyce, 2000; Owen et al., 1997). For them, regulated CSR could develop the democratic functioning of information flows and serve to empower economically weaker stakeholder groups. This led to a series of debates in the literature about the change potential of CSR. CSR proponents were often accused of naïvety in their belief that CSR could lead to forms of organizational or societal change given extant structural realities and the extent of corporate power. Rather than challenging corporate power, the skeptics viewed CSR as potentially extending it by allowing corporations to present a picture of concern and openness while at the same time ignoring fundamental societal concerns (Puxty, 1986, 1991; Tinker et al., 1991). These arguments pervaded throughout much of the 1990s with CSR proponents forced to deliver robust defences of their position (Bebbington, 1997; Gray, 2002; Gray et al., 1996; Owen et al., 1997). Eco-feminist (Cooper, 1992) and deep green (Gray, 1992) perspectives on CSR also emerged and added to what was fast becoming an exciting arena of debate in interdisciplinary accounting about the actual and potential impacts of CSR.

Parallel to the above debates, scholars were also involved in exchanges about whether accountants and accounting academics should be involved in researching CSR-related issues at all. While scholars like Gray et al. (1996) felt that engaging in the development of accountable CSR offered the accounting discipline an opportunity to adopt a different perspective, and to assist in undoing some of the environmental damage caused by short-term policies aided by financial accounting which failed to value externalities (Parker, 2005), others subscribing to the tenets of traditional neo-classical economics summarily dismissed this notion (Benston, 1982, 1984).

A further significant academic development was the evolution, from about 1989 onwards (Guthrie and Parker, 1989), of various, often overlapping social and political theoretical perspectives aimed at interpreting the growing CSR practice. Scholars adapted variants of organizational legitimacy theory, political economy theory, and stakeholder theory to illustrate how emerging CSR had little to do with enhancing accountability (see Gray et al., 1995; Deegan, 2002). As the 1990s drew to a close, so-called legitimacy theory had gained prominence as an explanatory theory of CSR practice although many studies used it in a somewhat limited vein (for some exceptions to this, see Deegan, 2002).

Leading Edge Environmental Reporting Practice:
A Critical Appraisal

Whilst the above, of necessity exceedingly brief, analysis provides some flavour of the broad-ranging debate taking place in the academic literature throughout the 1980s and 1990s concerning CSR issues in general, in this section we narrow down the focus of attention in order to critically appraise the environmental reporting practices which, as we have already noted, emerged in the 1990s and indeed persist to date. This precedes our discussion (in the following section) of its evolution towards broader sustainability reporting in the early part of this decade.

The series of Judges' Reports emanating from the ACCA and EERA schemes in recent years have been most instructive in terms of drawing attention to environmental reporting weaknesses which persisted throughout the 1990s and beyond. One particular recurring theme has been that reporters too often do not make sufficiently clear their strategic priorities, and thereby fail to prioritize targets, with the result that a mass of over-aggregated data is produced which it is difficult for the reader to navigate his, or her, way through. Additional problems typically identified are that links to financial reporting are often unclear and explanations of performance variations lacking. Of course, it may be argued that reporting weaknesses such as these are only to be expected at this relatively early stage of 'stand-alone' environmental reporting and, judging by the experience of recent years, improvement can be confidently expected. However, certain problem areas appear to be somewhat more intractable.

One such problem area centers on a general lack of clarity as to the stakeholder groups the company is seeking to communicate with via the environmental reporting process, and, equally fundamentally, how such groups are able to use the information provided in order to hold management accountable for their actions. Crucially, there has been a discernible failure to prioritize particular stakeholder interests within the environmental reporting exercise and to direct reports more specifically towards the information requirements of the selected stakeholder group(s). Should, for example, shareholders be identified as the primary constituency for environmental reports, weaknesses identified above, such as a failure to identify strategic priorities and to clearly spell out the financial, 'bottom line', implications of the company's environmental management strategy, must be addressed. Indeed, serious reservations can be expressed as to the usefulness of a stand-alone environmental report for communicating with the shareholder, and financial analyst, group, whose primary focus is always likely to be on the annual financial report.

Significantly, even a casual reading of the overwhelming majority of corporate environmental reports produced suggests that shareholders are not the only, or indeed primary, stakeholder group of concern within the reporting exercise. On the contrary, an apparent desire is expressed, at least implicitly if not always sufficiently explicitly, to address a much wider audience. This observation gives rise to the identification of the most fundamental problem concerning the initial wave of environmental reporting exercises, namely a tendency to privilege the physical environmental dimension to the almost complete exclusion of the social one.

Companies engaging in environmental reporting invariably claim this to be part of a commitment to pursuing *sustainable* business practices in response to the agenda set out in the Brundtland Report (World Commission on Environment and Development, 1987). Omission of any consideration of the social ramifications of corporate performance must therefore be considered a fundamental weakness in view of the Report's stressing of the fact that the environment cannot be considered in isolation from human actions, ambitions, and needs, and that, '... links between poverty, inequality and environmental degradation formed a major theme in our analysis and recommendations' (p. xii). Additionally, of course, for stakeholders other than shareholders, their assessment of the sustainability, or otherwise, of business performance is highly likely to be informed by social as well as purely environmental concerns. Consideration of issues such as fair employment practice, observance of human rights, product safety and quality, and responsiveness to community needs can, for example, dramatically alter perceptions from those derived purely from looking at single (physical) dimensional environmental reports.

In addition to stakeholder information needs not being fully met in the environmental reporting process, corporate governance mechanisms have not evolved so that stakeholders can effectively use the information provided, or highlight information not provided, with a view to influencing corporate decision-making. In essence, stakeholders within the environmental process, unlike shareholders within the financial reporting process, appear largely disenfranchised, and therefore unable to hold management accountable in any meaningful sense. A new wave of corporate sustainability reporting which arose in the late 1990s, and appeared as largely an extension of earlier environmental reporting initiatives, seems, at least on the surface, to offer the potential to address both the problems of information deficiency and stakeholder exclusion. It is to a consideration of this new phenomenon that we now turn our attention.

The Move Towards Sustainability Reporting

Pioneering the move towards a more socially rounded reporting, somewhat reminiscent of the German *socialbilanz* of the 1970s, were a number of 'values-based' organizations espousing a wide set of social and ethical objectives rather than simply being concerned with seeking profits. Prominent amongst these were Traidcraft, the Co-operative Bank, and Body Shop in the UK and the Danish Sbn Bank

(Sparekassen Nordjylland), whose initial reporting forays in the early to mid-1990s were increasingly taken up by more mainstream companies by the end of that decade. At the forefront of this movement were companies such as the oil giants Shell and BP and privatized utilities, of which BT provides a particularly prominent example, which some years previously had been equally proactive in the early years of environmental reporting. A perusal of the latest three (1999, 2002, 2005) of KPMG's triennial surveys of international corporate responsibility reporting practice bears testimony to the growth of this phenomenon in that it may be noted that whereas in 2002 approximately one-third of their top 100 companies samples had incorporated social (and economic) issues into what had been previously a purely environmental report, by 2005 the proportion had grown to almost half. Indeed, amongst the G250 companies the trend is even more marked, with 68% of reporters producing a 'sustainability' report in 2005.

Intriguingly, the terminology applied to these reporting initiatives varies greatly, although 'corporate responsibility' appears to be displacing 'sustainability' and 'social and environmental' as the preferred report title. Nevertheless, the initiatives do have broadly two themes in common. First, some attempt is made to address the environmental, social, and (usually) economic dimension within the confines of one report, a process for which Elkington (1997) memorably coined the phrase 'triple bottom line reporting'. Second, a commitment is expressed to employ stakeholder engagement and dialogue procedures in order to inform the reporting process. This latter aspect is particularly prominent in the series of Reporting Guidelines (2000, 2002, 2006) issued by the Global Reporting Initiative (GRI), the most comprehensive in scope, and influential in terms of guiding reporting practice, of all the ever-growing number of standards and guidelines for sustainability reporting produced in recent years. For example, at the outset in discussing the issue of defining report content it is noted that: 'Identification of stakeholders and consideration of their needs is of central importance ... since the stakeholders who are expected to use the report will become the reference point for many decisions regarding the preparation of the report' (GRI, 2006: 6).

Originally convened by the Coalition for Environmentally Responsive Economies (CERES) in partnership with the United Nations Environment programme (UNEP), the GRI has evolved into a multi-stakeholder international initiative incorporating the active participation of corporations, NGOs, consultancies, trade unions, and accountancy bodies amongst other interest groups. Its overriding aim is unequivocally stated as being to enhance 'the quality, rigour and utility of sustainability reporting' (GRI, 2002, p. i), with such reporting entailing 'measuring, disclosing *and being accountable for* organisational performance towards the goal of sustainable development' (GRI, 2006: 4, emphasis added).

The Guidelines comprise a comprehensive set of reporting principles and structured report content incorporating performance indicators for the economic, environmental, and social performance dimensions. In the latest (2006) version of the guidelines, the reporting principles laid down are designed both to guide decisions for determining issues and associated performance indicators to be included in the report and to ensure quality and appropriate presentation of reported information. Significantly, the former set of principles displays a profound stakeholder orientation. For example, 'inclusivity' calls for the organization to 'identify its stakeholders and explain how it has responded to their needs'; 'relevance and materiality' requires coverage in the report of 'issues and indicators that would substantively influence the decisions of stakeholders' whilst 'completeness' entails providing information 'sufficient to enable stakeholders to assess ... economic, environmental and social performance in the reported period'. The principles laid down to secure information quality, for their part, comprise widely promulgated basic accounting concepts (e.g. comparability, accuracy, timeliness) but also lay stress on 'assurability' in that 'information and processes used in the preparation of a report should be recorded, compiled, analysed and disclosed in a way that could be subject to review and assurance'.

Following on from the elaboration of principles, the Guidelines go on to specify a recommended reporting format and report content, comprising both an outline of the approach adopted towards managing economic, environmental, and social performance issues together with related specific performance indicators. Whilst the environmental indicators, which are able to draw upon a considerable body of extant practice, are not surprisingly the most highly developed, the social indicators prescribed are by no means insignificant. This latter set of indicators addresses the key areas of labor practices and decent work, human rights, society (including community impact, anti-competitive behavior and corruption), and product responsibility. Taken together, the social indicators prescribed present a most demanding agenda for companies to follow, particularly in the latest (2006) version of the Guidelines which calls for a greater degree of quantitative disclosure than its predecessors, which were rather more confined to qualitative issues such as policy and associated programs description.

KPMG's (2005) survey of corporate responsibility reporting practice suggests that the GRI Guidelines are having a considerable practical impact, with 40% of reporting companies referring to them as a tool used in deciding report content. How far the essential spirit of the Guidelines is being endorsed, however, is open to question in that only 21% claimed to systematically undertake stakeholder engagement in order to identify information needs, whilst a mere 11% went on to give actual details of engagement processes. Unfortunately, as Erusalimsky, Gray, and Spence (2006) point out, there is a dearth of systematic studies collating detailed data from stand-alone reports, so that it is impossible to arrive at an overall global picture of how many, and which particular, GRI indicators are finding favor with reporting organizations. Early work by Larrinaga-Gonzalez (2001), focusing on reports produced by 14 US, Canadian, and European multinationals pilot-testing the first draft version of the Guidelines, indicated, not surprisingly, that most space was devoted to environmental issues (about double that for social issues) whilst least attention was paid to the economic dimension. Reports from the panel of judges for the ACCA UK sustainability reporting awards (2001, 2002) paint a similar picture. However, our own casual evidence, as members of the judging panels for the UK and European award schemes, suggests that the social dimension is steadily achieving greater prominence. Even here, though, not all aspects are receiving equal degrees of attention, with Erusalimsky *et al.* (2006) suggesting on the basis of their examination of a sub-sample (34 out of a total of 84) of reports submitted to the 2005 UK awards scheme that social disclosure is massively dominated by reporting on and about employees. Indeed, 'the space devoted to employees was more than that devoted to communities, customers and suppliers (the next three biggest stakeholder groups) combined' (p. 17).

In contrast to the absence of survey data offering detailed analysis of corporate sustainability reporting practices, there are a growing number of field-based studies which seek to illuminate the processes underpinning the reporting process and to elicit the views of management and stakeholder groups as to its purpose and usefulness. A further strand of research analyzes in detail the practices of individual reporting organizations. A common feature of both these types of study lies in their attempt to evaluate the success, or otherwise, of corporate sustainability reporting initiatives in making truly transparent their social and environmental impacts whilst also delivering enhanced levels of accountability to those affected by them.

Sustainability Reporting: Transparency and Accountability or Corporate 'Spin'?

Whereas the GRI Guidelines, as we have noted, view sustainability reporting as being essentially an exercise in stakeholder accountability, a notion to which many reporting organizations apparently subscribe (see Owen, 2005), it would nevertheless appear that economic considerations provide its main driving force. Indeed, from the outset, advocates of sustainability reporting have generally been keen to advance the 'business case' for its adoption. SustainAbility's (1999) *Social Reporting Report*, for example, draws particular attention to benefits in terms of identifying weaknesses in management control of high risk activities, and enhanced stability enabling the organization to militate against unexpected shocks. For their part Gonella, Pilling, and Zadek (1998) suggest that: 'A stakeholder-based company is one that in many respects is most fit to take advantage of the technological and regulatory changes that underpin and enable the globalisation of trade, production and marketing' (p. 15).

Perhaps not surprisingly, in the light of the fallout from Enron and similar embarrassing episodes, issues of reputation and risk management have come even more to the fore in recent times. For example, Business in the Community's (2003) 'business case' for reporting notes that it offers: '... a means by which companies can manage and influence the attitudes and perceptions of stakeholders, building their trust and enabling the benefits of positive relationships to deliver business advantage' (p. 3).

The question, of course, arises here as to whether reporting motivated primarily by a desire to reap reputational gains and manage stakeholder expectations can, at the same time, effectively discharge accountability to affected parties. This is a question that has increasingly exercised academic writers in recent years, who have in particular questioned the degree of influence that the stakeholder engagement initiatives apparently underpinning a number of 'leading edge' reporting exercises actually do have on the contents of the report itself, and, more fundamentally, corporate decision-making processes.

For Swift (2001), current stakeholder dialogue and engagement activity can only, at best, deliver a 'soft' form of accountability, as with no rights to information built into the process, power differentials between the organization and its stakeholders remain unaltered. Furthermore, there is a failure to recognize that stakeholder conflict, rather than harmony, permeates much economic activity and, as Jones (1999) argues, that such conflict is invariably resolved in favor of shareholders as a powerful combination of external financial hegemony and internal bureaucratic control conspire to prevent organizations from being socially responsible in anything but an instrumental sense. Empirical evidence in support of this contention is offered by O'Dwyer's (2003) interview-based examination of the perceptions of corporate social responsibility held by a group of 29 senior executives employed by Irish public limited companies. Significantly here, O'Dwyer is able to point to a process of 'managerial capture' taking place with, despite instances of individual resistance, managers exhibiting a clear tendency to interpret CSR concepts in a highly constricted fashion consistent with corporate goals of shareholder wealth maximization.

Later case study work by O'Dwyer (2005) examining the evolution of a social accounting process in an Irish overseas aid agency, the Agency for Personal Service Overseas (APSO), provides a graphic illustration of managerial capture of CSR concepts extending to the reporting process itself. Key factors drawn to attention in the analysis include the denying of a voice to key stakeholders (most notably local communities in developing countries); distrust of management, together with fear of the consequences of dissenting opinions being voiced, inhibiting dialogue; and an absence of board-level commitment to acting on stakeholder concerns evident in a resistance to including any critical comment in the published social report.

Further evidence of managerial control and manipulation of stakeholder dialogue processes is provided by the work of Thomson and Bebbington (2005) and Unerman and Bennett (2004). The former draw upon their own extensive interactions over many years with reporting organizations in arguing that a perceived 'one way' managerial communication process, and associated lack of responsiveness to stakeholder concerns, greatly limits the potential for the reporting process to lead to change in organizational priorities. In similar vein, Unerman and Bennett's analysis of Shell's internet-based stakeholder dialogue web forum ('Tell Shell') points to one fundamental flaw being that it is not possible to tell the extent, if any, to which views expressed on the forum by stakeholders have actually affected corporate decisions.

> ... internal decision making might be informed by stakeholder views expressed through the web forum [as Shell claims]. However, in the absence of transparency in decision making processes, the web forum might just be a public relations exercise aimed at enhancing Shell's competitive advantage by attempting to convince economically powerful stakeholders that Shell behaves in a morally 'desirable' manner by taking account of all stakeholder views'.

> (p. 703).

In contrast to the somewhat pessimistic picture painted by the above studies, Deegan and Bloomquist (2006) provide case study evidence of a non-financial stakeholder group having some influence on, in this case environmental, reporting practice. The case in question utilizes a wealth of interview-based material, drawing on the views of all concerned parties, in order to illustrate how intervention by the environmental non-governmental organization (NGO) WWWF-Australia led to revisions in both the Australian Minerals Industry Code for Environmental Management and, subsequently, reporting practices of individual companies. However, the authors go on to strike a cautious note when considering the question as to whether the change in reporting practice actually reflects any substantial change in business priorities. The possibility is raised here that fairly modest changes within a 'business as usual' framework took place, whilst the support of a 'moderate' NGO together with the reporting changes introduced were useful legitimizing devices in deflecting the concerns of more critical stakeholder groups.

The question of which stakeholder groups take part in engagement exercises, and more particularly which are excluded (or exclude themselves), is clearly of central relevance when considering the credibility of the whole reporting process. Moerman and Van Der Laan (2005), for example, in a highly critical commentary on British American Tobacco's social reporting practices, point to the patchy nature of the stakeholder engagement process employed, in terms of both geographical scope, with the process being dominated by Western industrialized nations, and interests represented. In the latter context, one significant view omitted was that of health groups who turned down the company's invitation to participate. This led, in Moerman and Van Der Laan's view, to a selective report being produced, which whilst addressing some contentious issues, such as under-age smoking, ignored others, notably the harmful effects of the product itself.

Research undertaken by the New Economics Foundation (NEF, 2000) and Adams (2004) provides further evidence of the partial nature of (some) corporate social and sustainability reporting practice. The NEF study, in a particularly hard-hitting polemic, suggests that reporting has been captured by company marketing departments, with the result that: 'There are huge discrepancies between what some of the leading reporting companies say vs. what they actually do. Some are guilty of excluding relevant information, while others could be accused of outright corporate lies' (p. 2).

In support of this contention, the study contrasts statements appearing in the social reports of half a dozen major multinational companies seemingly signaling a corporate commitment to particular social objectives with evidence gleaned from external, independent sources which fundamentally questions the sincerity of the corporate views expressed. Adams, for her part, undertakes a particularly rigorous piece of empirical work which contrasts disclosures made by a large (un-named) chemical company with an alternative information set drawn from a wide range of media sources including databases, reference books, and internet sites. The discrepancies between the two versions of performance offered lead Adams to question the completeness of the company's report of its performance, which appears notably one-sided in skirting around a number of key concerns raised by external parties, whilst also exhibiting a clear tendency to avoid coverage of negative social and environmental impact. For Adams, this 'reporting-performance portrayal gap' is of such significance that it calls into question the transparency and accountability credentials of the company's whole reporting initiative.

For a number of commentators the lack of completeness of much corporate reporting practice is an inevitable result of its concentration on the interests of powerful stakeholders to the exclusion of those of the economically weak. This, it is suggested, is itself indicative of a focus placed on issues of stakeholder management rather than stakeholder accountability (see, e.g., Unerman and Bennett, 2004; O'Dwyer, Unerman, and Bradley, 2005). A practical illustration of this process is provided by Rahaman, Lawrence, and Roper's (2004) study of the social and environmental reporting practices undertaken by the Volta River Authority in Ghana. Attention here is drawn to the overriding focus placed on physical environmental impacts in response to information demands emanating from the international agencies funding a large-scale public sector electricity generation project being undertaken by the Authority. By contrast, the less visible social and economic impacts on Ghanaian rural communities unable to afford the charges dictated by the required commercial return imposed on the project are ignored.

Despite concerns expressed in the literature over the deficiencies of stakeholder dialogue processes, and strong reservations expressed over how successfully corporate sustainability reporting practices meet the information needs of less

economically powerful stakeholders, there is a relative dearth of studies directly investigating the perceptions of the latter group towards current disclosure practice.[4]
Some recent research (O'Dwyer, Unerman, and Bradley, 2005; O'Dwyer, Unerman,
and Hession, 2005) begins to address this deficiency in employing interview and
questionnaire-based approaches to analyze the views of a number of prominent
Irish social and environmental NGOs regarding the adequacy and potential of
sustainability reporting practice to meet their information needs and help them
to hold corporations to account.

Significantly, respondents in both the above studies expressed severe reservations
over the credibility of current reporting practice, suggesting, in particular, that
companies too often failed to provide crucial information on adverse social and
environmental impacts. Therefore, in their view, the public's 'right to know' about
the effect of corporate activities on their lives is not being satisfied. Rather, the
overriding consensus was that disclosure is primarily motivated by corporate self-
interest and stakeholder management rather than a genuine desire to account to
less powerful stakeholders. The only way reporting deficiencies can be meaningfully addressed, respondents suggested, was via the introduction of mandatory,
standardized, and externally verifiable corporate sustainability reporting.

As far as the introduction of mandatory corporate sustainability reporting is
concerned, it must be said the prospects are somewhat bleak. Such regulatory
practices that have been established so far, in both the United States and Europe,
as we have noted tend to privilege the environmental domain, or merely oblige
companies to make brief disclosures and sometimes just at site level. Additionally,
within Europe a climate of voluntarism dominates matters of CSR policy in general
(see Commission of the European Communities, 2002). Indeed, a particularly stark
illustration of this was recently provided in the UK with the recent cavalier ditching
by Chancellor Gordon Brown of the mandatory requirement for quoted companies
to publish an Operating and Financial Review, which it was envisaged would feature
a fairly modest amount of social and environmental information, within the annual
reports and accounts. Quite instructive is the reasoning offered by Brown for this
decision in a speech to the Confederation of British Industry (28 Nov. 2005):

Best practice is, of course, for companies to report on social and environmental strategies
relevant to their business. But I understand the concerns about the extra administrative
cost...So we will abolish this requirement and reduce the burdens placed upon you—the
first of a series of regulatory requirements which by working together we can abolish in the
interests of the British economy.

However, as far as companies producing externally verified information are
concerned, via the inclusion of an independent assurance statement within

[4] Research into user perspectives on sustainability reporting has tended to focus on economically
powerful stakeholders, notably the investment community (see O'Dwyer, Unerman, and Hession,
2005).

sustainability reports, the prospects seem far less bleak. Indeed recent survey evidence (ACCA, 2004; KPMG, 2005) indicates that a growing number of companies
are already going down this route.

SUSTAINABILITY ASSURANCE PRACTICE: A CRITICAL OVERVIEW

ACCA and CorporateRegister.com's (ACCA, 2004) comprehensive study of sustainability reporting practices worldwide points to a particularly significant growth in
provision of external assurance statements within sustainability reports. Drawing
on the latter's comprehensive database of significant corporate non-financial reports, it is noted that in 2003 nearly 40% included such statements, compared with
only 17% ten years previously. Whilst KPMG's (2005) survey suggests a slower rate
of growth taking place in recent years, it would nevertheless appear that around a
third of reports from both the Global 250 and top 100 companies' samples carry
some form of external assurance. The latter survey also draws attention to similar
geographical and industrial sector differences in assurance provision as was the case
with sustainability reporting in general, which we outlined earlier. In the former
context, whereas European countries exhibit a significant increase, with over 50%
of the Italian and UK samples providing assurance statements, the practice is largely
conspicuous by its absence in the United States. Turning to sectoral differences in
assurance provision, utilities, financial services, and oil and gas lead the way, whilst
for other sectors such practice is very much a minority pursuit.

It would appear that the key driving force for companies seeking external assurance lies in an aim to enhance the credibility of their sustainability reports.
Indeed, according to the ACCA and CorporateRegister.com study it: '... represents
the next stage of development in sustainability reporting as approaches become
more developed and demands of report users more sophisticated. Organisations
which fail to obtain assurance for their reports are likely to face issues of credibility'
(ACCA, 2004: 15).

However, the extent to which the provision of assurance statements does succeed
in enhancing the credibility of reporting has been called into question by a number
of academic studies appearing over the past few years.

Early studies (Ball *et al.*, 2000; Kamp-Roelands, 2002) focusing on assurance
practice applied to environmental reports produced throughout the 1990s raised
fundamental concerns about its rigor and usefulness. Kamp-Roelands, for example,
highlighted major inconsistencies in terms of subject matter addressed, scope of the
exercise carried out, objectives, assurance criteria and procedures adopted, level

of assurance provided, and wording of opinions offered. Yet more fundamental questions were raised by Ball *et al.*, over the key issues of assuror independence and degree of thoroughness with which their work was carried out. Attention was particularly drawn to managerial control over the whole assurance process, together with emphasis being placed on management systems as opposed to performance-based issues. This, the researchers suggested, greatly limited the potential of the assurance process as a means of enhancing corporate transparency and accountability to stakeholder groups.

The question of whether similar weaknesses in assurance provision are apparent in the more recent wave of sustainability reporting practice has been addressed in work carried out by CPA Australia (2004) and O'Dwyer and Owen (2005, 2007). One development that may lead one to expect substantial improvements to have been made has been the issuing of sustainability assurance practice guidelines by influential bodies in recent years, most notably FEE (2002), the GRI (2002), and ISEA (1999, 2003, 2005).

The guidelines issued by FEE and the GRI have much in common, being based on a somewhat cautious 'accountancy' based approach, largely concerned with confirming the accuracy of published data. Emphasis here is placed on identifying the scope of work undertaken, in particular highlighting any limitations, and the respective responsibilities of reporter and assurance provider, whilst clearly stating the criteria underpinning the work and any assurance standards employed. This particular approach has been more recently re-inforced by the publication of the International Auditing and Assurance Standards Board's (IAASB) 'International Framework for Assurance Engagements' (IFAC, 2004). Applying to all assurance work other than that concerned with historical financial statements, the framework (ISAE 3000) provides detailed guidance in terms of procedures to be employed from initial acceptance of the engagement through to issuance of the final statement.

In general, engagements carried out under the above approach result in low levels of assurance being offered with very little attention being paid to specific stakeholder concerns. By contrast, in the ISEA series of AA1000 assurance standards an overriding obligation is placed on the organization 'to account for its actions to . . . stakeholders in the light of their interests' (ISEA, 2005: 11). For their part, assurance providers are required to address in their statement the key issues of *materiality* of performance information to stakeholders (i.e. whether sufficient information is supplied so as to enable stakeholders to make informed judgments); the ability of the organization to report in a *complete* fashion; and the *responsiveness* of the organization to stakeholder concerns. A further feature that distinguishes the AA1000 approach lies in its encouragement to assurance providers to adopt a strategic stance in offering evaluative comment on issues concerning the reporting organization's systems and processes, together with the highlighting of perceived strengths in both the reporting and performance domains.

Despite the introduction of authoritative guidance described above for carrying out sustainability assurance engagements, empirical research points to a continued ambiguity and variability inherent in current practice. The particularly comprehensive study from CPA Australia (2004) which draws on assurance statements from 170 Australian, UK, mainland European, and Japanese companies published between 2000 and 2003, pinpoints a number of problem areas. These include variability in title of statements; a tendency not to identify an addressee; a wide range of objectives for, and scope of, the assignment (with the latter typically prescribed by company management); variation in extent of description of the nature, timing, and extent of procedures employed; a reluctance to disclose reporting criteria against which the report is assured and assurance standards employed; and variability in the wording of any conclusions offered. Indeed, on the basis of the evidence they produce, the study's authors are able to conclude that report readers would '. . . often have great uncertainty in understanding how the assurance provider undertook the engagement, what they reviewed and what was the meaning of their conclusion' (p. 67).

O'Dwyer and Owen's (2005) smaller scale study of 41 assurance statements appearing in reports of 'leading edge' reports short-listed for the 2002 ACCA and European Sustainability Reporting Awards observes a similar variability in practice. In particular, distinct approaches adopted towards the exercise from the two main types of assurance provider, accountants and consultancy firms, are highlighted. The former tend to adopt a cautious approach aimed at providing low levels of assurance, focusing largely on the issue of consistency of information appearing in the organization's report with underlying data sets, and are often limited in scope. By contrast, the latter are to the fore in using AA1000, and thus appear to provide a higher level of assurance addressing performance issues and focused on aiding corporate strategic direction. This approach, whilst arguably 'adding value' to the assurance process, does, of course, risk compromising the assurance provider's independence from company management. Such a risk is all the greater in that O'Dwyer and Owen point to a large degree of management control pervading the whole assurance process, with assurance providers being appointed by management, who can place any restrictions they wish upon the exercise. Indeed, they further note that to the (very limited) extent statements are addressed to anyone, it is overwhelmingly to corporate management. Additionally, despite a discernible improvement in extent and rigor of the assurance process itself to that observed by Ball et al. (2000), stakeholder participation appears minimal and in the, relatively rare, instances of specific mention being made of issues of materiality, completeness, and responsiveness, these are generally not addressed from a stakeholder perspective.

The two studies considered above suggest that sustainability assurance practice is characterized by inconsistencies in approach, whilst also providing little in terms of promoting greater levels of stakeholder accountability. Some hope for improvement is offered by ongoing attempts to develop comprehensive assurance standards that combine the procedural and presentational rigor of ISAE 3000 with the emphasis on stakeholder responsiveness of AA1000 (see, eg., Iansen-Rogers and Oelschlaegel, 2005). Further prospects for a more avowedly stakeholder-orientated approach being adopted by accountant assurance providers are encouraged by FEE's (2004) appeal for assurance standard setters to adopt a more pro-active approach to stakeholder engagement. Significantly, this appeal appears to have been heeded by the Dutch accountants body Royal NIVRA in their draft Standard for Assurance Engagements Relating to Sustainability Reports (ED 3410) issued in December 2004 (see Owen, forthcoming). Additionally, O'Dwyer and Owen's (2007) study of assurance statements appearing in reports short-listed for the 2003 ACCA UK and European Sustainability Reporting Awards Scheme is able to discern the beginnings of a more holistic stakeholder-centered approach, with AA1000 being increasingly used as a reference point. However, a note of caution is sounded here in that a continued lack of stakeholder involvement in the actual assurance process was observed, together with a paucity of evaluations of responsiveness to stakeholder concerns and continued reluctance to address statements to stakeholders.

The need for caution is re-enforced when one considers that, despite the apparent emerging consensus on the need to at least consider the interests of stakeholders in the reporting process, we are still a long way from reaching a position where true stakeholder accountability can be considered to have been meaningfully established. Management continues to control the assurance process, and indeed the whole exercise is largely sold to them on the basis of its efficacy as a driver of improved financial performance (see Zadek *et al.*, 2004). As Adams and Evans (2004) point out, enhancing stakeholder accountability entails transferring some degree of power over the process from management to stakeholders. Suggestions they offer include enabling stakeholders to appoint assurance providers and to determine the scope of the exercise. However, scope is still likely to be restricted in view of management's apparent reluctance to commit significant funding, with Park and Brorson's (2005) study indicating that fee levels for sustainability assurance work are a small fraction (typically 4–6%) of those for the financial audit.[5] Furthermore, even if, in the unlikely event, cost constraints were to be overcome, the fundamental problem remains that, in the context of the majority of prevailing corporate government structures, it is mightily difficult to envisage how stakeholders could use the assurance findings an a way that might influence corporate decision-making.

---

[5] A recent significant development in this context has been Shell's dropping of its long-standing external assurance provision in its 2005 Sustainability Report in favor of the far cheaper option of a 'commentary' from a five-person review committee made up of sustainability 'experts'.

CONCLUSION

We began this chapter by charting the emergence of social and environmental reporting practice in the 1970s, and subsequently noted its relative decline in the 1980s and re-birth, initially in the guise of environmental reporting, from the early 1990s onwards. The latest stage in the development process has witnessed the re-introduction of a social (and economic) dimension with the advent of sustainability reporting. Current trends strongly suggest that sustainability reporting will continue to displace more narrowly conceived environmental reporting and is also highly unlikely to wither as readily as did its 1970s predecessor. However, reporting, and associated assurance practice, is likely to remain predominantly confined to large companies operating in 'sensitive' industrial sectors.

A key factor in the growth of sustainability reporting practice appears to lie in an acceptance on the part of reporters that there is a strong 'business case' for its adoption. Certainly, there appears little prospect in the current economic and political climate for large-scale mandatory imposition of reporting requirements. The question inevitably arises here as to whether a predominantly voluntary reporting regime, despite an avowed commitment to notions of stakeholder engagement and dialogue, can effectively discharge accountability. It was, of course, a desire to hold economically powerful organizations accountable to those affected by their actions that drove the activities of early social reporting and auditing pioneers such as Social Audit Ltd. Evidence from a growing body of academic work reviewed in this chapter certainly calls into question the stakeholder accountability credentials of much current reporting practice, and indeed its completeness in painting a true 'warts and all' picture of corporate sustainability performance. Additionally, as we have seen, the success of assurance practice in lending much-needed credibility to reporting initiatives is itself highly questionable.

The key problem area that arises in terms of developing higher levels of corporate accountability for sustainability performance lies in the fact, which we alluded to in the previous section of this chapter, that no institutional forum is provided by which any meaningful form of stakeholder power may be utilized. The essential point here is that administrative reform, in the shape of new reporting systems, in isolation can do little to achieve real social change. Rather, it must be accompanied by institutional reform designed to empower shareholders by instituting more participatory forms of corporate governance (Owen *et al.*, 1997). In the absence of this happening, we are simply left with a corporate-led dialogue, or indeed monologue, agenda prevailing. In such a situation, whilst sustainability reporting and assurance practice may well represent a useful corporate reputation-building vehicle, although one that runs a real risk of falling into increased disrepute, it does little to demonstrate true transparency and accountability for corporate actions.

REFERENCES

ABT, C. C. and ASSOCIATES. 1972 ff. *Annual Report and Social Audit*. Cambridge, Mass.: Abt and Associates.

ADAMS, C. A. 2004. 'The Ethical, Social and Environmental Reporting-Performance Portrayal Gap'. *Accounting, Auditing and Accountability Journal*, 15(2): 223–50.

——and EVANS, R. 2004. 'Accountability, Completeness, Credibility and the Audit Expectations Gap'. *Journal of Corporate Citizenship*, (14): 97–115.

American Accounting Association. 1973a. 'Report of the Committee on Environmental Effects of Organisational Behaviour'. *Accounting Review Supplement*: 72–119.

——1973b. 'Report of the Committee on Human Resource Accounting'. *Accounting Review Supplement*: 169–85.

——1975. 'Report of the Committee on Social Costs'. *Accounting Review Supplement*: 51–89.

American Institute of Certified Public Accountants (AICPA). 1977. *The Measurement of Corporate Social Performance*. New York: AICPA.

Association of Chartered Certified Accountants (ACCA). 2001, 2002. *ACCA UK Awards for Sustainability Reporting: Report of the Judges*. London: ACCA.

——and CorporateRegister.com. 2004. *Towards Transparency: Progress on Global Sustainability Reporting*. London: ACCA.

BALL, A., OWEN, D. L., and GRAY, R. H. 2000. 'External Transparency or Internal Capture? The Role of Third Party Statements in Adding Value to Corporate Environmental Reports'. *Business Strategy and the Environment*, 9(1): 1–23.

BEBBINGTON, J. 1997. 'Engagement, Education and Sustainability: A Review Essay on Environmental Accounting'. *Accounting, Auditing and Accountability Journal*, 10(3): 365–81.

BENSTON, G. J. 1982. 'Accounting and Corporate Accountability'. *Accounting, Organizations and Society*, 7(2): 87–105.

——1984. 'Rejoinder to "Accounting and Corporate Accountability: An Extended Comment"'. *Accounting, Organizations and Society*, 9(3–4): 417–19.

BOYCE, G. 2000. 'Public Discourse and Decision Making: Exploring Possibilities for Financial, Social and Environmental Accounting'. *Accounting, Auditing and Accountability Journal*, 13(1): 27–64.

Business in the Community (BITC). 2003. *Indicators that Count*. London: BITC.

Commission of the European Communities. 2002. *Corporate Social Responsibility: A Business Contribution to Sustainable Development*. Brussels: Commission of the European Communities.

Context. 2006. *Global Corporate Responsibility Trends*. London: Context.

COOPER, C. 1992. 'The Non and Nom of Accounting for (M)other Nature'. *Accounting Auditing and Accountability Journal*, 5(3): 16–39.

CPA Australia. 2004. *Triple Bottom Line: A Study of Assurance Statements Worldwide*. Melbourne: CPA Australia.

DEEGAN, C. 2002. 'Introduction: The Legitimising Effect of Social and Environmental Disclosures—A Theoretical Foundation'. *Accounting, Auditing and Accountability Journal*, 15(3): 282–311.

——and BLOMQUIST, C. 2006. 'Stakeholder Influence on Corporate Reporting: An Exploration of the Interaction between WWF-Australia and the Australian Minerals Industry'. *Accounting, Organizations and Society*, 31(4–5): 343–72.

ELKINGTON, J. 1997. *Cannibals with Forks: The Triple Bottom Line of 21st Century Business.* London: Capstone.

ERNST & ERNST. 1978. *Social Responsibility Disclosure.* Cleveland: Ernst & Ernst.

ERUSALIMSKY, A., GRAY, R., and SPENCE, C. 2006. 'Towards a More Systematic Study of Stand-Alone Corporate Social and Environmental Reporting: An Exploratory Pilot Study of UK Reporting'. *Social and Environmental Accounting Journal*, 26(1): 12–19.

ESTES, R. W. 1976. *Corporate Social Accounting.* New York: Wiley.

Federation des Experts Comptables Européens (FEE). 2002. *Providing Assurance on Sustainability Reports.* Brussels: FEE.

——2004. *FEE Call for Action: Assurance for Sustainability.* Brussels: FEE.

FREDERICK, W. C. 1994. 'From CSR1 to CSR2: The Maturing of Business and Society Thought'. *Business and Society*, 33(2): 150–64.

GERDE, V. W., and LOGSDON, J. M. 2001. 'Measuring Environmental Performance: Use of the Toxics Release Inventory (TRI) and other US Environmental Databases'. *Business Strategy and the Environment*, 10(5): 269–85.

Global Reporting Initiative (GRI). 2000, 2002, 2006. *Sustainability Reporting Guidelines.* Amsterdam: GRI.

GONELLA, C., PILLING, A., and ZADEK, S. 1998. *Making Values Count: Contemporary Experience in Social and Ethical Accounting.* London: ACCA.

GRAY, R. H. 1992. 'Accounting and Environmentalism: An Exploration of the Challenge of Gently Accounting for Accountability, Transparency and Sustainability'. *Accounting, Organizations and Society*, 17(5): 399–426.

——2002. 'The Social Accounting Project and *Accounting Organizations and Society*: Privileging Engagement, Imagination, New Accountings and Pragmatism over Critique?' *Accounting, Organizations and Society*, 27(7): 687–708.

——KOUHY, R., and LAVERS, S. 1995. 'Corporate Social and Environmental Reporting: A Review of the Literature and a Longitudinal Study of UK Disclosure'. *Accounting, Auditing and Accountability Journal*, 8(2): 47–77.

————ADAMS, C. A. 1996. *Accounting and Accountability: Changes and Challenges in Corporate Social and Environmental Reporting.* Harlow: Prentice-Hall.

——OWEN, D. L., and MAUNDERS, K. T. 1987. *Corporate Social Reporting: Accounting and Accountability.* Hemel Hempstead: Prentice-Hall.

————1988. 'Corporate Social Reporting: Emerging Trends in Accountability and the Social Contract'. *Accounting, Auditing and Accountability Journal*, 1(1): 6–20.

GUTHRIE, J., and PARKER, L. D. 1989. 'Corporate Social Reporting: A Rebuttal of Legitimacy Theory'. *Accounting and Business Research*, 19: 343–52.

HARTE, G., and OWEN, D. L. 1987. 'Fighting De-Industrialisation: The Role of Local Government Social Audits'. *Accounting, Organizations and Society*, 12(2): 123–41.

IANSEN-ROGERS, J., and OELSCHLAEGEL, J. 2005. *Assurance Standards Briefing: AA1000 Assurance Standard and ISAE 3000.* London: Institute of Social and Ethical Accountability and KPMG.

Institute of Social and Ethical Accountability (ISEA). 1999. *AA1000 framework: Standard, Guidelines and Professional Qualification.* London: ISEA.

——2003. *AA1000 Assurance Standard.* London: ISEA.

——2005. *AA1000SES, AA1000 Stakeholder Engagement Standard.* London: ISEA.

International Auditing and Assurance Standards Board (IAASB). 2004. *International Standard on Assurance Engagements 3000: Assurance Engagements on Other than Audits or Reviews of Historical Information*. New York: International Federation of Accountants (IFAC).

JONES, M. T. 1999. 'The Institutional Determinants of Social Responsibility'. *Journal of Business Ethics*, 20: 163–79.

KAMP-ROELANDS, N. 2002. Towards a Framework for Auditing Environmental Reports. Unpublished doctoral dissertation, Tilberg University, The Netherlands.

KPMG. 1999. *International Survey of Environmental Reporting*. Amsterdam: KPMG.

—— 2002. *International Survey of Corporate Sustainability Reporting*. Amsterdam: KPMG.

—— 2005. *International Survey of Corporate Responsibility Reporting*. Amsterdam: KPMG.

LARRINAGA-GONZALEZ, C. 2001. 'The GRI Sustainability Reporting Guidelines: A Review of Current Practice'. *Social and Environmental Accounting Journal*, 21(1): 1–4.

LINOWES, D. F. 1972. 'An Approach to Socio-economic Accounting'. *Conference Board Record*, November: 58–61.

MEDAWAR, C. 1976. 'The Social Audit—A Political View'. *Accounting, Organizations and Society*, 1(4): 389–94.

MOERMAN, L., and VAN DER LAAN, S. 2005. Social Reporting in the Tobacco Industry: All Smoke and Mirrors?' *Accounting, Auditing and Accountability Journal*, 18(3): 374–89.

New Economics Foundation (NEF). 2001. *Corporate Spin: The Troubled Teenage Years of Social Reporting*. London: NEF.

O'DWYER, B. 2003. 'Conceptions of Corporate Social Responsibility: The Nature of Managerial Capture'. *Accounting, Auditing and Accountability Journal*, 16(4): 523–57.

—— 2005. 'The Construction of a Social Account: A Case Study in an Overseas Aid Agency'. *Accounting, Organizations and Society*, 30(3): 279–96.

—— 2006. 'Theoretical and Practical Contributions of Social Accounting to Corporate Social Responsibility', in J. Allouche (ed.), *Corporate Social Responsibility: Concepts, Accountability and Reporting*. London: Macmillan.

—— and OWEN, D. L. 2005. 'Assurance Statement Practice in Environmental, Social and Sustainability Reporting: A Critical Evaluation'. *British Accounting Review*, 37(2): 205–29.

—— —— 2007. 'Seeking Stakeholder-Centric Sustainability Assurance: An Examination of Recent Sustainability Assurance Practice'. *Journal of Corporate Citizenship*.

—— UNERMAN, J., and BRADLEY, J. 2005. 'Perceptions on the Emergence and Future Development of Corporate Social Disclosure in Ireland: Engaging the Voices of Non-governmental Organizations'. *Accounting, Auditing and Accountability Journal*, 18(1): 14–43.

—— —— and HESSION, E. 2005. 'User Needs in Sustainability Reporting: Perspectives of Stakeholders in Ireland'. *European Accounting Review*, 14(4): 759–87.

OWEN, D. L. (ed.) 1992. *Green Reporting: Accountancy and the Challenge of the Nineties*. London: Chapman & Hall.

—— 2005. *Corporate Social Reporting and Stakeholder Accountability: The Missing Link*. ICCSR Research paper No. 32–2005, Nottingham University Business School.

—— 2007. 'Assurance Practice in Sustainability Reporting', in J. Unerman, B. O'Dwyer, and J. Bebbington (eds.), *Sustainability Accounting and Accountability*. Abingdon: Routledge.

—— GRAY, R. H., and BEBBINGTON, J. 1997. 'Green Accounting: Cosmetic Irrelevance or Radical Agenda for Change?' *Asia Pacific Journal of Accounting*, 4(2): 175–98.

PARK, J., and BRORSON, T. 2005. 'Experiences of and Views on Third-Party Assurance of Corporate Environmental and Sustainability Reports'. *Journal of Cleaner Production*, 13: 1095–106.

PARKER, L. D. 2005. 'Social and Environmental Accountability Research: A View from the Commentary Box'. *Accounting, Auditing and Accountability Journal*, 18(6): 842–60.

PUXTY, A. G. 1986. 'Social Accounting as Immanent Legitimation: A Critique of A Technicist Ideology'. *Advances in Public Interest Accounting*, 1: 95–111.

——1991. 'Social Accountability and Universal Pragmatics'. *Advances in Public Interest Accounting*, 4: 35–45.

RAHAMAN, A. S., LAWRENCE, S., and ROPER, J. 2004. 'Social and Environmental Reporting at the VRA: Institutional Legitimacy or Legitimation Crisis?' *Critical Perspectives on Accounting*, 15(1): 35–56.

ROBERTS, C. B. 1990. *International Trends in Social and Employee Reporting*. London: ACCA.

SustainAbility. 1999. *The Social Reporting Report*. London: SustainAbility.

SWIFT, T. A. 2001. 'Trust, Reputation and Corporate Accountability to Stakeholders'. *Business Ethics: A European Review*, 10: 16–26.

THOMSON, I., and BEBBINGTON, J. 2005. 'Social and Environmental Reporting in the UK: A Pedagogic Evaluation'. *Critical Perspectives on Accounting*, 16(5): 507–33.

TINKER, A. M., LEHMAN, C., and NEIMARK, M. 1991. 'Falling Down the Hole in the Middle of the Road: Political Quietism in Corporate Social Reporting'. *Accounting, Auditing and Accountability Journal*, 4(1): 28–54.

UNERMAN, J., and BENNETT, M. 2004. 'Increased Stakeholder Dialogue and the Internet: Towards Greater Accountability or Reinforcing Capitalist Hegemony?' *Accounting, Organizations and Society*, 29(7): 685–707.

World Commission on Environment and Development. 1987. *Our Common Future*. Oxford: Oxford University Press.

ZADEK, S., RAYNARD, P., FORSTATER, M., and OELSCHLAEGEL, J. 2004. *The Future of Sustainability Assurance*. London: ACCA.

PART VI

CORPORATE SOCIAL RESPONSIBILITY IN GLOBAL CONTEXT

....

GLOBALIZATION AND CORPORATE SOCIAL RESPONSIBILITY

....

ANDREAS GEORG SCHERER

GUIDO PALAZZO

GLOBALIZATION AND CORPORATE SOCIAL RESPONSIBILITY—ANYTHING NEW?

....

IN the present chapter we will focus on the problem of globalization and its consequences for theorizing on corporate social responsibility (CSR). The social responsibilities of business in a market society have been discussed for decades, long before globalization became a catchword (see, e.g., Baumhart, 1961; Bowen, 1953; Donham, 1927). The capitalist system, i.e. voluntary exchange on free and open markets, is widely considered the best societal coordination measure for contributing to individual freedom and the well-being of society (Friedman, 1962; Hayek, 1996). Though the functions of the state system have always been a matter of debate (see, e.g., Block, 1994), it is generally acknowledged that in capitalist societies it is the task of the state to establish the preconditions for the proper working of markets, i.e. to define legal rules such as property rights and contractual rights, to erect an enforcement body, to provide public goods, and to reduce or avoid the consequences of externalities. At the same time, private firms are entitled to own means of production and to run a business, i.e. to supply goods and services in return for private profits, as it is the 'invisible hand' of the market which directs the behavior of firm owners towards the common good. The state, it was assumed, is capable of setting the rules in such a way that the consequences of market exchange contribute to (or at least do not harm) the well-being of society.

Business firms have to obey the law—this has always been a precondition and has been accepted as a minimum social responsibility of businesses, even by the harshest critics of CSR (see, e.g., Friedman, 1970; Levitt, 1970). However, as the system of law and the enforcement apparatus of the state are incomplete there is a high possibility of regulation gaps and implementation deficits which have to be filled and balanced by diligent managers with pro-social behavior and an aspiration to the common good (e.g. Stone, 1975). In as much as the state apparatus does not work perfectly, there is a demand for business to be socially responsible, i.e. corporations are asked to comply with the law when the enforcement body is weak and even to go beyond what is required by law, when the legal system is imperfect or legal rules are incomplete.

With globalization, it seems, the negative consequences of businesses have intensified (see, e.g., Mokhiber and Weissman, 1999; Korten, 2001), as has the public call for corporate responsibility (Parker, 1998). Several scholarly journals have dedicated special issues to the relationship between globalization and CSR (see, e.g., *Business Ethics Quarterly*, 2004, 2006; *Journal of Business Ethics*, 2005). Paradoxically, today, business firms are not just considered the 'bad guys', causing environmental disasters, financial scandals, and social ills. They are at the same time considered the solution to global regulation and public goods problems (e.g. Margolis and Walsh, 2003; Matten and Crane, 2005) as in many instances state agencies are completely overtaxed or unwilling to administer citizenship rights or contribute to the public good.

We hold that the solution to globalization problems is not just a matter of the degree of engagement in CSR, i.e. of more or less investment by business firms in CSR projects (McWilliams and Siegel, 2001). Rather we suggest that with globalization a *paradigm shift* is necessary in the debate on CSR. Current discussions in CSR are based on the assumption that responsible firms operate within a more or less properly working political framework of rules and regulations which are defined by governmental authorities. With globalization, we suggest, this assumption does not hold any more. The global framework of rules is fragile and incomplete. Therefore, business firms have an additional political responsibility to contribute to the development and proper working of global governance.

This chapter will be organized as follows: First, we will explain the concept of globalization. We will describe its conceptual variants and point to some of the phenomena that are associated with this process. Next we will describe the traditional paradigm of CSR where the responsibilities of businesses are discussed vis-à-vis a more or less properly working nation-state system and a homogeneous moral (cultural) community. We will argue that both these assumptions become problematic in the current 'post-national constellation' (Habermas, 2001). We describe the new situation of regulatory gaps in global regulation (Braithwaite and Drahos, 2000), an erosion of national governance (loss of national sovereignty and the extraterritorial application of national law) (Kobrin, 2001; Strange, 1996), and a loss of moral and cultural homogeneity in the corporate environment. We discuss the consequences of the post-national constellation with the help of two recent observations of business firms' behavior which call for a fresh view of the concept of CSR. Finally, we describe the necessary paradigm shifts toward a new politically enlarged concept of CSR in a globalized world.

GLOBALIZATION: A SOCIAL AND ECONOMIC PHENOMENON

What is Globalization?

Globalization is one of the most cited catchwords of our time and is used to describe a process of social change at the macro level of societies. Today, many social and economic phenomena such as peace, crime, migration, production, employment, technological developments, environmental risks, distribution of income and welfare, and social cohesion and identity are considered to be affected by the process of globalization (see e.g. Brakman *et al.*, 2006; Cohen and Kennedy, 2000; Held *et al.*, 1999; Scholte, 2005). We define *globalization* as the process of intensification of cross-area and cross-border social relations between actors from very distant locations, and of growing transnational interdependence of economic and social activities (see, e.g., Beck, 2000; Giddens, 1990). Giddens (1990: 64) holds that with globalization 'the modes of connection between different social contexts or regions become networked across the earth's surface as a whole'.

During this process the nation-state loses much of its political steering capacity (e.g. Beck, 2000; Habermas, 2001; Strange, 1996). The state's enforcement power is bound to its territory while the subjects of state regulation, especially the business firms, have massively expanded their activities beyond national borders. At the same time, new social and environmental challenges emerge which are transnational in scope and cannot be regulated or governed unilaterally (e.g. global warming, crime and terrorism, diseases, etc). Also, new actors and institutions, such as international organizations, transnational corporations, non-governmental organizations, and civil society groups, gain political influence. Their activities are not limited to a certain territory. Their influence stems from the political power they can exert inside and outside the traditional institutions of nation-state politics, for example, by lobbying, public relations, campaigning, knowledge, and competence, offering material or symbolic support, or threatening with disinvestments or the retreat of resources. As a result we observe new forms of governance below, above, and beyond the nation-state (Beck, 2000; Zürn, 2002).

This definition of globalization emphasizes the process aspect of change and is related to other concepts that describe how the status quo develops vis-à-vis this change process ('globality'), and the normative claims that are related to this process. The concept of *'globalism'* is used to describe an *ideology*, i.e. a normative attitude towards the process of globalization. While globalization protesters and skeptics reject the idea that the globalization process will lead to more prosperity and social well-being in the world ('anti-globalism') (see, e.g., Klein, 2000), the adherents of globalism are convinced that an unconstrained and borderless world economy will make everybody better off (e.g. Irwin, 2002; Krauss, 1997; Norberg, 2003). They advocate a primacy of market imperatives over political regulation via the nation-state. The central idea of modernity—that nation-state politics shall define the legal, social, and ecological framework and the restrictions within which market transactions take place—is abandoned in favor of the dominance of economic rationality (see, critically, Beck, 2000; Giddens, 1990).

What are the Causes of Globalization?

One could suggest that the globalization process was to some extent started deliberately by political decisions. However, it was also caused and/or supported by technological, social, and economic developments. The intensified cross-border transfer of resources, such as assets, capital, and knowledge, is in part a result of the liberalization policy of many nation-state governments after World War II. The growing cross-area and cross-country social exchange was also made possible through technological inventions and achievements (e.g. telecommunications, mass media, the Internet, transportation, etc.). The exchange processes are accompanied by a growing interdependence between citizens from different communities through the emergence of global risks (e.g. nuclear weapons, global warming, global diseases, etc.) which connect the destinies of peoples with each other. In the following we will describe some dimensions of globalization.

Dimensions of Globalization

Political Decisions and Disruptions

The General Agreement on Tariffs and Trade (GATT) at the end of World War II was certainly an important factor in the liberalization of the world economy (see e.g. Hoekman and Kostecki, 1995). At the end of World War II in Bretton Woods politicians from over twenty countries decided on the postwar economic order. They shared the conviction that free and open trade would lead to worldwide prosperity and would in turn reduce the possibility of war and forceful conflicts. The GATT (and later the World Trade Organization (WTO)) member states decided to reduce tariffs and decrease non-tariff barriers to trade step by step. This process of liberalization in cross-country trade and investments was accompanied by a policy of liberalization and privatization in many of the industrial states in the Western world. Highly regulated industries with state-owned or controlled firms and monopolies such as telecommunications, public transport, electricity, and water were privatized. In the 1980s, the collapse of Communism in Eastern Europe, and in many other countries in the world, led to another breakdown of trade barriers and encouraged intensified cross-border trade and investments.

Technological Developments and Achievements

The rapid technological development in the communication industry led to a significant decline in communication costs. Perraton *et al.* (1998: 143) reported that the cost of a three minute phone call from New York to London dropped from US$ 244.65 in 1930 to US$ 3.32 in 1990 (measured in 1990 US$). Advances in telecommunications and in computer technology, along with the invention and growth of the Internet, have made it possible for people to communicate with each other from virtually all points on the earth. Along with the decrease in communication costs there has been a dramatic drop in transportation costs (Perraton *et al.*, 1998: 143).

Socio-cultural Developments

As a result of globalization, the more or less homogeneous cultures of the pre-globalization world were dissolved. New values and lifestyles have entered the static world of traditional cultures: values, attitudes, and social practices that were once taken for granted have lost their certainty. This process is accompanied by the various migration processes which lead to a pluralism of cultures and values and to a growing heterogeneity of social expectations.

At the same time we observe the emergence of new social movements, civil society groups, and NGOs which aggregate diverse and disparate opinions and concerns into shared interests and thus create new identities for people who lose the backing of their traditional home culture and their reliance on the capacity of official state agencies to resolve issues of public concern. These new social movements can gain political currency outside and beyond the traditional institutions of the state system (such as e.g. political parties, parliaments etc.).

Economic Developments

On the macro level, the liberalization of trade, investments, and financial transactions has led to a huge increase both in foreign direct investments and in cross-border trade (see e.g. Brakman, *et al.*, 2006; Held *et al.*, 1999). Though some authors suggest that with regard to certain macroeconomic measures the situation today is not much different than it was a hundred years ago (see e.g. Hirst and Thompson, 1996), we hold that we are confronted with a new situation without precedent in history. First, economic measures show that for several decades the growth rate in the volume of world merchandise exports has been much higher than the growth rate of world GDP and that intra-firm trade has expanded dramatically (Held *et al.*, 1999). Second, the unprecedented interconnectedness of the destiny of people from different social settings and distinct locations has created new challenges.

Also, at the firm level, one can observe an entirely new situation. Business firms are able to split up their value chain and to source where the production of goods and services is most efficient. By means of technology they are able to collect information about sources, qualities, and prices, and to coordinate the various value chain processes inside and outside the boundaries of the firm.

Today, large multinational corporations (MNCs) have become very powerful economic and social agents. The world's biggest corporations have revenues that equal or even exceed the gross domestic product of some developed states (Chandler and Mazlish, 2005). The power of MNCs is not just based on the enormous amount of resources they control. Their power is further enhanced by their mobility and their capacity to shift resources to locations where they can be used most profitably and to choose among suppliers, applying criteria of efficiency. In effect this gives multinational firms the latitude to choose locations and the legal systems under which they will operate (Roach, 2005; Scherer *et al.*, 2006).

However, the power of the MNCs and their leaders is not unlimited. Rather, top managers increasingly feel the pressure of global financial markets when they have to respond to the profitability demands of investors and protect their firms from hostile takeovers. Institutional investors direct their attention and money to profitable firms and investments. Corporations that do not earn a high enough profit are sanctioned with disinvestment. Managers who do not focus on a high stock price may become the targets of takeovers. All in all the global financial market pressures business firms to stress profit and to engage only in such projects as will lead to a satisfactory return. Altruistic managers with pro-social attitudes may therefore be suspect in the emerging shareholder society and may be forced to adapt their behavior to the expectations of profit-seeking investors.

The Emergence of Transnational Risks

The process of globalization is accompanied by the emergence of global risks (Beck, 1992, 1999): citizens from very different communities and countries realize that their destiny is bound together and depends on how economic and political actors in other countries behave, though they often have no influence over regulating or determining their behavior. Environmental disasters (Chernobyl, global warming, overfishing of oceans, loss of biodiversity, etc.), global diseases (bird flu, mad cow disease, etc.) and social problems (drugs, organized criminality, terrorism, etc.) do not halt at national borders but affect the lives of people, who become aware that their traditional nation-state institutions have become incapable of protecting them from harm.

Consequences and Challenges of Globalization: A New Phenomenon

What is new about the current globalization? It is a new phenomenon that our everyday life and activities expand over national borders, that new social networks with mutual dependences are created which lead to emerging new responsibilities. Community, work, and capital are losing their home and locus and we are confronted with different cultures and lifestyles, while society is pluralized and common traditions, cultural values, and social certainties emerge into a melting pot of various values and lifestyles. At the same time, we find ourselves in a world society without a world state and without a world government (Beck, 2000).

In this new situation the traditional division of labor between nation-state politics and private business may not be sufficient to guarantee the efficient and peaceful integration of society. We hold that with globalization business firms become political actors that have social responsibilities beyond their economic role, and mere compliance with the law and the rules of common decency is not the appropriate response to the new challenges. Next we will describe the traditional paradigm of CSR that was implicitly based on the separation of political and economic responsibilities. Following that we will describe the new 'post-national constellation' that calls for a new understanding of CSR.

THE TRADITIONAL PARADIGM OF CSR

In 1993, Shell was confronted with a massive but non-violent protest by the Ogoni People in Nigeria. Led by the writer Ken Saro Wiwa, the Ogoni protested against the fact that the money for the oil extracted from their land disappeared into the pockets of the corrupt Nigerian military junta while for them there was nothing left but a wasted and highly polluted territory. When Saro Wiwa was arrested as a rebellion leader, human rights groups urged Shell to use its influence on the Nigerian government to prevent them from executing him. At that time, Shell Group Chairman Herkströter argued that the corporation as an economic actor had no license to interfere with political processes and that Shell preferred to remain politically neutral (Livesey, 2001).

Whatever the scope of corporate responsibility in management theory and practice, it implicitly builds upon the neoclassical concept of a strict division of labor between political and economic actors and domains. As the Shell anecdote suggests, this neoclassical thinking is deeply embedded in managerial perceptions of societal responsibilities. The corporation as a private actor should focus on profit seeking and public problems should be dealt with by the state and its institutions (Friedman, 1962; Sundaram and Inkpen, 2004). While corporations act on markets, the state provides the stable contexts for these markets by making the required infrastructural investments.

Paradoxically, even in the scholarly debate on CSR, this neoclassical focus is salient. Large parts of the literature operate with an instrumentalist understanding of corporate responsibility, thereby reducing it to another success factor in the corporate pursuit of profits (see e.g. Jones, 1995). Whether CSR pays in the long run is a key question in the debate (e.g. Aupperle *et al.*, 1985; Berman *et al.*, 1999; Cochran and Wood, 1984; see, for a critical viewpoint, Margolis and Walsh, 2003; Scherer and Palazzo, 2007). While normative approaches to CSR criticize the economically narrow world perception of purely instrumental research and attempt to ethically embed questions of societal responsibility (e.g. Donaldson and Dunfee, 1999; Solomon, 1993), they often leave aside political aspects of the CSR issue and do not consider the underlying institutional political order of society and the concept of democracy (see, for a critical perspective Scherer and Palazzo, 2007). Being enmeshed in the tradition of neoclassical thinking, the theory and practice of CSR still builds upon the idea of an intact nation-state that provides a stable context for market activities. Corporations should follow the rules of the game as established by the political system and the moral customs of a given community (see, e.g., Carroll, 1979; Swanson, 1999; Whetten *et al.*, 2002, and even Friedman, 1970). Corporate legitimacy, understood as 'a generalized perception or assumption that the actions of an entity are desirable, proper or appropriate within some socially constructed system of norms, values, beliefs, and definitions' (Suchman, 1995: 574), therefore follows from corporate compliance with societal expectations. Such an institutional isomorphistic approach (DiMaggio and Powell, 1983) understands responsibility as a kind of adaptation process in which the organization reacts to external expectations (Palazzo and Scherer, 2006; Strand, 1983).

What is the concept of democratic institutions that forms the common starting point of many of the contemporary conceptions of societal responsibility? In the liberal model of democracy[1] (Elster, 1986), corporations are considered private and

[1] Note that we use the terminology of political philosophy. We use the word 'liberal' to refer to the historic liberal tradition in political philosophy and economics. This school of thought considers individual liberties as the main concern of social theory. This is different from the common-sense use of the word in the United States where liberal in political terms means 'left of center'.

thus non-political actors. Whenever they step into the political arena in order to participate in processes of political deliberation or political problem solving, it is/should be either to lobby for their profit interests (Hillman *et al.*, 2004) or as voluntary acts of discretionary philanthropy (Carroll, 1979) that serve, however, strategic corporate goals (Porter and Kramer, 2002). Without doubt, corporations then and now occasionally enter the political sphere and attempt to influence decision-making by official political institutions in favor of their interests. However, seen from a liberal point of view, this does not transform them into political actors who have to justify their behavior towards the citizens of their respective communities. As private actors in the market, corporations are freed from any immediate legitimacy demands and thus are not required to expose themselves to public scrutiny and justify their behavior as long as they comply with the law (Friedman, 1962). Only the state as a public and political actor is held accountable by the polity.

The role of the state in a liberal conception of democracy is to reduce interference in private interactions to a minimum in order to guarantee the (mainly economically understood) freedom of the citizens. The main task of the state is to guarantee the stability of the societal context in which private interaction takes place. The state system and the political actors in the administration and in parliament earn their legitimacy from (*a*) maximizing the freedom of the private actors by minimizing regulatory pressure and (*b*) by periodic elections that confirm or replace those who hold power (Elster, 1986). While elections can hold political actors directly accountable, the legitimacy of the economic actor, due to its private character, is conceptualized in a much more indirect way. The markets themselves are regarded as 'essentially democratic' (Barber, 2000: 286), because as Barber argues, 'private power, unencumbered by law, regulation or government, is the essence of freedom' (2000: 284). Thus, overloading the market with legal or moral prescriptions is considered a threat to democracy itself (Friedman, 1962; Baumol and Blackman, 1991). Via the invisible hand of the market, self-interested transactions increase the welfare of society as a whole (Friedman, 1962; Jensen, 2002). Therefore, corporations are automatically legitimized by the output they produce (see for a critical view, Peters, 2004) as long as they consider laws and moral customs as parameters restricting their essentially economic decisions.

Considering the legal and moral rules of nationally bound communities as the point of reference for corporate legitimacy becomes a challenge against the background of a globally expanded corporate playing field (Palazzo and Scherer, 2006). As Barber has argued, 'we have managed to globalize markets in goods, labor, currencies and information, without globalizing the civic and democratic institutions that have historically comprised the free market's indispensable context' (Barber, 2000: 275). On the global playing field, the societal environment that grants legitimacy to corporations consists of a multiplicity of legal and moral demands that confront corporations with contradictory expectations (Young, 2004). Outside the national box and given the rising level of societal complexity, it seems to be much more demanding to answer questions of responsibility (Kostova and Zaheer, 1999). Obviously, there are no globally enforceable legal standards or broadly accepted moral rules that might circumscribe the legitimate activities of multinational corporations (Huntington, 1998; Rawls, 1993). However, the debate on CSR has only begun to discuss the consequences of globalization (Matten and Crane, 2005; Rondinelli, 2002; Spar and La Mure, 2003).

Post-national Constellation

Liberal democracy has developed under a national constellation with a clear division of labor between civil society, government and business (Habermas, 2001). Solidarity, power, and money are their respective contributions to the stability and flourishing of democracy: through their interaction, citizens create shared values, traditions, and cultural identities (solidarity). By formulating and enforcing laws, government provides a framework of peaceful conflict resolution (power). By their market activities, corporations contribute to the well-being of society by providing goods and jobs and paying taxes (money). The interaction of individual actors and organizational actors on a national playing field is oriented to the limiting parameters of legal prescriptions and moral custom. On the global playing field the authority of both forms of regulation seems to erode. The transnationalization of political, economic, and cultural problems and activities does not only question the efficiency and legitimacy of the established division of labor between civil society, government, and business, it furthermore seems to change the dynamic between these three pillars of democratic stability. Therefore, Habermas (2001) has described the emerging 'postnational constellation' as a key challenge to democracy.

Globalization is weakening the power of (national) political authorities to regulate the activities of corporations that globally expand their operations. This erosion of the regulatory power of (national) hard law has two effects: it forces national governments into a race to the bottom; and it opens a regulatory vacuum for transnationally expanded corporate activities.

(a) Race to the bottom effect Corporate activities by global players take place in a transnational context inhabited by political authorities whose sovereignty remains limited nationally and who are losing their influence on corporate behavior (Waters, 1995; Beck, 2000; Monbiot, 2000; Habermas, 2001). Multinational corporations can split their operations and shift them to those regions that promise the optimum contribution to profit maximization. In search of cost advantages, they can for instance deliberately determine the places that minimize tax burdens as well as those that minimize the costs of producing goods. Since they are able to arbitrate

among alternative regulations (Ghemawat, 2003), they can decide to produce in a country with low wages and weak unions and pay taxes in offshore countries. As a result, national governments may be forced into a race to the bottom in order to win the competition to attract corporate investments against other countries (Roach, 2005; Scherer and Smid, 2000). In their search for cost advantages, multinational corporations thereby undermine the ability of the public authorities to set rules, regulate economic activities, and to enforce specific behaviors within their jurisdictions (Reinicke *et al.*, 2000; Beck, 2000; Kobrin, 2001).

(b) Regulatory vacuum effect While the sovereignty of political authorities remains nationally limited, some of the key problems of today's world are transnational problems: global warming, AIDS, corruption, deforestation, and human rights are issues that have a strong transnational dimension and/or impact. They cannot be solved unilaterally by national governments within their geographically limited sphere of influence. Multinational corporations are criticized for being a principal source of these problems. They are perceived as the driving forces behind global warming (Le Menestrel *et al.*, 2002), ecological problems in general (Shrivastava, 1995), corruption (Nesbit, 1998), poverty (Jenkins, 2005), human rights violations (Taylor, 2004), and cooperation with repressive regimes (Taylor, 2004).

However, beyond the nation-state, there are not yet sufficiently strong global governance institutions that could define and impose rules and mechanisms for coping with these challenges and penalize the deviant behavior of corporations. International law has been developed as a legal framework for the interactions of the nation-states themselves (Kingsbury, 2003). Its direct application to non-state actors such as corporations is not yet broadly acknowledged in legal studies (for a critical discussion, see Kinley and Tadaki, 2004). As a result, no specific regulations exist that could be used to hold corporations to account for human rights violations or the support of repressive regimes (Ranald, 2002; Taylor, 2004). International conventions such as the United Nations (UN) Convention on Human Rights and the International Labour Organization (ILO) Conventions on the Fundamental Rights of Workers might provide a model for universal standards for corporations, but they cannot be enforced on them.

However, in recent years, the US government and US courts have began to develop laws or apply existing laws beyond their own national borders, punishing even non-US companies for corruption via the Foreign Corrupt Practices Act (Avi-Yonah, 2003), for human rights violations via the Alien Tort Claim Act (Taylor, 2004), and for financial fraud via the Sarbanes–Oxley Act (Vagts, 2003). On the one hand this seems to diminish the space for deviant corporate behavior thus reducing the transnational legal vacuum. On the other hand, such a transnational application of US law weakens all other national governments (Kobrin, 2001).

Shared values can be regarded as a second source of orientation for corporate actors within a society. The more homogeneous these values are, the less often conflicts occur and the stronger the overlap of interpretations of what should be done in a given situation. However, the pluralization of modern society (understood as the threefold process of individualization, the devaluation of tradition, and the globalization of society) results in a loss of cultural homogeneity. Industrial society in the twentieth century was characterized by relative cultural homogeneity and individuals were caught in a network of stable expectations (Giddens, 1990; Beck *et al.*, 1995). In the transition from industrial to post-industrial society, choices instead of traditions began to dominate the process of defining and shaping identities (Giddens, 1990). Norms, values, and interests were pluralized, and the cultural background of Western societies became more heterogeneous. Globalization with its deconstruction of boundaries confronted individual actors with even more alternative ways of life, thus promoting the pluralization of national cultures even further.

While operating on a more or less homogeneous playing field, corporations can consider shared moral values and shared mental maps as taken for granted (Strand, 1983; Suchman, 1995). In a global and pluralistic context, the taken-for-grantedness of shared convictions is lost (Palazzo and Scherer, 2006). While being confronted by more and more ethical questions that arise within their business operations (e.g. child labor, fair wages, slave labor, deforestation), multinational corporations are expected to find convincing answers on their own (Scherer *et al.*, 2006; Scherer and Palazzo, 2007).

CORPORATE BEHAVIOR ON THE GLOBAL PLAYING FIELD

The above-described regulatory vacuum is abused by some multinationals who demonstrate unacceptable or unethical behavior in their global activities, especially in those areas where states are weak or almost non-existent (e.g. Mokhiber and Weissman, 1999; Korten, 2001). As we have argued, the ongoing process of globalization creates a comparable context of transition (national to global economy) with weak governance mechanisms. Some multinational corporations are criticized for abusing the regulatory vacuum. Corporations such as De Beers have for instance been accused of profiting from the legal vacuum in African civil wars (Roberts, 2003; Dunfee and Fort, 2003). Exxon Mobil has been accused of collaborating with the military forces of corrupt political regimes in Indonesia and elsewhere. Mass graves of Indonesians executed by the military forces of the regime were found on Exxon Mobil's property (Taylor, 2004). Child labor and slave labor have reappeared in the modern sweatshops of the supply chains of many multinational corporations. As a consequence, some multinational companies such as Wal Mart have been described as the symbol of 'what is wrong with twenty-first century capitalism' (Beaver, 2005: 159).

However, the questionable behavior of some multinational companies has evoked a response. The post-national constellation is propelling a new distribution of power between national governments, economic actors, and civil society (Mathews, 1997). The smaller influence of national governments on large corporations is—at least partly—balanced by the politicization of civil society. What has been labeled 'globalization from below' (Beck, 2000: 68) describes the growing power of civil society actors to influence decision-making processes in governments and corporations. 'NGOs' role and influence have exploded in the last half-decade' (Mathews, 1997: 53). With the Internet forcing an ever-growing transparency in corporate behavior, more and more of these civil society activities are directed against corporations (Dryzek, 1999: 44; Klein *et al.*, 2004) whose business practices are scrutinized suspiciously (Spar and La Mure, 2003) and who are confronted with growing demands (Walsh *et al.*, 2003) and changing conditions of legitimacy (Palazzo and Scherer, 2006).

Under the pressure of changing societal expectations, some global corporations have started to intensify their CSR engagement. Many corporate initiatives intrude into domains that have traditionally belonged to the sphere of political responsibilities of state actors (Walsh *et al.*, 2003). Corporations start human rights initiatives (Matten and Crane, 2005) such as the Business Leaders' Initiative on Human Rights of British Petroleum, ABB, and other companies. They engage in public health, addressing issues such as AIDS or malnutrition (Margolis and Walsh, 2003). Furthermore, they have begun to engage in initiatives of self-regulation in order to fill the vacuum of global governance described above (Scherer *et al.*, 2006). These activities go beyond the mainstream CSR discussion with its intact division of labor between state actors and economic actors (see, critically, Scherer and Palazzo, 2007). While the traditional understanding of CSR still builds upon the isomorphic approach that demands compliance with society's moral and legal standards, some corporations have started to set or redefine those standards, thereby assuming a politically enlarged responsibility (Scherer *et al.*, 2006).

Toward a New Paradigm of CSR for the Global Economy

Current theorizing in CSR is still dominated by an economic view of the firm and an instrumental view of CSR projects (e.g. Jones, 1995). The stakeholder management approach (e.g. Agle *et al.*, 1999; Frooman, 1999; Mitchell *et al.*, 1997),

as well as the widely accepted attempt to justify CSR with an empirical argument that social performance contributes to financial performance (e.g. Berman *et al.*, 1999; Aupperle *et al.*, 1985; see, for a critical discussion, Vogel, 2005), are common expressions of the underlying economic rationality in contemporary CSR research. Seen from this perspective, a 'business case' for CSR is made, i.e. the engagement of business firms in social responsibility is considered similar to an investment in any other product attributes, such as quality, service, or reputation, that contribute to the profit-making of the firm (McWilliams and Siegel, 2001). The behavior of the business firm is directed towards profit-making and this is justified as long as the firm complies with the rules of the game set by the state and defined by the morality of the circumscribing social community. It is assumed that it is finally the 'invisible hand' of the well-functioning and well-defined market that directs economic behavior towards the common good. However, as we have seen, in a globalized world the capacity of the state to regulate economic behavior and to set the conditions for market exchange is in decline. We observe failures by the state apparatus of all sorts (e.g. public goods in short supply, gaps in regulation, lack of enforcement, externalities of market exchange without provisions from the state, etc.). In addition, due to the individualization and pluralization of values in social communities, the moral standards for business behaviour get fuzzy and lose their restrictive power. Under these conditions, economic forces are set free without appropriate restrictions in legal or moral terms. As a consequence, the sole emphasis on economic rationality will not contribute to public welfare, but rather may worsen the situation. Therefore, we have to consider new forms of political regulation above and beyond the nation-state in order to re-establish the political order and circumscribe economic rationality by new means of democratic institutions and procedures (Habermas, 1996; Scherer and Palazzo, 2007). And, in fact, with the intensified engagement of social movements and the growing activities of international institutions a new form of transnational regulation is emerging: global governance, the definition and implementation of standards of behavior with global reach (Fung, 2003, Habermas, 2001). There are not only public actors such as national governments and international governmental institutions (e.g. the UN, ILO, OECD, etc.) that contribute to this new world order, but also private actors such as NGOs, civil society groups, and even business firms that play a key role (Scherer *et al.*, 2006). Corporations become politicized in two ways: they operate with an enlarged understanding of responsibility and help to solve political problems in cooperation with state actors and civil society actors. Furthermore, they submit their growing power and political engagement to democratic processes of control and legitimacy. The challenge of CSR in a globalizing world is to engage in a political deliberation process that aims at setting and resetting the standards of global business behavior. While stakeholder management deals with the idea of internalizing the demands, values, and interests of those actors that affect or are affected by corporate decision-making, we argue that political CSR can be understood as a movement of the corporation into environmental and social challenges such as human rights, global warming, or deforestation. The politicization of the corporation translates into stronger connections of the corporation with those ongoing public discourses on 'cosmopolitan' or 'higher-order' interests (Teegen *et al.*, 2004: 471) and a more intensive engagement with transnational processes of policy-making and the creation of global governance institutions such as the Forest Stewardship Council or the Marine Stewardship Council or the numerous human rights initiatives that are emerging. As we wanted to demonstrate, political solutions for societal challenges are no longer limited to the political system but have become embedded in decentralized processes that include non-state actors such as NGOs and corporations. This new phenomenon goes beyond the mainstream understanding of corporate responsibility. On the global playing field, corporations have to be understood as economic *and* political actors with the consequences for the conceptualization of CSR described above (Scherer and Palazzo, 2007).

REFERENCES

AGLE, B. R., MITCHELL, R. K., and SONNENFELD, J. A. 1999. 'Who Matters to CEOs? An Investigation of Stakeholder Attributes and Salience, Corporate Performance, and CEO Values'. *Academy of Management Journal*, 42: 507–25.

AUPPERLE, K. E., CARROLL, A. B., and HARTFIELD, J. D. 1985. 'An Empirical Examination of the Relationship between Corporate Social Responsibility and Profitability'. *Academy of Management Journal*, 28: 446–63.

AVI-YONAH, R. S. 2003. 'National Regulation of Multinational Enterprises: An Essay on Comity, Extraterritoriality, and Harmonization'. *Columbia Journal of Transnational Law*, 42: 5–34.

BARBER, B. 2000. 'Can Democracy Survive Globalization?' *Government and Opposition*, 3: 275–301.

BAUMHART, R. C. 1961. 'How Ethical are Businessmen?' *Harvard Business Review*, 39(4): 6–12, 16, 19, 156–76.

BAUMOL, W. J. with BLACKMAN, S. A. B. 1991. *Perfect Markets and Easy Virtue: Business Ethics and the Invisible Hand*. Cambridge, Mass.: Blackwell.

BEAVER, W. 2005. 'Battling Wal Mart: How Communities Can Respond'. *Business and Society Review*, 110(2): 159–69

BECK, U. 1992. *Risk Society: Towards a New Modernity*. London: Sage.

——— 1999. *World Risk Society*. Cambridge: Polity Press.

——— 2000. *What is Globalization?* Cambridge: Polity Press.

——— GIDDENS, A., and LASH, S. 1995. *Reflexive Modernization*. Stanford, Calif.: Stanford University Press.

BERMAN, S. L., WICKS, A. C., KOTHA, S., and JONES, T. M. 1999. 'Does Stakeholder Orientation Matter? The Relationship between Stakeholder Management Models and Firm Financial Performance'. *Academy of Management Journal*, 42: 488–506.

BLOCK, F. 1994. 'The Roles of the State in the Economy', in N. J. Smelser and R. Swedberg (eds.), *The Handbook of Economic Sociology*. Princeton: 691–710.

BOWEN, H. R. 1953. *Social Responsibilities of the Businessman*. New York: Harper & Row.

BRAITHWAITE, J., and DRAHOS, P. 2000. *Global Business Regulation*. Cambridge: Cambridge University Press.

BRAKMAN, S., GARRETSEN, H., VAN MARREWIJK, C., and VAN WITTELOOSTUIJN, A. 2006. *Nations and Firms in the Global Economy. An Introduction to International Economics and Business*. Cambridge: Cambridge University Press.

Business Ethics Quarterly, 2004. Special issue on 'Business Ethics in a Global Economy', guest eds.: M. Calkins and S. L. Berman. *Business Ethics Quarterly*, 14(4).

——— 2006. Special forum on 'Voluntary Codes of Conduct for Multinational Corporations', guest ed.: S. P. Sethi. *Business Ethics Quarterly*, 16(2).

CARROLL, A. B. 1979. 'A Three-Dimensional Conceptual Model of Corporate Performance'. *Academy of Management Review*, 4: 497–505.

CHANDLER, A. D., and MAZLISH, B. (eds.). 2005. *Leviathans: Multinational Corporations and the New Global History*. Cambridge: Cambridge University Press.

COCHRAN, P. L., and WOOD, R. A. 1984. 'Corporate Social Responsibility and Financial Performance'. *Academy of Management Journal*, 27: 42–56.

COHEN, R., and KENNEDY, P. 2000. *Global Sociology*. London: Macmillan Press.

DiMAGGIO, P. J., and POWELL, W. W. 1983. 'The Iron Cage Revisited: Institutional Isomorphism and Collective Rationality in Organizational Fields'. *American Sociological Review*, 48: 147–60.

DONALDSON, T., and DUNFEE, T. 1999. *Ties that Bind: A Social Contract Approach to Business Ethics*. Boston: Harvard Business School Press.

DONHAM, W. B. 1927. 'The Social Significance of Business'. *Harvard Business Review*, 4(4): 406–19.

DRYZEK, J. S. 1999. 'Transnational Democracy'. *Journal of Political Philosophy*, 7(1): 30–51.

DUNFEE, T. W., and FORT, T. L. 2003. 'Corporate Hypergoals, Sustainable Peace, and the Adapted Firm'. *Vanderbilt Journal of Transnational Law*, 36: 563–617.

ELSTER, J. 1986. 'The Market and the Forum: Three Varieties of Political Theory', in J. Elster and A. Hylland (eds.), *Foundations of Social Choice Theory*. Cambridge: Cambridge University Press, 103–32.

FRIEDMAN, M. 1962. *Capitalism and Freedom*. Chicago: University of Chicago Press.

——— 1970. 'The Social Responsibility of Business is to Increase its Profit'. *The New York Times Magazine*, 13 Sept. Reprint in T. Donaldson and P. H. Werhane (eds.), *Ethical Issues in Business: A Philosophical Approach*. Englewood Cliffs, NJ: Prentice Hall, 217–23.

FROOMAN, J. 1999. 'Stakeholder Influence Strategies'. *Academy of Management Review*, 24: 191–205.

FUNG, A. 2003. 'Deliberative Democracy and International Labor Standards'. *Governance*, 16: 51–71.

GHEMAWAT, P. 2003. 'The Forgotten Strategy'. *Harvard Business Review*, 81: 76–84.

GIDDENS, A. 1990. *Consequences of Modernity*. Cambridge: Polity Press.

HABERMAS, J. 1996. *Between Facts and Norms: Contributions to a Discourse Theory of Law and Democracy*. Cambridge, Mass.: MIT Press.

——— 2001. *The Postnational Constellation*. Cambridge, Mass.: MIT Press.

HAYEK, F. A. VON. 1996. *Individualism and Economic Order*. Chicago: Chicago University Press.

HELD, D., McGREW, A., GOLDBLATT, D., and PERRATON, J. 1999. *Global Transformations: Politics, Economics and Culture*. Stanford, Calif.: Stanford University Press.

HILLMAN, A. J., KEIM, G. D., and SCHULER, D. 2004. 'Corporate Political Activity: A Review and Research Agenda'. *Journal of Management*, 30: 837–57.

HIRST, P., and THOMPSON, G. 1996. *Globalization in Question*. London: Polity Press.

HOEKMAN, B., and KOSTECKI, M. 1995. *The Political Economy of the World Trading System: From GATT to WTO*. Oxford: Oxford University Press.

HUNTINGTON, S. P. 1998. *Clash of Civilizations and the Remaking of World Order*. New York: Simon & Schuster.

IRWIN, D. A. 2002. *Free Trade under Fire*. Princeton: Princeton University Press.

JENKINS, R. 2005. 'Globalization, Production and Poverty'. United Nations University. World Institute for Development Economics Research. Research Paper No. 2005/40.

JENSEN, M. C. 2002. 'Value Maximization, Stakeholder Theory, and the Corporate Objective Function'. *Business Ethics Quarterly*, 12: 235–56.

JONES, T. M. 1995. 'Instrumental Stakeholder Theory: A Synthesis of Ethics and Economics'. *Academy of Management Review*, 20: 404–37.

Journal of Business Ethics. 2005. Special issue on 'Voluntary Codes of Conduct for Multinational Corporations', guest ed.: S. P. Sethi. *Journal of Business Ethics*, 59(1–2).

KINGSBURY, B. 2003. 'The International Legal Order', in P. Cane and M. Tushnet (eds.), *The Oxford Handbook of Legal Studies*. Oxford: Oxford University Press, 271–97.

KINLEY, D., and TADAKI, J. 2004. 'From Talk to Walk: The Emergence of Human Rights Responsibilities for Corporations at International Law'. *Virginia Journal of International Law*, 44: 931–1022.

KLEIN, J. G., SMITH, N. C., and JOHN, A. 2004. 'Why we Boycott: Consumer Motivations for Boycott Participation'. *Journal of Marketing*, 68: 92–109.

KLEIN, N. 2000. *No Logo: No Choice, No Space, No Jobs*. New York: Picador.

KOBRIN, S. J. 2001. 'Sovereignity@bay: Globalization, Multinational Enterprise, and the International Political System', in A. M. Rugman and T. L. Brewer (eds.), *The Oxford Handbook of International Business*. New York: Oxford University Press, 181–205.

KORTEN, D. C. 2001. *When Corporations Rule the World*. San Francisco: Berret-Koehler.

KOSTOVA, T., and ZAHEER, S. 1999. Organizational Legitimacy under Conditions of Complexity: The Case of the Multinational Enterprise. *Academy of Management Review*, 24: 64–81.

KRAUSS, M. 1997. *How Nations Grow Rich*. New York: Oxford University Press.

LE MENESTREL, M., VAN DEN HOVE, S., and DE BETTIGNIES, H.-C. 2002. 'Processes and Consequences in Business Ethical Dilemmas: The Oil Industry and Climate Change'. *Journal of Business Ethics*, 41(3): 251–66.

LEVITT, T. 1970. 'The Dangers of Social Responsibility', in T. Meloan, S. Smith, and J. Wheatly (eds.), *Managerial Marketing Policies and Decisions*. Boston: Houghton Mifflin, 461–75.

LIVESEY, S. 2001. 'Eco Identity as Discursive Struggle: Royal Dutch/Shell, Brent Spar, and Nigeria'. *Journal of Business Communication*, 38(1): 58–91.

McWILLIAMS, A., and SIEGEL, D. 2001. 'Corporate Social Responsibility: A Theory of the Firm Perspective'. *Academy of Management Review*, 26: 117–27.

MARGOLIS, J. D., and WALSH, J. P. 2003. 'Misery Loves Companies: Rethinking Social Initiatives by Business'. *Administrative Science Quarterly*, 48: 268–305.

MATHEWS, J. T. 1997. 'Power Shift'. *Foreign Affairs*, Jan./Feb.: 50–66.

MATTEN, D., and CRANE, A. 2005. 'Corporate Citizenship: Towards an Extended Theoretical Conceptualization'. *Academy of Management Review*, 30: 166–79.

MITCHELL, R. K., AGLE, B. R., and WOOD, D. J. 1997. 'Toward a Theory of Stakeholder Identification and Salience: Defining the Principle of Who and What Really Counts'. *Academy of Management Review*, 22: 853–86.

MOKHIBER, R., and WEISSMAN, R. 1999. *Corporate Predators: The Hunt for Mega-Profits and the Attack on Democracy.* Monroe, Me: Common Courage Press.

MONBIOT, G. 2000. *Captive State: The Corporate Takeover of Britain.* New York: Macmillan.

NESBIT, J. B. 1998. 'Transnational Bribery of Foreign Officials: A New Threat for the Future of Democracy'. *Vanderbilt Journal of Transnational Law*, 31: 1273–1319.

NORBERG, J. 2003. *In Defence of Global Capitalism.* Washington: Cato Institute.

PALAZZO, G., and SCHERER, A. G. 2006. 'Corporate Legitimacy as Deliberation: A Communicative Framework'. *Journal of Business Ethics*, 66: 71–88.

PARKER, B. 1998. *Globalization and Business Practice: Managing Across Borders.* London: Sage.

PETERS, F. 2004. 'Choice, Consent, and the Legitimacy of Market Transactions'. *Economics and Philosophy*, 20: 1–18.

PERRATON, J., GOLDBLATT, D., HELD, D., and McGREW, A. 1998. 'Die Globalisierung der Wirtschaft', in U. Beck (ed.), *Politik der Globalisierung.* Frankfurt am. Main.: Suhrkamp, 134–68.

PORTER, M. E., and KRAMER, M. R. 2002. 'The Competitive Advantage of Corporate Philanthropy'. *Harvard Business Review*, Dec.: 57–68.

RANALD, P. 2002. 'Global Corporations and Human Rights: The Regulatory Debate in Australia'. *Corporate Environmental Strategy*, 9(3): 243–50.

RAWLS, J. 1993. *Political Liberalism.* New York: Columbia University Press.

REINICKE, W. H., and DENG, F., with WITTE, J. M., BENNER, T., WHITAKER, B., and GERSHMAN, J. 2000. *Critical Choices: The United Nations, Networks, and the Future of Global Governance.* Ottawa: International Development Research Centre.

ROACH, B. 2005. 'A Primer on Multinational Corporations', in Chandler, A. D., and Mazlish, B. (eds.), *Leviathans: Multinational Corporations and the New Global History.* Cambridge: Cambridge University Press, 19–44.

ROBERTS, J. 2003. *Glitter and Greed: The Secret World of the Diamond Cartel.* New York: Disinformation.

RONDINELLI, D. A. 2002. 'Transnational Corporations: International Citizens or New Sovereigns?' *Business and Society Review*, 107(4): 391–413.

SCHERER, A. G., and PALAZZO, G. 2007. 'Toward a Political Conception of Corporate Responsibility. Business and Society Seen from a Habermasian Perspective'. *Academy of Management Review*, 32: 1096–120.

——— and BAUMANN, D. 2006. 'Global Rules and Private Actors. Towards a New Role of the Transnational Corporation in Global Governance'. *Business Ethics Quarterly*, 16: 505–32.

——— and SMID, M. 2000. 'The Downward Spiral and the U.S. Model Principles: Why MNEs Should Take Responsibility for the Improvement of World-Wide Social and Environmental Conditions'. *Management International Review*, 40: 351–71.

SCHOLTE, J. A. 2005. *Globalization: A Critical Introduction*, 2nd edn. New York: Palgrave.

SHRIVASTAVA, P. 1995. 'The Role of Corporations in Achieving Ecological Sustainability'. *Academy of Management Review*, 20: 936–60.

SOLOMON, R. C. 1993. *Ethics and Excellence: Cooperation and Integrity in Business*. New York: Oxford University Press.

SPAR, D. L., and LA MURE, L. T. 2003. 'The Power of Activism: Assessing the Impact of NGOs on Global Business'. *California Management Review*, 45: 78–101.

STONE, C. D. 1975. *Where the Law Ends*. New York: Harper & Row.

STRAND, R. 1983. 'A Systems Paradigm of Organizational Adaptations to the Social Environment'. *Academy of Management Review*, 8: 90–6.

STRANGE, S. 1996. *The Retreat of the State: The Diffusion of Power in the World Economy*. Cambridge: Cambridge University Press.

SUCHMAN, M. C. 1995. 'Managing Legitimacy: Strategic and Institutional Approaches'. *Academy of Management Review*, 20: 571–610.

SUNDARAM, A. K., and INKPEN, A. C. 2004. 'The Corporate Objective Revisited'. *Organization Science*, 15: 350–63.

SWANSON, D. L. 1999. 'Toward an Integrative Theory of Business and Society: A Research Strategy for Corporate Social Performance'. *Academy of Management Review*, 24: 506–21.

TAYLOR, K. M. 2004. 'Thicker than Blood: Holding Exxon Mobil Liable for Human Rights Violations Committed Abroad'. *Syracuse Journal of International Law and Commerce*, 31(2): 274–97.

TEEGEN, H., DOH, J. P., and VACHANI, S. 2004. 'The Importance of Nongovernmental Organization (NGOs) in Global Governance and Value Creation: An International Business Research Agenda'. *Journal of International Business Studies*, 35(6): 463–83.

VAGTS, D. F. 2003. 'Extraterritoriality and the Corporate Governance Law'. *American Journal of International Law*, 97(2): 289–94.

VOGEL, D. J. 2005. 'Is There a Market for Virtue? The Business Case for Corporate Social Responsibility'. *California Management Review*, 47, summer: 19–45.

WALSH, J. P., WEBER, K., and MARGOLIS, J. D. 2003. 'Social Issues and Management: Our Lost Cause Found'. *Journal of Management*, 29: 859–81.

WATERS, M. 1995. *Globalization*. New York: Routledge.

WHETTEN, D. A., RANDS, G., and GODFREY, P. O. 2002. 'What are the Responsibilities of Business to Society?' in A. Pettigrew, H. Thomas, and R. Whittington (eds.), *Handbook of Strategy and Management*. London: Sage, 373–408.

YOUNG, I. M. 2004. 'Responsibility and Global Labor Justice'. *The Journal of Political Philosophy*, 12: 365–88.

ZÜRN, M. 2002. 'From Interdependence to Globalization'. in W. von Carlsnaes, T. Risse, and B. Simmons (eds.), *Handbook of International Relations*. London: Sage, 235–54.

....

CHAPTER 19

CORPORATE SOCIAL RESPONSIBILITY AND THEORIES OF GLOBAL GOVERNANCE

STRATEGIC CONTESTATION IN GLOBAL ISSUE ARENAS

....

DAVID L. LEVY

RAMI KAPLAN

INTRODUCTION: THE RISE OF CORPORATE SOCIAL RESPONSIBILITY IN GLOBAL ISSUE ARENAS

THE rise of corporate social responsibility (CSR) is one of the more striking developments of recent decades in the global political economy. Calls for multinational corporations (MNCs) to demonstrate greater responsibility, transparency, and accountability are leading to the establishment of a variety of new governance structures—rules, norms, codes of conduct, and standards—that constrain and shape MNCs' behavior (Kolk and van Tulder, 2005; Levy and Newell, 2006). MNCs are not only under pressure to respond to these new sources of authority, they are also increasingly engaged in their development (Cashore *et al.*, 2004; Haufler, 2001; Newell and Levy, 2006). Frequently, the new forms of governance entail bargaining, conflict, as well as collaboration among business, civil society actors, governmental agencies, and international organizations (Cutler *et al.*, 1999; Teegen *et al.*, 2004). Haufler (2001: 2) describes CSR as 'a potential new source of global governance, that is, mechanisms to reach collective decisions about transnational problems with or without government participation'.

A number of factors accounts for the rise of CSR in the international arena. Foremost is the renewed concern in the 1990s with the power and influence of MNCs, in particular their impact in developing countries on human rights (Cutler, 2006; Utting, 2000; Winston, 2002), the environment (Levy and Newell, 2005; Livesey, 2001), and employment (DeWinter, 2001; Goodwin, 2005). These concerns had come to prominence in the 1970s (Barnet and Muller, 1974; Vernon, 1977), but subsided in the 1980s. There is now growing recognition that the production and marketing operations of large MNCs have a critical impact on environmental stresses, labor market practices, regional economic development, and the broader culture (Barnet and Cavanagh, 1994; Rondinelli and Berry, 2002). MNCs are frequently seen as vehicles of a process of globalization that is, on the one hand, characterized by economic integration and convergence, and on the other by social tensions, uneven development, and growing inequality (Kaplinsky, 2005). As they weave global production networks that bridge geographic, economic, and political divides, they highlight and sometimes exacerbate spatial differences in living and labor standards, health care, and individual rights (Henderson *et al.*, 2002; Levy, 2005). Simultaneously, they induce processes of cultural hybridization and diffusion that threaten local identities (Tomlinson, 1999). MNCs can easily, therefore, become symbols of a new age of exploitation, imperialism, and colonialism (Banerjee and Linstead, 2001; Litvin, 2003).

MNCs have, *de facto*, become part of the fabric of global governance. Matten, Crane, and Chapple (2003) argue that, under the guise of 'corporate citizenship', large corporations are displacing states as providers and protectors of civil and political rights. MNCs, in their role as investors, innovators, experts, manufacturers, lobbyists, and employers, play a key role in shaping every aspect of society, from media and entertainment to the environment and employment conditions. For example, the research and marketing decisions of pharmaceutical companies determine who has access to treatments for which diseases and at what prices (Sell and Prakash, 2004; Vachani and Smith, 2004). While this expansion of corporate power is widely viewed as problematic, the growing recognition that corporate power is accompanied by substantial organizational, technological, and financial resources has stimulated consideration of ways to direct these resources toward social goals.

The embrace of corporate capacity has been fuelled by growing concern at an international 'governance deficit'. International economic integration, with its associated transnational environmental and social impacts, creates greater demand for coordinated responses that strain existing institutional capacity (Slaughter, 2004). Newell and Levy (2006: 161) note that 'the transnationalization of production and capital and the removal of trade barriers have themselves created the need for orchestrated institutional responses from states. For example, it is the global and transboundary nature of the trade in genetically modified organisms (GMOs) that gave rise to the need for a protocol on biosafety.' Governance is frequently portrayed as a public good subject to problems of collective action. Haas (2004: 2) suggests that a 'new geopolitical reality is the growing complexity of a globalizing world, whose management requires more holistic or comprehensive policies'.

Despite the apparent need for more global coordination, states have tended to restrict their roles (Strange, 1996). Ougaard (2006) points to a global trend toward deregulation and privatization, exacerbating the undersupply of governance. Pressures for 'global competitiveness' have constrained resources and eroded the welfare state (Cashore and Vertinsky, 2000; Midttun, 2005). State regulatory powers are increasingly directed toward structuring markets in ways that advance the agenda of national competitiveness by enhancing market-based forms of resource allocation (Braithwaite and Drahos, 2000). In their relations with MNCs, governments of developing countries have moved from restrictive toward more collaborative positions (Murtha and Lenway, 1994), including the encouragement of CSR (Moon, 2004).

The framework of international law and institutions pertaining to social and environmental impacts is somewhat precarious (Cutler, 2006). Efforts in the 1970s by the United Nations Centre for Transnational Corporations to create a binding code of conduct for multinational corporations (MNCs) ended in failure (Kolk and van Tulder, 2005). The inadequacy of existing institutions has received particular notice in the environmental area, where externalities such as acid rain and greenhouse gas emissions are starkly obvious. The environment only receives tangential attention in the major international trade and investment agreements, while a dedicated organization such as the United Nations Environmental Program 'is now under-funded, overloaded and remote' (Haas, 2004). To plug the 'governance gap', some have made a spirited argument for a Global Environmental Organization, equivalent in scope to the World Trade Organization (WTO) (Bierman, 2001), while others call for strengthening the emerging system of 'loose, decentralized, dense networks of institutions and actors' (Haas, 2004: 6). Even in the European Union, where an emerging institutional framework has both facilitated and regulated integration, there remains disquiet regarding a 'democratic deficit' of EU-wide governance mechanisms (Coen, 1997).

Business is increasingly filling this void in global governance. The International Chamber of Commerce (ICC) has forcefully asserted industry's significance in the case of climate change:

Industry's involvement is a critical factor in the policy deliberations relating to climate change. It is industry that will meet the growing demands of consumers for goods and services. It is industry that develops and disseminates most of the world's technology.... It is industry, therefore, that will be called upon to implement and finance a substantial part of governments' climate change policies. (International Chamber of Commerce, 1995)

The quotation is remarkable for the way it constructs a business role in governance out of society's dependence on business. In assuming this role, business has tended to adopt a more constructive stance on many issues. From the World Business Council for Sustainable Development to the Fair Labor Association, many corporations are engaging with organizations that acknowledge the existence of social and environmental problems.

Business engagement with issues of social responsibility is generally attributed to two broad motivations, financial and political-institutional. It is by now conventional wisdom for management texts and CSR advocates to assert that taking care of a broad range of stakeholders is in a firm's best long-term interests (Lawrence et al., 2004). The economic rewards of CSR have been explored in depth in the environmental area (Hart, 1997; Prakash, 2000; Reinhardt, 2000); on the demand side, there are attractive niche markets for premium 'green' products, while on the production side, there are opportunities for reducing costs of energy, materials, and waste disposal. More broadly, CSR can generate positive market image, improve employee morale, and reduce liability, insurance, and legal compliance costs. MNCs, in particular, could benefit from supporting growth and market expansion in developing countries (Prahalad and Doz, 1987) and from the standardization of reporting requirements across countries (Ougaard, 2006). Despite plenty of anecdotal evidence supporting these claims, more rigorous empirical studies generally find a weak or insignificant relationship between measures of social responsibility and financial performance (Griffen and Mahon,

1997; Guerard, 1997; Waddock and Graves, 2000). Vogel (2005) argues that market demand for CSR is limited to narrow niche segments, while it is difficult to re-alize monetary value derived from 'supplying CSR' to stakeholders other than consumers.

The weakness of the economic argument for CSR suggests its political character. Utting (2000: 27) cites a former executive of a large oil company as remarking at a UN-sponsored CSR workshop that if the win-win argument were so compelling, 'then we wouldn't be sitting around this table'. The executive reminded participants that it was NGO and consumer pressure that had changed corporate behavior. For Utting (2002: 62), CSR 'reflects changes that are occurring in the balance of social forces—notably the growth of NGO and consumer pressures'. Companies have a political motivation to engage proactively with societal pressures, to 'allow business to not only deflect or dilute certain pressures but also be in the driving seat to ensure that change took place on terms favorable to business' (Utting, 2002: 68). In a similar vein, Levy (1997: 132) has framed corporate environmental management as an effort to maintain 'political sustainability' in the face of social and regulatory challenges. In this view, CSR is a means to accommodate pressures, construct the corporation as a moral agent (DeWinter, 2001; Marchand, 1998), reduce the threat of regulation, and marginalize more radical activists. Likewise, Shamir (2004) argues that MNCs have sought to shape the meaning of CSR in ways that deflect its radical potential, by stressing voluntarism rather than legal obligation or public accountability.

MNCs face particular challenges in sustaining their legitimacy, as they present opportunities for activists to highlight the stark contrasts across regions in con-sumption patterns and working conditions (Kostova, 1999; Levy, 2005). In devel-oping countries, MNCs often carry the baggage of popular resentment against colonialist histories and contemporary global inequalities (Ougaard, 2006), while local governments might have reason to encourage these resentments. In industri-alized countries, large MNCs such as Nike, Starbucks, and Wal-Mart have come to symbolize discontent with the environmental, social, and economic impacts of global economic forces (Klein, 2000). MNCs have been put in the spotlight by the confluence of the rise of CSR discourse combined with the growth of social movements with the capacity to monitor and publicize MNC operations (Keck and Sikkink, 1998; O'Neill, 2004; Winston, 2002). As Utting (2000: 27) notes:

the capacity of environmentalists, human rights organizations, consumer and other social interest groups to put TNCs under the spotlight and mount national and international campaigns has increased tremendously in the 1990s. This reflects not only the quantita-tive growth of civil society organizations around the world, but also the communications revolution.

Business in Global Governance

The term 'global governance' refers to the emerging multi-layered and multi-actor system of global authority. We define global governance broadly here to mean the rules, institutions, and norms that order, channel, and constrain economic activity and its impacts in relation to international issues of public concern. It therefore includes not only national level regulation and formal international agreements, but also private mechanisms such as codes of conduct, discursive and normative frames, and market structures (Levy and Newell, 2006; Prakash and Hart, 1999; Slaughter, 2004).

Governance structures take many forms. Multilateral institutions have long provided governance mechanisms for 'market-enabling' (Levy and Prakesh, 2003) regimes which provide the structure, stability, and secure property rights required for markets to function. It is only quite recently, however, that international governance structures are emerging around more 'regulatory' regimes. Global governance implies rule creation, institution-building, and enforcement. Yet it also implies a soft infrastructure of norms and expectations in processes that engage the participation of a broad range of stakeholders. Dauvergne (2005) describes the emergent informal governance structure for tropical forests, noting how the mixture of local politics, industry structures, and certification standards provides a weak system of protection. This conception of governance displaces government from its traditional, sovereign role in securing order. For Rosenau (1992: 2), governance 'embraces governmental institutions, but it also subsumes informal, non-governmental mechanisms...Governance is thus a system of rule that is as dependent on intersubjective meanings as on formally sanctioned constitutions and charters.'

The concept of global governance builds from the well-developed literature on regime theory in international relations (Young, 1994). Regime theory concerns itself with 'norms, rules, principles and decision-making procedures around which actors' expectations converge in a given area of international relations' (Krasner, 1983: 2). Regime theory has been subject to critique for its state-centric bias, though it increasingly recognizes the significance of private actors and informal, normative structures (Higgott et al., 2000). More troubling is the tendency to portray regimes as rational, technical solutions that successfully overcome problems of collective action among states in pursuit of the common good (Prakash and Hart, 1999). In doing so, it tends to neglect the significance of broader power relations and resulting asymmetries (Levy and Newell, 2005). Indeed, an observer of many complex, protracted negotiations could easily be forgiven for concluding that distributional impacts are far more important to participants than the ostensible goal of a regime. The Kyoto Protocol, for example, is likely to fail dismally in slowing greenhouse gas emissions, but does provide funding for technology transfers to developing countries, as well as valuable emission credits.

CSR, as a multi-actor and multi-level system of rules, standards, norms, and expectations, exemplifies this broad conception of global governance. In organizational terms, CSR constitutes an institution, defined as 'socially constructed, routine-reproduced programs or rule systems' (Jepperson, 1991: 149). Institutional theory has traditionally sought to explain aspects of corporate behavior that could not be attributed to competitive market pressures (Scott, 1987). Clemens and Cook (1999: 445) define institutions as 'models, schemas, or scripts for behavior. Consequently, institutions endure because these models become "taken-for-granted" through repeated use and interaction or "legitimate" through the endorsement of some authoritative or powerful individual or organization'. Doh and Guay (2006) argue that the legitimacy of CSR is conditioned by the national context, so that the 'relatively more advanced awareness of and support for CSR in Europe', in contrast to the United States, 'provides an environment that is more responsive to NGO influence in a number of contemporary public policy issue-areas, such as global warming, trade in GMOs, and pricing of anti-viral pharmaceuticals in developing countries'. The Global Compact, a CSR initiative sponsored by the United Nations, is designed to leverage institutional pressures in order to diffuse best CSR practices within a 'learning network' of major MNCs (Ruggie, 2002).

Institutions are increasingly understood from a poststructural perspective as discursive formations that constitute people's identities and subjectivities (Phillips et al., 2004). Global governance can likewise be viewed as a pervasive mode of power that emanates from the constitutive and disciplinary effects of discourse (Hewson and Sinclair, 1999). CSR, in this framework, represents a set of discursive texts and practices that construct corporate subjectivity and the fields within which corporate operations take place as domains of socially responsible action. Practices of social auditing and reporting represent a form of discipline that functions to standardize, rank, and categorize CSR performance. The surveillance of corporate activities thus translates CSR from an abstract set of norms and expectations 'into a quantifiable and standardized audit instrument that lends itself to objective and consistent measurement' (Sethi, 2002). This moment of 'examination' represents, for Foucault (1977: 184), 'a normalizing gaze, a surveillance that makes it possible to qualify, to classify and to punish'.

The rapidity with which large corporations have adopted various CSR standards and reporting mechanisms, such as ISO 14000, the Global Reporting Initiative (GRI), and annual social reports, is quite astonishing, given the absence of financial inducements or regulatory coercion (Kolk, 2005b; Kolk and van Tulder, 2005). One attraction of these standards is that many are based on the documentation of managerial processes rather than assessment of outcomes. Compliance can thus provide a degree of legitimacy without necessarily imposing substantial costs.

Accounting firms eager to expand their auditing business have become advocates of the standards. A Foucauldian perspective suggests that the imperative to classify and tabulate represents a deeper and more fundamental logic of modernity. Moreover, the specific form taken by these standards and reporting mechanisms reflects their discursive lineage from corporate financial accounting systems and regulatory oversight mechanisms.

Yet CSR is clearly not the only structure of global economic governance with discursive legitimacy. Indeed, CSR might well conflict with what Gill (1995) terms 'disciplinary neo-liberalism'. Firms, workers, consumers, and even states are subject to a governance system that combines economic forces of competition with consumerist and free-market ideologies, and the discursive discipline of credit ratings and financial accounting. This system is actively maintained within a political economy of corporate lobbying and influence, and is reproduced within the ideational realm of advertising, mass media, universities, and consultancies (Carroll and Carson, 2003; Morgan, 2001). The tensions inherent in the coexistence CSR and neoliberalism highlight the contested terrain of global governance. In the following sections we point to two distinct perspectives on CSR; as a more socially embedded and democratic form of governance that emanates from civil society, or alternatively, as a privatized system of corporate governance that lacks public accountability.

CSR as More Democratic Governance

The rising discursive currency of CSR can be viewed in the context of the emergence of global civil society and the diffusion of state authority to more decentralized networks of actors. Brown *et al.* (2000: 275) define civil society as 'an area of association and action independent of the state and the market in which citizens can organize to pursue purposes that are important to them, individually and collectively'. Teegen *et al.* (2004: 466) view NGOs as the 'organizational manifestations of civil society interests', defining them as 'private, not-for-profit organizations that aim to serve particular societal interests by focusing advocacy and/or operational efforts on social, political and economic goals, including equity, education, health, environmental protection and human rights'. Civil society is clearly growing in importance as an element of global governance. Haas (2004: 3) notes that a key feature of the 'new geopolitical reality is the proliferation of new political actors and the diffusion of political authority over major governance functions, particularly in the environmental sphere. These new actors include NGOs, MNCs, organized transnational scientific networks known as epistemic communities, global policy networks, and selective international institutions that are capable of exercising discretionary behavior independently of the wishes of their dominant member states'.

This diffusion of authority is widely perceived to represent a positive development that promises greater democracy, accountability, and capacity in solving problems requiring collective action at the international level (Lipschutz, 2005; Slaughter, 2004). Bruyn's (1999) vision of a 'moral economy' revives the liberal utopian promise of a self-regulating cooperative civil society. Keck and Sikkink (1998) argue that the networks constructed by economic actors, firms, scientists, and activists multiply channels of political access and make international resources available to actors in domestic struggles, leveling the playing field to some extent. Similarly, Florini (2000: 28) contends that 'the information revolution increases the capacity of non-state actors relative to states' and corporate actors. Falk (1995: 1–2) insists that a dramatic extension of democracy and a growing sense of allegiance to global civil society, though unlikely, would offer the most promising path to 'humane governance', which he defines in terms of addressing four key global social problems: poverty, lack of human rights, the prevalence of violent conflict, and environmental degradation.

In relation to CSR, Murphy and Bendell (1999) coin the term 'civil regulation' to refer to the pressure exerted on business to comply not only with governmental regulations but also with norms and standards advocated by civil society actors: 'We believe that civil society organizations are also playing significant roles in promoting environmental and social management. The evidence of anti-logging, anti-oil and anti-child labor protests illustrates that NGOs are increasingly setting the political agenda within which business must work' (1999: 57). Murphy and Bendell argue that the phenomenon of CSR should not be celebrated as an expression of corporate altruism or the discovery of win-win opportunities; instead, they acknowledge that CSR is a political response by business to social pressure. Rather than view this as a fundamental limitation, however, they find room for optimism in locating the source of agency and authority in the organizations of civil society, claiming that 'the challenge is therefore to seize the opportunities afforded by corporate environmental politics, not lament its existence' (1999: 57).

CSR AS PRIVATIZED GOVERNANCE

Locating CSR as part of a trend toward the privatization of governance provides a more critical perspective that views the locus of authority within the corporate sector rather than in elements of civil society. Critics argue that terms such as CSR, corporate citizenship, and sustainable development reflect a corporate-economic rather than a social or ecological rationality (Banerjee, 2003; Matten *et al.*, 2003). Cutler *et al.* (1999: 3) observe that 'a significant degree of global order is provided by individual firms that agree to cooperate, either formally or informally, in establishing an international framework for their economic activity'. In relation to CSR, these frameworks might comprise codes of conduct such as the 4C industry code for coffee (Kolk, 2005*a*), standards for social reporting and auditing such as the Global Reporting Initiative (Ougaard, 2006), or product labeling standards such as the Forestry Stewardship Council (Dauvergne, 2005). The concept of governance extends to the norms and authority structures in which these agreements are embedded. Acknowledging this, Cutler *et al.* (1999: 9) use the term 'private regime' to refer to 'an integrated complex of formal and informal institutions that is a source of governance for an economic issue area as a whole'. Though they recognize that private authority ultimately derives sanction and legitimacy from the state and society, they express concern with the blurring of boundaries between the state and private authority. Ougaard (2006: 243) echoes this point in emphasizing the public, political character of CSR but a lack of democratic accountability: 'When corporations engage in voluntary efforts, they make decisions on the allocation of scarce resources for public purposes'.

The enforcement of private regimes frequently takes place through reporting, auditing and inspection by other private authorities (Kolk *et al.*, 1999). Sanctions include withdrawal of a product or facility from certification and, more importantly, damage to public reputation and brand name. Not bound by the same customs and expectations as state-based regimes, with their requirements for consultation, representation, and transparency, private regimes allow for faster decision-making, some insulation against state regulation, favorable publicity, reduced transaction costs, and access to markets. States might also favor self-regulation because it lowers the financial and political costs of forging and enforcing policy (Prakash and Hart, 1999). In some cases, industry initiatives lead to the emergence of hybrid private–public governance systems. For example, private initiatives to develop trading systems for carbon emissions are likely to serve as templates for later regulatory structures (Rabe, 2004). Industry-level codes such as the ISO 14001 environmental management standards began life as a private initiative but were later incorporated into governmental trade and purchasing requirements (Clapp, 1998).

The privatization of governance can also be seen in the substantial corporate influence over more formal global regimes. Levy and Egan (1998) have argued that the unprecedented influence of the fossil fuel lobby over US climate policy derives from a combination of three sources of power: instrumental power, operating through a dense network of relationships between business and the state; structural power, derived from the state's dependency on business for investment, employment, and tax revenues; and discursive power, stemming from the construction and framing of scientific, economic, and policy dimensions of an issue.

In a similar way, Andrée (2005) has described how the economic, political, and discursive strategies of biotechnology companies helped shape a conducive global regime, in the face of significant opposition. Some issues motivate diverse sectors to pursue a unified political strategy. MNCs in the software, entertainment, and pharmaceutical industries were very active in drafting accords that strengthened and extended international protection of intellectual property rights under the auspices of the WTO (Sell, 2002).

A broad notion of governance extends beyond corporate engagement with external institutions, rules, and standards. The day-to-day production, employment, research and marketing practices of large companies play a critical role in shaping environmental impacts, labor market practices, income distribution, and even consumer identities. In the coffee sector, for example, the branding and production strategies of companies such as Nestlé and Starbucks have successfully shored up their market power in the 'value chain', with deleterious consequences for developing country growers (Kolk, 2005a; Talbot, 2004). In the case of ozone depletion, the technological strategies of leading chemical companies helped shape the content and implementation of the Montreal Protocol for ozone-depleting gases, a phenomenon that Falkner (2005) terms 'technological power'. The privatization of entire sectors in some countries in recent years, such as water and energy, signifies a broad transfer of governance functions to the corporate sector, frequently to foreign MNCs. Significant consequences are likely for quality, reliability, access, and pricing (Levy and Newell, 2006).

CSR as Contested Governance

CSR, we contend, encompasses contradictory moments, with tendencies toward greater democratic accountability as well as toward privatized, unaccountable power. In the following sections, we develop the argument that CSR represents contested political terrain as well as a strategic tool deployed in political struggles over corporate governance. As Ougaard (2006: 236) puts it, 'the CSR movement is a discursive and material struggle about business practice; it represents a politicization of the social content of the institutions that govern private economic activity'. Indeed, we argue that CSR entails a political struggle that extends beyond particular business practices to include the nature of corporate governance. The meaning of CSR itself is a key point of political struggle, reflecting the ambiguous meaning of 'responsibility'; business could assume a degree of responsibility *for* social outcomes, while retaining full authority and autonomy, or it could be held responsible and accountable *to* society in a way that cedes substantive authority to multiple stakeholders, including labor and elements of civil society. Here we examine CSR as contested global governance through the theoretical lenses of Karl Polanyi and Antonio Gramsci.

POLANYI AND GRAMSCI ON CONTESTED GOVERNANCE

Polanyi's (1944) insights into societal responses to the failures of 19th century market liberalism provide a valuable historical context for understanding contemporary CSR. Polanyi documents how the English Industrial Revolution was accompanied by the development of an economic and political theory of market liberalism, which claimed that unfettered markets could successfully self-regulate to achieve prosperity, stability, and political freedom. Polanyi (1944: 57) recognizes that market liberalism represented a fundamental historical transformation: 'Instead of economy being embedded in social relations, social relations are embedded in the economic system'. Polanyi argues, however, that market liberalism is a dangerous utopian myth. Real markets, once disembedded from society, tend toward unstable booms and depressions, and impose massive social and environmental costs. 'Such an institution could not exist for any length of time without annihilating the human and natural substance of society' (1944: 3). Consequently, the imposition of *laissez-faire* required a paradoxical expansion of the repressive powers of the state.

Inevitably, contends Polanyi, society reacted by engaging in a 'double movement', in which 'a network of measures and policies was integrated into powerful institutions designed to check the action of the market' (1944: 76). The Keynesian welfare state, however, lost ground and legitimacy during the latter part of the 20th century, which saw 'an intellectually and politically powerful renaissance of neo-*laissez-faire*' (Offe, 1984: 149). The neoliberal movement has successfully managed to legitimize and institutionalize a process of economic liberalization, deregulation, and privatization (Crouch and Streeck, 1997; Harvey, 2005).

The rise of CSR can be understood as a contemporary double-movement against global neoliberalism. Soaring disparities in income, the emergence of global environmental problems, and the outsourcing of increasingly skilled operations to developing countries, are all leading to demands for protection against the anarchy of unregulated market forces. In Polanyi's terms, CSR is an attempt to establish a more socially embedded form of economic governance. As with earlier manifestations of the double-movement, CSR has been embraced by 'enlightened' elements of business concerned with the systemic instabilities generated by the radicalization of discontented groups, erosion of the global environmental commons, or financial crises.

Where CSR differs most sharply from historical efforts to restrain markets is in its reliance on the private realm rather than the state. NGOs increasingly adopt strategies that bypass states and attempt to pressure businesses directly through 'non-state market driven governance systems' (Cashore, 2002). CSR can shape assumptions regarding consumer behavior, competitors' reactions, and regulatory responses, thus molding the market environment within which corporate strategy is developed. Crucially, CSR does not compromise the fundamentals of the market system; indeed, it proclaims the harmony of financial and social interests. 'Under non-state-market-driven governance, the relatively narrow institution of the market and its supply chain provides the institutional setting within which governing authority is granted and through which broadly based political struggles occur' (Cashore, 2002: 504).

Though CSR has clearly achieved considerable success in shifting corporate practices and attitudes regarding many issues, a private governance system carries considerable risks. The state still remains an immensely powerful source of authority, without whose sanction any effort to constrain corporate behavior will be limited. NGOs have also been challenged regarding their representational legitimacy and public accountability (O'Rourke, 2003). The extent to which CSR re-embeds markets within the social realm is thus highly questionable. Indeed, the CSR movement has avoided challenging the core economic structures and managerial prerogatives of contemporary market societies, which retain a high degree of legitimacy.

Polanyi's depiction of the double-movement as an inevitable reaction to the vicissitudes of the market underplays the significance of political struggles against particular manifestations of market-based governance. A Gramscian perspective, by contrast, understands CSR in the context of strategic contests among interested actors around politically charged issue arenas (Levy and Egan, 2003). Rather than presume broad social consensus on the need to constrain market forces, the Gramscian concept of hegemony suggests that constructing this consensus is a political project of building alliances, strategic negotiation, and public debates. The stability of a governance system relies on a combination of coercive power, economic incentives, and normative and cognitive frames that coordinate perceptions of interest. The particular practices of CSR that emerge around an issue therefore reflect the balance of forces among competing interest groups.

The harmony of business and social interests posited by CSR advocates is thus not something to take for granted, but rather represents a discursive accommodation and material compromise that emerges from the strategies of various parties. NGOs pragmatically couch their demands discursively in win-win terms as they try to draw some elements of business into a progressive coalition supporting CSR objectives. Business frequently embraces CSR discourse and practice because it sustains corporate legitimacy and autonomy in the face of challenges from civil society while deflecting and marginalizing demands for more radical change (Levy, 1997). The contestation between industry, environmentalists, and state agencies over the evolving global system for governing greenhouse gas emissions illustrates this perspective on CSR (Levy and Egan, 2003). CSR thus represents a classic Gramscian accommodation between unfettered market forces and pressures for greater social control. CSR can achieve this hegemonic status precisely because it embodies elements of Polanyi's double-movement as well as the business response to the double-movement. Typically, business agrees to concessions that modify corporate practices at the margin, but which do not challenge the fundamentals of managerial authority or market rationality. As a mode of governance, CSR accords a measure of legitimacy to external stakeholders, but reserves to corporate management the role of benign stewardship of societal resources. CSR is also constrained by the nesting of governance systems within the global financial and trade system. Business hegemony at this level is generally more firmly entrenched and less permeable to the discourse of CSR. Various WTO rulings, for example, reflect the precedence of free-trade principles over environmental concerns.

CONCLUSIONS AND IMPLICATIONS

This chapter has developed a framework in which CSR represents the contested terrain of global governance. Advocates view CSR as a move toward a form of civil regulation that is more responsive and accountable to social concerns, while critics see it as a privatized system of corporate governance that displaces the regulatory authority of the state and is frequently more geared toward public relations than substantive change. Our framework draws from Polanyi and Gramsci to argue that CSR is an emergent form of governance that can redress, to some degree, the governance deficit that exists in the international arena, and that reflects strategic contests as well as common ground among competing social forces. CSR is emerging as a set of discourses and practices that reflects the particular balance of forces in a contested issue arena. This political-strategic approach stands in sharp contrast to more conventional perspectives that develop a normative and ethical case for CSR, backed up with positivist arguments asserting a financial case for such behavior.

Activists and academics have found CSR to be a powerful discourse that can be deployed strategically to influence corporate norms and practice. Advocating for CSR can generate legitimacy for stakeholders, shift societal expectations of business, create media attention, directly pressure business, bring attention to win-win opportunities, and even shape market environments to expand those opportunities. For business, CSR comprises an element of corporate political strategy that offers social legitimacy, some attractive market opportunities, and protection against more severe activist demands and regulatory pressure. CSR therefore rests on a rather precarious balance of conflict and cooperation. At the same time, CSR is limited by the logic of the marketplace. It relies primarily on the pressure exerted by NGOs and consumer activism in affluent countries on MNCs with vulnerable brand names. CSR does little to empower workers in developing countries, neither has it reversed adverse labor market trends in industrialized countries, such as wage stagnation, rising inequality, and the erosion of health care and pensions.

From a Gramscian perspective, it is not surprising that CSR, as a hegemonic accommodation, largely reflects the dominant cultural, economic, and political role of business in society, and the permeation of the discourse of competitiveness and free markets into state and social structures. Yet Gramsci offers us 'optimism of the will', the conviction that collective action, organization, and smart strategy could overcome conventional sources of power. Rather than view the current status of CSR as a disappointing endpoint, CSR can be viewed as a long-term strategy that challenges corporate power on numerous fronts. A particular CSR arrangement, such as a code of conduct, might dampen pressures for change, but it might also prepare the stage for a new round of struggle in which NGOs build on their successes to demand effective monitoring and enforcement. Indeed, some elements of the CSR movement are increasingly using the language of business *accountability to* society rather than *responsibility for* society (Newell and Wheeler, 2006). CSR is thus not just a struggle over practices, but over the *locus* of governance authority, offering a potential path toward the transformation of stakeholders from external observers and petitioners into legitimate and organized participants in decision-making.

References

ANDRÉE, P. 2005. 'The Genetic Engineering Revolution in Agriculture and Food: Strategies of the "Biotech Bloc"', in Levy and Newell (2005), 135–68.

BANERJEE, S. B. 2003. 'Who Sustains Whose Development? Sustainable Development and the Reinvention of Nature'. *Organization Studies*, 24(2): 143–80.

—— and LINSTEAD, S. 2001. 'Globalization, Multiculturalism and Other Fictions: Colonialism for the New Millennium?' *Organization*, 8(4): 683–722.

BARNET, R. J., and CAVANAGH, J. 1994. *Global Dreams: Imperial Corporations and the New World Order*. New York: Simon & Schuster.

—— and MULLER, R. E. 1974. 'Global Reach: The Power of the Multinational Corporations'. New York: Simon & Schuster.

BIERMAN, F. 2001. 'The Emerging Debate on the Need for a World Environment Organization'. *Global Environmental Politics*, 1(1): 45–55.

BRAITHWAITE, J., and DRAHOS, P. 2000. *Global Business Regulation*. Cambridge: Cambridge University Press.

BROWN, L. D., KHAGRAM, S., MOORE, M. H., and FRUMKIN, P. 2000. 'Globalization, NGOs and Multisectoral Relations', in J. S. Nye and J. D. Donahue (eds.), *Governance in a Globalizing World*. Washington: Brookings Institution Press, 271–86.

BRUYN, S. T. 1999. 'The Moral Economy'. *Review of Social Economy*, 57: 25–46.

CARROLL, W. K., and CARSON, C. 2003. 'The Network of Global Corporations and Policy Groups: A Structure for Transnational Capitalist Class Formation?' *Global Networks*, 3(1): 29–57.

CASHORE, B. 2002. 'Legitimacy and the Privatization of Environmental Governance'. *Governance*, 15(4): 503–29.

——AULD, G., and NEWSOM, D. 2004. *Governing Through Markets*. New Haven: Yale University Press.

——and VERTINSKY, I. 2000. 'Policy Networks and Firm Behaviors: Governance Systems and Firm Responses to External Demands for Sustainable Forest Management'. *Policy Sciences*, 33: 1–33.

CLAPP, J. 1998. 'The Privatization of Global Environmental Governance: ISO 14000 and the Developing World'. *Global Governance*, 4: 295–316.

CLEMENS, E. S., and COOK, J. M. 1999. 'Politics and Institutionalism: Explaining Durability and Change'. *Annual Review of Sociology*, 25(1): 441–66.

COEN, D. 1997. 'The Evolution of the Large Firm as a Political Actor in the European Union'. *Journal of European Public Policy*, 4(1): 91–108.

CROUCH, C., and STREECK, W. (eds.). 1997. *Political Economy of Modern Capitalism*. London: Sage.

CUTLER, C. A. 2006. 'Transnational Business Civilization, Corporations, and the Privatization of Global Governance', in C. May (ed.), *Global Corporate Power*. Boulder, Colo.: Lynne Rienner.

——HAUFLER, V., and PORTER, T. (eds.). 1999. *Private Authority and International Affairs*. Albany, NY: SUNY Press.

DAUVERGNE, P. 2005. 'The Environmental Challenge to Loggers in the Asia-Pacific: Corporate Practices in Informal Regimes of Governance', in Levy and Newell (2005).

DEWINTER, R. 2001. 'The Anti-sweatshop Movement: Constructing Corporate Moral Agency in the Global Apparel Industry'. *Ethics & International Affairs*, 15(2): 99–115.

DOH, J. P., and GUAY, T. R. 2006. 'Corporate Social Responsibility, Public Policy, and NGO Activism in Europe and the United States: An Institutional-Stakeholder Perspective'. *Journal of Management Studies*, 43(1): 47–73.

FALK, R. A. 1995. *On Humane Governance*. University Park, Pa.: Pennsylvania State Press.

FALKNER, R. 2005. 'The Business of Ozone Layer Protection: Corporate Power in Regime Evolution', in Levy and Newell (2005).

FLORINI, A. M. 2000. 'Who Does What? Collective Action and the Changing Nature of Authority', in Higott *et al.* (2000), 15–31.

FOUCAULT, M. 1977. *Discipline and Punish: The Birth of the Prison*. New York: Random House.

GILL, S. 1995. 'Globalisation, Market Civilisation, and Disciplinary Neoliberalism'. *Millennium: Journal of International Studies*, 24(3): 399–423.

GOODWIN, N. 2005. 'The Social Impacts of Multinational Corporations: An Outline of the Issues with a Focus on Workers', in A. D. Chandler, and B. Mazlish (eds.), *Leviathans: Multinational Corporations and the New Global History*. Cambridge: Cambridge University Press, 135–65.

GRIFFEN, J. J., and MAHON, J. F. 1997. 'The Corporate Social Performance and Corporate Financial Performance Debate: Twenty-five Years of Incomparable Research'. *Business and Society*, 36(1): 5–31.

GUERARD, J. B. 1997. 'Is there a Cost to being Socially Responsible in Investing?' *The Journal of Investing*, 6: 11–18.

HAAS, P. M. 2004. 'Addressing the Global Governance Deficit'. *Global Environmental Politics*, 4(4): 1–15.

HART, S. L. 1997. 'Beyond Greening: Strategies for a Sustainable World'. *Harvard Business Review*, 75: 66–76.

HARVEY, D. 2005. *A Brief History of Neoliberalism*. Oxford: Oxford University Press.

HAUFLER, V. 2001. *A Public Role for the Private Sector: Industry Self-Regulation in a Global Economy*. Washington: Carnegie Endowment for International Peace.

HENDERSON, J., DICKEN, P., HESS, M., COE, N., and WAI-CHUNG YEUNG, H. 2002. 'Global Production Networks and the Analysis of Economic Development'. *Review of International Political Economy*, 9(3): 436–64.

HEWSON, M., and SINCLAIR, T. J. (eds.). 1999. *Approaches to Global Governance Theory*. Albany, NY: SUNY Press.

HIGGOTT, R., UNDERHILL, G., and BIELER, A. (eds.). 2000. *Non-state Actors and Authority in the Global System*. London: Routledge.

International Chamber of Commerce. 1995. Statement by the International Chamber of Commerce before COP1, 29 Mar. Berlin.

JEPPERSON, R. L. 1991. 'Institutions, Institutional Effects, and Institutionalism', in W. W. Powell and P. J. DiMaggio (eds.), *The New Institutionalism in Organizational Analysis*. Chicago: University of Chicago Press, 143–63.

KAPLINSKY, R. 2005. *Globalization, Poverty and Inequality: Between a Rock and a Hard Place*. Cambridge: Polity.

KECK, M. E., and SIKKINK, K. 1998. 'Transnational Advocacy Networks in International Politics: Introduction', in M. E. Keck and K. Sikkink (eds.), *Activists Beyond Borders: Advocacy Networks in International Politics*. Ithaca, NY: Cornell University Press.

KLEIN, N. 2000. *No Logo*. London: Flamingo.

KOLK, A. 2005a. 'Corporate Social Responsibility in the Coffee Sector: The Dynamics of MNC Responses and Code Development'. *European Management Journal*, 23(2): 228–36.

—— 2005b. 'Environmental Reporting by Multinationals from the Triad: Convergence or Divergence?' *Management International Review*, 45(1): 145–66.

—— and VAN TULDER, R. 2005. 'Setting New Global Rules? TNCs and Codes of Conduct'. *Transnational Corporations*, 14(3): 1–27.

—— —— and WELTERS, C. 1999. 'International Codes of Conduct and Corporate Social Responsibility'. *Transnational Corporations*, 8(1): 143–80.

KOSTOVA, T. 1999. 'Transnational Transfer of Strategic Organizational Practices: A Contextual Perspective'. *Academy of Management Review*, 24(2): 308–24.

KRASNER, S. (ed.). 1983. *International Regimes*. Ithaca, NY: Cornell University Press.

LAWRENCE, A. T., WEBER, J., and POST, J. E. 2004. *Business and Society: Stakeholders, Ethics, Public Policy*. New York: McGraw-Hill.

LEVY, D. L. 1997. 'Environmental Management as Political Sustainability. *Organization and Environment*, 10(2): 126–47.

—— 2005. *Hegemony in the Global Factory: Power, Ideology, and Value in Global Production Networks*. Paper presented at the Best Paper Proceedings of the Sixty-Fifth Annual Meeting of the Academy of Management (CD), ISSN 1543–8643.

—— and EGAN, D. 1998. 'Capital Contests: National and Transnational Channels of Corporate Influence on the Climate Change Negotiations'. *Politics and Society*, 26(3): 337–61.

—— —— 2003. 'A Neo-Gramscian Approach to Corporate Political Strategy: Conflict and Accommodation in the Climate Change Negotiations'. *Journal of Management Studies*, 40(4): 803–30.

—— and NEWELL, P. J. 2005. *The Business of Global Environmental Governance*. Cambridge, Mass.: MIT Press.

—— —— 2006. 'Multinationals in Global Governance', in S. Vachani (ed.), *Transformations in Global Governance: Implications for Multinationals and other Stakeholders*. Cheltenham: Edward Elgar.

—— and PRAKESH, A. 2003. 'Bargains Old and New: Multinationals in International Governance'. *Business and Politics*, 5(2): 131–51.

LIPSCHUTZ, R. 2005. *Regulation for the Rest of Us: Globalization, Governmentality and Global Politics*. London: Routledge.

LITVIN, D. 2003. *Empires of Profit: Commerce, Conquest, and Corporate Responsibility*. London: Texere.

LIVESEY, S. M. 2001. 'Eco-Identity as Discursive Struggle: Royal Dutch Shell, Brent Spar, and Nigeria'. *Journal of Business Communication*, 38(1): 58–91.

MARCHAND, R. 1998. *Creating the Corporate Soul: The Rise of Public Relations and Corporate Imagery in American Big Business*. Berkeley: University of California Press.

MATTEN, D., CRANE, A., and CHAPPLE, W. 2003. 'Behind the Mask: Revealing the True Face of Corporate Citizenship'. *Journal of Business Ethics*, 45(1): 109–20.

MIDTTUN, A. 2005. 'Realigning Business, Government and Civil Society'. *Corporate Governance*, 5(3): 159–74.

MOON, J. 2004. *Government as a Driver of Corporate Social Responsibility: The UK in Comparative Perspective*. Nottingham: International Centre for Corporate Social Responsibility.

MORGAN, G. 2001. 'Transnational Communities and Business Systems'. *Global Networks: A Journal of Transnational Affairs*, 1(2): 113–30.

MURPHY, D. F., and BENDELL, J. 1999. 'Partners in Time? Business, NGOs, and Sustainable Development'. Geneva: United Nations Reserach Institute for Social Development.

MURTHA, T. P., and LENWAY, S. A. 1994. 'Country Capabilities and the Strategic State: How National Political Institutions Affect Multinational Corporations' Strategies'. *Strategic Management Journal*, 15: 113–29.

NEWELL, P. J., and LEVY, D. L. 2006. 'The Political Economy of the Firm in Global Environmental Governance', in C. May (ed.), *Global Corporate Power*. Boulder, Colo.: Lynne Rienner.

—— and WHEELER, J. (eds.). 2006. *Rights, Resources and the Politics of Accountability*. London: Zed Books.

OFFE, C. 1984. 'Some Contradictions of the Modern Welfare State', in J. Keane (Ed.), *Contradictions of the Welfare State*. Cambridge, Mass.: MIT Press.

O'NEILL, K. 2004. 'Transnational Protest: States, Circuses, and Conflict at the Frontline of Global Politics'. *International Studies Review*, 6(2): 233–52.

O'ROURKE, D. 2003. 'Outsourcing Regulation: Analyzing Nongovernmental Systems of Labor Standards and Monitoring'. *Policy Studies Journal*, 31(1): 1–29.

OUGAARD, M. 2006. 'Instituting the Power to Do Good?' in C. May (ed.), *Global Corporate Power*. Boulder, Colo.: Lynne Rienner.

PHILLIPS, N., LAWRENCE, T. B., and HARDY, C. 2004. 'Discourse and Institutions'. *Academy of Management Review*, 29(4): 635–52.

POLANYI, K. 1944. *The Great Transformation: The Political and Economic Origins of our Time*. Boston: Beacon Press.

PRAHALAD, C. K., and DOZ, Y. L. 1987. *The Multinational Mission: Balancing Local Demands and Global Vision*. New York: Free Press.

PRAKASH, A. 2000. 'Responsible Care: An assessment. *Business & Society*, 39: 183–209.

—— and HART, J. (eds.). 1999. *Globalization and Governance*. London: Routledge.

RABE, B. G. 2004. *Statehouse and Greenhouse: The Emerging Politics of American Climate Change Policy*. Washington: Brookings Institution Press.

REINHARDT, F. L. 2000. *Down to Earth: Applying Business Principles to Environmental Management*. Boston: Harvard Business School Press.

RONDINELLI, D. A., and BERRY, M. A. 2002. 'Environmental Citizenship in Multinational Corporations: Social Responsibility and Sustainable Development. *European Management Journal*, 18(1): 70–84.

ROSENAU, J. N. 1992. 'Governance, Order, and Change in World Politics', in J. N. Rosenau, and E. O. Czempiel (eds.), *Governance without Government: Order and Change in World Politics*. Cambridge: Cambridge University Press, 1–29.

RUGGIE, J. G. 2002. 'The Theory and Practice of Learning Networks: Corporate Social Responsibility and the Global Compact'. *Journal of Corporate Citizenship*, 5: 27–36.

SCOTT, R. W. 1987. 'The Adolescence of Institutional Theory. *Administrative Science Quarterly*, 32: 493–511.

SELL, S. K. 2002. *Private Power, Public Law*. Cambridge: Cambridge University Press.

—— and PRAKASH, A. 2004. 'Using Ideas Strategically: The Contest between Business and NGO Networks in Intellectual Property Rights'. *International Studies Quarterly*, 48(1): 143–75.

SETHI, P. 2002. 'Corporate Codes of Conduct and the Success of Globalization'. *Ethics & International Affairs*, 16(1): 89–106.

SHAMIR, R. 2004. 'The De-radicalization of Corporate Social Responsibility'. *Critical Sociology*, 30(3): 669–89.

SLAUGHTER, A.-M. 2004. *A New World Order*. Princeton: Princeton University Press.

STRANGE, S. 1996. *The Retreat of the State: The Diffusion of Power in the World Economy*. Cambridge: Cambridge University Press.

TALBOT, J. M. 2004. *Grounds for Agreement: The Political Economy of the Coffee Commodity Chain*. Lanham, Md.: Rowman & Littlefield.

TEEGEN, H., DOH, J. P., and VACHANI, S. 2004. 'The Importance of Nongovernmental Organizations in Global Governance and Value Creation: An International Business Research Agenda. *Journal of International Business Studies*, 35(6): 463–83.

TOMLINSON, J. 1999. *Globalization and Culture*. Chicago: University of Chicago Press.

UTTING, P. 2000. 'Business Responsibility for Sustainable Development'. Geneva: United Nations Research Institute for Social Development.

—— 2002. 'Regulating Business via Multistakeholder Initiatives: A Preliminary Assessment', in P. Utting (ed.), *Voluntary Approaches to Corporate Responsibility*. Geneva: United Nations Non-Governmental Liaison Service, 61–130.

VACHANI, S., and SMITH, C. N. 2004. 'Socially Responsible Pricing: Lessons from the Pricing of AIDS Drugs in Developing Countries'. *California Management Review*, 47(1): 117–44.

VERNON, R. 1977. *Storm over the Multinationals*. Cambridge, Mass.: Harvard University Press.

VOGEL, D. J. 2005. *The Market for Virtue: The Potential and Limits of Corporate Social Responsibility*. Washington: Brookings Institution Press.

WADDOCK, S., and GRAVES, S. 2000. 'Performance Characteristics of Social and Traditional Investments'. *Journal of Investing*, 9(2): 27–38.

WINSTON, M. 2002. 'NGO Strategies for Promoting Corporate Social Responsibility'. *Ethics & International Affairs*, 16(1): 71–87.

YOUNG, O. R. 1994. *International Governance: Protecting the Environment in a Stateless Society*. Ithaca, NY: Cornell University Press.

....

CHAPTER 20

CORPORATE SOCIAL RESPONSIBILITY IN A COMPARATIVE PERSPECTIVE

....

CYNTHIA A. WILLIAMS
RUTH V. AGUILERA

INTRODUCTION

....

COMPARATIVE studies of corporate social responsibility (CSR) are relatively rare, certainly as contrasted with other related fields, such as comparative corporate governance or comparative corporate law. This is to be expected in a field, CSR, that is still 'emergent' (McWilliams *et al.*, 2006). While theoretical perspectives on corporate social performance or stakeholder management have been developed for over two decades (Carroll, 1979; Freeman, 1984; Donaldson and Preston, 1995; Clarkson, 1995; McWilliams and Siegel, 2001), it is only in the last decade that businesses have begun to exhibit serious evidence of CSR in their strategic management and stakeholder socialx reporting.

Moreover, the field of empirical CSR research generally has been hampered by the lack of a consistent definition of the construct of CSR, as well as its operationalization and measurement, as recently pointed out by McWilliams *et al.* (2006) and Rodríguez *et al.* (2006). This lack of consistency of CSR definitions across studies makes it difficult to evaluate and compare the findings from different studies because they usually refer to different dimensions of CSR. Most research on CSR has focused on the consequences of CSR implementation—or lack of implementation—on financial performance with little attention to comparative issues (e.g. McWilliams and Siegel, 2000; Margolis and Walsh, 2003; Barnett and Salomon, 2006), the main exception being a meta-analysis which includes studies conducted in the context of different countries (Orlitzky *et al.*, 2003). We know, however, from existing research that individuals are likely to have distinct expectations and attitudes towards CSR contingent on the industry (Bansal and Roth, 2000; Strike *et al.*, 2006) or societal culture (Waldman *et al.*, 2006) in which they are embedded.

Notwithstanding these difficulties, comparative studies of CSR illuminate theories of corporate governance and relationships amongst the various actors that both comprise and influence companies. Thus it is of value to attend to the studies that have been conducted, and to develop research protocols to encourage further comparative work.

Studies that are comparative in this field differ in how they define the comparative unit of analysis, and such differences often have methodological implications. Where countries or other geographical units such as continents are used as the basis for comparing CSR environments, studies then tend to use either comparative legal analysis or comparative institutional analysis. Fewer studies than might be expected use individual countries as the unit of analysis, but this is likely inherent in the nature of the CSR challenge itself. CSR as a rapidly developing business strategy (and not simply a theory in the management literature), is a response to globalization and the extension of global multinational enterprises ('MNEs') across countries, with the implication that state control over such enterprises is rapidly fragmenting (Logsdon and Wood, 2002; Zumbansen, 2006). Thus, broader units of analysis that reflect these global challenges are often used.

One approach that has used both comparative legal analysis and comparative institutional analysis has been to compare the perspectives and strategies on CSR inherent in different corporate governance systems, such as contrasting Anglo-American versus Continental European approaches to CSR. A number of these studies will be discussed in the next section. Other studies have used a 'most similar case' approach to show differences in companies' approaches to CSR in countries with seemingly similar socio-political traditions within these corporate governance systems. Comparisons between the United States and the UK are of particular note because they have implications for theories about corporate governance systems in addition to CSR, as discussed in below.

Other comparative approaches examine pressures on companies across a broad range of countries at one level of analysis or on one dimension. A developing body of scholarship compares, across countries, the actions or perspectives of employees, consumers, institutional investors or non-governmental organizations (NGOs) to engage in CSR initiatives. Some of these studies will be summarized below, with a particular emphasis on differences in perspectives of top management teams (TMT) and consumers between geographic regions. Other approaches look at companies' CSR actions more directly, such as studies of differences in corporate social reporting across countries or differences in companies' community partnerships or partnerships with NGOs across countries. A number of these studies will be discussed below. Recent research in international business discusses the strategic management of CSR issues by global companies operating in different countries, summarized in the penultimate section. A conclusion follows.

COMPARISONS OF LEGAL AND INSTITUTIONAL FACTORS SHAPING CSR

Comparative Legal Analysis regarding CSR

Today, scholarship at the intersection of law and sociology 'decenters' the state as a locus of regulatory power in favor of a more nuanced view of various systems of control that have an impact on conduct, including law, norms, industry and professional practices, markets and even architecture (Lessig, 1999; Scott, 2003). And yet comparative legal analysis still has much to offer in understanding CSR, since the laws governments pass to encourage CSR are uniquely powerful, in at least three respects. First, the standards established by laws and mandatory regulation, while not immediately translated into action in any realistic portrait of global organizational practice, have a particularly strong influence on establishing social expectations about responsible corporate behavior. The social expectations then act as a 'focal point' around which firms structure their behavior (McAdams and Nadler, 2005). Second, once the social expectation is created, a number of other forces, including consumer demands, institutional investor demands, community demands, and NGO demands, interact to create incentives for firms to meet the standards set out in the law (Kagan et al., 2003), whether enforcement is a realistic threat or not. Third, the laws and policies that governments enact send a strong signal about the importance of a subject—a signal that, as regards CSR, is amplified by the business culture in the country, consumers' interests, institutional investors' actions, the corporate governance regime, NGOs' effectiveness, and the individualistic versus collectivist nature of the country's underlying political and social philosophy.

An example of these factors, given government leadership in the administration of Prime Minister Tony Blair, is the emphasis by the UK government in promoting CSR (Moon, 2004; Aaronson and Reeves, 2002). In 1996, the Blair administration promulgated regulations, since followed by Belgium, France, Germany, and the Netherlands, that require the trustees of occupational pension funds to adopt Statements of Investment Principles detailing the way social and environmental information is taken into account in constructing investment portfolios. This law has had an important effect on the behavior of the largest pension funds, causing them to ask questions of asset managers about their CSR records, and in turn fueling greater interest in, and investment in, socially responsible investment (SRI) (Williams and Conley, 2005). As one example of its policy encouragement, the UK government was persuaded that extractive industry revenue transparency would help to promote government accountability, political stability, and reduce poverty in many 'resource rich yet poor' countries. It also realized that such political stability would be advantageous to two of its flagship companies, BP and Shell, but only so long as BP and Shell did not suffer competitive disadvantages from losing oil concessions to companies that did not require revenue transparency. As a result, Prime Minister Tony Blair became a leader in the recent Extractive Industry Transparency Initiative to encourage companies in the oil, gas, and mining industry to 'Publish What They Pay', that is to publish the payments companies have made to countries to obtain concessions to extract oil, gas, or minerals (Williams, 2004).

Given the UK's leadership role in encouraging CSR, it is not surprising that comparative studies show that companies in the UK have higher rates of stakeholder engagement and social reporting than companies in every other European country except Norway, even as European companies generally lead the world on these metrics (Welford, 2005). Future work that investigates the effect of government laws and policies in the UK in producing these high rates of reporting, and that differentiates between legal factors and institutional factors such as institutional investor pressures, top management team (TMT) leadership, labor or NGO activism, in producing these high rates of stakeholder engagement and social reporting, would be valuable.

With respect to developing countries, one predominant CSR concern is that governments will ignore corporate irresponsibility or refuse to enforce protective labor or environmental standards in the law as an inducement to foreign investment (Aman, 2001). China, for instance, has strong rights to collective bargaining, by law, and yet thousands of people in jail for trying to exercise those rights (Diamond, 2003). Yet, some developing country governments are promulgating laws requiring higher standards of responsible environmental or social conduct in order to compete for foreign capital and institutional investment, in addition to competing on the more familiar 'rule of law' issues of contract and property law rights, financial transparency, intellectual property protection, and reduced government corruption (Hebb and Wojcik, 2004). Comparing these legal developments in different emerging economies would be valuable as a basis for further understanding of the relationship of law and development and of the contribution of CSR, if any, to economic development.

Chapple and Moon (2005) have found that CSR in Asia is unrelated to pre-existing levels of economic development, but is related to the extent to which domestic companies engage in international trade, even where that trade is with other Asian nations. Conversely it would be useful to study whether 'imports' of CSR standards into developing countries lead to greater economic development or enhance rule of law norms. This strand of comparative legal analysis of CSR would take up the suggestion of Ahlering and Deakin (2005) to examine more carefully the complementarities between legal and economic institutions in promoting economic development.

Comparative Institutional Analysis

Comparative institutional analysis proceeds from the assumption that formal institutions, such as constitutions, laws, and government policies, interact with both informal institutions such as social norms and 'mental modes of analysis' (Doh and Guay, 2006), and organizations such as business entities, labor organizations, and civil society, to produce unique cultural and institutional frameworks for company action (Aguilera and Jackson, 2003; Campbell, 2005; Ahlerling and Deakin, 2005). One such recent study is that of Doh and Guay, which explored differences in the institutional environments in the European Union (EU) versus the United States with respect to government policy-making, corporate strategies to affect government policy-making, and NGO activism (Doh and Guay, 2006). Doh and Guay looked at differences in NGO strategies and power in the EU versus United States with respect to three CSR policy issues, those of genetically modified foods, climate change, and HIV/AIDS drug pricing. They conclude that the more influential position of NGOs in the EU is explained by differences in the processes of policy-making in the EU, in that there are explicit avenues for including the views of business, labor, and civil society as important policies are being developed at the EU level, and by differences in the political legacies of the two regions, given the social-democratic traditions in the EU versus the more individualistic and libertarian strands of political thought in the United States (Doh and Guay, 2006).

Another comparative institutional study that evaluates the legal requirements and market incentives to engage in CSR throughout the EU, with a particular emphasis on Spain, is Cuesta González and Valor Martinez (2004). Their article includes a comprehensive description of regulations and government policies across the EU to encourage CSR initiatives and to require greater disclosure of social and environmental information that should be useful to future researchers. The authors view the most important aspects of CSR, labor relationships, and environmental protection, as incorporated into the regulatory framework in Europe, but that social and environmental information and company responsibility for subsidiaries' actions or their supply chains are 'gaps' in the framework that leave room for voluntary CSR. Cuesta González and Valov Martínez (2004) note that most of the laws in Europe to address these gaps seek to create market incentives to encourage CSR, such as recognition of best practices, awareness campaigns, and the like, designed to encourage consumers to use their purchasing power to promote CSR, which the authors conclude is indicative of governments 'not strongly committed to these [CSR] initiatives' (p. 284) The authors evaluate the disclosure requirements as an effort to overcome information asymmetries about companies' CSR activities, such that capital and consumer markets can respond with greater precision to companies' records. Generally, though, the authors conclude that consumer and investor market incentives are too weak in Spain, the specific country they examine in detail, and so specific regulations would be required to increase the value of required disclosure, to expand fiduciary duties of company directors and managers, and to hold the public sector accountable for its social, economic and environmental performance.

A trenchant suggestion to extend institutional comparative work of this type comes from Zumbansen (2006: 18), who posits that the questions of defining companies' social responsibilities and examining convergence and divergence in corporate governance cannot fully be answered until companies themselves are examined as 'institutions of social learning' within unique socio-economic and regulatory contexts, each shaped by national path dependencies and international comparisons. While some comparative social responsibility work is starting in that direction, by combining attention to comparative institutional and regulatory context with examining companies' actions in those different contexts, Zumbansen is undoubtedly correct to call for more systematic attention to how companies respond and 'learn' within different regulatory and institutional environments.

Implications of Comparative CSR for Understanding Corporate Governance Systems

Studies of comparative CSR have implications for our understanding of theories of corporate governance. Corporate governance scholars have roughly divided the world into the Anglo-American 'outsider' system versus the Continental European and Japanese 'insider' systems, which divisions have been suggested to map onto shareholder versus stakeholder views of the firm and onto different cognitive styles in various cultures (Licht, 2004). Yet, recent studies of comparative CSR suggest that these conceptual demarcations need substantial qualification. In particular, a number of studies show that legal developments and institutional contexts in Britain concerning CSR show important similarities with Europe, and related contrasts with the United States, thus casting doubt on a unified 'Anglo-American' system of corporate governance.

Matten and Moon (2004) have compared CSR in Europe to that in the United States, and have proposed a conceptual framework of 'explicit' versus 'implicit' CSR, while recognizing that these are matters of emphasis, not wholly dichotomous states. They define explicit CSR as that seen in the United States, where companies volunteer to address important social and economic issues through their CSR policies, in significant part because of less stringent legal requirements than in Europe for such things as health-care provision, employee's rights, environmental protection, and so on (p. 9). In contrast, in Europe and the UK, responsibility for these issues is undertaken as part of a company's legal responsibilities, and thus CSR is 'implicit' in the way the company does business (ibid). The results of their work suggests that Britain shares with Europe institutional and legal features that reflect its European character, so that business is assigned, by law, 'an agreed share of responsibility for society's interests and concerns' (Matten and Moon, 2004: 9). In this analysis, Matten and Moon (2004) have implicitly interrogated the question of whether there is an 'Anglo-American' system of corporate governance, at least at the level of agreed conclusions on the perennial debates of the corporate purpose, and whether shareholders only, or stakeholders in addition, should comprise the full ambit of managerial strategy and concern.

Similarly, Armour et al. (2003) and Deakin (2005) have looked critically at the claim that the UK's system of corporate governance shares with the United States primacy for the interests of shareholders. They find considerable support for the idea that the institutional context in Britain—particularly protections of employees in insolvency law and in labor law—casts doubt on a unitary 'Anglo-American' view of corporate governance. They also describe some influential pension fund shareholders in London as concerned with broader stakeholder interests, observing that '[s]ome institutional investors are beginning to use their influence to monitor performance by companies across a range of social and environmental issues that impact upon stakeholders' (Armour et al., 2003).

Williams and Conley (2005) and Aguilera et al. (2006) have followed Armour et al. (2003) in evaluating legal and institutional factors in the UK and the City of London that are encouraging a divergence between the United States and the UK in the emphasis given in the two countries' capital markets to companies' social and environmental role. Legal factors include more required disclosure of social and environmental information by publicly listed companies in the UK than in the United States; and the required disclosure by pension fund trustees of the extent to which social and environmental issues are considered in constructing their investment portfolios (Williams and Conley, 2005). Institutional factors include: (a) differences in the composition of institutional investors in the two markets, with a higher percentage of institutional investors in the UK being pension funds and insurance companies with longer time-horizons for investment than the mutual funds that have dominated in the United States; (b) 'soft law' encouragement in the UK by the highly influential Cadbury Commission of institutional investor engagement with portfolio companies; and (*c*) encouragement of attention to CSR issues by the Institutional Shareholders Committee, which represents over 80% of institutional investment in the UK (Aguilera *et al.*, 2006; Williams and Conley, 2005). Further research should re-evaluate these institutional factors as private equity investors and hedge funds become a more substantial percentage of each market, in order to determine if the time-frames for investment are being affected by shifts in the composition of the two markets, since concern with longer-term risks is part of investors' concerns with CSR. It would be particularly important to evaluate if the priority given to CSR issues by City of London investors, as previously described, is being eroded.

ACTOR-CENTERED CROSS-NATIONAL COMPARISONS: ATTITUDES OF MANAGERS AND CONSUMERS TOWARDS CSR

As remarked above, comparative research can be approached from multiple perspectives. For example, it can compare a given issue, such as CSR transparency, across different countries or different industries. Another route is to take an actor-centered perspective where one analyzes the differences and similarities in the strategy and capacity of different stakeholders to influence CSR issues at the firm, government, or societal level. A third comparative route might be to combine the two comparative methods, looking at different CSR issues as well as stakeholder reactions across regions, as did Doh and Guay (2006) in the research discussed above. Thus, in conducting comparative and qualitative research using a case study methodology to assess the roles of NGOs in the United States and Europe in exercising influence on three CSR issues (trade and regulation of genetically modified organisms, relaxation of intellectual property protection for HIV/AIDS medications, and the Kyoto Agreement on climate change), they were able to show that differences in these two regions in the structure of political institutions and the strategies of interests groups directly determined how CSR is perceived and put into practice by the different firms, activists, and governments. This type of comparative research is difficult to conduct, given the complexity of data collection, and the research design is challenging if we are to rely on survey methodology.

One CSR research question which has received some comparative attention and hence is worthwhile synthesizing and discussing is how stakeholders across different institutional and cultural settings approach and react to CSR issues. In particular, there is some interesting work looking at the role of managers and consumers across countries. We discuss each of them in turn.

Comparative TMT Attitudes towards CSR

There is an extensive literature which conceptually justifies why managerial values and attitudes towards CSR in a given organization, industry, or national context are likely to have a strong influence on firm-level CSR outcomes (e.g. Hay and Gray, 1974; Hemingway and Maclagan, 2004; Hemingway, 2005; Aguilera *et al.*, forthcoming). In addition, the research finding that individual and organizational values, regardless of country-level factors, are significant predictors of CSR managerial behavior has also been confirmed by multiple empirical studies in different national and industry contexts. For example, Vitell and Paolillo's (2004) cross-cultural study of the antecedents of the perceived role of social responsibility in the decision-making process of managers from Spain, Turkey, Great Britain, and the United States shows that managerial CSR decisions and likelihood of success are shaped by the managers' individual ethical perspective and their organizational culture. Similarly, Waldman *et al.*'s (2006) cross-national and longitudinal study of culture and leadership precursors shows that both CEO visionary leadership and individual integrity are key factors associated with corporate social responsibility values. Finally, in the context of one emerging country, Branzei *et al.*'s (2004) study of 360 Chinese firms uncovers that leaders' cognitions influence the formation of novel responses to much-needed corporate greening strategies. One of the implications of these three empirical studies is that individual and organizational contexts do matter.

In light of these findings at the individual level, we would like to turn our attention to how managers might display different attitudes and values towards CSR given the cultural and historical differences across countries, regions, and even industrial fields. In other words, we seek to introduce a more systematic comparative perspective as well as to explore the distinct expectations that society (and societal actors) are likely to impose on TMTs as a team and as individual managers on their engagement in CSR issues. In effect, we expect a wide range of variation despite increasing global convergence in business practices. That expectation is based on the extensive evidence developed by international management scholars showing that managers, and more generally top management teams (TMTs), behave differently across countries because they are highly influenced by the national cultural norms of work (e.g. Hofstede, 1980, 2001; Schwartz, 1994; Triandis, 1995), organizational culture (O'Reilly and Chatman, 1996; Schein, 1992), or profession (Sirmon and Lane, 2004) in which they are embedded. Hence, these managers tend to make distinct strategic decisions and also have diverse constraints and capabilities in their decision-making process, depending on the country in which they are operating.

We know from the more established business ethics literature that there is a strong relationship between the likelihood that a manager will engage in corrupt business behavior and the extent to which managers operate in countries with high power distance, masculinity, and uncertainty (Husted, 1999). In this regard, one conceptual framework to compare how managers' attitudes towards CSR might vary across countries can be done by testing the cross-national validity of Donaldson and Dunfee's (1999) integrative social contracts theory as extended to CSR. This research could explore whether *hypernorms* or fundamental principles such as 'people should not be forced to work excessive hours and under inhumane conditions' are constant across societies, but *local norms* such as 'allowing some degree of child labor in very controlled circumstances is acceptable'—vary across countries. In addition, there are a number of empirical studies systematically comparing managerial ethical reasoning across countries which the CSR field could use as a benchmark. For example, Spicer *et al.* (2004) have conducted an empirical analysis that compares responses on an ethics survey from Americans working in Russia and in the United States. They show that location had little effect on these managers' attitudes towards hypernorms, but it did have a significant effect on their attitudes towards local norms and how expatriates address ethical dilemmas outside the United States. And Cullen *et al.* (2004) draw on institutional anomie theory, which takes into account cultural values and social institutional effects on individuals' behavior, and use the World Values Survey, to test managers' unethical conduct in 28 countries. They find significant nation-level effects, for instance, that industrialization weakens social norms and triggers a win-at-all-costs mentality, or that in societies with strong cultural values such as universalism and materialism managers tend to engage in more egoistic ethical reasoning.

There exist a few empirical studies which show cross-national differences in managerial attitudes towards CSR. We discuss four of them below to illustrate the distinct dimensions that comparative CSR has taken and ultimately to encourage other scholars to continue this research venue (the comparative CSR field), which remains fairly unexplored. The work that we discuss exemplifies the variety of research designs and countries covered. Then, we conclude this section by discussing another set of studies which do not see country-level variables as main drivers of CSR managerial attitudes and strategies, and point us towards somewhat mixed findings. This lack of consistent findings can be explained, in part, by the lack of a universal definition of CSR. It is not surprising that when individuals fill in surveys in different countries they have very distinct mental maps and expectations of what CSR is and is not, what it should be in an ideal world, and who should be involved in CSR issues. As Fukukawa and Moon (2004) have brought to our attention, even the definition of such terms as 'business' varies between countries, such that the Japanese word for business is a 'compound of the words kei, meaning "governing the world in harmony while bringing about the well-being of the people," and ci, meaning making "ceaseless efforts to achieve"'.

First, Orpen (1987) conducted a survey among senior managers in South Africa and the United States to uncover their attitude towards CSR. One part of the survey was designed to assess managers' 'major arguments for and against involvement in social responsibility activities by business' (p. 90) and another part of the survey was designed to assess managers' 'perceptions of the extent to which their society regards it as desirable that business engage in various socially responsible activities' (p. 91). Orpen (1987) finds that US managers hold a much more positive attitude towards CSR activities than South African managers. In other words, US managers agreed more with pro-responsibility statements while South African managers tended to support more anti-responsibility arguments, and differences were stronger when referring to social as opposed to environmental issues. Moreover, it is also shown that US managers felt more pressure to get involved in CSR strategies than their counterparts in South Africa.

Second, Maignan and Ralston (2002)'s cross-national study shows that businesses' communication about CSR, as evaluated by the information displayed in the 100 largest company web pages in 1999 in France, the Netherlands, the UK, and the United States, varies significantly. Maignan and Ralston concluded that businesses in these four countries do not ascribe the same importance to managing their image as a socially responsible organization, and that businesses draw on different mechanisms in different countries to communicate the nature of their CSR principles, processes, and stakeholder issues. For example, US and UK firms tended to be more eager to show that they 'cared' about CSR issues, at least, on the surface, whereas Dutch and French firms were more likely to include CSR issues in their websites only as a response to stakeholders' scrutiny and pressures. Maignan and Ralston (2002) also show variance across these four industrialized OECD countries in the principal motivations for CSR, whether these were mostly performance-driven, as in the UK, an extension of their core company values, as in the United States, or a combination of performance-driven, values-driven, and stakeholder-driven, as was the case with Dutch and French firms. Lastly, stakeholders' pressure on companies to address CSR issues also differed across countries. Maignan and Ralston (2002) show that communities and consumers were the primary stakeholder drivers in the UK, while customers and regulators were more salient in France and the Netherlands.

More recently, Waldman et al. (2006) published an extensive cross-national study of 561 firms based in 15 countries, on five continents, which examines the relation between CSR values of top management team members and two country-level societal cultural constructs, institutional collectivism and power distance, among other individual-level constructs. Their societal culture values are based on the Global Leadership and Organizational Behavior Effectiveness (GLOBE) research project (House et al., 2004), where institutional collectivism is defined as 'the extent to which a collective should believe in encouraging and rewarding the collective distribution of resources and collective action, and emphasizes group performance and rewards' (p. 826); and power distance refers to the degree which a culture believes that power should be unequally distributed. (High power distance societies tend to be more stratified economically, socially, and politically.) For example, Brazil scores high in institutional collectivism and China scores high in power distance, according to the GLOBE scores. In addition, managerial CSR values are conceptualized and measured as a multidimensional construct where managers can identify with three different dimensions of CSR: shareholder/owner, stakeholder issues, or community/state welfare. Waldman *et al.* (2006) show that managers in countries which esteem institutional collectivism traits such as obtaining gratification for addressing long-term concerns, and devalue high power distance traits, are more likely to manifest managerial behaviors positively associated with the three dimensions of CSR. In addition, they show that managers in wealthier countries are mostly concerned with shareholder/owner CSR issues, that is, CSR strategies which maximize economic returns.

Similarly, Egri *et al.* (2006) have conducted an extensive multi-level study which looks at the individual and national effects on attitudes towards corporate responsibilities (CR) in 28 countries. One of the key differences with Waldman *et al.* (2006) is that Egri *et al.*'s macro-level variable draws on two different societal cultural values included in the World Values Survey developed by Inglehart (1997), which are: traditional/secular-rational and survival/self-expression cultural values. The additional contribution of this study is that in their analysis of what influences corporate responsibility outcomes across countries, the authors differentiate three different types of corporate responsibility (social, environmental, and economic) and also account for three country-level factors (societal culture, degree of government intervention, and trade openness). In addition to reporting that personal values have a direct relationship with the type of CR that managers are likely to support in different countries, Egri *et al.* (2006) show that managers in traditional cultures that promote ethical idealism and communitarian norms, and tend to have a Roman Catholic heritage (e.g. Colombia and Italy) were more supportive of social CR than environmental or economic CR. Secular-rational and survival societies such as ex-Communist countries (e.g. Croatia and Hungary) or Confucian-oriented societies (e.g. Taiwan and Hong-Kong) were more likely to support economic CR initiatives.

As mentioned before, other comparative studies have not so clearly concluded that national cultural and market settings are strong predictors of managerial CSR behavior. Instead, they put more weight on the values of individuals and organizations regardless of country or regional institutional and cultural context. For example, Quazi (1997) and a follow-up study by Quazi and O'Brien (2000) comparing textile and food manufacturers in two very different countries, Australia and Bangladesh, find that managerial CSR decision-making in these two countries tends to be more universal than country-driven and that individual differences are mostly two-dimensional in terms of the span of corporate responsibility and the range of outcomes of social commitments of businesses, as opposed to culturally driven.

Similarly, Bansal and Roth (2000) have conducted an excellent qualitative study which looked at two broad conceptual categories of determinants of managerial ecological responsiveness in two countries, the UK and Japan. On the one hand, they examine corporate-level motivations such as competitiveness, legitimation, and degree of overall environmental responsibility, and on the other hand, they explore the contextual determinants defined as the level of cohesion within a given industry, the salience of the given CSR issue, and the managerial individual concern for CSR issues. They are able to conclude that managers and firms in these two countries are driven by distinct factors to pursue positive CSR actions although there is not an explicit country-level cleavage. Instead, the authors remind us that ecological responsiveness exemplifies *configurational equifinality*, that is, firms, regardless of their country of origin, can reach the same final state of responsiveness from differing contextual and motivational conditions and taking distinct paths to reach that same outcome.

Comparative Consumer Attitudes towards CSR

Consumers are an important stakeholder in the context of CSR and can become strategic nightmares for companies, as Nike experienced when it became a lightning rod for concerns over labor practices in Asia, or as Royal Dutch Shell experienced with the Brent Spar environmental imbroglio. Marketing research has demonstrated that corporate social performance information shapes consumer purchase intentions (e.g. Brown and Dacin, 1997; Creyer and Ross, 1997). There also exits a fascinating literature drawing on social movement theory which discusses consumers' capabilities, strategies and ultimately power as an organized group to impact firms' CSR behavior (e.g. Kozinets and Handelman, 2004; O'Rourke, 2005; Schurman, 2004; Sharma and Vredenburg, 1998). However, the research on comparative consumer attitudes toward CSR is less developed, and certainly less abundant, than the comparative managerial work reviewed in the previous section.

Isabelle Maignan and her colleagues have offered pioneering insights into the field of marketing research and CSR, or the so-called 'socially responsible buying' behavioral literature, by asking what differences there are across countries regarding the extent to which consumers support socially responsible business. For example, Maignan's (2001) study is one of the first cross-national comparative studies of consumer attitudes towards CSR and of the demands that this group of stakeholders is willing to make on firms. Maignan (2001) collected consumer survey data in France, Germany, and the United States, and concluded that American consumers are mostly concerned with corporate economic responsibilities, agreeing with such statements as business must 'maximize profits' and 'control their production costs strictly' (p. 64), as opposed to statements emphasizing companies' legal, ethical, and philanthropic responsibilities. Meanwhile, French and German consumers generally tend to put more value on supporting socially responsible organizations conforming with legal and ethical standards, and have better mechanisms and tactics in place to monitor and influence the behavior of organizations as a consumer group (see also Maignan and Ferrell, 2003 for a follow-up study).

More recently, Schuler and Cording (2006) have developed a conceptual model of consumer behavior based on the process by which consumers make purchasing decisions, as affected by different characteristics of information intensity, such as information source, degree of diffusion, and corporate reputation, to explain the complex relationship between corporate social performance (CSP) and corporate financial performance. It would be worthwhile to test their consumer behavioral model in different industry and national settings. In addition, some researchers have examined the role of marketing professionals and their perception of consumers in CSR issues. For example, Singhapakdi *et al.* (2001) compare the attitudes of marketing professionals when assessing consumer preferences in Australia, Malaysia, South Africa, and the United States. This might be another interesting route to take in exploring consumer attitudes and behavior towards firms' CSR. Finally, it is important to note that while there are societies that place a lot of emphasis on consumers' voice and have in place direct mechanisms where they can express their concerns, such as in the France, this is not the case in other societies, such as in Japan, where the consumer movement has been relatively weak (Wokutch, 1990).

BEHAVIOR-CENTERED CROSS-NATIONAL COMPARISONS

A different comparative approach is to examine companies' CSR behaviors, such as sustainability reporting or NGO/company partnerships, across countries. A number of these studies have looked at companies' sustainability reporting, evaluating differences across countries in reporting rates, in the issues discussed, and in how CSR issues are framed. Studies consistently find that reporting rates are highest in Europe, followed by Japan, and with the United States showing the lowest rates of reporting among comparable companies (Kolk, 2003; KPMG, 2005; Kolk, forthcoming; Welford, 2005). Kolk's most recent study shows that 90% of European companies in the Fortune Global 250 publish sustainability reports, followed by 83% of Japanese companies, as contrasted with 35% of American companies. Kolk suggests that this dramatic differential between Europe and the United States reflects cross-national differences in public discussion of CSR and sustainability reporting and European leadership in CSR (Kolk, forthcoming: 6), while it must be noted that Europe requires social and environmental reporting, albeit without being specific about the format. Of course, the fact that Europe requires some aspects of sustainability reporting can also be understood as evidence of its leadership on CSR.

Interesting differences emerge in what issues are emphasized in companies' sustainability reports and how those issues are framed. Kolk finds that about 60% of sustainability reports now discuss the corporate governance of sustainability within the organization, while surveys of similar sets of companies only a few years ago (2002 reports) did not discuss this topic (Kolk, forthcoming). Kolk also finds that European and Japanese companies are more specific than US companies about 'the organizational aspects and responsibilities for sustainability' (Kolk, forthcoming: 8). Differences also emerge in external verification of sustainability reports, with 45% of European reports being externally verified, as contrasted with 24% of Japanese reports and 3% of American reports (Kolk, 2006: 10 and table 3). As Kolk recognizes, American disclosure patterns and lack of verification may reflect the greater concern with litigation in the United States, and the difficulties of a purely voluntary approach to expanded sustainability disclosure in such a context. Further comparative research that investigates the decisions by TMTs to produce sustainability reports, and their understanding of their own motivations for the structure, contents, and verification of such reports, would be of value.

Country of origin also has an impact on how multinationals as legal entities incorporated in a given home country behave around the world through their subsidiaries. For example, Meek *et al.* (1995) have conducted a study of voluntary annual report disclosure by US, UK, and Continental European multinational firms. They are able to show that the country of origin has a significant effect not only on the degree of voluntary disclosure but also on what type of information (i.e. strategic, non-financial, and financial) is most likely to be covered in these MNCs' annual reports.

Despite the transnational efforts to design and implement universal CSR standards connected to 'triple bottom line' thinking (Waddock *et al.*, 2002), in practice international hard regulation on and enforcement of how MNCs should behave around the world is non-existent. It is interesting to examine to what degree MNCs from different parts of the world comply with soft international regulation. For example, Christmann and Taylor (2006) look at MNCs' compliance with ISO 9000 (a set of international environmental standards) in China, which allows them to control for the host country enforceability of regulation. They discover that MNC compliance with this environmental standard, whether it is substantive or symbolic, is determined by customer preferences, customer monitoring, and expected sanctions from customers in their home countries. This study suggests a fruitful line of inquiry evaluating the relative efficacy of legal versus market 'enforcement' of standards.

Another comparative approach to the study of CSR within MNCs is to examine whether there are differences in practices not only between the home MNC and the subsidiaries, but also across the different subsidiaries of a given MNC. Husted and Allen (2006) have investigated how CSR is managed within MNCs, and studied the relationship between global and local (country-specific) CSR. Building upon Donaldson and Dunfee (1994: 260), they define global CSR issues as those 'issues that transcend national boundaries and about which considerable consensus is emerging', such as human rights and environmental protection (Husted and Allen, 2006: 840). Local CSR issues are those that respond to the specific needs and concerns of particular communities, such as HIV/AIDS in Africa: it is an issue that every company doing business in Africa needs to address, but it has not become part of the global CSR agenda. Husted and Allen (2006) surveyed firms in Mexico, and found that the firms followed different patterns of management of global and local CSR issues depending on whether they were firms with many, semi-autonomous subsidiaries (multi-domestic); were organized from a central office with lean subsidiaries (global); or combined elements of central organization and local responsiveness (transnational). Following Husted and Allen's (2006) sugges-tion, these results can be useful in evaluating government policies in developing countries to encourage greater economic development. For instance, comparative research might study whether decisions about valuable licenses to operate or to extract local resources would best be granted to specific types of firms (global, multi-domestic, transnational), depending on the mix of local versus global CSR issues in the region or industry at issue.

CONCLUSION

The field of comparative CSR, ultimately, addresses a research question of critical practical importance: how best to structure global enterprise to import best practice in CSR in order to produce economic development that is consistent with raising labor standards and encouraging environmental protection. Strike *et al.* (2006) have produced empirical evidence that clearly states the challenge, by virtue of their findings that international diversification of firms increases both CSR as well as corporate irresponsibility, given the difficulties of managing semi-autonomous subsidiaries in different countries. Further comparative investigations of the respec-tive roles of government; institutional actors such as labor unions, investors, and NGOs; and actors within the firm, such as TMTs and employees, are necessary to further our understanding of the differing pressures from consumers, cultures, and political entities towards responsible corporate actions. Such research may provide an empirical and theoretical basis for developing policies to encourage CSR and for conceptualizing which kinds of pressures are likely to be effective in encouraging a positive relationship between international businesses and society.

REFERENCES

AARONSON, S., and REEVES, J. 2002. *Corporate Responsibility in the Global Village: The Role of Public Policy*. Washington: National Policy Association.

AGUILERA, R. V., and JACKSON, G. 2003. 'The Cross-National Diversity of Corporate Governance: Dimensions and Determinants'. *Academy of Management Review*, 28: 447–65.

—— WILLIAMS, C., CONLEY, J., and RUPP, D. 2006. 'Corporate Governance and Corporate Social Responsibility. A Comparative Analysis of the U.K. and the U.S.'. *Corporate Governance: An International Review*, 14(3): 147–57.

—— RUPP, D., WILLIAMS, C., and GANAPATHI, J. Forthcoming. 'Putting the S Back in CSR: A Multi-level Theory of Social Change in Organizations'. *Academy of Management Review*.

AHLERING, B. and DEAKIN, S. 2005. 'Labour Regulation, Corporate Governance and Legal Origin: A Case of Institutional Complementarity?' European Corporate Governance Institute, Law Working Paper No. 72/2006.

AMAN, A., JR. 2001. 'Privatization and the Democracy Problem in Globalization: Making Markets More Accountable through Administrative Law'. *Fordham Urban Law Journal*, 28: 1477–506.

ARMOUR, J., DEAKIN, S. and KONZELMANN, S. J. 2003. 'Shareholder Primacy and the Trajectory of UK Corporate Governance'. *British Journal of Industrial Relations*, 41(3): 531–55.

BANSAL, P., and ROTH, K. 2000. 'Why Companies Go Green: A Model of Ecological Responsiveness'. *Academy of Management Journal*, 43: 717–36.

BARNETT, M. L., and SALOMON, R. M. 2006. 'Beyond Dichotomy: The Curvilinear Relationship between Social Responsibility and Financial Performance'. *Strategic Management Journal*, 1101–22.

BRANZEI, O., URSACKI-BRYANT, T. J., , VERTINSKY, I., and ZHANG, W. 2004. 'The Formations of Green Strategies in Chinese Firms: Matching Corporate Environmental Responses and Individual Principles'. *Strategic Management Journal*, 25: 1075–95.

BROWN, T. J., and DACIN, P. A. 1997. 'The Company and the Product: Corporate Associations and Consumer Product Responses'. *Journal of Marketing*, 61: 68–84.

CAMPBELL, J. 2005. *Institutional Change and Globalization: Exploring Problems in the New Institutional Analysis*. Princeton: Princeton University Press.

CARROLL, A. 1979. 'A Three-Dimensional Model of Corporate Performance'. *Academy of Management Review*, 4: 497–505.

CHAPPLE, W., and MOON, J. 2005. 'Corporate Social Responsibility (CSR) in Asia: A Seven-Country Study of CSR'. *Business and Society*, 44(4): 415–41.

CHRISTMANN, P., and TAYLOR, G. 2006. 'Firm Self-Regulation through International Certifiable Standards: Determinants of Symbolic versus Substantive Implementation. *Journal of International Business Studies*, 37: 863–78.

CLARKSON, M. 1995. 'A Stakeholder Framework for Analyzing and Evaluating Corporate Social Performance'. *Academy of Management Review*, 20: 92–117.

CREYER, E. H., and ROSS, W. T. 1997. 'The Influence of Firm Behavior on Purchase Intention: Do Consumers really Care about Business Ethics?' *Journal of Consumer Marketing*, 14: 421–32.

CUESTA GONZÁLEZ, M., and VALOR MARTÍNEZ, C. 2004. 'Fostering Corporate Social Responsibility through Public Initiative: From the EU to the Spanish Case'. *Journal of Business Ethics*, 55: 273–93.

CULLEN, J. B., PARBOTEEAH, K. P., and HOEGL, M. 2004. 'Cross-National Differences in Managers' Willingness to Justify Ethically Suspect Behaviors: A Test of Institutional Anomie Theory'. *Academy of Management Journal*, 47: 411–21.

DEAKIN, S. 2005. 'The Coming Transformation of Shareholder Value'. *Corporate Governance: An International Review*, 13(1): 11–18.

DIAMOND, S. F. 2003. 'The "Race to the Bottom" Returns: China's Challenge to the International Labor Movement'. *University of California at Davis Journal of International Law and Policy*, 10: 39–74.

DOH, J. P., and GUAY, T. R. 2006. 'Corporate Social Responsibility, Public Policy, and NGO Activism in Europe and the United States: An Institutional-Stakeholder Perspective'. *Journal of Management Studies*, 47–73.

DONALDSON, T., and DUNFEE, T. W. 1994. 'Toward a Unified Conception of Business Ethics: Integrative Social Contracts Theory'. *Academy of Management Review*, 19: 252–84.

————1999. *Ties that Bind. A Social Contracts Approach to Business Ethics*. Boston: Harvard Business Review.

——and PRESTON, L. 1995. 'The Stakeholder Theory of the Corporation: Concepts, Evidence, and Implications'. *Academy of Management Review*, 20: 65–91.

EGRI, C. P., RALSTON, D. A., MILTON, L., CASADO, T., PALMER, I., RAMBURUTH, P., WANGENHEIM, F., FU, P. P., KUO, M. H., CARRANZA, M. T. G., GIRSON, I., DABIC, M., BUTT, A., SRINVASAN, N., FURRER, O., HALLINGER, P., DALGIC, T., RICHARDS, M., ROSSI, A. M., DANIS, W., GUTIREZ, J. R., REYNAUD, E., BROCK, D., MOLTENI, M., STARKUS, A., CASTRO, F., CHIA, H. B., DARDER, F. L., WALLACE, A., NAOUMOVA, I., ANSARI, M., RIDDEL, L., POTOCAN, V. V., and THANH, H. V. 2006. 'The Influence of Personal Values and National Contexts on Attitudes towards Corporate Responsibilities'. Presented at the Third BC Organizational Behaviour Conference, Vancouver, Canada.

FREEMAN. R. E. 1984. *Strategic Management: A Stakeholder Perspective*. Englewood Cliffs, NJ: Prentice Hall.

FUKUKAWA, K., and MOON, J. 2004. 'A Japanese Model of Corporate Social Responsibility? A Study of Website Reporting'. *Journal of Corporate Citizenship*, 16: 45–60.

HAY, R., and GRAY, E. 1974. 'Social Responsibilities of Business Managers'. *Academy of Management Journal*, 17: 135–43.

HEBB, T., and WOJCIK, D. 2004. 'Global Standards and Emerging Markets: The Institutional Investor Value Chain and CALPERS' Investment Strategy'. *University of Oxford Working Paper 04–05*, available at <http://www.ssrn.com/author=202581>.

HEMINGWAY, C. A. 2005. 'Personal Values as a Catalyst for Corporate Social Entrepreneurship'. *Journal of Business Ethics*, 60(3): 233–49.

——and MACLAGAN, P. W. 2004. 'Managers' Personal Values as Drivers of Corporate Social Responsibility'. *Journal of Business Ethics*, 50(1): 33–44.

HOFSTEDE, G. 1980. *Culture's Consequences: International Differences in Work-Related Values*. Beverly Hills, Calif.: Sage.

—— 2001. '*Culture's Consequences: Comparing Values, Behaviours, Institutions, and Organizations across Nations* 2nd edn. Thousand Oaks, Calif.: Sage.

HOUSE, R. J., HANGES, P. M., JAVIDAN, M., DORFMAN, P., and GUPTA, V. 2004. *Culture, Leadership and Organizations: The GLOBE Study of 62 Societies*. Thousand Oaks, Calif.: Sage.

HUSTED, B. W. 1999. 'Wealth, Culture and Corruption'. *Journal of International Business Studies*, 30: 339–60.

HUSTED, B. W., and ALLEN, D. B. 2006. 'Corporate Social Responsibility in the Multinational Enterprise: Strategic and Institutional Approaches'. *Journal of International Business Studies*, 37: 838–49.

INGLEHART, R. 1997. *Modernization and Postmodernization: Cultural, Economic, and Political Change in 43 Societies*. Princeton: Princeton University Press.

KAGAN, R. A., GUNNINGHAM, N., and THORNTON, D. 2003. 'Explaining Corporate Environmental Performance: How does Regulation Matter?' *Law and Society Review*, 37: 51–90.

KOLK, A. 2003. 'Trends in Sustainability Reporting by the Fortune Global 250'. *Business Strategy and the Environment*, 12: 279–91.

—— Forthcoming. 'Sustainability, Accountability and Corporate Governance: Exploring Multinationals' Reporting Practices'. *Business Strategy and the Environment*.

KOZINETS, R. V., and HANDELMAN, J. M. 2004. 'Adversaries of Consumption: Consumer Movements, Activism, and Ideology'. *Journal of Consumer Research*, 31: 691–704.

KPMG. 2005. 'KPMG International Survey of Corporate Responsibility Reporting 2005'. Amsterdam: KPMG Global Sustainability Services.

LESSIG, L. 1999. *Code and other Laws of Cyberspace*. New York: Basic Books.

LICHT, A. N. 2004. 'The Maximands of Corporate Governance: A Theory of Values and Cognitive Style'. *Delaware Journal of Corporate Law*. 29: 649–746.

LOGSDON, J., and WOOD, D. J. 2002. 'Business Citizenship: From Domestic to Global Level of Analysis'. *Business Ethics Quarterly*, 12: 155–88.

McADAMS, R., and NADLER, J. 2005. 'Testing the Focal Point Theory of Legal Compliance: The Effect of Third-Party Expression in an Experimental Hawk/Dove Game'. *Journal of Empirical Legal Studies*, 87–123.

McWILLIAMS, A., and SIEGEL, D. 2000. 'Corporate Social Responsibility and Financial Performance: Correlation or Misspecification?' *Strategic Management Journal*, 21: 603–10.

—— —— 2001. 'Corporate Social Responsibility: A Theory of the Firm Perspective', *Academy of Management Review*, 26: 117–27.

—— —— and WRIGHT, P. 2006. 'Corporate Social Responsibility: Strategic Implications'. *Journal of Management Studies*, 43: 1–18.

MAIGNAN, I. 2001. 'Consumers' Perception of Corporate Social Responsibilities: A Cross-Cultural Comparison'. *Journal of Business Ethics*, 30: 57–72.

—— and FERRELL, O. C. 2003. 'Nature of Corporate Responsibilities: Perspectives from American, French and German Consumers'. *Journal of Business Research*, 56: 55–67.

MAIGNAN, I., and RALSTON, D. 2002. 'Corporate Social Responsibility in Europe and the U.S.: Insights from Businesses' Self-Presentations'. *Journal of International Business Studies*, 33: 497–514.

MARGOLIS, J. D., and WALSH, J. P. 2003. 'Misery Loves Companies: Rethinking Social Initiatives by Business'. *Administrative Science Quarterly*, 48: 655–89.

MATTEN, D., and MOON, J. 2004. ' "Implicit" and "explicit" CSR: A Conceptual Framework for Understanding CSR in Europe', in A. Habisch, J. Jonker, M. Wegner and R. Schmidpeter (eds.), *CSR across Europe*. Berlin: Springer-Verlag, 335–56.

MEEK, G., ROBERTS, C., and GRAY, S. 1995. 'Factors Influencing Voluntary Annual Report Disclosures by U.S., U.K. and Continental European Multinational Corporations'. *Journal of International Business Studies*, 26: 555–73.

MOON, J. 2004. 'Government as a Driver of Corporate Social Responsibility: The UK in Comparative Perspective'. *International Centre for Corporate Social Responsibility Research Paper No. 20–2004*, Nottingham: Nottingham University Business School.

O'REILLY, C., and CHATMAN, J. 1996. 'Culture as Social Control: Corporations, Cults, and Commitment'. *Research in Organizational Behavior,* 18: 157–200.

ORLITZKY, M., SCHMIDT, F. L., and RYNES, S. L. 2003. 'Corporate Social and Financial Performance: A Meta-analysis'. *Organization Studies,* 24: 403–41.

O'ROURKE, D. 2005. 'Market Movements. Nongovernmental Organization Strategies to Influence Global Production and Consumption'. *Journal of Industry Ecology,* 9: 1–14.

ORPEN, C. 1987. 'The Attitudes of United States and South African Managers to Corporate Social Responsibility'. *Journal of Business Ethics,* 6: 89–96.

QUAZI, A. M. 1997. 'Corporate Social Responsibility in Diverse Environments: A Comparative Study of Managerial Attitudes in Australia and Bangladesh'. *Business and Professional Ethics Journal,* 16: 67–84.

——and O'BRIEN, D. 2000. 'An Empirical Test of a Cross-National Model of Corporate Social Responsibility'. *Journal of Business Ethics,* 25: 33–51.

RODRÍGUEZ, P., SIEGEL, D. S., HILLMAN, A., and EDEN, L. 2006. 'Three Lenses on the Multinational Enterprise: Politics, Corruption, and Corporate Social Responsibility'. *Journal of International Business Studies,* 37: 733–46.

SCHEIN, E. H. 1992. *Organizational Culture and Leadership.* San Tranciso: Jossey-Bass.

SCHULER, D. A., and CORDING, M. 2006. 'A Corporate Social Performance-Corporate Financial Performance Behavioral Model for Consumers'. *Academy of Management Review,* 31: 540–58.

SCHURMAN, R. 2004. 'Fighting "Frankenfoods": Industry Opportunity Structures and the Efficacy of the Anti-biotech Movement in Western Europe'. *Social Problems,* 51: 243–68.

SCHWARTZ, S. H. 1994. 'Cultural Dimensions of Values: Towards an Understanding of National Differences', in H. C. Kim, C. Triandis, C. Kagitcibasi, S. C. Choi, and G. Yoon (eds.), *Individualism and collectivism: Theoretical and Methodological Issues.* Thousand Oaks, Calif.: Sage, 85–119.

SCOTT, C. 2003. 'Regulation in the Age of Governance: The Rise of the Post-regulatory State', in J. Jordana and DD. Levi-Faur (eds.), *The Politics of Regulation.* Cheltenham: Edward Elgar.

SHARMA, S., and VREDENBURG, H. 1998. 'Proactive Corporate Environmental Strategy and the Development of Competitively Valuable Organizational Capabilities'. *Strategic Management Journal,* 19: 729–53.

SINGHAPAKDI, A., KARANDE, K., RAO, C. P., and VITELL, S. J. 2001. 'How Important are Ethics and Social Responsibility? A Multinational Study of Marketing Professionals'. *European Journal of Marketing,* 35(1–2): 133–45.

SIRMON, D. G., and LANE, P. J. 2004. 'A Model of Cultural Differences and International Alliance Performance', *Journal of International Business Studies,* 35: 306–19.

SPICER, A., DUNFEE, T. W., and BAILEY, W. J. 2004. 'Does National Context Matter in Ethical Decision Making? An Empirical Test of Integrative Social Contracts Theory'. *Academy of Management Journal,* 47: 610–20.

STRIKE, V. M., GAO, J., and BANSAL, P. 2006. 'Being Good While Being Bad: Social Responsibility and the International Diversification of US Firms. *Journal of International Business Studies,* 37: 850–62.

TRIANDIS, H. C. 1995. *Individualism and Collectivism.* Boulder, Colo.: Westview Press.

VITELL, S. J., and PAOLILLO, J. G. 2004. 'A Cross-Cultural Study of the Antecedents of the Perceived Role of Ethics and Social Responsibility'. *Business Ethics,* 13(2–3): 185–99.

WADDOCK, S. A., BODWELL, C., and GRAVES, S. B. 2002. 'Responsibility: The New Business Imperative'. *Academy of Management Executive*, 16: 132–48.

WALDMAN, D. A., SULLY DE LUQUE, M., WASHBURN, N., and HOUSE, R. J. 2006. 'Cultural and Leadership Predictors of Corporate Social Responsibility Values of Top Management: A GLOBE Study of 15 countries'. *Journal of International Business Studies*, 37: 823–37.

WELFORD, R. 2005. 'Corporate Social Responsibility in Europe, North America and Asia'. *Journal of Corporate Citizenship*, 17: 33–52.

WILLIAMS, C. A. 2004. 'Civil Society Initiatives and 'Soft Law' in the Oil and Gas Industry'. *New York University Journal of International Law and Politics*, 36: 457–502.

—— and CONLEY, J. 2005. 'An Emerging Third Way? The Erosion of the Anglo-American Shareholder Value Construct'. *Cornell International Law Journal*, 38(2): 493–551.

WOKUTCH, R. E. 1990. 'Corporate Social Responsibility Japanese Style'. *Academy of Management Executive*, 42: 56–74.

ZUMBANSEN, P. 2006. 'The Conundrum of Corporate Social Responsibility: Reflections on the Changing Nature of Firms and States', in R. Miller and R. Bratspies (eds.), *Transboundary Harm: Lessons from the Trail Smelter Arbitration*. Cambridge: Cambridge University Press.

CORPORATE SOCIAL RESPONSIBILITY IN DEVELOPING COUNTRIES

WAYNE VISSER

INTRODUCTION

The challenge for corporate social responsibility (CSR) in developing countries is framed by a vision that was distilled in 2000 into the Millennium Development Goals—'a world with less poverty, hunger and disease, greater survival prospects for mothers and their infants, better educated children, equal opportunities for women, and a healthier environment' (UN, 2006: 3). Unfortunately, these global aspirations remain far from being met in many developing countries today. The question addressed by this chapter, therefore, is: What is the role of business in tackling the critical issues of human development and environmental sustainability in developing countries?

To begin with, it is worth clarifying my use of the terms *developing countries* and *CSR*. There is an extensive historical and generally highly critical debate in the development literature about the classification of countries as *developed* and *less developed* or *developing*. Without reviving that debate here, suffice to say that I use *developing countries* because it is still a popular term used to collectively describe nations that have relatively lower per capita incomes and are relatively less industrialized.

This is consistent with the United Nations Developments Program's (2006) categorization in its summary statistics on human development and is best represented by the World Bank's classification of lower and middle income countries.[1] It should be noted, however, that the UNDP's classification of high, medium and low development countries produces a slightly different picture than the World Bank's list of which countries are developed and developing.

CSR is an equally contested concept (Moon, 2002*b*). However, for the purposes of this chapter, I use *CSR in developing countries* to represent 'the formal and informal ways in which business makes a contribution to improving the governance, social, ethical, labour and environmental conditions of the developing countries in which they operate, while remaining sensitive to prevailing religious, historical and cultural contexts' (Visser *et al.*, 2007).

The rationale for focusing on CSR in developing countries as distinct from CSR in the developed world is fourfold:

1. developing countries represent the most rapidly expanding economies, and hence the most lucrative growth markets for business (IMF, 2006);
2. developing countries are where the social and environmental crises are usually most acutely felt in the world (WRI, 2005; UNDP, 2006);
3. developing countries are where globalization, economic growth, investment, and business activity are likely to have the most dramatic social and environmental impacts (both positive and negative) (World Bank, 2006); and
4. developing countries present a distinctive set of CSR agenda challenges which are collectively quite different to those faced in the developed world.

The latter claim is explored further in the sections which follow and is summarized at the end of the chapter. The chapter begins by proposing different ways to categorize the literature on CSR in developing countries. It then reviews the research which has been conducted at a global and regional level, before considering the main CSR drivers in developing countries. Finally, a model of CSR in developing countries is proposed, before concluding with a summary and recommendations for future research.

---

[1] See <http:www.worldbank.org>.

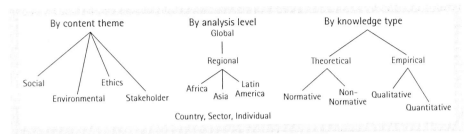

Fig. 21.1 Classification of literature on CSR in developing countries

CLASSIFICATION

There are various ways to classify the literature on CSR in developing countries, including in terms of content (thematic coverage), type (epistemological approach), and level (focus of analysis), as depicted in Figure 21.1. These will each be briefly considered in turn.

Content Theme

Using the same classification of content as Lockett *et al.* (2006), the CSR literature can be grouped into four dominant CSR themes: social, environmental, ethics, and stakeholders. What is immediately evident in applying this categorization to the literature on CSR in developing countries is that, in contrast to Lockett *et al.*'s (2006) findings that most CSR articles in top management journals focus on ethical and environmental themes, most scholarly work on CSR in developing countries focuses on the social theme.

In part, this reflects the fact that *corporate social responsibility* is the preferred term in the literature to describe the role of business in developing countries, as opposed to, say, business ethics, corporate citizenship, corporate sustainability, or stakeholder management. More than this, however, social issues are generally given more political, economic, and media emphasis in developing countries than environmental, ethical, or stakeholder issues (Schmidheiny, 2006). And there is also still a strong emphasis on the philanthropic tradition in developing countries, which is often focused on community development.

Knowledge Type

Lockett *et al.* (2006) also classify CSR papers by epistemological approach and find a roughly even split between theoretical and empirical research, which is also the case in the literature on CSR in developing countries, although the latter has a slight weighting towards empirical work.

What is interesting is that, whereas Lockett *et al.* (2006) find that 89% of theoretical CSR papers are non-normative, in the CSR in developing countries literature, the balance is far more evenly split. This is largely due to the relatively large number of papers on the role of business in development, which tend to adopt a normative, critical perspective (Blowfield and Frynas, 2005).

In terms of empirical research, there are also differences. According to Lockett *et al.* (2006), the CSR literature is dominated by quantitative methods (80%). In contrast, CSR papers on developing countries are more likely to be qualitative. Lockett *et al.* (2006) suggest that their findings probably reflect the positivist editorial tendencies of many of the top management journals, rather than the inherent epistemological preference of CSR scholars. And indeed, the CSR and development journals in which most developing country papers are published seem to have more interpretive or epistemologically flexible editorial policies.

ANALYSIS LEVEL

Most research on CSR in developing countries to date has either generalized about all developing countries (e.g. Frynas, 2006), or focused at a national (rather than a regional) level. In terms of generic literature, *Corporate Citizenship in Developing Countries* (Pedersen and Huniche, 2006) is a useful compendium, as are special issues on CSR in developing countries that have appeared in the *Journal of Corporate Citizenship* (issue 24, 2006), *International Affairs* (81(3), 2005) and *Development* (47(3), 2004).

Despite the focus on countries in the literature, only about a fifth of all developing countries have had any CSR journal articles published on them. Of these, the most commonly analyzed and written about countries are China, India, Malaysia, Pakistan, South Africa, and Thailand. Analysis at a regional level (notably Africa, Asia, and Latin America) is becoming more common, but papers at the sector, corporate, or individual level remain relatively scarce.

Global

Although the literature often frames the debate about CSR in a global context, there is very little empirical research on the nature and extent of CSR in developing countries. One notable exception is Baskin's (2006) research on the reported corporate responsibility behavior of 127 leading companies from 21 emerging markets[2] across Asia, Africa, Latin America, and Central and Eastern Europe, which he compares with over 1,700 leading companies in high-income OECD countries.

Looking at three generic indicators of CSR, Baskin (2006) finds that emerging market companies have a respectable representation in the Dow Jones Sustainability Index and show rising levels of take-up of the Global Reporting Initiative and ISO 14001. More specifically, over two-thirds of the emerging market companies in the sample either produced a sustainability report or had a specific section on their website or in their annual report covering CSR. Interestingly, emerging market companies are also more inclined to report extensively on corporate social investment activities than OECD companies.

Other areas of reported CSR performance examined by Baskin (2006) show that emerging markets lag the OECD significantly on reporting on business ethics and equal opportunities (with the exception of South Africa), are roughly on a par for environmental reporting, and show comparable reporting variance on women on company boards (e.g. high in Norway and South Africa, low in Japan and Latin America), training and occupational health and safety (e.g. high in South Africa and Western Europe, low in North America and Asia).

Despite the limitations of using reporting as an indicator of CSR performance and the danger of representing regions by just a few countries (e.g. only two of the 53 countries in Africa were included in the sample), the Baskin (2006) study does provide some insight into the level of CSR activity in developing countries, concluding that 'there is not a vast difference in the approach to reported corporate responsibility between leading companies in high income OECD countries and their emerging-market peers. Nonetheless, corporate responsibility in emerging markets, while more extensive than commonly believed, is less embedded in corporate strategies, less pervasive and less politically rooted than in most high-income OECD countries' (p. 46).

Regional

Asia

Asia is the region most often covered in the literature on CSR in developing countries, with a significant focus on China (e.g. Zhuang and Wheale, 2004), India (e.g. Balasubramanian *et al.*, 2005), Indonesia (e.g. Blowfield, 2004), Malaysia (e.g. Zulkifli and Amran, 2006), Pakistan (e.g. Lund-Thomsen, 2004), and Thailand

---

[2] Argentina, Brazil, Chile, China, Colombia, Czech Republic, Egypt, Hungary, India, Indonesia, Malaysia, Morocco, Mexico, Pakistan, Peru, Philippines, Poland, Russia, South Africa, Thailand, and Turkey.

(e.g. Kaufman *et al.*, 2004). Other countries that have had less attention include Bangladesh (Nielsen, 2005), the Pacific Forum Islands (Prasad, 2004), Sri Lanka (Luken and Stares, 2005), and Vietnam (Prieto-Carron, 2006*b*).

The *Journal of Corporate Citizenship* special issue on CSR in Asia (issue 13, spring 2004) provides a good overview of the status of the debate. Editors Birch and Moon (2004) note that CSR performance varies greatly between countries in Asia, with a wide range of CSR issues being tackled (e.g. education, environment, employee welfare) and modes of action (e.g. foundations, volunteering, and partnerships).

A number of quantitative studies confirm this picture of CSR variance. In a survey of CSR reporting in Asia, Chapple and Moon (2005) find that nearly three-quarters of large companies in India present themselves as having CSR policies and practices versus only a quarter in Indonesia. Falling somewhere between these two extremes are Thailand (42%), Malaysia (32%), and the Philippines (30%). They also infer from the research that the evolution of CSR in Asia tends to occur in three waves, with community involvement being the most established form of CSR, following by successive second and third waves of socially responsible production processes and employee relations.

In a comparative survey of CSR in 15 countries across Europe, North America, and Asia, Welford (2005) speculates that the low response rates from countries like Hong Kong, Malaysia, Mexico, and Thailand may in itself be an indicator of CSR being less prevalent in developing countries. This seems to be borne out by the research findings, in which these countries fairly consistently underperform when compared with developed countries across 20 aspects of CSR measured by the survey. More specifically, Malaysia is generally the weakest in terms of CSR performance, with Thailand being relatively strong on external aspects (such as child labor and ethics) and Hong Kong being generally better on internal aspects (such as non-discrimination and equal opportunities).

Africa

The literature on CSR in Africa is heavily dominated by South Africa (Visser, 2005*a*), while other pockets of research exist for Côte D'Ivoire (e.g. Schrage and Ewing, 2005), Kenya (e.g. Dolan and Opondo, 2005), Nigeria (e.g. Amaeshi *et al.*, 2006), Tanzania (e.g. Egels, 2005), and Mali and Zambia (e.g. Hamann *et al.*, 2005). Very few papers are focused on industry sectors, with traditionally high impact sectors like agriculture (e.g. Blowfield, 2003), mining (e.g. Kapelus, 2002), and petrochemicals (e.g. Acutt *et al.*, 2004) featuring most prominently.

Two good sources of literature on the region are *Corporate Citizenship in Africa* (Visser *et al.*, 2006) and the *Journal of Corporate Citizenship* special issue on CSR in Africa (issue 18, summer 2005). The latter concludes that 'academic institutions and researchers focusing specifically on corporate citizenship in Africa remain few and under-developed' (Visser *et al.*, 2005: 19).

This is confirmed by a review of the CSR literature on Africa between 1995 and 2005 (Visser, 2006a), which found that that only 12 of Africa's 53 countries have had any research published in core CSR journals, with 57% of all articles focused on South Africa and 16% on Nigeria. The latter partly reflects the high media profile generated around corporate citizenship issues and the petrochemical sector, especially focused on Shell and their impacts on the Ogoni people (Ite, 2004).

My review also found that, in contrast to the socially oriented focus of the literature on CSR in developing countries more generally, business ethics dominates as a research topic in the region, accounting for 42% of all articles on CSR in Africa over the past decade. Partly, this reflects the collective weight of the ethics-focused journals in the study. But it is also because CSR debates in Africa have historically been framed in terms of the ethics of colonialism and apartheid and the prevalence of corruption and fraud on the continent.

This pattern is unsurprisingly also reflected in CSR research on South Africa. For example, in a previous review I found that, of the pre-1994 literature, most dealt with the ethical investment issues relating to apartheid; and since the transition to democracy in 1994, many papers now focus on the individual ethics of South African managers (Visser, 2005a). I expect that other themes, such as stakeholder engagement, social responsibility, and health (including HIV/AIDS) will move up the agenda as CSR increasingly addresses these issues in an African context. In practice, however, it is likely that the economic and philanthropic aspects of CSR (rather than the legal and ethical responsibilities) will continue to dominate CSR conceptualization and practice in Africa (Visser, 2007).

Latin America

CSR in Latin America is the least covered of the developing country regions (Haslam, 2007), with the focus mainly on Argentina (e.g. Newell and Muro, 2006), Brazil (e.g. Vivarta and Canela, 2006) and Mexico (e.g. Weyzig, 2006), although Nicaragua (Prieto-Carron, 2006a) and Venezuela (Peindado-Vara, 2006) also feature. One helpful collection of papers is the *Journal of Corporate Citizenship* special issue on CSR in Latin America (issue 21, spring 2006).

De Oliveira (2006) notes that the CSR agenda in Latin America has been heavily shaped by socio-economic and political conditions, which have tended to aggravate many environmental and social problems such as deforestation, unemployment, inequality, and crime. Schmidheiny (2006) frames this in a constructive way, claiming that CSR is seen by many Latin Americans as the hope for positive change in the face of persistent poverty, environmental degradation, corruption, and economic stagnation.

The trend towards increasing CSR in the region has been generally upward. For example, Correa *et al.* (2004), cited in Schmidheiny (2006), reported that by 2004, there were more 1,000 Latin American companies associated with EMPRESA (the hemisphere-wide CSR network), 300 were members of the World Business Council for Sustainable Development, 1,400 had obtained ISO 14001 certification, and 118 had signed up to the UN Global Compact. Furthermore, the CSR debate is alive and well, with the CSR track in Brazilian Academy of Management (ENANPAD) in 2005 attracting the largest number of articles (De Oliveira, 2006).

Araya's (2006) survey of CSR reporting among the top 250 companies in Latin America also gives some indication of practices in the region. Overall, 34% of the top companies publish sustainability information in a separate report, the annual report, or both, mostly from the energy and natural resources sectors. The annual report is the more common format (27%, versus 16% using separate reports), with Brazilian companies being the most likely to report (43% disclose sustainability information in annual reports and 22% in sustainability reports), as compared with Mexico (33% and 25%) and Chile (22% and 16%). Even companies with European and American origins are less likely to be reporters than Brazilian companies.

The picture for small and medium-sized enterprises (SMEs) is slightly different. In a survey of over 1,300 SMEs in Latin America, Vives (2006) found that SMEs in Chile and Argentina have the highest level of CSR activity, while those in Brazil and El Salvador have the lowest. Most CSR by SMEs is focused on internal activities (especially employee welfare), whereas external (philanthropic) and environmental activities are less common.

DRIVERS

Having sketched a broad overview of the ways in which the literature on CSR in developing countries can be classified, as well as giving a flavour of CSR in a regional context, I now want to address the central question of what makes CSR in developing countries different from its typical manifestation in the developed world, as defined by America and Europe. One powerful way to do this is by examining the various drivers for CSR in developing countries. Although they are not all unique to developing countries, together they build up a distinctive picture of how CSR is conceived, incentivized, and practiced in emerging economies. I have identified ten major drivers for CSR in developing countries, as illustrated in Figure 21.2 and discussed below. Internal drivers refer to pressures from within the country, while external drivers tend to have a global origin.

Cultural Tradition

While many believe CSR is a Western invention (and this may be largely true in its modern conception), there is ample evidence that CSR in developing countries

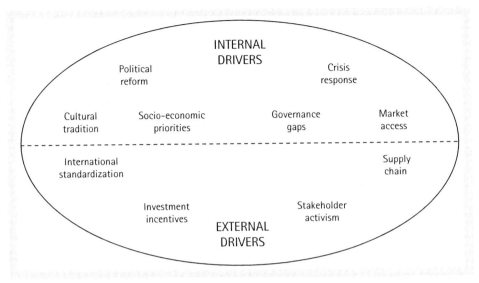

Fig. 21.2 Drivers of CSR in developing countries

draws strongly on deep-rooted indigenous cultural traditions of philanthropy, business ethics, and community embeddedness. Indeed, some of these traditions go back to ancient times. For example, Visser and Macintosh (1998) recall that the ethical condemnation of usurious business practices in developing countries that practice Hinduism, Buddhism, Islam, and Christianity dates back thousands of years. Similarly, Frynas (2006) notes that 'business practices based on moral principles were advocated by the Indian statesman and philosopher Kautilya in the 4th century BC' (p. 17).

In a Latin American context, Sanborn (2002), quoted in Logsdon *et al.* (2006) reminds us that 'varied traditions of community self-help and solidarity stretch back to the region's pre-Hispanic cultures, and include the mutual aid societies, trade unions and professional associations that emerged in the 19th and early 20th centuries' (p. 2). This is consistent with Logsdon *et al.*'s (2006) myths of CSR in Mexico that need debunking: 'One myth is that CSR in Mexico is new, another is that US firms brought CSR to Mexico, and a third is that CSR as practised by Mexican firms simply reflects the CSR patterns and activities of US firms' (p. 51).

Looking at more modern applications of CSR, in Vives's (2006) survey of over 1,300 small and medium-sized enterprises in Latin America, he finds that the region's religious beliefs are one of the major motivations for CSR. Similarly, Nelson (2004) shows how Buddhist traditions in Asia are aligned with CSR.

In Asia, Chapple and Moon (2005) reach a similar conclusion, namely that 'CSR does vary considerably among Asian countries but that this variation is not explained by [levels of] development but by factors in the respective national business systems' (p. 415), a finding consistent with Birch and Moon's (2004) review of CSR papers for the *Journal of Corporate Citizenship* special issue on CSR in Asia.

In an African context, Amaeshi *et al.* (2006) find that CSR in Nigeria is framed by socio-cultural influences like communalism, ethnic religious beliefs, and charitable traditions, while Visser (2005*b*) suggests that the values-based traditional philosophy of African humanism (*ubuntu*) is what underpins much of the modern, inclusive approaches to CSR on the continent.

Political Reform

CSR in developing countries cannot be divorced from the socio-political reform process, which often drives business behavior towards integrating social and ethical issues. For example, De Oliveira (2006) argues that the political and associated social and economic changes in Latin America since the 1980s, including democratization, liberalization, and privatization, have shifted the role of business towards taking greater responsibility for social and environmental issues.

In South Africa, the political changes towards democracy and redressing the injustices of the past have been a significant driver for CSR, through the practice of improved corporate governance (Roussouw *et al.*, 2002), collective business action for social upliftment (Fourie and Eloff, 2005), black economic empowerment (Fig, 2005), and business ethics (Malan, 2005). Visser (2005*a*) lists more than a dozen examples of socio-economic, environmental, and labor-related legislative reform in South Africa between 1994 and 2004 that have a direct bearing on CSR.

Likewise, more recently, the goal of accession to European Union membership has acted as an incentive for many Central and Eastern European countries to focus on CSR, since the latter is acknowledged to represent good practice in the EU (Baskin, 2006).

Socio-economic Priorities

There is a powerful argument that CSR in developing countries is most directly shaped by the socio-economic environment in which firms operate and the development priorities this creates.

Amaeshi *et al.* (2006), for example, argue that CSR in Nigeria is specifically aimed at addressing the socio-economic development challenges of the country, including poverty alleviation, health-care provision, infrastructure development, and education. This, they argue, stands in stark contrast to many Western CSR priorities such as consumer protection, fair trade, green marketing, climate change concerns, or socially responsible investments.

Similarly, Schmidheiny (2006) questions the appropriateness of imported CSR approaches, citing examples from Latin America, where the most pressing issues like poverty and tax avoidance are typically not included in the CSR conceptions, tools, and methodologies originating in developed countries. By contrast, locally developed CSR approaches are more likely to respond to the many social and environmental problems in the region, such as deforestation, unemployment, income inequality, and crime (De Oliveira, 2006).

Michael Spicer, CEO of the South Africa Foundation and former senior executive for the mining conglomerate Anglo American, argues that having CSR guided by the socio-economic priorities of the country or region is simply good business. Furthermore, he suggests that companies in developing countries have to actively shape the socio-economic and political landscape in order to create an operating environment which is conducive for business (Middleton, 2005). The business response to the socio-economic challenge of HIV/AIDS is a case in point (Brennan and Baines, 2006).

Governance Gaps

CSR as a form of governance or a response to governance challenges is discussed elsewhere in this book (Levy and Kaplan, Chapter 19). However, of particular relevance for developing countries is the fact that CSR is often seen as a way to plug the 'governance gaps' left by weak, corrupt, or under-resourced governments that fail to adequately provide various social services (housing, roads, electricity, health care, education, etc.).

Matten and Moon (forthcoming) see this as part of a wider trend in developing countries with weak institutions and poor governance, in which responsibility is often delegated to private actors, be they family, tribe religion, or, increasingly, business. Furthermore, 'as many developing country government initiatives to improve living conditions falter, proponents of [CSR and bottom of the pyramid] strategies argue that companies can assume this role'.

Such proponents of CSR, Blowfield and Frynas (2005) observe, see it as 'an alternative to government' (p. 502) which is 'frequently advocated as a means of filling gaps in governance that have arisen with the acceleration of liberal economic globalisation' (p. 508). A survey by the World Business Council for Sustainable Development (WBCSD 2000) illustrates this perspective: when asked how CSR should be defined, Ghanaians stressed 'building local capacity' and 'filling in when government falls short'.

Moon (2002a) argues that this is part of a broader political shift towards 'new governance' approaches, whereby governments are increasingly seeking to share responsibilities and to develop new modes of operation, whether as a result of overload or of a view that they do not have a monopoly of solutions for society. This is often in the form of social partnerships with non-profit and for-profit organizations. Moon et al. (2005) cite this as an example of corporations acting in a 'civic republicanism' mode.

In addition to being encouraged to step in where once only governments acted, through the mechanism of either privatization or welfare reform, Matten and Crane (2005) also suggest that companies enter the arena of citizenship where government has not as yet administered citizenship rights, for example, improving working conditions in sweatshops, ensuring for employees a living wage, and financing the schooling of child laborers in the absence of legislation requiring this.

However, there are many critics of this approach. Hamann et al. (2005) argues that CSR is an inadequate response to these governance gaps and that more proactive involvement in moving local governance towards accountability and inclusiveness is necessary. Blowfield and Frynas (2005) also question the logic: 'Is CSR a stepping-stone on the path to better national regulation in developing countries? Or is it part of a longer term project for overcoming the weaknesses of territorially prescribed judicial and welfare mechanisms, that is, addressing the limitations of the nation-state in regulating a global economy?' (p. 509)

There are also serious questions about the dependencies this governance gap approach to CSR creates, especially where communities become reliant for their social services on companies whose primary accountability is to their shareholders. Hence, multinationals may cut expenditure, or disinvest from a region if the economics dictates that they will be more profitable elsewhere. There is also the issue of perceived complicity between governments and companies, as Shell all too painfully experienced in Nigeria (Ite, 2004).

Crisis Response

Various kinds of crises associated with developing countries often have the effect of catalyzing CSR responses. These crises can be economic, social, environmental, health-related, or industrial. For example, Newell (2005) notes that the economic crisis in Argentina in 2001–2 marked a significant turning point in CSR, prompting debates about the role of business in poverty alleviation. Others see climate change (Hoffman, 2005) and HIV/AIDS (Dunfee, 2006) as crises that are galvanizing CSR in developing countries.

Catastrophic events with immediate impact are often more likely to elicit CSR responses, especially of the philanthropic kind. The corporate response to the Asian tsunami is a classic case in point (Fernando, 2007). However, industrial accidents may also create pressure for CSR. Examples include Union Carbide's response to the 1984 Bhopal disaster in India (Shrivastava, 1995) and Shell's response to the hanging of human rights activist Ken Saro-Wiwa in Nigeria in 1995 (Wheeler *et al.*, 2002).

Market Access

The flipside of the socio-economic priorities driver is to see these unfulfilled human needs as an untapped market. This notion underlies the now burgeoning literature on 'bottom of the pyramid' strategies, which refer to business models that focus on turning the four billion poor people in the world into consumers (Prahalad and Hammond, 2002; London and Hart, 2004; Rangan *et al.*, 2007). As we have previously noted, this straying of business into the development arena is not without its critics or problems (Hardcourt, 2004).

CSR may also be seen as an enabler for companies in developing countries trying to access markets in the developed world. For example, Baskin (2006) identifies competitive advantage in international markets as one of the key drivers for CSR in Central and Eastern Europe and Asia. Similarly, Araya's (2006) survey of CSR reporting among the top 250 companies in Latin America found that businesses with an international sales orientation were almost five times more likely to report than companies that sell products regionally or locally.

This is especially relevant as more and more companies from developing countries are globalizing and needing to comply with international stock market listing requirements, including various forms of sustainability performance reporting and CSR code compliance (Visser, 2005a). This is echoed in Chapple and Moon's (2005) study of seven countries in Asia, which found that there is a strong relationship between international exposure, either in terms of international sales or foreign ownership, and CSR reporting.

CSR is also sometimes used as a partnership approach to creating or developing new markets. For example, the AED/Mark Partnership with Exxon Mobil was created on the basis of developing a viable market for insecticide-treated mosquito nets in Africa, while improving pregnant women's access to these nets, through the delivery of targeted subsidies (Diara *et al.*, 2004). Similalry, ABB used a partnership approach to CSR to deliver a rural electrification project in Tanzania (Egels, 2005).

International Standardization

Despite the debate about the Western imposition of CSR approaches on the global South, there is ample evidence that CSR codes and standards are a key driver for CSR in developing countries. As already noted, Baskin's (2006) survey of CSR practices in emerging markets indicates growing adoption rates of ISO 14001 and the Global Reporting Initiative's Sustainability Reporting Guidelines.

Codes are also frequently used as a CSR response in sectors that are prevalent in developing countries, such as horticulture (Dolan and Opondo, 2005), cocoa (Schrage and Ewing, 2005), and textiles (Kaufman *et al.*, 2004), as well as to deal with pressing social issues in developing countries, such as child labor (Kolk and Van Tulder, 2002) or the role of women in the workplace (Prieto-Carron, 2004).

Often, CSR is driven by standardization imposed by multinationals striving to achieve global consistency among its subsidiaries and operations in developing countries. For example, the Asia study by Chapple and Moon (2005) found that 'multinational companies are more likely to adopt CSR than those operating solely in their home country, but that the profile of their CSR tends to reflect the profile of the country of operation rather than the country of origin' (p. 415).

Investment Incentives

The belief that multinational investment is inextricably linked with the social welfare of developing countries is not a new phenomenon (Gabriel, 1972). However, increasingly these investments are being screened for CSR performance. Hence, socially responsible investment (SRI) is becoming another driver for CSR in developing countries. As one indicator of this, Baskin (2006) notes that approximately 8% of emerging market companies on the Dow Jones World Index are included in the Dow Jones Sustainability Index, compared with around 13% of high-income companies.

In some developing countries, like South Africa, the SRI trend is well documented (AICC, 2002). In addition to featuring prominently in the SRI movement in the 1980s through the anti-apartheid disinvestment phenomenon, since 1992, South Africa has introduced more than 20 SRI funds nationally which track companies' social, ethical, and environmental performance (Visser, 2005a). According to research by the African Institute of Corporate Citizenship (AICC) (2002), the size of the South African SRI market in 2001 was already 1.55% of the total investment market. In a significant development, in May 2004, the Johannesburg Securities Exchange also launched its own tradable SRI Index, the first of its kind in an emerging market (Sonnenberg *et al.*, 2004). A similar index has also subsequently been introduced in Brazil.

Closely linked to the literature on SRI in developing countries is the debate about the business case for CSR. Although very few instrumental studies have been done, a Thailand survey by Connelly and Limpaphayom (2004) shows that environmental reporting does not negatively impact on short-term profitability and has a positive relationship with firm valuation. More generally, a report by SustainAbility (2002) uses case studies to illustrate various business benefits associated with addressing sustainability in developing countries. Furthermore, Goyal

(2006) contends that CSR may serve as a signaling device for developing countries seeking to assess foreign direct investment proposals by unknown foreign firms.

Stakeholder Activism

In the absence of strong governmental controls over the social, ethical, and environmental performance of companies in developing countries, activism by stakeholder groups has become another critical driver for CSR. Lund-Thomsen (2004) describes this as 'an outcome of micro-level struggles between companies and communities over the distribution of social and environmental hazards which are created when global political and economic forces interact with local contexts around the world' (p. 106).

In developing countries, four stakeholder groups emerge as the most powerful activists for CSR, namely development agencies (Jenkins, 2005), trade unions (Kaufman *et al.*, 2004), international NGOs (Christian Aid, 2005), and business associations (WBCSD, 2000). These four groups provide a platform of support for local NGOs, which are not always well developed or adequately resourced to provide strong advocacy for CSR. The media is also emerging as a key stakeholder for promoting CSR in developing countries (Vivarta and Canela, 2006).

Stakeholder activism in developing countries takes various forms, which Newell (2001) classifies as civil regulation, litigation against companies, and international legal instruments. Of these, civil regulation is perhaps the most common and effective. Bendell (2000) describes this as the theory that 'businesses are being regulated by civil society, through the dual effect of negative impacts from conflict and benefits from collaboration [which] provides new means for people to hold companies accountable, thereby democratising the economy directly'.

There are numerous examples of civil regulation in action in the developing world of which South Africa is a rather striking case in point (Visser, 2005*a*). This has manifested itself mainly through community groups challenging companies over whether they are upholding the constitutional rights of citizens. Various landmark cases between 1994 and 2004 suggest that, although civil society still tends to lack capacity and resources in South Africa, this has been an effective strategy. Stakeholder activism has also taken a constructive approach towards encouraging CSR, through groups like the National Business Initiative and partnerships between business and NGOs.

Stakeholder activism can also be a source of criticism of CSR, arguing that it is an inadequate response to the social and environmental challenges of developing countries. The Christian Aid (2005) report *Behind the Mask: The Real Face of Corporate Social Responsibility* epitomizes this critical approach, and may be a driver for an enlarged conception and practice of CSR in developing countries.

Supply Chain

Another significant driver for CSR in developing countries, especially among small and medium-sized companies, is the requirements that are being imposed by multi-nationals on their supply chains. This trend began with various ethical trading initiatives (Blowfield, 2003, 2004), which led to the growth of fair trade auditing and labelling schemes for agricultural products sourced in developing countries (Dolan and Opondo, 2005; Schrage and Ewing, 2005). Allegations of poor labor conditions and human rights abuses in several high profile multinational supply chains in the sporting and clothing sectors were also a significant catalyst for greater attention to CSR requirements (Hussain-Khaliq, 2004; Kaufman *et al.*, 2004; Nielsen, 2005).

One response has been the development of certifiable standards like SA 8000, which is now widely used as a screening mechanism for multinationals in selecting their suppliers in developing countries (Kolk and Van Tulder, 2002). Major change has also been achieved through sector-based initiatives such as the Forest Stewardship Council for sustainable forestry and the Marine Stewardship Council for sustainable fishing. More recently, this driver has been scaled up due to the so-called 'Wal-Mart effect' whereby major global and national retailers are committing to promoting sustainability and responsibility through their suppliers (Johnson, 2004).

A CSR PYRAMID FOR DEVELOPING COUNTRIES

Having considered the various drivers for CSR in developing countries, the question is: Are current Western conceptions and models of CSR adequate for describing CSR in developing countries? If we consider the most popular model—Carroll's (1991) CSR Pyramid, comprising economic, legal, ethical, and philanthropic responsibilities—this is almost entirely based on research in an American context. Even so, several empirical studies suggest that culture may have an important influence on perceived CSR priorities (Pinkston and Carroll, 1994; Edmondson and Carroll, 1999; Burton *et al.*, 2000).

Crane and Matten (2007*a*) address this point explicitly by discussing CSR in a European context using Carroll's CSR Pyramid. They conclude that 'all levels of CSR play a role in Europe, but they have different significance, and furthermore are interlinked in a somewhat different manner' (p. 51). In the same way, I believe

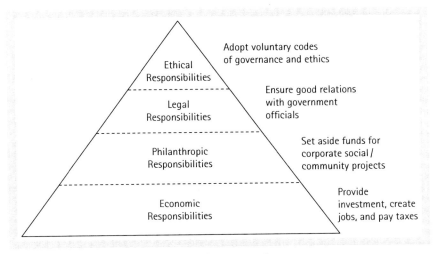

Fig. 21.3 CSR pyramid for developing countries

Carroll's four-part pyramid construct can be useful to look at how CSR is manifested in a developing country context.

Taking this approach, my contention is that the order of the CSR layers in developing countries—if this are taken as an indicator of the relative emphasis assigned to various responsibilities—differs from Carroll's classic pyramid (Visser, 2006b). Hence, in developing countries, economic responsibilities still get the most emphasis. However, philanthropy is given second highest priority, followed by legal and then ethical responsibilities. This is illustrated in Figure 21.3. Each element will be briefly discussed in turn.

Economic Responsibilities

It is well known that many developing countries suffer from a shortage of foreign direct investment, as well as from high unemployment and widespread poverty. It is no surprise, therefore, that the economic contribution of companies in developing countries is highly prized, by governments and communities alike. Fox (2004) argues that this should not be seen in a negative light, but rather as a more development-oriented approach to CSR that focuses on the enabling environment for responsible business in developing countries and that brings economic and equity aspects of sustainable development to the forefront of the agenda.

This is similar to the approach to economic responsibility taken by companies in Europe, in contrast to the more narrow focus on profitability in the USA (Crane and Matten, 2007a). Hence, in developing countries, CSR tends to stress the importance of 'economic multipliers', including the capacity to generate investment and in-come, produce safe products and services, create jobs, invest in human capital, establish local business linkages, spread international business standards, support technology transfer and build physical and institutional infrastructure (Nelson, 2003). For this reason, companies that operate in developing countries increasingly report on their economic responsibilities by constructing 'economic value added' statements.

It is worth re-emphasizing as a caveat that economic responsibility has two faces—economic contribution on the one side and economic dependence on the other. When communities or countries become overly dependent on multinationals for their economic welfare, there is the risk of governments compromising ethical, social, or environmental standards in order to retain their investment, or suffering huge social disruption if those businesses do decide to disinvest, as occurred with Anglo American in Zambia.

Philanthropic Responsibilities

Crane and Matten (2007a) suggest that philanthropic responsibility in Europe tends more often to be more compulsory via the legal framework than discretionary acts of successful companies or rich capitalists as in the United States In this respect, developing countries have more in common with the American model, although philanthropy generally gets an even higher priority as a manifestation of CSR (Arora and Puranik, 2004; Fig, 2005; Ahmad, 2006; Amaeshi et al., 2006; Weyzig, 2006).

Partly, this is a result of strong indigenous traditions of philanthropy in develop-ing countries, as previously discussed. However, there are several other reasons as well. In the first instance, the socio-economic needs of the developing countries in which companies operate are so great that philanthropy is an expected norm—it is considered the right thing to do by business.

Second, companies realize that they cannot succeed in societies that fail, and philanthropy is seen as the most direct way to improve the prospects of the communities in which their businesses operate. HIV/AIDS is a case in point, where the response by business is essentially philanthropic (it is not an occupa-tional disease), but clearly in companies' own medium- to long-term economic interest.

Third, over the past 50 years, many developing countries have become reliant on foreign aid or donor assistance. Hence, there is often an ingrained culture of philanthropy. And a final reason for developing countries' prioritization of philan-thropy is that they are generally still at an early stage of maturity in CSR, sometimes even equating CSR and philanthropy, rather than embracing the more embedded approaches now common in developed countries.

Legal Responsibilities

In developing countries, legal responsibilities generally have a lower priority than in developed countries. This does not necessarily mean that companies flaunt the law, but there is far less pressure for good conduct. This is because, in many developing countries, the legal infrastructure is poorly developed, and often lacks independence, resources, and administrative efficiency.

Many developing countries are also behind the developed world in terms of incorporating human rights and other issues relevant to CSR into their legislation (Mwaura 2004). Admittedly, there are exceptions and some developing countries have seen significant progress in strengthening the social and environmental aspects of their legislation (Visser, 2005b). However, government capacity for enforcement remains a serious limitation, and reduces the effectiveness of legislation as a driver for CSR.

Hence, several scholars argue that tax avoidance by companies is one of the most significant examples of irresponsible business behavior in developing countries, often contradicting their CSR claims of good conduct (Christensen and Murphy, 2004).

Ethical Responsibilities

Crane and Matten (2007a) suggest that ethical responsibilities enjoy a much higher priority in Europe than in the United States. In developing countries, however, ethics seems to have the least influence on the CSR agenda. This is not to say that developing countries have been untouched by the global trend towards improved governance (Reed, 2002). In fact, the 1992 and 2002 King Reports on Corporate Governance in South Africa have both led the world in their inclusion of CSR issues.

For example, the 1992 King Report was the first global corporate governance code to talk about 'stakeholders' and to stress the importance of business accountability beyond the interests of shareholders (IoD, 1992). Similarly, the 2002 revised King Report was the first to include a section on 'integrated sustainability reporting', covering social, transformation, ethical, safety, health, and environmental management policies and practices (IoD, 2002).

This progress is certainly encouraging, but in general, it is still the exception rather than the rule. For instance, in Transparency International's annual Corruption Perception Index and Global Corruption Barometer, developing countries usually make up the bulk of the most poorly ranked countries. Furthermore, survey respondents from these countries generally agree that corruption still affects business to a large extent. The World Bank's (2005) Investment Climate Survey paints a similar picture.

One of the attempts to address corruption in developing countries has been the UK-led Extractive Industries Transparency Initiative (EITI), which aims to increase transparency over payments by companies to governments and government-linked entities, as well as transparency over revenues by those host country governments. This is clearly a step in the right direction, but the refusal of countries like Angola to even participate shows that there is still a long way to go in embedding ethical responsibilities in developing countries.

An Ideal CSR Pyramid

The descriptive approach adopted in the previous sections was used to illustrate how CSR actually manifests in developing countries, rather than presenting an aspirational view of what CSR in developing countries *should* look like. For example, it is not proposed that legal and ethical responsibilities *should* get such a low priority, but rather that they do in practice.

By contrast, if we are to work towards an ideal CSR Pyramid for CSR in developing countries, I would argue that improved ethical responsibilities, incorporating good governance, should be assigned the highest CSR priority in developing countries. It is my contention that governance reform holds the key to improvements in all the other dimensions, including economic development, rule of law, and voluntary action. Hence, embracing more transparent, ethical governance practices should form the foundation of CSR practice in developing countries, which in turn will provide the enabling environment for more widespread responsible business.

CONCLUSIONS

To summarize, I have argued that CSR in developing countries has the following distinctive characteristics (Visser *et al.*, 2007):

- CSR tends to be less formalised or institutionalized in terms of the CSR benchmarks commonly used in developed countries, i.e. CSR codes, standards, management systems and reports.
- Where formal CSR is practiced, this is usually by large, high profile national and multinational companies, especially those with recognized international brands or those aspiring to global status.
- Formal CSR codes, standards, and guidelines that are most applicable to developing countries tend to be issue specific (e.g. fair trade, supply chain, HIV/AIDS) or sector-led (e.g. agriculture, textiles, mining).

- In developing countries, CSR is most commonly associated with philanthropy or charity, i.e. through corporate social investment in education, health, sports development, the environment, and other community services.
- Making an economic contribution is often seen as the most important and effective way for business to make a social impact, i.e. through investment, job creation, taxes, and technology transfer.
- Business often finds itself engaged in the provision of social services that would be seen as government's responsibility in developed countries, for example, investment in infrastructure, schools, hospitals, and housing.
- The issues being prioritized under the CSR banner are often different in developing countries, for example, tackling HIV/AIDS, improving working conditions, provision of basic services, supply chain integrity, and poverty alleviation.
- Many of the CSR issues in developing countries present themselves as dilemmas or trade-offs, for example, development versus environment, job creation versus higher labour standards, strategic philanthropy versus political governance.
- The spirit and practise of CSR is often strongly resonant with traditional communitarian values and religious concepts in developing countries, for example, African humanism (*ubuntu*) in South Africa and harmonious society (*xiaokang*) in China.
- The focus on CSR in developing countries can be a catalyst for identifying, designing and testing new CSR frameworks and business models, for example, Prahalad's Bottom of the Pyramid model and Visser's CSR Pyramid for Developing Countries.

Research into CSR in developing countries is still relatively underdeveloped and tends to be adhoc with a heavy reliance on convenience-based case studies or descriptive accounts. The focus is often on high profile incidents or branded companies and a few select countries (e.g. Brazil, China, India, South Africa), with a general lack of comparable benchmarking data.

Hence, there is an urgent need for further research on CSR in developing countries at the international, regional, national and sectoral levels, as well as on theoretical constructs. There is a dearth of international research which surveys the nature and extent of CSR in developing countries, as compared with developed countries. Next to this need for more data in general, there is need for more comparative work which analyses CSR between regions (e.g. Africa, Latin America, Asia) and between countries within regions. On a more national or regional level, there is need for detailed national research on CSR, especially on the more than 100 developing countries that appear to have had no academic papers published about them in CSR journals. Alongside these efforts there seems to be a specific need for more sectoral research on CSR codes and practices, especially for the lesser covered industries like chemicals, financial services, infrastructure (including construction), manufacturing (including motor), media, retail, telecommunications, and travel and leisure. Finally, all these different streams of empirical research should inform more conceptual work on CSR conceptions, frameworks, or models that are more applicable to developing countries.

What is clear from this chapter, therefore, is that CSR in developing countries is a rich and fascinating area of enquiry, which is becoming ever more important in CSR theory and practice. And since it is profoundly under-researched, it also represents a tremendous opportunity for improving our knowledge and understanding about CSR.

REFERENCES

ACUTT, N., MEDINA-ROSS, V., and O'RIORDAN, T. 2004. 'Perspectives on Corporate Social Responsibility in the Chemical Sector: A Comparative Analysis of the Mexican and South African Cases'. *Natural Resources Forum* 28(4): 302–16.

AHMAD, S. J. 2006. 'From Principles to Practice: Exploring Corporate Social Responsibility in Pakistan'. *Journal of Corporate Citizenship*, 24 winter: 115–29.

AICC. 2002. *Socially Responsible Investment in South Africa*. Johannesburg: African Institute for Corporate Citizenship (AICC).

AMAESHI, K. M., ADI, B. C., OGBECHIE, C., and OLUFEMI, O. A. 2006. 'Corporate Social Responsibility in Nigeria: Western Mimicry or Indigenous Influences?' *Journal of Corporate Citizenship*, 24, winter: 83–99.

ARAYA, M. 2006. 'Exploring Terra Incognita: Non-financial Reporting in Latin America'. *Journal of Corporate Citizenship* 21, spring: 25–38.

ARORA, B., and PURANIK, R. 2004. 'A Review of Corporate Social Responsibility in India'. *Development*, 47(3): 93–100.

BALASUBRAMANIAN, N. K., KIMBER, D., PUSSAYAPIBUL, N., and DAVIDS, P. 2005. 'Emerging Opportunities or Traditions Reinforced? An Analysis of the Attitudes Towards CSR, and Trends of Thinking about CSR, in India'. *Journal of Corporate Citizenship*, 17, spring: 79–92.

BASKIN, J. 2006. 'Corporate Responsibility in Emerging Markets'. *Journal of Corporate Citizenship*, 24, winter: 29–47.

BENDELL, J. (ed). 2000. *Terms for Endearment: Business, NGOs and Sustainable Development*. Sheffield: Greenleaf.

BIRCH, D., and MOON, J. 2004. 'Introduction: Corporate Social Responsibiity in Asia'. *Journal of Corporate Citizenship*, 13, spring: 18–23.

BLOWFIELD, M. 2003. 'Ethical Supply Chains in the Cocoa, Coffee and Tea Industries'. *Greener Management International*, 43, autumn: 15–24.

—— 2004. 'Implementation Deficits of Ethical Trade Systems: Lessons from the Indonesian Cocoa and Timber Industries'. *Journal of Corporate Citizenship*, 13, spring: 77–90

—— and FRYNAS, J. G. 2005. 'Setting New Agendas: Critical Perspectives on Corporate Social Responsibility in the Developing World'. *International Affairs*, 81(3): 499–513.

BRENNAN, R., and BAINES, P. 2006. 'Is There a Morally Right Price for Anti-retroviral Drugs in the Developing World?' *Business Ethics: A European Review*, 15(1): 29–43.

BURTON, B. K., FARH, J.-L., and HEGARTY, W. H. 2000. 'A Cross-Cultural Comparison of Corporate Social Responsibility Orientation: Hong Kong vs. United States Students'. *Teaching Business Ethics*, 4(2): 151–67.

CARROLL, A. B. 1991. 'The Pyramid of Corporate Social Responsibility: Toward the Moral Management of Organizational Stakeholders'. *Business Horizons*, 34: 39–48.

CHAPPLE, W., and MOON, J. 2005. 'Corporate Social Responsibility in Asia: A Seven-Country Study of CSR Web Site Reporting'. *Business & Society*, 44(4): 415–41.

CHRISTENSEN, J., and MURPHY, R. 2004. 'The Social Irresponsibility of Corporate Tax Avoidance: Taking CSR to the Bottom Line'. *Development*, 47(3): 37–44.

Christian Aid. 2005. *Behind the Mask: The Real Face of Corporate Social Responsibility*. London: Christian Aid.

CONNELLY, J. T., and LIMPAPHAYOM, P. 2004. 'Environmental Reporting and Firm Performance: Evidence from Thailand'. *Journal of Corporate Citizenship*, 13, spring: 137–49.

CORREA, M. E., FLYNN, S., and AMIT, A. 2004. 'Responsibilidan Social Corporative en América Latina: Una visión empresarial'. *Série CEPAL Medio Ambiente y Desarrollo*, 85. Santiago de chile: CEPAL.

CRANE, A., and MATTEN, D. 2007a. *Business Ethics*, 2nd edn. Oxford: Oxford University Press.

———— (eds.). 2007b. *Corporate Social Responsibility*, 3 vols. London: Sage.

DE OLIVEIRA, J. A. P. 2006. 'Corporate Citizenship in Latin America: New Challenges to Business'. *Journal of Corporate Citizenship*, 21 spring: 17–20.

DIARA, M., ALILO, M., and McGUIRE, D. 2004. 'Corporate Social Responsibility and Public-Private Partnership: The Case of the Academy for Educational Development and Exxon-Mobil'. *Development*, 47(3): 69–77.

DOLAN, C. S., and OPONDO, M. 2005. 'Seeking Common Ground: Multi-stakeholder Processes in Kenya's Cut Flower Industry'. *Journal of Corporate Citizenship*, 18, summer: 87–98.

DUNFEE, T. W. 2006. 'Do Firms with Unique Competencies for Rescuing Victims of Human Catastrophes have Special Obligations? Corporate Responsibility and the Aids Catastrophe in Sub-Saharan Africa'. *Business Ethics Quarterly*, 16(2): 185–210.

EDMONDSON, V. C., and CARROLL, A. B. 1999. 'Giving Back: An Examination of the Philanthropic Motivations, Orientations and Activities of Large Black-Owned Businesses'. *Journal of Business Ethics*, 19(2): 171–9.

EGELS, N. 2005. 'CSR in Electrification of Rural Africa: The Case of ABB in Tanzania'. *Journal of Corporate Citizenship*, 18 summer: 75–85.

FERNANDO, M. 2007. 'Corporate Social Responsibility in the Wake of the Asian Tsunami: A Comparative Case Study of Two Sri Lankan Companies'. *European Management Journal*, 25(1): 1–10.

FIG, D. 2005. 'Manufacturing Amnesia: Corporate Social Responsibility in South Africa'. *International Affairs*, 81(3): 599–617.

FOURIE, A., and ELOFF, T. 2005. 'The Case for Collective Business Action to Achieve Systems Change: Exploring the Contributions Made by the Private Sector to the Social, Economic and Political Transformation Process in South Africa'. *Journal of Corporate Citizenship*, 18, summer: 39–48.

Fox, T. 2004. 'Corporate Social Responsibility and Development: In Quest of an Agenda'. *Development*, 47(3): 29–36.

Frynas, J. G. 2006. 'Corporate Social Responsibility in Emerging Economies'. *Journal of Corporate Citizenship*, 24, winter: 16–19.

Gabriel, P. P. 1972. 'MNCs in the Third World: Is Conflict Unavoidable?' *Harvard Business Review*. 50(4): 93–102.

Goyal, A. 2006. 'Corporate Social Responsibility as a Signalling Device for Foreign Direct Investment'. *Journal of Corporate Citizenship*, 13(1): 145–63.

Hamann, R., Kapelns, P., Sonnenberg, D., Mackenzie, A., and Hollesen, P. 2005. 'Local Governance as a Complex System: Lessons from Mining in South Africa, Mali and Zambia'. *Journal of Corporate Citizenship*, 18, summer: 61–73.

Hardcourt, W. 2004. 'Editorial: Is CSR Rewriting Development?' *Development*, 47(3): 1–2.

Haslam, P. A. 2007. 'The Corporate Social Responsibility System in Latin America and the Caribbean', in Crane and Matten (2007*b*).

Hoffman, A. J. 2005. 'Climate Change Strategy: The Business Logic Behind Voluntary Greenhouse Gas Reductions'. *California Management Review*, 47(3): 21–46.

Hussain-Khaliq, S. 2004. 'Eliminating Child Labour from the Sialkot Soccer Ball Industry: Two Industry-Led Approaches'. *Journal of Corporate Citizenship*, 13, spring: 101–7.

IMF. 2006. *World Economic Outlook: Financial Systems and Economic Cycles*. Brussels: International Monetary Fund.

IoD. 1992. *King Report on Corporate Governance in South Africa*. Johannesburg: Institute of Directors in Southern Africa.

——2002. *King Report on Corporate Governance in South Africa*. Johannesburg: Institute of Directors in Southern Africa.

Ite, U. E. 2004. 'Multinationals and Corporate Social Responsibility in Developing Countries: A Case Study of Nigeria'. *Corporate Social Responsibility and Environmental Management*, 11(1): 1–11.

Jenkins, R. 2005. 'Globalization, Corporate Social Responsibility and Poverty'. *International Affairs*, 81(3): 525–40.

Johnson, M. 2004. 'Marks & Spencer Implements an Ethical Sourcing Program for its Global Supply Chain'. *Journal of Organizational Excellence*, 23(2): 3–16.

Kapelus, P. 2002. 'Mining, Corporate Social Responsibility and the Case of Rio Tinto, Richards Bay Minerals and the Mbonambi'. *Journal of Business Ethics*, 39: 275–96.

Kaufman, A., Tiantubtim, E., Pussayapibul, N., and Davids, P. 2004. 'Implementing Voluntary Labour Standards and Codes of Conduct in the Thai Garment Industry'. *Journal of Corporate Citizenship*, 13, spring: 91–9.

Kolk, A., and Van Tulder, R. 2002. 'Child Labour and Multinational Conduct: A Comparison of International Business and Stakeholder Codes'. *Journal of Business Ethics*, 36: 291–301.

Lockett, A., Moon, J., and Visser, W. 2006. 'Corporate Social Responsibility in Management Research: Focus, Nature, Salience, and Sources of Influence'. *Journal of Management Studies*, 43(1): 115–36.

Logsdon, J. M., Thomas, D. E., and Van Buren III, H. J. 2006. 'Corporate Social Responsibility in Large Mexican Firms'. *Journal of Corporate Citizenship*, 21, spring: 51–60.

London, T., and Hart, S. L. 2004. 'Reinventing Strategies for Emerging Markets: Beyond the Transnational Model'. *Journal of International Business Studies*, 35(5): 350–70.

LUKEN, R., and STARES, R. 2005. 'Small Business Responsibility in Developing Countries: A Threat or an Opportunity?' *Business Strategy and the Environment*, 14: 38–53.

LUND-THOMSEN, P. 2004. 'Towards a Critical Framework on Corporate Social and Environmental Responsibility in the South: The Case of Pakistan'. *Development*, 47(3): 106–113.

MALAN, D. 2005. 'Corporate Citizens, Colonialists, Tourists or Activists? Ethical Challenges facing South African Corporations in Africa'. *Journal of Corporate Citizenship*, 18, summer: 49–60.

MATTEN, D., and CRANE, A. 2005. 'Corporate Citizenship: Toward an Extended Theoretical Conceptualization'. *Academy of Management Review*, 30(1): 166–79.

——and MOON, J. (forthcoming). '"Implicit" and "Explicit" CSR: A Conceptual Framework for a Comparative Understanding of Corporate Social Responsibility'. *Academy of Management Review*.

MIDDLETON, C. 2005. 'Interview with Michael Spicer, Chief Executive, South Africa Foundation'. *Journal of Corporate Citizenship*, 18, summer: 21–4.

MOON, J. 2002a. 'Business Social Responsibility and New Governance'. *Government and Opposition*, 37(3): 385–408.

——2002b. 'Corporate Social Responsibility: An Overview. in C. Hartley, *The International Directory of Corporate Philanthropy*. London and New York: Europa Publications, 3–14.

——CRANE, A., and MATTEN, D. 2005. 'Can Corporations be Citizens? Corporate Citizenship as a Metaphor for Business Participation in Society'. *Business Ethics Quarterly*, 15(3): 427–51.

MWAURA, K. 2004. 'Corporate Citizenship: The Changing Legal Perspective in Kenya'. Interdisciplinary CSR Research Conference, Nottingham, International Centre for Corporate Social Responsibility (ICCSR).

NELSON, J. 2003. *Economic Multipliers: Revisiting the Core Responsibility and Contribution of Business to Development*. London: International Business Leaders Forum (IBLF).

NELSON, J. A. 2004. 'A Buddhist and Feminist Analysis of Ethics and Business'. *Development*, 47(3): 53–60.

NEWELL, P. 2001. 'Managing Multinationals: The Governance of Investment for the Environment'. *Journal of International Development*, 13: 907–19.

——2005. 'Citizenship, Accountability and Community: The Limits of the CSR Agenda'. *International Affairs*, 81(3): 541–57.

——and MURO, A. 2006. 'Corporate Social and Environmental Responsibiity in Argentina: The Evolution of an Agenda'. *Journal of Corporate Citizenship*, 24, winter: 49–68.

NIELSEN, M. E. 2005. 'The Politics of Corporate Responsibility and Child Labour in the Bangladeshi Garment Industry'. *International Affairs*, 81(3): 559–80.

PEDERSEN, E. R., and HUNICHE, M. (eds.) 2006. *Corporate Citizenship in Developing Countries*. Copenhagen: Copenhagen Business School Press.

PEINDADO-VARA, E. 2006. 'Corporate Social Responsibility in Latin America'. *Journal of Corporate Citizenship*, 21, spring.

PINKSTON, T. S., and CARROLL, A. B. 1994. 'Corporate Citizenship Perpectives and Foreign Direct Investment in the US'. *Journal of Business Ethics*, 13(3): 157–69.

PRAHALAD, C. K., and HAMMOND, A. 2002. 'Serving the World's Poor, Profitably'. *Harvard Business Review*, 80(9): 48–57.

PRASAD, B. C. 2004. 'Globalisation, Free Trade and Corporate Citizenship in Pacific Forum Island Countries'. *Journal of Corporate Citizenship*, 13, spring: 65–76.

PRIETO-CARRON, M. 2004. 'Is there Anyone Listening? Women Workers in Factories in Central America, and Corporate Codes of Conduct'. *Development*, 47(3): 101–5.

—— 2006a. 'Corporate Social Responsibility in Latin America: Chiquita, Women Banana Workers and Structural Inequalities'. *Journal of Corporate Citizenship*, 21, spring: 85–94.

—— 2006b. 'Critical Perspectives on CSR and Development: What we Know, what we Don't Know, and what we Need to Know'. *International Affairs*, 82(5): 977–87.

RANGAN, V. K., QUELCH, J. A., HERRERO, G., and BARTON, B. (eds.) 2007. *Business Solutions for the Global Poor: Creating Social and Economic Value*. San Franciso: Jossey-Bass.

REED, D. 2002. 'Corporate Governance Reforms in Developing Countries'. *Journal of Business Ethics*, 37: 223–47.

ROUSSOUW, G. J., VAN DER WATT, A., and MALAN, D. P. 2002. 'Corporate Governance in South Africa'. *Journal of Business Ethics*, 37(3): 289–302.

SANBORN, C. 2002. 'Latin American Phil in Changing Times'. *Revista: Harvard Review of Latin America* 1(3), spring. <http://www.fas.harvard.edu/~drclas/publications/revista/Volunteering/charity2Solidarity.html>.

SCHMIDHEINY, S. 2006. 'A View of Corporate Citizenship in Latin America'. *Journal of Corporate Citizenship*, 21, spring: 21–4.

SCHRAGE, E. J., and EWING, A. P. 2005. 'The Cocoa Industry and Child Labour'. *Journal of Corporate Citizenship*, 18, summer: 99–112.

SHRIVASTAVA, P. 1995. 'Industrial/Environmental Crises and Corporate Social Responsibility'. *Journal of Socio-Economics*, 24(1): 211–27.

SONNENBERG, D., REICHARDT, M., and HAMANN, R. 2004. 'Sustainability Reporting in South Africa: Findings from the First Round of the JSE Socially Responsible Index'. Interdisciplinary CSR Research Conference, Nottingham, International Centre for Corporate Social Responsibility.

SustainAbility. 2002. *Developing Value: The Business Case for Sustainability in Emerging Markets*. London: SustainAbility.

UN. 2006. *Millennium Development Goals Report 2006*. Brussels: United Nations.

UNDP. 2006. *Beyond Scarcity: Power, Poverty and the Global Water Crisis*. Brussels: United Nations Development Programme.

VISSER, W. 2005a. 'Corporate Citizenship in South Africa: A Review of Progress Since Democracy'. *Journal of Corporate Citizenship*, 18, summer: 29–38.

—— 2005b. 'Is South Africa World Class in Corporate Citizenship?' in A. Freemantle (ed.), *The Good Corporate Citizen*. Johannesburg: Trialogue.

—— 2006a. 'Research on Corporate Citizenship in Africa: A Ten-Year Review (1995–2005). in Visser *et al.* (2000b).

—— 2006b. 'Revisiting Carroll's CSR Pyramid: An African Perspective'. in Pedersen and Huniche (2006), 29–56.

—— 2007b. 'Revisiting Carroll's CSR Pyramid'. in Crane and Matten.

—— and MACINTOSH, A. 1998. 'A Short Review of the Historical Critique of Usury'. *Accounting, Business & Financial History*, 8(2): 175–89.

—— McINTOSH, M., and MIDDLETON, C. 2006. *Corporate Citizenship in Africa: Lessons from the Past; Paths to the Future*. Sheffield: Greenleaf.

—— MATTEN, D., POHL, M., and TOLHURST, N. 2007. *The A to Z of Corporate Social Responsibility*. London: Wiley.

—— MIDDLETON, C., and McINTOSH, M. 2005. 'Introduction to the Journal of Corporate Citizenship Special Issue on Corporate Citizenship in Africa'. *Journal of Corporate Citizenship*, 18, spring: 18–20.

VIVARTA, V., and CANELA, G. 2006. 'Corporate Social Responsibility in Brazil: The Role of the Press as Watchdog'. *Journal of Corporate Citizenship*, 21, spring: 95–106.

VIVES, A. 2006. 'Social and Environmental Responsibility in Small and Medium Enterprises in Latin America'. *Journal of Corporate Citizenship*, 21, spring: 39–50.

WBCSD. 2000. *Corporate Social Responsibility: Making Good Business Sense*. Geneva: WBCSD.

WELFORD, R. 2005. 'Corporate Social Responsibility in Europe, North America and Asia'. *Journal of Corporate Citizenship*, 17, spring: 33–52.

WEYZIG, F. 2006. 'Local and Global Dimensions of Corporate Social Responsibility in Mexico'. *Journal of Corporate Citizenship*, 24, winter: 69–81.

WHEELER, D., FABIG, H., and BOELE, R. 2002. 'Paradoxes and Dilemmas for Stakeholder Responsive Firms in the Extractive Sector: Lessons from the Case of Shell and the Ogoni'. *Journal of Business Ethics*, 39(3): 297–318.

World Bank. 2005. *Investment Climate Survey*. Washington: World Bank.

—— 2006. *World Development Report 2007: Development and the Next Generation*. Washington: World Bank.

WRI. 2005. *World Resources 2005—The Wealth of the Poor: Managing Ecosystems to Fight Poverty*. Washington: D.C., World Resources Institute, UNDP, UNEP, World Bank.

ZHUANG, C., and WHEALE, P. 2004. 'Creating Sustainable Corporate Value: A Case Study of Stakeholder Relationship Management in China'. *Business and Society Review*, 109(4): 507–47.

ZULKIFLI, N., and AMRAN, A. 2006. 'Realising Corporate Social Responsibility in Malaysia: A View from the Accounting Profession'. *Journal of Corporate Citizenship*, 24, winter: 101–14.

PART VII

FUTURE
PERSPECTIVES
AND
CONCLUSIONS

....

CHAPTER 22

EDUCATING FOR RESPONSIBLE MANAGEMENT

....

DUANE WINDSOR

THIS chapter reviews theories of management education and current coverage of corporate social responsibility (CSR) concepts in the United States, Europe, and elsewhere (Crane and Matten, 2004). It then examines prospects for responsible management education in the 21st century. Responsible management is the most important theory-development and educational issue facing business schools and the most important question facing businesses. Companies morally educate personnel as executives promote ethical climates and corporate codes of conduct. The term responsible management covers honesty and integrity of managers, corporate citizenship and corporate social responsibility, fairness and justice in stakeholder relationship management, ecological sustainability of the planet, a rising global concern for human and also animal rights, and sustainable development for a growing world population.

The remainder of this chapter proceeds in four main sections. First, the chapter addresses management education theories. Several prominent academics have raised serious questions about the conventional model of management education. Second, the chapter assesses the state of knowledge concerning responsible management. Very different approaches prevail in North America, Western Europe, and elsewhere. Responsibility involves profound controversy, ranging from a view that management should focus on the financial bottom line to a view that the corporate bottom line involves multiple dimensions of planet and people as well as profits. Third, the chapter examines the state of knowledge concerning education for responsible management. Views range from the impossibility of changing the moral character of adults and the uselessness of responsibility education through identification of profit incentives for responsibility activities to demands for business schools and corporations to try harder in the wake of recent corporate scandals. Fourth, the chapter discusses the effect of the Association to Advance Collegiate Schools of Business (AACSB) International accreditation standards on responsibility education. A concluding section summarizes the chief points.

MANAGEMENT

Parallel debates over management education and responsibility education have occurred in the context of the great worldwide expansion in the number of business schools, as well as in the wake of recent corporate scandals. Stimulating the debates in part has been the emergence of journalistic rankings of business schools. While the reports associated with these rankings arguably improve customer information and promote continuous performance improvement (Danko and Anderson, 2005), they also foster curricular and intellectual turmoil as schools periodically change appearance and reduce core requirements to offer more electives to remain competitive. Fundamental 'industry' change may be unavoidable (Friga et al., 2003). Change is not, however, automatically improvement. Also stimulating the debates are long-standing discussions over the balance between social science research (Gordon and Howell, 1959) and leadership and management skill development (Porter and McKibbin, 1988); and between the science model and contrasting humanities traditions of philosophical ethics and business history.

After a global economic downturn, 'just as the market value of an MBA is reviving, its academic credibility is being attacked' (The Economist, 2005; Ellin, 2006). Leading academics—Pfeffer and Fong (2002, 2004), Ghoshal (2003, 2005), Mintzberg (2004), and Bennis and O'Toole (2005)—have issued provocative calls for fundamental transformation of MBA education.

In the 1950s, there were complaints that business schools were merely trade schools doing little more than vocational (not professional) training. The Gordon and Howell (1959) report, for the Ford Foundation, recommended that business schools needed to shift to social science foundations. The recommendation continues to have substantial merit. There has been, coincident with the expansion in the number of business schools, deep investment in economics, psychology, and quantitative methods (i.e. statistics and operations research). This orientation has profoundly affected business applications such as finance, marketing, organizational behavior, and strategy. The emphasis has been on social scientific research (theory building and empirical verification) as distinct from case material development (which still exists at a number of schools). Adherents of the former often frown on the latter as not scientific research.

By the 1980s, there was developing concern over neglect of the behavioral and professional skill development aspects of management (Boyatzis, 1982). Criticisms of the scientific model emphasize the desirability of a professional model of leadership and management (Bennis and O'Toole, 2005). The Porter and McKibbin (1988) report surveyed administrators of all AACSB member schools, about 10% of faculty, and many business executives together with students and alumni. Business executives reported they were generally happy with subject matter and analytical preparation, but were far less satisfied with individual influence skills such as communications (Stolzenberg et al., 1986) and leadership.

Pfeffer and Fong (2002) argued that business schools are not very effective in terms of either career success or influence of research on management practice. They suggested that economic value was largely restricted to the very top schools. The evidence offered for teaching ineffectiveness is that neither an MBA degree nor grades earned correlate with salaries or career success (Livingston, 1971). It is difficult to disentangle educational effects from entering quality of the student body. The evidence offered for research ineffectiveness is that intellectual influence among managers tends to be commanded by journalists and executives rather than by academics. While the author accepts the thrust of this evidence, the narrowly gauged argument does neglect indirect and long-term influence. The continuing demand for MBA degrees and reviving economic growth prospects suggest that the declining economic value argument is overstated (Connolly, 2003), although the high tide of business school success may well have passed. In any case, Pfeffer and Fong raise serious questions about the long-term viability of the MBA industry, and the prospects for a future shake-out. Such prospects must serve to promote 'hypercompetition' among schools for absolute survival and relative position.

Ghoshal (2003, 2005) argued that pseudo-scientific pretensions underpinning MBA education fostered recent corporate scandals (Thompson and Williams, 2006). Linked economic assumptions of individual self-interest maximization and corporate shareholder value maximization have encouraged a conception of un-trustworthy agents and release from moral responsibility. These simplistic as-sumptions permit theoretical modeling and empirical verification that promote academic respectability. 'In business research...the things routinely ignored by academics on the grounds that they cannot be measured—most human factors and all matters relating to judgment, ethics, and morality—are exactly what make the difference between good business decisions and bad ones' (Bennis and O'Toole, 2005: 100). Pfeffer and Fong (2004) cautioned non-US programs against following the example of US business schools, which combine a strong market orientation with lack of professional ethos (Armstrong, 2005; Cowton and Cummins, 2003; Maclagan, 2002). Pfeffer (2005) argued that Ghoshal understated the pernicious effects of economic assumptions (Ferraro *et al.*, 2005). Even if arguably overstated (Nord, 2005*a*; Greenwood, 2003), Ghoshal's criticisms warrant close attention.

Mintzberg (2004) offered a broad critique of both management and management education (Nord, 2005*b*). He argues that MBA education emphasizes management science at the cost of the art and craft of management practice. Mintzberg presents a case for building organizations rather than shareholder value. (The difference is between long-term sustainable business and short-term earnings pressures.) Mintzberg also argues that MBA programs admit the wrong students: relatively young individuals with little or no management experience are focused primarily on analysis and technique as distinct from leadership and management. Education should focus on experienced managers who learn from their experiences in a class-room setting (Dreher and Ryan, 2004). Mintzberg's critique at least directs attention to the segmentation of MBA programs that have occurred among full-time and evening programs (usually attended by relatively inexperienced individuals) and executive programs (usually attended by experienced managers).

The essence of this multi-pronged assault on conventional MBA education is that a pseudo-scientific posture grounded in economics and psychology and directed at relatively young individuals turns out mis-educated technicians or functionaries rather than managers or leaders. Steve Jobs of Apple, like Bill Gates of Microsoft and Michael Dell a college dropout, quipped that MBAs 'knew how to manage but they didn't know how to *do* anything' (Farrell, 2006: 66). On the other hand, Ebbers (WorldCom) and Scrushy (HealthSouth), found not guilty in one trial, had no formal business education qualification (*The Economist*, 2005). Additionally, pseudo-scientific education leaves these technicians lacking any appropriate sense of moral responsibility. Kozlowski (Tyco) reportedly falsely claimed having an MBA on a *Who's Who in America* questionnaire (Bianco *et al.*, 2002; *The Economist*, 2005).

These arguments do not support abandonment of the scientific model, which has an important role. Young students may develop and mature through on-the-job training and experience. The difficulty has been that the scientific model, more suitable for Ph.D. than MBA students, tends to dominate business school education to the detriment of the professional model (Bennis and O'Toole, 2005). Leadership is about ethics, responsibilities, and values—at least as much as strategy and or-ganizational development. The professional model incorporates this conception, omitted from the scientific model. How to combine the scientific and professional models is, given the reality of academic focus on disciplines as opposed to multi-disciplinary collaboration and interdisciplinary integration, almost unavoidably an increasingly fierce competition among those disciplines for a place in the curriculum, status/prestige, and resources.

RESPONSIBILITY

Responsibility is the fundamental management issue of the 21st century. As noted earlier, responsibility is a broad rubric term embracing business ethics, CSR, stakeholder management, and ecological sustainability. Academic reality bears adversely on responsibility research and education with a vengeance. Fundamentally differing views of markets, personal and managerial responsibility, government regulation, and moral virtues reinforce marked interdiscipline competition. Responsibility has the weakest scientific reputation and the weakest status/prestige in the business school, dominated by the scientific model. The technical language of philosophical ethics is arguably impenetrable for managers and business students (without deep study); and also next to useless for practical decision calculations in business. (That many of the same managers and students may find economics and psychology equally impenetrable is offset by the circumstance that those disciplines can be more readily reduced to pseudo-scientific formulas for choice applied without theoretical understanding.) The concept of responsibility involves broad (and difficult to delimit) consequences and duties (Carroll, 1999). 'Responsibility' is best understood as an 'umbrella term' (Matten and Moon, 2004) for a set of responsibilities of management to various stakeholders including society at large.

There are considerable differences in the conception of responsibility across countries (Enderle, 1996, 1997; Spence, 2002). In North America, emphasis rests on economic responsibility (goods and services, jobs and wages, and profits) to primary stakeholder groups (customers, employees, and investors). This concept of economic responsibility readily reduces in the scientific model to fiduciary responsibility of management to investors, while deferring all other considerations to public policy (to be influenced, of course, by management and investors to their economic self-interest). Corporate citizenship, increasingly regarded as strategic philanthropy for enhancing corporate reputation (Moskowitz, 2002), has tended to supplant CSR. The recent emphasis on business ethics in US business tends to reflect a cost-benefit calculation about the necessity of legal compliance rather than concern for moral integrity, and to reflect an orientation toward just skirting legal rules rather than implementing ethical principles (see Paine, 2000). An illustration of this distinction concerns Jeffrey Skilling of Enron notoriety. A Harvard Business School professor reported that in an MBA class then student Skilling supported the position that he would keep selling a harmful product for profit maximization unless the government prohibited such conduct (Fusaro and Miller, 2002: 28).

In Western Europe, a broader conception of CSR is gaining greater sway. European CSR combines ecological sustainability and stakeholder participation in corporate governance. The European Commission (2001, 2002) chaired a voluntary European Multi-stakeholder Forum on Corporate Social Responsibility, which presented its final report in June 2004. In March 2006, the EC launched a voluntary European Alliance for Corporate Social Responsibility. The 'triple bottom line' model of corporate social performance theorizes that managers of publicly owned companies face multiple responsibilities for people, planet, and profit. Stakeholder management is ultimately about fairness and justice in the context of tough decisions about conflicts of interest (citing Norman Augustine, then CEO of Martin Marietta and later of Lockheed Martin, quoted in Paine, 1992: 1).

Outside the advanced economies, the emerging concern is more with sustainable development. The ten principles of the UN Global Compact define this concern in terms of human rights, labor rights, ecological sustainability, and corruption control. The International Standards Organization (ISO) is developing ISO 26000 guidelines for global CSR. The target release date is presently October 2008. The guidelines will not be certification standards—reinforcing the argument made above that CSR is not a computational formula or algorithm, but rather amounts to a heuristic for thinking about multiple responsibilities. The underlying assumption is that business ethics and responsibility create conditions favorable to sustainable business profitability.

Today's manager faces a complex multi-task situation. Four tasks can be identified as professional responsibility for a sustainable organization, handling conflicts among multiple stakeholders, compliance with laws and customary ethics, and addressing the long-term public interest.

One approach to this multi-task situation is to make long-term wealth creation for investors the primary objective. Stakeholders, laws and ethics, and the public interest are then simply channels for and/or constraints on that primary business objective (Gentile and Samuelson, 2005).

The alternative approach is to view the four tasks as trade-offs or balancing judgments. If one depicts the mutual interdependency situation as two partly overlapping Venn spaces labeled business and society, then the overlap is where business and social values can be and should be created jointly to mutual benefit (Gentile and Samuelson, 2005). Obviously, it would be highly desirable for this overlap to handle much of business–society relations. There are, however, strong attitudes and preferences that may lead managers to treat society as a problem for government. Furthermore, there are strong financial incentives for managers to ignore both investor and stakeholder responsibilities in favor of personal self-interest. Business misconduct incensing mobilized, powerful stakeholders may tend to expand the society space at business expense.

Much of the recent criticism concerning management education and responsibility education focuses on the increasing prominence of economics in fields such as finance, marketing, organizational behavior, and strategy (as elsewhere broadly in the social sciences). Finance and marketing are coming to dominate the scientific model of management. The criticism tends to combine two issues or problems. One issue is whether technical analysis alone, and particularly without practical experience, can substitute for management judgment. Another issue is whether economics education negatively affects business students' understanding of ethics and social responsibility.

Critics of MBA education complain (Matten and Moon, 2004) of 'brainwashing' in 'shareholder value ideology' (Adler, 2002; Caulkin, 2004; Ghoshal, 2003, 2005; Gioia, 2005; Willen, 2004). The shareholder value position is a constellation of positions that are mutually reinforcing. The constellation includes, of course, fiduciary responsibility of managerial agents to investor principals and relatively free (i.e. unregulated) markets. Fiduciary responsibility is a purely legal and not remotely an ethical concept. (No private contract can violate public policy. The business corporation is a governmentally licensed activity.) Relatively free markets depend on an economic theory predicting that such markets will in the longer run outperform excessive governmental regulation generating economic wealth. (The theory must assume that there are no significant negative externalities, such as environmental degradation, and that markets are workably competitive and innovative.) Economic history supports the prediction so far (neglecting negative externalities, of course), but the issue in the 21st century is whether the past record will continue under the burden of global warming, population growth, and resource deterioration. Fiduciary responsibility, strictly interpreted, excludes any discretionary altruism. Corporate philanthropy should be purely strategic, whether in terms of generating future corporate wealth or functioning as a kind of political 'hedge' against increased governmental regulation. The constellation includes a position that all social issues should be deferred to the government for solution. The preference is for government to absorb social costs and to avoid generating additional (i.e. costly) business regulations. The position suggests that businesses strategically should influence public policy against competitors and in favor of economic self-interest without consideration for various stakeholders. This position concerning government becomes the posture abroad that the laws of all countries must be strictly obeyed, even if those laws are immoral (a matter of moral judgment) or inconsistent with the core values of a business. The only question is strategic: does the firm need to operate in a particular country? The constellation rests on tacit 18th and 19th century assumptions concerning private property rights, libertarianism, self-interest rationalism, personal autonomy, and individual achievement. The complaint raised here is not that the assumptions are wrong—a matter to be evaluated—but that the assumptions are typically tacit and thus barely considered.

The position of economics as a premier social science is a function of both its methodological rigor and its importance in business and public policy. There are many policy disagreements among economists stemming from differing views concerning both values and parameters (Fuchs et al., 1997). There are two dimensions to economics as a science.

First, economics is a logical analysis of human behavior. This logical analysis deduces implications from assumptions. John Maynard Keynes regarded economics as 'a branch of logic, a way of thinking' and opposed attempts 'to turn it into a pseudo-natural science' (Moggridge, 1976: 21). Alfred Marshall commended short chains of deductive reasoning (1920: 771, 773, 781). However, he also accepted Cournot's view that an economic problem is not a chain of causation but a set of mutually determining elements (Marshall, 1920, pp. ix–x, 'Preface to the First Edition,' 1890). 'Economic language seems technical and less real than that of common life. But in truth it is more real, because it is more careful and takes more account of differences and difficulties' (Marshall, 1920: 759). 'Adam Smith saw clearly that while economic science must be based on a study of facts, the facts are so complex, that they generally can teach nothing directly; they must be interpreted by careful reasoning and analysis' (Marshall, 1920: 759 n. 2). Human behavior is not necessarily a fixed phenomenon like physical nature. Behavioral economics is beginning to challenge the conventional assumptions.

Second, Keynes held that 'economics is essentially a moral science and not a natural science. That is to say, it employs introspection and judgements of value. . . .' (Moggridge, 1976: 22). A. C. Pigou emphasized that Marshall viewed economics 'as a handmaid of ethics and a servant of practice' (Moggridge, 1976: 21). J. M. Clark's view (1916, 1924) was that value assumptions of neoclassical economics promoted irresponsibility toward the public interest. For Marshall, 'economic man' is not perfectly selfish; '. . . ethical forces are among those of which the economist has to take account' (1920, p. vi, 'Preface to the First Edition', 1890).

Economic assumptions may become self-fulfilling and reshape behavior toward the egoistic (Ferraro et al., 2005). Empirical evidence on this matter is disputed. Self-selection bias may lead more self-interested students to study business and economics. Pfeffer (2005: 97) cites three interesting studies. The Aspen Institute (2001) reported that student 'values' changed toward shareholder value and away from customers and employees. McCabe and Treviño (1995: 210, 211) reported that business school students report the most academic cheating and place the least importance on matters such as knowledge, justice, and 'a meaningful philosophy of life'. Williams et al. (2000: 706) suggested that citations for violations of health and safety regulations rise with the proportion of a company's top managers holding an MBA. Such evidence suggests that business and economics education may tend to reinforce, or at least not contradict, 'values' and 'attitudes' already held.

EDUCATION

The recent debate over responsibility education has focused on 'business ethics' (which will serve here as an illustrative dimension of responsibility). Critics of conventional MBA education complain, with reasonable accuracy, of an 'intellectual bias against business ethics' (Hosmer, 1999: 91, 102). The bias is pro-science (i.e. anti-philosophical) and pro-realism (i.e. anti-idealism). Such bias creates difficulties, because 'Principled leadership is neither easy nor simple' (Schmalensee (Dean, MIT Sloan School of Management), 2002). There is relentless pressure for bottom line results.

The minimum case for business ethics education is public expectation of legal compliance and moral integrity in business (Adler, 2002; Caulkin, 2004; Kelly, 2003). This minimum case should match with academic self-defense (Willen, 2004): no school today can afford to have its alumni stating when under indictment they received no instruction concerning ethics. The essential case for CSR education, more broadly defined, is that it can enlighten management to possibilities for creating business and social value simultaneously. Edward Tuck (1842–1938), the founding donor of the Amos Tuck School of Business, the first graduate management school (1900), argued that not only are absolute values of truth, honesty, and honor critically important in business but further that 'altruism is the highest form of egoism'.[1]

Plainly 'If business schools have encouraged such [bad] behavior, we need to fix it' (Schmalensee, 2002). In the wake of recent corporate scandals, a commonplace defense for business schools continuing to practice conventional MBA education as usual has been that schools were not at fault for the moral character defects of a few 'bad apples' (Willen, 2004). This defense has three defects. One defect is that the recent prosecutions are not about ethical issues at all but about plain dishonesty and lack of integrity (Schmalensee, 2002). Another defect is that the vital issue is not 'guilt' for past misdeeds—no one can guarantee a perfect set of law-abiding much less ethical graduates (Schmalensee, 2002)—but proactive responsibility going forward. 'We must integrate a concern for ethics and values, for responsibility and professional behavior throughout the curriculum' (Schmalensee, 2002). 'Guilt' simply argues a backward-looking case for assuming responsibility going forward. The responsibility case can be stated directly; the consequences of not acting at all are already known. A third defect is that conventional business school education permits not just a few 'bad apples' but rather fosters a general climate that effectively denigrates ethics in favor of bottom line profitability. If 'bad apples' are attracted to this climate, the situation is thereby compounded. 'One of the most consistent findings is that good people do bad things. We're not talking about an issue of character; that oversimplifies matters. Good people do horrendous things in the workplace because they don't see the situation as an ethical dilemma. They see it as a business problem to be solved' (Professor Arthur Brief, quoted in Teuke, 2004: 58).

Two considerations bear on education for responsibility. One consideration is that 'responsibility' is more a professional practice theme than an academic

---

[1] Letter of 12 Oct., 1904, to Dartmouth College President William J. Tucker, <http://www.tuck.dartmouth.edu/news/features/ethics.html>—'Business Ethics at Tuck' (accessed 31 May, 2006).

discipline. The business school is organized around scientific disciplines such as accounting, economics, finance, marketing, organizational behavior, and strategy. A scientific discipline has a more or less unified theory core and empirical verification methodology and a set of widely respected academic journals. While philosophical ethics and business history, although in the humanities, can meet this discipline standard, 'responsibility' (notwithstanding Keynes's notion of a 'moral science') more broadly does not. The notion is a rubric for a variety of social and stakeholder issues. Responsibility can certainly be taught as a set of subject matters and management problems. The question is what to teach.

Matten and Moon (2004) report the results of a 2003 survey of CSR education in Europe. The survey identified some 669 institutions in 20 countries, with something like a 24.8% response rate (n = 166 respondents). The survey indicates a broad definition of CSR encompassing various educational approaches including business ethics, CSR, environmental management, and sustainable development.

A second consideration is that management is a 'profession incorporate' (Bedeian, 2004: 92) rather than a true, governmentally licensed profession (e.g. accountants, doctors, and lawyers). In the absence of a true profession with strong incentives for voluntary self-regulation and stewardship of public interests, individuals with an economics or finance education may tend to eschew any ethics beyond a purely instrumental or strategic tool for protecting the bottom line through safeguarding the reputation of the business. Fiduciary agency dominates student perspective on professionalism. This instrumental approach may of course result in socially desirable behavior, but the issue is whether instrumentalism in the absence of ethics is sufficient to sustain such behavior. The deeper challenge is somehow to blend the agency model and the stewardship model (Hambrick, 2005: 107).

How to 'educate' MBAs in 'responsible management' is the vital matter of controversy. There are several key disputes. An issue concerns whether 'business and society' should in some form (e.g. business ethics, business–government relations, businesses in societies, corporate social responsibility, environmental management, legal environment, and/or sustainable development) be required universally or left to school discretion. An issue concerns whether a universal requirement should be handled as a stand-alone course (i.e. an independent subject) or be 'mainstreamed' (i.e. systematically integrated) throughout the required curriculum (Matten and Moon, 2004). The former is unlikely to be effective; the latter is unlikely to be feasible. An issue concerns whether moral character of an adult can be influenced by education; and thus whether moral character, as distinct from moral sensitivity and ethical decision-making procedure and corporate social responsiveness, is the proper target of education. An issue concerns pedagogy. What are the advantages or disadvantages of action learning, case discussions, executive visitors, gaming, preaching, service assignments, Socratic dialogue, and/or white-collar criminal visitors (Morrell, 2004; Ricci and Markulis, 1990)? There are several different targets for ethics education (Stewart, 2004). (1) Experiencing fear from listening to an ex-convict may accomplish Pavlovian conditioning as an emotional deterrent to misconduct. (2) Moral character may be formed early in life, or may be subject to subsequent modification. (3) Moral imagination and sensitivity may be heightened. (4) Ethical judgment focuses on moral dilemmas for which answers are not immediately obvious. (5) Fostering an ethical climate and designing a corporate code of conduct are important dimensions of leadership.

'Responsibility' suffers among academics, managers, and students as a result of its 'philosophical' appearance. Moral 'science' is, however, inherently of this character. Gentile and Samuelson (2005) argue that the issue is neither a separate course nor special modules within existing courses, but the condition that ethics is often taught about ethics rather than about business. 'The students use the tools of ethical analysis—deontological reasoning, utilitarianism, Rawls' veil of ignorance—instead of using the tools of business analysis. And they pit business objectives *against* moral objectives, instead of revealing the interdependence of the two' (Gentile and Samuelson, 2005: 499). These authors, affiliated with The Aspen Institute Business and Society Program, urge a shift from ethics or corporate social responsibility to social impact management, defined as management of the unavoidable interdependency of business and society to mutual benefit. This interdependency involves managing multiple stakeholders.

The debate suggests that what has been happening in business schools is the relative academic success of the scientific model for management education in combination with shareholder value obsession. This combination marches with managers' compensation and performance evaluation. The whole line of argument against ethics and responsibility education is automatically suspect because self-serving (see Hooker, 2004): 'If we believe we can't make a difference, you can be quite certain that we won't' (Gioia, 2002: 144). In contrast, what is alleged or perceived is the relative failure of the philosophical model for business ethics education in combination with preaching about corporate social responsibility. '...[S]tudents learn there are various philosophies of ethics, such as utilitarianism or deontology. Yet philosophy is notorious for leading to no firm conclusions; rather students learn to criticize each of the philosophical positions. Applied to ethics, the philosophical method can easily lead to skepticism about any ethics' (Donaldson, 2005: 112). If so, the effort should be on imparting moral values rather than resolving moral dilemmas (Donaldson, 2005: 112). But Treviño and Brown (2004) take the opposite view. They argue that (1) ethical decisions are complex, (2) business misconduct is not simply a few 'bad apples,' (3) formal ethics codes and programs do not manage the problem, (4) ethical leadership is not simply about leader integrity, and (5) people are not less ethical than previously. The pro-science position is that philosophy (i.e. non-science) produces unhealthy skepticism leading to denigration or deterioration of moral values. The anti-science position is that science (i.e. non-philosophy) produces unhealthy focus on narrowly definable measurability and obsession with shareholder value. The case for philosophical skepticism is that it encourages testing of assumptions and tacit beliefs promoting superficial thinking (Morrell, 2004).

Whether responsibility can be learned, in the sense of acquired, by adults is not strictly the vital question. 'You may not be able to change character, but you can teach people what's expected of them as professional managers. They may choose not to meet those expectations, but we have an obligation to make sure they at least recognize an ethical problem when it arises' (Schmalensee, 2002). A number of prominent CSR and ethics specialists argue the merits of educating for moral character and imagination (Andre and Velasquez, 1987; Bebeau, 1991, 1994; Callahan and Bok, 1980; Carroll, 2003). Alsop (2003), quoting Professor Lynn Paine, reported that Harvard Business School retained a developmental psychologist for advice concerning the ethics education receptivity of MBA students. The psychologist advised that MBA students in their mid to late twenties were particularly receptive to discussions about moral issues (see Rest, 1982, 1986, and 1988).

The Tuck website published an interview with adjunct professor of business ethics Richard S. Shreve (Harvard MBA and a former managing director of Morgan Stanley), who joined the Tuck faculty in 1992.

The difficulty of integrating ethics into the core curriculum of a business school is well recognized. Harvard Business School wrote a book on the subject [Piper et al., 1993], and Columbia Business School published a candid essay acknowledging that their efforts had failed ['Can Ethics Be Taught?' by John Doran]. The principal impediment to success is the reluctance of the core faculty to teach a subject that is outside their area of expertise. And the common approach of inviting an ethics professor as a guest lecturer to address the ethical issues in a finance case, for instance, sends a powerful message to the students that ethics is not a mainstream concern in finance.

Shreve reported that his attention focused on 'practical business skills, rather than molding moral character.' These practical skills include making decisions about moral dilemmas and using the language of ethics to defend a position against doing something wrong. Shreve reported that media attention following recent corporate scandals has focused on moral character and not on practical skill development. Tuck has begun addressing moral character through a five-point program: (1) top corporate attention to ethical values; (2) faculty–student mentoring relationships; (3) celebrating moral exemplars; (4) service learning; and (5) highlighting bad effects of misconduct. For example, an ex-convict explains what life will be like in a federal prison.

ACCREDITATION

Likely less than half of US business schools ever had much responsibility education in their core curricula (Buchholz, 1979; Collins and Wartick, 1995; Hosmer,

1985, 1988). The Aspen Institute–World Resource Institute 'Beyond Grey Pinstripes' survey reports periodically on the state of MBA education for 'social and environmental stewardship.' The author has argued a case for foundation responsibility education in a separate course followed by 'mainstreaming' of responsibility topics throughout the rest of the core curriculum (Windsor, 2004). That case draws on the experiences of the Harvard Business School, where such an approach was recommended (Piper *et al.*, 1993).

AACSB, acting in the wake of recent corporate scandals, in its most recent accreditation standards revision (promulgated Apr. 2003) re-emphasized ethics without resolving how to handle operationally increased emphasis (Windsor, 2002). The AACSB 2003 revision focused operationally on assurance of learning through demonstration of direct educational achievement (Blood, 2004: 429) associated with greater school flexibility (Blood, 2004: 430). The approach seeks to encourage continuous improvement in measurable outcomes (Blood, 2004: 431). AACSB's hesitation in compelling a stronger educational stance on ethics and responsibility skirts the academic realities described above. In effect, AACSB (whether intentionally or inadvertently) has wound up promoting 'mainstreaming' (without requiring any foundation courses in responsibility) and codes of conduct for faculty and students.

Blood suggested that one 'overriding...consequence' of the AACSB approach will be 'a greater sense of community among the faculty, staff, and students in the school' centered on contribution to mission (2004: 432). The suggestion ignores two potential negative effects. First, the school administration acting with the backing of a majority of the faculty determines mission. Anyone disagreeing is subject to forced compliance or exit. Ethics faculty will always be a small group. A school's approach depends on the values of the controlling faculty majority. Second, competitive pressures dictate that individuals with highest teaching evaluations from students handle core instruction. If ethics and CSR receive systematically lower teaching evaluations than deemed essential for purely competitive purposes, those courses and instructors are in danger. Disagreement with mission or over values and parameters may be viewed as professional irresponsibility. The odds favor increased conflict or enforced conformity rather than 'a greater sense of community.' Business school faculty are under unremitting pressure to publish in a pre-defined set of top ('A') academic journals, to teach at extraordinarily high levels of student satisfaction, to provide community, professional, and academic service as uncompensated organizational citizenship behavior, and to promote the school in any media and through consulting activities.

Three key examples depict the range of solutions, from relatively little to pretty solid. The information below comes from 2005–6 websites and is thus subject to the author's misinterpretation.

The University of Chicago's Graduate School of Business, founded in 1898, is one of the world's premier schools. In 2005–6, the two-year full-time MBA degree involved ten required quarter courses (whether full credit or less), and eleven electives. The degree requirements included a required course on Leadership Effectiveness and Development (LEAD) featuring, on a cohort basis, communication and leadership skills. This course included a section on ethics (Cohen and Burns, 2006). There were some elective courses for business ethics, corporate governance, and legal environment. Ethics and/or law might already be 'mainstreamed' in some manner, but such is not immediately evident from the Chicago website descriptions.

The Tuck School, at Dartmouth College, was the first graduate school of management (1900). In 2005–6, the Tuck MBA operated in four ten-week terms. In contrast to Chicago, Tuck used a very strong core (most of the first year is required) emphasizing leadership and teamwork. There was a single elective slot in the first year (in the last term). The second year was wholly elective. The approach to ethics in business was characterized as 'multi-faceted.' Tuck reported that 'nonprofits and ethics'—including the James M. Allwin Initiative for Corporate Citizenship—was a popular special interest area for students. There was no required course in the business and society area. There were second-year electives in Ethics in Action (a mini-course in which faculty from various disciplines participated) and Corporate Social Responsibility. Tuck had a required series of four panels of visitors that operated within other required courses to address 'Ethics at Tuck'.

The Wharton School, at the University of Pennsylvania, was the first collegiate school of business (1881). In 2005–6, operating on a quarter system, the MBA (on which the Executive MBA was modeled) emphasized a strong first-year core curriculum, following a month-long pre-term preparation, with some additional required courses in the second year. The core included under the rubric of 'a leadership essential' a half-credit course in Ethics and Responsibility (which could not be waived) and a full-credit course in the Governmental and Legal Environment of Business (which could be waived). Majors were available in Business and Public Policy and in Environmental and Risk Management.

CONCLUSION

The prospects for responsible management education in the 21st century are mixed. In the United States, attention remains focused on compliance rather than responsibility. In Western Europe, a broader concern for triple bottom line performance is spreading. In other countries, the overriding consideration is sustainable development. The chapter concludes that there is good reason to be concerned about the content and process of conventional management education, even though some criticisms advanced by prominent academics arguably may be overdrawn. Conventional education has been and remains dominated by a scientific model, grounded in economics and psychology, applied to major dimensions of business analysis. This scientific model, while having its merits and role, makes development of a satisfactory professional model emphasizing leadership and management difficult. An essential core dimension of the professional model for the 21st century is indisputably responsible management. There is a controversy concerning why and how to educate managers for broadly defined responsibilities. The weight of considerations bears in favor of a curricular approach to educating MBAs in which required foundation preparation in legal, ethical, and political dimensions of management is followed by 'mainstreaming' of those dimensions throughout the rest of the required core curriculum. Pure 'mainstreaming' is unlikely to prove satisfactory. The author's proposed approach, in combination with leadership and management education, will involve major (and definitely not elective) surgery on the conventional MBA curriculum.

References

ADLER, P. S. 2002. 'Corporate Scandals: It's Time for Reflection in Business Schools'. *Academy of Management Executive*, 16: 148–9.

ALSOP, R. 2003. 'Right and Wrong: Can Business Schools Teach Students to be Virtuous? In the Wake of All the Corporate Scandals, They Have No Choice But to Try'. *Wall Street Journal*, 17 Sept.

ANDRE, C., and VELASQUEZ, M. 1987. 'Can Ethics be Taught'? *Issues in Ethics* (Markkula Center for Applied Ethics, Santa Clara University), 1(1), fall, <http://www.scu.edu/ethics/publications/iie/v1n1>.

ARMSTRONG, S. 2005. 'Postgraduate Management Education in the UK: Lessons From or Lessons for the U.S. Model'? *Academy of Management Learning & Education*, 4: 229–34.

Aspen Institute. 2001. *Where Will They Lead? MBA Student Attitudes about Business and Society*. New York: Aspen Institute for Social Innovation through Business.

BEBEAU, M. J. 1991. 'Can Ethics be Taught? A Look at the Evidence'. *Journal of the American College of Dentists*, 58(1): 100–15.

——1994. 'Can Ethics be Taught? A Look at the Evidence: Revisited'. *NY State Dental Journal*, 60(1): 51–7.

BEDEIAN, A. G. 2004. 'The Gift of Professional Maturity'. *Academy of Management Learning & Education*, 3: 92–8.

BENNIS, W., and O'TOOLE, J. 2005. 'How Business Schools Lost their Way'. *Harvard Business Review*, 83(5) May: 96–104.

BIANCO, A., SYMONDS, W., and BYRNES, N., WITH POLEK, D. 2002. 'The Rise and Fall of Dennis Kozlowski'. *BusinessWeek Online*, 23 Dec.

BLOOD, M. 2004. 'A Conversation with Milton Blood: The New AACSB standards'. *Academy of Management Learning & Education*, 3: 429–39.

BOYATZIS, R. 1982. *The Competent Manager: A Model for Effective Performance*. New York: John Wiley.

BUCHHOLZ, R. A. 1979. *Business Environment/Public Policy: A Study of Teaching and Research in Schools of Business and Management*. Washington: AACSB and St. Louis: Center for the Study of American Business, Washington University, Working Paper No. 41 (Feb.).

CALLAHAN, D., and BOK, S. (eds.). 1980. *Ethics Teaching in Higher Education*. New York: Plenum Press.

CARROLL, A. B. 1999. 'Corporate Social Responsibility: Evolution of a Definitional Construct'. *Business & Society*, 38: 268–95.

——— 2003. 'Can Ethics be Taught?' 17 Feb. (Forum essay), <http://www.uga.edu/columns/030217/news12.html.>

CAULKIN, S. 2004. 'Business Schools for Scandal. *Observer*, 28 Mar.: 9 (Business).

CLARK, J. M. 1916. 'The Changing Basis of Economic Responsibility'. *Journal of Political Economy*, 24: 209–29.

CLARK, J. M. 1924. 'The Socializing of Theoretical Economics'. in R. G. Tugwell (ed.), *The Trend of Economics*. New York: Alfred A. Knopf, 73–105.

COHEN, J. S., and BURNS, G. 2006. 'Can You Teach a Person Ethics?' Iraqi Allegations, Hiring Probes, Enron: Right and Wrong Seem to be Elusive Concepts'. *Chicago Tribune*, 7 June.

COLLINS, D., and WARTICK, S. L. 1995. 'Business and Society/Business Ethics Courses: Twenty Years at the Crossroads'. *Business & Society*, 34: 51–89.

CONNOLLY, M. 2003. 'The End of the MBA As We Know It?' *Academy of Management Learning & Education*, 2: 365–7.

COWTON, C. J., and CUMMINS, J. 2003. 'Teaching Business Ethics in UK Higher Education: Progress and Prospects'. *Teaching Business Ethics*, 7: 37–54.

CRANE, A., and MATTEN, D. 2004. 'Questioning the Domain of the Business Ethics Curriculum'. *Journal of Business Ethics*, 54: 357–69.

DANKO, J. M., and ANDERSON, B. L. 2005. 'In Defense of the MBA'. *BizEd* (AACSB), 5(1), Nov./Dec.: 24–8.

DONALDSON, L. 2005. 'For Positive Management Theories while Retaining Science: Reply to Ghoshal'. *Academy of Management Learning & Education*, 4: 109–13.

DREHER, G. F., and RYAN, K. C. 2004. 'A Suspect MBA Selection Model: The Case Against the Standard Work Experience Requirement'. *Academy of Management Learning & Education*, 3: 87–91.

The Economist. 2005. 'Business Schools Get a Bad Rap'. Reprinted in *National Post*, 7 May, Financial Post, Weekend: FW10 (Toronto edn).

ELLIN, A. 2006. 'Was Earning that Harvard M.B.A. Worth It?' *New York Times*, 11 June. <http://www.nytimes.com/2006/06/11/business/yourmoney/11harvard.html>.

ENDERLE, G. 1996. 'A Comparison of Business Ethics in North America and Continental Europe'. *Business Ethics: A European Review*, 5(1): 33–46.

——— 1997. A Worldwide Survey of Business Ethics in the 1990s'. *Journal of Business Ethics*, 16: 1475–83.

European Commission Directorate-General for Employment and Social Affairs. 2001. *Promoting a European Framework for Corporate Social Responsibility*. Luxembourg: Office for Official Publications of the European Communities.

——Commission of the European Communities. 2002. Communication from the Commission concerning Corporate Social Responsibility: A Business Contribution to Sustainable Development. Brussels: Commission of the European Communities.

FARRELL, L. 2006. 'You have to be a Bet-the-Ranch Type: Just One of the Myths Behind Being an Entrepreneur'. *Across the Board*, 43(2), Mar./Apr.: 65–6.

FERRARO, F., PFEFFER, J., and SUTTON, R. I. 2005. 'Economic Language and Assumptions: How Theories Can Become Self-Fulfilling'. *Academy of Management Review*, 30: 8–24.

FRIGA, P. N., BETTIS, R. A., and SULLIVAN, R. S. 2003. 'Changes in Graduate Management Education and New Business School Strategies for the 21st Century'. *Academy of Management Learning & Education*, 2: 233–49.

FUCHS, V. R., KRUEGER, A. B., and POTERBA, J. M. 1997. 'Why do Economists Disagree about Policy? The Roles of Beliefs about Parameters and Values'. National Bureau of Economic Research (NBER) Working Paper No. W6151, <http://ssrn.com/abstract=225914>.

FUSARO, P. C., and MILLER, R. M. 2002. *What Went Wrong at Enron: Everyone's Guide to the Largest Bankruptcy in U.S. History*. New York: John Wiley.

GENTILE, M. C., and SAMUELSON, J. F. 2005. Keynote Address to the AACSB International Deans Conference, 10 Feb. 2003: 'The State of Affairs for Management Education and Social Responsibility'. *Academy of Management Learning & Education*, 4: 496–505.

GHOSHAL, S. 2003. 'Business Schools Share the Blame for Enron'. *Financial Times*, 18 July.: 19.

——2005. 'Bad Management Theories are Destroying Good Management Practices'. *Academy of Management Learning & Education*, 4: 75–91.

GIOIA, D. A. 2002. 'Business Education's Role in the Crisis of Corporate Confidence'. *Academy of Management Executive*, 16: 142–44.

GORDON, R. A., and HOWELL, J. E. 1959. *Higher Education for Business*. New York: Columbia University Press.

GREENWOOD, W. 2003. 'Timely Plea Misrepresents the Facts'. *Financial Times*, 23 July: 12 (Letter to the Editor).

HAMBRICK, D. C. 2005. 'Just How Bad Are Our Theories? A Response to Ghoshal'. *Academy of Management Learning & Education*, 4: 104–7.

HOOKER, J. 2004. 'The Case against Business Ethics Education: A Study in Bad Arguments'. *Journal of Business Ethics Education*, 1: 75–88.

HOSMER, L. T. 1985. 'The Other 338: Why a Majority of our Schools of Business Administration Do Not Offer a Course in Business Ethics'. *Journal of Business Ethics*, 4: 17–22.

——1988. 'Adding Ethics to the Business Curriculum'. *Business Horizons*, 31(4) July–Aug.: 9–15.

——1999. 'Somebody Out There Doesn't Like Us: A Study of the Position and Respect of Business Ethics at Schools of Business Administration'. *Journal of Business Ethics*, 22: 91–106.

KELLY, J. 2003. 'It's a Heckuva Time to be Dropping Business Ethics Courses'. *Bizlife*, June: 44–46.

LIVINGSTON, J. S. 1971. 'Myth of the Well-Educated Manager'. *Harvard Business Review*, 49(1) Jan.–Feb.: 79–89.

McCABE, D. L., and TREVINO, L. K. 1995. 'Cheating Among Business Students: A Challenge for Business Leaders and Educators'. *Journal of Management Education*, 19: 205–18.

MACLAGAN, P. 2002. 'Reflections on the Integration of Ethics Teaching into a British Under-graduate Management Degree Programme'. *Teaching Business Ethics*, 6: 297–318.

MARSHALL, A. 1920. *Principles of Economics: An Introductory Volume*. 8th edn. London: Macmillan.

MATTEN, D., and MOON, J. 2004. 'Corporate Social Responsibility Education in Europe. *Journal of Business Ethics*, 54: 323–37.

MINTZBERG, H. 2004. *Managers not MBAs: A Hard Look at the Soft Practice of Managing and Management Development*. London and New York: Financial Times Prentice Hall.

MOGGRIDGE, D. E. 1976. *John Maynard Keynes*. New York: Penguin Books.

MORRELL, K. 2004. 'Socratic Dialogue as a Tool for Teaching Business Ethics'. *Journal of Business Ethics*, 53: 383–92.

MOSKOWITZ, M. 2002. 'What Has CSR Really Accomplished? Much of the Movement Has been a Public Relations Smokescreen'. *Business Ethics*, May–June and July–August: 4.

NORD, W. 2005*a*. 'Comments on Ghoshal's Paper'. *Academy of Management Learning & Education*, 4: 92–113 (Kanter, Pfeffer, Gapper, Hambrick, Mintzberg, Donaldson).

—— 2005*b*. 'Comments on Mintzberg's *Managers Not MBAs*'. *Academy of Management Learning & Education*, 4: 213–47 (Miles, Feldman, Barnett, Armstrong, Tyson, Klein-richert, Lewicki, Mintzberg).

PAINE, L. S. 2000. 'Does Ethics Pay?' *Business Ethics Quarterly*, 10: 319–30

—— with CHOY, A., and SANTORO, M. 1992 (rev. 1994). 'Martin Marietta: Managing Corporate Ethics (A)'. Harvard Business School Case 9-393-016.

PFEFFER, J. 2005. 'Why Do Bad Management Theories Persist? A Comment on Ghoshal'. *Academy of Management Learning & Education*, 4: 96–100.

—— and FONG, C. T. 2002. 'The End of Business Schools? Less Success than Meets the Eye'. *Academy of Management Learning & Education*, 1: 78–95.

—— —— 2004. 'The Business School "Business": Some Lessons from the US Experience'. *Journal of Management Studies*, 41: 1501–20.

PIPER, T. R., GENTILE, M. C., and PARKS, S. D. 1993. *Can Ethics be Taught? Perspectives, Challenges, and Approaches at Harvard Business School*. Boston, MA: Harvard Business School.

PORTER, L. W., and McKIBBIN, L. 1988. *Management Education and Development: Drift or Thrust into the Twenty-First Century?* New York: McGraw-Hill.

REST, J. R. 1982. 'A Psychologist Looks at the Teaching of Ethics'. *Hastings Center Report*, 12 Feb.: 29–36.

—— 1986. 'Moral Development in Young Adults'. in R. A. Mines and K. S. Kitchener (eds.), *Adult Cognitive Development: Methods and Models*. New York: Praeger, 92–111.

—— 1988. 'Can Ethics be Taught in Professional Schools? The Psychological Research.' *Easier Said than Done*, winter: 22–6.

RICCI, P., and MARKULIS, P. M. 1990. 'Can Ethics be Taught? A Simulation Tests a Traditional Ethics Pedagogy'. *Developments in Business Simulation & Experiential Exercises*, 17: 141–5.

SCHMALENSEE, R. 2002. 'Without Ethics, Business Can't be Done—or Taught'. *Boston Globe*, 30 Aug.: A19. <http://mitsloan.mit.edu/newsroom/2002-dean-on-ethics.php.>

SPENCE, L. 2002. 'Is Europe Distinctive from America? An Overview of Business Ethics in Europe'. in H. von Weltzien Hoivik (ed.), *Moral Leadership in Action*. Cheltenham, UK: Edward Elgar, 9–25.

STEWART, C. S. 2004. 'A Question of Ethics: How to Teach Them?' *The New York Times*, 21 Mar.

STOLZENBERG, R., GIARUSSO, R., and ABOWD, J. M. 1986. 'Abandoning the Myth of the Modern MBA Student'. *Selections: The Magazine of the Graduate Management Admission Council*, autumn: 9–21.

TEUKE, MOLLY R. 2004. 'Teach the Right Thing: Debating the Place of Ethics in the Business Curriculum'. *Continental*, Sept.: 57–9.

THOMPSON, J. R., and WILLIAMS, E. E. 2006. 'Future Enrons Await, Unless...: Business Schools Must Stop Teaching Faulty Formulas'. *Houston Chronicle*, 105(227), 28 May.: E4 (Outlook).

TREVIÑO, L. K., and BROWN, M. E. 2004. 'Managing to be Ethical: Debunking Five Business Ethics Myths'. *Academy of Management Executive*, 18: 69–81.

WILLEN, L. 2004. 'Kellogg Denies Guilt as B Schools Evade Alumni Lapses (Bloomberg News). <http://www.cba.k-state.edu/departments/ethics/docs/bloombergpress.htm.>

WILLIAMS, R. J., BARRETT, J. D., and BRABSTON, M. 2000. 'Managers' Business School Education and Military Service: Possible Links to Corporate Criminal Activity'. *Human Relations*, 53: 691–712.

WINDSOR, D. 2002. 'An Open Letter on Business School Responsibility', Publ. 8 Oct., available at <http://iabs.net.>

—— 2004. 'A Required Foundation Course for Moral, Legal and Political Education'. *Journal of Business Ethics Education*, 1: 137–64.

CHAPTER 23

CORPORATE SOCIAL RESPONSIBILITY

DEEP ROOTS, FLOURISHING GROWTH, PROMISING FUTURE

WILLIAM C. FREDERICK

WHAT are Corporate Social Responsibility's (CSR) prospects for the future? Will it, and should it, guide business decisions and policies during the 21st century? This chapter argues that CSR's prospects are anchored in its early beginnings, in its ever-expanding acceptance as a legitimate business practice, and in the looming necessities and crises spawned by unprecedented global expansion of economic enterprise.

CSR's Meaning

CSR occurs when a business firm, through the decisions and policies of its executive leaders, consciously and deliberately acts to enhance the social well-being

Corporation As Organic Unit/Institution/Entity: Societal Function to Create Economic Value
    CSR = Corporation–Society Interactions Benefiting Both
    CSR = Public Policy/Regulation/Law Defining Public Interest
    CSR = Shareholder–Stakeholder Balance of Interests
    CSR = Integrity of Business Functions
    • Capital acquisition and management: Transparency, full disclosure
    • Production: Product integrity, job creation, environmental impact
    • Marketing: Fair pricing, honest advertising
    • Finance/Accounting: GAAP, audits, operational safeguards
    • Supply-chain relations: Competitive, non-coercive, non-exploitive
    • Human resources: Wages, hours, workplace safety-health, pensions, etc.
    • Corporate governance: Diversity, insider-outsider balance
    • Corporate strategy: Location, sourcing, sustainability
Company's CSR status = f (Institutional Actions of Board of Directors and Top Executives)

Individual Managers and Employees as Corporate Agents: Personal Actions, Motives, and Intentions
    CSR = Agents act virtuously to create a good company and society: Aristotelian ethics
    CSR = Agents respect rights, duties, and obligations to all stakeholders: Kantian ethics
    CSR = Agents favor social equity, fairness, and justice in the workplace: Rawlsian ethics
    CSR = Agents create and support an ethical corporate mission, goals, and strategies
Company's CSR status = f (Personal Actions of individual agents)

Fig. 23.1 The dual meaning of CSR

of those whose lives are affected by the firm's economic operations. In this way, CSR blends and harmonizes economic operations with a human community's social systems and institutions, creating an organic linkage of Business and Society. The goal of this relationship is to achieve a balance between the firm's economic operations and the society's aspirations and requirements for community welfare.

Social responsibility takes many different forms and is expressed in numerous ways, varying from firm to firm. As Figure 23.1 reveals, a company that enjoys mutually beneficial relations with its host communities, obeys laws and public policies, balances stakeholder claims, and conducts business with integrity would be considered to be a socially responsible corporate citizen. Some corporations score well on all counts while others attain a CSR stature in fewer areas.

Figure 23.1 also identifies two distinct ways of determining a company's CSR standing: looking at *the company as a whole*, or examining *the individuals* who make decisions and set policies for the company. When things go wrong, who should be blamed—the company? or the executives who made the wrong decisions? When the auditing firm, Arthur Andersen, was convicted of condoning illegal behavior by its officials, federal court action put the whole company out of business. In such cases, a firm's CSR status is an outcome of *institutional/organizational actions* taken by the company as a distinct, identifiable legal entity.

On the other hand, individual top executives of Enron, Tyco, and WorldCom—not the companies themselves—were jailed and fined for criminal acts these executives committed in the company's name. Here, the companies' CSR status is an outcome of the *personal actions and character* of the offending executives. When a company's agents or representatives act legally and ethically, that could be counted as a form of CSR as shown in the lower half of Figure 23.1. Encouraging and rewarding virtuous behavior toward others, respecting their rights, treating employees and customers fairly, and supporting ethical corporate goals mark a company and its leaders as being ethically and socially responsible.

CSR's Stages of Development

CSR has a longer history in the United States than in most other nations. The primary reason is the prevalence of a market-style economy, supported by free-market ideology and limited government regulations. These conditions generate an increased expectation of social awareness and social services from private enterprise rather than from government-provided social guidance. CSR ideas in the United States emerged in the early decades of the 20th century—coming from the corporate sector itself, especially the top executives of major companies (Heald, 1970; Frederick, 2006).

From that early beginning, CSR evolved in four chronological phases described next and illustrated in Figure 23.2. In this four-stage emergence of CSR, individual firms may be positioned at different points on the phased trend line. Not all companies pass through all four phases, although many of today's leading CSR enterprises manifest all of them simultaneously.

CSR$_1$: Corporate Social Stewardship (1950s–1960s)

The Basic Idea: Corporate Managers as Public Trustees and Social Stewards

In this early version of CSR, three core principles stand out: corporate managers as public trustees and stewards of broad-scale economic interests; an executive duty to balance the competing claims of employees, customers, owners, and the public; and philanthropic support of worthy social causes. These duties and obligations, carried out by top-level executives, are entirely voluntary, supporting a belief that those who hold power incur reciprocal responsibilities to society (Abrams, 1951).

The mainstay of this first, and voluntarily assumed, approach to CSR is philanthropy—the allocation of company funds to support worthy community projects. Philanthropic contributions could, in a marginal way, help reduce the

CSR₁: CORPORATE SOCIAL STEWARDSHIP (1950s–1960s)
   Guiding CSR Principle: Corporate managers are public trustees and social stewards
   Main CSR Action: Corporate philanthropy
   CSR Drivers: Executive conscience and company reputation
   CSR Policy Instruments: Philanthropy and public relations

CSR₂: CORPORATE SOCIAL RESPONSIVENESS (1960s–1970s)
   Guiding CSR Principle: Corporations should respond to legitimate social demands
   Main CSR Action: Interact with stakeholders and comply with public policies
   CSR Drivers: Stakeholder pressures and government regulations
   CSR Policy Instruments: Stakeholder negotiations and regulatory compliance

CSR₃: CORPORATE/BUSINESS ETHICS (1980s–1990s)
   Guiding CSR Principle: Create and maintain an ethical corporate culture
   Main CSR Action: Treat all stakeholders with respect and dignity
   CSR Drivers: Human rights and religio-ethnic values
   CSR Policy Instruments: Mission statements, ethics codes, social contracts

CSR₄: CORPORATE GLOBAL CITIZENSHIP (1990s–2000s)
   Guiding CSR Principle: Accept responsibility for corporate global impacts
   Main CSR Action: Adopt and implement global sustainability programs
   CSR Drivers: Globalization disruptions of economy and environment
   CSR Policy Instruments: International code compliance, sustainability policy

Fig. 23.2 Four stages of CSR

gap between rich and poor, the haves and have-nots, thereby moving towards a more just and balanced social outcome. Authorizing these redistributive gifts from corporate treasuries is a responsibility, not to say a privilege, of public trusteeship (Bowen, 1953).

CSR₂: Corporate Social Responsiveness (1960s–1970s)

The Basic Idea: Responding to Social Demands

CSR took on an entirely new meaning during the 1960s and 1970s. Under the hammer blows of rising social protests, corporations were expected to go beyond voluntary philanthropy and take practical steps to help solve society's problems. The general public demanded *response* to their social demands, not just a continuation of the *voluntary* stewardship of CSR₁.

This new social agenda required businesses to correct racial and sexual discrimination in the workplace, reduce industrial pollution, upgrade health and safety conditions in plants and offices, charge fair prices for consumers, insure the reliability and effectiveness of products, provide full information for investors, avoid bribery of foreign officials, treat suppliers fairly, and refuse to engage in price-fixing with competitors. Other critics condemned weapons production, war profiteering, and business support of militant foreign policy. Some reformers proposed federal chartering of corporations and a more socially diverse board of directors.

In all of this social turmoil, business was expected *to do something tangible* in response to these social demands. Executive minds reacted by adopting a socially pragmatic attitude emphasizing *response* rather than a passive, voluntary *responsibility*. No longer was it a question of *whether* business should pay attention to social issues because public opinion and new government regulations had answered affirmatively.

This new social activism by business firms led to big changes internally. New incentives and sanctions encouraged socially responsible behavior by managers and employees. Corporate strategy incorporated socially responsible goals. Stakeholders affected by company operations were identified and brought into negotiations. Newly enacted government regulations aimed at curbing social ills became a new managerial mandate. Leading corporations moved from passive responsibility to active social response (Ackerman, 1975; Preston and Post, 1975; Freeman, 1984).

CSR$_3$: Corporate/Business Ethics (1980s–1990s)

The Basic Idea: Fostering Ethical Corporate Culture

Beginning around 1980, CSR took on a new meaning that went beyond CSR$_1$'s philanthropy and CSR$_2$'s social activism. A CSR$_3$ company could be recognized by the quality of its corporate culture, the type of ethical climate it displays, and the normative principles that guide the company's policies, strategies, and decisions.

Every business firm has a distinctive organizational culture that exerts a strong influence on the company's behavior, the goals it seeks, and the human beings who work there (Deal and Kennedy, 1982). Since it plays such a dominant role in shaping company practices, culture holds the key to charting a socially responsible path for the firm. Especially influential is the ethical climate present in the workplace, i.e. managers' and employees' beliefs and attitudes about what constitutes right and wrong on-the-job behavior (Victor and Cullen, 1988).

A CSR$_3$ company strives to create an ethical climate based on the ethics principles shown previously in Figure 23.1: positive outcomes in community relationships; respect for stakeholders' rights; fairness and justice in all business transactions, and promoting socially responsible goals (Phillips, 2003). Companies that explicitly and consciously make these principles an integral part of their culture and organizational climate move well beyond the two earlier CSR phases to become normatively focused CSR$_3$ corporations. A whole array of tools is available for these purposes: mission statements committing the company to ethical goals; a company code of ethics defining the core values and ethical principles to be followed by all employees; a chief ethics officer to police wrongful actions; ethics audits, ethics training workshops, ethics hot-lines for reporting misconduct; and positive rewards for outstanding ethical behavior on the job (Murphy, 1998).

This panoply of CSR_3 policy instruments invokes the concept of a 'social contract' between company and community where specific responsibilities are defined for each side. Donaldson and Dunfee (1999) propose a unique kind of social contract between business and society that embodies universal human rights principles vital to society while granting economic enterprises the degree of flexibility and practicality needed for successful market operations.

CSR_4: Corporate Global Citizenship (1990s–2000s)

The Basic Idea: Accept and Attain Global Citizenship Responsibility

Corporations, as legal entities, have the same duties and obligations as other members of civil society: to obey the law, contribute to the commonweal, participate in governance, and demonstrate respect for other citizens. As citizens, they are responsible for their actions, and their owners and directors are charged with fiduciary oversight of company operations and assets. This basic meaning of Corporate Citizenship is present in all three of the CSR phases described above. However, globalization of trade has greatly expanded the citizenship duties of corporations. Today's multinational corporations are citizens, not just of one or two nations, but of all the societies where they conduct business. Their social responsibility has become worldwide in scope and magnitude, going far beyond philanthropy (CSR_1), social activism (CSR_2), and organizational ethics (CSR_3). CSR_4 companies are truly Corporate *Global* Citizens (McIntosh *et al.*, 2003; Waddock, 2006).

Globalization—the penetration of market-driven corporate enterprise into societies everywhere—has been accompanied by disruptive and often ruinous environmental and ecological damage: despoliation of air, rivers, oceans, arable land, forests, natural habitats, potable water supplies, food stocks, and depletion of mineral caches. Small and medium-sized local firms (SMEs) are driven out by the competition of bigger, more powerful multinational enterprises (MNEs). National labor policies, social welfare programs, health care institutions, public taxes, currency systems, communication and transportation networks face review and painful reform by local governments. Some lesser developed regions are lifted up economically by a surge of new jobs while formerly prosperous locales suffer precipitous decline. The consequent political unrest and instability following these massive economic transitions render the governance of civil society increasingly complicated.

An issue of even greater importance generated by globalization—perhaps even the central issue—is the quest for the long-term *sustainability* of individual companies, national economies, and the world's ecological systems that nurture life on the entire planet.

Corporate Global Citizens respond to these complex challenges in several ways: seeking solutions through a collective dialogue with affected stakeholders, government representatives, and non-governmental organizations (NGOs); and by pledging compliance with global codes of conduct regarding human rights, environmental impacts, transparency of operations, and financial integrity (McIntosh *et al.*, 2003). Some scholars have proposed a new role for global corporations as peacemakers in a world of rising tensions (Fort and Schipani, 2002).

CSR's Global Prospects

CSR is an idea whose time has arrived, not just in the United States but wherever markets and corporate enterprise comprise the foundation of a society's economic endeavors. Unevenly developed and experienced across the grand arc of 21st century societies, CSR is infiltrating into corporate consciousness and corporate culture, finds expression in the workplace, sparks stakeholder involvement, molds company strategy, enriches the quality of community life, broadens business vision, and seeks to humanize economic enterprise wherever it is found.

A cardinal principle of CSR's spread throughout the globe is that each society and each business firm shall, and indeed should, find its own unique way of expressing and realizing CSR's core meaning. In achieving an integrity of business operations, equal regard should be had for the integrity of each society's core values and moral standards. While globalization has forcefully thrust the face of corporate enterprise into societies everywhere, CSR continues, as it should, to be discovered and expressed in varying ways that parallel the sociocultural diversity of values found throughout the world. For these reasons, it would be unwise to embrace the four stages of CSR development found in the United States as a model to be followed everywhere.

As Figure 23.3 reveals, there is a complex mosaic of forces both permitting as well as discouraging the emergence of CSR. What is thought to be socially responsible business behavior in Poland, Estonia, or Turkey varies greatly from US experience, while sharing some similarities (Habisch *et al.*, 2005; Kooskora, 2006). The same can be said of business enterprise in the nations of Asia, Africa, and Latin America (Minus, 1993; Dunfee and Nagayasu, 1993; Werhane and Singer, 1999). Diverse

- Firm size: MNE/SME differences
  Scale and magnitude of corporate social impact
  Comparative resource capability
  Competitive pressures and market strength
- Politico–governmental system
  Government-sponsored social programs
  Private business-sponsored CSR activities
- Economic development stage
  CSR affordability in developed nations
  Marginal CSR focus in developing nations
- Geopolitical events and transitions
  North-South prosperity/poverty gap
  East-West religio-political tensions
  Development pressures on resources and environment
- Diverse societal value systems
  Differential commitment to utilitarian-instrumental values
  Historical experience with market-centered business practice
- Environmental and natural forces
  Climatological disasters
  Human habitat preservation
  Viral pandemics

Fig. 23.3 Factors shaping CSR's future

religious traditions alone powerfully shape both private and public conceptions of right and wrong business behavior. Smaller businesses (SMEs)—by far the largest number of firms worldwide—necessarily confront CSR issues in ways distinct from multinational firms (MNEs) (Spence, 1999; Enderle, 2004; Worthington *et al.*, 2006). Recently, an enlivened philanthropic impulse among leading corporate executives promises to drive CSR more forcefully to broader levels and higher purposes (Hechinger and Golden, 2006).

Common problems and shared ways of coping with them do exist in the midst of sociocultural diversity, signaling that a global CSR consciousness is needed and achievable. Global compacts, policy regimes, and codes of conduct—all of them forms of social contracts between Business and Society—are a first step (Williams, 2000; Leipziger, 2003; Sethi, 2003), but see Roger Scruton's warning that this Western concept lacks the needed behavioral underpinning in large swaths of the world (Scruton, 2002). CSR, as a concept and as operational practice, now far exceeds in planetary significance its earlier struggles to gain acceptance of social justice and community well-being. Foremost now is the gargantuan struggle to balance business's economizing impulse and the world's ecologizing communitarian needs— that is, to secure and sustain not just the economic base, the business firms, and the moral systems of each nation but to preserve and prolong planetary life itself (Frederick, 1995). The prospect of not rising to this challenge is as frightening as it is unlikely, so long as businesses everywhere continue to cultivate the seeds of CSR planted long ago and in many lands.

References

ABRAMS, F. 1951. 'Management's Responsibilities in a Complex World'. *Harvard Business Review*, 29(3), May: 29–34.

ACKERMAN, R. 1975. *The Social Challenge to Business*. Cambridge, Mass.: Harvard University Press.

BOWEN, H. R. 1953. *Social Responsibilities of the Businessman*. New York: Harper.

DEAL, T. E., and KENNEDY, A. A. 1982. *Corporate Cultures: The Rites and Rituals of Corporate Life*. Reading, Mass.: Addison-Wesley.

DONALDSON, T., and DUNFEE, T. W. 1999. *Ties that Bind: A Social Contracts Approach to Business Ethics*. Boston, Mass.: Harvard Business School Press.

DUNFEE, T. W., and NAGAYASU, Y. (eds.). 1993. *Business Ethics: Japan and the Global Economy*. Dordrecht: Kluwer.

ENDERLE, G. 2004. 'Global Competition and Corporate Responsibilities of Small and Medium-Sized Enterprises'. *Business Ethics: A European Review*, 13(1): 51–63.

FORT, T. L., and SCHIPANI, C. A. (eds.), 2002. 'Corporate Governance, Stakeholder Accountability, and Sustainable Peace: A Symposium'. *Vanderbilt Journal of Transnational Law*, 35(2): 389–436.

FREDERICK, W. C. 1995. *Values, Nature, and Culture in the American Corporation*. New York: Oxford University Press.

—— 2006. *Corporation, Be Good! The Story of Corporate Social Responsibility*. Indianapolis: Dog Ear Press.

FREEMAN, R. E. 1984. *Strategic Management: A Stakeholder Approach*. Boston, Mass.: Pitman.

HABISCH, A., JONKER, J., WEGNER, M., and SCHMIDPETER, R. (eds.) 2005. *Corporate Social Responsibility across Europe*. Berlin: Springer.

HEALD, M. 1970. *The Social Responsibilities of Business: Company and Community, 1900–1960*. Cleveland: Case Western Reserve University Press.

HECHINGER, J., and GOLDEN, D. 2006. 'The Great Giveaway'. *Wall Street Journal*, 8–9 July: A-1/A-8.

KOOSKORA, M. 2006. 'Perceptions of Business Purpose and Responsibility in the Context of Radical Political and Economic Development: The Case of Estonia'. *Business Ethics: A European Review*, 15(2), Apr.: 183–99.

LEIPZIGER, D. 2003. *The Corporate Responsibility Code Book*. Sheffield: Greenleaf.

MCINTOSH, M., THOMAS, R., LEIPZIGER, D., and COLEMAN, G. 2003. *Living Corporate Citizenship: Strategic Routes to Socially Responsible Business*. London: Prentice-Hall/Financial Times.

MINUS, P. M. (ed.). 1993. *The Ethics of Business in A Global Economy*. Dordrecht: Kluwer.

MURPHY, P. E. (ed.) 1998. *Eighty Exemplary Ethics Statements*. Notre Dame, In.: Notre Dame University Press.

PHILLIPS, R. 2003. *Stakeholder Theory and Organizational Ethics*. San Francisco: Berrett-Koehler.

PRESTON, L. E., and POST, J. E. 1975. *Private Management and Public Policy*. Englewood Cliffs, NJ: Prentice-Hall.

SCRUTON, R. 2002. *The West and the Rest: Globalization and the Terrorist Threat*. Wilmington, Del.: Intercollegiate Studies Institute.

SETHI, S. P. 2003. *Setting Global Standards: Guidelines for Creating Codes of Conduct in Multinational Corporations*. New York: John Wiley & Sons.

SPENCE, L. J. 1999. 'Does Size Matter? The State of the Art in Small Business Ethics'. *Business Ethics: A European Review*, 8(3), July: 163–74.

VICTOR, B., and CULLEN, J. B. 1988. 'The Organizational Bases of Ethical Work Climates'. *Administrative Science Quarterly*, 33: 101–25.

WADDOCK, S. 2006. *Leading Corporate Citizens: Vision, Values, Value Added*, 2nd edn. New York: McGraw-Hill/Irwin.

WERHANE, P. H., and SINGER, A. E. (eds.). 1999. *Business Ethics in Theory and Practice: Contributions from Asia and New Zealand*. Dordrecht: Kluwer.

WILLIAMS, O. F. (ed.). 2000. *Global Codes of Conduct: An Idea whose Time has Come*. Notre Dame, Ind.: Notre Dame University Press.

WORTHINGTON, I., RAM, M., and JONES, T. 2006. 'Giving Something Back: A Study of Corporate Social Responsibility in UK South Asian Small Enterprises'. *Business Ethics: A European Review*, 15(1): 95–108.

CHAPTER 24

SENIOR MANAGEMENT PREFERENCES AND CORPORATE SOCIAL RESPONSIBILITY

ALISON MACKEY

TYSON B. MACKEY

JAY B. BARNEY

WHILE interest in the causes and consequences of socially responsible corporate actions continues to grow, several issues central to our understanding of this phenomenon remain largely unaddressed in the prior literature. Among these are the role that senior managers play in formulating and implementing socially responsible policies for their firms.

On the one hand, it seems reasonable to expect that senior managers who are, themselves, personally committed to socially responsible causes are more likely to champion activities that further these causes in the firms they manage. However, that senior managers with these preferences may be predisposed to implementing socially responsible activities in their firms does not mean that having these kinds of senior managers is either necessary, or sufficient, for a firm to pursue these activities. Necessity would suggest that not having these kinds of senior managers would insure that a firm did not implement socially responsible activities. Sufficiency would suggest that having these kinds of senior managers, by itself, would always lead a firm to implement socially responsible activities.

Hence, the purpose of this chapter is to examine whether or not having senior managers who are personally committed to socially responsible causes is either necessary or sufficient for firms to implement socially responsible activities. While not denying that having such senior managers may increase the probability that a firm will pursue a socially responsible agenda, the chapter concludes that senior manager commitment to socially responsible causes is neither necessary nor sufficient for a firm to implement socially responsible activities.

While this discussion is theoretically important, it is not just an academic exercise. In fact, this chapter has important practical implications for those seeking to increase the amount of socially responsible corporate behavior in the economy. In particular, the arguments developed here suggest that efforts that focus exclusively on changing the social responsibility preferences of senior managers in firms may be misguided, and at the least should be augmented by efforts focused on different firm stakeholders. The chapter begins by defining a few critical terms in the analysis.

Assumptions and Definitions

Any analysis that includes the concept of social responsibility must begin with a definition of this concept. Rather than adding to the ever growing list of definitions of this term, this chapter adopts a definition that has already been established in the literature. Hence, corporate social responsibility is defined, in this chapter, as voluntary firm actions designed to improve social or environmental conditions (e.g. Aguilera et al., 2007; Davis, 1973; Wood, 1991; Wood and Jones, 1995; Waddock, 2006).

What is somewhat different in this chapter is the recognition that there are two types of corporate social responsibility: Socially responsible actions that increase the present value of a firm's cash flows and socially responsible actions that reduce the present value of a firm's cash flows (Mackey et al., 2007). The former has been labeled by some as 'compensated altruism', while the latter has been described as 'costly philanthropy'. The relationship between senior manager commitment to social cause and corporate social responsibility will be examined for both the case of compensated altruism and costly philanthropy.

Finally, in this chapter, senior managers are said to be committed to a particular social cause when they seek to implement firm activities that address this cause regardless of the impact of those activities on a firm's performance. Senior managers are described as traditional profit maximizers when they are only willing to implement socially responsible activities that increase their firm's performance.

SENIOR MANAGEMENT PREFERENCES AND COMPENSATED ALTRUISM

While several corporate social responsibility theorists have argued that sometimes firms need to set aside the wealth-maximizing interests of a firm's shareholders to pursue responsible courses of action that benefit other stakeholders of a firm (e.g. Swanson, 1999; Whetten *et al.*, 2001), most empirical research in the field has sought to establish a positive correlation between a firm's socially responsible activities and its economic performance (see Margolis and Walsh, 2003; Orlitzky *et al.*, 2003 for a review of the empirical literature in this area). Several different measures of a firm's economic performance have been used in this empirical literature. However, most of these measures are based either directly or indirectly on the present value of a firm's cash flows (Margolis and Walsh, 2003). Thus, in the case of compensated altruism, questions about the relationship between senior management commitments and socially responsible firm activities can be accurately restated as follows:

Are senior managers with strong personal commitments to socially responsible causes either necessary or sufficient for a firm to pursue socially responsible activities that increase the present value of a firm's cash flows?

Necessity

Imagine a firm headed by senior managers whose only interest was maximizing the present value of their firm's cash flows. Would this firm ever engage in socially responsible activities? If the answer to this question is yes, then having senior managers committed to social causes is not necessary for firms to implement socially responsible activities.

In fact, it seems reasonably clear that even senior managers that are purely profit maximizing will engage in socially responsible activities that increase the present value of a firm's cash flows. At least three ways in which this can occur have been identified in the literature. First, firms can use their socially responsible activities to differentiate their products in the marketplace. If consumers prefer to purchase goods and services from firms that engage in socially responsible activities, such activities can have the effect of increasing the willingness of customers to pay (McWilliams and Siegel, 2001; Waddock and Graves, 1997). If an increase in the willingness of customers to pay is greater than the cost of engaging in socially responsible activities, then these socially responsible activities will have the effect of increasing the present value of a firm's cash flows. In this setting, traditional profit-maximizing managers will find it in their self-interest to engage in socially responsible activities.

Second, by engaging in socially responsible activities, firms may be able to avoid large government-imposed fines (Belkaoui, 1976; Bragdon and Marlin, 1972; Freedman and Stagliano, 1991; Shane and Spicer, 1983; Spicer, 1978). Here, social responsibility has little or nothing to do with differentiating a firm's products or services. Rather, cash flow is enhanced because firms are able to avoid paying large fines. If the value of these avoided fines is greater than the cost of the socially responsible activities used to avoid them, then social responsibility in this context can also increase the present value of a firm's cash flows, and traditional profit-maximizing managers will find it in their self-interest to engage in socially responsible activities.

Third, engaging in socially responsible activities can be thought of as investing in an insurance policy against socially irresponsible activities sometime in the future (Godfrey, 2005). Specifically, corporate philanthropy is argued to build moral capital with a firm's stakeholders such that if the firm later engages in activities that adversely impact certain stakeholders and that might threaten relational assets of the firm, the negative impact of these acts is mitigated by moral capital. In other words, engaging in corporate social responsibility can serve as an insurance policy for firms when things go wrong. This insurance protection is valuable to shareholders and will therefore add value to a firm.

As before, it is not necessary for managers to be highly committed to these socially responsible activities in order for a firm to pursue them. Rather, purely-profit-maximizing managers would pursue them as well.

Sufficiency

While it is not necessary for senior managers to be committed to socially responsible activities for a firm to pursue those activities when they increase the present value of a firm's cash flows, these commitments might be sufficient for firms to pursue these activities. As suggested earlier, sufficiency implies that having senior managers that are personally committed to socially responsible causes will, by itself, lead firms to pursue socially responsible activities. To demonstrate sufficiency, it must be shown that there are no reasonable circumstances under which senior managers who are personally committed to socially responsible causes will not lead a firm to implement socially responsible activities, even when those activities increase the present value of a firm's cash flow.

Traditional logic from financial economics suggests that firms should pursue all activities that increase the present value of their cash flows, unless those activities are somehow mutually exclusive. When these activities are mutually exclusive, traditional profit-maximizing firms should pursue those activities that have the highest present value (Copeland et al., 1994). This logic gives us a clue about conditions under which senior managers who are personally committed to socially responsible causes will not lead a firm to implement socially responsible activities, even when those activities increase the present value of a firm's cash flow.

Consider the following. Suppose a firm can pursue two activities: The first is not socially responsible but generates very large positive cash flow for a firm; the second is socially responsible and generates positive cash flow for a firm, but not nearly as large as the first activity. Also, suppose these two activities are mutually exclusive—the firm can do one but not both of them. An example of this scenario might be a mining firm that has a choice between two mining technologies: one that has adverse environmental effects but enables the extraction of a great deal of valuable ore and one that does not have adverse environmental effects but extracts much less valuable ore.[1] Traditional economic logic suggests that a firm will always choose the first option. The corporate social responsibility literature suggests that the firm should choose the second option, or at least, that firms that are led by senior managers that are committed to social responsibility are more likely to choose the second option rather than the first.

However, the notion that senior managers that are committed to socially responsible causes will generally choose the second option fails to recognize that there can be adverse consequences to individuals who make this choice when higher value alternatives are available. In particular, even though the socially responsible option in this case increases the present value of a firm's cash flows (i.e. the conditions of compensated altruism hold), the value of opportunities foregone may be large enough such that failure to exploit the first option could put the employment and career of senior managers committed to socially responsible activities at risk. In this setting, even senior managers committed to socially responsible causes, where activities associated with those causes actually increase the present value of a firm's cash flows, may not choose to implement socially responsible activities in their firms.

In principle, only those senior managers who would choose the socially responsible strategy 'no matter what' can be reliably counted on to always choose to implement socially responsible activities. However, even this does not mean that the firm these senior managers lead will always implement the policies chosen

---

[1] It is assumed that these cash flows are net of any fines, the cost of environmental clean-up, and so forth.

by its senior managers. It is not unusual for there to be significant disconnects between the policies and activities endorsed by a firm's senior managers and the actions taken by other firm employees. Indeed, this phenomenon has been described for firms that announce socially irresponsible policies, only to see their employees engage in socially responsible activities that violate corporate directives. But the disconnect between senior management decisions and actual firm activities could go the other way as well—senior managers could call for socially responsible activities and employees could engage in systematically less responsible activities.

Thus, senior management commitment to socially responsible causes is not likely to be sufficient for firms to implement socially responsible activities, even when those activities increase the present value of a firm's cash flows. Sometimes the value of non-responsible opportunities forgone may be so large so as to counterbalance the value of responsible opportunities taken. Moreover, decisions taken by senior managers to implement socially responsible actions may not be fully implemented throughout a firm.

None of this denies the real likelihood that firms with senior managers committed to socially responsible causes are more likely to engage in socially responsible activities than firms without these kinds of senior managers. This is especially likely when these socially responsible activities increase the present value of a firm's cash flows. However, this logic does suggest that simply having such managers will not always lead a firm to engage in socially responsible activities, even when those activities increase the present value of a firm's cash flows.

SENIOR MANAGEMENT PREFERENCES AND COSTLY PHILANTHROPY

So far, only the relationship between the preferences of senior managers and socially responsible activities that increase the present value of a firm's cash flows have been examined. In this section, the impact of the commitment of senior managers to social causes and firm decisions to implement socially responsible activities that reduce the present value of a firm's cash flow is examined. As before, both necessity and sufficiency arguments will be examined. Also, the questions addressed in this section can be more precisely stated as:

Are senior managers with strong personal commitments to socially responsible causes either necessary or sufficient for a firm to pursue socially responsible activities that decrease the present value of a firm's cash flows?

Necessity

At first, it seems likely that senior management commitment to social causes will be necessary for firms to implement socially responsible activities that reduce the present value of a firm's cash flows. After all, in this costly philanthropy setting, traditional profit-maximizing managers cannot rely on the increased cash flow associated with implementing a socially responsible activity. It seems reasonable to expect then that such managers would not implement costly philanthropy. Thus, not having senior managers committed to social causes is likely to lead a firm to not implement socially responsible activities, a condition consistent with necessity.

However, Mackey et al. (2007) develop an argument that specifies conditions under which even traditional profit-maximizing managers will pursue socially responsible activities that reduce the present value of their firm's cash flows. This suggests that even in the case of costly philanthropy, having senior managers that are committed to social causes is not necessary for firms to implement socially responsible activities.

Mackey et al.'s (2007) argument focuses on the relationship between a firm and its shareholders. Suppose two kinds of shareholders exist, those that prefer to maximize their wealth in making their investment decisions and those that prefer to invest in socially responsible firms in making their investment decisions. In this setting, firms that engage in socially responsible activities can be thought of as selling the opportunity to invest in a socially responsible firm to current and potential shareholders. Importantly, because this argument is developed in the context of costly philanthropy, socially responsible firms gain no net cash flow advantages from product differentiation, fine avoidance, or insurance from their responsible activities. This means that in comparing two otherwise identical firms, the firm implementing socially responsible activities will have lower cash flows than the firm not pursuing these activities.

However, lower cash flows need not always be reflected in the market value of a firm. Market value is a function of the demand for and supply of opportunities to invest in particular types of firms (Karpoff, 1987; Wang, 1994). In particular, if demand for opportunities to invest in socially responsible firms increases or if the supply of socially responsible firms decreases, then there can be a shortage of opportunities to invest in socially responsible firms. In this setting, profit-maximizing managers can be motivated to engage in socially responsible activities—even when those activities reduce the present value of a firm's cash flows—because demand for opportunities to invest in these firms exceeds supply. In these supply and demand conditions, engaging in costly philanthropy can increase a firm's market value even though it reduces a firm's cash flows. Profit-maximizing managers will implement costly philanthropy in this setting. Thus, having senior managers that are committed to particular social causes is not a necessary condition for firms to pursue socially responsible activities that reduce the present value of a firm's cash flows.

In the end, Mackey *et al.*'s (2007) argument depends critically on separating the present value of a firm's cash flows from the market value of a firm. These two concepts are only equivalent under the restrictive assumption that all of a firm's current and potential shareholders have the same interest in how they would like to see a firm managed, i.e. in a way that maximizes their wealth. As soon as account is taken of the possible existence of a set of shareholders who have interests in addition to maximizing their wealth when they make their investment decisions, then it is possible to disconnect the idea of maximizing a firm's cash flows from the idea of maximizing a firm's market value (Brealey and Myers, 2003).

Sufficiency

Mackey *et al.*'s (2007) argument also has implications for the sufficiency question concerning the relationship between senior management commitment to social causes and costly philanthropy. In particular, all the arguments regarding the sufficiency of senior management commitment and corporate social responsibility in the case of compensated altruism can be applied in the case of costly philanthropy with one critical change. Instead of those arguments being couched in terms of cash flows, they would have to be restated in terms of the market value of a firm.

For example, suppose a firm was faced with two mutually exclusive activities, the first not socially responsible but with a very positive impact on a firm's value, the second socially responsible but with a somewhat smaller, but still positive, impact on a firm's value. Note that this second activity could reduce the present value of a firm's cash flows, but still have a positive impact on a firm's market value if there is sufficient demand for opportunities to invest in socially responsible firms. The economic consequences of the first, non-responsible, activity can be understood in classic cash flow terms. If the impact of the first activity on a firm's market value (through its cash flows) is much larger than the impact of the second activity on a firm's market value (because it gives investors an opportunity to invest in a socially responsible firm), then it is not at all clear that senior management's commitment to socially responsible causes will be enough to ensure that a firm chooses social responsibility over wealth maximization.

In addition, the earlier arguments that socially responsible policies implemented at the firm level may not be evenly implemented throughout the firm apply here as well. Indeed, in this case, since these socially responsible activities reduce the present value of a firm's cash flow, one suspects that even more employees throughout a firm will be tempted to void the socially responsible efforts of senior managers in favor of more traditional decision criteria.

IMPLICATIONS

This chapter acknowledges that having senior managers who are personally committed to social causes probably increases the probability that the firms they lead will engage in socially responsible activities. Indeed, there is some emerging empirical support for this conclusion (Whetten and Mackey, 2007). However, that there is this correlation between senior management commitment to social causes and corporate social responsibility does not mean that such commitments are either necessary or sufficient for corporate social responsibility. Traditional profit-maximizing managers may find it in their self-interest to engage in compensated altruism and costly philanthropy (the necessity arguments). Moreover, fully committed senior managers may not always be able to implement either compensated altruism or costly philanthropy forms of social responsibility.

As a matter of theory, these arguments suggest a much more subtle relationship between senior management preferences and firm behavior—much more consistent with the behavioral theory of the firm (Cyert and March, 1963)—than the traditional corporate social responsibility literature proposes. In fact, there is little data to suggest that just because a senior manager in a large and complex firm wants to implement a particular policy, then it automatically happens. The process of decision-making, influence, and politicking have been shown to be important in the implementation of a wide variety of corporate policies—from pricing to capital investments. It seems likely that, if anything, these processes are going to be more important in implementing socially responsible corporate activities, especially in the case of costly philanthropy. Ultimately, the implementation of corporate social policies by firms may be a particularly fruitful venue within which to study the implications of the behavioral theory of the firm.

As a matter of practice, these arguments suggest that a single-minded focus on influencing the preferences of senior managers towards socially responsible activities seems limited. Surely, if such managers exist in a firm already, then their preferences can be used to help implement socially responsible corporate activities. This is probably why the positive correlation between these kinds of senior managers and corporate social responsibility exists.

But what about firms that do not currently have such managers? Getting these managers to 'convert' to socially responsible causes in order to get their firms to change policies seems difficult. Moreover, as has been suggested here, it is neither necessary nor sufficient to actually see socially responsible corporate policies being implemented. That is, activists seeking to increase the amount of corporate social responsibility in the world do not have to change 'the hearts and minds' of senior managers to see this happen, and even if they did, it may not have the broad effects on the level of social responsibility they had been hoping for.

What, then, can be done? Mackey *et al.*, (2007) suggest that efforts to increase demand among investors to invest in socially responsible firms can have an independent, and probably much greater, effect on the level of social responsibility in a society, compared to trying to 'convert' non-responsible senior managers into responsible senior managers. This probably explains the reported higher level of socially responsible activities among firms that trade in European markets compared to firms that trade in the United States. If demand for opportunities to invest in socially responsible firms is greater in Europe than in the United States, the arguments developed here suggest that there will be more socially responsible activities in Europe than in the United States. Marketing efforts designed to increase this demand in markets where it is currently low seem to hold significant potential for increasing the level of social responsibility in a country in the long run.

In the end, the assertion that senior managers with strong personal commitments to social causes lead firms to implement socially responsible corporate activities is a self-limiting theory of corporate social responsibility. According to this theory, corporate social responsibility can only spread as fast as senior managers in organizations change their perceptions of their fiduciary responsibilities. On the other hand, if it is recognized that such senior managers—while they can be helpful—are neither necessary nor sufficient for the development of corporate social responsibility, then it becomes possible for more firms, with more traditional senior managers, to at least consider the possibility of engaging in some socially responsible activities.

References

AGUILERA, R. V., RUPP, D. E., WILLIAMS, C. A., and GANAPATHI, J. 2007. 'Putting the S Back in Corporate Social Responsibility: A Multilevel Theory of Social Change in Organizations'. *Academy of Management Review*, 32: 836–63.

BELKAOUI, A. 1976. 'The Impact of the Disclosure of the Environmental Effects of Organizational Behavior on the Market'. *Financial Management*, 5: 26–31.

BRAGDON, J. H., JR., and MARLIN, J. A. T. 1972. 'Is Pollution Profitable?' *Risk Management*, 19: 9–18.

BREALEY, R., and MYERS, S. 2003. *Principles of Corporate Finance*, 3rd edn. New York: McGraw-Hill.

COPELAND, T., MURRIN, J., and KOLLER, T. 1994. *Valuation*, 2nd edn. New York: John Wiley & Sons.

CYERT, R. M., and MARCH, J. G. 1963. *The Behavioral Theory of the Firm*. Englewood Cliffs, NJ: Prentice-Hall.

DAVIS, K. 1973. 'The Case For and Against Business Assumption of Social Responsibilities'. *Academy of Management Journal*, 16: 312–22.

FREEDMAN, M., and STAGLIANO, A. J. 1991. 'Differences in Social-Cost Disclosures: A Market Test of Investor Relations'. *Accounting, Auditing and Accountability Journal*, 4: 68–83.

GODFREY, P. C. 2005. 'The Relationship between Corporate Philanthropy and Shareholder Wealth: A Risk Management Perspective'. *Academy of Management Review*, 30(4): 777–98.

KARPOFF, J. M. 1987. 'The Relation between Price Changes and Trading Volume: A Survey'. *Journal of Financial and Quantitative Analysis*, 22: 109–26.

MACKEY, A., MACKEY, T. B., and BARNEY, J. B. 2007. 'Corporate Social Responsibility and Firm Performance: Investor Preferences and Corporate Strategies'. *Academy of Management Review*, 32(3): 817–35.

MCWILLIAMS, A., and SIEGEL, D. 2001. 'Corporate Social Responsibility: A Theory of the Firm Perspective'. *Academy of Management Review*, 26: 117–27.

MARGOLIS, J. D., and WALSH, J. P. 2003. 'Misery Loves Companies: Rethinking Social Initiatives by Business'. *Administrative Science Quarterly*, 48: 268–305.

ORLITZKY, M., SCHMIDT, F. L., and RYNES, S. 2003. 'Corporate Social and Financial Performance: A Meta-analysis'. *Organization Studies*, 24: 403–11.

SHANE, P. B., and SPICER, B. H. 1983. 'Market Response to Environmental Information Produced Outside the Firm'. *Accounting Review*, 58: 521–38.

SPICER, B. H. 1978. 'Investors, Corporate Social Performance and Information Disclosure: An Empirical Study'. *Accounting Review*, 53: 94–110.

SWANSON, D. L. 1999. 'Toward an Integrative Theory for Business and Society: A Research Strategy for Corporate Social Performance'. *Academy of Management Review*, 24: 506–21.

WADDOCK, S. A. 2006. 'What will it Take to Create a Tipping Point for Corporate Responsibility?' in M. Epstein and K. O. Hansen (eds.), *The Accountable Corporation*, vol. 4. Greenfield, Conn.: Praeger, 75–96.

—— and GRAVES, S. B. 1997. 'The Corporate Social Performance–Financial Performance Link.' *Strategic Management Journal*, 18: 303–19.

WANG, J. 1994. 'A Model of Competitive Stock Trading Volume'. *Journal of Political Economy*, 102(1): 127–68.

WHETTEN, D. A., and MACKEY. A. 2007. 'An Identity-Congruence Explanation of Consistently High Corporate Social Performance Ratings'. Working Paper, Marriott School of Management, Brigham Young University.

—— RANDS, G., and GODFREY, P. C. 2001. 'What are the Responsibilities of Business to Society?' in A. Pettigrew, H. Thomas, and R. Whittington (eds.), *Handbook of Strategy and Management*. London: Sage Publications, 373–410.

WOOD, D. J. 1991. 'Corporate Social Performance Revisited'. *Academy of Management Review*, 16(4): 691–718.

—— and JONES, R. E. 1995. 'Stakeholder Mismatching: A Theoretical Problem in Empirical Research on Corporate Social Performance'. *International Journal of Organizational Analysis*, 3(3): 229–67.

CHAPTER 25

THE TRANSATLANTIC PARADOX

HOW OUTDATED CONCEPTS CONFUSE THE AMERICAN/EUROPEAN DEBATE ABOUT CORPORATE GOVERNANCE

THOMAS DONALDSON

CRAFTSMEN caution us to 'use the right tools'. As we debate models of corporate governance, and especially the so-called 'American' versus 'European' model of the corporation, we seem blind to this advice.

The concept of the corporation is not separable from the systems of incorporation and regulation that instantiate it. This is true of both the 'American' model of the corporation, with its dominant emphasis on shareholder rights (no matter how imperfectly those rights are protected), and of the 'European' model, with its attention to community interests, especially employment issues. The former is frequently attacked by Europeans for its neglect of the interests of key stakeholders, while the latter is attacked by Americans for its neglect of economic efficiency. I want to show why too much journalistic and academic debate has been wasted defending the American conception over the European and vice versa. Given the conceptual tools that both sides tend to employ defending their conceptions, the debate is irresolvable. It is, in effect, a puzzle with missing pieces.

Recent resorts to normative pluralism and the idea that different cultures require different corporate models don't solve the transatlantic problem. To be sure, no monolithic, cosmopolitan concept of the corporation can be fixed because cultural differences should influence to some extent economic policy. But this normative pluralism accounts for only a small part of the normative variance in the corporate concept. Americans, just as Europeans, endorse job satisfaction and low levels of unemployment. Europeans, just as Americans, want to see wealth enhanced.

The tools used in the transatlantic debate about the corporation are largely either purely *political* concepts or purely *economic* ones. These concepts, and the traditional theories from which they derive, were put to good use when critiquing the aristocratic, feudal systems that preceded the emergence of the modern, industrialized democracies or when critiquing the mercantilist or state-authoritarian systems that stifled commercial initiative. They remain useful even today when examining broad questions of political order and a number of specific economic questions, such as how to effectively limit monopolies. But these economic and political concepts are ill-suited for critiquing the form of the modern corporation, and only serve to confuse the debate about the American and European corporation.

We should, instead, develop approaches today that focus squarely on the nature and function of the modern corporation. Both the American and European models must adjust to new, corporation-specific concepts. Such approaches remain largely in their infancy, but desperately need further development. Two examples are the 'social contract' analysis of the corporation and the 'team production' analysis of the corporation (Blair and Stout, 1999a, 1999b). In the end, corporation-specific concepts such as these alone hold promise for solving the paradox of the American versus European model.

The debate between American and European conceptions of the corporation is probably more accurately described as a debate between Anglo-American and Continental conceptions. The UK is closer in its interpretation to the United States than it is to France, Germany, or other European states. For convenience, however, I shall most often refer to the distinction through the terms 'European' and 'American'. It is a distinction that institutional theory helps us understand (Matten and Moon, forthcoming). Entrenched and longstanding institutions of government, finance, and education surround and define corporate entities in Europe and America. A key distinguishing feature of the European system, in contrast to the American one, is the power of the state. 'In America there is greater scope for corporate discretion as government has been less active therein. Even where American governments have been active this has often been through the creation of incentives to employers to provide social benefits through negative tax expenditures' (Matten and Moon, forthcoming). For corporations in Europe this has meant heavier regulation of the corporation, especially for issues of employment.

But differences in the relative power of the state is only one of the characteristics that separate US from European ideas of the corporate governance. Scandinavian and Continental European countries have far more direct ownership or alliance ownership, i.e. ownership through networks of banks, governments, or insurance companies. As John Coffee notes, 'European governance systems have...tended toward a hierarchical and centrally dominated structure that is a barrier to new entrants and entrepreneurship' (Coffee, 1999). This contrasts with the US system, which while using a stricter system of securities regulation has stronger equity markets and more dispersed ownership of corporations. The more concentrated form of ownership common in Europe is reflected in popular moral conceptions that citizens hold about corporations. Europeans who criticize corporations often base their critiques on the entrenched wealth they represent. By an 'entrepreneur' European critics appear to mean a rich owner of a bank or factory, while Americans usually mean a newcomer, an outsider, who means to unsettle the status quo (Phelps, 2006). Finally, we note that more employees are unionized in Europe, with the result that European corporations are constantly forced to confront labor issues that their American counterparts do not.

In the United States, self-organization triumphs over collective organization. As Moon and Matten write,

In the USA, greater prominence has been given to market self-organization, upheld by governments and the courts through anti-trust laws...[whereas] in Europe markets tended to be organized by producer group alliances which either reflect consensual representation and mediation of labor and capital or, particularly in the case of France, strong government-leadership. (Matten and Moon, forthcoming)

In countries such as France and Germany where share ownership is much less dispersed among the public than in the United States, the citizenry views the main issue of corporate governance not to be the rights of shareowners, but the rights of the community in relationship to the corporation (Salacuse, 2002). 'Europe's emphasis on "social solidarity," its skepticism about the merits of unfettered competition, and its formal inclusion of labor in corporate management', Salacuse writes, 'all manifest the greater importance that European culture attaches to the community, particularly as opposed to American culture' (ibid.).

More differences exist between the American and the European corporate governance institutions than these, but for the time being we may summarize most differences by contrasting the extent to which the respective institutions of the United States and Europe either embed or fail to embed the interests of the community in the governance of the corporation. We see, in short, that Europe's corporations are far more deeply *embedded in the community* than are those in the United States. This happens through its producer alliances, union involvement, government regulation of labor, and ownership arrangements. So different is the European system that it has its own name: the 'social market economy' in Germany, 'social democracy' in France, and 'concertazione' in Italy (Phelps, 2006).

The different American and European institutions that define the governance of their respective corporations have been themselves shaped by different traditions of political and economic beliefs. Americans are somewhat more focused on issues of individual liberty and economic freedom, while Europeans are more occupied with those of class difference and community solidarity. The influence of philosophers and economists such as Rousseau, Marx, and Hegel is ubiquitous in Europe, even as that of Locke, Jefferson, Smith, and Mill is in the Anglo-sphere. Even modern economic literature reflects these forces. The writings of American industrial organization economists have been shown statistically to exhibit more confidence in the market's capability to allocate resources than those of their European counterparts (Aiginger *et al.*, 2001).

We must keep in mind the tasks these philosophical and economic theories were historically designed to serve. They were designed to address longstanding problems of economic inefficiency and political injustice. Rousseau and Locke advanced their social contract analyses of government in times when monarchies dominated the political landscape and when the interests of the citizenry were often subordinated to those of the landed aristocracy. Marx and Smith advanced their conceptions of economic relationships at a time when property was dominated by either the royalty or the new industrial barons, where the barriers to entrepreneurship were enormous, and when nation states such as France embraced a philosophy of Mercantilism that treated all economic activity as a zero-sum game in which trade barriers were the preferred route to national wealth. To a large extent these emerging theories of economy and politics succeeded in correcting longstanding problems. The Industrial Revolution, as well as the later advent of national social systems (e.g. by Bismarck in Germany) succeeded in freeing economic activity for more entrepreneurship, and protecting the individual from the capricious control of the state and the market.

But these economic and political theories and the concepts they embody, such as 'liberty', 'class', 'entrepreneurship', and 'socialism', were not designed to confront the modern corporation. The political and economic concepts that are nowadays commonly used in critiquing corporate models arose long before the corporation assumed its current dominant position in the economic landscape. Adam Smith's work is emblematic of the rise of modern, liberal economic theory. But in his landmark book, *The Wealth of Nations*, Smith relegates the discussion of the corporation to two paragraphs, in which he predicts that the future of corporations is limited, and will be constrained mostly to the areas of banking and canal building. Smith could not have imagined the present dominant position of the corporation in the global economy; one in which the revenues of some corporations eclipse those of many of the world's nation states. Craftsmen advise that we should use tools that are suited to the task at hand, and with this in mind it is noteworthy that these theories that provide the conceptual bedrock for the modern conception of society are ill-suited to address the issue of the modern corporation.

What is equally important for present purposes is that in critiquing aristocratic power and Mercantilism's inefficiency, Europeans chose—largely by accident of the author's nationality—to salute different intellectual banners. Those on the Continent drew more heavily upon the ideas of theorists such as Rousseau, Hegel, and Marx as they criticized the status quo, even as those in the Anglo-sphere used the ideas of Locke, Jefferson, and Smith. Again, while these thinkers were all united in critiquing what would soon become the 'ancien regime', they had no clear picture of a future world in which the corporate entity, often held in the form of widely dispersed ownership, would become the engine of the modern economy. Hence, as these ideas came later to inform discussions of modern corporations, their underlying differences spawned awkward and sometimes conflicting views of the corporation.

Consider John Locke and Adam Smith, two philosophers who have strongly influenced the interpretation of corporations in the Anglo-sphere (Locke, 1948; Smith, 1976). Arguably the two most popular views of the modern corporation in American business literature today are the 'agency' model and the 'transaction-cost' model. Both find their genesis in concepts from Locke and Smith. In John Locke's famous critique of the aristocratic state he makes axiomatic not only the right to individual freedom, but the right to personal property. This 'two-termed' view of property (i.e. owner/property), in which an individual owner has certain rights over a piece of property, lies at the core of the agency model of the corporation. Hence, insofar as property rights in the corporation can be shown to be analogous to my rights in owning a car or a piece of land, it follows that managers can be viewed as 'agents' of the 'principals', i.e. the shareowners. With this simple Lockean conception in hand, the function of the modern corporation is easily interpreted as essentially the efficient use and protection of its owners' rights in the hands of their agents, the managers.

The transaction cost analysis of the modern corporation (Williamson, 1976, 1985) similarly draws directly from the model of free market efficiency spawned by the writings of English classical economists such as Adam Smith and James Mill. Insofar as hierarchies can solve some of the efficiency problems obvious in free markets, and insofar as corporations serve as more efficient institutions by reducing transaction costs, corporations can be seen as natural developments of free market activity. Their role, in short, is to render markets more efficient.

The picture of the corporation from the European Continent is very different. Rousseau spoke famously when critiquing the aristocratic regime that sometimes people had to be 'forced to be free' (Rousseau, 1997) That is to say, when Rousseau critiqued the existing monarchical conceptions of the state in the eighteenth century, he envisaged a situation in which, even absent kings and princes, people might still need the benevolent force of the collective will, of the body politic. Sometimes individuals are confused and see only dimly the requirement of the collective will. His conceptions enshrine an important role for government regardless of the form of government, and have influenced modern European conceptions of the government's relationship to the modern corporation. As we have seen, the modern European corporation is far more imbedded in the social collective than is its American counterpart and far more liable to direct government regulation.

Marx and his intellectual predecessor, Hegel, also criticized existing conceptions of government and economics, but couched their critiques in terms of collectives rather than individuals. Hegel's famous 'spirit' is fundamentally a collective phenomenon in which each individual person embodies within him the historical spirit of preceding generations (Hegel, 1807) And Marx, as is well known, viewed history as a class struggle in which the group of 'haves' must be steadily reconciled with the group of 'have-nots'. Despite his repudiation of all forms of government institutions in his idealistic rendering of future 'communism', Marx in the *Manifesto* promotes the role of a strong-handed state in the present world, notably, arguing on behalf of social security systems for the aged and the formation of national banks. It is not accidental that Europeans view corporations warily from the standpoint of the wealth and power they embody. They possess a vital tradition of political criticism originating from Marx that critiques the concentration of wealth and which, in turn, elevates the role of a benevolent state. The two-tiered board, or co-determination model of modern Germany, as well as the prominent status of labor unions in modern Europe, is not unconnected with the concern for worker welfare evident in the writings of Marx and others.

The point is that while Locke, Marx, Hegel, Smith, and the other intellectual forbears of modern political thinking were successful in transforming the pre-twentieth century world, and although we may still validly debate their conceptions on their own terms, their ideas were designed to address issues of politics, *not corporations*. Moreover, their different starting points have made debates about corporations conceptually confusing if not un-winnable. Which conception of the corporation most enhances liberty? It is an almost unanswerable question. Most of our conceptions of liberty deal with the limits of the power of the state over the individual, not the corporation over the individual. Issues of freedom of speech and of freedom of worship, central issues in traditional political theory, are at best peripheral issues in current debates about corporate governance. And shall we ask which conception of the corporation most enhances efficiency? This, too, is an almost unanswerable question given that the corporation exists, by almost all accounts, as more than a simple agent in a conceptual Pareto optimum, i.e. more than a simple actor in an idealized order of free transactions among human individuals.

In order to find better conceptual tools with which to address the modern corporation, we should take a leaf from the book of those who so effectively foreshadowed our modern political institutions. We should focus upon the problem at hand rather than earlier problems that challenged our intellectual forbears. The problem at hand is the identification of the role and function of the modern corporation. In turn, we should refrain from asking how the modern corporation satisfies or fails to satisfy one or another conception of pure political theory or pure economics, but what role this unique entity can and should play in modern society.

Such approaches remain in their infancy at this stage of history, but desperately need further development. Two requirements exist for any such theory: (1) the theory must embody normative and not merely descriptive principles, and (2) the theory must be capable of dealing with the corporation *qua* corporation. In other words, it must first embody principles that do more than merely describe and explain the facts of corporations but that paint a picture of the role that corporations *should* play in society. Second, it must analyze the corporation on its own terms and as more than a second-order phenomenon of economics or political behavior.

I mention briefly two current examples of promising approaches that seem to satisfy these two conditions. Perhaps not surprisingly, one example comes from work I have undertaken with others. It is the 'social contract' analyses of the corporation that have been growing in complexity over the past two decades (Dunfee, 1998; Husted, 1999; Donaldson and Dunfee, 1999). These are attempts to reflect on the implicit 'contract' between corporations and society that reasonable citizens would be willing to honor. Much as Hobbes, Locke, and Rousseau envisioned a state of nature without governments and asked what the terms of the contract should be between the state and its citizens, so we too should ask what the economic state of nature would be like without corporations (or more broadly, productive organization[1]), i.e. where all production and exchange is through individuals, and ask what the terms of that contract should be .(Donaldson, 1982). In other words, what are the terms of the implied contract that will guide the post-state-of-nature world in which productive organizations exist, that is, in which two or more people combine their labor to produce a good or service? Much of what should persuade citizens to enter into a contract with corporations is their unrivaled efficiency, especially their ability to organize labor. For this reason, economic efficiency should stand as one of the central terms of the social contract, and as one of the guiding moral dictums for corporate management. But surely rational citizens will also require other terms in the contract, such as terms that relate to avoiding injustice and to protecting the environment.

The second promising strain of thought for interpreting the modern corporation begins in a similar way by seeking to define the uniqueness of the corporation

---

[1] Productive organizations are defined as those in which two or more people combine their labor to produce a good or service (Donaldson, 1982).

as a social institution. Margaret Blair and Lynn Stout have recently advanced the 'team production' model of the corporation (Blair and Stout, 1999*a*, 1999*b*;). Economic production, Blair and Stout posit, sometimes requires a team. In other words, production requires the combined inputs of time, money, or other valuable resources of two or more individuals. Second, they posit that team members must invest some resources that are 'team-specific', i.e. that have a higher value when used in the team than in their next best use. And finally, they assume that some of the economic rents flowing from the team production are joint or inseparable, 'making it difficult to attribute any particular portion of the gains to any single team member's contribution' (Blair and Stout, 1999*a*, 1999*b*).

Clearly the insights from applying, say, the social contract model or the team production model to the corporation will be very different from applying those of, say, the 'agency' model. On the team production model, questions arise immediately about how, apart from explicit contractual agreements, the fruits of team production should be divided. On the social contract model, questions arise immediately about how society should respond to corporations that break the terms of the social contract. Should the response always be a legal one or are there other avenues of redress?

I have argued, then, that the American and European models of corporate governance must adjust to new, corporation-specific concepts. Too much journalistic and academic debate has pitted the American conception of the corporation against the European. The conceptual tools used on both sides are drawn from traditional notions of purely political or purely economic theory, and these are tools outdated by the very existence and prominence of the modern corporation. The benefits and risks of the corporation for European society are remarkably similar to its benefits and risks for American society. We should abandon purely economic and political concepts in favor of approaches that focus squarely on the nature and function of the modern corporation, and in this way utilize new tools appropriate to our new task.

REFERENCES

AIGINGER, KARL, MCCABE, MARK, MUELLER, DENNIS C., and WEISS, CHRISTOPH 2001. 'Do American and European Industrial Organization Economists Differ?' *Review of Industrial Organization*, 19: 383–405.

BLAIR, MARGARET, and STOUT, LYNN. 1999*a*. 'Team Production in Business Organizations: An Introduction'. *Journal of Corporation Law*, 24(4): p. 743.

———— 1999*b* 'A Team Production Theory of Corporate Law'. *Virginia Law Review*, 85(2): 247–328.

COFFEE, JOHN C., JR. 1999. 'The Future as History: The Prospects for Global Convergence in Corporate Governance and its Implications'. *Northwestern University Law Review*, 93(3): 641–707.

DONALDSON, THOMAS. 1982. *Corporations and Morality*. Englewood Cliffs, NJ: Prentice-Hall.

——and DUNFEE, THOMAS. 1999. *Ties that Bind: A Social Contracts Approach to Business Ethics*. Cambridge, Mass.: Harvard Business School Press.

DUNFEE, THOMAS W. 1998. 'Social Contract Theory', in Gary L. Cooper and Chris Argyris (eds.), *Encyclopedia of Management*. Oxford: Blackwell, 603–5.

HEGEL, G. W. F. 1807. *Phenomenology of Spirit*, trans. A. V. Miller, 1977. Oxford: Clarendon Press.

HUSTED, B. W. 1999. 'A Critique of the Empirical Methods of Integrative Social Contracts Theory'. *Journal of Business Ethics*, 20(3): 227–35.

LOCKE, JOHN. 1948. *The Second Treatise of Civil Government and a Letter Concerning Toleration*. Oxford: Basil Blackwell.

MATTEN, DIRK., and MOON, JEREMY (2008). ' "Implicit" and "Explicit" CSR: A Conceptual Framework for a Comparative Understanding of Corporate Social Responsibility'. *Academy of Management Review* April 33(2).

PHELPS, EDMUND S. 2006. 'Dynamic Capitalism'. *The Wall Street Journal*, 10 Oct.: sect. A.

ROUSSEAU, JEAN-JACQUES. 1997. *Rousseau—The Social Contract and Other Later Political Writings*, trans. Victor Gourevitch. Cambridge Texts in the History of Political Thought. Cambridge: Cambridge University Press.

SALACUSE, JESWALD W. 2002. 'European Corporations American Style? Governance, Culture and Convergence'. *Transatlantic Perspectives on US–EU Economic Relations: Convergence, Conflict and Cooperation*. Cambridge, Mass.: John F. Kennedy School of Government, 1–18.

SMITH, ADAM. 1976. *The Glasgow Edition of the Works and Correspondence of Adam Smith*. Oxford: Oxford University Press.

WILLIAMSON, OLIVER E. 1985. *The Economic Institutions of Capitalism: Firms, Markets, Relational Contracting*. New York: Free Press.

——1996. *The Mechanisms of Governance*. New York: Oxford University Press.

....

CHAPTER 26

SPIRITUALITY AS A FIRM BASIS FOR CORPORATE SOCIAL RESPONSIBILITY

....

PETER PRUZAN

INTRODUCTION

....

AFTER more than a decade where corporate leaders, often subjected to pressure from the media and influential trend-setters, considered whether they should embrace the concept of corporate social responsibility (CSR), there is now a fairly broad acceptance of the so-called 'business case' for CSR. In particular many larger companies motivate the implementing of a CSR-strategy with a rationale of protecting corporate reputation and earnings. This can be seen as building upon similar earlier activities regarding 'business ethics' where the underlying focus was not on how to define and promote ethical behavior but to avoid being attacked by stakeholders for *un*ethical behavior.

Thus, the current focus is primarily on how to operationalize CSR—how to integrate it into the corporation's vocabulary, policies, stakeholder communications, and reporting systems.[1] In this rush towards pragmatism something very important is missing: a sincere inquiry into what corporate leaders really mean when they speak of responsibility at the individual and organizational level. It is my conviction that the CSR agenda will develop, slowly but surely, such that social responsibility will be considered to be as fundamental and overarching an obligation as profitability. This will entail a far broader and more inclusive concept of the firm, its purposes and relations to societal development than characterizes the modern corporation. *This development will be characterized by organizational existential inquiry as to corporate identity, success, and responsibility.*

In line with this, I argue that in order for an organization and its members to be able to experience an obligation to live up to their social responsibility, an organization must address the following three fundamental questions (Pruzan and Miller, 2006):

- *What* is responsibility?
- *Can* organizations be responsible?
- *Why* be responsible?

This chapter briefly addresses these inquiries. In particular, based on theoretical reasoning and empirical research in the form of interviews with leaders from six continents and 15 countries,[2] it is argued that true responsibility, both by leaders and their organizations, is grounded in a perspective on leadership—*spiritual-based leadership*—that transcends the (self-imposed) limitations of economic rationality. From this perspective, neither individual nor organizational social responsibility are means to an end; responsibility is fundamentally important in its own right and provides a foundation for the development of identity, purpose, and success at both an individual and organizational level.

WHAT IS 'RESPONSIBILITY'?

Most of us have an intuitive feeling or understanding of what it means to be responsible—or to be irresponsible. Often we justify our behavior when faced with complex ethical dilemmas by referring to our conscience, and we experience discomfort when witnessing our own irresponsible behavior as well as that of others, including corporations.

---

[1] This explicit focus is particularly true in the case of larger corporations; in small and medium-sized operations where the distance from top leadership to employees and other stakeholders is smaller, work with CSR is far more implicit.

[2] See the description of the Spiritual-Based Leadership Research Programme in (Pruzan and Pruzan Mikkelsen, 2007).

According to *Webster's Deluxe Unabridged Dictionary*, 'responsibility' is derived from the late-Latin *responsabilis*—requiring an answer. The word can be seen as having two parts: response + able, i.e. the ability to respond, to be able to answer for one's conduct and obligations. Ultimately it means: 'expected or obligated to account (*for* something, *to* someone)...involving duties...able to distinguish between right and wrong...trustworthy, dependable, reliable'.

But this definition raises questions, such as why be accountable, for what, and to whom?

Before considering possible answers to such questions, it is necessary to consider whether only individual human beings, characterized as we are by consciousness, can be responsible.

CAN ORGANIZATIONS BE RESPONSIBLE?

Increasingly, management rhetoric speaks of a company's visions, values, and virtues. But is it meaningful to ascribe qualities that are ordinarily attributed to individuals—including the ability and obligation to behave responsibly—to organizations? Individuals are conscious beings with a conscience, with the inherent ability to empathize, and with the ability to analyze, reflect, and to make rational choices, and therefore with the ability to 'act responsibly'. Does an organization also have this competency?

This line of questioning is a fundamental precursor for being able to deal with the other basic question posed here: *Why* should organizations be responsible?

There are fundamentally two possible affirmations of the idea that organizations can be responsible (Pruzan, 2001a). The first argues that organizations are 'judicial persons' with legal responsibilities, and that this responsibility is borne by the leadership of the organization. This legalistic perspective also contends that companies can also have obligations that arise from norms other than strictly legal rules, including expectations from owners, guidelines from branch organizations, and company codes of conduct. Responsibility is thus impersonal and defined by explicit, formal, and structural relationships.

The second affirmative answer is a more complex response. It is based on the perspective that an organization is a social system—created not just via legal documents and financial transactions, but also by an ongoing, identity-creating dialogue among its members. In such a participative, self-referential corporate culture, employees speak of 'we' when they refer to the company. As such, the organization has the characteristic of being a community. Just as an 'I', a sense of personal identity, is a precondition for an individual to feel a sense of responsibility, so is the existence of a 'we', a sense of identity as a community, a precondition for an organization as a whole to 'feel' that it has responsibilities (Pruzan, 2001*b*).

In contrast to the legalistic perspective, the norms that regulate behavior here tend to be implicit. Nevertheless they provide guideposts for responsible behavior as well as sanctions for behavior that is considered to be irresponsible. Such norms will typically be imbedded in the corporate culture, in its special vocabulary, traditions, and rituals, and its reward and recognition systems.

WHY BE RESPONSIBLE?

Only infrequently is this question brought to the level of conscious reflection in organizations, even amongst leaders in major corporations. The debates that characterized the earlier stages of CSR in the 1990s tended to deal with potential impacts of an explicit CSR policy on reputation and earnings, rather than with more fundamental issues of duty and obligation. The outcome of these debates was primarily an instrumental response, the so-called 'business case for CSR'; responsibility was—and still is—considered to be subservient to an economic or utilitarian rationale that asks: does it 'pay' to be responsible? Responsibility was not considered to be important in its own right, a fundamental precondition for well-functioning individuals, corporations, and societies.

In fact answers to the 'why be responsible' question are not nearly as obvious as the business case would argue. An ongoing inquiry into the 'why-question' is a precondition for corporations being able to successfully and sustainably integrate 'responsibility' into their own and the organization's self-awareness—and therefore into the policies, processes, and practices that promote socially responsible behavior.

It is instructive here to very briefly consider four overarching and progressively more inclusive perspectives on the question of 'why be responsible?' each with its own history, logic, and language (Pruzan and Miller, 2006):

(1) The *rational perspective* answers that a leader or a company should only be responsible if this serves some other, higher priority goals—typically the classical business goals of growth, market capitalization, and shareholder value. This instrumental perspective on responsibility originally emerged at the beginning of the 20th century (Taylor 1911/1998). Perhaps its clearest and most often quoted expression is the (in)famous statement by Nobel laureate Milton Friedman (1962):

'Few trends could so thoroughly undermine the foundations of our free society as the acceptance by corporate officials of a social responsibility other than to make as much money for their shareholders as possible'. This utilitarian argument is readily accepted by most leaders in major corporations today and is the foundation of the so-called 'business case' that has dominated debates about CSR.

(2) The *humanist perspective* is based on the assumption that to be responsible is a natural consequence of being human—it is part of our human nature. From this perspective—which first gained momentum in the 1950s and 1960s (MacGregor, 1960), and became the norm for many major corporations by the 1980s—a leader's responsibility includes providing a working environment that motivates employees to be responsible and helps them to become self-actualized.

There are two versions of this humanist perspective on 'Why be responsible?' One is the *empathy* argument which presumes the existence of an inherent human capacity to sympathize and empathize, a capacity that is more fundamental than our competence for rational choice. The second version can be referred to as the *integrity* argument. Its essence is that we are primarily responsible to ourselves and therefore that we should carry out our leadership function so that we live up to our own values. This focus on one's self as the ultimate object of responsibility can appear to be similar to the 'what's in it for me?' rational perspective. Nevertheless, there is a significant difference. The rational perspective focuses on living up to demands by others to generate financial wealth, while the humanist perspective focuses on living up to one's own values and humanness.

(3) The *holistic perspective* on responsible business behavior was first voiced in the late 1960s and gained momentum in the 1980s and 1990s (Freeman, 1984). Its starting point is that we are all interdependent, which implies a duty to respect the rights of others. Support for this perspective can be found in religious norms. For example, all major religions have some form of the 'Golden Rule'—that you should 'do unto others as you would have them do unto you'.[3] Support can also be found in cultural norms such as the Universal Declaration of Human Rights (UN, 1948).

From this holistic perspective, the responsibility of business leadership evolves beyond wealth creation for shareholders, as in the rationalist perspective, to wealth creation for the benefit of all stakeholders. At present, a growing minority of larger corporations are in the process of integrating this holistic perspective on identity, purpose, and duty into their self-reference, and are employing it to supplement (not replace) more traditional viewpoints about success and responsibility. Many are experimenting with new forms of reporting such as 'triple-bottom-line-reporting' in accord with international guidelines, such as those of the Global Reporting Initiative (2007). Although this holistic perspective to 'Why be responsible?' is

---

[3] See e.g. The Holy Bible, Luke 6: 31, Luke 10: 27, Matthew 7: 12.

more inclusive than the rational and humanist perspectives on responsibility, it still neglects the deeper, more fulfilling spiritual aspects of human and organizational life.

(4) The *spiritual-based perspective* holds that responsibility is grounded in our nature as spiritual beings who have an inherent longing (whether or not we are aware of it) to realize who we truly are, individually and collectively. Thus, our most intrinsic motivation is to realize our essential spiritual nature and purpose, not to fill an ever-present set of need-based desires. Although this perspective first emerged in writings on leadership from the 1990s (Harman and Porter, 1997), its basis is wisdom handed down over the ages by those who have been recognized for their spiritual accomplishments (Huxley, 1946/1985).

A basic tenet of this perspective is that once leaders have developed their own spiritual self-awareness, they naturally exercise it in some form of service beyond self-interest (Greenleaf, 1998). The dualistic distinction between one's self and others becomes replaced by a deeply felt connectivity—and the ordinary distinction between responsibility to one's self and to others attenuates.

Thus, when responsibility becomes more inclusive, traditional concepts of managerial power expand from controlling others to serving them (Pruzan, 2001c). It follows from this perspective that the nature of business itself is transformed. Wealth creation is no longer the *goal*; it becomes a *means* for enabling and sustaining *spiritual fulfilment* and *service to society*. Corporations and their leaders become responsible for promoting the well-being and spiritual fulfilment of those touched by business.

The following is a selection of replies from the leaders interviewed for the research program that underlies this exposition as to the meaning of 'spirituality' (Pruzan and Pruzan Mikkelsen, 2007):

- Spirituality is inspired responsibility towards people, other living beings, and the world...seeing and relating with Divinity in every aspect. Self-improvement plus world service equals spirituality.
- Spirituality is attunement with a universal spirit. It is being so in tune with that spirit that you are not acting from a place of ego or desire or greed, but you are acting from a place that is on behalf of the welfare of the totality.
- Spirituality is our deep connection with a force greater than ourselves; it is a very individual, lived experience that includes longing and belonging, for which the fruits are love and compassion.

In the rational, humanist, and holistic perspectives on responsibility, if 'spirituality' is considered at all, it is only considered to be one of many aspects of life, along with work, family, leisure time, health, etc. That is, if life were a pie, spirituality would be one slice of the pie. From the spiritual-based perspective, however, spirituality is the pie itself; the spiritual perspective of responsibility includes yet transcends the other three perspectives.

CONCLUSION

There are many business leaders today who are eager to try to project an image of social responsibility—for example, by developing 'triple-bottom-line' reports. Often, this is simply an economically instrumental way of reacting to pressures from an increasing number of challenges from internal and external stakeholders. One might say that this is a pattern of adopting the ethic of 'responsibility' from 'the outside in'.

But rather than writing off this pattern as a cynical representation of responsible corporate behavior, I suggest that we can instead be optimistic. The very fact that corporate leaders are introducing the word 'responsibility' into their business vocabulary and are attempting to operationalize this concept is highly encouraging. If a company maintains this effort for an extended period of time, even as a reaction to pressures, it is likely to lead to a greater awareness of and sensitivity to the need for responsible behavior (Zadek, 2004).

Beyond this, I am optimistic that there is a new generation of leaders who sincerely ascribe to corporate social responsibility from an ever-broadening sense of I-dentity. As they identify with not just themselves and their companies, but with their communities and society at large, with the environment and with future generations, they will naturally embody responsibility from 'the inside out'.

In the evolution from the rational perspective on responsibility to the spiritual-based perspective, we find an increasingly inclusive sense of responsibility—a spiritual oneness that ultimately embraces humanity and the planet. Professor Steven C. Rockefeller, Chairman of the Rockefeller Brothers Fund, stated in a speech at the University of the Philippines, 31 August 2004 that this responsibility requires an evolution of our spiritual consciousness (Rockefeller, 2004):

Some would argue that it is humanity's spiritual destiny to build a just, sustainable and peaceful world community. I believe that. However, to achieve this ideal a further development in the evolution of our ethical and spiritual consciousness must occur. ... It is doubtful whether humanity can find any lasting solution to the big problems it faces without taking this spiritual challenge to heart.

Ultimately, when leaders and organizations are operating from the spiritual-based perspective—from a deep awareness of their spiritual nature—they naturally behave responsibly beyond their own self-interest. A result will be business leadership that is spiritually uplifting to all, tangible in its results for all, humanly respectful to all, and socially responsible to all.

References

FREEMAN, E. 1984. *Strategic Management: A Stakeholder Approach*. Boston: Pitman.

FRIEDMAN, M. 1962. *Capitalism and Freedom*, Chicago: University of Chicago Press.

Global Reporting Initiative (GRI) 2007. *RG Sustainability Reporting Guidelines*. <http://www.globalreporting.org/ReportingFramework/G3Guidelines>.

GREENLEAF, T. 1998. *The Power of Servant Leadership*, ed. L. Spears. San Francisco: Berrett-Koehler.

HARMAN, W., and PORTER, M. 1997. *The New Business of Business: Sharing Responsibility for a Positive Global Future*. San Francisco: Berritt-Koehler.

HUXLEY, A. 1946/1985. *The Perennial Philosophy*. London: Triad Grafton Books, 1985; 1st pub. 1946.

MACGREGOR, D. 1960. *The Human Side of Enterprise*. New York: McGraw-Hill.

PRUZAN, P. 2001*a*. 'The Question of Organizational Consciousness: Can Organizations have Values, Virtues and Visions?' *Journal of Business Ethics*, 29: 271–84.

—— 2001*b*. 'Corporate Reputation: Image and Identity'. *Corporate Reputation Review*, 4(1): 47–60.

—— 2001*c*. 'The Trajectory of Power: From Control to Self-Control', in S. K. Chakraborty and P. Bhattacharya (eds.), *Leadership and Power—Ethical Explorations*. Delhi: Oxford University Press, 166–81.

—— and MILLER, W. 2006. 'Spirituality as the Basis of Responsible Leaders and Companies', in T. Maak and N. Pless (eds.), *Responsible Leadership*. London: Routledge, 68–92.

—— and PRUZAN MIKKELSEN, K. 2007. *Leading with Wisdom: Spiritual-Based Leadership in Business*, Delhi: Sage/Response Books and Sheffield: Greenleaf Publishing.

ROCKEFELLER, S. C. 2004. 'Interdependence and global Ethics' lecture at the University of the Philippines, Aug. 31, 2004; now available as: http://www.rmaf.org.ph/Foundation/Press-Releases/LectureRockefeller.html

TAYLOR, F. W. 1911/1998. *The Principles of Scientific Management*. New York: Dover, 1998, 1st pub. 1911.

UN 1948. Universal Declaration of Human Rights. <http://www.un.org/Overview/rights.html>.

ZADEK, S. 2004. 'The Path to Corporate Responsibility', *Harvard Business Review*, 82(12): 125–32.

FUTURE PERSPECTIVES OF CORPORATE SOCIAL RESPONSIBILITY

WHERE WE ARE COMING FROM? WHERE ARE WE HEADING?

ULRICH STEGER

THIS contribution not only tries to place the current debate in the context of developments over the last 25 years, but also exhorts academics to design less 'holistic' concepts (which easily degenerate into propaganda used in political debate), to contribute to transparency by providing sober empirical evidence, and to express more appreciation for marginal yet continuous incremental improvements in the business world.

I would like to thank Aileen Ionescu-Somers, Heike Leitschuh-Fecht, and Oliver Salzmann for their valuable feedback on an earlier draft of this chapter.

WHERE ARE WE COMING FROM?

When I was Secretary of State for Industry and Technology in Hessia in the mid-1980s, in the first 'red-green' coalition in Germany, I suffered from industry's often clumsy response to the environmental concerns of citizens and green initiatives. When I moved into academia, it was not only to recover from the intellectual exhaustion after ten years in politics but also to design new concepts for companies in response to the environmental agenda, at that time the dominant topic.

Therefore on 1 September 1987, I took up a newly established academic chair for 'Environment and Business Administration' (*Ökologie und Unternehmensführung*) at one of the few private universities in Germany, the European Business School (EBS). Until then, the (natural) environment had predominantly been a mere regulatory issue (and thus mainly a governmental responsibility), as it was usual to 'internalize externalities'. The new chair reflected a paradigm shift: a move away from regulation as the only solution, to ask instead, from the corporate strategy point of view, how environmental management could be used as a tool for competitive advantage (Steger, 1988/1993 reflected this new paradigm, that of integrating the environmental dimension into all management functions).

In 1990, the CEO of Volkswagen brought me in as a new member of the Managing Board, with responsibility for the development and implementation of a worldwide environmental strategy and the development of new systems of transportation. Volkswagen wanted to reap a first-mover advantage by becoming the economic market leader and invest for the future with a view to ultimately becoming a 'Mobility Company'. The first Earth Summit in Rio in 1992, which prompted the creation of what is now the World Business Council for Sustainable Development (WBCSD), brought together a first wave of industrial leaders proactively calling for workable strategies that would allow companies to assume responsibility for their externalities beyond regulatory compliance.

This change of tune within industry was not only because of rational enlightenment. Industry, particularly the most risk-exposed energy, chemical, car, and steel/metal sectors, was facing a series of heavy political defeats in all OECD countries. Smarter executives realized that their lobbying—based on arguments related mainly to competitiveness and employment—could at best delay regulation, but at the heavy price of lost reputation and credibility and cumbersome regulatory regimes. They therefore decided to try tackling the issues using a managerial approach and to see to what extent this learning and innovation process could contribute to a solution. However, this proactive stance was never the universal attitude in industry, but that of relatively few, often very visible 'best-practice' companies. The majority expressed their view through industry associations—with few exceptions—by means of traditional lobbying.

I returned to academia in the mid-1990s, during which an economic recession (with persistent high unemployment and an emerging competitive threat from low-cost countries in Eastern Europe and Asia) pushed environmental topics down the agenda. In addition, the 'clean up' of industry in the OECD countries had virtually come to an end and all remaining issues—such as global warming—were scientifically controversial, politically uncertain, and relatively intangible. The second half of the 1990s brought with it a new 'low' on discussion about the broader responsibilities of companies. Excitement about the rich pickings of the 'New Economy' dominated public discourse: 'Greed is good' (and maybe even 'green') was the mantra of the day. But it was also a time when the dominant environmental agenda was being extended to include the social dimension of Sustainable Development. The integration of social, ecological and economic goals became the conceptual mantra of the day (cynics called it the 'new trinity').

Subsequently, political resistance to globalization, the bursting of the dot.com bubble, along with all manner of revelations of fraud, massive conflicts of interest, and misleading information changed the situation again: now ethics was in vogue (as is the case after all major excesses) and topics of Corporate Social Responsibility (CSR) became more visible in public discussion. The 'War on Terror' also brought renewed efforts against corruption, money laundering, and so on, and with them a focus on conditions in developing countries, where the supply chains of multinational companies were extending on an unprecedented scale. Moreover, after the end of the Cold War, there were no longer any reasonable alternatives or threats to capitalism, and therefore there was a corresponding decline in the need to show the 'human face' of capitalism. However, in today's highly uncertain and competitive world, fighting on several fronts is avoided in favour of 'internal peace'—also via good 'corporate citizenship'.

Now, Where do we Stand?

If you believe the empirical evidence (for an overview see Steger, 2004 and 2006), the public rhetoric about CSR (or whatever else it is termed) has not had any significant effect on everyday life in the corporate sector, nor has the wealth of currently available academic research and suggestions. To put it in a nutshell: even for the most risk-exposed companies or industries, everything beyond the (hard-) core business is of secondary importance. At best, global companies are interpreting their current business model in a more responsible way and cautiously choosing an incremental but continuous, improvement path to increase their environmental and social performance. Over time this can produce some results (e.g. behavior of multinationals in developing countries), but the impacts of such efforts currently remain significantly below the academic expectations of break-through innovation and new business models. However, there are reasons for this risk-averse behavior.

The influence of financial institutions on companies has increased, not de-creased, and with it, short-term financial performance has become even more dom-inant than a decade ago. Customers—the second most important stakeholder—have very limited interest in CSR-related topics, resulting in a certain paradox: every company complains about its own customers' lack of social and environmental awareness and (purchasing and use) behavior. But if you look closely at how the same company behaves as a customer towards its suppliers, you will most probably find exactly the same type of more or less ignorant conduct.

Moreover, our empirical evidence dictates the following rule—the more interest stakeholders have in CSR (e.g. NGOs), the less important (economically speaking) they are to companies.

Optimists point to increasing levels of CSR reporting, but tend to mistake report-ing for performance. It is true that companies need to be much more transparent than they were a decade ago, especially towards their shareholders. More detailed reporting on social and environmental activities fits this trend. But what is new in terms of substance? Not much . . . if you look at the current 'corporate feudalism' in continental Europe or at formerly regulated industries. To be fair: given current economic conditions, the tendency of companies to cautiously evolve their business model at the margins is a rational approach. Anything else would mean putting the company at risk and 'up for grabs'.

Of course, reality is always more nuanced than the bottom line findings of empirical investigations might indicate. In market niches in particular, you will always find examples to the contrary. However, mainstreaming has failed so far or—smartly—has not been tried, since it dispels the first-mover advantage that is so often claimed from CSR actions. In most cases, companies remain reactive (focusing on value protection rather than value enhancement).

Large and highly visible multinationals are particularly vulnerable.

One can clearly see that NGOs—and the media along with them—are focusing on real or perceived shortcomings of multinationals. They can hurt corporate repu-tation by attacking image, credibility, and well-recognized brands. However, things have also evolved in this 'department': In recent years, companies have learned to manage their reputation, issues, and stakeholders much better. It is no coincidence that all of the huge PR disasters—Shell Brent Spar, Nike, Monsanto, and so on—happened a decade or more ago (see Steger, 2003 for more details). Neverthe-less, companies are still able to damage themselves through internal corruption, mass layoffs, and so on (as the recent examples of Siemens and Deutsche Bank illustrate).

WHERE ARE WE HEADING?

Any empirical evidence is—of course—only a snapshot of the status quo. Identifying drivers for change and emerging trends is a more compelling challenge than simply describing the current state of affairs.

To overcome the inertia of the current trajectory, powerful drivers to push developments in a new direction are required. It is not easy to identify them. In fact, in a complex world it is very much like looking into a crystal ball, something that academics are notoriously not good at. To compensate for this shortcoming, they invent scenarios. One of the most important change drivers currently—the emergence of Asian world-class competitors—is unlikely to have a positive impact on CSR. For the years to come, countries like China, India, and Thailand will be in 'catch-up' mode. Being suspicious of Western intentions, particularly those of the United States, they tend to view the whole rhetoric on sustainable development more as a means of denying them what the West has already been enjoying for decades. For example, in the emerging new Cold War for natural resources, particularly energy, these countries show little concern for human rights, landscape protection, or biodiversity. They often regard them as Western concepts designed to maintain Western competitive advantage and to suppress their own development.

The required change of direction must therefore be triggered by negative impacts of current trends in the Western world, in other words, a crisis. This is because organizational or human changes are rarely driven by reason (with the exception of the individual driven by love ...) but mostly by pressure.

Where can the 'required' negative impacts originate? Let us look at the three main players: financial institutions, governments, and individual customers as the nominal 'kings' of a market economy.

The power that financial markets wield over companies has never been stronger than today's unprecedented level. Investment banks push for major M&A (merger and acquisition) projects (which invariably end up destroying shareholder value rather than creating it). Private equity investors shake up companies and whole industries (consider the trend towards consolidation in the car supply industry). Financial analysts dissect every (real or supposed) corporate inefficiency and hedge funds earn money when others lose. The different players in the financial markets have—with few exceptions—two things in common: (1) a complete ignorance about any longer-term, broader perspective beyond narrow, short-term financials (in other words, everything under the heading of 'sustainable development' or similar concepts); and (2) a herd-like mentality and behavior. Since money as the ultimate commodity can be shifted in staggering amounts by no more than a mouse click, we should not be surprised that a major financial bubble has occurred at least every five to ten years. Consider what happened with Latin America in the late 1980s, Asia in the late 1990s, and the dot.com bubble in 2001. What will be next:

housing markets, possibly, or private equity or the triple debt line of the United States? Such bubbles have the capacity to spread rapidly around the globe, and thus an increasing number of local markets are also likely to oscillate between boom and bust. The bursting of one of these financial bubbles would clearly have far-reaching repercussions for financial institutions and cause significant collateral damage in the 'real' economy and amongst innocent bystanders.

In the process of globalization, national governments—with the exception of the United States and China—have seen a decline in their ability to ensure the well-being of their nation. Many drivers of this development are—for better or worse—simply beyond their control (and the two governments mentioned above are currently not inclined to show much interest in sustainable development). Alliances beyond the individual nation state have been formed—such as the EU—to get still more leverage, but at the price of cumbersome and slow decision-making processes. The 'War on Terror' has demonstrated two things. First, there is as yet no substitute for the nation state as the ultimate source of power. Second, a lot can be achieved quickly if, in the face of pressure or threats, national governments stand together. One of the few cases in which the global financial industry was regulated swiftly and effectively was after 9/11/2001, when, for example, the option of using hedge funds for money laundering (since they required no personal identities) was closed. Ironically, before these events, Wall Street had been successfully lobbying against the US government signing the UN Convention against terrorism financing.

Similar concerted efforts could possibly occur (e.g. via the International Energy Agency (IEA)) if the price of oil exceeds $100 per barrel (thus, for example, significantly reducing the use of fossil fuel). However, there is also potential for an entirely opposite scenario whereby there would be a 'new Cold War' and where every nation fights to secure its own energy supply. Moreover, the first signs of such a conflict are actually clearly identifiable already (take US and Chinese foreign policies as cases in point). To date, it is by no means clear which way the world will go, but it is certainly by no means a 'given' that future action will go in a favorable direction from the point of view of sustainable development.

The third player—the customer—has, on average, shown little to no environmental or social conscience. Opinion polls are full of commitment to all kinds of 'ethically sensitive' consumption—but markets are littered with environmentally friendly and socially desirable products that have ultimately failed to please the consumer. The fact remains that customers—as individuals and as organizations—are not willing to pay environmental or social premiums—unless, that is, they benefit immediately and significantly from so doing. The well-known 'free-rider' theorem explains why this behavior is inevitable. And it illustrates why products that deliver these perceived private benefits can be successful in larger market segments. Two examples are bio-food (bringing personal health benefits) and the Toyota Prius (bringing the status of driving a cutting-edge hybrid car). Otherwise the empirical evidence is clear: if customers show any interest at all, they are more willing to punish laggards than to reward pioneers. And even then, their impact can be negligible, as the case of Exxon Mobil illustrates. To the despair of many environmental NGOs that have been fighting Exxon as a primary target for some decades, it continues to be the most financially successful company in its industry (and Exxon's executives leave no doubt whatsoever about the fact that that is what counts for them...)

In Praise of Incremental Improvements

Overall, this leaves us with a pretty sobering if not pessimistic picture: in the absence of one or several major (and then likely catastrophic) 'external' events, we are most likely to see a continued 'muddling-through' based on 'more of the same': a public attention cycle here, a progress there, a backlash here, and all within a highly complex and dynamic system in which we really do not know where the limits are and what the potential outcomes might be. Clearly, decision-makers will opt to be risk-averse in such circumstances. Much will depend on the agendas and actions of key players. For example, will we see an 'Alliance of the Bold' (governments, companies, and NGOs) that will protect 'beyond-compliance' social and environmental practices in developing countries (and hence indirectly in industrial countries too) against players that are unaccountable at home and careless abroad? This is probably unlikely. But we should look more favorably upon the marginal improvements that companies favor in their risk-averse approach towards corporate sustainability (again: a rational behavior). Granted, it is far from the 'holistic' strategies and the 'leading the revolution' type of rhetoric that is favored by academics and—in even shriller tones—by consultants. But it has the considerable advantage of being realistic and of showing long-lasting results, even if attained sometimes over a longer time period than expected by players outside the company. The—already quoted—improvements in the behavior of many multinational companies are the most convincing examples (take the incarnation of corporate imperialism in 'Banana Republics' by a company that was previously called United Fruits Company, now Chiquita, that even turned its bankruptcy crisis into a role model in that respect).

To support these developments from the academic side, we need to highlight the complex web of actions and impacts in a more transparent manner and input sober empirical evidence in all areas of academic research (and not just from the 'sustainability' experts).

As the Law of Unintended Consequences teaches us, we may ultimately also be driven by the unexpected: awareness about global warming is rising, and so is the probability of a nuclear revival (probably an outcome that environmental campaigners least intended). As Friedrich August von Hayek once remarked, 'History is the result of our decisions, not our intentions'.

REFERENCES

STEGER, ULRICH. 1988/1993. *Umweltmanagement—Erfahrungen und Instrumente einer umweltorientierten Unternehmensstrategie.* Wiesbader: Gabler, 1st. edn., 1988; 2nd edn., 1993. (English translation, 1997; a shortened version also appeared in Japanese and Chinese.)

——— 2003. *Corporate Diplomacy.* Chichester: John Wiley.

——— (ed.) 2004. *The Business of Sustainability.* Houndmills: Palgrave Macmillan.

——— (ed.) 2006. *Inside the Mind of the Stakeholder.* Houndmills: Palgrave Macmillan.

....

CHAPTER 28

CONCLUSION

....

ANDREW CRANE

ABAGAIL McWILLIAMS

DIRK MATTEN

JEREMY MOON

DONALD SIEGEL

INTRODUCTION

....

As a field of inquiry, corporate social responsibility (CSR) is still in an embry-onic stage. The study of CSR has been hampered by a lack of consensus on the definition of the phenomenon, unifying theory, measures, and unsophisticated empirical methods. Globalization has also added to the complexity of CSR issues to be addressed.

Despite these concerns, there is still some excellent research on this topic, which we have gathered in this volume. Specifically, the volume contains findings from numerous experts in a wide variety of social science disciplines and fields in busi-ness administration, who have summarized the body of CSR literature and also outlined an agenda for additional research.

Given that we have included many perspectives on CSR, readers with a specific ideological or disciplinary orientation will encounter chapters that correspond with their view of CSR. At the same time, they will also be exposed to new perspectives on CSR.

We suspect that most business schools academics who teach courses in CSR or who conduct research on this topic will find the conclusion that firms can 'do well by doing good' quite appealing. Neoclassical economists will also accept this argument, especially if it can be framed in such a way as to justify the existence of a rational, economic justification for 'doing good' (McWilliams and Siegel, 2001). Conversely, such academics will dislike the call for broader involvement in social responsibility, such as corporate citizenship implies.

On the other hand, those academics who advocate government intervention in the realm of CSR may 'dislike' the positive relationship between doing good and doing well, because it obviates the need for additional regulation vis-à-vis CSR. Conversely, they will support the notion, which was discussed in several chapters, for additional discretionary spending on CSR by business.

We hope this heterogeneity in perspectives and paradigms results in rich discussion and additional interdisciplinary research on this topic. From a practitioner standpoint, there may be very different reactions from US businesses (which emphasize stockholder rights) and non-US businesses (which may emphasize a balance of stakeholder rights). Some mutual understanding may lead to more consistency of CSR actions globally.

The authors in this volume provide insights on many concepts and descriptions of the state of knowledge and practice of social responsibility over a wide range of countries and regions. With that in mind, we review some of the important contributions of this volume.

Defining Corporate Social Responsibility and Related Concepts

In addition to having no consensus definition of CSR, there are multiple related concepts and terms that are sometimes used interchangeably with CSR. CSR is typically used to consider and or evaluate the effects of business on society, beyond the traditional role of seeking to maximize profits. These may include such effects as support of charitable and educational organizations, hiring and training of hard-core unemployed, non-discrimination in employment, improved workplace safety, development of green technologies, use of non-animal testing processes, increased consumer protection, and transparency in reporting. Definitions of CSR can be found in this volume in the chapters by Carroll; Dunfee; Frederick; Mackey, Mackey, and Barney; Orlitzky; and Salazar and Husted.

The definition of CSR often depends on motivation, that is, whether an effect such as the development of a green technology was motivated by a concern for the environment or simply as a means to reduce the cost of environment compliance (deceasing costs and increasing profits). Motivation is inherently unobservable, therefore a related concept, corporate social performance (CSP), which is defined in terms of observed CSR policies, processes, and outcomes, was developed. This concept has several weaknesses, not least of which is its reliance on the concept of the ill-defined CSR. However, many researchers have used this concept, rooted in sociology, to test the relationship between firms doing good (CSP) and doing well (corporate financial performance or CFP). Definitions of CSP are found in chapters by Melé and Orlitzky, while definitions of CFP are found in chapters by Carroll and Orlitzky.

While also sometimes used interchangeably with CSR, corporate citizenship (CC), which has its roots in political science, is a broader concept than CSR. It considers the role of corporations as social institutions and their ability to respond to non-market pressures, especially in a global context. In this volume, discussions of CC are found in the chapters by Frederick, Melé, Orlitzky, and Windsor.

Another related, but not synonymous concept, is that of socially responsible investing (SRI), which has roots in religion, ethics, economics, and political science. SRI differs from the other concepts addressed in this volume, because it is a way for stakeholders to control the socially responsible behavior of managers by determining the incentives for such behavior. A definition of SRI is found in the chapter by Kurtz.

Reviewing and Expanding Perspectives on Corporate Social Responsibility

A dominant perspective in CSR research and practice is the business case, which has its roots in economics, especially the theory of the firm. The business case is that firms 'do well' (financially) by 'doing good' (acting responsibly). The mechanism by which 'doing good' is translated into 'doing well' has been open to discussion, both from a theoretical perspective and based on a critique of the empirical evidence. Kurucz, Colbert, and Wheeler address the means by which firms benefit by 'doing good' and argue for 'building a better case', which 'would extend beyond the economic' in their chapter.

Another economic concept, agency theory, has been used to argue against managers engaging in CSR. This perspective, advanced by Friedman (1970), asserts that managers who engage in CSR are acting in their own self-interest, rather than in the interest of shareholders (the owners of the firm). Therefore, CSR is not good business practice. Salazar and Husted extend this analysis by outlining an agency theory model, where the pursuit of CSR can be an appropriate business practice.

An alternative theory is that of stakeholder management, which has its roots in ethics (rights and justice). Stakeholder theory posits that many stakeholders, not just shareholders, are affected by the actions of firms, and therefore also have rights.

The chapters by Melé and Carroll constitute an in-depth analysis of stakeholder theory.

A more extensive and inclusive theory of CSR (sometimes referred to as CC) has its roots in political science and argues that business firms are citizens, with both rights and responsibilities. The responsibilities of firms include both the economic and social welfare of other citizens. This concept extends the responsibilities of firms beyond those of stakeholders to all citizens. This conceptualization is especially important in developing countries where the governments might not offer protection of human rights and there may be insufficient regulation of environmental, employment, and consumer impacts. A discussion of these issues is found in the chapters by Frederick, Levy and Kaplan, Melé, Millington, Scherer and Palazzo, and Visser.

Levels of Analysis

One of the most challenging aspects of developing a unified theory of CSR is that studies of this phenomenon have been conducted at numerous levels of aggregation: individual actor (manager or employee), organization, industry, nation, region, and global. Each of these levels of analysis is represented in this volume.

Individual actors are at the center of the controversy surrounding CSR. While firms may be legal entities and may be thought of as having identities and citizenship rights, it is individual managers who make decisions about firms' actions, including allocating resources to CSR. Several motives for engaging in CSR have been recognized, including personal preference, career enhancement, stakeholder coercion, moral leadership, reputation building and profit enhancement. Mackey, Mackey, and Barney examine the correlation between managers' commitment to socially responsible causes and the activities of the firm, while Salazar and Husted propose a model for creating incentives for managers to engage in CSR. Windsor's chapter is devoted to examining how responsible management is taught.

Most CSR studies have been based on the firm as the unit of observation. This is entirely appropriate, since most CSR-related decisions are made at the corporate level. Furthermore, while there is substantial turnover among senior managers, large firms continue to operate and affect our lives. It is also easier to identify actions with the firm rather than with individual decision-makers. Carroll presents a comprehensive history of firm-level CSR. In examining the business case for CSR, Kurucz, Colbert, and Wheeler analyze the creation of firm value through CSR. Kurtz examines the foundations of SRI and how shareholders can affect the behavior of the firms they own, that is, the role of shareholder activism in promoting CSR by the firm.

In recent years, differences in the provision of CSR across countries have been of interest to both researchers and managers. Donaldson examines differences in corporate governance between American firms (where shareholder interests dominate) and European firms (where other groups' interests are also considered). Moon and Vogel examine differences in the business and government interface between the United States and Western European countries and how these differences affect the provision of CSR in these countries. Visser offers an analysis of CSR in developing countries and draws several conclusions regarding how CSR provision differs in developed and developing countries.

The incidence and nature of CSR in a global context is also a fruitful area of research and discourse because technology improvements have opened up markets throughout the world to Western-style business with its attendant benefits and costs. Because many countries do not provide sufficient government and legal protection for consumers, employees, and the environment, businesses or firms that operate globally are expected to recognize and respond to greater responsibilities than they may have to in their (developed) home country. Scherer and Palazzo explain these expectations. Millington explains how the recent phenomenon of the global supply chain has created pressure on large multinational firms to set the standards for CSR behavior by their suppliers that often operate in developing countries—what he terms ethical supply chain management (ESCM).

Drivers of CSR

One of the issues central to CSR, but often left unexamined, is what 'drives' CSR? That is, where does the idea of responsibility originate? Several of the chapters in this volume address this issue in some detail.

One relatively well-recognized driver of CSR is the consumer. Smith examines how consumers can drive CSR behavior through both positive ethical consumerism (support for products that are produced by responsible firms) and negative ethical consumerism (boycotting firms that act irresponsibly). Steger is more reserved in his support for consumers as drivers, pointing out that consumers are still generally reluctant to support CSR and may punish laggards, but not reward pioneers in CSR. Williams and Aguilera compares consumer attitudes towards CSR across cultures, postulating that there are significant differences.

Another well-recognized driver of CSR is the manager. The manager as agent for the stockholders (principals) of the firm has control over the resources and can determine how those resources are allocated. Therefore, managers, and especially CEOs, can strongly influence CSR behavior (Waldman et al., 2006). This is at the heart of most of the controversy surrounding CSR. Proponents of CSR assert that managers should exercise moral leadership, as proposed in Swanson's chapter. Opponents believe that there is an agency problem when managers engage in CSR or more generally, that 'investment' in CSR constitutes an inefficient use of corporate resources. Salazar and Husted examine this tension. Williams and Aguilera discuss differences in CSR attitudes and behaviors across different cultures. Pruzan discusses a spiritual-based perspective of CSR which implies that managers are—and should be—the drivers of CSR.

The lack of government regulation and legal protections in much of the world is another recognized driver of CSR. In developing countries and regions, firms must take over many of the social functions of government so that there is a stable economy, a viable workforce, and a globally sustainable environment in which to conduct commerce. This driver is discussed in several chapters, but most explicitly analyzed in the Visser chapter. Hanlon argues that unmet social needs create a means for firms to develop relationships with stakeholders that benefit the firm (building reliance on firms rather than governments).

In developed countries, government may be a driver of CSR. Moon and Vogel discuss ways in which governments can actively encourage firms to engage in CSR, for example, through the establishment of non-binding codes and standards. Alternatively, firms might choose CSR as a way to escape formal regulation. Whether through the stick or the carrot, governments may be effective in encouraging CSR.

Social Auditing and Reporting

One area where proponents of CSR have prevailed is in auditing and reporting. The premise behind the support for reporting is that managers will be encouraged to perform more responsibly if they must report on results, and shareholder activists can use the information in reports to invest responsibly. Owen and O'Dwyer discuss the growth and development of corporate social and environmental reporting. Kuhn and Deetz outline the critical theorists' critique of social audits and reports. Buchholtz, Brown, and Shabana discuss the role of legislation in establishing standards for auditing and reporting and the need for global guidelines.

Information Asymmetry and the Strategic Use of CSR

These chapters underscore the importance of information relating to CSR practices. More generally, we believe that the role of information asymmetry in CSR is a fruitful area of research (see Baron, 2001, and Fedderson and Gilligan, 2001, for theoretical analyses and Siegel and Vitaliano, 2007, for empirical evidence). It is important to note that CSR practices and product features are not always totally transparent and observable to the consumer and other stakeholders. This makes it

difficult for consumers and other stakeholders to evaluate the firm's social performance.

As noted in Fedderson and Gilligan (2001), the degree of asymmetric information regarding internal operations can be mitigated by the company or by 'activists'
and/or/'non-governmental organizations' (NGOs). It is interesting to note that
McDonalds, Motorola, and Nike now publish 'annual CSR reports'. One can view
this activity as a form of advertising, especially for more general types of CSR.
However, stakeholders may perceive this information as biased, since it is presented
by incumbent managers and not an independent source. Therefore, NGOs may
emerge to fill this gap. Additional evidence is needed on how consumers and other
stakeholders respond to these efforts.

More generally, the field would greatly benefit from more research on precisely
how firms matrix decisions regarding CSR into their business and corporate-
level strategies. There is now mounting empirical evidence (Russo and Fouts,
1997; Reinhardt, 1998; Siegel and Vitaliano, 2007) that it is consistent with strategic theories of CSR and rational, profit-seeking management decision-making.
However, others may view this evidence quite differently. They may perceive this
stylized fact as indicative of the notion that CSR is a 'fraud' or a 'smokescreen',
used to disguise other irresponsible behavior. In this regard, it is interesting to
note that firms such as Enron and Philip Morris were actively involved in social
responsibility.

An interesting recent paper by Strike, Gao, and Bansal (2006) examines
this tension between responsibility and irresponsibility. The authors assert that
firms can simultaneously be socially responsible and socially irresponsible (e.g.
Philip Morris). Based on a strategic/resource-based-view framework, they examine
whether international diversification influences the propensity of firms to be socially responsible and socially irresponsible. More specifically, the authors demonstrate that firms diversifying internationally create value by acting responsibly and
destroy value by acting irresponsibly.

The field of CSR remains wide open and we hope that these authors have expanded your horizons. Hope springs eternal.

REFERENCES

Baron, D. 2001. 'Private Politics, Corporate Social Responsibility and Integrated Strategy'.
    Journal of Economics and Management Strategy, 10: 7–45.
Feddersen, T., and Gilligan, T. 2001. 'Saints and Markets: Activists and the Supply of
    Credence Goods'. *Journal of Economics and Management Strategy*, 10: 149–71.
Friedman, M. 1970. 'The Social Responsibility of Business is to Increase its Profits'. *New York
    Times Magazine*, 13 Sep.

McWilliams, A., and Siegel, D. 2001. 'Corporate Social Responsibility: A Theory of the Firm Perspective'. *Academy of Management Review*, 26(1): 117–27.

Reinhardt, F. 1998. 'Environmental Product Differentiation'. *California Management Review*, 40, summer: 43–73.

Russo, M. V., and Fouts, P. A. 1997. 'A Resource-Based Perspective on Corporate Environmental Performance and Profitability'. *Academy of Management Journal*, 40: 534–59.

Siegel, D. S., and Vitaliano, D. 2007. 'An Empirical Analysis of the Strategic Use of Corporate Social Responsibility'. *Journal of Economics and Management Strategy*, 17(3): 773–92.

Strike, V. M., Gao, J., and Bansal, T. 2006. 'Being Good while Being Bad: Social Responsibility and the International Diversification of U.S. Firms'. *Journal of International Business Studies*, 37(6): 850–62.

Waldman, D., Siegel, D. S., and Javidan, M. 2006. 'Components of CEO Transformational Leadership and Corporate Social Responsibility.' *Journal of Management Studies*, 43(8): 1703–25.

INDEX

....